Building a Successful Palestinian State

The RAND Palestinian State Study Team

Supported by a gift from
David and Carol Richards

RAND
CORPORATION

Research for this study was carried out from September 2002 through May 2004 by a multidisciplinary team of RAND researchers, working under the direction of the RAND Health Center for Domestic and International Health Security in conjunction with the Center for Middle East Public Policy (CMEPP), one of RAND's international programs. RAND Health and CMEPP are units of the RAND Corporation. Primary funding for the project was provided by a generous gift from David and Carol Richards. This research in the public interest was also supported by RAND, using discretionary funds made possible by the generosity of RAND's donors and the earnings on client-funded research.

Library of Congress Cataloging-in-Publication Data

Building a successful Palestinian state / the Rand Palestinian State Study Team.
   p. cm.
   "MG-146."
   Includes bibliographical references.
   ISBN 0-8330-3532-0 (pbk. : alk. paper)
   1. Arab-Israeli conflict—1993– —Peace. 2. Palestine—Politics and government.
3. Legitimacy of governments. 4. Education—Palestine. 5. Health care reform. I. Rand
Palestinian State Study Team.

   DS119.76.B85 2005
   956.05'4—dc22

                           2005005242

The RAND Corporation is a nonprofit research organization providing objective analysis and effective solutions that address the challenges facing the public and private sectors around the world. RAND's publications do not necessarily reflect the opinions of its research clients and sponsors.

RAND® is a registered trademark.

Cover design by Stephen Bloodsworth and Doug Suisman
Cover photo: "The Olive Tree: Hi Mama, I'm Home!"
Photographer: Steve Sabella at www.sabellaphoto.com

Published 2005 by the RAND Corporation
1776 Main Street, P.O. Box 2138, Santa Monica, CA 90407-2138
1200 South Hayes Street, Arlington, VA 22202-5050
201 North Craig Street, Suite 202, Pittsburgh, PA 15213-1516
RAND URL: http://www.rand.org/
To order RAND documents or to obtain additional information, contact
Distribution Services: Telephone: (310) 451-7002;
Fax: (310) 451-6915; Email: order@rand.org

Study Group Directors

Steven N. Simon, C. Ross Anthony, Glenn E. Robinson, David C. Gompert, Jerrold D. Green, Robert E. Hunter, C. Richard Neu, Kenneth I. Shine

RAND Research Staff by Task

Introduction
C. Ross Anthony
Glenn E. Robinson
Michael Schoenbaum
Steven N. Simon
Cynthia R. Cook

Governance
Glenn E. Robinson

Internal Security
Kevin Jack Riley
Seth G. Jones
Steven N. Simon
David Brannan
Anga R. Timilsina

Demography
Kevin F. McCarthy
Brian Nichiporuk

Economics
Justin L. Adams
Kateryna Fonkych
Keith Crane
Michael Schoenbaum

Water
Mark Bernstein
David G. Groves
Amber Moreen

Health
Michael Schoenbaum
Adel K. Afifi
Richard J. Deckelbaum

Education
Charles A. Goldman
Rachel Christina
Cheryl Benard

Cost Team
Keith Crane
Michael Schoenbaum
Cynthia R. Cook

Communications Support
Barbara Meade
Mary E. Vaiana

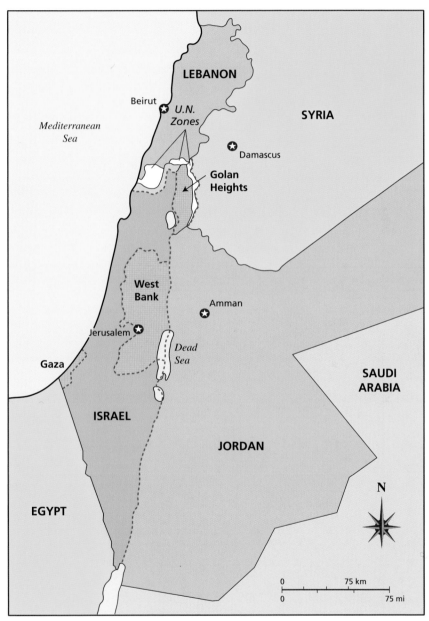

LEBANON

Beirut

*U.N.
Zones*

SYRIA

*Mediterranean
Sea*

Damascus

**Golan
Heights**

**West
Bank**

Amman

Jerusalem

Gaza

*Dead
Sea*

**SAUDI
ARABIA**

ISRAEL

JORDAN

EGYPT

N

| 0 | 75 km |
| 0 | 75 mi |

Israel/Palestine Region

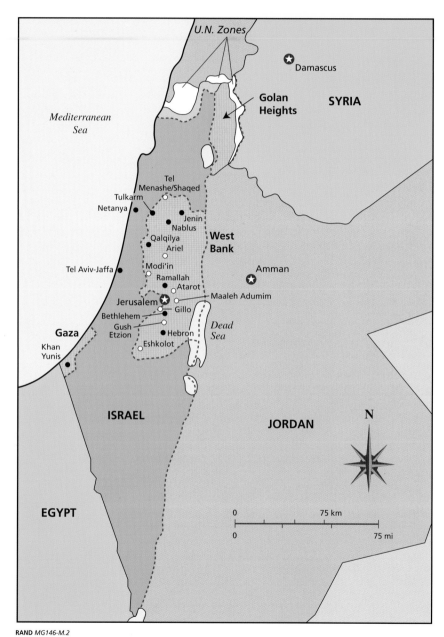

U.N. Zones

Damascus

SYRIA

Golan
Heights

Mediterranean
Sea

Tel
Menashe/Shaqed

Tulkarm

Netanya

Jenin

Nablus

West
Bank

Qalqilya

Ariel

Modi'in

Tel Aviv-Jaffa

Ramallah

Amman

Atarot

Jerusalem

Maaleh Adumim

Bethlehem

Gillo

Gush
Etzion

Hebron

Dead
Sea

Gaza

Eshkolot

Khan
Yunis

ISRAEL

JORDAN

N

EGYPT

0   75 km

0   75 mi

RAND *MG146-M.2*

Israel/Palestine Region with City Detail

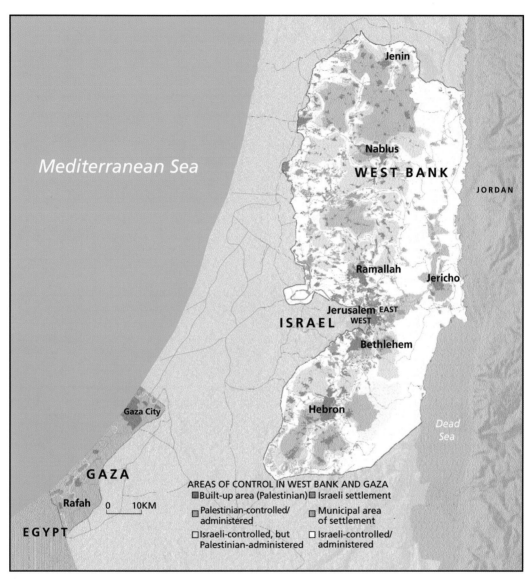

NOTE: The Green Line—control of the regions within these borders has been contested since Israel seized the West Bank and Gaza in 1967.

RAND *MG146-M.3*

Israeli Settlements in the West Bank

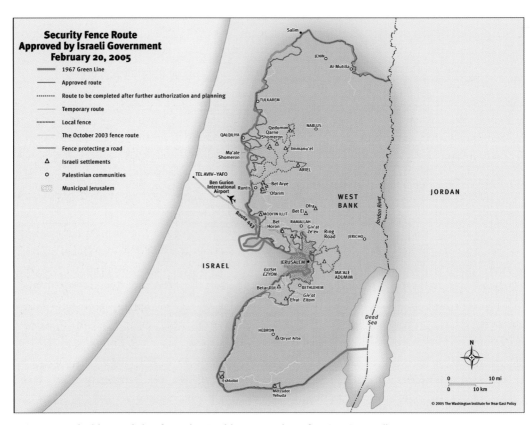

SOURCE: Used with permission from the Washington Institute for Near East Policy.

RAND *MG146-M.4*

Security Fence Route Approved by the Israeli Government as of February 20, 2005

Preface

The Palestinian Authority, Israel, the United States, the European Union, Russia, and the United Nations all officially support the establishment of an independent Palestinian state. This book focuses on a single analytical question: How can an independent Palestinian state be made successful? We do not examine how the parties could reach a settlement that would create such a state. Rather, we develop recommendations, based on rigorous analysis, about steps that Palestinians, Israel, the United States, and the international community could take if a state were established, to promote the state's success.

Once established, the new state must grapple with many difficult issues, including establishing effective and accepted democratic governing institutions, rebuilding a devastated country, establishing an economy that grows rapidly to provide increased income and jobs for its citizens, dealing with a rapidly growing population and declining water resources, providing basic services such as health care and education, and, above all, ensuring security both within its borders and in relation to its neighbors. This study examines what must be done in the first ten years of independent statehood to address most of these issues and to establish a state with the capacity to succeed.

The book first defines success and then examines internal security and governance—areas that must be successfully addressed from the first day of a new state. We then turn our attention to demography, economics, and water before considering two keys determinants of social well-being—health and education. Each chapter analyzes the relevant issues, makes recommendations where appropriate, and provides estimates in the areas discussed of the costs of achieving a successful state. Two companion reports are also forthcoming. The first, *The Arc: A Formal Structure for a Palestinian State* (RAND Corporation, 2005), explores options for addressing local housing, transportation, and related requirements of returning refugees and part of the rapidly growing Palestinian population. The second, entitled *Building a Successful Palestinian State: Security,* examines security issues in more detail.

We hope this study will spur additional research and that the document will be continuously updated as the situation and information change. A number of key areas were beyond the scope of the present study including roads, energy, and ports; we hope to address them in future editions of this work. In each chapter, we have also identified issues demanding further analysis that we hope to pursue over time.

This study should be of interest to the Palestinian and Israeli communities; to policymakers in the Roadmap Quartet (the United States, the European Union, the United Nations, and Russia); to foreign policy experts; and to organizations and individuals committed to helping establish and sustain a successful state of Palestine. It should also be of interest to the negotiating teams charged with the responsibility of establishing the new state. Certainly, recent experience in Iraq and Afghanistan underscores both how hard nation-building can be, particularly in a situation such as the one in the West Bank and Gaza today, and the necessity of having plans in place for the eventuality of an independent Palestine.

Research for this study was carried out from September 2002 through May 2004 by a multidisciplinary team of RAND researchers, working under the direction of the RAND Health Center for Domestic and International Health Security in conjunction with the Center for Middle East Public Policy (CMEPP), one of RAND's international programs. RAND Health and CMEPP are units of the RAND Corporation.

Primary funding for the project was provided by a generous gift from David and Carol Richards. This research in the public interest was also supported by RAND, using discretionary funds made possible by the generosity of RAND's donors and the earnings on client-funded research.

Acknowledgments

Many people both within and outside RAND contributed to this book. The authors are deeply indebted to the numerous Palestinian and Israeli experts who graciously donated their time and expertise to provide source material for this analysis. We are equally indebted to Laurie Brand, Bruce Hoffman, Lawrence Freeman, Itamar Rabinovich, Yezid Sayigh, David Aaron, and Carl Bildt, who carefully reviewed several drafts of this entire study. Their thoughtful comments and in-depth knowledge of the Middle East helped us analyze and refine the policy implications of our research.

In addition to the reviews of the entire study mentioned above, each sector chapter was also reviewed by at least two external reviewers, as well as by a variety of technical experts within RAND. We wish to extend our thanks and gratitude to all of these individuals, whose critiques greatly helped to sharpen our analyses. These reviewers included Amitzur Barak, Sue Bodilly, Robert Bowker, Nathan Brown, Louay Constant, Julie DaVanzo, Sir Lawrence Freedman, Osman Galal, Sir Timothy Garden, Shimon Glick, Debra Knopman, Ellen Laipson, Robert Malley, Itamar Rabinovich, Alan Richards, Andrew Rigby, Yezid Sayigh, Avraham Sela, Khalil Shikaki, and Tarik Yousef. Of course, the final research and findings are the responsibility of the authors.

All authors would like to thank our RAND colleagues. We would especially like to thank Barbara Meade and Mary Vaiana, who reviewed the entire volume for clarity and structure, and Jane Ryan and Peter Hoffman, who coordinated book design and production. Christina Pitcher and Miriam Polon edited the manuscript and produced a greatly improved final version. Stephanie Griffith, Jacelyn Cobb, and Christine Carey's effective project management enabled us to keep track of each chapter through the lengthy writing and review cycles.

Work on this study would not have been possible without the support of David and Carol Richards, whose generous funding for this project reflects their deep commitment to peace in the Middle East. We are also grateful to RAND's corporate management team, whose encouragement and financial support enabled publication of this book. We extend special thanks to Michael Rich, RAND's Executive Vice President, and Robert Brook, Vice President and Director of RAND Health, for their timely reviews of the study and unflagging encouragement to the authors.

Contents

CHAPTER SEVEN
Health

CHAPTER EIGHT

Education

Figures

Tables

Summary

This study focuses on a single analytical question: How can an independent Palestinian state be made successful?

Identifying the requirements for success is a pressing policy need if a new Palestinian state is established. Currently, the United States, Russia, the European Union, and the United Nations remain committed to the establishment of a Palestinian state, as do a critical mass of Palestinians and Israelis according to surveys. The "Roadmap," which these parties have all officially supported, calls for the establishment of a new Palestinian state by 2005.[1] President Bush recently revised this timetable for the United States, calling for a new state by 2009. As this book is published, prospects for an independent Palestine are uncertain, although the recent passing of Yasser Arafat has opened up new dialogue and new opportunities. Nevertheless, recent history in nation-building clearly indicates that in the absence of detailed plans, such efforts almost always fail. It is this void that the present volume seeks to fill.

In this study, we explore options for structuring the institutions of a future Palestinian state, so as to promote the state's chances of success. We do not examine how the parties could reach a settlement that would create an independent Palestinian state. Rather we develop recommendations, based on analysis, about steps that Palestinians, Israel, the United States, and the international community can begin to take now to increase the likelihood that a new Palestinian state will thrive.

It should be emphasized that nation-building even under ideal circumstances is a very difficult undertaking. If a peace is agreed to, significant distrust will still exist between Palestinians and Israelis, and some elements in both countries will not accept a peace settlement and instead will actively seek to disrupt progress toward a successful Palestinian state. Success will require good planning; significant resources; fortitude; significant sustained involvement of the international community; and courage, commitment, and hard work on the part of the Palestinian people.

---

[1] The full title of the Roadmap is *A Performance-Based Roadmap to a Permanent Two-State Solution to the Israeli-Palestinian Conflict* and can be found at http://www.state.gov/r/pa/prs/ps/2003/20062pf.htm, as of June 2004.

Approach

We begin our discussion by considering the essentials of a successful new state—the nature of the institutions that will govern it and the structures and processes that will ensure its security. We then describe the demographic, economic, and environmental resources on which a Palestinian state can draw, while also identifying factors that can limit the state's ability to use these resources effectively. Finally, we consider what a Palestinian state must do to ensure that its citizens are healthy and educated.

In each substantive area, we draw on the best available empirical data to describe the requirements for success, to identify alternative policies for achieving these requirements, and to analyze the consequences of choosing different alternatives. We also provide initial estimates of the costs associated with our recommendations over the first decade of independence. The methodology used in each chapter differs depending on the nature of the analytic questions and the availability of data. Each chapter describes its individual approach and identifies the constraints and uncertainties that accompany the analysis.

Defining Success

In our view, "success" in Palestine will require an independent, democratic state with an effective government operating under the rule of law in a safe and secure environment that provides for economic development and supports adequate housing, food, education, health care, and public services for its people. To achieve this success, Palestine must address four fundamental challenges:

- **Security:** Palestinian statehood must improve the level of security for Palestinians, Israelis, and the region.
- **Governance:** A Palestinian state must govern effectively and be viewed as legitimate by both its citizens and the international community.
- **Economic development:** Palestine must be economically viable and, over time, self-reliant.
- **Social well-being:** Palestine must be capable of feeding, clothing, educating, and providing for the health and social well-being of its people.

Conditions for Success

Security
The success of an independent Palestinian state is inconceivable in the absence of peace and security for Palestinians and Israelis alike. Adequate security is a prerequisite to achieving all other recommendations in this volume. An independent Palestinian state

must be secure within its borders, provide for the routine safety of its inhabitants, be free from subversion or foreign exploitation, and pose no threat to Israel. Moreover, these conditions must be established from the moment of independence: Unlike infrastructure or industry, security is not something that can be built gradually.

Successful security arrangements range from protecting borders that surround the state to maintaining law and order within it. Success, even under the most favorable conditions, will probably require extensive international assistance; close cooperation between any international security personnel and their Palestinian counterparts; and Israeli-Palestinian security cooperation, bolstered by at least international financial assistance.

Governance

Good governance will be a key measure of success of a new Palestinian state. From our perspective, this must include governance that is representative of the will of the people, practices the rule of law, and is virtually free of corruption. The government must also enjoy the support of the people. To gain the support of the majority of Palestinians—three-fourths of whom public opinion surveys suggest support reconciliation with Israel and the establishment of an independent Palestinian state—a new state must be seen as legitimate by its citizens and practice the good governance that is necessary to maintain public respect and support.

The thoroughness with which democratic institutions and processes, including the rule of law, are established will be vital from the outset—indeed, it is already critical. The death of Yasser Arafat in November 2004 will yield new challenges and opportunities for Palestinians trying to establish the institutional foundation for an independent state.

Economic Development

An independent Palestinian state cannot be considered successful unless its people have good economic opportunities and quality of life. Palestinian economic development has historically been constrained, and per-capita national income peaked in the late 1990s in the range of "lower middle income" countries (as defined by the World Bank). Since then, national income has fallen by half or more following the start of the second intifada (uprising) against Israel in September 2000. An independent Palestinian state will need to improve economic conditions for its people just as urgently as it will need to improve security conditions.

Our analysis indicates that Palestine can succeed only with the backing, resources, and support of the international community—above all, the United States, the European Union, the United Nations, the World Bank, and the International Monetary Fund. Resource requirements will be substantial for a decade or more. Of course, the availability of such resources cannot be taken for granted. The possible limited availability of resources intensifies the need for the state to succeed quickly, especially in the eyes of those who provide private investment capital.

During the period of international assistance, the Palestinian state should invest aid, not merely consume it. Ultimately, an independent Palestinian state cannot be characterized as successful until the state becomes largely self-reliant.

Social Well-Being

A fourth condition for the success of an independent Palestinian state is that the living conditions of its people improve substantially over time. Many observers have suggested that disappointment about slow improvement in living conditions under Palestinian administration after 1994—and sharp declines in some years—contributed significantly to the outbreak of the second intifada.

In addition to the conditions for success described above, the Palestinian health and education systems must be strengthened. Options for such improvements are discussed in the final chapters of this book. Both systems start with considerable strengths. But both will also need considerable development, which will require effective governance and economic growth, as well as external technical and financial assistance. In the area of health, the state can be seen as successful if it is able to provide its citizens with access to adequate primary and tertiary care services while being able to carry out the basic public health functions of a modern state, including immunization programs for children. In education, all children need to be assured access to educational opportunities to enable them to achieve their potential while contributing to the economic and social well-being of the society.

Crosscutting Issues: Permeability, Contiguity, and Security

Our analysis identified three crosscutting issues that will strongly influence prospects for the success of a Palestinian state:

- How freely people can move between Israel and an independent Palestinian state, which we refer to as "*permeability*" of borders.
- Whether the state's territory (apart from the separation of Gaza from the West Bank) is *contiguous*.
- The degree to which *security* is achieved.

These issues affect all of the other issues examined in this book. It is important to understand how they are interlinked, how they affect key goals, and how they might be reconciled. This study concludes that none of the major conditions of success—security, good governance, economic viability, and social welfare—can be realized unless Palestinian territory is substantially contiguous. In a territorially noncontiguous state, economic growth would be adversely affected, and the resulting poverty would aggravate political discontent and create a situation where maintaining security would be very difficult, if not impossible. In any case, a Palestine divided into several or many parts would present its government with a complex security challenge since a noncontiguous state would hamper law enforcement coordination; require duplicative and, therefore, expensive capabilities; and risk spawning rivalries among security officials, as happened between Gaza and the West Bank under the Palestinian Authority. Greater border permeability is essential for economic development but significantly complicates security.

Key Findings from the Analyses

Below key findings from our analyses are summarized. Most areas examined include estimates of the financial costs associated with implementing each chapter's recommendations. Costs are presented in constant 2003 U.S. dollars, unless otherwise noted, with no attempt to adjust the estimates for future trends in inflation or exchange rates.

These estimates are not based on detailed cost analyses. Rather, we intend them to suggest the scale of financial assistance that will be required from the international community to help develop a successful Palestinian state. More precise estimates will require formal cost studies (involving detailed needs assessments), which were outside the scope of the present project. Moreover, we did not estimate the costs of all the major institutional changes and improvements in infrastructure that would be required for a successful Palestinian state, so summing the cost estimates across the chapters of this book will fall considerably short of the "total" financial requirements for successful Palestinian development.

Governance

A successful Palestinian state will be characterized by good governance, including a commitment to democracy and the rule of law. A precondition to good governance is that the state's citizens view their leaders as legitimate. An important source of legitimacy will be how well Palestinian leaders meet the expectations of their people in negotiations with Israel on key issues such as the size of the new state, its territorial contiguity, and the status of Jerusalem, as well as the form and effectiveness of governance, economic and social development, and the freedom of refugees to resettle in Palestine or be compensated.

Good governance will be more easily achieved if Palestine's borders are open, its economy prosperous, its refugee absorption manageable, its security guaranteed, and its early years bolstered by significant international assistance. Good governance will not be achieved without significant effort and international assistance. It will depend heavily on the reform of government institutions and practices. At a minimum, Palestine must take actions that (1) promote the rule of law including empowering the judiciary, (2) give greater power to a Palestinian parliament, (3) significantly reduce corruption, (4) promote meritocracy in the civil service, and (5) delegate power to local officials. Among other actions, a currently pending constitution that recognizes the will of the people and clearly defines the powers of various branches of government must be wisely completed. Finally, the authoritarian practices and corruption that has characterized rule under the Palestinian Authority must be eliminated.

Strengthening Palestinian governance will entail real costs, for instance for conducting elections and for establishing and operating the legislative and executive branches of government. Our analysis does not explicitly estimate the costs of these institutional changes. These costs are addressed in some instances, however, particularly those relating to administration of justice in Chapter Three.

Internal Security

The most pressing internal security concern for a Palestinian state will be the need to suppress militant organizations that pose a grave threat to both interstate security (through attacks against Israel and international forces) and intrastate security (through violent opposition to legitimate authority). Public safety and routine law enforcement—administration of justice—will also need to be put on a sound footing as quickly as possible.

Assistance for the administration of justice would facilitate the emergence of an independent judiciary and an efficient law enforcement agency capable of investigating and countering common criminal activity and ensuring public safety. Both of these broad objectives would require funds for rebuilding courthouses and police stations; supplying equipment and materials necessary for training, such as legal texts, computers, and other office equipment; and providing forensic and other training and the equipment that police need to carry out their day-to-day patrolling duties. A more comprehensive program aimed at accelerating the reform process and creating a sense of security for Palestinian citizens more swiftly would include deploying international police and vetting and recruiting judges, prosecutors, and police officers.

As in the realms of counterterrorism and counterintelligence, internal security requirements would demand restructured security services and up-to-date equipment, monitoring, training, and analytical support. Depending on the severity of the domestic terrorist threat and the speed with which Palestinian capacities develop in this area, a more intensive program might be needed.[2]

We estimate general internal security reconstruction costs to be at least $600 million per year, and as much as $7.7 billion over ten years.

Demography

There are almost 9 million Palestinians, nearly 40 percent of them living within the boundaries of what is likely to become a new Palestinian state (the West Bank and

---

[2] A forthcoming RAND companion study to this one, entitled *Building a Successful Palestinian State: Security,* will explore security issues in more depth.

Gaza). The population's fertility rate is high. If there is large-scale immigration by Palestinian diaspora, the population in the Palestinian territories will grow very rapidly for the foreseeable future.

Rapid population growth will stretch the state's ability to provide water, sewerage, and transportation to Palestinian residents, and it will increase the costs of doing so. It will tax the physical and human capital required to provide education, health care, and housing, and it will place a heavy financial burden for funding these services on a disproportionately smaller working-age population. A new Palestinian state will also be hard-pressed to provide jobs for the rapidly growing number of young adults who will be entering the labor force.

There are clear signs that Palestinian fertility rates are declining, but the rate of decline is uncertain. In the short run, births will certainly increase since the number of Palestinian women in the prime childbearing years will more than double. How much fertility rates decline over the long term will probably depend on the degree to which the education levels and labor force participation of Palestinian women rise.

There is also considerable uncertainty surrounding the number of diasporic Palestinians who might move to a new Palestinian state. The Palestinian Central Bureau of Statistics and the United States Census Bureau estimate between 100,000 and 500,000 returnees. Our own estimates, based on assumptions about which groups of Palestinians will be most likely to return and under what conditions, are somewhat higher. Ultimately, the number of Palestinians returning will depend on the terms of the final agreement and on social, political, and economic developments in the new Palestinian state. These demographic realities greatly affect the likely economic and social development of the new state.

Water

A viable Palestinian state will need adequate supplies of clean water for domestic consumption, commercial and industrial development, and agriculture. These requirements are not being met today. Current water and waste management practices are degrading both surface streams and rivers and underground water resources.

Most of Palestine's water is provided by springs and wells fed by underground aquifers that are shared with Israel. Current water resource development provides only about one-half of the World Health Organization's per-capita domestic water requirement and limits irrigation and food production. In addition, current water use is unsustainable: The amount of water that the Palestinians and Israelis extract from most of the region's aquifers exceeds the natural replenishment rate.

Options for increasing the water supply that were examined include increasing groundwater use, accommodated by Israel's reduction in use; increasing rain and storm water capture; and increasing desalination capabilities where no other options exist. Demand can be managed through the wise application of water efficiency technologies, water reuse methods, and infrastructure improvements.

We estimate a base case cost of more than $4.9 billion for supplying water and sanitation through 2014. Improved water management strategies could save $1.3 billion to $2 billion.

Health

The health system of a future Palestinian state starts with many strengths, including a relatively healthy population, a high societal value placed on health, many highly qualified health professionals, national plans for health system development, and a strong base of governmental and nongovernmental health care institutions.

Important areas of concern include poor system-wide coordination and implementation of policies and programs across geographic areas and between the governmental and nongovernmental sectors of the health system, many underqualified health care providers, weak systems for licensing and continuing education, and considerable deficits in the operating budgets of the Palestinian Ministry of Health and the government health insurance system (the principal source of health insurance).

Our analysis focused on major institutions that the health care system would need in the first decade of an independent state. In addition, we identified several urgently needed programs for preventive and curative care.

We examined and recommended that priority be given to initiatives in two areas:

- Integrating health system planning and policy development more closely, with meaningful input from all relevant governmental and nongovernmental stakeholders.
- Improving public and primary health care programs, including an updated immunization program, comprehensive micronutrient fortification and supplementation, prevention and treatment of chronic and noninfectious disease, and treatment of developmental and psychosocial conditions.

We estimate that the Palestinian health system would require between $125 million and $160 million per year in external support over the first decade of an independent state.

Education

The future state's education system begins with a strong foundation, especially in the areas of access, quality, and delivery. Access strengths include a commitment to equitable access and success in achieving gender parity, strong community support for education, and leadership that is supportive of both system expansion and system reform. Strengths in the area of quality include willingness to engage in curricular reform, strong interest in and resources for improving pedagogy, commitment to improving the qualifications and compensation of staff, and the perception of schools as a key location for developing students' civic skills and social responsibility. The system is relatively well managed and has some solid data collection capabilities.

Nevertheless, the system faces notable challenges. In the area of access, these include rising levels of malnutrition, homelessness, and general poor health; inadequate facilities and supplies; unsafe schools and routes to schools; lack of special education options for students with special needs; lack of informal education options for school-age students; and the absence of lifelong learning opportunities. Quality challenges include a lack of clear goals and expectations for the system; limited relevance of secondary, vocational, and tertiary programs to Palestine's economic needs; limited research and development capacity and activity; low staff compensation and an emerging administrative "bulge"; and difficulty in monitoring process and outcomes. Delivery is hobbled by a severely underfunded and donor-dependent system, and the limited data on the system are not effectively linked to reform.

Our analysis examined ways in which access, quality, and delivery could be improved, with a long-term goal of positioning Palestine as a powerful player in the region's knowledge economy. We recommend the following three primary goals for the system over the next ten years:

- Maintaining currently high levels of access, while also working within resource constraints to expand enrollments in secondary education (particularly in vocational and technical education and the academic science track) and early childhood programs.
- Building quality through a focus on integrated curricular standards, assessments, and professional development, supported by long-term planning for system sustainability.
- Improving delivery by working with donors to develop streamlined and integrated funding mechanisms that allow the administration to focus on the business of meeting student needs, informed by strong evaluation and backed by significant sustained investment.

We estimate that the Palestinian education system will require between $1 billion and $1.5 billion per year in financing over the first decade of statehood if it is to operate at a level that will support national ambitions for development. (We do not distinguish between donor and national investments.) We recognize that these investment levels are substantial, both in absolute terms and relative to historical spending levels in Palestine (which averaged around $250 million per year during 1996–1999). Our recommendations are based on international benchmarks for spending per pupil in successful education systems. We also offer options for reducing costs should it be necessary to do so.

Economic Development

We examined possible economic development trajectories in an independent Palestinian state during the 2005 to 2019 timeframe, focusing on Palestine's prospects for sustaining growth in per-capita incomes. Prerequisites for successful economic development include adequate security, good governance, adequate and contiguous territory, stable access to adequate supplies of power and water, and an adequate transportation infrastructure. In addition to the prerequisites, four critical issues—transaction costs, resources including internal resources and financing and external aid, the Palestinian trade regime, and the access of Palestinian labor to employment in Israel—will primarily determine the conditions under which the Palestinian economy will function.

Since Palestinian territory has limited natural resources, economic development will depend critically on human capital, with stronger systems of primary, secondary, and vocational education as indispensable down payments on any future economic success. Other important conditions will include Palestinian access to Israeli labor markets and substantial freedom of movement of people and products across the state's borders, including the border with Israel. However, brittle Israeli-Palestinian relations are likely to constrain cross-border movement of Palestinians into Israel for some time after a peace agreement.

Strategic choices made by policymakers at the outset of the new state will markedly affect its economic development. Decisions about *geographic contiguity*—the size, shape, and territorial coherence of a future Palestinian state, the inclusion of special sites or areas, and control over land and resources—will determine the resources that the new state's leaders will have to foster growth and the ease with which Palestinians can engage in business. Decisions about the degree of *economic integration* with Israel in terms of trade and the mobility of Palestinian labor will shape the Palestinian economy, the rate of economic growth, and prospects for employment.

We analyze four development scenarios, each determined by decisions about geographic contiguity and economic integration. We estimate the levels of economic growth that might be achieved under each scenario, given specific levels of international investment.

Under each scenario except the low-contiguity/low-integration case, Palestine could surpass its 1999 per-capita gross national income by 2009 and double it by 2019. Achieving such growth would require significant investment in Palestinian capital stock: Between 2005 and 2019, the Palestinian private and public sectors and the international community would have to invest about $3.3 billion annually, for a cumulative total of some $33 billion over the first decade of independence (and $50 billion over the period 2005–2019).

Under any scenario, domestic private employment would have to grow at a substantial pace (perhaps at an annual average of 15 to 18 percent) between 2005 and 2009 to reach rates of employment last seen during the summer of 2000. These employment rates should be possible once Palestinian businesses are able to operate in a relatively unrestricted environment and are fully able to utilize available resources.

We note that the assumed level of capital investment of $3.3 billion per year is in the same range as the total cost estimates for a port, airport, and connecting road; improvements in the electric power system; the capital costs of expanding water and sewage systems; and even costs of improving health and education, many of which are operating, not investment costs. Thus, the economic analysis of the Palestinian economy provides some comfort that the total of the individual cost estimates is not out of line with overall investment needs.

Donor Funding and the Costs of Creating a Viable Palestinian State

As a frame of reference for the magnitude of funding that may be required from international donors to ensure successful Palestinian development, we considered the cases of Bosnia and Kosovo, two areas where the international community has recently invested very large sums for post-conflict reconstruction. Like the West Bank and Gaza, these two entities suffered considerable damage from conflicts. Both have attracted considerable international interest and assistance. Both have had some success in creating democratic governments and revitalizing the local economies. In the first two years following the signing of peace accords in Bosnia and Kosovo, foreign assistance (grants and loans) averaged $714 and $433, respectively, per person per year.

Applying these per-capita figures to the projected population of West Bank and Gaza, an analogous annual inflow of assistance of $1.6 billion to $2.7 billion would be required in the first year. The level of required assistance would rise to between $2.1 to $3.5 billion by 2014 because of increases in population (see Table S.1). Over

Table S.1
Aid Flows Analogous to Bosnia and Kosovo

Year	Estimated Palestinian Population	Total Aid (millions of 2003 dollars)	
		Bosnia Analogy	Kosovo Analogy
2005	3,761,904	2,688	1,627
2006	3,889,249	2,779	1,683
2007	4,018,332	2,871	1,738
2008	4,149,173	2,964	1,795
2009	4,281,766	3,059	1,852
2010	4,416,076	3,155	1,910
2011	4,547,678	3,249	1,967
2012	4,676,579	3,341	2,023
2013	4,807,137	3,434	2,080
2014	4,939,223	3,529	2,137
Total		31,068	18,813

SOURCE: World Bank, *West Bank and Gaza Update,* Washington, D.C., April–June 2003.
NOTE: The World Bank figures are in then-year U.S. dollars.

the ten-year period between 2005 and 2014, flows of foreign assistance to a new Palestinian state analogous to levels that have been granted to Kosovo and Bosnia would run from $18.8 billion to $31.1 billion. Those levels of foreign investment would be enough to cover the areas examined by our study, with some left over for other areas that were outside the scope of our study (e.g., transportation).

Looking to the Future

At the time of this writing, the prospects for establishing an independent Palestinian state are uncertain. U.S. attention, without which a negotiated settlement between Palestinians and Israelis seems unlikely, has been focused primarily on Iraq and elsewhere to date. However, President Bush recently called for a new state by 2009. U.S. experience in Iraq and Afghanistan can only reinforce the value of having plans in place for the eventuality of an independent Palestine. The death of Yasser Arafat in November 2004, which spurred both Palestinians and the wider world to focus on the future of the region, may yet turn this eventuality into a more imminent reality.

Our book is not a prediction that peace will come soon. However, we believe that thoughtful preparation can help make peace possible. And when peace comes, this preparation will be essential to the success of the new state. This book is designed to help Palestinians, Israelis, and the international community—the United States, its Quartet partners, and Palestine's Arab neighbors—prepare for the moment when the parties are ready to create and sustain a successful Palestinian state.

Abbreviations

ARIJ	Applied Research Institute Jerusalem
CM	cubic meter
CME	continuing medical education
EDZs	economic development zones
EIA	Energy Information Agency
EU	European Union
GDP	gross domestic product
g/l	grams per liter
GNI	gross national income
GNP	gross national product
ha	hectare
HDIP	Health, Development, Information and Policy Institute
ICITAP	International Criminal Investigative Assistance Program (U.S. Justice Department)
IDF	Israeli Defense Forces
IMF	International Monetary Fund
I/PCRI	Israel/Palestine Center for Research and Information
l/d	liters (of water) per day
M&I	municipal and industrial
MAS	Palestine Economic Policy Research Institute
MCM	million cubic meters
MoE	Palestinian Ministry of Education
MOH	Palestinian Authority Ministry of Health
N.A.	not available
NGO	nongovernmental organization
NIS	Israeli shekels

NWC	National Water Council
PA	Palestinian Authority
PASSIA	Palestinian Academic Society for the Study of International Affairs
PCBS	Palestinian Central Bureau of Statistics
PCDC	Palestinian Curriculum Development Center
PFLP	The Popular Front for the Liberation of Palestine
PHG	Palestinian Hydrology Group
PIJ	Palestinian Islamic Jihad
PLO	Palestinian Liberation Organization
PMA	Palestinian Monetary Authority
ppm	parts per million
PR	proportional representation
PRCS	Palestinian Red Crescent Society
PWA	Palestinian Water Authority
QI	quality improvement
QIP	Quality Improvement Project (of the Palestinian Authority Ministry of Health)
RSC	Regional Security Committees
TFP	total factor productivity
TIPH	Temporary International Presence in Hebron
UFW	unaccounted for water
UN	United Nations
UNCTAD	United Nations Conference on Trade and Development
UNDOF	United Nations Disengagement Observer Force
UNDP	United Nations Development Programme
UNEF	United Nations Emergency Force
UNEP	United Nations Environmental Programme
UNESCO	United Nations Educational, Scientific, and Cultural Organization
UNRWA	United Nations Relief and Works Agency for Palestine Refugees in the Near East
UNSCO	United Nations Office of the Special Coordinator in the Occupied Territories
UNSCR	United Nations Security Council Resolution

USAID	The United States Agency for International Development
USBC	U.S. Bureau of the Census
WB	West Bank
WHO	World Health Organization

Glossary

1948 war—first in a series of wars in the Arab-Israeli conflict. It established the state of Israel as an independent state and divided the remaining parts of the British Mandate of Palestine into areas controlled by Egypt and Transjordan

1967 borders—Israel's borders after the 1967 Six-Day War

1967 Six-Day War—war fought in 1967 by Israel on one side and Egypt, Syria, and Jordan on the other. Israel took over the Golan Heights, the Jordanian portion of Jerusalem, the Jordanian West Bank of the Jordan River, and a large piece of territory in northeastern Egypt. Israel still occupies all of these territories except the Sinai Peninsula, which it gave back to Egypt in 1982

1991 Madrid Peace Conference—hosted by the Government of Spain and cosponsored by the U.S. and Russia (then the USSR); proposed two separate but parallel tracks for Israeli-Palestinian peace negotiations, the bilateral track and the multilateral track

1993 Declaration of Principles on Interim Self-Government Arrangements (Oslo I)—*see* Oslo Accords

1994 Protocol on Economic Relations (Paris Protocol)—agreement between Israel and the PLO that laid the groundwork governing the economic relations between the two sides

1995 Israeli-Palestinian Interim Agreement on the West Bank and the Gaza Strip (Oslo II)—*see* Oslo Accords

al-Aqsa intifada—*see* second intifada

Al-Aqsa Mosque—mosque on top of Haram al-Sharif

aquifers—rain-fed underground stores of water that can be utilized through wells and springs

Arab League initiative—plan put forth at the Arab League summit in March 2002 calling for full Israeli withdrawal from all territories occupied since June 1967 and Israel's acceptance of an independent Palestinian State with East Jerusalem as its capital, in return for the establishment of normal relations in the context of a comprehensive peace with Israel

basic education—grades 1–10 (current system)

diaspora—dispersion of a people from their original homeland *distributive* or *rentier* **states**—states that derive all or a substantial portion of their revenue from natural resources, such as petroleum, or from other bulk transfers to their treasury

Fatah—the largest faction of the Palestine Liberation Organization first intifada ("uprising") against Israel. 1987–1993

Geneva Accord (October 2003)—unofficial peace treaty drafted by a group of Israelis and Palestinians and issued in October 2003

graywater—household wastewater from sinks and showers

Green Line—name given to the 1949–1967 division between Israel and the West Bank

Hamas—acronym of Harakat al-Muqawamah al-Islamiyyah (Arabic: Islamic Resistance Movement), a Palestinian Islamist paramilitary and political organization

Haram al-Sharif (Temple Mount)—site in Jerusalem holy to both Muslims and Jews

higher education—formal schooling following completion of secondary school (includes community colleges, colleges, and universities)—*see also* tertiary education

Hizballah—a political and military organization in Lebanon founded in 1982 to fight Israel in southern Lebanon

Mandate Palestine—Palestine governed by the British under a mandate from the League of Nations, 1922–1948

net enrollment rate—number of enrolled same-age children divided by all school-age children, and excluding over-aged and under-aged children

Oslo Accords—The two agreements signed between Israel and the Palestine Liberation Organization in 1993 and 1995

Oslo II (the Taba Agreement)—interim agreement signed in Taba, Egypt, in September 1995

"permeable borders"—can include some limitations on the number of crossing points between Israel and Palestine, as opposed to "open" or "unrestricted" borders.

preparatory education—grades 8–10 (prior system, still a common reference, especially in UNRWA schools

Roadmap—*A Performance-Based Roadmap to a Permanent Two-State Solution to the Israeli-Palestinian Conflict.* Online at http://www.state.gov/r/pa/prs/ps/2003/20062pf.htm, as of June 2004

second intifada (al-Aqsa intifada)—uprising against Israeli in September 2000

secondary education—grades 11–12 (current system)

security barrier—barrier being constructed by Israel between Israel and Palestine

Taba Agreements—*see* Oslo II

tawjihi—graduation examination following grade 12

tertiary education—formal schooling following completion of secondary school (includes community colleges, colleges, and universities)—*see also* higher education

two-state solution—according to UNSCR 1397 (2002), two states, Israel and Palestine, living side by side within secure and recognized borders.

UN Security Resolutions 242 and 338—UNSCR 242 (1967) of 22 November 1967; UNSCR 338 (1973) of 22 October 1973.

CHAPTER ONE

Introduction

C. Ross Anthony, Glenn E. Robinson, Michael Schoenbaum, Steven N. Simon,
and Cynthia R. Cook

This study focuses on a single analytical question: How can an independent Palestinian state be made successful?

Identifying these requirements became a pressing policy need for the United States with the adoption of the "Roadmap,"[1] which calls for a Palestinian state in 2005. President Bush recently revised this timetable and is now calling for a new state by 2009. Following a March 2002 UN Security Council Resolution, which called for the creation of a Palestinian state and was supported by the United States—in June 2002, President George W. Bush expressed explicit U.S. support for creating a Palestinian state.[2] To this end, the United States joined the European Union, Russia, and the United Nations to pursue the Roadmap initiative in 2003. The same year, the Israeli government under Prime Minister Ariel Sharon also formally endorsed the eventual creation of an independent Palestinian state.

When President Bush made his initial declaration, he called for creation of an independent Palestinian state within three years, and the Roadmap was designed to meet this timetable. As this chapter is written, however, the prospect of an independent Palestine is uncertain.[3] Nevertheless, a critical mass of Palestinians and Israelis, as well as the United States, Russia, the European Union, and the United Nations, remains committed to the establishment of a Palestinian state.

This book proposes options for structuring the institutions of a future Palestinian state, so as to ensure as far as possible the state's success. This study does not examine how an independent Palestinian state might be created, nor does it explore the process or terms of a settlement that would lead to its creation. In fact, one of the book's strengths is that by concentrating on factors that are key to making an established

---

[1] The full title of the Roadmap is *A Performance-Based Roadmap to a Permanent Two-State Solution to the Israeli-Palestinian Conflict* and can be found at http://www.state.gov/r/pa/prs/ps/2003/20062pf.htm, as of June 2004.

[2] The Bush administration's support for a Palestinian state represents the culmination of gradual U.S. policy changes dating to the 1991 Madrid Peace Conference and the 1993 Declaration of Principles.

[3] Indeed, in an interview with the Egyptian newspaper *Al-Ahram* published on May 7, 2004, President Bush said that "the timetable of 2005 isn't as realistic as it was two years ago." *The Washington Post,* in an article by Mike Allen and Glenn Kessler (November 13, 2004, p. A01), reported that on November 12, 2004, President Bush set a new goal of "ensuring the creation of a peaceful, democratic Palestinian state alongside of Israel before he leaves office in 2009." "'I'd like to see it done in four years,'" Bush said. "'I think it is possible.'"

Palestinian state successful, it develops conclusions about what must be present both at the beginning and throughout the process to achieve success.

This work should be seen as a living document that will need to respond to the constantly changing realities in the region and that will need to be expanded to cover areas that were beyond the scope of this study. In particular, key areas such as housing, transportation, and energy are not dealt with in this study, although a companion study[4] will deal with them at a community level. A second companion study will deal with security issues not dealt with here.[5] Furthermore, the rapidly changing dynamics in the region and the death of Yasser Arafat demand a deeper analysis of the option for establishing good governance in a new state. The chapter on internal security must also be updated as geopolitical and security realities change and because of changes in international, Palestinian, and Israel leadership.

U.S. experience in Afghanistan and Iraq since 2001 has underscored our conviction that nation-building can only benefit from detailed consideration of governance, security, economic development, health, education, and natural resources, among other factors. Recent experience also clearly demonstrates the need for thoughtful detailed planning if nation-building experiences are to succeed. Furthermore, the lessons of U.S. experience in Iraq indicate clearly that, in order to seize the opportunity to build a state when it arises, advance planning is extremely important. Failure to have feasible options on the shelf can result in lost opportunity at the least and disaster at the extreme. Many of the policy options laid out here—including those in the areas of health, education, and water—can be initiated even before the establishment of a state.

Creating a state of Palestine does not ensure its success. But for Palestinians, Israelis, and many around the world, it is profoundly important that the state succeed. If the failed or failing states of recent years—Somalia, Yugoslavia, the Democratic Republic of the Congo, and Afghanistan—have endangered international security, consider the perils in the Middle East and beyond of a failed Palestine, or the costs and risks of one so weak that it must be propped up and policed by the United States and others. The true challenge for a Palestinian state is not that it exist, but that it succeed.

Organization of This Book

In our discussion, we first consider the essentials of a successful state—the nature of the institutions that will govern it and the structures and processes that will ensure its internal security. We then describe the demographic, economic, and critical water resource on which a Palestinian state can draw, while also identifying factors that can

---

[4] Doug Suisman, Steven N. Simon, Glenn E. Robinson, C. Ross Anthony, and Michael Schoenbaum, *The Arc: A Formal Structure for a Palestinian State,* Santa Monica, Calif.: RAND Corporation, MG-327-GG, 2005.

[5] See RAND's forthcoming *Building a Successful Palestinian State: Security.*

limit the state's ability to use these resources effectively. Finally, we consider what a Palestinian state must do to strengthen its human capital, through ensuring its citizens health care and educational opportunities.

In each substantive area examined, we draw on the best available empirical data to describe the requirements for success, to identify alternative policies for achieving these requirements, and to describe the consequences of choosing each alternative. We also provide initial estimates of the costs associated with our recommendations over the first decade of independence. The specific methodology in each chapter differs with the nature of the analytic questions and the availability of data. Each chapter describes its individual approach and identifies the constraints and uncertainties that accompany the analysis.

In the remainder of this chapter, we consider goals for a successful Palestinian state in more detail. We then turn our attention to three major issues that cut across all parts of our book: the degree to which movement of people and goods is possible between an independent Palestinian state and other countries, which we refer to as "permeability"; the degree to which the territory of an independent Palestinian state is integral or fragmented, which we refer to as "contiguity"; and the nature of the security arrangements for Palestinians, Israelis, and the region. Finally, we describe the methodology we have used to estimate the costs of the options put forward in the various chapters.

Defining "Success"

In our view, "success" in Palestine will require an independent, democratic state with an effective government operating under the rule of law in a safe and secure environment that provides for economic development and supports adequate housing, food, education, health, and public services for its people. To achieve this success, Palestine must succeed in addressing four fundamental challenges:

- *Security:* Palestinian statehood must improve the level of security for Palestinians, as well as that for Israelis and the region as a whole.
- *Good Governance and Political Legitimacy:* A Palestinian state must be governed effectively and be viewed as legitimate by both its citizens and the international community.
- *Economic Viability:* Palestine must be economically viable and, over time, self-reliant.
- *Social Well-Being:* Palestine must be capable of feeding, clothing, educating, and providing for the health and social well-being of its people.

When a Palestinian state is established, its success is not only important as an end in itself; it could influence the course of political and social reform in the greater Middle East. The failure of a Palestinian state might discourage efforts to bring about reform in the region.

Conditions for Success

Security

The success of an independent Palestinian state—indeed, its very survival—is inconceivable in the absence of peace and security for Palestinians and Israelis alike. Thus an independent Palestinian state must be secure within its borders, provide for the routine safety of its inhabitants, be free from radical subversion or foreign exploitation, and pose no threat to Israel. Moreover, these conditions must be established from the moment of independence. Security is not something that can be built gradually, like infrastructure or industry, but must be in place at the beginning of a new state if that state is to have a chance of succeeding. In fact, as shown in the security chapter (see Chapter Three), it is clear that even before a new state can be established, the present situation will need to improve considerably. Because of the breakdown in security within areas of Palestinian control in recent years, it is hard to see how Palestinians can assume the responsibility and gain the ability to provide adequate security, objectively and in Israeli eyes, without international support and involvement.

Successful security arrangements range from patrol and protection of the borders themselves to workable justice and public safety systems within them. There is no room in this chain for weak links: Internal leniency toward violent extremists will likely lead to Israeli reactions; and failure to monitor and manage who and what enters Palestine can only weaken internal public safety. The borders of an independent Palestinian state, including the degree of territorial contiguity and whether Palestinian territory surrounds Israeli settlements, will significantly affect the success of any security arrangements.

It will take more than Palestinian good faith and effort to meet such standards of security, even under the most favorable conditions. It will also require extensive international assistance and close cooperation among security personnel.

Good Governance and Political Legitimacy

Palestinian national aspirations have evolved over time since the creation of Israel in 1948. Through the establishment of the Palestine Liberation Organization (PLO) in 1964, Palestinians formally rejected the existence of Israel and called for a Palestinian state in the whole of all the territory that was governed by the British under the League of Nations mandate of 1920 (excluding Transjordan). As the "two-state solution" gained legitimacy internationally and among Palestinians living in the West Bank and

Gaza, the PLO formally changed course in 1988, recognized Israel, and proclaimed a Palestinian state based on the earlier UN partition resolution. This evolution in Palestinian goals was pushed further with the 1993 exchange of recognition letters between Israel and the PLO and the establishment of the Palestinian Authority (PA) by the Oslo Accords. Since 1994, however, the PLO has formally committed itself to a two-state solution.[6] Moreover, surveys suggest that some three-fourths of Palestinians in the West Bank and Gaza would support reconciliation with Israel following a peace treaty and the establishment of an independent Palestinian state.[7]

Of course, even a small number of rejectionists can be dangerous, as the past decade has shown. Such factions could target Israel or the Palestinian state and its leadership. In practice, the willingness and ability of the Palestinian state to resist or co-opt such factions will depend on its political legitimacy. Legitimacy, in turn, will depend on a number of factors, including the form and effectiveness of governance; economic and social development; territorial size and contiguity; the status of Jerusalem; and the status and the treatment of Palestinian refugees, particularly those currently living in Lebanon, Syria, and Jordan.[8]

Finally, the way that Palestinians govern themselves will affect the political viability of the new state (as well as its economic vitality and security). The thoroughness with which democratic institutions and processes are established will be critical from the outset—indeed, they are already critical even before the state has been created. Finally, the passing of Yasser Arafat is likely to generate new challenges and opportunities.[9]

Economic Viability

An independent Palestinian state cannot be considered successful unless its people have good economic opportunities and quality of life. Palestinian economic development has historically been constrained, and per-capita national income peaked in the late 1990s in the range of "lower middle income" countries (as defined by the World Bank). Since then, national income has fallen by half or more following the start of the second intifada ("uprising") against Israel in September 2000. An independent Pales-

---

[6] The official Palestinian position today is to create a Palestinian state in the entirety of the West Bank and Gaza, with East Jerusalem as its capital, and living side by side with Israel. Palestinians have also accepted the principle of "land swaps" on a one-to-one basis.

[7] See, for instance, polls conducted by the Palestinian Center for Policy and Survey Research during November 14–20, 2002 (http://www.pcpsr.org/survey/polls/2002/p6a.html, as of May 2004), and during March 14–17, 2004 (http://www.pcpsr.org/survey/polls/2004/p11a.html, as of May 2004).

[8] There are approximately 612,000 Palestinians living in refugee camps in Lebanon, Syria, and Jordan, according to the Palestinian Central Bureau of Statistics.

[9] The pivotal role of sound political and social institutions has been acknowledged by the United States and the European Union and explored by key public policy research groups. RAND has built, in particular, on the work of the Council on Foreign Relations Independent Task Force on Strengthening Palestinian Public Institutions, whose 1999 report was updated in 2003 by its chairman, Henry Siegman. (The update can be accessed at www.cfr.org/pubs/5536_english.pdf as of March 15, 2005.)

tinian state will need to improve economic conditions for its people as immediately and urgently as it will need to improve security conditions.

As we describe in this book (see Chapter Five), there are a number of prerequisites for successful economic development in a Palestinian state. These include security; adequate and contiguous territory (although we assume that the West Bank and Gaza will remain physically separate); stable access to adequate supplies of power and water; adequate infrastructure for transporting goods, both domestically and internationally, and the ability to use it; and an improved communication infrastructure. Since Palestinian territory has limited natural resources, economic development will depend critically on human resources, with stronger systems of primary, secondary, and vocational education as crucial down payments on any future economic success.

Historically, income from Palestinians working in Israel has been an important component of Palestinian national income. However, the degree of access by Palestinians to Israeli labor markets has fluctuated greatly and is minimal at the time of this writing. The extent of such access in the future is another important variable discussed in this book that will affect Palestinian economic development under independence.

A new Palestinian state will not be successful without significant economic development. Such development will require considerable external assistance in the form of investment capital in addition to good governance and human capital formation. It is also difficult to see how the Palestinian economy can flourish unless there is substantial freedom of movement of people and products across the state's borders, including the border with Israel.

Our study indicates that Palestine can succeed only with the backing and assistance of the international community—above all, the United States, the European Union, the United Nations, the World Bank, and the International Monetary Fund. Resource requirements will be substantial for a decade or more. During that period, aid should be invested, not merely consumed. Palestine's institutions and policies should be prepared to absorb many forms of foreign help—e.g., for external and internal security, health care and education, financing needs, and good governance. At the same time, an independent Palestinian state cannot be truly characterized as successful until the amount and scope of external assistance diminishes and the state becomes largely self-reliant.

The requirements for external assistance estimated in this study are considered essential to enable a Palestinian state to succeed. However, the availability of such resources should not be assumed at a time when many donor countries around the world are in, or are just coming out of, a recessionary period that has resulted in very tight budgets. This limited availability of resources places a special burden on the new state and intensifies the need for it to succeed quickly in the eyes of the international community—particularly among providers of private investment capital.

Social Well-Being

A fourth condition for the success of an independent Palestinian state is that the social well-being of its people improve substantially over time. Living conditions and provision of social services including health care and education have declined with Palestinian national income since the outbreak of the second intifada.

The final chapters of this book focus particularly on options for strengthening the Palestinian health care and education systems (see Chapters Seven and Eight). Both systems start with considerable strengths, but also require considerable development in the future. Such development will require effective governance and economic growth, as well as external technical and financial assistance.

Crosscutting Issues: Permeability, Contiguity, and Security

The following discussion highlights three crosscutting issues that will have special influence on the ability of a Palestinian state to achieve the essential conditions for success:

- how freely can people travel to and from an independent Palestinian state, which we refer to as *permeability* of borders
- whether its territory (apart from Gaza's separation from the West Bank) is *contiguous*
- the prevailing degree of *security* and public safety.

These issues affect all of the other issues examined in this book, and they interact with each other as well. It is important to understand how they are intertwined, how they affect key goals, and how they might be reconciled in some optimal way. As a rule, the greater the permeability, contiguity, and security of Palestine, the more likely Palestine will succeed as a state.

Permeability

Movement of people between Israel and Palestine will be crucial to the Palestinian economy by giving labor, products, and services access to a vibrant market and by encouraging foreign (Western and perhaps Israeli) investment in Palestine. On the other hand, a sealed border will undoubtedly affect political viability of the state and its economy. There are also some one million Palestinian citizens of Israel, who will desire access to family, friends, colleagues, and business associates in a Palestinian state and vice versa. An impermeable border would separate them from the Palestinian state.

Obviously, permeability has major implications for security. The more freedom of movement between a Palestinian state and Israel, the more opportunities there will be for the infiltration of terrorists into Israel. Such threats, in turn, will undermine the stability of a final status accord, especially if they lead to Israeli incursions into Palestinian territory.

On the surface, then, permeability could foster economic viability and political legitimacy at the cost of security. Of course, it is not that simple. Better economic and political conditions, thanks in part to permeability, could enhance stability and increase Palestinians' stake in security. On the other hand, sealing off Palestine from Israel will substantially reduce but probably not eliminate suicide attacks or other terrorist threats against Israeli civilians altogether.

In sum, permeability is basic to economic and political viability, as well as to long-term security. But it raises major security issues. If Israel itself deals with the dangers inherent in permeable borders, the potential for conflict would be high. If Israel is to be convinced to entrust others with responsibility for the security of permeable Israeli-Palestinian borders, the demands on the United States and its partners could be substantial and long lasting.

Contiguity

Palestinian political legitimacy and economic viability will depend on contiguity of land no less than and perhaps more than on the permeability of its borders. A Palestine of enclaves is likely to fail. Moreover, political and social development requires that Palestinians be free to move within and among Palestinian territories (e.g., between the West Bank and Gaza). Successful economic development further requires that movement of goods within and among Palestinian territories be as free as possible.

This study concludes that none of the major conditions of success—security, political legitimacy, economic viability, social welfare—can be realized unless Palestinian territory is substantially contiguous. In a territorially noncontiguous state, economic growth would be adversely affected, resulting in poverty that would aggravate political discontent and create a situation where maintaining security would be very difficult if not impossible. In any case, a Palestine divided into several or many parts would present its government with a complex security challenge since a noncontiguous state would hamper law enforcement coordination; require duplicative and, therefore, expensive capabilities; risk spawning rivalries among security officials, as happened between Gaza and the West Bank under the PA; and result in immense operational security problems. Even the most challenging peacekeeping experiences—Cyprus, Bosnia, and Kosovo—might seem easy by comparison.

Security

We explicitly describe options for structuring internal security arrangements in a subsequent chapter of this book. Here, we provide a brief overview of options facing an independent Palestinian state, Israel, and the international community.

Security is a precondition for successful establishment and development of all other aspects of a Palestinian state. The challenge is how to ensure security in order to advance Palestine's economic and political goals while recognizing that extreme security measures inhibit political and economic development.

One critical dimension of security is the trust of Palestinian citizens in the stability of their new state. They must be confident that they live under the rule of law. In our analysis, we explore how to build a judicial and police system on which citizens can rely for safety and equitable treatment.

The other key dimension of security for a new Palestinian state will be protection against political violence. Various groups may reject the validity of the accord with Israel and continue to try to attack Israel to undermine the peace agreement and the Palestinian government that agreed to it. Such groups might also rekindle internal violence. It is to address these possibilities that we will examine external security issues in a forthcoming volume.

Accordingly, we explore how the United States and other countries might reorganize, train, equip, and directly support an internal security force that could defeat challenges to the new state's authorities without resorting to repressive methods.

Estimating the Costs of Success

This book differs from other studies of Palestinian state building because we have estimated the costs of developing institutions for some of the areas we examine. Below we describe the estimating approaches we used. We emphasize that the estimates are approximations; with better data and more clarity about the approaches to be taken, the estimates can be improved. Furthermore, our analysis could not cover all relevant sectors of a Palestinian state. Some important development areas, such as transportation and energy, were outside the scope of the volume but will certainly require considerable resources in their own right. (Some of these issues are discussed at a community level in a forthcoming RAND publication.[10])

RAND has an extensive history of estimating the costs of both U.S. and non-U.S. defense and nondefense projects and, in the process, has developed some of the basic tools and approaches used in creating cost estimates.[11] There are three primary ways in which cost estimating is done, which we refer to as "bottom-up," "parametric," and

---

[10] Suisman et al., 2005.

[11] Much of RAND's research on cost has been undertaken for military weapons systems. See, for example, Harold Asher, *Cost-Quantity Relationships in the Airframe Industry*, R-291, 1956; Brent D. Bradley, R. E. Clapp, and R. L. Petruschell, *A New Cost Model to Support Air Force Long-Range Planning*, P-3133, 1965; David Novick, *Beginning of Military Cost Analysis, 1950–1961*, P-7425, 1988; Ronald W. Hess and H. P. Romanoff, *Aircraft Airframe Cost Estimating Relationships: Study Approach and Conclusions*, R-3255-AF, 1987. RAND has also conducted a great deal of research using cost analysis techniques to estimate the costs for a wide range of civilian projects. See, for example, Edward W. Merrow, Lorraine McDonnell, and R. Y. Argüden, *Understanding the Outcomes of Mega-Projects: A Quantitative Analysis of Very Large Civilian Projects*, R-3560-PSSP, 1988; Bridger M. Mitchell, *Incremental Capital Costs of Telephone Access and Local Use*, R-3764-ICTF, 1989; Craig B. Foch, *The Costs, Effects, and Benefits of Preventive Dental Care: A Literature Review*, N-1732-RWJF, 1981; John L. Birkler and William Micklish, *Comparing Project Investment Costs: A Methodology and Baseline for the Refining Industry*, N-2389-PSSP, 1986.

"analogy." The three methodologies have different levels of data requirements and are appropriate in different situations; all three methods have been used in this book. A brief discussion of the three methods helps to illuminate the complexities of developing cost estimates for this analysis.

Bottom-up estimating involves identifying all of the individual items involved in a project, which are then summed to produce a final estimate for the entire project. Bottom-up estimating for social programs can be an extremely costly process and requires a great deal of research and robust data. For example, in the field of education, bottom-up estimating would ideally start with a needs assessment. Analysts could determine the educational goals of the state, the desired level of education and the fields of study, and the number of students who will need schooling over the next few decades. The next step would be to determine existing current assets and identify any additional assets that would be needed. Data might include the number of existing schools, their physical condition, and the number of students they can serve. Insight would be needed about the number of available teachers, their training, and ways to recruit and train additional teachers. What school supplies—including books, computers, and Internet connections—are available or would be needed?

As the list is developed, costs of incremental investment can be estimated, perhaps by getting bids from construction companies for the cost of schools. This information is collected, the costs are estimated and added, and a total cost estimate is reached.

Parametric estimation involves developing an equation (using some form of regression analysis) in which the changes in the information desired—the dependent variable—are modeled based on known relationships to some group of independent or explanatory variables. These equations are referred to as cost estimating relationships.

Generally, the parametric approach involves developing a database of historical information that can be used as inputs to the model. For example, if the decision were made to invest in a shipping port in Gaza, the costs of such a port could be estimated by taking information from other port construction projects and developing a model including key variables that affected cost. In this case, cost may be affected by the desired size and capacity of the port and the depth of the relevant body of water. Information from the construction of other port projects, the specific details of the site, and the requirements could be used to estimate a likely cost.

Another example of the use of parametric estimating is the development of the cost of educating a student for one year. Large school systems often have these costs available in their budget systems. Thus, to estimate the cost of a school system, the number of students per year would be the independent variable and the dependent variable would be the total cost of educating the group per year. The parametric approach avoids the detail required for a bottom-up estimate but in this case requires gathering data from other school systems on costs per pupil per year and adjusting them for the Palestine case (for example, changing the average teacher's salary).

An approach related to the parametric method is to estimate by analogy. With this approach, an analyst selects a similar or related situation and makes adjustments for differences. Analogy works well when there are reasonable comparisons, or for derivative or evolutionary improvements. Its main advantage over the bottom-up approach is that only the changes or differences must be separately estimated—thus saving time and cost.

However, analysts must have a good starting baseline of similar projects to use this method. For example, they may have a lot of information about the costs of an internal security system in Iraq. Although there are many key differences between Iraq and a likely Palestinian state, the baseline information from the Iraqi case can be adjusted for these differences to derive an estimate using reasoning by analogy. Similarly, knowing the differences between the existing Palestinian security capabilities and the desired ones may allow for the development of an evolutionary cost assessment.

From this discussion, it may seem that the bottom-up approach would provide the greatest fidelity. Indeed, if all the required data could be perfectly captured, that would be the case. However, given the many unknown factors, the difficulty of collecting accurate data, and the difficulties involved in predicting future needs, the bottom-up approach may not necessarily yield a better estimate than the other two methodologies. In addition, omitting requirements is often the largest risk in using this approach. Because of its costs and extensive data, using the bottom-up approach to estimate the costs of a new Palestinian state would require resources far beyond the scope of this study.

Parametric estimating is commonly used in developing cost estimates for new weapons systems where cost estimating relationships between such inputs as weight and material and such outcomes as cost have been developed over a number of years with many data points. The building of a Palestinian state can be compared to situations such as those in Kosovo, Bosnia, and Iraq. However, the number of variables that affect cost is large enough that any relationships developed using this relatively limited number of cases would be of questionable validity.

For the most part, the authors in this volume use the analogy approach, with cost estimates that either assess the cost of evolutionary or derivative changes from the current situation, or they use case studies of situations that are comparable along one or more dimensions. The analogy approach is used in the "Internal Security" and "Health" chapters. Some chapters also list the detailed cost elements that would need to be collected in a bottom-up approach. These elements provide insight into the complex nature of the state-building task. The "Education" chapter provides some bottom-up information. The "Water" chapter uses a previously developed parametric model that the authors have modified based on the scenarios they develop. The "Economics" chapter uses a simple growth model to estimate Palestinian economic growth under different assumptions about economic integration with Israel and territorial contiguity. Two of the chapters ("Governance" and "Demography") do not involve cost estimates, although some of the institutional structures called for in the "Governance" chapter, such as certain issues relating to the justice system, are estimated in the "Internal Security" chapter.

CHAPTER TWO

Governance

Glenn E. Robinson

Summary

To be successful, a new Palestine state will need to be characterized by good governance, including a commitment to democracy, the rule of law, and elimination of the present corruption. An important precursor for good governance is for the state to enjoy a high level of political support and legitimacy in the eyes of its own people. The key variables that will determine such support and the state's legitimacy in the eyes of Palestinians are: the size of the state, the contiguity of its lands, and the nature of its presence in Jerusalem.

Good governance will likewise be enhanced if Palestine's borders are permeable, its economy prosperous, its refugee absorption manageable, its security guaranteed, and its early years bolstered by significant international assistance. Given their mutually reinforcing relationship, the actual practice of good governance in Palestine will contribute to the long-term legitimacy of the state.

To achieve good governance, authoritarian practices and corruption that characterized rule under the Palestinian Authority must not be repeated.

If good governance is to be achieved in a Palestinian state, a number of issues must be addressed: the promotion of the rule of law, the empowerment of parliamentary democracy, and the promotion of meritocracy in the civil service. Specific recommendations on how to promote these goals in Palestine are discussed.

Introduction

The success of Palestinian statehood will depend, in large part, on whether it is characterized by good governance, including a commitment to democracy and the rule of law. A number of factors will help determine the prospects for good governance in Palestine initially.[1] The most important of these is whether or not the state is legitimate in the eyes of the Palestinian people. While the shape and characteristics of any Palestinian state will not please everyone (particularly rejectionists who will

---

[1] Throughout this chapter, "Palestine" refers to a newly created state of Palestine.

settle for nothing less than all of historic Palestine), opinion polls consistently show that a large majority of Palestinians in the West Bank and Gaza are prepared to live in peace with Israel.[2] It is for this critical population mass that the new state must pass the legitimacy test.

A Palestinian state's legitimacy in the eyes of most Palestinians will be based fundamentally on three factors. Those factors are the size and contiguity of the lands of a new Palestinian state and the nature of its presence in Jerusalem. A new Palestinian state is likely to be seen as more legitimate in the eyes its people the more closely its borders follow the "Green Line" (the Green Line is the name given to the 1949–1967 division between Israel and the West Bank), the more contiguous those lands are (apart from the unavoidable separation of the West Bank from Gaza), and the more credible its presence in Jerusalem.[3]

Assuming that basic state legitimacy is secured in a final status agreement with Israel, the foundations and practices of good governance must be established in the new state. This will mean the dealing with many important issues and reversing common practices of the present corrupt and authoritarian Palestinian Authority (PA).[4]

The correction of existing problems needs to be coupled with a vision of what good governance should entail in an independent state of Palestine. The third section of this chapter focuses attention on positive requirements for the rule of law and democratic governance in an independent Palestinian state.[5] We focus on specific recommendations that would help promote the rule of law, empower parliamentary democracy, and bolster bureaucratic meritocracy.

---

[2] Polls conducted by the Palestinian Center for Policy and Survey Research (www.pcpsr.org) and the Jerusalem Media and Communications Center (www.jmcc.org) regularly include questions pertaining to Palestinian acceptance of Israel in the framework of a two-state solution. Typically, about 70 percent of Palestinians in the West Bank and Gaza support such a framework.

[3] These requirements are met in the unofficial Geneva Accord announced in October 2003. The Roadmap for Peace (developed by the United States in cooperation with Russia, the European Union, and the United Nations and presented to Israel and the PA on April 30, 2003) is less clear on these critical elements of Palestinian statehood.

[4] The PA has executive, legislative, and judicial branches. However, for simplicity's sake and conforming to standard practice, we use the acronym PA to refer exclusively to the executive branch of government. References to legislative and judicial branches are clear in context.

[5] The task of reforming PA institutions has received significant attention in recent years. Indeed, such reforms became a prerequisite for restarting peace negotiations between Palestinians and Israelis. Because this book seeks to take the long view of Palestinian governance, we do not discuss near-term considerations in this chapter. Near-term issues have been well covered elsewhere. See, for example, Brown (2002); Shikaki (2003); and various reports by the Independent Task Force on Strengthening Palestinian Public Institutions, sponsored by the Council on Foreign Relations.

The Relationship Between State Legitimacy and Good Governance

State legitimacy and good governance are synergistic. As policymakers and negotiators create an independent Palestinian state in the coming years, it will be essential that this synergy be fully understood if Palestine is to succeed. The greater the legitimacy of the state at its founding, the more likely good governance will take hold; the better governance is in an independent Palestinian state, the more likely the state will retain and consolidate its legitimacy.

A discontinuous and isolated state with control over a relatively small area of the West Bank and without a credible sovereign presence in Jerusalem would likely be rejected by most Palestinians.

The Importance of the 1967 Borders[6]

There is nothing particularly "natural" about the two parts of historical Palestine that remained in Arab hands at the conclusion of the 1948 war. Indeed, it was an article of Palestinian nationalism until the 1970s that the West Bank and Gaza bore no particular significance apart from the whole of mandate Palestine. In part as a reaction to what has been a strong international consensus in support of Israel's 1967 borders, the Palestine Liberation Organization (PLO) gradually changed its policies, beginning haltingly in 1974, to accept the 1967 borders as the basis for a two-state solution. The acceptance of the 1967 borders is now part of a broad Palestinian national consensus, as reflected in numerous surveys and case studies. Rejecting the 1967 borders would bring into serious doubt the basis upon which the Palestinians have recognized Israel and have entered into negotiations to end the conflict permanently.

The foundational documents noted in the 2003 Roadmap for Peace, including UN Security Council Resolutions 242 and 338 and the Arab League peace initiative, either explicitly or implicitly adopt the 1967 borders as the borders separating Israel and Palestine, leaving open the possibility of small and mutually acceptable land swaps. The negotiations that took place in Taba, Egypt, in January 2001 discussed an Israeli annexation of about 4 percent of the West Bank in exchange for an equal amount of swapped land annexed to Palestine from Israel. The unofficial "Geneva Accord" announced in October 2003 posited an Israeli annexation of about 2 percent of the West Bank in exchange for ceding to Palestine an equal amount of territory adjacent to Gaza.[7]

Maximizing the land area of an independent Palestinian state has practical consequences beyond state legitimacy. While this book finds that large and rapid refugee

---

[6] The 1967 borders (West Bank, Gaza, and East Jerusalem) comprise about 23 percent of the lands of historic Palestine, as delineated under the British Mandate for Palestine.

[7] The actual percentages vary according to how one defines the West Bank, which may or may not include East Jerusalem and the northwest section of the Dead Sea. For a good discussion of competing percentages, see Pressman (2003).

settlement in Palestine would pose serious problems for the new state, some resettlement will no doubt occur. In addition, Palestinians in the West Bank and Gaza have one of the highest birth rates in the world. Land, and the resources that come with it, will be needed to accommodate potentially large increases in population following statehood (see Suisman et al., 2005).

Contiguity of Land

Also, basic land contiguity in Palestine will be essential not only for the pragmatic operation of the state, but for its sense of legitimacy as well. A discontinuous Palestine will not enjoy popular legitimacy, and will therefore risk greater levels of internal dissent.

The construction of large numbers of Israeli settlements in the occupied territories has made the construction of a contiguous and viable new independent state vastly more difficult. The U.S. government and the larger international community view these settlements as "illegal" under international law.[8] Certainly the expansion of settlements helped undermine the Oslo peace process and made the already distant prospect of good governance in Palestine even more remote.

Jerusalem and State Legitimacy

Jerusalem will also play a key role in Palestine's legitimacy in the eyes not only of Palestinians, but also of Arabs and Muslims more generally. A new Palestinian state that does not have a viable sovereign presence in Jerusalem will likely lack basic state legitimacy in the eyes of its people. This is true for two reasons. First, as noted above, the 1967 boundaries—which include East Jerusalem—have gained a central place in the Palestinian national consensus over peace. Second, given the religious importance to all Muslims of the Haram al-Sharif, or Temple Mount, in Jerusalem, particularly the al-Aqsa Mosque, no Muslim leader of Palestine could afford to formally relinquish all of Jerusalem. Indeed, some form of Muslim-Palestinian sovereignty over the Muslim holy sites in Jerusalem will almost certainly be critical to selling a peace deal to the larger Muslim world.

There have been numerous plans conceived over the years concerning the best way to share Jerusalem between Israel and Palestine, including split sovereignty in East Jerusalem or shared sovereignty over the whole of the city of Jerusalem. Some have proposed redrawing the municipal boundaries of Jerusalem to make the sharing of sovereignty more appealing to both sides.[9] We make no recommendation in this book

---

[8] Official U.S. policy holds that these settlements violate the Fourth Geneva Convention of 1949 and are "inconsistent with international law." Excerpts from the State Department's legal finding may be found at http://www.fmep.org/documents/opinion_OLA_DOS4-21-78.html. While political language has softened over time (e.g., settlements as "an obstacle to peace"), the United States has never repudiated its formal opinion that such settlements are illegal and, indeed, has reconfirmed it on a number of occasions at the United Nations. President Bush's April 2004 letter to Prime Minister Sharon indicated that a final negotiated peace would likely leave in place some Israeli settlements in the West Bank, but did not renounce the official legal opinion set out above.

[9] See, for example, IPCRI (1999).

over which plan for Jerusalem is best. Rather, we observe that without a credible sovereign presence in Jerusalem, the new state of Palestine will suffer a serious legitimacy deficit among its people that, in addition to other problems, will make the emergence of good governance and a stable state problematic.

Legitimacy and Violence

A negotiated solution that fails to achieve political support is likely to exacerbate political violence in at least two ways. First, the various Islamist and nationalist groups that have carried out violence in recent years will feel free to continue, and perhaps increase, the violence. If the legitimacy of the new state is doubtful, they would likely find a more supportive population. A second source of renewed political violence would be the regional Palestinian refugee community, primarily in Lebanon, Jordan, and Syria. Since effective refugee absorption would be impossible under these conditions, refugees would express their opposition to a settlement that in their eyes is "unsatisfactory" and to the Palestinian government that negotiated it. While most of this opposition would no doubt be political in nature, it might lead to an increase in violence against local states where refugees are concentrated. Hashemite rule in Jordan would be especially susceptible to such instability.

Good Governance Bolsters Legitimacy. Just as state legitimacy is a necessary ingredient for good governance, good governance is vital to state legitimacy. Poor governance has contributed to the failure of many states. However, the "tools" of legitimacy are not enough. Good decisions are also crucial, as are strong, transparent, and accountable institutions and a healthy and vibrant civil society.

Although the impact of perceptions of state legitimacy on governance may be felt immediately, the effect of governance on legitimacy would only be apparent over a longer period of time. However, even with the time lapse, there is still no question that, if endemic corrupt and authoritarian political practices continue, they will drain Palestine of its political legitimacy, both in the eyes of its own people and in the eyes of the international community.

Other Variables Affecting Good Governance

In addition to land and its contiguity, and security, which have all been discussed, other factors noted below also will affect the legitimacy and a new Palestinian state including:

- **Permeability.** The permeability of the borders of the new state will significantly affect its economic development.
- **Security Arrangements.** The arrangements that govern security inside Palestine, and between Palestine and its neighbors, will critically affect all sectors of Palestinian life, including governance. Good governance in the absence of adequate security is difficult to envisage (see Chapter Three).

- **Refugee Return.** The issue of refugees returning to Palestine after statehood will also complicate the challenges of good governance. There are nearly four million UN-registered Palestinian refugees and their descendants.[10] After statehood is established, up to a million refugees may wish to "return" to the West Bank. Many will likely come from Lebanon.[11] Palestinians in Lebanon are the poorest and least educated of all the diaspora Palestinian populations and will constitute a significant strain on the ability of the new state to prosper.[12]

Refugee return has three important components. First is the *scale* of the return, ranging anywhere from tens of thousands to over a million. Second is the *quality* of the returnees. Educated, middle-class Palestinians returning from Jordan pose a very different set of issues from the more likely scenario of the Lebanese return. Third, and most important, is the *timing* of the return: a rapid return versus a gradual return over many years.

The worst-case scenario in terms of straining Palestinian governance is a large, rapid return of the most destitute Palestinians in the diaspora. Such a scenario would have obvious and deleterious effects on all sectors under consideration. Conversely, a relatively small and gradual return of refugees would put far less strain on new state institutions in Palestine. Indeed, if the scale of return is small and the timing of the return gradual, then the quality of the returnees matters less.

Over the long run, returning Palestinians will no doubt provide a source of vitality and dynamism to the state. And refugee absorption will provide a legitimacy litmus test for the new state. Inevitably, a Palestine that is seen to be dragging its heels on refugee absorption will likely lose some of its legitimacy in the eyes of the diaspora community. This catch-22 is unavoidable.

In the short run, however, the stresses and strains of a large returning population will degrade the ability of new state institutions to function well. Indeed, one can imagine a state of emergency arising if the new state institutions are overwhelmed. Certainly a significant and immediate return from Lebanon must be anticipated, even with the likely negative consequences for governance and security it would entail in the near term.

---

[10] About 750,000 Palestinian refugees were created in the 1948 war. Only those refugees who met the UN's definition of a Palestinian refugee and who registered in a timely manner with the UN are formally considered refugees. They and their direct descendants currently number about four million. In addition, about 300,000 Palestinians, some of whom were refugees from 1948, were displaced in the 1967 war. The "displaced persons" from 1967 have a different legal status than the "refugees" from the 1948 war. For an interesting overview of the Israeli-Palestinian negotiations on this issue, see Tamari (1996).

[11] The vast majority of Palestinian refugees hail from what is now Israel proper, so speaking of a "return" to the West Bank is not exactly accurate. Palestinian refugees in Lebanon come mostly from northern Israel, especially the Galilee region.

[12] We need not concern ourselves with the issue of refugees returning to Israel proper. Such a return, if it happens at all, is likely to be small and should not affect the viability of a Palestinian state in the West Bank and Gaza.

- **Economic Development.** Almost always, greater per-capita wealth leads to a higher likelihood of democratic governance. Economic development in Palestine will increase the chances for good governance in the new state; however, for political as well as economic reasons, it is important that economic development in Palestine not be entirely state-directed, but rather occur primarily in the private sector; this will help reduce corruption and cronyism. Resource flows into Palestine can help or hinder economic development and good governance, depending on where they are directed.

- **International Support.** As with economic development, sustained international support will be critical if a new Palestine is to be democratic. That support takes two forms. First, and most obviously, Palestine will need significant international aid to overcome its present stagnation and to deal successfully with the world's largest refugee population. Such an aid package would be most effective if it is part of the settlement itself.

  However, the international community must carefully balance its aid to Palestinian state and society. Both state and society will have legitimate needs for assistance. Funneling all or most assistance through the Palestinian government directly, however well-intentioned, will diminish the prospects for democracy and good governance. International aid is critically important, but it needs to be distributed carefully to have the desired impact.

PA Authoritarianism

If authoritarianism in the PA were a "natural" condition, then trying to create good governance in Palestine would be a hopeless task. Fortunately, such need not be the case. Although the Palestinian national movement under Yasser Arafat always had a strong authoritarian streak—not uncommon in revolutionary or underground movements—three political factors in the 1990s and the first few years of the new century reinforced this tendency. Two of them were transitional in nature. While a full discussion of PA authoritarianism can be found elsewhere (e.g., Robinson, 1997, chapter 7), a brief overview of the problem is necessary in order to gauge the problems and prospects of reforming such a system. We argue that given the transitional nature of much of PA authoritarianism, reform is possible. However, policymakers must be cognizant of a third, structural, cause of PA authoritarianism that can be ameliorated with prudent assistance.

A first transitional cause of PA authoritarianism concerned the consolidation of power by the new Palestinian regime created by the Oslo Accords. The Oslo Accords led to the return to Palestine from Tunisia of the PLO power structure and bureaucracy, along with about 100,000 supporters of this outside elite.[13] While PLO officials both inside Palestine and those returning from decades of exile shared many familial and

---

[13] A good overview of this elite split based on survey polls can be found in Shikaki (2002). Shikaki uses the term "Old Guard" instead of Oslo elite and the analytic categories vary somewhat, but the basic distinction is the same.

political ties, they tended to have evolved on different political trajectories. "Inside" Palestinian leaders tended to favor more institutionalized and less personalized politics, and they were considerably more committed to democracy in theory and in practice than their "outside" or "Tunisian" counterparts. In order to neutralize the power of potential rivals, the "old guard" (to use Khalil Shikaki's phrase) adopted authoritarian practices. As the integration of the "outsiders" into West Bank/Gazan society strengthens and post-Arafat politics are sorted out, it is likely that this distinction—and the authoritarian practices it produced—will diminish with time.

A second transitional cause of PA authoritarianism concerned the vast imbalance of power between the PA and Israel. As a weak "term taker," the PA was powerless to stop Israel from creating more settlements, which generated significant ill will among Palestinians both toward Israel and toward their government's impotence. The doubling of settlers during the Oslo years is another example of the results of the power imbalance. The PA responded in two authoritarian ways: It quashed voices of dissent directed at the PA, and it engaged in populist demagoguery itself to deflect criticism. While the imbalance of power will not disappear with the establishment of a successful Palestinian state, its political importance will be mitigated. In other words, the significant international intervention needed to launch a Palestinian state and see it through will itself displace the consequences of the power imbalance.

A third cause of PA authoritarianism concerns the type of political economy built in Palestine in the 1990s. As more than 70 percent of PA government revenues came from bulk transfers to the treasury—and not from the direct taxation of its own people—the PA's political economy came to look increasingly like those of the oil states in the region.[14] In such "rentier"[15] or "distributive" states, no social contract is developed between state and society over the relationship between taxation and expenditures. Instead, the one-way flow of resources from state to society tends to promote personalized authoritarianism. It is critical for the democratic development of Palestine's political economy that steps be taken to reverse this trend. Primarily, this means that capital transfers to Palestine should go increasingly to nongovernmental and local government sectors and less into central government coffers.

Requirements for Good Governance in Palestine

Good governance will most easily emerge out of the existing reality and existing institutions. The Oslo Accords created, altered, and empowered a series of institutions,

---

[14] Jordan has been particularly adept at securing strategic rents from the United Kingdom, the Gulf states, and the United States, depending on the era. Typically, Jordan relied on strategic rents to cover half of its government budget every year, and its foreign policy would shift depending on who was providing the rents. For a fascinating study of this history, see Brand (1994).

[15] An excellent review essay on the rentier argument may be found in Cooley (2001).

laws, rules, and relationships governing the West Bank and Gaza. Policymakers will be best served by fixing these extant institutions (in some cases radically), as opposed to trying to apply a boilerplate solution from scratch. The institutional base for creating a functioning democracy in the Arab world is present in Palestine. Finally, the recent death of Yasser Arafat provides a rare opportunity to strengthen Palestinian institutions in order to ameliorate the excessively personalized nature of PA governance under Arafat.

According to evidence presented at a recent World Bank conference[16] the Palestinian Authority's effectiveness, ability to control corruption, and institution of a viable rule of law have plummeted over the past several years. As Figure 2.1 indicates, by 2002 the Palestinian Authority was in the bottom 16 percent of countries worldwide in controlling corruption, among the bottom 12 percent in government effectiveness, and in the bottom 50 percent in the effectiveness of the rule of law. As Figure 2.2 illustrates, the percentage of Palestinians who believe there is significant corruption in Palestinian Authority institutions has increased from approximately 50 percent in 1996 to 85 percent in 2004.

By way of overview, the Oslo Accords created a strong office of the presidency (*ra'is*) and an 88-member parliament, neither of which had existed in the West Bank

Figure 2.1
Governance Indicators for the West Bank and Gaza

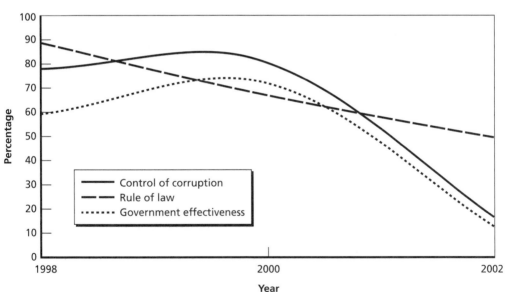

SOURCE: World Bank Governance Research Indicators Dataset.
RAND *MG146-2.1*

---

[16] Douglas Ierley, *Law and Judicial Reform in Post-Conflict Situations: A Case Study of the West Bank Gaza,* World Bank Conference, July 2001, p. 17.

Figure 2.2
Palestinian Perceptions of Corruption

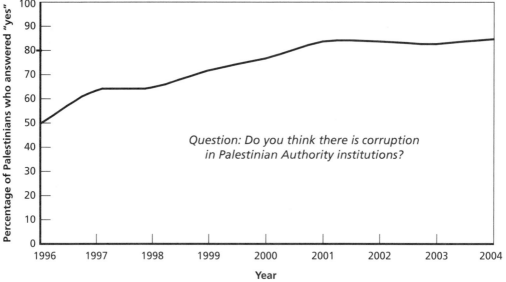

SOURCE: Palestinian Center for Policy and Survey Research.
RAND *MG146-2.2*

and Gaza under Israeli occupation. Elections judged free and fair by international observers were held in January 1996. While the parliament (Palestinian Legislative Council, or PLC) had significant powers on paper, in reality it was actually subservient to the president and his cabinet. A prime minister's office was added in 2003 with an eye toward diminishing the power of the president and creating more of a parliamentary system rather than a presidential one. The system remains a hybrid one today. A Palestinian judicial system that included both civil and criminal courts predated the Oslo Accords but had largely become irrelevant under Israel's occupation. Reviving a judicial branch of government was a major challenge during the 1990s and remains a key challenge today. Ministries reporting to the executive branch of government became large and influential under the Oslo Accords. They were highly politicized at the top levels, and employment within the ministries served as a principal source of regime patronage.

In short, Palestine already has executive, legislative, and judicial branches of government in place. The main challenge, therefore, is not to create new institutions but to reform, strengthen, and make functional existing institutions by taking existing realities into account. We find that there are three basic challenges to reforming Palestine's governmental framework so that it can promote and sustain good governance: promoting the rule of law, empowering parliamentary democracy, and promoting meritocracy in the civil service. We treat each topic in turn and raise critical questions that will need to be answered before a new state can be governed successfully.

Promoting the Rule of Law

There is no substitute for the rule of law as the cornerstone of good governance. Among other things, the rule of law enhances accountability in governance, bolsters trade and promotes economic growth, and provides citizens the security to lead productive lives. Given the right political context, Palestine has the necessary attributes to sustain the rule of law. Its reasonably educated population; middle class sensibilities; and an increasingly distant history of civil courts, secular law, and a (relatively) independent judiciary make it feasible to create a society based on the rule of law. However, the growing political and social fragmentation in Palestine over the past four years will impede a transition to rule of law. Two elements will be essential to the development of rule of law in Palestine: empowering the judiciary and adopting a good constitution.

Empowering the Judiciary. A non-shari'a judiciary charged with applying secular civil and criminal law has existed in Palestine since the mid-19th century, although its modern variant dates from the British Mandate. A major judicial problem in recent decades, including under the PA, has been the lack of true authority vested in the judiciary. Reforms are required to empower the judiciary and are within the realm of the possible. Creating a strong and independent judicial branch that can check executive power will require four steps.

Step 1: Empower Judges. Judges have been underpaid and disempowered by the PA (and under Israeli military rule as well). Although Supreme Court justices are supposed to have lifetime appointments, the PA has dismissed several chief justices. While a judicial council is supposed to oversee the judiciary, in practice those powers were usurped by the executive branch, often through fiat.[17]

Under strong internal and external pressure, Arafat took steps in 2002–2003 to reverse the degradation of judicial independence, especially through the promulgation of the law on judicial independence that had been sitting on his desk for four years. This effort needs to be expanded by his successors. In structuring a Palestinian state, a firm commitment to the empowerment and independence of the judiciary is a necessary step toward the realization of the rule of law.

An empowered judiciary (and concomitant enforcement of judicial decisions) will also be a boon to private property rights in Palestine. The institution of private property is firmly rooted in Palestinian law, in both the West Bank and Gaza.[18] Private property rights exist on paper and are zealously guarded by Palestinian citizens. However, respect for the rule of law concerning those property rights has not always been practiced by the PA. For example, the PA's heavy-handed confiscation of private property to establish the Gaza airport remains a powerful symbol of distrust of government

---

[17] For an overview of the legal system under PA rule, see Brown (2003), chapter 2; and Robinson (1997).

[18] The Ottoman Land Law of 1858 explicitly recognized large private land holdings, an institution continued during the British Mandate and its successors. Small private land holdings known as *mulk* lands were codified in Islamic law centuries earlier and were enforced by the Ottomans in Palestine and elsewhere. In short, the institution of private property has a long history in Islam.

in Gaza. The new government of Palestine must do better than the PA in protecting property rights.

It should be stressed that enforcement of commercial law, particularly contracts, is an important and necessary component of the respect for private property. Indeed, this is the sine qua non for building a prosperous and fair private-sector economy. A vibrant, independent, and strong judicial branch is essential for the protection of private property and commercial activities already guaranteed under law.[19]

Step 2: Integrate the West Bank and Gaza Legal Systems into a Single Set of Laws. In brief, Gazan law is a holdover from British common law introduced under the British Mandate in the 1920s, whereas West Bank law is primarily a reflection of the French Napoleonic law adopted by Jordan and implemented in the West Bank during Jordanian rule (1950–1967).[20] A number of steps have been taken in recent years to try to integrate these two very different systems into a unified whole, some developed under World Bank, U.S., and Australian auspices. Much remains to be done, however, and this must be a high priority in the new Palestinian state in order to promote the rule of law.

Step 3: Repair the Infrastructure. An appropriate physical infrastructure is necessary for the proper functioning of courts. Put bluntly, the physical infrastructure of the judicial system is decrepit. The two major courthouses in Gaza and Ramallah are in severe disrepair; the regional courthouses are worse. It is difficult to cultivate respect for rule of law when the physical symbols of the law are in a state of disrepair. In addition to the poor condition of courthouses, many important internal functions (such as archiving documents and transcribing trials and decisions) are in dramatic need of modernization. Some improvements to the physical infrastructure were made under the PA, but much more needs to be done. Indeed, a large international investment in building new courthouses using modern technologies would go a long way toward providing tangible, physical proof of the commitment to the rule of law in the new state.

Step 4: Enforce Legal Decisions. Legal decisions should be enforced in a consistent and transparent manner. The inconsistent and politically driven enforcement of both civil and criminal legal decisions breeds contempt for the rule of law. The judiciary is incapable of compelling enforcement of decisions alone, and the executive branch has been at the root of this problem. Lecturing executive authorities on respect for the rule of law is not the remedy. Rather, the key to compelling enforcement of legal decisions is to make police and security forces accountable to the legislative branch of government.

---

[19] A number of studies have focused on these issues. Private-sector development has been a major concern of the World Bank; see, for example, World Bank (2002). Likewise, the Israel/Palestine Center for Research and Information (I/PCRI) focused its attention on private property and commercial law in the PA during the 1990s. See, for example, Molkner and Hamid (1994) and Kalman et al. (1997). These and other works can be found at www.ipcri.org.

[20] Both areas also have an overlay of Israeli military orders, but those laws were enforced by Israeli tribunals and officials, not by Palestinian civil and criminal courts.

Answering to parliament in an open fashion would lead to higher levels of enforcement than is currently the case in a closed system dominated by the executive branch.

Adopting a Good Constitution. A well-constructed constitution is necessary for the rule of law to succeed. A Basic Law was promulgated by President Arafat in the spring of 2002, having been passed by the Palestinian Legislative Council five years earlier. In many states, including Israel and the United Kingdom,[21] a Basic Law is a functional substitute for a constitution. Nevertheless, a draft constitution was released a month later by the PLO under Nabil Sha'th's direction. A more current iteration of the draft constitution was released in February 2003 and was amended the next month in order to accommodate a new office of prime minister.[22]

There are two schools of thought about a final Palestinian constitution. The first school wants the Palestinian constitution to look a lot like constitutions elsewhere in the Arab world, with an overly strong executive branch and a substantive formal recognition of Islam as the official religion of the state. The second school wants a truly liberal, democratic constitution along Western lines that does not merely mimic uninspired Arab constitutions. The Palestinian legal and legislative communities prefer the second model, but face considerable political opposition from other quarters.

The current draft constitution leaves many significant powers in the hands of the president, among them foreign affairs (including negotiations with Israel), military and security matters (as "supreme commander"), the power to appoint and dismiss the prime minister, and the power to dissolve parliament. Most Palestinian reformers seek to have the presidency become a more ceremonial office, but that has not yet occurred. In November 2004, as Arafat was on his deathbed, top PLO and PA officials stripped the presidency of key powers, especially regarding control over security forces, and gave them to the office of the prime minister. It falls to the parliament to codify constitutionally these and other steps to transform the relationship between president and prime minister.

Empowering Parliamentary Democracy[23]

The idea that a functioning democracy is essential to good governance has become orthodox. On paper, Palestine currently has a relatively democratic system—indeed, relatively free and fair elections were held in 1996. However, three steps must be taken to enhance parliamentary democracy in the context of actual statehood: empower-

---

[21] Indeed, the PA's Basic Law was superior to those of the United Kingdom and Israel. Unlike the UK's, the PA's Basic Law is written, and it is more comprehensive than Israel's. Also, it should be noted that several Arab countries, including Saudi Arabia, preferred the use of the term "Basic Law" over "Constitution" for their own political reasons. We thank Nathan J. Brown for this insight.

[22] The current draft constitution can be found at www.jmcc.org.

[23] There is a robust debate in academic circles concerning sociocultural barriers to democracy in the Arab-Islamic world. Some authors argue that elements within Islam and/or tribal-clan cultures militate against the adoption of modern democratic institutions. Other scholars have rebutted these assertions, primarily on the grounds that they

ing the legislature, adopting a single-district proportional representation system, and strengthening the powers of the new office of prime minister.

Empowering the Legislature. The Palestinian Legislative Council, like all parliaments in the Arab world, is an important venue for discussion and debate, but it lacks significant real powers. To have a functioning democracy, Palestine must have a parliament with real powers, and parliamentary power anywhere can be judged by a single criterion: the power of the purse. Parliaments that have real budgetary authority have real power; parliaments that lack real budgetary authority lack real power. Although the executive branch of the PA is legally mandated to submit budgets to the PLC, it has often done so late and as a mere formality. PLC votes have mattered little. In short, the PA, not the PLC, made most important budget decisions. Thus, for democracy to emerge in Palestine, the parliament must be given true budgetary authority.

Adopting a Single-District Proportional Representation System. Electoral districts have emerged as a significant issue in Palestinian legislative elections. The major problem is that Palestinian electoral districts are highly fragmented. For example, Israel has twice the population and four times the geographic size as Palestine. Yet while Israel is a single district in a proportional representation (PR) system, Palestine has 16 electoral districts, each with its own "first-past-the-post" winner-take-all system. The Palestinian electoral system devised for the 1996 elections is chaotic and needs to be reformed. Slicing a tiny country like Palestine up into 16 electoral districts has complicated the political process because it has encouraged tribalization. Local familial notables without national standing could be—and were—elected to parliament under such a system. Conversely, national movements with broad support suffer under such a system and are thus more inclined to take their politics outside the legal process. Palestine would be better served by a single district proportional representation electoral system.

Empowering broad national movements at the expense of tribal chiefs and clan elders has an added benefit. It will compel these movements to have a vested interest in settling their political differences within the confines of parliamentary rules,

---

reify abstractions and do not give enough credence to the pragmatic and evolving ways in which any religious or cultural group actually practices its belief system. Still other scholars reject such cultural approaches to understanding democracy as inconsequential when compared with more important and more explanatory variables. Without entering this broader debate, we assume that neither the fact that most Palestinians are Muslim nor that most Palestinians enjoy strong extended family (clan, tribe) networks will decisively work against democracy in Palestine. In other words, while there are serious obstacles to democracy in Palestine, neither Islam nor familial structures count among them. We posit this based on the actual experience of elections in the West Bank and Gaza over many years. In addition to the parliamentary and presidential elections of 1996, Palestinians in the West Bank and Gaza have participated in vigorous and democratic elections in universities, professional associations, and local jurisdictions for three decades. Islamic groups have not only participated in these elections, they have often done quite well, and have accepted the results. The same thing is true for members of Palestinian clans (singular, *hamula*), although Palestinians have rarely politically mobilized in elections along clan lines. In sum, whatever the truth of general arguments of Islam and democracy in the Arab-Muslim world, at least in the case of the Palestinians, such sociocultural realities have not inhibited democratic practices. The boldest statement of sociocultural impediments to democracy in the Arab world can be found in Kedourie (1992). More-scholarly treatments of the subject can be found in Salame (1994); Brynen, Korany, and Noble (1995 and 1998); and Esposito and Voll (1996).

which often include compromise through coalitional politics. Put more bluntly, adopting a single-district PR system may make it possible to tame the politics of those in Hamas willing to work within a legitimate system. A PR approach would enhance the prospects for co-opting Hamas into participating in Palestine's governance, rather than encouraging further radicalization and violence. Playing electoral games—such as micro-districting—intended to disempower national movements like Hamas will only encourage the polarization of Hamas in the new Palestinian state.

A further advantage of a PR system in Palestine would be to downplay the cleavage between the West Bank and Gaza. The current system locks in a structural division between the two, further aggravating centrifugal forces between them. Under the current system, the West Bank has twice the population of Gaza, 11 districts to Gaza's 5, and 51 seats in parliament to Gaza's 37. The population disparity will likely grow in the future because refugees will most likely be resettled in the West Bank. Such a situation could engender resentment among Gazans at the West Bank's domination of politics, even though on a percentage basis Gaza has greater parliamentary representation than its population share alone would warrant.

A two-district PR system in which both the West Bank and Gaza have their own single districts would present the same disadvantages. That is, such a system would tend to aggravate the existing cleavage rather than to lessen any differences. Devising a two-district system would create a series of practical problems as well. Assigning each district an equal number of seats in parliament would disadvantage the more populous West Bank. Assigning the number of seats on a straight population split would tend to encourage the West Bank bloc to act in concert, out-voting Gaza on all important issues. Moreover, refugee absorption will likely be done entirely in the West Bank, rapidly altering the population balance and creating new tensions with Gaza as the West Bank increases its percentage of representatives.

Under a PR system, each political party would have the flexibility to adjust its electoral lists according to different criteria, including geographic origin. No doubt this would still lead to more representation from the West Bank, as befits its larger population, but the cleavage would not be codified structurally. Moreover, political parties that are based on ideologies and philosophies instead of familial ties and geography are by nature less concerned about the geographic origins of their candidates. Thus, by privileging ideology over primordial ties, a political culture that reflects this advantageous hierarchy is more likely to emerge and be strengthened.

Strengthening the Office of Prime Minister. Under pressure internally from Palestinian reformers and externally from the United States and Israel, the PA created the position of prime minister in March 2003. As noted above, the powers of the prime minister were significantly strengthened on the eve of Yasser Arafat's death. However, these changes have not been codified by the parliament, nor do they go far enough. To enhance the prospects for good governance in Palestine, the distribution of powers between the president and prime minister will need to be clarified and reordered.

Consistent with the type of parliamentary democracy described above, Palestine will need to have a more empowered prime minister and a more ceremonial position of president. This would also be consistent with the political system Palestinians know well—Israel—where the prime minister is the head of government and the president is the ceremonial head of state. An added benefit of advocating an empowered prime minister is that this is consistent with the wishes of the internal reform movement in Palestine. However, given the Palestinian conviction that a strong president is essential in negotiations with Israel, a fully empowered prime minister should not be expected until after statehood.

Promoting Meritocracy in the Civil Service

Good governance requires that those who make and implement policies be competent in their duties and transparent in their actions. Palestine has an abundance of highly trained and capable technocrats both inside the West Bank and Gaza and in the diaspora. A number of these technocrats have been employed by the PA, although many more have been reluctant to serve in the PA's ministries.

Those who have served have often been ineffectual due to the overtly politicized and personalized decisionmaking process. By the end of 2002, 84 percent of Palestinians viewed the PA as corrupt, a number that had doubled in only six years.[24] The corruption is grounded in the personalized nature of power and appointments, where rank in the hierarchy was trumped by ties to Arafat. A dramatic example of this was the departure of the Palestinian Minister of Agriculture, who resigned in protest because his deputy—a man close to Arafat—kept countermanding his orders without penalty.

A merit-based civil service in Palestine is essential for good governance. Creating such a service is not impossible; it has been done in many countries around the world. Indeed, Palestine does have a merit-based civil service on paper, but its full implementation has been blocked to date. A patronage-driven bureaucracy allows leaders to maintain power through the distribution of jobs and resources based on personal loyalty. Creating an atmosphere that ensures a certain level of autonomy for technocrats to carry out their duties relatively free of intrusive politicking is a necessary condition for good governance to materialize in Palestine.[25]

Costs

Most chapters in this book present estimates of the costs required to strengthen the specific Palestinian institutions discussed in those chapters. This chapter does not, for several reasons.

---

[24] Shikaki (2003), p. 6.

[25] Palestine would do well to learn from Japan about building an autonomous technocratic civil service protected from the winds of politics. See Johnson (1982).

Many government activities, while important, are beyond the scope of this study. For example, the Palestinian Foreign Ministry or Ministry of Finance will need a budget for attracting investments from abroad. The government will also need to hold elections and set up and operate a national parliament. However, these activities represent just a small portion of the total costs of governance.

Some of the largest governance-related costs are discussed in other chapters. For example, costs associated with strengthening the Palestinian judicial system, including the courts and police, appear in Chapter Three. Chapters Six, Seven, and Eight discuss and provide cost estimates for various functions that the Palestinian government will either perform directly or oversee, such as regulating water safety, health care facilities and providers, and the educational system. Chapter Five discusses how government policies can encourage economic and social development, and provides growth estimates for a variety of scenarios.

Good governance will affect nearly every area of Palestinian life. The following chapters provide greater detail.

Conclusion

Our findings on good governance in Palestine may be summarized as follows:

- State legitimacy is a most important element for promoting good governance in Palestine. Without a high level of legitimacy in the eyes of its own people, Palestine will have no chance to practice good governance. The most important elements for state legitimacy will be determined in the negotiations: the size of Palestine, its territorial contiguity and border permeability, and the status of Jerusalem.
- The actual practice of good governance including the elimination of corruption, will help ensure Palestine's long-term legitimacy both in the eyes of its own people and in the view of the international community. Good governance in this context means full democracy under the rule of law.
- A Palestine that is crafted in a way that fails to promote good governance and basic state legitimacy will likely be an endemic source of violence and instability.
- Good governance will also be affected by the vitality of the economy, the level of security, the size and rate of refugee absorption, and the amount and nature of international assistance.
- For the rule of law to be practiced, Palestine must legally empower the judiciary, fully integrate and unify the legal systems in Gaza and the West Bank, significantly upgrade the physical infrastructure of its courts, and enforce legal decisions in a consistent and transparent manner.

- Good governance in Palestine will be positively affected by the adoption of a liberal constitution as advocated by the professional legal establishment in Palestine.
- Parliamentary democracy will be enhanced by giving the legislature full budgetary authority; adopting a single district, proportional representation electoral system; strengthening the office of the prime minister as the head of government; and transforming the office of the president to a largely ceremonial, head-of-state position.
- Good governance will be strengthened through the promotion of meritocracy in the Palestinian civil service.

Bibliography

Brand, Laurie A., *Jordan's Inter-Arab Relations: The Political Economy of Alliance Making,* New York: Columbia University Press, 1994.

Brown, Nathan J., "The Palestinian Reform Agenda," *Peaceworks,* No. 48, Washington, D.C.: United States Institute of Peace, December 2002.

———, *Palestinian Politics After the Oslo Accords: Resuming Arab Palestine,* Berkeley: University of California Press, 2003.

Brynen, Rex, Bahgat Korany, and Paul Noble, eds., *Political Liberalization and Democratization in the Arab World,* Volumes 1 and 2, Boulder and London: Lynne Rienner, 1995 and 1998.

Cooley, Alexander A., "Booms and Busts: Theorizing Institutional Formation and Change in Oil States," *Review of International Political Economy,* Vol. 8, No. 3 (Spring 2001), pp. 163–180.

Esposito, John L., and John O. Voll, *Islam and Democracy,* New York and Oxford: Oxford University Press, 1996.

Ierley, Douglas, *Law and Judicial Reform in Post-Conflict Situations: A Case Study of the West Bank Gaza,* St. Petersburg, Russia: World Bank Conference, July 2001.

Israel/Palestine Center for Research and Information's (IPCRI), *Projections for Jerusalem's Future,* Jerusalem: IPCRI, May 1999.

Johnson, Chalmers A., *MITI and the Japanese Miracle: The Growth of Industrial Policy, 1925–1975,* Stanford, CA: Stanford University Press, 1982.

Kalman, Daniel, et al., *Commercial Contract Enforcement in the Palestinian Territories,* Jerusalem: IPCRI, February 1997.

Kedourie, Elie, *Democracy and Arab Political Culture,* Washington, D.C.: The Washington Institute Press, 1992.

Molkner, Keith, and Ra'ed Abdul Hamid, *The Legal Structure for Foreign Investment in the West Bank and Gaza Strip,* Jerusalem: IPCRI, October 1994.

Pressman, Jeremy, "Visions in Collision: What Happened at Camp David and Taba?" *International Security,* Vol. 28, No. 2, Fall 2003, pp. 5–43.

Robinson, Glenn E., *Building a Palestinian State: The Incomplete Revolution,* Bloomington and Indianapolis: Indiana University Press, 1997.

Salame, Ghassan, ed., *Democracy Without Democrats? The Renewal of Politics in the Muslim World,* London and New York: IB Tauris, 1994.

Shikaki, Khalil, *Building a State, Building a Peace; How to Make a Roadmap that Works for Palestinians and Israelis,* Washington, D.C.: The Saban Center for Middle East Policy at the Brookings Institution, December 2003.

———, "Palestinians Divided," *Foreign Affairs,* January/February 2002, pp. 89–105.

Suisman, Doug, Steven N. Simon, Glenn E. Robinson, C. Ross Anthony, and Michael Schoenbaum, *The Arc: A Formal Structure for a Palestinian State,* Santa Monica, Calif.: RAND Corporation, MG-327-GG, 2005.

Tamari, Salim, *Palestinian Refugee Negotiations: From Madrid to Oslo II,* Washington, D.C.: Institute for Palestine Studies, 1996.

The World Bank, *Long-Term Policy Options for the Palestinian Economy,* Washington, D.C.: July 2002.

CHAPTER THREE

Internal Security

Kevin Jack Riley, Seth G. Jones, Steven N. Simon,
and David Brannan with Anga R. Timilsina

Summary

Internal security will be critical to the viability of a Palestinian state. However, it is unlikely that the Palestinians will be able to set up an effective internal security system on their own; the United States and the international community will need to help. In this chapter we examine the Palestinian internal security system and offer options that the United States and the international community could pursue to help the Palestinians develop an effective internal security system capable of providing public order and domestic stability, as well as improving peace with Palestine's neighbors. We conclude the following:

- The Palestinian internal security system is in disarray. Though it was never highly functional, its capacity has been further eroded in recent years. Facilities have been destroyed, a number of personnel have been killed. Many internal security functions have been assumed by Israel.
- Terrorist and militant organizations pose a grave threat to both interstate security (through attacks against Israel and multinational troops that might be sent there) and intrastate security (through violent opposition to legitimate authority). Suppression of these organizations, to the extent they cannot be co-opted into the political process, will be the most pressing internal security concern.
- Two areas in which the United States and the international community could make valuable contributions are supporting the administration of justice and the formation of a competent and law-abiding internal security capacity. By "internal security," we mean dismantling groups that seek to undermine constitutional authority or use violence to change the political order. Support for the administration of justice and internal security will require the reorganization of the existing welter of security services and the separation of law enforcement departments that investigate common crimes and patrol the streets from counterterrorist, counterintelligence and counter-subversion agencies.
- In the broadest terms, options for U.S. and international assistance in these areas range from financial support for construction of new facilities, equipment, and training to the deployment of police or military personnel.

- More specifically, assistance for the administration of justice should aim to facilitate the emergence of an independent judicial system by funding construction of courthouses, police stations and jails, and providing legal texts, computers, forensic laboratories, and the kind of equipment that police need to carry out their law enforcement duties. A more intensive program would include deployment of international police, and vetting and recruiting judges, prosecutors, police officers, and others involved in the administration of justice.
- Assistance in the realm of internal security would entail technical advice on how best to restructure the existing labyrinth of security services as well as transfer or procurement of essential equipment. The United States and others could conduct training, monitor and evaluate performance, and assess compliance with human rights standards.
- RAND estimates overall reconstruction costs to be at least $600 million per year, and as much as $7.7 billion over ten years.

Introduction

Perhaps the most important indicator of Palestine's success will be the degree to which security prevails there. If the halting and uncertain transition to stable democracy in Iraq has shown anything, it is that in the absence of security, civil society cannot survive, let alone thrive. This means, first and foremost, that Palestinian citizens must feel safe in the streets and in their homes. In a successful state, they would be confident that they enjoy equal recourse to law enforcement if they are robbed or injured by criminals, that crimes will be investigated swiftly and professionally, and that a criminal justice system will adjudicate such cases fairly and with due process. Citizens of the new state would be correspondingly confident that they will not be subjected to political persecution under cover of judicial or police authority.

At this point, Palestinians are far from enjoying this sort of security. Thus, the first objective of this chapter is to show how a structure for the effective and impartial administration of justice can be built in Palestine. Among other factors, the analysis explores the infrastructural, training, equipping, staffing, and monitoring requirements for the development of a judicial and police system in a society that has never had one.

Just as the citizens of Palestine must enjoy a palpable sense of personal security, the democratic political order that will—hopefully—be established prior to independence must be secured against the challenge of political violence. Given the level of internecine violence that now marks Palestinian society and the striking incapacity of the Palestinian Authority to monopolize the use of force, the possibility of armed confrontation between opposition movements and the state after independence cannot be disregarded. The proliferation of heavily armed militias and gangs and a spreading ethos that favors suicidal violence as a mode of political self-expression are harbingers of a potentially grim and turbulent future. The increasingly permeable boundary between authorized law enforcement and paramilitary entities and terrorist organizations darkens this picture even more.

The present study, which focuses on the decade following independence, assumes that much of this intramural violence will have been stanched prior to statehood. Indeed, if it is not, there is unlikely to be a Palestinian state. Nevertheless, the possibility that constituent groups will reject the validity of the final status accord with Israel that created the state—and by implication the Palestinian government that was party to it—is undeniable. It is also possible that a well-established opposition group, like Hamas, will support an insurgency in pursuit of a religiously based political and social order that a majority of Palestinian voters would reject. A variety of other such rationales for insurrection could plausibly be postulated, especially in an environment where poverty is widespread, and there is no recent tradition of trust in governmental authority or belief in its primacy.

Hence the focus in this chapter is on the requirements for state security. Specifically, we ask how best to restructure the existing welter of security-related entities, ensure that they are not only well-trained and equipped, but accountable and transparent in their operations and in the strongest position possible to stave off or counter violent challenges to the constitutional authorities of the new state.

Our discussion has four parts. First, we provide a historical overview that highlights key issues since the 1993 Oslo Accords. Second, we identify the most important challenges confronting the Palestinian internal security system, including conditions that might engender renewed internal strife. Third, we outline options for an effective internal security system that helps promote domestic order and a durable peace with Israel. Fourth, we discuss the costs associated with those options.

Historical Overview

This section offers a brief overview of the key historical issues since the September 1993 *Declaration of Principles on Interim Self-Government Arrangements* (Oslo Accords) and the May 1994 *Agreement on the Gaza Strip and the Jericho Area*. The dates are important because they mark the beginning of limited Palestinian autonomy in the area of internal security. Prior to the Oslo Accords, the Palestinians lacked an autonomous police force and criminal justice system, both of which functions were provided by the Israeli government.

Phases of Internal Security

The evolution of the Palestinian internal security system can be divided into three phases. During the first period, lasting from the Oslo Accords until approximately late 1995, Palestinian security forces were constituted mostly from members of the Palestinian Liberation Army and Gaza refugees. However, the Palestinian Authority failed to create effective institutions and the security forces gradually lost support. Corruption, mismanagement, and human rights violations quickly eroded their credibility.

During the second period, lasting from approximately 1996 to the beginning of the al-Aqsa intifada in 2000, there were sporadic efforts at reform. However, the Palestinian security institutions suffered from a notable lack of "process." Corruption was still rampant, and people with resources were able to establish their own private justice. Security courts became the preferred method of prosecuting accused spies, opposition figures, and many criminals. Such trials were not subject to public oversight and disregarded due process.

The third major period began with the al-Aqsa intifada in 2000, during which members of the Palestinian internal security forces participated in anti-Israeli violence. These actions enjoyed strong public support. In consequence, however, Israeli Defense Forces (IDF), took over virtually all security functions, destroyed much of the police infrastructure, and killed police officers involved in the uprising.

Terrorist and Militant Groups

The salient internal security issue has been the activity of numerous terrorist and militant organizations.[1] Between 1993 and 2003, 1,188 people were killed by terrorist attacks in Israel, the West Bank, and Gaza; over 60 percent of those were between 2001 and 2003.[2] Several major organizations have been active over the last decade: Tanzim, al-Aqsa Martyrs Brigades, Hamas, Palestinian Islamic Jihad, the Popular Front for the Liberation of Palestine, the Democratic Front for the Liberation of Palestine, and Hezbollah.

Tanzim is a loosely organized militia of Fatah, the largest faction of the Palestine Liberation Organization (PLO). The organization has been involved in violence during the al-Aqsa intifada, and its members played prominent roles in two previous cycles of violence: the Nakba riots of May 2000 and the "Tunnel Riots" of September 1996.

---

[1] Used in this context, *terrorist group* refers to any substate organization that uses violence—or the threat of violence—against noncombatants to achieve political aims or motives. Defining terrorism and terrorist groups is a highly contentious endeavor, particularly in the context of the Israeli-Palestinian conflict. We have designated Hamas, PIJ, Tanzim, al-Aqsa Martyrs Brigades, PFLP, and Hezbollah as terrorist groups because they use violence (including suicide attacks) against noncombatants. This is consistent with the U.S. government's definition. See, for example, U.S. Department of State (2003), p. 99.

[2] The figures are from the Casualties and Incidents Database. They include the following years and numbers: 1993 (25), 1994 (215), 1995 (46), 1996 (78), 1997 (42), 1998 (21), 1999 (9), 2000 (31), 2001 (193), 2002 (356), 2003 (172).

The *al-Aqsa Martyrs Brigades* are an armed faction affiliated with Fatah, which emerged after the start of the al-Aqsa intifada. They have carried out numerous attacks on Israelis, worked closely with other groups, and deployed the first female suicide bomber of the intifada.

Hamas, whose declared goal is an Islamic state in Palestine, has been a key combatant since the early stages of the first intifada. Its robust social and political infrastructure has since enabled it to expand its support base from Gaza into the West Bank.[3] This organization is an important rival for power within Palestine and has periodically challenged the supremacy of the Fatah-oriented Palestinian Authority. In the wake of Yasser Arafat's death, Hamas has declared that it still will not participate in elections, raising again the question of its transformation into a normal political party. Since the late 1970s, several radical Palestinian Islamic factions have acted under the rubric of *Palestinian Islamic Jihad* (PIJ). The PIJ Fathi Shikaki faction, which likewise calls for an armed struggle to establish an Islamic state in Palestine, has been active as well.

Violent groups of a secular bent exist as well. *The Popular Front for the Liberation of Palestine* (PFLP), a Marxist-Leninist group founded in 1967 by George Habash, has conducted attacks against Israelis—including the October 2001 assassination of Israeli Tourism Minister Rehavam Ze'evi. It sees itself as "a progressive vanguard organization of the Palestinian working class," with the aim of "liberating all of Palestine and establishing a democratic socialist Palestinian state."[4] The *Democratic Front for the Liberation of Palestine,* which was founded in 1969 when it broke away from the PFLP, is a secular Marxist-Leninist group whose members believe that Palestinian goals can only be achieved by a popular uprising throughout the Arab world led by the proletariat.

Finally, *Hezbollah,* a Shi'ite militant organization and Lebanese political party, has targeted Israel from Lebanon with the support of Syria and Iran since the early 1980s. It has adopted a "strategic partnership" with Palestinian groups through joint training in Lebanon on guerrilla warfare, political coordination, intelligence-sharing, and the transfer of some weapons and financial assistance.[5] Hezbollah is judged by the United States and Israel to be the most capable of the terrorist organizations now operating in the region.

The IDF asserts that it has severely degraded the capacity of these terrorist groups. (This claim does not apply to Lebanese Hezbollah.) In particular, the army believes that Palestinian bomb-making capabilities have been severely reduced by capturing or killing of some of the most experienced bomb engineers.[6] According to IDF staff, roughly 90 percent of the terrorist attacks for which there is pre-incident intelligence are thwarted. Jaffee Center expert Shlomo Brom (BGen ret.) argued that, "'Defensive

---

[3] Mishal and Sela (2000); Hroub (2000).

[4] For an excellent review of these and other Palestinian rejectionist organizations, see Strindberg (2000).

[5] Strindberg (2003); Sobelman (2003).

[6] Interview with senior officials, Israeli Defense Forces, May 23, 2003.

Shield' has accomplished most of its aims. Much of the terrorist infrastructure has been destroyed. And while precise figures are not yet known, it appears that hundreds of Palestinian gunmen have been killed and many others wounded."[7] Some IDF officers went further, stating that Operation Defensive Shield was successful in reestablishing Israeli deterrence.[8] Nevertheless, attacks by Hamas, PIJ, al-Aqsa Martyrs Brigades, and other groups continued throughout 2004, although at a vastly lower tempo.[9] The persistence of attacks is an indicator of powerful motivation and the ability, albeit degraded, to replace personnel who are removed from the scene through death or capture.

The Palestinian Security Structure

The domestic security forces were officially created in May 1994 following the signing of the Israeli-Palestinian Agreement on the Gaza Strip and the Jericho Area.[10] The agreement established several branches: Civil Police, Public Security, Intelligence, Emergency Services and Rescue, and the Coastal Police. In September 1995, the Israeli-Palestinian Interim Agreement added two more branches: the Preventive Security Service, which dealt with subversion, and the Amn al-Ri'asah, which was charged with protecting Yasser Arafat, then president of the Palestinian Authority (PA).[11] By 2004, the security apparatus in the West Bank and Gaza had expanded to include additional services such as military intelligence and military police.

Despite the upheaval of the intifada, as well as strong European, American, and domestic pressure for security sector reform, Yasser Arafat retained virtually exclusive control over the Palestinian security forces until his death in November 2004. To prevent challenges to his authority, he encouraged conflict and competition between the various branches and individual leaders of the security services.[12] Following Arafat's death, the Palestinian Authority leadership controlled the security forces.

Table 3.1 illustrates the functions of Palestinian security institutions as of 2004.[13] The Civil Police handles routine law enforcement functions, e.g., traffic control and public safety; the National Security Force patrols borders, but also has municipal patrol duties; the Preventive Security Service deals with subversion and violent political dissidents; the Coast Guard's mission is to detect and stop smuggling of contraband and ensure maritime safety; and the Civil Defense serves as the fire and rescue service. In addition, there are several intelligence services: General Intelligence gathers intel-

---

[7] Brom (2002).

[8] Goodman (2002); Henkin (2003); Levitt and Wilkas (2002).

[9] See, for example, the data from the Casualties and Incidents Database.

[10] *Agreement on the Gaza Strip and the Jericho Area* (1994), Article VIII, Article IX, and Annex I.

[11] Usher (1996); Weinberger (1995); Sayigh (1995).

[12] Luft (2000, 2002); Blanche (2001).

[13] For a description of the Palestinian security services, see Luft (1999).

Table 3.1
Palestinian Internal Security Forces

Security Force	Function
Civil Police (Al-Shurta)	Keeps public order, directs traffic, and arrests common criminals
National Security Force (Al-Amn al-Watani)	Guards checkpoints, patrols borders, and conducts joint patrols
Preventive Security Service (Al-Amn al-Wiqa'i)	Handles subversion, counterespionage, and dissident organizations
Coast Guard (Shurta Bahariya)	Patrols territorial waters off of Gaza Strip
Civil Defense (Al-Difa'aal-Madani)	Conducts rescue and fire services
General Intelligence (Mukhabarat Salamah)	Gathers intelligence and conducts counterespionage operations
Military Intelligence (Istikhabarat al-Askariya)	Arrests and interrogates opposition activists and investigates other security bodies
Special Security Force (Al-Amn al-Khass)	Gathers information about opposition groups and monitors other security bodies
Presidential Security Service, Force 17 (Al-Amn al-Ri'asah)	Protects Arafat and other top PA officials, and arrests opposition activists and suspected collaborators with Israel

ligence inside and outside the Palestinian territories and conducts counterespionage operations; Military Intelligence arrests and interrogates opposition activists; and the Special Security Force gathers intelligence on the Palestinian Authority's other security services and monitors their activity. Finally, the Presidential Security Service, (PSS or Force 17), serves as the personal security of top PA leaders. The PSS also suppresses opposition activists and individuals accused of clandestine collaboration with Israeli security services. The duplicative nature of this grab bag of police and paramilitary organizations reflects their fundamentally political origins and purposes.

Administration of Justice

During the period of Israeli administration from 1967 to 1994, Palestinian courts did not handle security or political cases. Rather, East Jerusalem came under the jurisdiction of Israeli domestic law, and Israeli military courts and military committees retained jurisdiction over criminal matters in the West Bank and Gaza.[14] This changed in 1993 following the Oslo Accords, when a Palestinian criminal justice system was created that included a legal system, courts, and a ministry of justice.[15]

The current Palestinian legal system is an amalgam of British, Ottoman, Jordanian, and Israeli laws. All of Palestine practiced a form of British common law during

---

[14] Zureik (1988).

[15] For an overview of the Palestinian justice system, see UNSCO (1999).

the Mandate period. However, in the years following 1948, the legal systems in the West Bank and Gaza Strip diverged. The West Bank, then under Jordanian control, followed the Hashemite Kingdom in adopting French-based civil law. The legal system in Gaza, which was under Egyptian military administration, retained its British flavor. The Palestinian Authority has also established comprehensive laws that apply to both Gaza and the West Bank, while a number of Ottoman and Israeli laws and decrees persist in both regions. The Palestinian Legislative Council has the authority to draft and adopt laws that apply to the whole Palestinian Authority. Furthermore, the judicial system encompasses an array of courts—Conciliation, District, Municipal, and High Courts—that have jurisdiction over all levels of criminal infractions and civil claims. In addition, the State Security Courts and Military Courts have jurisdiction over cases involving threats to internal and external security, including crimes by civilians against security forces and suspected Israeli collaborators. Islamic shari'a courts adjudicate personal status cases. Finally, the Ministry of Justice oversees the administration and structure of the courts and judiciary and is home to an attorney general who is appointed by the president.

Internal Security Challenges

By any objective measure, Palestinian security and justice institutions are deficient in their structure and operation. The general problems include a lack of independence from the political structure, a lack of oversight by and accountability to democratically elected legislative structures, political patronage, and a lack of resources to create professional security organizations that meet modern standards of performance. (These deficiencies and their consequences are covered in more detail in other places throughout this section.) These serious problems will not be remedied overnight.

The physical capital of the security forces has been destroyed since the al-Aqsa intifada began in September 2000.[16] Despite Palestinian Authority promises to restructure the security forces and reduce the number of services, there is no evidence that this has been done. Installations such as police stations in the West Bank and Gaza have been closed or destroyed by the Israeli Defense Forces. For instance, after Hamas gunmen entered an Israeli settlement in Gaza in October 2001 and killed two Israelis, the IDF responded by demolishing ten Palestinian police posts located nearby.[17] Israel has justified these attacks against Palestinian installations by accusing members of the Palestinian security forces of taking up arms against Israelis and failing to crack down on organizations such as Hamas and PIJ.[18] Indeed, there is significant evidence of

[16] Luft (2001, 2002).

[17] Dudkevitch and Lahoud (2001).

[18] On Fatah and the al-Aqsa intifada, see Rabbani (2001) and Paz (2001).

collusion between the Palestinian Authority security forces and anti-Israeli terrorists. Examples include cooperation between PIJ, Hamas, and the PA's General Intelligence and Preventive Security Service in the Jenin area, Tulkarm, Ramallah, and Nablus.[19] Furthermore, the Israeli reoccupation of significant portions of the West Bank has crippled the security forces' ability to perform even such perfunctory duties as directing traffic, patrolling cities, or investigating nonterrorist-related crimes.

In sum, the Palestinian security forces, which were never highly effective to begin with, have been weakened in at least three ways: Their physical infrastructure (buildings, weapons caches, police posts) has been destroyed; they have lost control and authority over significant portions of the West Bank and Gaza; and the Palestinian Authority has neglected to consolidate the vast security apparatus. The lack of institutional reforms to the security apparatus in Palestine, combined with the physical damage to the infrastructure, ensures the need for much reorganization and rebuilding.

Against the backdrop of these significant incapacities, the new state may find itself beset by intensified internecine violence. One or any combination of three plausible scenarios could bring this about. First, most conceivable variations on a Palestinian-Israeli final status accord will leave one or another rejectionist group unsatisfied and prepared to continue the fight against Israel.[20] Indeed, if a large part of the Palestinian population believes that a peace settlement failed to meet the minimum requirements of statehood, it will be difficult for a Palestinian government to co-opt members of militant groups. Recognizing that the Hamas charter may well be revised or reinterpreted in the wake of a peace accord, its currently accepted text warns: "Initiatives, the so-called peaceful solutions, and international conferences to resolve the Palestinian problem all contradict the beliefs of the Islamic Resistance Movement. Indeed, giving up any part of Palestine is tantamount to giving up part of its religion. There is no solution to the Palestinian problem except by Jihad."[21] Some militants are dedicated to the destruction of Israel and the reconstitution of pre-1948 Palestine. The IDF estimates that several hundred Palestinian militants are dedicated to combat against Israel and several thousand more actively support the infrastructure by offering money, transportation, housing, religious indoctrination, equipment, or training, and occasionally attacking IDF forces.[22]

Several factors may complicate efforts to counter irredentist violence. Deteriorating economic conditions in a Palestinian state, worsened by the return of refugees competing for scarce resources, could strengthen the leverage of organizations, such as

---

[19] See, for example, the documents captured by the IDF during Operation Defensive Wall, which are published on the IDF's web site at www.idf.il.

[20] These "rejectionist groups" would invariably lose power and prestige in the event of the formation of a Palestinian state. For a review of these groups and their individual focus, see Strindberg (2000).

[21] Hamas (1988), Article 13.

[22] Interview with senior official, Israeli Defense Forces, May 23, 2003.

Hamas, that sponsor both armed wings and massive social service efforts.[23] Under these conditions Hamas, in combination with other disaffected factions, could exploit social and economic dislocation in Palestine and win support for a violent challenge to the authority of the elected leadership. Another trigger for violence could be supplied by the large international presence that would descend on Palestine after independence. The UN and NGO presence, already large, would probably balloon. The deployment of U.S. or other international peacekeeping forces along the borders of a Palestinian state or in other areas could lead to violent attacks by armed groups against such troops, bases, or other symbolic structures—as happened in Lebanon in the 1980s and now in Iraq, where international NGO personnel are targeted by Sunni terrorists.

Competition for control of the new state and/or disputes over its ideological foundation could spark internecine fighting or even a civil war, with neighboring countries proffering support for rival factions. Khalil Shikaki maintains that if the Palestinian Authority suppresses internal opponents, it risks "being seen, if successful, as an Israeli lackey or even another Sa'd Haddad [the commander of the South Lebanon Army created by Israel in the late 1970s to provide security for northern Israel]."[24] If unsuccessful, it faces civil war. Although the PA and Palestinian militant organizations have worked assiduously to avoid armed confrontation with each other over the past decade, the PLO has historically been involved in violent confrontations with the Jordanian and Syrian armies, Lebanese militias, and Palestinian factions, such as those led by Abu Musa and Abu Nidal.[25] There were also sporadic periods of confrontation in the 1990s, such as after the February and March 1996 suicide bombings in Israel.[26]

Although the Palestinian Authority has maintained good relations with Egypt and Jordan, several other states could threaten the power of a Palestinian government, depending on the nature of a peace settlement and the makeup of the government. Syria and Iran, for example, have provided financial support, training, safe haven, and weapons to such organizations as Hamas, Palestinian Islamic Jihad, and PFLP.[27] There is also evidence that Saudi Arabia and other Arab states have supplied funding and encouragement to Palestinian militant organizations.[28] Consequently, these states could become disaffected with a Palestinian government and attempt to destabilize or overthrow it through covert activity, perhaps through Iran and Syria's relationship with Hezbollah.[29] A peace accord that resolves the status of the West Bank and Gaza but not the Golan Heights may increase the likelihood of Syrian intervention.

---

[23] Mishal and Sela (2000).

[24] Shikaki (2002a), p. 104.

[25] Kimmerling and Migdal (2003), pp. 240–273; Rubin and Rubin (2003), pp. 37–99.

[26] Mishal and Sela (2000), pp. 75–76; Davis (1996); Battersby (1996a).

[27] On Iranian and Syrian support for Palestinian groups see U.S. Department of State (2003), pp. 77, 81; Jane's Terrorism Intelligence Center; Levitt (2002, 2003).

[28] Mishal and Sela (2000).

[29] On Hezbollah's relations with Syria and Iran, see Warn and Strindberg (2003) and Goldberg (2002).

These challenges could be compounded by the territorial configuration agreed upon as part of a final status accord, which in turn will set the overall context for Palestinian internal security and administration of justice arrangements. As noted elsewhere in this report, the greater Palestine's territorial contiguity the more efficiently it can be administered. Conversely, the costs of a noncontiguous state are demonstrable. Palestinian authorities, for example, have dealt with the division of Palestine between the West Bank and Gaza by duplicating services. Many ministries, including those responsible for internal security, have deputies for both areas. The construction of a land corridor connecting Bayt Hanun in the northern part of Gaza with Hebron in the West Bank, which was discussed during the Camp David and Taba negotiations, would improve contiguity challenges by facilitating movement between the areas without eliminating them entirely.[30]

Although the continuing presence of Israeli settlements in an independent Palestine is unlikely, and it is somewhat improbable that Palestine would agree to the sort of territorial dispensation that would retain Israeli sovereignty over settlements within the West Bank, these contingencies cannot be ignored. If the settlements remain, the Israelis would face the challenge of securing their safety. The Palestinians would need either to create self-standing security forces in the Palestinian areas that are isolated by the settlements or to address the logistical challenges of quickly moving Palestinian police and security forces through Israeli checkpoints to respond to incidents in Palestine. As one planning representative argued: "It is very difficult to plan, let alone complete, Palestinian infrastructure with the settlements."[31] Although in theory it is possible to build connecting corridors through the settlements, such an approach would be expensive and difficult to maintain. If some Israeli settlements remained and international peacekeeping forces were deployed to Palestinian territory to assist the government, these forces would need to liaison with the Israeli forces securing the settlements.

A final issue is the security barrier that is currently being constructed near the Green Line[32] separating Israel from Palestinian territory, around Jerusalem, and in various areas within Palestinian territory. The barrier was officially approved by the Israeli Defense Cabinet in July 2001, following the recommendations of a steering committee headed by the director of the National Security Council. Construction began shortly thereafter to prevent the infiltration of terrorists and criminals into Israel.[33]

The barrier has the potential to both exacerbate and improve the security situation. Supporters argue that it will increase Israel's ability to deny entry to suicide attackers.[34] Reducing suicide attacks would remove a major irritant in Palestinian-

---

[30] See, for example, "Moratinos Nonpaper" (2002), p. 83.

[31] Interview with senior Palestinian planning official, May 21, 2003.

[32] The Green Line is the name given to the 1949–1967 division between Israel and the West Bank.

[33] *Seam Zone* (2003). Also see B'Tselem (2002b) and Sheehan (2003).

[34] Elizur (2003); Steinberg (2003); Bennet (2002); *Seam Zone* (2003).

Israeli relations and, on balance, reduce the security burden on the Palestinian internal security service.[35]

Administration of Justice

States derive much of their legitimacy from their ability to maintain public order. The Palestinian Authority's law enforcement and judicial infrastructure has been eroded beyond what can remotely be considered effective.[36] As a World Bank report concluded: "Legal development, despite public statements to the contrary, has not been a priority of the Palestinian Authority."[37] The justice system has little independent power and accountability over the Palestinian security forces. The security forces have consistently and systematically ignored orders of the Palestinian High Court to release detainees, judges have been removed from office without reasonable cause, and the courts are powerless to prosecute security officers who commit crimes.

Moreover, the absence of external accountability over the security forces has led to numerous allegations of human rights abuses.[38] For example, Human Rights Watch argues that the security forces have frequently detained Palestinians without charges or trial, arrested alleged collaborators without sufficient evidence and warrants, denied prisoners access to lawyers and independent doctors, tortured prisoners under interrogation, and refused to prosecute vigilante killings against suspected Israeli collaborators.[39] According to the Palestinian Human Rights Monitoring Group, at least 28 detained prisoners have been killed while in custody since 1995.[40] A number of the detained prisoners who were killed in custody were accused of collaborating with Israel.

The emergence of an empowered Palestinian Authority has not significantly altered the legal landscape. In many ways it has simply substituted one system of patrimony with another.[41] The absence of synchronized laws has compounded the serious shortcomings in the current system, including a lack of consistency in the application of the rule of law as well as the proliferation of judicial bodies with significant overlap in their mandates.[42] There are eight types of Palestinian courts: the Magistrates Court, District Court, Municipal Court, Court of Appeals, High Court of Justice, Supreme

---

[35] Palestinian militant groups would likely adopt countermeasures to a barrier. They could, for example, increase efforts to enter Israel by sea, recruit militants from the Arab community in Israel, or fire Katyusha or Qassam rockets over the barrier.

[36] Luft (2001, 2002).

[37] Ierley (2001), p. 17.

[38] Shikaki (2002b).

[39] Human Rights Watch (2001).

[40] Palestinian Human Rights Monitoring Group (www.phrmg.org).

[41] For a fuller account of this phenomenon, see Brynen (1995).

[42] Interview with Hiba I. Husseini, Palestinian Attorney, Ramallah, PA territories, May 21, 2003.

Judicial Council, Military Courts, and the State Security Courts.[43] In reality, few of these courts are currently functioning, and there is little indication that they were effective, even at the height of Palestinian court effectiveness between 1996 and 1999.

The Palestinian legal community is under-resourced and ill-trained. The entire Palestinian legal profession comprises just 1,000 lawyers to service the approximately three million people living under the administration of the Palestinian Authority.[44] Similar shortfalls affect judges, as well as the staffing of the court's necessary administrative positions. Criminal cases routinely take three to five years for initial adjudication, a length that far exceeds international standards.[45]

An effective Palestinian state must be able to perform a number of such basic law enforcement tasks as patrolling cities and towns, investigating crimes, directing traffic, and punishing criminals. Palestinian police have already had to deal with a wide array of crimes, such as murder, kidnapping, theft, and arson, and the creation of a Palestinian state may increase the challenges to public order. First, the potential flow of Palestinians from overcrowded and impoverished Gaza to the West Bank could increase policing problems in the West Bank. The establishment of a state will likely cause a net flow of people from Gaza to the West Bank. Because Gaza has a higher unemployment rate, lower per-capita income, and lower levels of educational attainment,[46] a significant movement of Palestinians from Gaza to the West Bank could increase both the likelihood of intercommunal conflict and the number of incidents of common crime.

Second, as noted earlier, the return of Palestinian refugees following a peace settlement could also increase public order challenges.[47] About 2.5 million registered refugees reside outside of the West Bank and Gaza, primarily in Jordan, Lebanon, and Syria.[48] Many are poor, and the repatriation of even a small percentage of those refugees may raise crime rates because of their economic marginalization.

Third, the absence of competent institutions has strengthened the role of informal, tribal, and unofficial modes of enforcement and administration of justice at the expense of the limited progress made between 1994 and 2000. The refugee camps are a particular locus for patron-based forms of dispute resolution and maintenance of public order.

---

[43] The initial six are described in LAW (1999), with the final two noted as recent additions in Sayigh and Shikaki (1999), p. 42.

[44] Ierley (2001), p. 7.

[45] Al-Haq (2002).

[46] World Bank (2002).

[47] Sayigh (2000/2001).

[48] UNRWA (2003).

Internal Security Options

To create an effective and workable system for the administration of justice and what the United States might call homeland security, a Palestinian state will require external assistance. However, it will be up to Palestinians themselves to implement the substantial institutional changes—establishing an independent judiciary, eliminating executive control over the security forces, and reducing corruption and patrimonialism—that will be required if U.S. and international assistance is to be effective. In this section, we focus on constructing a viable Palestinian administration of justice system and accountable "homeland security" services, and we discuss the critical role that the United States and the international community should play in providing assistance and fostering reforms.

Administration of Justice

The long-term goal of the United States and the international community should be to ensure that a Palestinian government has robust and self-sustaining capacities in the administration of justice. Critical objectives include

- increasing the independence, transparency, and accountability of security and justice institutions in Palestine
- improving human rights conditions
- encouraging capital investments in court buildings, police stations, prisons, and detention facilities
- unifying the myriad laws in the West Bank and Gaza
- improving the competency of judges, prosecutors, and police officers through training
- providing such necessary equipment as legal texts, computers, forensic tools, and basic paraphernalia of routine law enforcement.

This subsection examines areas in which the United States and international community can encourage restructuring of the justice system and provide financial assistance, equipment, training, and other aid to a Palestinian government without becoming directly involved in the implementation of policies. We concentrate on three topics: staffing levels for major justice administration functions; capital investments; and basic reforms for judges and courts, police, prosecutors, and detention facilities.

Staffing Levels. Although choices about assistance to a Palestinian government—in the form of training, technical aid, and related support—will in part be dictated by the security environment, they will largely be determined by the capacity of the Palestinian institutions to receive assistance. Put another way, the amount of indirect aid required will be proportional to, or at least a function of, the size and efficiency of the internal security institutions that the Palestinians create. States and organizations providing assistance will also look closely at the Palestinians' commitment to respecting human rights and the Palestinian institutions' resistance to corruption.

The available evidence tells a confusing and incomplete story about the nature of Palestinian internal security institutions. For example, Jenin's Magistrate Court has been cited as particularly shorthanded, with just one judge serving a jurisdiction of 250,000 people.[49] In contrast, Palestinian law enforcement ratios have been high. The ratio of police to citizens in Palestinian-controlled areas has been estimated at 1:50, whereas the United States averages a ratio of 1:400.[50]

To clarify staffing levels that might be appropriate for Palestinian internal security, we examined staffing ratios in other countries. For comparison purposes, we chose Afghanistan, Bosnia, Bulgaria, Egypt, Haiti, Jordan, Kosovo, Poland, and Turkey. Each of these countries bears some similarity to Palestine. Many (Afghanistan, Bosnia, Bulgaria, Haiti, Kosovo, and Poland) have been through recent seminal transitions in the structure and operation of their national governments. Others, such as Jordan, Egypt, and Turkey, are primarily Muslim and offer potential important cultural comparisons. Because good data on the United States are generally available, we also use it as a point of comparison.

Table 3.2 shows that there is considerable variation in the staffing levels of the comparison countries. Egypt, for example, maintains an estimated 37.7 police per 100,000 population, while Bosnia maintains more than 700.[51] Fewer data are available on prosecution functions, but Turkey appears to have the lowest staffing ratio, while Egypt has the highest. Similar ranges are found in the area of the courts and detention facility staff. We were unable to find information about how other countries staff their counterterrorism and counterinsurgency functions.

The wide variation in internal security staffing ratios across these countries suggests that there is no absolute level of staffing associated with internal security. To further clarify the choices, we developed "low," "medium," and "high" staffing levels in relation to the estimated population of Palestine. We present these findings in Table 3.3.

The data from Table 3.3 help define the choices available for the development of Palestinian public safety institutions. If Palestine staffed policing at the same per-capita ratio as Egypt, 1,369 officers would be needed; if it staffed at the same ratio as Bosnia, 25,940 officers would be needed. The number of Palestinian prosecutors could range from a low of 160 to over 1,000. If a Palestinian government pushed for judges and court staff at the same ratio as Egypt, it would need a total of 57; using the ratio for Bosnia it would be nearly 800. Finally, the total number of jail and prison staff could range from a low of 53, using the per-capita ratio for Egypt, to a high of nearly 3,000,

---

[49] LAW (1999), p. 38.

[50] Luft (1999).

[51] The Bosnian figure is probably inflated by the inclusion of security personnel in the count of policing staff.

Table 3.2
Staffing Ratios for Internal Security Functions, Selected Countries

	Number of Personnel per 100,000 Population			
	Police	Prosecution	Judges and Court Staff	Jail and Prison Staff
Afghanistan	187	NA	NA	NA
Bosnia	714	NA	22	75
Bulgaria	NA	11	NA	NA
Egypt	38	28	2	2
Haiti	68	NA	NA	NA
Jordan	83	NA	20	NA
Kosovo	143	NA	14	53
Palestinian Territories	370	2	2	NA
Poland	260	11	15	NA
Turkey	254	4	9	39
United States	244	10	10	141

SOURCES: United Nations Surveys of Crime Trends and Operations of Criminal Justice Systems, covering the period 1990–2000, http://www.unodc.org/pdf/crime/seventh_survey/567sc.pdf; Jordanian police figures modified with data from http://www.1upinfo.com/country-guide-study/jordan/jordan143.html.

Table 3.3
Palestinian Internal Security Staffing Needs, by Function

Population: 3,634,495	Estimated Number of Personnel			
	Low	Medium	High	U.S.
Police	1,369[c]	9,465[e]	25,940[a]	8,863
Prosecution	160[f]	410[b]	1,016[c]	343
Judges and court staff	57[c]	496[d]	789[a]	379
Jail and prison staff	53[c]	1,937[e]	2,732[b]	5,132

NOTES: These figures were extrapolated from the staffing levels of the selected countries presented in Table 3.2, taking into account the population of Palestinian territory. Letters correspond to the country from which the staffing estimate is derived: [a]Bosnia; [b]Bulgaria; [c]Egypt; [d]Kosovo; [e]Poland; [f]Turkey. "Low," "high," and "U.S." represent the lowest, highest, and U.S. staffing ratios among the countries for which data are available. "Medium" represents the staffing ratio for the country closest to the average among countries for which data are available.

using the ratio for Bulgaria. The figures are also useful for thinking about cost and timing factors, which are discussed in the last section of this chapter.

Capital Investment. It is important not to underestimate the needs of the various components of the Palestinian justice system. A USAID evaluation described the system as in "a state of virtual collapse" and "moribund and decapitated."[52] The capabilities and infrastructure of the Palestinian police and security forces have been

---

[52] U.S. Agency for International Development survey quoted in UNSCO (1999), p. 12.

destroyed during the al-Aqsa intifada. In 2003, over 40 Palestinian police installations that housed prisons, training centers, and forensic laboratories were destroyed. Some Palestinians estimate the cost of the damages at $27 million.[53]

Although a host of countries and global institutions have embarked on over $100 million worth of projects to address the needs of the Palestinian justice system, only one-tenth of total aid has been earmarked for construction and refurbishment of physical infrastructure.[54] The destruction of the physical infrastructure necessitates significant capital investment. By functional area, the key capital investment requirements are the following:

- *Judges and courts:* Work facilities, courts, and office space. In addition, a training facility that allows judges and court personnel to remain current on international adjudication standards is required.
- *Police:* Work facilities and equipment, including office space, uniforms, patrol cars, communication gear, and protective gear such as helmets and flak jackets. Also, a training facility is required to ensure that the Palestinian police are current on basic practices in patrol, investigation, dispute resolution, use of force, and respect for human rights.
- *Prosecutors:* Work facilities, such as office space. In addition, a case-tracking system is required.
- *Detention facilities:* The Palestinians need prisons, jails, and pretrial detention facilities. Ideally, these facilities would separate those arrested for serious felonies from misdemeanants during pretrial custody and segregate violent and nonviolent offenders. A training facility on custodial matters is also needed. The training facility would emphasize basic human rights, the provision of basic medical care, and an understanding and commitment to the rule of law.

Basic Reforms. The Palestinians' greatest justice needs are in such areas as creating and maintaining an independent judiciary; improving the operational capacity of law enforcement; reconstituting effective forensic capacity; operating secure detention facilities; and improving the capabilities of judges, police, and prosecutors through training. We discuss four areas in detail: judges and courts, police, prosecutors, and detention facilities.

In general, structural reform is needed to ensure that justice and security functions are distinct and under the domain of separate ministries. The Ministry of Justice should have broad responsibility for the administration of justice in Palestine. The civil police, court system, and civil defense programs would operate under the Ministry of Justice's control. The civil police would work in close contact with the court system

---

[53] Leggett (2003).

[54] UNSCO (1999).

both to investigate criminal acts and to prosecute arrested subjects. It is important that civil police forces, which are dedicated to traditional criminal concerns, be controlled by a ministry that has a strong basis in law enforcement and a strong connection to the courts, and that these functions be distinctly separated from the internal security functions of domestic intelligence, border patrol, and other quasi-military functions.

Judges and Courts. Creating an independent judicial system and developing an effective rule of law have not been central concerns for the Palestinian Authority. Consequently, the United States and international community should strongly encourage steps to create an independent judiciary. A functioning judicial system in Palestine would be responsive and accountable to the populace. Responsiveness would ensure that the Palestinian state pursues criminal cases on the behalf of all victims of codified crimes, regardless of their political affiliations and resources. Accountability would include transparent processes for judicial review and appeal.

An independent judicial system is fundamental to good governance and a viable internal security system. High-priority reforms include the unconditional acceptance by the executive branch of judicial independence as laid out in the Palestine Basic Law and the Judicial Authority Law, in addition to an independent Ministry of Justice.[55] A possible litmus test would be the cessation of presidential decrees, which are widely interpreted as superseding established law. In addition, there is a need to empower and reorganize the Supreme Judicial Council, a body whose responsibility for nominating and promoting judges is vital to the strengthening of judicial authority vis-à-vis the executive and legislative branches.[56]

Another step should be to unify the myriad laws and procedures in the West Bank and Gaza. This might include establishing a permanent secretariat to coordinate the various law commissions working in these areas, and providing them with technical and support staff, office space, legal materials, and supplies.[57] A Palestinian government would also need to unify the separate court systems and their overlapping jurisdictions in the West Bank and Gaza. This might include abolishing the Military and State Security Courts, which conduct extrajudicial trials, are closed to the public, and offer no right of appeal—despite the fact that these courts handle many routine criminal cases. As an interim first step, the executive authority should clearly define the functions of these courts, make them transparent, permit credible defense, and provide for appeal.[58]

---

[55] The Palestine Basic Law (Article 89) states: "Judges shall be independent, and shall not be subject to any authority other than the authority of law while exercising their duties. No other authority may interfere in the judiciary or in the justice affairs." On establishing an independent judiciary, also see LAW (1999).

[56] Sayigh and Shikaki (1999, 2003).

[57] The construction of a Legal Databank System, or Al-Muqtafi, at Birzeit University's Institute of Law is a laudable step in efforts to unify legislation by compiling all legislation enacted in Palestine since the middle of the nineteenth century. For access to the Al-Muqtafi online, see lawcenter.birzeit.edu.

[58] Sayigh and Shikaki (1999), pp. 9–10.

The United States and the international community can play an important role in supplying equipment and providing training for judges and staff. A greater number of trained, well-paid, and independent judges will be critical in creating a viable administration of justice, as will training for bailiffs and clerks and the establishment of a national judicial training facility.[59] In the past, the PA has had insufficient revenue to pay judges enough to mitigate the possibility of corruption.

Police. The United States and the international community can be of significant service in encouraging police reform and providing financial assistance and training. Structural reform and financial assistance will be required to develop the two major elements of democratic policing—responsiveness and accountability—that are missing from Palestinian policing.[60] *Responsiveness* is the ability of the police to take its cues from individual members of the public, not from state and government. The most obvious example of responsiveness is a 911-type call system. Such a system demonstrates the power of the individual to summon police assistance, regardless of social and political standing. Responsiveness brings two advantages. First, it shows that police are accountable to diverse interests, including those of minority ethnic background or political opinions. Second, it shows that the authority of the state will be used in the interest of the people. *Accountability* is the police authority's submission to and acceptance of outside supervision. Courts, legislatures, the media, ombudsmen, and complaint processes are all forms of accountability. Accountability is critical because it demonstrates, transparently, that police are responsible to laws, not governments. Several steps should be taken to develop the responsiveness and accountability of the Palestinian police system.

Palestinian law enforcement must be held accountable by an independent and effective judiciary. This not only includes preventing police impunity from prosecution but also involves such steps as requiring police to secure warrants from a judge before conducting such activities as wiretapping. A weak judicial system that is corrupt and plagued by patrimonialism will increase the likelihood of human rights violations by Palestinian police.[61]

Palestinian law enforcement would also benefit from foreign training in police management, investigative techniques, crime scene investigations, riot control, traffic control, juvenile justice, and proper interview and interrogation techniques. Such training helps make responsiveness part of the organization's core values. Training police forces has been common in past nation-building operations. For example, beginning in 1994 the U.S. Justice Department's International Criminal Investigative Assistance Program (ICITAP) trained Haitian law enforcement officials in administrative and

---

[59] A national judicial training facility might include training in such areas as juvenile justice, labor issues, and fiscal and administrative law. See, for example, UNSCO (1999), p. 25.

[60] National Institute of Justice (1997).

[61] On patrimonialism in Palestinian territory, see Brynen (1995).

managerial capabilities, as well as in such specialized skills as investigative policing and forensics.[62] (Of course, foreign assistance programs must be tailored to local Palestinian traditions and practices.) Also necessary would be the construction of a national training institution with a systematized curriculum that incorporates human rights and other international standards.[63]

Finally, it will be important to develop an independent forensic science capacity. Immediate needs include the ability to conduct fingerprint identification and basic evidentiary forensic testing. Also important would be the construction of forensic crime labs and the training of relevant police officials in basic explosive detection and in preserving evidence for prosecution.

Prosecutors. A Palestinian state should be strongly encouraged to improve the prosecutorial system. There will likely be a need to increase the number of Palestinian lawyers and improve their training.[64] Aid will be required to establish a more universal training program designed to regulate the profession and ensure that basic competencies are achieved before lawyers are fully licensed to practice.[65] Such a program would serve to institutionalize accepted procedures and to create the potential for continuity in the application of law between the West Bank and Gaza. Licensing procedures should also include the passage of a bar association law that addresses at least minimum criteria for admission to the bar. International donor assistance for the construction of law university facilities will be necessary to mitigate the strain on existing infrastructure. In the past, support for the Palestinian prosecutorial system has come from Germany (through the Konrad Adenauer Foundation), Norway, the United Nations, and Birzeit University's Institute of Law.

Detention Facilities. Structural reform and assistance will be necessary for detention facilities. Palestinian detention custodians require training in the proper treatment of prisoners. This training should include such factors as respecting detainees' human rights and giving them basic medical care. International assistance will be necessary to supply such basic necessities as blankets, kitchen facilities, and medical facilities. The creation of an independent judiciary is also critical for the establishment of effective detention facilities, since Palestinian jail and prison staff have generally answered to the executive branch rather than to the courts.[66]

The international community can greatly improve the prospects for successful reform of the justice system by deploying international police and helping to vet and

---

[62] Bailey, Maguire, and Pouliot (1998); Perito (2002).

[63] On the Palestinian police and human rights violations, see Human Rights Watch (2002).

[64] Legal professionals have frequently requested training and further development of the technical capacity of their staff. See, for example, UNSCO (1999), p. 19.

[65] The current system requires a law degree from a licensed university and a two-year apprenticeship; however, the latter is largely unstructured and provides no established benchmarks indicating proficiency in the field.

[66] Brown (2002), p. 31.

recruit judges, attorneys, police officers, and others involved with the administration of justice.[67] This relatively intrusive approach would be warranted by the extremely limited Palestinian capacity to follow through on reforms and the fact that the judicial selection process is currently tainted. A buildup time will likely be needed to establish optimum capabilities and force-to-population ratios. During this interim period, the international community might need to play a more direct role in such areas as law enforcement, detention facilities, and the justice system.

Several potential roles might be envisioned:

- Vetting, recruiting, and selecting judges and police
- Monitoring and supervising local law enforcement officials
- Training and mentoring local police forces through joint patrols
- Occasionally performing law enforcement functions
- Assisting in detention facilities and monitoring human rights conditions.

In its mildest form, direct involvement in the Palestinian judicial system might take the form of helping to vet, recruit, and approve judges. This has been done in several nation-building operations and would involve sending a team of U.S. or international jurists to work with the Palestinian government to help select judges, take inventory of courts, and catalogue the qualifications of judges. Experienced jurists would need to interview potential judges and perhaps prosecuting attorneys to make a judgment about their competence and qualifications. The current absence of appropriately trained legal professionals in Palestinian territory suggests that outside expertise would be beneficial.

The team of outside judicial experts might also be used to recruit qualified candidates rather than waiting or relying on those suggested by the administration. Though perhaps more difficult for outsiders to perform, this task might be completed through personal interviews with members of the bar, other portions of the legal system, and Palestinian advocacy groups who have monitored the legal system.

An international panel could play a similar role in helping to select, train, and monitor key officials with responsibility for law enforcement, including leaders of the police and security services. In this case, the vetting panel would be drawn from serving and retired U.S. and international police, intelligence, and other government sectors with security expertise. In addition to the vetting panel, personnel for monitoring ongoing effectiveness might be necessary. This task would be important to prevent known human rights abusers, criminals, and terrorists from serving in Palestinian law enforcement.

A stronger form of direct aid would involve the use of U.S. or international police to assist Palestinian police in such functions as patrol, investigation, arrest, and ensuring safe passage of returning refugees or displaced persons. This has been done in a

---

[67] On direct intervention in past nation-building operations, see Schmidl (1998) and Perito (2002), pp. 1–10.

number of nation-building operations, such as Haiti, Bosnia, and Kosovo, with the assistance of American police, Italian *carabinieri,* French *gendarmerie,* Spanish *guardia civil,* Dutch *marechaussee,* and others.[68] These cases have included the deployment of armed international police to monitor, train, mentor, and sometimes substitute for indigenous forces until a proficient domestic police force is created. In Haiti, for example, several thousand international police, armed with weapons and given the power to arrest, were deployed in support of military peacekeepers. They assisted the Haitian National Police by conducting joint patrols, mentoring, and establishing standardized reporting forms to evaluate police performance and effectiveness.[69]

As Figure 3.1 illustrates, if countrywide deployment of international police were attempted in a Palestinian state on the same scale as in Kosovo, Somalia, Bosnia, or Haiti beginning in 2003, the force could range from zero to a high of more than 8,000 per year.

Finally, a third party could play a significant role in detention, as occurred after the Oslo Accords. One of the primary functions for U.S. observers was to ensure that terrorists and criminals convicted by the PA remained in custody. A direct aid role might involve allowing international prison guards and jailers to assist in the custodial care of inmates, monitor human rights conditions, and perhaps take inventory of detention facilities.

Reform of the Security Services

One of the most important internal security challenges for a nascent Palestinian state will be to restructure the Palestinian security services and curb the activity of terrorist

Figure 3.1
International Police Projections for West Bank and Gaza

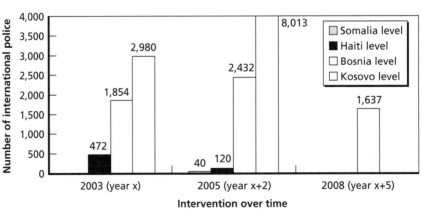

RAND *MG146-3.1*

---

[68] Perito (2002); Dobbins et al. (2003); Oakley, Dziedzic, and Goldberg (1998).

[69] Perito (2002), pp. 38–47.

organizations and other militant groups that may seek to attack Israel, undermine a peace accord, or destabilize the Palestinian government.

The long-term goal of the United States and the international community should be to ensure that the Palestinian government has a self-sufficient capability to counter militant organizations operating from its territory. To reach this goal, Palestinians, working with the United States and other countries, must

- restructure the security services by decreasing their total number
- eliminate executive control over them
- establish an oversight mechanism
- improve a range of vital capabilities including airport security, bomb detection, monitoring of terrorist financing, VIP protection, hostage rescue, and crisis management
- develop a tactical capability sufficient to disrupt terrorist cells and dismantle terrorist infrastructure within Palestine territory
- establish productive intelligence liaison relationships with key regional countries, including Israel, and with the United States.

Currently, internal security institutions operate largely under the control of the Palestinian Authority leadership. There are few checks and balances on these security institutions, and their functioning is opaque to external observers. Palestinian internal security forces are generally organized by the "rule of the perceived patron" rather than by the rule of law. An additional problem with the current structure is that it tends to blend quasi-military and justice administration functions either under a single ministry or with overlapping lines of authority. Thus, even if the Palestinian Authority ultimately invests its ministers with true executive authority, internal security forces are still structured, and thus likely to perform, in a suboptimal manner. It is important to separate the military and intelligence functions of the internal security apparatus from those departments that are strictly responsible for the administration of justice.

Restructuring the Security Services. It is necessary to separate administration of justice and security functions in the executive hierarchy. The realignment proposed below for the security functions is drawn from the current list of internal security forces presented in Table 3.1. A revamped Ministry of Interior should be created. In past agreements, the Palestinian Authority has been specifically denied the ability to maintain a Ministry of Defense. A Ministry of Defense might normally be seen as the appropriate part of government to direct organizations such as the various intelligence agencies and preventive security forces that are likely to deal with terrorism. In the absence of this option, the Ministry of Interior is the next-likely place from which to direct these organizations.

The major components grouped under the Ministry of Interior are outlined in Table 3.4. They exclude the police and Civil Defense (rescue and fire services), which should be organized within the Ministry of Justice.

Under this realignment, the National Security Force would guard checkpoints and patrol borders. Its mandate would necessitate ongoing interaction and coordination with border patrol, military, and intelligence bodies from Israel, Egypt, Jordan, and other relevant parties. The Preventive Security Service would handle issues related to subversion, counterespionage, and dissident organizations within the Palestinian state. General Intelligence would gather intelligence and conduct counterespionage operations. Although not designed as exclusively counterterrorist in nature, this service would need to work with counterterrorism agencies in other countries such as Israel, Jordan, and Egypt to be effective. The Presidential Security Service would protect various leaders within the government, including the president and prime minister. The Coast Guard would patrol territorial waters off of Gaza and monitor activity in the Dead Sea. In this proposed realignment, the Special Security Force and Military Intelligence would be eliminated because their functions largely overlap with the Preventive Security Service, and the judicial and legislative branches would ideally have oversight over the security services.

In the United States, these security functions typically receive a high degree of oversight from the U.S. Congress. Other democratic countries generally exert some combination of executive and legislative oversight over such forces, and the judicial branch holds them accountable. Given the degree to which political—as opposed to genuine executive—control has been a problem in Palestine, a model of strong legislative oversight seems appropriate.

Table 3.4
Proposed Security Service Realignment

Security Service	Function	Size[a]
National Security Force (Al-Amn al-Watani)	Guard checkpoints and patrol borders	18,000
Preventive Security Service (Al-Amn al-Wiqa'i)	Handle subversion, counterespionage, and dissident organizations	3,500
General Intelligence (Mukhabarat Salamah)	Gather intelligence and conduct counterespionage operations	3,000
Presidential Security Service (Al-Amn al-Ri'asah)	Protect top Palestinian officials	500
Coast Guard (Shurta Bahariya)	Patrol territorial waters off of Gaza	200
Total		25,200

[a] These numbers are based on past estimates of their size taken from International Strategic Studies Association (2002), pp. 1320–1321 and IISS (2002), p. 115.

Improving Capabilities. The United States and the international community can also provide equipment, monitoring, training, and other assistance to the Palestinian security services. Since the long-term goal should be to establish Palestinian self-sufficiency, the international role should be a temporary one. A Palestinian government will need to adopt a combination of two strategies—co-option and enforcement—to deal with terrorist and other militant organizations. *Co-option* involves offering inducements to militants to wean them from the use of violence, guarantees regarding participation in the political process if they jettison their commitment to armed struggle, amnesties and early release from prison, or jobs in the public or private sector. Indeed, since organizations such as Hamas have political arms, it is conceivable that a portion of them may decide to participate in the political process if a Palestinian state is created.

However, it is plausible to assume that there will be some rejectionists who will not give up armed struggle because they are unhappy with a peace settlement, are frustrated with the organizational makeup or policies of a Palestinian government, or wish to continue jihad against Israel. This means that a Palestinian government will need to adopt an *enforcement* strategy as well, especially the arrest and prosecution of militants.

For much of the 1990s, the Palestinian Authority was somewhat effective at dealing with organizations such as Hamas and PIJ when it wanted to be.[70] The PA demonstrated some willingness to confiscate arms and to arrest, jail, and even kill individuals. For example, following the February and March 1996 suicide bombings in Israel, Palestinian forces led by Muhammad Dahlan, head of the Palestinian Preventive Security Service, targeted Hamas's Ezzedin al-Qassam wing in Gaza that was planning attacks against both Israelis and PA leaders. In a six-week sweep in March and April 1996, Palestinian police arrested more than 600 Islamic militants.[71] In April 1997, the IDF and the Palestinian Authority, led by West Bank security chief Jibril Rajoub, dismantled the Hamas "Halhoul" cell in the West Bank. This led to violent clashes between Palestinian police and Palestinian demonstrators in Hebron. In October 1998, the PA placed Hamas spiritual leader Sheikh Ahmed Yassin under house arrest following a bombing in Gush Katif, and Dahlan organized the arrest of dozens of Hamas activists.[72]

These steps were often taken in coordination with Israeli intelligence services.[73] However, the Palestinian Authority's actions were neither comprehensive nor frequent enough throughout the 1990s, and the police and security forces often violated basic human rights by resorting to torture or assassination.

---

[70] See Mishal and Sela (2000), especially pp. 49–112.

[71] Davis (1996) p. 2; Battersby (1996b).

[72] Harman and Dudkevitch (1998); Kershner (1999).

[73] Black (1997).

Since a Palestinian government is likely to utilize an enforcement strategy against rejectionists, the United States and the international community can assist in at least three areas: providing capacity-building training, offering military and other counterterrorism assistance, and improving intelligence cooperation and provide intelligence monitoring.

Capacity Building. Security and combat training would improve the capacity of the Palestinian security and law enforcement personnel to take strong, decisive action against terrorist and militant organizations.[74] Of particular importance will be training in such areas as bomb detection, sniper training, firearms training, VIP protection, covert communications, terrorist financing, interrogation techniques, and human rights. Indeed, the United States has provided this type of assistance since the early 1990s, when the CIA's Middle East operations chief Frank Anderson resurrected U.S. contact with the PLO. The Central Intelligence Agency subsequently trained members of the Palestinian Preventive Security Services and General Intelligence in Jericho, Ramallah, and the United States. The training covered a wide range of areas from firearms training to interrogation techniques and bomb disposal.[75] The U.S. State Department's Anti-Terrorism Assistance (ATA) Program, managed by the Bureau of Diplomatic Security, also provides such training to foreign governments.[76] The Egyptian and Jordanian intelligence services could also offer security and other training to the Palestinian security services, as they have in the past.[77]

Military and Counterterrorism Assistance. The United States and the international community should supply equipment and financial aid to the Palestinians. Nonlethal assistance might include navigation equipment, such as global positioning systems, radios, and other communications equipment; protective gear, such as helmets and flak jackets; and handcuffs, night-vision devices, intelligence equipment, and all-terrain vehicles.[78] Appropriate lethal aid might include sniper rifles, submachine guns, light semiautomatic rifles, and ammunition. Since the Oslo Accords, the CIA and U.S. government have supplied a wide range of sophisticated equipment to Palestinian security and intelligence services, including miniature listening and observation devices, night-vision equipment, photography equipment, and communications scanners.[79] It

---

[74] Indyk (2003).

[75] Shapiro (2003); Blanche (2001); Toameh and Lahoud (2003); "What the CIA Can Teach the PLO" (1998); Weiner (1998).

[76] See, for example, U.S. Department of State (2002). Other U.S. counterterrorism programs include the International Law Enforcement Academies, in which the Departments of Treasury and Justice provide on-site training for foreign governments, and the Justice Department's Overseas Prosecutorial Development and Assistance Training Program (OPDAT) and the International Criminal Investigation Training Assistance Program.

[77] Anderson (2003); Lahoud (2002); Dunn (2002).

[78] In 1994 and 1995, for example, the Department of Defense provided the Palestinian police with trucks, jeeps, uniforms, and medical equipment. U.S. General Accounting Office (2001b), p. 4.

[79] Shapiro (2003).

is unlikely that Palestinian security and police forces will need to be heavily militarized to be effective, but good intelligence, light weapons, and sound counterterrorism tactics will be important.

The United States and the international community could also examine the viability of supplying or operating biometric or other technological aids for use along Palestinian borders and at border crossings. At Palestinian border crossings, such as the Allenby Bridge or Erez checkpoints, travelers are subject to background and bag checks using X-ray machines and material that can detect explosives.[80]

Current Palestinian identification cards are paper only. They are easily forged, and some Israeli observers report that Israeli intelligence devotes substantial resources to monitoring suspected forgers. One solution would be to embed identification cards with a biometric device (such as a fingerprint) that would allow authorities to verify the identities of border crossers. Palestinians willing to use such identification methods could conceivably be precleared for unchecked crossings, passively screened, or directed to special, faster screening points. Current technologies that might be considered along Palestinian borders and at checkpoints include remote sensing tools from satellites and aircraft, acoustic and ground-based sensors, and nonintrusive inspection equipment and radiation detection devices.[81]

Biometrics have been implemented to a limited degree in U.S. border control systems—especially by the INS at airports. Biometric technologies include facial recognition, fingerprint recognition, hand geometry, iris recognition, retina recognition, signature recognition, and speaker recognition. Using biometrics is appealing because biometric identification can help bind a traveler tightly to his or her physiological or behavioral characteristics, and it is less easily lost or fabricated than other forms of identification. However, biometrics are still at an early stage of development and there are potential drawbacks—high cost, longer waiting lines, technological flaws, and privacy concerns.[82] This is why the United States largely relies on visa and passport processing, as well as port-of-entry inspections, to examine travelers, trucks, and cargo along its borders with Mexico and Canada.

Intelligence Cooperation and Monitoring. The United States and the international community could provide assistance in the area of intelligence and monitoring. One way is to monitor Palestinian compliance in arresting terrorists and insurgents, as well as destroying their infrastructure. Organizations such as the Central Intelligence Agency can—and should—play an important role in monitoring whether terrorist and insurgent groups are being dismantled. Are individuals being jailed or is there a revolving-door policy? Are the capabilities of organizations increasing or decreasing?

---

[80] de Quetteville (2003).

[81] See, for example, United Nations Institute for Disarmament Research (1999).

[82] U.S. General Accounting Office (2002); Woodward et al. (2001); Lee (2003).

Are organizations being permitted to raise money or otherwise operate on Palestinian territory?

The United States—and especially the CIA—have had experience with monitoring as part of the Israeli-Palestinian peace process. In the 1990s, the Palestinian Authority agreed to share with the United States its working plan against militant groups and their infrastructure. A bilateral America-Palestinian committee was established to examine steps implemented by the PA to combat terror, and U.S.-Israeli-Palestinian committees were set up to monitor arms smuggling and political incitement.[83]

The United States and the international community could also help a nascent Palestinian state build and improve its intelligence collaboration with important partners such as Israel, Jordan, Egypt, and the United States. An effective counterterrorism campaign in a Palestinian state will require substantial cooperation with other governments regarding the transborder movement of terrorists, insurgents, and their goods; the location of weapons caches, hideouts, and other infrastructure; terrorist financial support; and links with criminal elements such as drug- and arms-trafficking organizations. Indeed, terrorist and militant organizations currently operating in Palestinian territory have connections with—or operate in—numerous countries, such as Jordan, Lebanon, Syria, Libya, Sudan, and Algeria.

In sum, the United States and the international community should assist a Palestinian state by providing training to police and security forces, offering military and other counterterrorism aid, and assisting with monitoring and intelligence cooperation. The fact that the United States has been willing to do this in the past is a good indication that it can—and will—provide assistance in the future. In 2003, for example, it provided approximately $300 million in assistance through the Central Intelligence Agency to Palestinian police and security forces for such purposes as training forces, constructing jails, and purchasing communications equipment and vehicles.[84] The European Union gave $8 million in 1997, $7 million in 2000, and $4 million in 2001 for a variety of counterterrorism purposes such as training the PA security services.[85]

Costing the Options

The preceding sections of this chapter outlined the challenges associated with creating effective internal security functions in a Palestinian state. This section estimates general reconstruction costs, such as training and equipping police and other internal security forces, rebuilding infrastructure, and providing other assistance.

---

[83] *The Wye River Memorandum* II A 1 (a); Tenet (1998); Shapiro (2003), pp. 100–106; O'Sullivan (1998); Gates (1998); Bearden (1998); Weiner (1996).

[84] Weisman (2003a,b); Zacharia (2003).

[85] European Commission (2003).

General Reconstruction Costs

One of the most significant costs in rebuilding the Palestinian internal security system will be operating, equipping, and training justice administration components and the various security forces: the police, national security force, civil defense force, preventive security force, and coast guard. *Operating* includes administration expenditures necessary to operate these agencies. *Equipment* incorporates the cost of uniforms and a range of lethal and nonlethal equipment from handcuffs to munitions. This will be necessary both because of the destruction that the Israelis have inflicted during the second intifada and because it is not clear that the Palestinians have ever adequately provided for their internal security. Several kinds of equipment may be particularly useful. For example, Palestinian police would benefit from state-of-the-art surveillance and forensic equipment for investigative purposes. A national security communications network would also be useful to facilitate communication within the Ministry of Interior agencies, as well as among them. Finally, *training* includes deploying and paying international advisers, building training academies, supplying training equipment, and providing necessary field support for advisers and trainers. Training is necessary to ensure that security and justice officials are current on effective standards and procedures and to improve the probability that effective reform of these institutions will occur.

Capital investments will also be necessary. These include building and refurbishing courts, Ministry of Justice buildings, prisons, detention centers, police stations, firehouses, and Ministry of Interior buildings. In general, we expect capital costs to be one-time charges (perhaps spread out over many years) associated with the construction or establishment of permanent assets.

It is not possible to make precise estimates for rebuilding the Palestinian internal security system in advance of a peace agreement, since it is impossible to predict infrastructure conditions and the availability of equipment at that time. However, it is possible to make reasonable estimates. This chapter assumes that the costs of rebuilding Palestine's internal security system will be roughly proportional to the costs of rebuilding Iraq's internal security system, in per-capita terms.[86] Both areas have suffered significant damage due to warfare, will require substantial internal security assistance, and will likely be well funded.[87] Consequently, we used Coalition Provisional Authority (CPA) budget figures on the cost of rebuilding Iraq's internal security system, calculated per person costs in a range of categories by dividing CPA estimates by Iraq's

---

[86] Some might argue that the U.S. reconstruction of Iraq has not been successful to date and that Iraq is thus a poor frame of reference for estimating the cost of successful development of an independent Palestinian state. In our view, however, the lack of success in Iraq has not principally been due to inadequate financial resources. In both absolute and per-capita terms, the resources available for Iraqi reconstruction have been high relative to other recent nation-building efforts. Rather, U.S. challenges have more likely been a result of the absence of planning for reconstruction and a variety of other factors. See, for example, Dobbins et al. (2003).

[87] For instance, external assistance per capita in Iraq is considerably higher than it has been in Afghanistan since 2002, and it is also higher in real terms than in several other U.S.-led nation-building efforts over the past two decades.

population, and then rescaled to Palestine by multiplying per-capita spending by West Bank and Gaza population figures.[88]

Based on the U.S. costs in rebuilding Iraq, it is reasonable to expect that at least $612.1 million per year would be necessary to rebuild a Palestinian state's internal security system.[89] The cost over ten years could range from $7.0 billion, assuming 3 percent population growth in Palestinian territory, to $7.7 billion, assuming 5 percent growth.

We note two important caveats to these estimates. First, we did not adjust Palestinian population figures to account for possible immigration of Palestinian refugees from outside the West Bank and Gaza to a Palestinian state. If such immigration is substantial, our estimates will understate the amount of assistance necessary for successful reconstruction. Second, our estimates for the cost of rebuilding Iraq may be slightly understated, since they include only U.S. costs. Although the United States has incurred the vast majority of international costs in rebuilding Iraq's internal security system, several other countries have also provided assistance.

Cost Summary

As Table 3.5 highlights, we estimate that general reconstruction costs for rebuilding the Palestinian internal security system could be approximately $612.1 million. The cost for general reconstruction over ten years could range from $7.0 billion, assuming 3 percent population growth in Palestinian territory, to $7.7 billion, assuming 5 percent growth (see Table 3.6).

---

[88] President of the United States (2004); Operating and Expenditure data are 2005 estimates from *Iraq Budget, 2004–2006* (2004).

[89] This estimate is slightly higher than current funding. Best estimates indicate that the United States and European nations provided more than $300 million in assistance beginning in 2003 for such purposes as training forces, constructing jails, and purchasing communications equipment and vehicles, with the CIA providing the vast bulk of that assistance. Weisman (2003a,b); Zacharia (2003); European Commission (2003).

Table 3.5
Annual Cost of Rebuilding the Palestinian Internal Security System (in millions of 2003 US$)

General Reconstruction Costs

Police force equipment and training	168.2
National security force equipment and training	39.8
Civil defense force equipment and training	17.4
Preventive security force, coast guard, intelligence equipment and training	177.1
Judge, prosecutor equipment and training	4.3
Forensic and other technical aid	0.7
National security communications network	12.8
Operating expenditures for police, security forces	118.1
Operating expenditures for justice (including prisons)	7.4
Rebuilding courts and other justice facilities	19.2
Rebuilding prison facilities	14.2
Rebuilding detention facilities	19.8
Rebuilding police stations, firehouses, Ministry of Interior buildings	13.1
Subtotal	612.1

Low Military Option: 1,000 Forces

Military personnel	43.4
Civilian personnel	1.1
Personnel support	9.4
Operating support	68.0
Transportation	15.8
Subtotal	137.7

High Military Option: 15,000 Forces

Military personnel	650.7
Civilian personnel	16.1
Personnel support	141.0
Operating support	1,020.0
Transportation	237.6
Subtotal	2,065.4

Total Annual Costs

Low estimate	749.8
High estimate	2,677.5

NOTES: Military and civilian personnel include the incremental costs of deploying forces into the Palestinian theater of operations—for example, hazard pay and costs associated with paying reserve personnel called to active duty. Personnel support includes food, water, equipment, and medical costs. Operating support includes the operation and maintenance of all forces involved in the Palestinian peace-enabling force. It comprises incremental costs for increasing flying hours; equipping and maintaining ground forces; buying equipment; maintaining command, control, and communications functions; and fixing or replacing damaged equipment. Transportation includes moving soldiers and equipment to the area of operations from bases in the United States and around the world.

Table 3.6
Ten-Year Cost of Rebuilding the Palestinian Internal Security System (in millions of 2003 US$)

General Reconstruction Costs	Ten-Year Total, 3% Population Growth	Ten-Year Total, 5% Population Growth
Police force equipment and training	1,928.0	2,115.4
National security force equipment and training	456.7	501.1
Civil defense force equipment and training	199.0	218.3
Preventive security force, coast guard, intelligence equipment and training	2,030.8	2,228.1
Judge, prosecutor equipment and training	48.9	53.7
Forensic and other technical aid	8.1	8.9
National security communications network	146.8	161.1
Operating expenditures for police, security forces	1,353.8	1,485.4
Operating expenditures for justice (including prisons)	84.8	93.1
Rebuilding courts and other justice facilities	220.2	241.6
Rebuilding prison facilities	163.1	179.0
Rebuilding detention facilities	226.7	248.8
Rebuilding police stations, firehouses, Ministry of Interior buildings	150.1	164.6
Total	7,017.0	7,699.1

Bibliography

Agha, Hussein, and Robert Malley, "The Last Negotiation: How to End the Middle East Process," *Foreign Affairs,* Vol. 81, No. 3, May/June 2003, pp. 10–18.

Agreement on the Gaza Strip and the Jericho Area, The Governments of the State of Israel and the Palestine Liberation Organization, May 4, 1994.

Al-Haq (Palestinian Organisation for Human Rights), *Special Report on the Palestinian Judiciary,* Ramallah, West Bank: Al-Haq, Spring 2002.

Amnesty International, *Shielded from Scrutiny: IDF Violations in Jenin and Nablus,* New York: Amnesty International, 2002.

Anderson, John Ward, "US-Backed Reforms for Palestinians Moved to Back Burner," *The Washington Post,* January 19, 2003, p. A18.

Bailey, Michael, Robert Maguire, and J. O'Neil G. Pouliot, "Haiti: Military-Police Partnership for Public Security," in Robert B. Oakley, Michael J. Dziedzic, and Eliot M. Goldberg, eds., *Policing the New World Disorder: Peace Operations and Public Security,* Washington, D.C.: National Defense University Press, 1998, pp. 215–252.

Battersby, John, "Arafat Tightens Screws on Hamas," *Christian Science Monitor,* March 25, 1996a, p. 6.

———, "Palestinian Police Force Meets Goals to Disarm, Disband Hamas Militants," *Christian Science Monitor,* April 8, 1996b, p. 8.

Bearden, Milt, "CIA as Honest Broker," *Jerusalem Post,* November 11, 1998, p. 8.

Bennet, James, "No Peace in Sight, Israelis Trust in a Wall," *New York Times,* December 17, 2002, p. A1.

Binnendijk, Hans, and Richard Kugler, "Transforming European Forces," *Survival,* Vol. 44, No. 3, Autumn 2002, pp. 117–132.

Black, Ian, "Spooky Alliance Bears Fruit," *The Guardian,* January 22, 1997, p. 11.

Blanche, Ed, "CIA Withdrawal Leaves Vacuum in Negotiating Process," *Jane's Intelligence Review,* May 2001, pp. 39–42.

Brom, Shlomo, "Operation 'Defensive Shield': An Interim Assessment," *Tel Aviv Notes,* No. 35, April 11, 2002.

Brown, Nathan J., *The Palestinian Reform Agenda,* Washington, D.C.: United States Institute of Peace, 2002.

Brynen, Rex, "The Neopatrimonial Dimension of Palestinian Politics," *Journal of Palestine Studies,* Vol. 25, No. 1, Autumn 1995, pp. 23–36.

B'Tselem, *Operation Defensive Shield: Soldiers' Testimonies, Palestinian Testimonies,* Jerusalem: B'Tselem, 2002a.

———, *The Separation Barrier: Position Paper,* September 2002, Jerusalem: B'Tselem, 2002b.

Casualties and Incidents Database, International Policy Institute for Counter-Terrorism at the Interdisciplinary Center, Herzliya. Online at www.ict.org.il (as of June 2004).

Congressional Budget Office, *The Long-Term Implications of Current Defense Plans: Summary Update for Fiscal Year 2005,* Washington, D.C., 2004.

Cordesman, Anthony H., *Iraq: Too Uncertain to Call,* Washington, D.C.: Center for Strategic and International Studies, 2003.

Davis, Douglas, "Hamas, Jihad: PA Preventing Us from Carrying Out Suicide Attacks," *Jerusalem Post,* October 25, 1996.

de Quetteville, Harry, "British Bombers Make Mockery of Israel's Security," *The Daily Telegraph,* May 5, 2003, p. 4.

Desch, Michael C., ed., *Soldiers in Cities: Military Operations on Urban Terrain,* Carlisle, PA: Strategic Studies Institute, 2001.

Dobbins, James, John G. McGinn, Keith Crane, Seth G. Jones, Rollie Lal, Andrew Rathmell, Rachel M. Swanger, Anga Timilsina, *America's Role in Nation-Building: From Germany to Iraq,* Santa Monica, Calif.: RAND Corporation, MR-1753-RC, 2003.

Dudkevitch, Margot, "Budget Cuts Force IDF to Close Judea HQ," *Jerusalem Post,* May 29, 2003a, p. 2.

———, "IDF Photographer, Five Palestinians Killed in Rafah," *Jerusalem Post,* April 21, 2003b, p. 1.

———, and Lamia Lahoud, "Six Palestinians Killed in IDF Incursion into Gaza," *Jerusalem Post,* October 4, 2001, p. 3.

Dunn, Ross, "CIA Hatches Plan to Revamp Palestine Security Forces," *Sydney Morning Herald,* August 10, 2002, p. 17.

Elizur, Yuval, "Israel Banks on a Fence," *Foreign Affairs,* Vol. 82, No. 2, March/April 2003, pp. 106–119.

European Commission, *European Community Assistance to the Palestinians and the Peace Process Since Oslo,* Brussels: European Commission, 2003.

Fisk, Robert, *Pity the Nation: Lebanon at War,* New York: Oxford University Press, 2001.

Gabriel, Richard A., *Operation Peace for Galilee: The Israeli-PLO War in Lebanon,* New York: Hill and Wang, 1984.

Gates, Robert M., "The CIA's Little-Known Resume," *New York Times,* October 29, 1998, p. A31.

Glenn, Russell W., ed., *The City's Many Faces: Proceedings of the RAND Arroyo-MCWL-J8 UWG Urban Operations Conference,* Santa Monica, Calif.: RAND Corporation, CF-148-A, 2000.

———, Jamison Jo Medby, Scott Gerwehr, Frederick J. Gellert, Andrew O'Donnell, *Honing the Keys to the City: Refining the United States Marine Corps Reconnaissance Force for Urban Combat Ground Operations,* Santa Monica, Calif.: RAND Corporation, MR-1628-USMC, 2003.

Goldberg, Jeffrey, "In the Party of God," *The New Yorker,* October 14, 2002, pp. 180–195.

Goodman, Hirsh, "Defensive Shield: A Post Mortem," *Insight: A Middle East Analysis,* New York: United Jewish Communities, June 2002.

———, and Jonathan Cummings, eds., *The Battle of Jenin: A Case Study in Israel's Communications Strategy,* Memorandum No. 3, Tel Aviv: Jaffee Center for Strategic Studies, 2003.

Hamas, *Covenant of 1988: The Covenant of the Islamic Resistance Movement, August 18, 1988.* Online at http://www.yale.edu/lawweb/avalon/mideast/hamas.htm (as of June 7, 2004).

Harel, Amos, and Arnon Regular, "IDF Cameraman, Five Palestinians Killed in Rafah," *Ha'aretz,* April 21, 2003, p. 1.

Harman, Danna, and Margot Dudkevitch, "PA Puts Yassin Under House Arrest," *Jerusalem Post,* October 30, 1998, p. 1.

Headquarters, Department of the Army, *Concept for Objective Force,* Washington, D.C.: Department of the Army, November 2001.

Henkin, Yagil, "The Best Way into Baghdad," *New York Times,* April 3, 2003, p. A21.

———, "Urban Warfare and the Lessons of Jenin," *Azure,* No. 5763, Summer 2003, pp. 33–69.

Hoffman, Bruce, *Insurgency and Counterinsurgency in Iraq,* Santa Monica, Calif.: RAND Corporation, OP-127-IPC/CMEPP 2004.

Hroub, Khaled, Hamas: *Political Thought and Practice,* Washington, D.C.: Institute for Palestine Studies, 2000.

Human Rights Watch, *Jenin: IDF Military Operations,* New York: Human Rights Watch, Vol. 14, No. 3, 2002.

Human Rights Watch, *Justice Undermined: Balancing Security and Human Rights in the Palestinian Justice System,* New York: Human Rights Watch, Vol. 13, No. 4, 2001.

Ierley, Douglas, "Law and Judicial Reform in Post-Conflict Situations: A Case Study of the West Bank Gaza," paper presented at the World Bank Conference on "Empowerment, Security, and Opportunity through Law and Justice" in St. Petersburg, Russia, July 2001.

Indyk, Martin, "A Trusteeship for Palestine?" *Foreign Affairs,* May/June 2003, Vol. 82, No. 3, pp. 51–66.

International Crisis Group, *Middle East Game II: How a Comprehensive Israeli-Palestinian Peace Settlement Would Look,* Washington: International Crisis Group, July 2002.

International Institute for Strategic Studies (IISS), *The Military Balance, 2002–2003,* London: Oxford University Press, 2002.

International Strategic Studies Association, *Defense and Foreign Affairs Handbook,* Alexandria, VA: International Strategic Studies Association, 2002.

Iraq Budget, 2004–2006, Baghdad: Coalition Provisional Authority, 2004.

Jane's Terrorism Intelligence Center. Online at jtic.janes.com (as of June 4, 2004).

Kershner, Isabel, "The Rise and Rise of Col. Dahlan," *Jerusalem Report,* February 1, 1999, p. 22.

Kimmerling, Baruch, and Joel S. Migdal, *The Palestinian People: A History,* Cambridge, MA: Harvard University Press, 2003.

Lahoud, Lamia, "U.S., Egypt, Jordan Will Guide PA Reforms," *Jerusalem Post,* August 11, 2002, p. 3.

LAW (Palestinian Society for the Protection of Human Rights and the Environment), *Executive Interference in the Judiciary: Independent Judiciary Unit,* Jerusalem: LAW, 1999.

Lee, Jennifer, "Passports and Visas to Add High-Tech Identity Features," *New York Times,* August 24, 2003, p. 26.

Leggett, Karby, "Palestinian Police Are Forced to Walk Fine Line in Jericho," *The Wall Street Journal,* April 18, 2003, p. 1.

Levitt, Matthew, "Palestinian Islamic Jihad: Getting By with a Little Help from Its Friends," *Peacewatch,* No. 396, September 3, 2002.

———, "Terror from Damascus, Part I," *Peacewatch,* No. 420, May 7, 2003.

———, and Seth Wilkas, "Defensive Shield Counterterrorism Accomplishments," *Peacewatch,* No. 377, April 17, 2002.

Loeb, Vernon, "Lessons from Israel: Drones and Urban Warfare," *The Washington Post,* September 23, 2002.

Luft, Gal, "Palestinian Military Performance and the 2000 Intifada," *Middle East Review of International Affairs,* Vol. 4, No. 4, December 2000, pp. 1–8.

————, "The Palestinian Security Services: Between Police and Army," *Middle East Review of International Affairs,* Vol. 3, No. 2, June 1999, pp. 47–63.

————, "The Mirage of a Demilitarized Palestine," *Middle East Quarterly,* Vol. 8, No. 3, Summer 2001, pp. 51–60.

————, "Reforming the Palestinian Security Services," *Peacewatch,* No. 382, May 15, 2002.

Medby, Jamison Jo, and Russell W. Glenn, *Street Smart: Intelligence Preparation of the Battlefield for Urban Operations,* Santa Monica, Calif.: RAND Corporation, MR-1287-A, 2002.

Milton, Lieutenant Colonel T. R., "Urban Operations: Future Warfare," *Military Review,* Vol. 74, No. 2, February 1994, pp. 37–46.

Mishal, Shaul, and Avraham Sela, *The Palestinian Hamas: Vision, Violence, and Coexistence,* New York: Columbia University Press, 2000.

"The Moratinos Nonpaper on the Taba Negotiations, Summer 2001," *Journal of Palestine Studies,* Vol. 31, No. 3, Spring 2002, pp. 81–89.

National Institute of Justice, *Civilian Police and Multinational Peacekeeping—A Workshop Series: A Role for Democratic Policing,* Washington, D.C.: U.S. Department of Justice, 1997.

Oakley, Robert, Michael J. Dziedzic, and Eliot Goldberg, eds., *Policing the New World Disorder: Peace Operations and Public Security,* Washington, D.C.: National Defense University Press, 1998.

Office of the Secretary of Defense, *Justification for Component Contingency Operations and the Overseas Contingency Operations Transfer Fund (OCOTF),* Washington, D.C., 2004.

O'Hanlon, Michael, "A Matter of Force—and Fairness," *Washington Post,* October 1, 2004, p. A29.

O'Sullivan, Arieh, "Calling in the CIA," *Jerusalem Post,* October 30, 1998, p. 14.

The Palestine Basic Law, Article 89. Online at www.mideastweb.org/basiclaw.htm (as of June 2004).

Palestinian Human Rights Monitoring Group, "Death of Prisoner No. 20 Held in Palestinian Custody," August 10, 1998. Online at www.phrmg.org (as of June 7, 2004).

Paz, Reuven, "Force-17: The Renewal of Old Competition Motivates Violence," *Peacewatch,* No. 316, April 5, 2001.

Perito, Robert M., *The American Experience with Police in Peace Operations,* Centre pour le Maintien de la Paix, Pearson Peacekeeping Centre Clementsport, Nova Scotia: Canadian Peacekeeping Press Publications, 2002.

Peters, Ralph, "Our Soldiers, Their Cities," *Parameters,* Vol. 26, No. 1, Spring 1996, pp. 43–50.

Pew Research Center for the People and the Press, *Views of a Changing World: June 2003,* Washington, D.C.: Pew Research Center for the People and the Press, June 2003.

Posen, Barry R., "Urban Operations: Tactical Realities and Strategic Ambiguities," in Michael C. Desch, ed., *Soldiers in Cities: Military Operations on Urban Terrain,* 2001, pp. 149–166.

President of the United States, *Second Quarterly Report, Emergency Appropriations Act for Defense and for the Reconstruction of Iraq and Afghanistan,* Washington, D.C.: Office of Management and Budget, April 2004.

Rabbani, Mouin, "Rocks and Rockets: Oslo's Inevitable Conclusion," *Journal of Palestine Studies,* Vol. 30, No. 3, Spring 2001, pp. 68–81.

Rees, Matt, "The Battle of Jenin," *Time,* May 8, 2002.

Rubin, Barry, and Judith Colp Rubin, *Yasir Arafat: A Political Biography,* New York: Oxford University Press, 2003.

Satloff, Robert B., ed., *International Military Intervention: A Detour on the Road to Israeli-Palestinian Peace,* Washington, D.C.: The Washington Institute for Near East Policy, Publication No. 45, September 2003.

Sayigh, Yezid, "Palestine's Prospects," *Survival,* Vol. 42, No. 4, Winter 2000/2001, pp. 5–19.

―――, "Redefining the Basics: Sovereignty and Security of the Palestinian State," *Journal of Palestine Studies,* Vol. 24, No. 4, Summer 1995, pp. 5–19.

―――, and Khalil Shikaki, *Strengthening Palestinian Public Institutions,* Council on Foreign Relations Independent Task Force Report, June 28, 1999.

―――, and Khalil Shikaki, *Reforming the Palestinian Authority: An Update,* New York: Council on Foreign Relations, January 2003.

Schmidl, Erwing A., "Police Functions in Peace Operations: An Historical Overview," in Oakley, Dziedzic, and Goldberg (eds.), *Policing the New World Disorder,* 1998, pp. 19–40.

Seam Zone, Tel Aviv: Israeli Ministry of Defense, 2003.

Shapiro, Shlomo, "The CIA as a Middle East Peace Broker?" *Survival,* Vol. 45, No. 2, Summer 2003, pp. 91–112.

Sharm el-Sheikh Fact-Finding Committee (The Mitchell Plan), April 30, 2001. Online at http://www.yale.edu/lawweb/avalon/mideast/mitchell_plan.htm (as of June 2004).

Sheehan, Edward R. F., "The Map and the Fence," *New York Review of Books,* Vol. 50, No. 11, July 3, 2003.

Shikaki, Khalil, "Palestinians Divided," *Foreign Affairs,* Vol. 81, No. 1, January/February 2002a, pp. 89–105.

―――, "Unrealized Reform: Learning from Past Mistakes," in Dennis Ross, ed., *Reforming the Palestinian Authority: Requirements for Change,* Washington, D.C.: Washington Institute, 2002b, pp. 7–19.

Sobelman, Daniel, "Hizbullah Infiltrates Israel," *Jane's Intelligence Review,* Vol. 15, No. 4, April 2003, pp. 26–27.

Steinberg, Gerald, "Separation Is Better Than Conflict," *Financial Times,* June 23, 2003.

Strindberg, N. T. Anders, "Assessing the Hizbullah Threat," *Jane's Intelligence Review,* Vol. 15, No. 3, March 2003, pp. 24–27.

———, "The Damascus-Based Alliance of Palestinian Forces: A Primer," *Journal of Palestine Studies,* Vol. 29, No. 3, Spring 2000, pp. 401–417.

Tenet, George J., "What 'New' Role for the CIA?" *New York Times,* October 27, 1998, p. A23.

Toameh, Khaled Abu, and Lamia Lahoud, "CIA Training PA Antiterror Force," *Jerusalem Post,* May 27, 2003, p. 2.

Trainor, Bernard E., "Military Operations in an Urban Environment: Beirut, 1982–84," in Michael Desch, ed., *Soldiers in Cities,* 2001, pp. 121–130.

"United Nations Peacekeeping Operations," Background Note, Washington, D.C.: Henry L. Stimson Center, April 15, 2002.

United Nations Institute for Disarmament Research, *The Potential Uses of Commercial Satellite Imagery in the Middle East,* Geneva, Switzerland: United Nations Institute for Disarmament Research, 1999.

United Nations Relief and Works Agency for Palestine Refugees in the Near East (UNRWA), "West Bank Refugee Camp Profiles." Online at www.un.org/unrwa/index.html, May 2003.

United Nations Special Coordinator in the Occupied Territories (UNSCO), *Rule of Law Development in the West Bank and Gaza Strip,* Jerusalem: May 1999.

U.S. Department of Defense, *Doctrine for Joint Special Operations,* Washington, D.C.: Joint Publication 3–05, April 17, 1998.

U.S. Department of State, *Combating Terrorism: Department of State Programs to Combat Terrorism Abroad,* Washington, D.C.: United States General Accounting Office, GAO-02–1021, 2002.

———, *Patterns of Global Terrorism 2002,* Washington, D.C.: United States Department of State, April 2003.

U.S. General Accounting Office, *Defense Trade: Information on U.S. Weapons Deliveries to the Middle East,* Washington, D.C.: GAO-01–1078, 2001a.

———, *Information on U.S. Weapons Deliveries to the Middle East,* Washington, D.C.: GAO-01–1078, 2001b.

———, *Technology Assessment: Using Biometrics for Border Security,* Washington, D.C.: GAO-03–174, 2002.

Usher, Graham, "The Politics of Internal Security: The PA's New Intelligence Services," *Journal of Palestine Studies,* Vol. 25, No. 2, Winter 1996, pp. 21–34.

Vick, Alan, David Orletsky, Bruce Pirnie, and Seth Jones, *The Stryker Brigade Combat Team: Rethinking Strategic Responsiveness and Assessing Deployment Options,* Santa Monica, Calif.: RAND Corporation, MR-1606-AF, 2002.

Warn, Mats, and Anders Strindberg, "Syria Retains Ties with Hizbullah Despite U.S. Pressure for Change," *Jane's Intelligence Review,* Vol. 15, No. 6, June 2003, pp. 22–25.

Weinberger, Naomi, "The Palestinian National Security Debate," *Journal of Palestine Studies,* Vol. 24, No. 3, Spring 1995, pp. 16–30.

Weiner, Tim, "CIA Officers, with Israel's Knowledge, Teach Palestinians the Tricks of the Trade," *New York Times,* March 5, 1998, p. A10.

———, "CIA Will Press Arafat and Israel on Anti-Terrorism," *New York Times,* March 9, 1996, p. 1.

Weisman, Steven R., "U.S. Eases Demand for Palestinians to Curb Militants," *New York Times,* August 2, 2003a, p. A1.

———, "U.S. Plans Fast Aid for Gaza Projects," *New York Times,* July 10, 2003b, p. A1.

"What the CIA Can Teach the PLO," *New York Times,* March 7, 1998, p. A12.

Woodward, John D., Katharine Watkins Webb, Elaine M. Newton, Melissa Bradley, David Rubenson, Kristina Larson, Jacob Lilly, Katie Smythe, Brian K. Houghton, Harold Alan Pincus, Jonathan M. Schachter, and Paul Steinberg, *Army Biometric Applications: Identifying and Addressing Sociocultural Concerns,* Santa Monica, Calif.: RAND Corporation, MR-1237, 2001.

World Bank, *West Bank and Gaza Update,* Washington, D.C.: The World Bank Group, April 2002.

The Wye River Memorandum, October 23, 1998. Online at www.mfa.gov.il/mfa/go.asp? MFAH07o10 (as of June 7, 2004).

Zacharia, Janine, "U.S. Mulls Direct Aid to PA," *Jerusalem Post,* July 2, 2003, p. 1.

Zureik, Elia, "Crime, Justice, and Underdevelopment: The Palestinians Under Israeli Control," *International Journal of Middle East Studies,* Vol. 20, No. 4, November 1988, pp. 411–412.

CHAPTER FOUR

Demography

Kevin F. McCarthy and Brian Nichiporuk

Summary

In the four and one-half decades since the 1948 Arab-Israeli War triggered the first wave of the Palestinian diaspora, the size of the Palestinian population has increased almost sixfold (from approximately 1.5 million to almost 9 million). Throughout the first three decades of this period, the dominant demographic feature of this population was its increasingly geographic dispersion. Today, almost 40 percent of the Palestinian population lives within the boundaries of what would be a new Palestinian state (the West Bank and Gaza); another 50 percent is living in the four states near the West Bank and Gaza; and about 10 percent is living farther abroad.

Over at least the last two decades, however, the Palestinian diaspora appears to have ended, primarily as a result of a growing reluctance of the traditional destination states to allow additional Palestinians to settle. As a result, the growth of the Palestinian population has become increasingly concentrated within the boundaries of the West Bank and Gaza, where the most prominent feature of Palestinian demography has been the population's very high fertility. When combined with the possibility of large-scale return migration by diaspora Palestinians, this high fertility increases the probability of rapid population growth in the Palestinian territories for the foreseeable future.

Such rapid growth rates (currently about three times the world's average) are almost certain to pose a host of problems for a new Palestinian state. For example, given the poor condition of its infrastructure and its limited natural resources (most especially land and water), rapid population growth will stretch the ability and increase the costs of providing basic resources (water, sewerage, transportation) to Palestinian residents. Similarly, the Palestinian population's extreme youth (a byproduct of its high fertility) will tax the physical and human capital required to provide such essential services as education, health care, and housing, as well as placing a heavy financial burden for funding these services on a disproportionately smaller working-age population. Finally, a new Palestinian state will be hard-pressed to provide jobs not just for its current workers but also for the rapidly growing number of young adults who will be entering the labor force.

Although dealing with these challenges will be difficult given the current size of the population, they could prove to be even more daunting if the current rapid pace of growth does not abate. As the projections of future population by both the Palestinian Central Bureau of Statistics (PCBS) and the United States Bureau of the Census (USBC) make clear, the prospects for future Palestinian population growth hinge on the future course of fertility and migration. Currently, total fertility rates, a measure of the average number of children per woman and the key indicator used to project future fertility, are 6.9 in Gaza and 5.6 in the West Bank. These rates are among the highest in the world and much higher than the 2.1 children per woman needed for a population to replace itself. Although there are clear signs that these fertility rates are declining, the rate of that decline is very uncertain. As a result, the projections of the growth on the population between 2005 and 2025 span a very wide range—from a low of 5.4 million (about 70 percent higher than at present) to a high of 8.1 million (160 percent higher than at present). How many Palestinians return to a new state and when they arrive will also affect the future growth of the population both directly (in the form of additional residents) and indirectly (in the form of the children they bear after they return).

What can we expect in terms of future changes in fertility and mortality? In the short run, regardless of any declines in fertility rates, the number of births seems certain to increase given the fact that the number of Palestinian women in the prime childbearing years will more than double. Over the longer term, however, fertility rates will begin to decline. Whether these declines will lower the total fertility rate to replacement levels (as we assume in our low projection), or by 50 percent (as we assume in our medium projection) or by only 30 percent (as we assume in our high projection) would seem to depend upon the degree to which Palestinian women's education levels and labor force participation rise—since education appears to play a major role in determining both desired and actual childbearing patterns.

There is also considerable uncertainty surrounding the number of diaspora Palestinians who might move to a new Palestinian state. In their population projections, the Palestinian Central Bureau of Statistics and the United States Census Bureau estimate between 100,000 and 500,000 returnees. Our own estimates, based on assumptions about which groups of Palestinians (those living in camps, registered refugees, etc.) will be most likely to return and under what conditions, are somewhat higher. Which set of estimates will prove to be most accurate will depend upon the terms of the final agreement and social, political, and economic developments in the new Palestinian state.

Introduction

It has been over five decades since one could unambiguously link Palestine as a geographically identified state with the Palestinians as a people. This situation may be changing. If Israeli-Palestinian negotiations follow the "Roadmap" for peace proposed by President Bush, an independent and territorially defined Palestinian state could emerge rapidly. But declaring independence and forming a government will be only the most visible components of building a Palestinian state. Government agencies must be established; the health and welfare of the population must be provided for; the population must be educated; infrastructure and basic resources such as water, sewer, and transportation must be made available; and a viable economy established.

As is true for any state, demographic issues will help shape this state-building process in at least four ways. First, at the most basic level, a nascent Palestinian state must address the question of who among those of Palestinian lineage will qualify for citizenship and, just as importantly, who will have the right to settle in the newly independent Palestine. The answers to these questions can be assumed for most countries, but—given the history of the Palestinian people and its diaspora, Palestinian relations with Israel, and the political cleavages within the Palestinian population—these questions are of central importance to the future of a Palestinian state and how it will be viewed by Palestinians and others. Second, how these questions are answered, and thus which and how many Palestinians qualify for residence in the new state, will help determine the state's practical viability in terms of the balance between numbers of residents and the availability of basic resources. Third, the political viability of future Palestinian governments will depend upon their ability to meet the service requirements of their citizens. In large part, the demand for these services and the state's ability to supply them will be determined by the future number and characteristics of Palestinian residents. Finally, a central requirement for any future Palestinian government will be its ability to ensure that its residents can make a living. Demographic factors will influence the economic viability of a new state both because they determine the number of jobs required to employ the labor force and because the labor force itself will be one of the new state's most important economic resources.

This chapter describes the demography of the Palestinian people and how the characteristics of that population will affect each of the four key issues mentioned above: the number of residents in the new state, the balance between residents and resources, the new state's service requirements, and the ability of residents to make a living. It begins with a review of the post-1948 history of the Palestinian population and estimates how many Palestinians there are and where they are located. It then describes in some detail the characteristics of the population currently living in the West Bank and Gaza, with a particular focus on those features of the population that are likely to affect the balance between resources and population, the service needs of that population, and the demands they are likely to impose on the economy. It next explores various projections of the future growth of the population in the West Bank and Gaza as well as the feasibility of the assumptions underlying those projections.

We then turn to the links between the demography of the Palestinian population and the four issues identified above. We first examine the issue of the carrying capacity of the new state, what resources are available, and what they imply about the feasible size and distribution of that population. Next, we examine how the size and characteristics of that population will affect social service demand. Then, we turn to the implications of demography for the economy of a new Palestinian state. This discussion examines both the implications for the number of new jobs that will need to be created and the short- and longer-term prospects for the viability of the Palestinian economy.

Finally, we explore the critical issue of return migration of diaspora Palestinians to the new state and the tensions that this issue will almost certainly create between the legitimacy of the state and the pressures that substantial return migration will impose on the state's carrying capacity, service demands, and economy.

The Palestinian Population and Its Post-1948 Diaspora

Questions about how to define the Palestinian population and which elements among that population will be entitled to settle in Palestinian territory arise because of the rapid growth of that population and its dramatic diaspora since the 1948 Arab-Israeli War and the creation of the state of Israel. Prior to that war, approximately 1.5 million Palestinians lived in what was then Mandate Palestine. Today, the roughly 8.8 million people of Palestinian lineage are scattered across the globe—although the vast majority remain in the West Bank, Gaza, and nearby countries (see Table 4.1).

A little less than 40 percent of the Palestinian population is currently located in the Palestinian territories (the West Bank and Gaza), and approximately 50 percent are in the four countries surrounding those territories, with the largest single concentra-

Table 4.1
Distribution of the Palestinian Population by Region of Residence, 1995 to 2002

Region	Population (millions)		1995–2002 % Change	Distribution 2002 (%)
	1995	2002		
Palestine Territories	2.51	3.39	35.1	38.7
West Bank	1.63	2.16	32.5	24.7
Gaza	0.88	1.23	39.8	14.0
Surrounding Countries	3.55	4.52	27.3	51.6
Jordan	1.98	2.72	37.4	31.1
Lebanon	0.39	0.40	2.6	4.6
Syria	0.36	0.40	11.1	4.6
Israel	0.82	1.00	22.0	11.4
Far Abroad	0.71	0.83	16.9	9.5
Balance of Middle East	0.51	0.54	5.9	6.2
Others	0.20	0.29	45.0	3.3
Total	6.77	8.76	29.4	100.00

SOURCE: 1995 estimates from Adlakha et al. (1995); 2002 estimates from PCBS (2002).

tion in Jordan (about one-third of the total Palestinian population). Slightly less than 10 percent of all Palestinians are located in "far abroad" regions. About two-thirds of the "far abroad" population is located in the Middle East and about one-third outside the Middle East, with the largest single concentration in the United States (about 200,000) and other sizable settlements in Europe and Canada.

Over the past seven years (1995 to 2002), the Palestinian population has increased very rapidly—by about 30 percent, which is more than three times as fast as the world's population grew during this period. However, the rate at which the Palestinian population is growing varies dramatically depending upon where that population is located. The most rapid growth has occurred in the West Bank, Gaza, and Jordan, where almost three-quarters of all Palestinians now live, and outside the Middle East, where only about 3 percent of the Palestinian population is located. Growth rates have been much lower in other Arab countries (Syria, Lebanon, and the balance of the Middle East). Growth rates in Israel, where about 10 percent of the Palestinians are located, fall between these two groups.

These differences in growth rates largely reflect different demographic dynamics. Rapid population growth in the Palestinian territories is largely a by-product of the extremely high fertility of the Palestinian population in the West Bank and Gaza. Total fertility rates (a measure of the average number of children per woman) are 6.9 in Gaza and 5.6 in the West Bank—many times higher than the 2.1 children per woman required for a population to replace itself (PCBS 2003b).

The Palestinian population in Jordan has also grown significantly due to the repatriation of close to 300,000 Palestinians who relocated to Jordan from Kuwait following the U.S.-led eviction of Iraq from Kuwait during Operation Desert Storm. The rapid increase in the number of Palestinians living outside the Middle East (although starting from a small base) is primarily a function of migration to these areas. The slower rates of growth in the balance of the Middle East reflect somewhat lower fertility rates in these countries (although still well above the level required for replacement) and what appears to be a reversal of the formerly rapid pace of in-migration by Palestinians to these areas.

Indeed, the increasing concentration of the Palestinian population in the West Bank, Gaza, and Jordan reflected in Table 4.1 represents a marked contrast to the increasing dispersal of the Palestinian population that characterized most of the post-1948 era. This dispersal, typically referred to as the Palestinian diaspora, is depicted in Figure 4.1, which plots the average annual rate of growth of the Palestinian population in five-year intervals from 1950 to 2002 in the five areas containing the vast majority of the Palestinian population.[1] Since Israel has tightly controlled migration into its territory, the growth rate of its Palestinian population provides a measure of the natural

---

[1] The surrounding states include Syria, Lebanon, and Jordan. Most of the Palestinians living in the balance of the Middle East live in the Gulf region.

Figure 4.1
Growth Rates of Palestinian Population by Area of Residence, 1950–2002

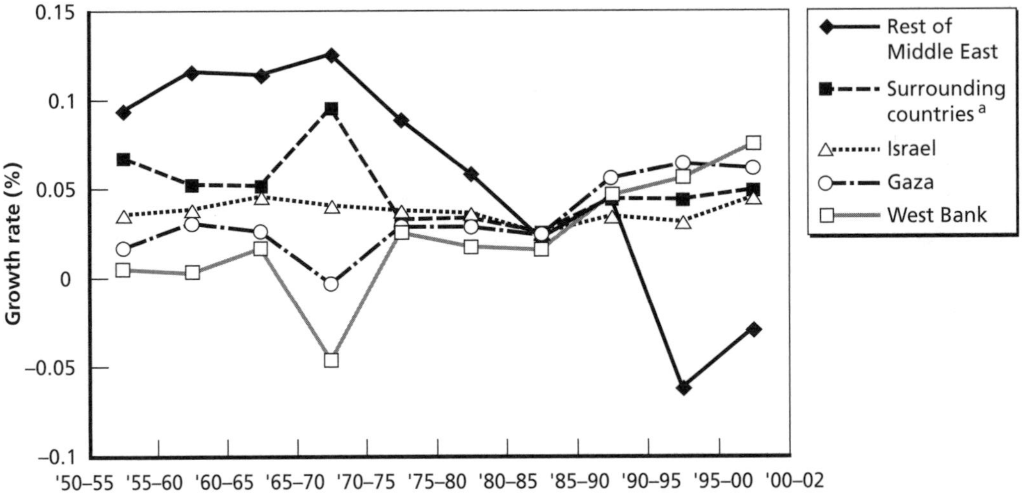

SOURCE: McCarthy (1996), USBC (1999; 2003a, b).

^aSyria, Lebanon, and Jordan.

RAND *MG146-4.1*

increase of the Palestinian population throughout this period.[2] Deviations around this line reflect the influence of migration and thus provide a history of the movement of the Palestinian population throughout the diaspora.

Although Figure 4.1 begins with 1950–1955, the first wave of refugees—approximately 700,000—actually left or were expelled during and shortly after the end of the 1948 war. These 1948 refugees and their descendants settled in the West Bank, Gaza, southern Lebanon, Jordan, and Syria.

Apparently, most of those who settled in Gaza came from Jaffa and villages south of Jaffa; those who lived in the northern half of what is now Israel, including a substantial group from Haifa, moved north into Syria and Lebanon.[3] Despite this outflow, over three-quarters of the initial Palestinian population was still located in the West Bank and Gaza in 1950 (McCarthy, 1996).

During the next 15 years (1950 to 1965), Gaza and especially the West Bank experienced very modest growth (well below the growth rate of the Palestinian population in Israel, which was driven almost exclusively by natural increase) suggesting that,

---

[2] The growth of Israel's Palestinian population no doubt understates the actual rate of natural increase, since there has certainly been some outmigration of Palestinians from Israel during this period. The most salient fact about the use of Israel's Palestinian population as a standard against which to measure natural increase, however, is the absence of any substantial amount of immigration.

[3] See historical review of Palestinian refugee movements at http://www.globalexchange.org/countries/palestine/refugeeFacts.

subsequent to their initial resettlement, there was considerable movement of the original refugees and their descendants to other areas of the Middle East. This movement is reflected in the rapid growth of the Palestinian populations both in the surrounding states and, in particular, in other areas of the Middle East. In fact, most of this growth took place in the Gulf states, which imported skilled Palestinians to fill managerial and professional jobs during the massive development programs that they began during this period. The number of Palestinians living in the balance of the Middle East increased almost fourfold during this period. In addition, Jordan's investment in East Bank development encouraged significant migration from the West Bank (annexed by Jordan in 1950) to the East Bank during this period.

The 1967 Six-Day War triggered a second major outflow of Palestinians from the West Bank and Gaza. Approximately 150,000 to 200,000 Palestinians were displaced by this war (reflected in the negative growth in the West Bank and Gaza during this period), most of whom moved to the surrounding Arab states, especially Jordan, and to a lesser extent elsewhere in the Middle East.

Since the 1970s, however, the rate of movement of Palestinians around the Middle East appears to have dropped off—a pattern that is apparent in the convergence of growth rates after 1980. Four major factors have influenced this reversal of prior migration patterns. First, the Gulf states became increasingly reluctant to import Arab labor, including Palestinian workers, during the late 1970s and 1980s—a phenomenon that is reflected in the steady decline in the growth rate of their Palestinian populations after 1970. Initially this reluctance was driven by security concerns about the political integration of Palestinian guest workers—a concern that culminated in the expulsion of more than 300,000 Palestinians from Kuwait after the Gulf War ended in 1991. More recently, it has been driven by rising unemployment among the indigenous populations of these countries and national policies designed to substitute native for foreign-born workers.

Second, with the exception of Jordan, where over half of the population is already of Palestinian origin and where most of the Palestinians expelled from Kuwait appear to have settled, the surrounding states have become considerably less willing to resettle Palestinians. This situation is most pronounced in Lebanon, where the Palestinian population has been marginalized both economically and politically as a result of its being caught in the middle of ethnic and religious divisions that have periodically erupted in armed conflict. Indeed, the Lebanese government has made it clear that it wants the Palestinian population to return to Palestine as soon as possible. Although the Palestinians living in Syria are better integrated into the local economy, their political rights remain circumscribed.

Third, although the Palestinian population outside the Middle East has never been large, the willingness of countries in North America and Europe to resettle substantial numbers has, no doubt, declined sharply since the events of 9/11.

Finally, the Oslo Accords and the establishment of the Palestinian Authority in the West Bank and Gaza have rekindled the prospect of a return to Palestine and, despite periodic intifadas and violence between Palestinians and Israelis, increased the attractiveness of Palestine as a final destination, particularly in contrast to what appears in general to be a growing reluctance of other Arab states to accept large numbers of Palestinian migrants.[4]

Several key points emerge from this brief history of the Palestinian population since the 1948 war. First, although war and civil turmoil have played a significant role in the dispersion of the Palestinian population over the past 55 years, there also appears to have been a considerable amount of economically motivated migration. This pattern suggests that political and economic prospects will play a significant role in determining where diaspora Palestinians choose to settle over the long run. Second, the diaspora—the movement of Palestinians around the world—appears to have terminated at least two decades ago. This change appears to be due less to the integration of the Palestinian population into the various countries in which they have settled than to a growing reluctance of the traditional destination countries to resettle additional Palestinians. Third, although much of the rhetoric surrounding the establishment of a Palestinian state has revolved around the return of Palestinian refugees from the 1948 and 1967 conflicts, in fact, the number of surviving refugees and displaced persons is likely to be dwarfed by the number of their descendants, many of whom will have never lived in Palestine. Using data for the first half of the 1990s, for example, we estimated that, at that time, the refugees were outnumbered by their descendants 7 to 1. That ratio has most likely increased substantially since then. Finally, as the movement of Palestinians across international borders has dropped off precipitously, the growth and distribution of that population has been increasingly shaped by natural increase. This has been particularly true of the Palestinian population in the West Bank and Gaza. As we will discuss below, the rapid growth of that population due to very high fertility levels will pose real challenges for a future Palestinian state. These challenges will only be intensified by the return of a substantial number of the diaspora Palestinian population.

A Profile of the Population in the West Bank and Gaza

Barring a large-scale return of Palestinians from abroad (a topic to which we will return in the section titled "Prospects for Return Migration"), the population most likely to affect the operation of a future Palestinian state is the one currently living in the West Bank and Gaza, along with its descendants. Three demographic factors stand out: the total size of that population, its future growth, and its age structure. Population size and growth are directly relevant to a state's carrying capacity; its age structure is particularly important in shaping both the demand for services and the state's ability to provide those services.

Virtually all demographic phenomena (births, deaths, marriage, childbearing, and migration), many economic behaviors (entering and retiring from the labor force), and

---

[4] Survey research conducted by Khalil Shikaki (2003) provides recent empirical data on the attractiveness of a new Palestinian state as the destination of choice for most refugees.

many other key decisions and behaviors (obtaining education and training, setting up a household) typically occur within certain age ranges. From a societal point of view, three age groups are particularly noteworthy: the young population (both preschoolers and those who are still in school); the working population; and those who have retired from the labor force. Although the services they use differ, both the young and the retired populations are intensive service users. The costs of providing those services are largely borne by the working-age population either directly (through cross-generational transfers) or indirectly (through taxes). Thus, the relative sizes of these different groups will directly affect both the nature and amount of services a population demands and the ability to provide those services.

As noted in Table 4.1, a little less than 40 percent of the total Palestinian population worldwide currently lives in the West Bank and Gaza. The total population of the West Bank is three-quarters larger than that of Gaza, but between 1995 and 2002, the growth rate in Gaza was 22 percent higher than in the West Bank. The higher growth rate in Gaza is due partly to the return of about 100,000 Palestinians to Gaza, where the seat of Palestinian government was initially located after the signing of the Oslo Accords, and partly to a higher fertility rate in Gaza (although different sources report different estimates of those rates[5]). Whatever the actual rates, they are clearly very high by any standard. The U.S. Census reports that the worldwide fertility rate in 1998 was 2.9; as we have already noted, a rate of 2.1 is sufficient for population replacement.[6]

A direct consequence of high Palestinian fertility is a very young age structure. Figures 4.2 and 4.3 present the age-gender structures of the West Bank and Gaza in the form of a population pyramid. Population pyramids show the size of each successive male and female age cohort of the population. These pyramids are typical of societies with high fertility and very rapid growth. This pattern is reflected in the fact that the youngest cohort is the largest single age grouping. As one moves up the age pyramid, each successive cohort is smaller than the one that preceded it. Both of these population pyramids are dominated by youth (those who are less than 20 years old), who make up the vast majority of the population. The median age of these populations, for example, is 16, meaning that half of the total population is 16 or younger.

A clearer picture of the implications of this age structure on the demand for social services in these populations can be obtained by combining these individual age groups into the five age categories identified above as most relevant to service demand: pre-

---

[5] The Palestinian Central Bureau of Statistics reports discrepant estimates of total fertility rates for the West Bank and Gaza. In an analytical report on fertility patterns in Palestine (PCBS, 2003b), the total fertility rates for the West Bank and Gaza are reported as 4.5 and 5.4 for the years 1997 to 1999. In its statistical fact sheet, the PCBS reports total fertility rates of 5.5 and 6.8 for the West Bank and Gaza, respectively, for 2002. The most recent population projections by the PCBS use total fertility rates of 5.6 and 6.9 for the West Bank and Gaza, respectively. The U.S. Bureau of the Census World Population Profile (1999) reports that the 1998 total fertility rates for West Bank and Gaza were 4.9 and 7.6, respectively. Its most recent projections use the 5.6 and 6.9 figures.

[6] The Census estimates that the average total fertility rate for the Middle East as a whole was 4.4, the highest for any region. For less-developed countries as a whole, the rate is 3.2; for the developed countries, 1.6 (U.S. Bureau of Census, 1999).

Figure 4.2
Age Pyramid for West Bank, 2000

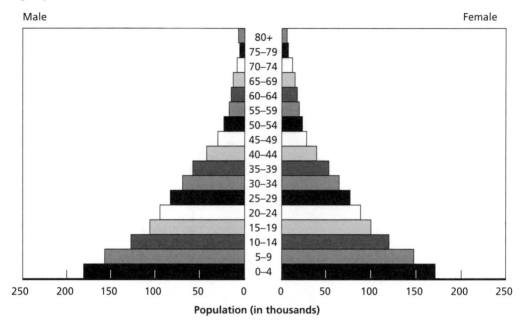

SOURCE: U.S. Census Bureau, International Data Base.
RAND *MG146-4.2*

Figure 4.3
Age Pyramid for Gaza, 2000

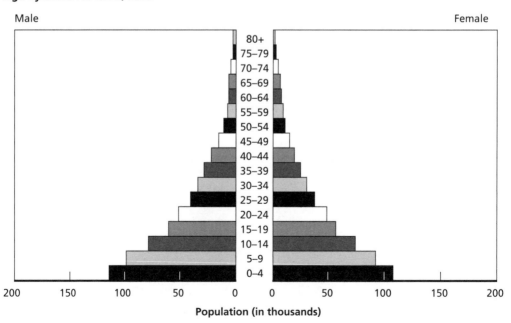

SOURCE: U.S. Census Bureau, International Data Base.
RAND *MG146-4.3*

schoolers (ages 0 to 4), the school-age population (ages 5 to 19), younger (ages 20 to 44) and older workers (ages 45 to 64), and retirees (age 65 and above), and comparing the size of these groups in the Palestinian territories to their counterparts in other areas. The three comparison groups used here are the Middle East (the fastest growing region of the world), the less-developed countries, and the more-developed countries. These comparisons are reported in Table 4.2.

As might be expected, this comparison highlights the sharp differences in age structure between the populations of the West Bank and Gaza and of developed countries. However, the data presented in Table 4.2 also reveal that the Palestinian population is significantly younger than that of less-developed countries as a whole, and younger than other populations in the rapidly growing Middle East. Not surprisingly, these differences are most pronounced on a percentage basis at the extremes of the age distribution—for example, there are more than three times as many preschool-age children on a percentage basis in the Palestinian territories as in the developed countries, but only one-fifth as many retirees. However, significant differences are also readily apparent among both the school and working-age populations. The school-age population is almost twice as large as that of developed countries and one-quarter larger than that of developing countries. Conversely, the proportion of the population of working age is significantly smaller than in all the other areas listed.

These differences in age structure are likely to have profound effects, at both the state and individual household levels. At the state level, for example, they not only will affect the types and cost of services that must be supplied but may also influence state-funded capital investments—resources allocated to current consumption cannot be devoted to investments. Similarly, larger household sizes (a direct by-product of high fertility) will affect household resource allocation decisions. The more money that must be devoted to meeting basic household needs (food, housing, clothes, etc.), the less that is available for investing in education, training, and accumulating private capital.

Table 4.2
Comparison of Selected Age Groups (% of total population)

Age Group	Palestinian Territories			Middle East	Less-Developed Countries	Developed Countries
	West Bank	Gaza	Total			
Preschool (0–4)	17.5	19.8	18.4	14.1	11.6	5.7
School age (5–19)	39.0	40.9	39.2	34.8	31.8	20.0
Early workers (20–44)	22.8	20.4	21.9	34.5	37.8	36.8
Late workers (45–64)	7.5	8.0	8.0	11.9	20.2	23.3
Retirees (65+)	3.3	2.5	2.9	4.3	4.9	14.2

SOURCE: Palestinian Population from 1997 Census of Population, PCBS (1999). Data for other countries from USBC (1999).

Given the youthfulness of the Palestinian population, we would expect that, at both the governmental and private levels, major expenditures will need to be made for housing, education, and health care (especially for young children and the elderly). Moreover, given the high dependency ratios in the Palestinian population, the resources required for these expenditures will pose a proportionately greater burden on the working-age population, through either taxes (if the state provides these services directly) or intergenerational transfers (if they are primarily provided within the family). The extent of that burden will, of course, vary with the level of expenditures, but there is no question that there are many fewer Palestinian workers per preschool and school-age child (the ratio is 0.73 workers per child in the West Bank and 0.60 in Gaza, compared with 3.1 in developed countries, 1.2 in developing countries, and 0.96 in the Middle East as a whole).

Prospects of Future Population Growth in the West Bank and Gaza

The pressures its population will pose for a new Palestinian state will depend not only on the population's current size and structure but also on how these features change in the future. As in all populations, such changes are produced in two ways: through natural increase (the difference between births and deaths), and net migration (moves into and out of the country). In this section, we first discuss the mechanics of population growth and how they will condition the timing and amount of future growth in the Palestinian territories. We next present different projections of future population growth. Finally, we discuss the assumptions underlying those projections and their implications for the actual course of growth.

Dynamics of Future Population Growth

Of the two determinants of natural increase, the future course of fertility in the West Bank and Gaza is considerably more uncertain than the future course of mortality. Indeed, in contrast to the much higher levels of fertility in Palestine than in other developing regions, mortality patterns are notably lower there than in the rest of the developing world. For example, the infant mortality rates in the West Bank and Gaza (27 and 24 per 1,000) lie between those in the developed countries (9 per 1,000) and those in both the Middle East (45 per 1,000) and the developing world (58 per 1,000). The same pattern is evident in comparisons of life expectancy.[7] In fact, the two most notable projections of future population growth in the West Bank and Gaza (those made by the Palestinian Central Bureau of Statistics and by the United States Census Bureau) both assume minor improvements in mortality for the foreseeable future.[8]

---

[7] Life expectancy is 71 years in Gaza and 72 in the West Bank, compared with 75 in developed countries, 69 in the Middle East as a whole, and 63 in the developing world.

[8] The USBC, for example, projects that life expectancy will increase by approximately 6 percent in both the West Bank and Gaza between 2000 and 2025.

Correspondingly, what happens to fertility patterns will principally determine the future growth of the population in a new Palestinian state. Both the PCBS and the USBC project that fertility rates among the Palestinian population will decline in the future, but these declines will not immediately result in fewer births. The number of births is a product of both a population's fertility rates and its age structure; the age structures of the populations in the West Bank and Gaza are particularly conducive to high birth rates. This pattern is reflected in Table 4.3, which compares relevant measures of both fertility behavior and age structure in the West Bank and Gaza with comparable measures in the remainder of the Middle East, developed countries, and developing countries. As we noted above, the total fertility rate among Palestinians is substantially higher than elsewhere, including the rest of the Middle East. In addition, a substantially larger fraction of Palestinian women are in the prime childbearing years (ages 15 to 44). Moreover, the number of women in the childbearing ages (all of whom are already born) will increase by over 40 percent in the West Bank and by almost 60 percent in Gaza during the current decade.

Projected Growth

Since the number of births to a population is a product of the rate at which women bear children and the number of women in the childbearing years, fertility rates would need to drop both very substantially and very rapidly to keep the number of births from rising from their current (already high) levels—at least for the next decade. In fact, both the PCBS and USBC projections assume that Palestinian fertility rates will decline by only between 20 and 25 percent during the current decade—substantially less than the much more certain rise in the number of women in the childbearing years. Thus, even if fertility rates follow the expected downward pattern, the number of births (and correspondingly, the absolute growth of the Palestinian population in the West Bank and Gaza) can be expected to expand for at least the next decade.

Although continued decline in fertility rates will eventually result in a decline in the number of women in the childbearing years, the size and timing of that decline will

Table 4.3
Selected Comparisons of Fertility Potential of the Palestinian Population, 1998

Area	Total Fertility Rate	Women in Childbearing Years (ages 15–44)	
		% Adult Women	% Change, 2000–2010
Gaza	6.8	84	58
West Bank	5.5	83	42
Middle East	4.4	80	31
Developed countries	1.6	60	−3
Developing countries	3.7	71	17

SOURCE: USBC (1999).

depend upon how quickly and how far fertility rates drop. This phenomenon is often referred to as the "momentum" of population growth and can take decades to play out. The importance of this momentum and the degree to which it will continue to operate in a new Palestinian state is particularly relevant in light of potential increases in economic growth and productivity that can result from the so-called "demographic bonus." This term refers to the drop in dependency ratio (the ratio of children and elderly to the working-age population) that occurs when rapidly declining fertility reduces the number of births relative to the working-age population before the effects of previously high fertility rates begin to increase the size of the elderly population. Such a decline in the dependency ratio can allow countries to increase the resources they devote to investment rather than consumption and thus increase productivity and economic growth. Although this bonus appears to have played a role in the growth of such countries as Korea and Taiwan and, some predict, may soon occur in other Middle Eastern countries, it will not begin to operate in Palestine before 2015 at the earliest.

The second major component of growth in Palestine is net migration. As we have already suggested, how many and which diaspora Palestinians return to a new Palestinian state will play an important role in determining the legitimacy of that state. How these issues are resolved will, of course, be determined by the political negotiation process. But the outcome of those political negotiations can have a significant influence on the future demography of a new state. This effect will have both direct and indirect components.

Clearly, the larger the number of diaspora Palestinians who move to Palestine, the larger the direct addition to the resident population. In addition to this direct effect, however, migrants will indirectly increase the size of the population through childbearing after they migrate. The importance of this indirect effect will depend upon the timing of the return migrants (the sooner the migrants return, the larger the effect), the characteristics of the migrants (the higher their fertility, the larger the effect), and, of course, the number of migrants (the more migrants, the larger the effect).

As we have already noted, both the PCBS and the USBC have made projections of future population growth in the West Bank and Gaza for the period 2000 to 2025.[9] Table 4.4 presents the results of the PCBS's medium projection. The assumptions underlying these projections are reported in the notes to the table. As the results make clear, the population of a new Palestinian state is projected to increase rapidly over the next 25 years. The population of the West Bank, for example, is projected to more than double, and, consistent with its higher fertility rate, Gaza's population is projected to increase by over 160 percent. The population of the combined West Bank and Gaza is projected to increase by 133 percent.

Although the total amount of growth is projected to remain at approximately 800,000 per five-year period during the 25 years covered by this projection, the overall

---

[9] The PCBS and the USBC appear to have used the same fertility and mortality assumptions in their projections. As we note below, they differ only in the assumptions about net migration.

Table 4.4
PCBS Medium Projections of Population Growth in West Bank and Gaza Between 2000 and 2025 (estimates in thousands)

Year	West Bank	Gaza	Total
2000	2,017	1,142	3,159
2005	2,541	1,472	4,013
2010	3,061	1,868	4,929
2015	3,517	2,241	5,758
2020	3,962	2,618	6,580
2025	4,409	2,993	7,402

NOTES: Key assumptions—Mortality: Infant mortality rate will decrease by 50 percent between 1995 and 2025 and life expectancy at birth will increase by 6 percent. Migration: Net migration into the Palestinian territories will total 500,000 between 1997 and 2011. Net migration between 2011 and 2025 is assumed to be zero. Fertility: The total fertility rate will decline by 50 percent by 2025.

growth rate in the Palestinian territories is expected to decline from its current annual rate of just under 4 percent to about 2.2 percent.[10] In both cases, however, the annual growth rate is expected to increase in the short term because the projections assume that approximately 500,000 net migrants will enter the Palestinian territories prior to 2011.[11]

As is true of all population projections, the accuracy of these projections depends upon the accuracy of the assumptions about the future course of fertility, mortality, and net migration that underlie the projection. In recognition of this fact, the PCBS has produced alternative projections using different assumptions about how rapidly total fertility rates will decline over the next 25 years. Although the USBC uses essentially the same set of assumptions as the PCBS about how fertility and mortality patterns will change over the next 25 years, each agency uses a different set of assumptions about net migration.[12] Combining these two sets of projections, we can see how the total population of a new Palestinian state might change under alternative assumptions. The results of this comparison are reported in Table 4.5.

Not surprisingly, the projected change in total population varies dramatically depending upon the assumptions that are made about the future course of fertility and migration in a proposed Palestinian state. Although the total population in the combined Palestinian territories will increase substantially regardless of the assumptions

---

[10] The respective declines in annual growth rates differ somewhat between the West Bank and Gaza in this projection. The rate in the West Bank is projected to drop from its current rate of 3.81 percent to about 2 percent. The rate in Gaza is projected to decline from its current rate of 4.3 percent to 2.49 percent (PCBS, 2003c).

[11] The accuracy of these migration assumptions is examined in more detail in the section entitled "Prospects for Return Migration," which compares these assumptions with estimates based on survey data on the location preferences of diaspora Palestinians.

[12] The PCBS assumes that 500,000 net migrants will enter the West Bank and Gaza between 1997 and 2011; the USBC assumes that the corresponding figure for that period will be 100,000. Both agencies have assumed zero net migration after 2010.

Table 4.5
Projections of Total Palestinian Population in 2025 Under Alternative Fertility and Migration Assumptions

	Net Migration 1997 to 2011 (thousands)	
Fertility	Low	High
Low	5,352	6,232
Medium	6,422	7,402
High	7,125	8,125
	% Change from 2000	
	Low	High
Low	69.4	97.3
Medium	103.3	134.3
High	125.5	157.2

NOTES: Fertility assumptions—Low: Total fertility rate will decline to replacement level (2.1) by 2025 in the West Bank and Gaza. Medium: Total fertility rate will decline by 50 percent in both West Bank and Gaza by 2025. High: Total fertility rate will decline by 30 percent in both West Bank and Gaza by 2025. Migration assumptions—Low: 100,000 net migrants between 2000 and 2010; High: 500,000 net migrants between 2000 and 2020.

used, the range between the lowest and highest projections of total population is over 50 percent (5.4 to 8.1 million). Correspondingly, the projected percentage growth in the total population between 2000 and 2025 might range from a little under 70 to almost 160 percent.

The magnitude of the expected decline in fertility and the scale of net migration will both make a substantial difference in the size of the Palestinian population in 2025. For example, if the fertility rate in the Palestinian territories were actually to decline to the replacement level, the total population would be almost 1.2 million smaller than if it declined by only 50 percent during that period. However, if fertility rates were to decline by 30 rather than 50 percent, the total population would be almost three-quarters of a million larger. Similarly, an increase of 400,000 migrants by 2010 would increase the total population by almost one million people.[13]

Accuracy of the Underlying Assumptions

As we suggested above, projections of future population growth are not predictions of what will actually occur. Instead, the accuracy of any projection depends upon the accuracy of the assumptions that drive it. Since we will discuss the issue of diaspora

---

[13] The difference in USBC and PCBS medium projections in 2025 is 980,000. This difference is due to the PCBS's assumption of 500,000 net migrants by 2010 versus the USBC's assumption of 100,000 net migrants. The fact that the total difference in these two projections substantially exceeds the difference in net migrants reflects natural increase among the migrants.

Palestinians returning to a new Palestinian state in "Prospects for Return Migration" below, we focus our discussion here on which of the alternative assumptions about the future course of Palestinian fertility appears to be most probable.

All of the projections discussed above assume that the fertility rates of Palestinian women will decline over the next 25 years. In fact, there is strong evidence to support this assumption because the number of children ever born to Palestinian women who are currently nearing the end of the reproductive years (ages 40 to 49) is significantly higher than current total fertility rates—a synthetic measure of projected total fertility.[14] The key questions about future fertility are how far and how fast fertility rates are likely to drop. The various projections reported above use very different assumptions about these two issues. The low projection, for example, assumes that total fertility rates in the West Bank and Gaza will decline to the replacement level (2.1 children per woman) over the next 25 years. This represents a 63 percent decline in fertility among women in the West Bank and a 70 percent decline in fertility among women in Gaza. The medium projection, on the other hand, assumes that total fertility rates in both the West Bank and Gaza will decline by 50 percent over the next 25 years (these declines would reduce the total fertility rate in the West Bank and Gaza to 2.8 and 3.45, respectively). Finally, the high projection assumes that total fertility rates will decline by 30 percent over the next 25 years (these declines would reduce total fertility rates in the West Bank and Gaza to 3.9 and 4.8, respectively). Which of these assumptions most closely matches reality will determine not only the size of the total population in 2025 but also how much growth will occur thereafter.

Demographers have shown that women's reproductive behavior is determined by a combination of demographic and social factors (Davis and Blake, 1956). We have already noted, for example, that the number of births is strongly influenced by how many women are of childbearing age. How many of those women will actually bear children will be affected by several other demographic factors, e.g., the percentage of women who marry, their average age at marriage, their use of contraceptives, and the effectiveness of the contraceptive methods.[15] Similarly, the number of children women bear is affected by what they consider their desired family size, which in turn varies depending upon what opportunities are available for women outside childbearing and childrearing, women's education levels, and their labor force patterns (McCarthy, 2001). Thus, to evaluate how plausible the various fertility assumptions used in these projections are, we now examine how Palestinian women compare across these various dimensions.

---

[14] Unlike the number of children ever born, which reflects actual fertility behavior, the total fertility rate assumes that women will continue to have children at the same rate as women of various ages are currently bearing children, i.e., it sums the age-specific birth rates of women across various ages. Currently, the mean number of children ever born among women age 40–49 is 6.05 in the West Bank and 7.04 in Gaza. The comparable total fertility rates for those two areas are 5.6 and 6.9, respectively.

[15] Another key factor in most cultures is the incidence of childbearing outside of marriage. However, we assume that this is very low in all Arab societies.

In several respects, marriage patterns among Palestinian women appear to fall between the patterns in the developed world and those in the balance of the Middle East and the rest of the less developed world. Among women of reproductive age (15 to 49), for example, about two-thirds are currently married, compared with about 60 percent in the developed countries and between 67 percent in developing countries and 71 percent in the Middle East as a whole. In addition, about 90 percent of all women eventually marry, as is true for the developed world. However, marriage patterns in Palestine differ sharply from those in the developed world in two respects. First, Palestinian women marry at much younger ages than in the developed world. The median age at which women marry in the Palestinian territories is 20, compared with 25 in the United States. Second, married women in Palestine appear much less likely to divorce or become separated from their husbands than those in developed countries. The PCBS, for example, reports that less than 4 percent of ever-married Palestinian women between the ages of 40 and 49 were divorced or separated from their husbands, compared with close to 18 percent of ever-married American women of similar ages.[16] The net effect of these differences in marriage patterns seems to be that Palestinian women not only are exposed to the risk of childbearing at significantly earlier ages but also are substantially less likely to have that exposure cut off by divorce or separation than are women in developed countries. Since rising ages at marriage and increased marital disruption rates appear to have played an important role in reducing fertility in the developed world, these differences in marriage patterns would seem to militate against rapid reductions in fertility among Palestinian women.

Marriage patterns among Palestinian women are, of course, likely to change as they have in the developed world over the past few decades. Of the two marriage patterns discussed above, however, the age of marriage is more likely to rise than the rate of marital disruption. But the key to that change would appear to be increasing education levels among Palestinian women, since marriage ages are notably higher among Palestinian women who have at least 13 years of schooling.

Contraceptive practices can, of course, offset prolonged exposure to childbearing among married women, and there is evidence that contraceptive usage, particularly the use of modern contraceptive methods, is increasing among Palestinian women (PCBS, 2001). However, that increase is most pronounced among older women (ages 30 to 49). Overall rates of contraceptive usage among Palestinian women appear to lie slightly below the mid-range of international patterns (USBC, 1999). Moreover, the rate of usage of modern contraceptive methods among married Palestinian women does not appear to be related to education levels.

Traditionally, the sustained declines in fertility rates in the developed countries have been associated with changed views of childbearing. In high-fertility societies, large families often represent a form of social security—a conscious investment in the

---

[16] The statistics reported here for Palestine come from the PCBS (2002); the data for the United States come from U.S. Department of Commerce (2001).

future. People tend to have many children to help with the labor of the family and to provide for the elderly when they can no longer work.[17] Low-fertility societies, on the other hand, have a very different view of children and focus not on having many children but rather on having a few well-educated ones—"quality" rather than quantity (McCarthy, 2001). This attitudinal shift reflects the increased importance of work and economic mobility as well as a profoundly transformed view of women's role. Such a view is typically reflected in increasing levels of education and labor-force participation among women, as well as reductions in their desired family sizes. Although this view is most pronounced in the developed world, it is also increasingly apparent in the developing world.

The most recent data on desired family size among Palestinian women were collected in a 1995 survey conducted by the PCBS. Although the results of that survey suggest that desired family size is lower for younger women than for older women,[18] the median ideal number of children per woman, 4.6, is still well above the total fertility rates used in the low and medium projections (between 2.1 and 3.5) and lies between the total fertility rates for the West Bank (3.9) and Gaza (4.8) used in the high projections. Of course, desired family size among Palestinian women may well decline during the next two decades. Indeed, although we have no information on desired family size by education level, the PCBS reports that Palestinian women with at least 13 years of schooling (the equivalent of some post-secondary training) have lower fertility rates than less well-educated women.[19] Thus, there is reason to believe that fertility rates in the Palestinian territories will decline as education levels of women increase—particularly if more Palestinian women receive post-secondary training.

Although current educational levels among Palestinian women appear to be high relative to the balance of the Middle East, they are well below the levels found in developed countries. The PCBS reports, for example, that only 19 percent of adult Palestinian women have completed 12 years of schooling (secondary school), compared with 84 percent of adult women in the United States, and only about 7 percent have completed some post-secondary training (at least 13 years of schooling), compared with 24 percent in the United States.[20] However, the general pattern of rising school enrollment

---

[17] In addition to these social and economic reasons for high fertility, Palestinian women may also be partly motivated by political reasons to the extent that high growth rates might be viewed as strengthening the Palestinian cause vis-à-vis Israel, which has much lower fertility.

[18] The median reported ideal was over five children per woman among those age 40 and older and about 4.6 for those under 40 (PCBS, 1995). It is also interesting to note that total fertility rates among Palestinian Christians are substantially lower than those of Moslems (2.6 versus 6.2). However, the percentage of Christians living in Palestine has declined progressively over the past 100 years and is now less than 5 percent of the total Palestinian population (Fargues, 1998).

[19] The total fertility rate among women with 13 or more years of schooling is 3.4, compared with over 5 for women with less education (PCBS, 2002).

[20] The figures for Palestine are derived from data reported in PCBS (2002). The U.S. figures are reported in U.S. Department of Commerce (2000).

rates in Palestine suggests that educational levels may rise sharply in the future, assuming that the disruptions caused by the current intifada are short term. Table 4.6, for example, compares school enrollment rates by age among Palestinian and American women. Although Palestinian girls start school on average a year later than American girls, their enrollment rates through age 13 are comparable. Female enrollment in the secondary-school years (ages 14 to 17) begins to drop off among Palestinian women—a difference that becomes more pronounced at older ages.[21] Nonetheless, these enrollment rates suggest that the percentage of women age 18 and above who will complete at least some post-secondary education is substantially higher than in the population as a whole.

The degree to which increased schooling will translate into lower fertility, however, may well be conditioned by whether employment opportunities are available for women. Currently, women's labor force participation in Palestine is low by most developing country standards (UN, 2001). However, the rate at which Palestinian women participate in the labor force is very strongly related to their education levels. For example, the PCBS reports that half of all working-age women with at least 13 years of schooling are in the labor force, compared with 18 percent of women with 10 to 12 years of schooling and 12 percent of women with less than 9 years.

In conclusion, although the fertility rates of Palestinian women seem certain to decline, the extent and pace of that decline appears to be contingent on increasing their education levels and employment opportunities. If these factors lag, so too will the pace and extent of their fertility decline. If, on the other hand, they can be expanded significantly, fertility rates will decline at a faster pace and so, correspondingly, will the rate of population growth.

Table 4.6
Comparison of Female School Enrollment Rates by Age in Palestine and the United States (%)

Ages	Palestine	United States
5–6	54	95
7–9	99	98
10–13	97	99
14–15	84	98
16–17	62	94
18–19	33	63
20–21	18	47
22–24	5	27

SOURCES: PCBS (2002), USBC (1999).

---

[21] Interestingly, female school enrollment rates are higher than those of males in Palestine until ages 18–19, when they lag behind. In the United States, females actually have higher enrollment rates than males—although the differences are not large.

Implications of Population for the State-Building Process

As we discussed above, the size and characteristics of the population in a new Palestinian state will affect the state-building process by determining the natural and physical resources needed to sustain the population; by influencing the demand for services and the ability to support those service levels; and by shaping the demands placed on the economy. In this section, we examine each of these issues in turn.

Carrying Capacity

Palestine will begin statehood with the second-highest population density in the Arab world: 567 persons per square kilometer, second only to Bahrain at 1,014 persons per square kilometer. And in light of the population projections described above, this density will increase to between 958 and 1,457 persons per square kilometer over the next 25 years. Moreover, these are averages for the entire Palestinian territory and thus mask the considerable difference between the West Bank and the much more densely settled Gaza, where population density is already 3,457 person per square kilometer—a figure that rivals Singapore and Hong Kong,[22] two of the most densely settled regions in the world.

These statistics raise the question as to whether a new Palestinian state has or will in the near future reach its "carrying capacity"—the total population that the nation's land and resources can sustain. However, as the comparison with Hong Kong and Singapore suggests, the challenge of coping with increasing population density depends less on physical limits and more on how a society and its economy are organized and what financial and technological resources it has at its disposal for coping with increasing population size and density. In other words, the real issues are costs and resources. In the years since Malthus predicted that population growth would eventually outstrip the growth of available resources in 1798, global population and income levels have both expanded multifold—exactly contrary to his theory.

Although the exact costs of adjusting to continued rapid population growth in Palestine are unknown, it is certain that they will be substantial and are likely to include not only financial resources but also economic and social adjustments. Major changes are likely to be required in three areas: water, land use, and infrastructure.

As Chapter Six makes clear, the pressures upon water sources and water infrastructure in the Palestinian territories are already severe and will probably worsen in the future. That analysis reveals that current Palestinian water consumption averages half the United Nations' per-capita minimum daily standard and that total consumption in the region (by Israelis and Palestinians combined) exceeds the renewable supply, with the most severe problem in Gaza. As Chapter Six also notes, several factors con-

---

[22] The population densities in Hong Kong and Singapore are 6,570 and 5,540, respectively (CIA, *World Factbook*, 1999).

tribute to this problem, including the greater share Israel takes of the available water stocks, the fact that agricultural irrigation uses about half of Palestine's water, and the deterioration of Palestine's water infrastructure. In light of expected population growth and the increased demand for water, it seems clear a new Palestinian state will need to take several steps to deal with its water problem, including negotiating with Israel for a larger allocation of shared water resources, upgrading its water infrastructure (including developing desalination facilities), reducing its dependence on irrigated agriculture, and using its available water resources more efficiently. Meeting the costs of such actions will require substantial international assistance.

A second critical resource that will be stressed by rapid population growth is land. The entire Palestinian territory comprises a total of 2,400 square miles—a little more than half the area of Qatar and about one-fifth the size of Belgium. The available land will need to accommodate a wide variety of uses, including infrastructure, other public uses, a variety of economic uses (approximately one-quarter of the total land is currently used for agriculture), housing, and open space. An expanding population will increase the demand for all these uses. For example, the PCBS reports that there are an average of 6.4 persons per housing unit in Palestine. Assuming that this occupancy rate, which is currently high by developed country standards, were to be maintained, then accommodating population growth of between 2.2 and 5 million new residents during the next 25 years would require adding between 310,000 and 780,000 new housing units to the existing stock. Clearly, the government of a new Palestinian state will face difficult choices in managing the allocation of land among competing uses.

Finally, the physical infrastructure of the West Bank and Gaza needs substantial upgrading. A 1993 World Bank report underscores the infrastructure problems of the West Bank and Gaza, including the shortage of water supply, low and sporadic electricity supplies, a solid waste collection and disposal system that is grossly inadequate and raises serious health and environmental concerns, a road system that has deteriorated to the point where past investment may be completely lost, and a low ratio of telephones to population (World Bank, 1993). This appraisal was made, of course, prior to the further damage that has been done to Palestine's infrastructure during the current intifada and does not consider the additional requirements that continued rapid population growth will bring. Moreover, even in areas where the existing infrastructure is in better condition (e.g., health care), the organization of that system relies too heavily on high technology delivered in small inefficient units and must be improved. In sum, added population growth will only increase the need for investment in what is already a problematic physical infrastructure.

Service Demand

As we noted in the Introduction, the political viability of a new Palestinian state will be affected by its ability to meet its citizens' service needs. Population growth of the magnitude we have discussed will, of course, increase demand for services across the spectrum. But, as we have also noted, a population's age structure is perhaps the most important factor in determining service demand. Both the young and the old are intensive service users, in contrast to the working-age population, who have the primary responsibility for paying for those services.

Three areas of service demand are especially prone to feeling the impact of rapid population growth: education, health care, and housing. Population growth affects the demand for physical infrastructure (new schools, health care facilities, and homes); the demand for trained personnel to staff the new schools and health facilities; and the political pressures to change policies that influence the quality and organization of the services delivered.

The Palestinian education system is known throughout the Arab world for its effectiveness, universality, and secular character.[23] It produces more university graduates per capita than almost any other Arab state and offers education to virtually all Palestinian youth who wish to attend primary and secondary schools. Moreover, before the current intifada, the level of academic achievement among adults and enrollment rates among youth appeared to have been increasing. Nonetheless, as we noted above, measures of completed schooling and current enrollment lag well behind comparable rates in the developed world.

Despite Palestine's current educational achievements, there are several reasons why increasing education levels further will be important to the country's future. First, given the small area of the Palestinian state and its limited natural resources, its human capital is likely to be its most important economic asset, so increasing the skill levels of its population will be the key to future economic development. Second, increasing enrollment rates among those currently of school age and those who will be of school age in the future can provide some short-term relief from what are certain to be growing pressures on the economy to provide employment to a rapidly expanding labor force. Finally, as we have discussed above, increasing educational achievement among Palestinian women can reduce future population growth by increasing age at marriage, reducing desired family size, and reducing actual fertility levels.

Currently, Palestine's primary and secondary schools have slightly over one million students divided among government schools (72 percent of total enrollment), United Nations Relief and Works Agency (UNRWA) schools (22 percent), and assorted private schools (8 percent). In addition, about 90,000 students are enrolled in Palestine's universities and colleges.[24] The system's primary and secondary schools are currently staffed by close to 38,000 teachers, in addition to about 3,500 who teach at the post-secondary level.

A new Palestinian state will be required to increase educational expenditures for both the physical infrastructure (schools and classrooms) and the human resources

---

[23] See Chapter Eight for more detail.

[24] These figures, which are based on data provided by the PCBS (2002), may overestimate current enrollment totals, which appear to have declined somewhat as a result of the current political problems in Palestine.

(teachers) needed to accommodate the dramatic increase in enrollment expected over the next few years. For example, during the current decade, the number of primary and secondary school students is expected to increase by 50 percent (at current enrollment rates)—a figure that will require the addition of over 15,000 new classrooms at the current ratio of 35 students per class.[25] Increasing enrollment at the post-secondary level would require a similar expansion of university and college facilities. Similarly, assuming that student/teacher ratios remain at current levels, accommodating the increased enrollments expected at the primary and secondary levels during the current decade will require the hiring of another 18,000 or so teachers.

Since the Palestinian population will continue to grow at a relatively high rate at least until 2025, these initial expenditures are likely to be a mere down payment on future educational expenditures. Whether a new Palestinian state will bear the full costs of these expected changes in educational service levels will depend upon the status of the UNRWA schools, which are funded by the United Nations, and the private schools, many of which are funded by international donors. If UNRWA ceases operations in Palestine subsequent to the establishment of a Palestinian state and if international donors reduce their financial support to the privately run system, then the financial impact on the new Palestinian state will be correspondingly greater.

In addition to the costs of accommodating these enrollment increases, a new Palestinian state will also be required to deal with a series of policy issues that may potentially influence service levels and expenditures. At the secondary level, for example, the Palestinian educational system suffers from a dearth of vocational training programs, which reduces both the school enrollment rates of those who do not wish to pursue academic training and the skill level of the labor force. Similarly, post-secondary students are disproportionately concentrated in the humanities and social sciences rather than the physical sciences and engineering. Addressing these imbalances will pose further financial and organizational challenges to the educational system.

As we have already indicated, the physical and human capital infrastructure of the Palestinian health care system appears to be in reasonably good shape.[26] Both the number of hospitals and the number of beds, for example, have been increasing steadily over the past decade. Indeed, the most significant problem with the current infrastructure is its inefficient geographic distribution—for instance, cancer centers are present in towns with a greater need for maternity facilities and vice versa. Nonetheless, the pace of population growth over the next decade will require a 60 percent increase in hospital beds and medical personnel to keep those indicators of service levels at their current ratios.[27]

---

[25] These additional students could, of course, be accommodated with fewer new schools by increasing class size or running multiple shifts—a phenomenon that has already been occurring.

[26] The state of Palestine's health care system is discussed in greater detail in Chapter Seven.

[27] We lack the current information on medical personnel needed to calculate what this expansion would require. However, data from PCBS (2002) indicate that about 3,000 new hospital beds (above the 5,000 currently available) would be required to keep the ratio of hospital beds per 1,000 population at its current level of 1.4 beds per 1,000 population.

In light of current levels of physical and human capital in the health sector, the greatest challenge facing the health system in a new Palestinian state in light of increasing population seems likely to be in the area of health finance. Currently, the Palestinian National Authority provides universal access to immunizations, pre- and postnatal care, and care for children under three. Other care, particularly secondary and tertiary care, requires government-sponsored health insurance, except for those patients who can afford to pay for care in private clinics and hospitals. In addition, the liabilities of the Palestinian Ministry of Health exceed its annual budget.[28] Thus, the capacity of the Palestinian health sector to continue providing financial access to health care may be in doubt without major infusions of international assistance.

Housing is a third area in which population growth is likely to place substantial stress on service delivery in a new Palestinian state. In our discussion of land use above, we noted that a Palestinian state will need to add between 310,000 and 780,000 new units of housing stock (above the current total of 390,000) to accommodate projected population growth. However, that figure does not take into account either current access to electricity, water, and sewer facilities or the degree of crowding. At present, only about one-third of all occupied housing units in Palestinian territories are connected to water, electricity, and sewage facilities; less than one-half have access to both electricity and running water.[29] Clearly, a Palestinian state will face pressures not simply to expand the current stock but also to upgrade the quality of its housing. Furthermore, a 1995 survey indicated that about one-third of all households in the Palestinian territories were living in housing units at a density of over three persons per room. Although about 80 percent of all housing units in the Palestinian territories appear to be owner-occupied,[30] a new state will no doubt feel pressure to provide access to financing to relieve this level of overcrowding. Finally, the preceding estimates of required new housing assume constant household sizes. Although this assumption is probably reasonably accurate in the short run, it is likely to increasingly underestimate the scale of new housing required as fertility levels decline and average household sizes become smaller.

Demographic Pressures on the Palestinian Economy

Finding gainful employment for its growing working-age population will be among the most pressing problems facing a new Palestinian state. Although a Palestinian state will no doubt rely initially on international aid, the long-term viability of the state will be contingent on the ability of individual Palestinians to earn an adequate living and on the state's ability to generate sufficient revenues to satisfy the service needs of its residents. Given its economic structure and history, this will not be an easy task—even without the rapid growth of its labor force in the future.

---

[28] See Chapter Seven.

[29] See table, "Occupied Housing Units by Availability of Public Services," PCBS, 2002.

[30] See Demographic Survey, PCBS, 1995.

Historically, Palestinians in the Palestinian territories have depended upon work in Israel and on remittances sent from Palestinian workers elsewhere in the Middle East for a significant share of their income. However, neither of these two sources of employment appear to be as viable in the future as they have been in the past. At its peak, the number of Palestinians making the daily commute to Israel for employment totaled 130,000 (Davoodi and von Allmen, 2001) but that number has dropped precipitously. Indeed, the number of Palestinians living in the West Bank and Gaza but working in Israel has dropped from almost one-quarter of all employed Palestinians in 1999 to less than 10 percent today.[31] Moreover, the perception that Palestinian workers represent a security threat to Israel has prompted the Israelis to replace low-wage Palestinians with other foreign workers. Even if a peace agreement is signed, it is unclear whether the number of Palestinians working in Israel will ever rebound to its earlier high point.

The prospects of Palestinian workers finding employment elsewhere in the Middle East also seem to have declined sharply. As we noted in our review of historical Palestinian migration patterns, the large-scale movement of Palestinian workers to the Gulf states terminated over three decades ago, as those countries became increasingly reluctant to import Arab labor in the face of rising unemployment among their own citizens. There are no signs that this reluctance will diminish in the foreseeable future.

The prospects for employment growth in the West Bank and Gaza are also uncertain. Although employment levels have dropped since the onset of the current intifada,[32] it is unclear which sectors of the economy are best suited to absorbing the existing labor force. Currently, the two largest employment sectors of the economy are agriculture (about 15 percent of total employment) and services (about 35 percent—a substantial fraction of which consists of public-sector employment). Growth in the agricultural sector is likely to face constraints due to limited natural resources (land and water), and international financial institutions like the World Bank are already demanding reductions in public-sector employment as a way to streamline the Palestinian economy. However, a study conducted in the late 1990s indicated that residential construction, tourism, consumer electronics, cut flowers, olive oil processing, software development, and stone and marble processing could all be viable industries in Palestine (Davoodi and von Allmen, 2001). Moreover, given the infrastructure needs described above, residential and commercial construction would seem to offer a significant source of employment,[33] at least in the short run.

---

[31] See "Number of Palestinians in Israel for Selected Years," www.pcbs.org/english/abs_pal/abs_pal2/Qudsb/1.2.htm.

[32] Although we lack data on total employment levels, the labor-force participation rate among prime-age men has declined to 65.5 percent (from 70.7 percent) and among females from 12.7 to 10.4 percent during the past four years (PCBS, 2002).

[33] A more detailed discussion of Palestine's economic prospects is contained in Chapter Five.

The challenges facing the Palestinian economy as it seeks to find adequate employment for its current labor force will, of course, be compounded by the fact that this labor force is growing rapidly and will continue to do so for the foreseeable future. One indication of this growth and the challenges it will pose is that the age group that will be entering the labor force over the next ten years (ages 10 to 19) is seven times as large as the age group that will be moving out of the working years (ages 55 to 64).[34] Although this ratio overstates the number of new jobs that must be found to accommodate labor force growth since it includes women (who have very low labor force participation rates) as well as males who, for schooling and other reasons, will not be looking for work, it does suggest the magnitude of the challenge facing the Palestinian economy. Moreover, the Palestinian economy could certainly benefit from increasing labor force participation rates—both among men, many of whom may have dropped out of the labor force due to the current political turmoil, and especially among women as an indirect means of reducing fertility and thus future population growth.

Ironically, in light of these employment challenges, the strongest economic asset of the new Palestinian economy is likely to be its human capital. Certainly, it is the only one of the principal factors of production (land and natural resources, technology, and labor) that Palestine has in abundance. Moreover, given the relatively high educational levels of Palestinians, if this labor force can be gainfully employed, it could be a major factor for promoting economic growth. To take advantage of this asset, however, the new state will need to continue to increase the education and training levels of the population, as well as find a solution to the daunting structural problems it faces.

Prospects for Return Migration

The number of diaspora Palestinians who move to a new Palestine state will be critical to the political and practical viability of that state. In this section, we first review the reasons why this issue is so important. Next, we discuss some of the technical aspects of the return migration from a negotiating perspective. Finally, we estimate the potential sizes of various return flows and the conditions under which they might occur, and we discuss the implications for a new Palestinian state.

Importance of the Issues

From a political perspective, the plight of diaspora Palestinians symbolizes the predicament of the Palestinian people. Palestinians lack a homeland. Other states and parties (e.g., Israel, the United States and the other Roadmap states, and the host states in which Palestinians live) control their fate. Until they gain statehood (sovereignty) and

---

[34] The current population ages 10 to 19 totals a little less than 600,000 whereas the population ages 55 to 64 is 84,000.

control over their fate, Palestinians will not have achieved their ends and their struggle will most likely continue. Thus, solving the refugee issue assumes a tremendous symbolic importance to Palestinians.

Given the symbolic importance of refugees and return migration to the Palestinian identity, how the Palestinian leadership deals with these issues will provide a critical test for that leadership's legitimacy for several reasons. First, the predicament of Palestinian refugees, particularly those living in camps in Lebanon, serves as a continuing source of discontent to all Palestinians and as an ongoing rationale for the armed struggle. Thus, a satisfactory solution to the refugee issue will play an important role in determining whether a negotiated settlement ends the ongoing violence. Second, how the Palestinian Authority deals with the refugee and return migration in the negotiation process will serve as a central test of its effectiveness as an advocate for the Palestinian people as well as how that settlement is viewed by Arab states and others. Third, as we discussed above, how many and which Palestinians migrate to Palestine will have tremendous practical economic and social implications for the future viability of the new state. In addition to the number and size of the return migration, the period over which it occurs will also affect the eventual size of the population in the new state.[35] Fourth, not only is the refugee issue of great importance to Palestinians, it is also of direct concern to Israelis since it could have a direct effect on Israeli security, the interests of Israeli settlers, and—depending upon how many Palestinians return and where they settle—on the essential Jewish character of the Israeli state.[36] Indeed, the importance of this issue to the Israelis was encapsulated in the statement by a prominent Israeli commentator who stated that "any settlement that fails to completely solve the refugee problem will not provide a realistic and durable settlement" (Gazit, 1995).

In sum, resolution of the refugee and return migration issues will be central to a successful conclusion to the peace negotiations. Indeed, given their importance to both parties, it is not surprising that the refugee issue was designated a final status issue in the original Oslo Accords and is thought to be one of the major reasons that the Palestinian Authority was unwilling to accept the peace agreement offered by the Barak government.

Key Issues

Although the formal terms on which the refugee issues will be negotiated are not altogether clear, a host of potential issues could be on the table. Who will be eligible to return and who should be given priority? Will eligibility be limited to registered refugees and their immediate descendants and, if so, which ones should be given priority—the original 1948 refugees, the 1967 displaced persons, or those currently living in refu-

---

[35] As the projections reviewed above indicate, natural increase among returnees could substantially increase the amount of population growth.

[36] All of the initial refugees were displaced from land that is now part of Israel. If return entails resettlement on that land, it could definitely affect the demographic balance between Jews and Arabs in Israel.

gee camps? Alternatively, should priority be given to those who might make the most immediate contribution to a new Palestinian state? As we have indicated above, the original refugees (both 1948 and 1967) are now outnumbered by their descendants. The number of registered refugees is only a fraction of the total Palestinian population outside the Palestinian territories, just as the number of refugees living in camps is only a fraction of the total number of registered refugees. Thus, how the eligible population is defined will help shape not only how many Palestinians may decide to return but also what effects they are likely to have on the economy and the service demands placed on the new state.

A second key issue is what is meant by "return." There are currently several viewpoints. Return may be defined as the physical return of refugees to their original homes and land in Mandate Palestine, including land in Israel that is currently occupied by Israelis. Or it may refer only to return to Palestinian territory in the West Bank and Gaza or in "swapped" land.[37] Alternatively (or in addition) it may refer to some kind of financial settlement for lost property in lieu of actual physical return. Finally, is it sufficient just to return to Palestine—even if this means moving returnees from a camp in Lebanon to a new camp in the West Bank and Gaza—or does it require that individuals be relocated outside refugee camps?

Third, what conditions and timetable will govern the return process? This question really encompasses a wide range of issues, such as the timetable for return, the conditions (for example, security levels) that must be met for return to proceed peacefully, who will administer and monitor the return process (the Palestinians, the Israelis, some neutral third party, or a multilateral commission), and what role, if any, UNRWA will play in the return process and in Palestinian refugee affairs in the future.

Finally, apart from the issue of who is eligible to return, there is the question of how many diaspora Palestinians might actually wish to return. The answer to this question is likely to depend upon many factors. For example, a survey conducted among Palestinians living in Jordan and Lebanon indicated that the proportion who might return would vary not only with the terms of the agreement but also with such factors as whether they have relatives currently living in Israel, the Palestinian territories, or elsewhere (e.g., in a third country); whether they currently live inside or outside refugee camps; their current incomes; and whether they own land in the country of their current residence (Shikaki, 2003). Other factors—such as economic and political conditions in the new Palestinian state, how these conditions compare with those in the countries of current residence, and the attitudes of host governments toward Palestinian residents remaining in their countries after statehood—will also play a role in determining how many and which diaspora Palestinians might choose to return.

---

[37] The December 2000 Clinton proposals, the January 2001 Taba negotiations, and the October 2003 Geneva accord all foresee land swaps whereby Israel annexes a small amount of West Bank land where settlements are concentrated in exchange for Palestine annexing current Israeli territory.

Estimates of Potential Returnees

Our estimates of the range of potential returnees are derived in two steps: First, we identify which groups of Palestinians are most likely to return; second, we estimate a range of potential return rates depending upon the options returnees might be given with regard to where they may settle. Potential return rates for different groups of Palestinians and under different conditions are estimated using results from a recent survey of Palestinian refugees living in the West Bank/Gaza, Jordan, and Lebanon.[38]

As we reported in Table 4.1 above, approximately 5.4 million people of Palestinian origin live outside the Palestinian territories. Close to 1 million of them live in what we have termed the "far abroad" regions. Since this particular group includes many of the most highly skilled and economically successful Palestinians, it seems unlikely that any substantial number would consider resettling in a new Palestinian state before a stable and nonviolent political climate is well-established, the government is up and running, and the prospects for a successful economy well-grounded. Instead, the most likely candidates for return, at least in the short run, will be found among the 3.5 million Palestinians living in the surrounding states of Lebanon, Syria, and Jordan.[39] Approximately 70 percent of these Palestinians (or roughly 2.5 million people) are registered refugees. Of this latter group, about one-quarter (or roughly 650,000 people) are currently living in refugee camps. Although the living conditions and political rights of Palestinians living in these surrounding states and in various refugee camps within these states differ,[40] it seems highly likely that the prime candidates for return will be the registered refugees in general and those living in refugee camps in particular. Thus, we estimate that the potential pool of returnees will be between 650,000 (those living in refugee camps) and 2.5 million (those who are registered refugees).

In the survey referenced above, respondents were asked a series of questions about how they might respond to different resettlement options, including what their first choice for permanent residence was; under what conditions they would consider moving to Israel; and whether they would move to Palestine if the refugee and resettlement issues were excluded from a peace agreement but resolved later (referred to subsequently as the "permanent minus" option). We used the responses to these questions to estimate a range of return rates that might apply under different return options. The resulting estimates of the number of returnees are listed in Table 4.7.

The first three rows of this table compare the size of different groups of Palestinians who currently live outside the West Bank and Gaza. The first row lists the total

---

[38] Shikaki (2003).

[39] Approximately 1 million Palestinians currently live in Israel. Although some of those Palestinians might consider moving to a new Palestinian state, the number of such migrants is not likely to be very large since, unlike the diaspora Palestinians, most are not refugees who were displaced from their original homes in Mandate Palestine.

[40] Palestinians living in Jordan have the benefits of citizenship and are well integrated into the Jordanian economy and society; Palestinians living in Syria are integrated into the Syrian economy but lack citizenship; and those living in Lebanon lack citizenship and are not integrated into the Lebanese economy or society.

Table 4.7
Estimates of Potential Return Migration by Area of Current Residence

	Potential Immigration (thousands)				
	Jordan	Lebanon	Syria	Other	Total
Total population	2,720	400	400	1,830	5,350
Registered	1,700	390	400	0	2,490
In camps	300	220	120	0	640
Low 1	75	70	40	0	185
Low 2	425	120	110	0	655
Medium	460	75	90	5	630
High 1	630	160	160	5	955
High 2	715	250	210	10	1,185

NOTES: Assumptions—Low 1: Population living in camps multiplied by the percentage who report that they would return to Palestine under the permanent minus option. Low 2: Registered refugees multiplied by the percentage who report that they would return to Palestine under the permanent minus option. Medium: Registered refugees multiplied by the percentage who report that their first choice is to move to Palestine. High 1: Registered refugees multiplied by the percentage who report that their first choice is either to move to Palestine or to swapped areas. High 2: Registered refugees multiplied by the percentage who report that their first choice is either to move to Palestine, to swapped areas, or to Israel.

number of Palestinians who live in each area. The second row lists the number of registered refugees in each area. The third row lists the number of refugees living in camps in each area. As the very different size of these groups suggests, the number of migrants who might return to a new Palestinian state will depend upon whether each of these groups is equally likely to move to a new state. As we indicated above, we do not believe equal rates of return migration to be likely. Instead, we expect that the propensity to migrate will be selective in two ways: first, by area of current residence; second, by refugee status. Specifically, we anticipate that the vast majority of returnees (at least in the short run) will come from the surrounding countries and, within those populations, predominately from registered refugees—particularly those currently living in refugee camps.

The next five rows of the table list a range of estimates of the number of migrants who might move to Palestine under various conditions. The rates used to calculate these estimates are based on the responses given to two questions in the survey described above. The first question asked respondents to identify their first choice of residence if they were free to move wherever they wanted. The range of options included Israel, the new Palestinian state, areas within Israel that would later be swapped with Palestine as part of a territorial exchange, remaining in their current country of residence, or moving to a third country. The second question asked respondents to indicate whether they would move to Palestine even if a formal peace agreement left the issue of refugee resettlement unresolved and subject to later negotiation. Since the permanence of such resettlement as well as the rights of the returnees would remain unresolved under this permanent minus condition, we assume that respondents who would nonetheless resettle in Palestine are the most likely to move under any circumstances. In making our estimates, we multiplied the various rates calculated from the data by two different populations: the number of refugees currently living in camps and the number of registered refugees. The pairing of populations and return rates is identified in the table notes. Since the survey data did not include Palestinians living in Syria, we calculated estimates for that country as the average of the rates from Jordan and Lebanon.[41]

The resultant estimates fall within a wide range—between a low of about 185,000 returnees and a high of close to 1.2 million. As reflected in the difference between the moderate and high estimates, how the issues of swapped land and Palestinian return to Israel proper are resolved could make a substantial difference in how many Palestinians actually return.[42] On the other hand, for reasons discussed above, we do not expect that many Palestinians currently living in the far abroad or Israel are likely to move to a new Palestinian state, at least in the foreseeable future.

These estimates, of course, are only as valid as the assumptions used to calculate them. Nonetheless, they can provide a rough guide as to how return migration to a new Palestinian state might affect population growth in that state as reflected in the population projections reported in Table 4.5. Since these estimates generally fall near the low end of the net migration assumptions used by the USBC and the PCBS in their projections, they suggest that the total population growth in a new Palestinian state may be more likely to fall at the high end of the medium fertility–high migration projection—in other words, close to 7.5 million by 2025.[43]

One issue that is not built into our migration estimates but is incorporated into the population projections discussed above is the timing of the potential return migration. The survey data used for our estimates also included information about the respondents' preferences as to the timing of any return migration. These data indicate that close to two-thirds of Palestinians currently living in the Palestinian territories and in Jordan would prefer that the return migration take place gradually. About 60 percent of the Palestinians living in Lebanon, on the other hand, want the return to happen all at once. Although this difference may be understandable given the living conditions in Lebanon, it not only could increase the adjustment problems that return migration

---

[41] The rationale for using the average of the Jordanian and Lebanese rates was the fact that the economic and political status of Palestinians living in Syria appears to lie between their status in Jordan and Lebanon.

[42] The conditions applied to Palestinian migrants to Israel would also make a substantial difference in the number who actually return. As Shikaki's (2003) data make clear, although approximately 235,000 Palestinians list Israel as their first choice, only about 10,000 would actually return if they were forced to become Israeli citizens.

[43] The USBC assumed 100,000 net migrants and the PCBS assumed 500,000. These estimates refer to net migration (immigrants minus outmigrants), whereas the estimates in Table 4.7 refer only to immigrants. However, we do not expect this difference to make a substantial difference in the size of the net flows.

might engender but also would have a larger multiplier effect on the eventual size of the Palestinian population (through natural increase to return migrants).

As the discussion in this chapter has made clear, estimates of the range of return migration to a new Palestinian state are wide. Moreover, they generally exceed the net migration assumptions upon which the population projections reported earlier are based. Thus they are likely to compound the problems of population growth in a new Palestinian state. Although there can be no definitive answer to the question of how many Palestinians might move to a new Palestinian state, it is clear that the more refugees Palestine absorbs, the greater the overall cost and the fewer the resources available for other needs. Conversely, fewer refugees means lower cost to the state and more resources available to provide for the needs of the existing population.

Bibliography

NOTE: Palestinian statistics cited in this paper that are not contained in the specific sources listed in the bibliography may be found at the Palestinian Central Bureau of Statistics' web site: www.pcbs.org.

Adlakha, Arjun L., Kevin G. Kinsella, and Marwan Khawaja, "Demography of the Palestinian Population with Special Emphasis on the Occupied Territories," *Population Bulletin of ESCWA,* No. 43, 1995, pp. 5–28.

Bard, Mitchell, "Homeless in Gaza: Arab Mistreatment of Palestinian Refugees," *Policy Review,* Vol. 47, Winter 1989, pp. 36–42.

Brand, Laurie, " Palestinians in Syria: The Politics of Integration," *The Middle East Journal,* Vol. 42, No. 4, Autumn 1988, pp. 621–637.

Central Intelligence Agency, "1999 World Factbook," www.geographic.org, 2000.

Courbage, Youssef, "Reshuffling the Demographic Cards in Israel/Palestine," *Journal of Palestine Studies,* Vol. 28, No. 4, Summer 1999, pp. 21–39.

Davis, Kingsley, and Judith Blake, "Social Structure and Fertility: An Analytical Framework," *Economic Development and Cultural Changes,* Vol. 4, No. 3, 1956, pp. 211–235.

Davoodi, Hamid R., and Ulric Erickson von Allmen, "Demographics and Long-Term Growth in the Palestinian Economy," in *West Bank and Gaza: Economic Performance, Prospect, and Policies,* Washington, D.C.: International Monetary Fund, 2001.

Efrat, Moshe, *The Palestinian Refugees: The Dynamics of Economic Integration in Their Host Countries,* Jerusalem, Israel: Israeli International Institute for Applied Economic Policy, September 1993.

Fargues, Phillipes, "The Arab Christians of the Middle East: A Demographic Perspective," in Andrea Pacini (ed.), *Christian Communities in the Arab Middle East: The Challenge of the Future,* Oxford, UK: Clarendon Press, 1998.

Gazit, Shlomo, *The Palestinian Refugee Problem: Final Status Issues: Israel-Palestinians, Study No. 2,* Tel Aviv, Israel: Jaffe Center for Strategic Studies, Tel Aviv University, 1995.

Gillespie, Kate, et al., "Palestinian Interest in Homeland Investment," *Middle East Journal,* Vol. 55, No. 2, Spring, 2001, pp. 237–255.

Global Exchange, www.globalexchange.org/countries/Palestine/refugeeFacts, accessed July 2003.

Heiberg, Marianne, and Geir Ovensen, *Palestinian Society in Gaza, West Bank and Arab Jerusalem,* Oslo: FAFO Report 151, 1993.

Kinsella, Kevin, "Palestinian Projections for 16 Countries/Areas of the World, 1990 to 2010," U.S. Bureau of the Census, Center for International Research, March 1991.

Kossaifi, George, "Forced Migration of Palestinians from the West Bank and Gaza Strip," *Population Bulletin of ESCWA,* Vol. 27, December 1985, pp. 73–108.

McCarthy, Kevin F., "World Population Shifts: Boom or Doom," Santa Monica, Calif.: RAND Corporation, DB-308-WFHF/DLPF/RF, 2001.

McCarthy, Kevin F., "The Palestine Refugee Issue: One Perspective," Santa Monica, Calif.: RAND Corporation, DRU-1358-GMESC, 1996.

Palestinian Central Bureau of Statistics (PCBS), "Family Formation in the Palestinian Territory: Analytical Report," www.pcbs.org, accessed May 2003a.

———, "Fertility in the Palestinian Territory: Analytical Report," www.pcbs.org, accessed May 2003b.

———, "Population Projections," www.pcbs.org, accessed May 2003c.

Population Reference Bureau, *2001 World Population Data Sheet,* Washington, D.C., 2001.

Shikaki, Khalil, "Attitudes and Behavior of Palestinian Refugees in the Permanent Status. Comprehensive Surveys in the West Bank and the Gaza Strip, Jordan and Lebanon," Briefing given at RAND, Washington, D.C., July 17, 2003.

U.S. Bureau of the Census (USBC), "IDB Summary Demographic Data for Gaza Strip," www.census.gov/ipc/www/idbnew.html, 2003a.

———, "IDB Summary Demographic Data for West Bank," www.census.gov/ipc/www/idbnew.html, 2003b.

———, "World Population Profile: 1998," www.census.gov/ipc/www/wp98.html, 1999.

U.S. Department of Commerce, "America's Families and Living Arrangements," Washington, D.C.: Current Population Reports, P20–537, 2001.

———, "School Enrollment-Social and Economic Characteristics," Washington, D.C.: Current Population Reports, P20–521, 1999.

United Nations (UN) Statistic Division, "Demographic, Social, and Housing Statistics," UN Department of Economic and Social Affairs, New York, 2001.

World Bank, *Developing the Occupied Territories: An Investment in Peace,* Volume 1: *Overview,* Washington, D.C.: World Bank, September 1993.

CHAPTER FIVE

Economics

Justin L. Adams, Kateryna Fonkych, Keith Crane, and Michael Schoenbaum

Summary

The economy of an independent Palestinian state will be the engine of opportunity for its citizens. To provide sustained growth in per-capita incomes, Palestine needs a dynamic private sector that can employ the current and future labor force. The economy will need to be diverse and resilient enough to withstand economic or political shocks and open enough to participate fully and competitively in the world economy. To foster such an economy, the future Palestinian government will need to

- surmount the many challenges facing the Palestinian economy, especially those posed by the need for regional security
- make strategic choices and choose policies that will contribute to the development of the Palestinian economy
- attract the investment needed to create the infrastructure and industrial base needed for sustained growth.

The Palestinian Economy

The Palestinian economy is very small. Palestinian gross national income (GNI) of $5.2 billion in 1999 yielded a per-capita income of nearly $1,800 annually, placing the West Bank and Gaza in the range of lower-middle-income countries. A significant portion of GNI (about 17 percent) over much of the past three decades has been derived from wages paid to Palestinians employed in Israel and the settlements.

The Palestinian economy is geared mostly to providing services and producing nontradable goods, and it is also highly dependent on trade. Israel is Palestine's main trading partner, having gained control of the West Bank and Gaza in 1967. Trade flows between them are skewed, however: Israel runs a very large trade surplus with the West Bank and Gaza. Israeli wage payments greatly exceed Palestinian exports as a means of funding Palestinian imports of Israeli goods and services.

Israeli control has made the Palestinian economy very sensitive to economic and political shocks emanating from Israel. During the 1970s through the 1990s, inflation and economic cycles in Israel strongly affected inflation in the West Bank and Gaza and demand for Palestinian labor. However, these economic effects have been superseded by the effects of Israeli security policies in the West Bank and Gaza that were taken in response to the intifadas. Restrictions on the movement of goods and people, the destruction of capital, and the construction of a road network restricted to Israeli access have had devastating effects on the economy of the West Bank and Gaza. Since 2000, per-capita incomes have declined by one-half.

Major Challenges and Issues

The Palestinian economy holds promise because of its substantial human capital, assuming that the international community is willing to invest in reconstruction. But the economy will face a number of significant challenges. First, sustained economic growth will require security and political stability. Second, the Palestinian authorities will have to create conditions for employing a large and rapidly growing labor force. Third, the West Bank and Gaza have little in the way of developed economic sectors: Many industries would need to be developed from scratch. Fourth, the Arab world provides a logical market for Palestinian products, but the West Bank and Gaza have weak economic relations with their Arab neighbors. Fifth, rapid population growth, the possible immigration by a large number of Palestinian refugees to the West Bank and Gaza, the destruction of physical infrastructure related to the intifada, and a poor initial infrastructure base will require substantial investments in roads, water, electric power, and other infrastructure. Sixth, Palestinian businesses lack access to private-sector capital. Finally, Palestinian governing institutions have yet to show signs that they can create a business environment conducive to rapid economic growth.

Strategic choices made by policymakers at the outset of the new state will markedly affect the path of its economic development. Decisions about *geographic contiguity*—the size, shape, and fragmentation of a future Palestinian state, the inclusion of special sites or areas, and control over land and resources—will determine the resources that the Palestinian Authority (PA) will have at its disposal to foster growth and the ease with which Palestinians can move and engage in business. Decisions about the degree of *economic integration* with Israel in terms of trade and the mobility of Palestinian labor will shape the Palestinian economy, the rate of economic growth, and prospects for employment.

Economic Scenarios and Implications

The future Palestinian state can be considered within the framework of four scenarios, determined by decisions about geographic contiguity and economic integration. We analyze these scenarios for the 2005–2019 time frame, quantifying what each scenario implies for economic growth and identifying the level of investment needed to achieve sustained economic growth and improved living standards.

Our analysis indicates that under each scenario except the low-contiguity/low-integration case, Palestine could reasonably surpass its 1999 per-capita GNI by 2009 and nearly double it by 2019. But achieving this income growth would require significant investment in Palestinian capital stock: Between 2005 and 2019, the Palestinian private and public sectors and the international community would have to invest around $50 billion under each scenario, averaging about $3.3 billion a year, to achieve these rates of growth.[1] Regardless of the scenario, domestic private employment would have to grow at a substantial pace (perhaps at an annual average of 15 to 18 percent) between 2005 and 2009 to reach rates of employment last seen around the summer of 2000. These employment rates should be possible once Palestinian businesses are able to operate in a relatively unrestricted environment and are fully able to utilize available resources.

Policy Options

We discuss best-practice economic policy options for Palestine that would help to support its economic development, regardless of the scenario in which it found itself. Policies fall into eight general categories:

1. Fostering free trade by minimizing the costs of commerce
2. Partnering with its neighbors to develop specific economic sectors and to leverage infrastructure
3. Investing in infrastructure for transportation, water and power, and communications
4. Facilitating Palestinian employment in Israel by implementing appropriate security measures that make employment feasible
5. Expanding access to capital through a program of industrial estates/economic development zones, reformed domestic banking policies, and an international insurance fund
6. Choosing currencies to minimize inflation and economic volatility
7. Improving the business climate through increased transparency and accountability of Palestinian governance
8. Investing in human capital by improving the education system.

Introduction: Overview of the Palestinian Economy

The economy of an independent Palestinian state will be the engine of opportunity for its citizens. To foster an economy that can provide sustained growth in per-capita incomes, Palestine needs a dynamic private sector that grows rapidly enough to employ the current and future labor force. The economy must also be diverse and resilient

---

[1] All dollar amounts in this chapter are 2003 U.S. dollars and are expressed approximately unless otherwise noted.

enough to withstand the effects of economic or political shocks, and, particularly in light of Palestine's small size, open enough to participate fully and competitively in the world economy.

In this chapter, we explore the issues surrounding how a Palestinian state can achieve such sustained economic growth over its first 15 years. We first examine the current state of the economy in the West Bank and Gaza, including development since 1967. Second, we describe the major challenges and issues confronting the generation of sustainable economic growth. Third, because the details of a Palestinian state have not yet been determined, we consider how different initial conditions are likely to influence the path and ultimate success of economic development. Fourth, we analyze the implications of these scenarios, with an eye to quantifying the amount of investment needed from the private sector and the international community to achieve sustained growth in per-capita incomes. Finally, we discuss a number of best-practice economic policies for Palestine that can help stimulate economic growth regardless of its initial conditions.

Snapshot of Palestinian Economy in 1999

The economy of the West Bank and Gaza is small. In 1999, the year before the onset of the second intifada, the West Bank and Gaza (excluding East Jerusalem) had a gross domestic product (GDP) of $4.3 billion. GNI was higher, $5.2 billion, because of the additional income earned by Palestinians employed in Israel. The resulting per-capita income of nearly $1,800 a year placed the Palestinian economy in the group of lower-middle-income countries (World Bank, 2002c, p. 8).[2] This figure is comparable to the per-capita income of Jordan but is only about 10 percent of Israel's per-capita income (World Bank, 2004). Although the West Bank and Gaza struggled with high unemployment and poverty throughout the 1990s, unemployment dropped to 10 percent (World Bank, 2000, p. 10) and the poverty rate dropped to 20 percent in 1999 (World Bank, 2002c, p. 8).[3]

The Palestinian economy is primarily oriented to providing services and producing nontradable goods. In 1999, service sectors, including government services, made

---

[2] By comparison, Israel in 2000 had a GDP of $110.4 billion (World Bank, 2002a), Egypt in 2001 had a GDP of $91.1 billion (World Bank, 2003a), and Jordan in 2000 had a GDP of $8.5 billion (World Bank, 2003b).

[3] Here, the World Bank uses a widely accepted definition of poverty as being household expenditures of less than $2 per person, per day. World Bank obtains unemployment figures from the Palestinian Central Bureau of Statistics (PCBS), which defines unemployment according to International Labour Organization standards as follows:

> Unemployed [Palestinian] persons are those individuals 15 years and over who did not work at all during the reference week, who were not absent from a job and were available for work and actively seeking a job during the reference week. [Palestinian] persons who work in Israel and were absent from work due to closure are considered unemployed, and also those persons [who] never work and [are] not looking for work but [are] waiting to return back to their [businesses] in Israel and [the] Settlements (PCBS, 2003).

up 63 percent of Palestinian GDP, including economic activity in East Jerusalem. The goods-producing sectors—mining, quarrying, and manufacturing (18 percent); construction (12 percent); and agriculture (7 percent)—constituted the remainder of GDP [Palestine Economic Policy Research Institute (MAS), 2000, p. 12]. Part of the difference in size between the service and goods-producing sectors stems from the structure of the manufacturing sector: It is dominated by small workshops that have little capital and that produce relatively unsophisticated goods. The disparity is also the result of a large public-sector apparatus. In 1999, public administration and services accounted for about 23 percent of all domestic employment, making it the largest segment in terms of employment.[4] The next largest employers were commerce, hotels, and restaurants (18 percent); manufacturing and quarrying (16 percent); and agriculture and fishing (14 percent). The total Palestinian workforce numbered nearly 630,000 in that year.

The Palestinian economy is very dependent upon trade; as a matter of fact, the total value of traded goods and services (both imports and exports) is equal to its GDP. This high reliance on trade stems from the small size of the economy and from the West Bank and Gaza's limited resources: Palestinians depend largely on imports, almost all of which come from or go through Israel, for raw materials and intermediate goods.[5] Palestinian merchandise trade runs heavily in deficit. Imports of goods and services were 81 percent of GDP in 1999, compared with only 18 percent for exports; imports as a share of GDP are the highest in the region. The resulting large trade deficit has traditionally been financed through wages earned abroad and through foreign aid; donor financing in the mid- to late 1990s was consistently between about 12 and 16 percent of GNI per year (Fischer, Alonso-Gamo, and von Allmen, 2001, pp. F256–F257).

A key feature of the Palestinian economy is its integration with the Israeli economy with respect to trade. Formalized in the Protocol on Economic Relations of 1994 (Paris Protocol), the West Bank, Gaza, and Israel form a customs union. The area imposes common (Israeli) tariffs, while Palestinian and Israeli goods are traded duty-free. In other words, Palestinian and Israeli goods receive preferential treatment in each other's markets, relative to the goods of other countries.

It is not surprising that Israel is the main trading partner of the West Bank and Gaza: In 1998, it accounted for 80 percent of the value of merchandise trade transactions (exports plus imports) with the West Bank and Gaza. In contrast, Jordan and Egypt (the second and ninth largest trading partners) accounted for only 2.4 percent and 1.0 percent, respectively, of total trade (UNSCO, 2000, p. 29). Palestinian trade with other countries often transits

---

[4] The Palestinian public sector is large for the region as well. In 1997, the civilian central government in the West Bank and Gaza made up 14.5 percent of the labor force, compared with 12.4 percent for Egypt, 10.1 percent for Jordan, 4.2 percent for Lebanon, 5.6 percent for Morocco, and 10.5 for Tunisia (World Bank, 1999b, p. 55).

[5] The West Bank and Gaza have little in the way of natural resources, necessitating imports of raw materials. In 1998, imports of energy and raw materials amounted to 29 percent of all imports. Investment goods (including those imported for donor-funded projects) ran 36 percent of imports (UNSCO, 2000, p. 28).

through Israel. Because Israel has a much larger economy and more developed economic relations with other countries, trade with Palestine is a much smaller proportion of Israel's total trade than of Palestine's total trade with Israel (MAS, 2001, p. 15).

Another historical feature of the Palestinian economy is the relatively large share of the labor force employed in Israel or Israel's settlements in the West Bank and Gaza. In 1999, higher Israeli wages and few domestic opportunities induced about 135,000 Palestinians, nearly 23 percent of the Palestinian labor force, to find employment in Israel or the settlements (MAS, 2000, p. 15). Most of these jobs involved relatively unskilled labor, such as for construction and agriculture.

Because of this dependence on Israel, the Palestinian economy is very vulnerable to Israeli policy decisions. Israeli security measures intended to deal with suicide bombings and shootings have repeatedly caused disruptions in production and labor and commodity flows, thereby severely affecting employment, income, and production in the West Bank and Gaza. Palestine is also very sensitive to economic shocks emanating from Israel. Recessions, periods of high inflation, and devaluations have an immediate impact on the Palestinian economy, although their effects have been moderated somewhat by Palestine's use of multiple currencies (rather than just the new Israeli shekel), which has helped to dampen inflation.[6] These shocks, which introduce uncertainty and volatility into the business environment, have been important factors in limiting investment in economic sectors (except for residential construction) throughout the West Bank and Gaza. On the other hand, periods of boom in Israel have a corresponding positive effect on demand for Palestinian labor and on wages.

Palestinian Economic Development from 1967 to the Oslo Accords in 1993[7]

Israeli control over the West Bank and Gaza since 1967 has had profound effects on the development of the Palestinian economy. Before 1967, the economy of the West Bank was tied to Jordan's, and the economy of Gaza was integrated with Egypt's. Following Israel's occupation of the West Bank and Gaza in 1967, however, Israel created a de facto customs union incorporating the West Bank and Gaza's economy. High Israeli tariffs and many nontariff barriers, reinforced by political factors such as Arab boycotts of Israeli products (which extended to products from the West Bank and Gaza), diverted Palestinian commerce away from its Arab neighbors toward Israel.

However, integrating the West Bank and Gaza's smaller, poorer economy into the more-developed Israeli economy also produced a number of benefits for Palestinians: Technology transfer (especially in agriculture) helped income and economic growth in the West Bank and Gaza to outpace Israel's in the late 1960s and early 1970s. At that time, many predicted that the two economies would eventually converge. By the late

---

[6] The West Bank and Gaza do not have their own currency but instead use three freely exchanged foreign currencies: the new Israeli shekel, the U.S. dollar, and the Jordanian dinar.

[7] This subsection is based on Naqib (2002) and World Bank (1999a, pp. 1–13).

1980s, over one-third of the West Bank and Gaza labor force commuted daily to Israel and the settlements, drawn by higher wages.

Economic growth in the West Bank and Gaza began to slow in the mid-1970s, in part because of Israeli policies and actions that restricted Palestinian commerce. Israel blocked some Palestinian goods from being exported to Israel while simultaneously promoting its own goods in Palestinian markets. Israel used water and land from the West Bank and Gaza for roads, settlements, and security purposes. Infrastructure investment in the West Bank and Gaza lagged that in Israel. These policies and the disruption of the Palestinian financial sector caused by the closure of Arab-owned banks in the West Bank and Gaza hurt economic development. Through the 1980s, the development of manufacturing industries in the West Bank and Gaza was very slow. Exports consisted mostly of unsophisticated, labor-intensive manufactured goods (e.g., furniture and textiles) produced under subcontracting arrangements with Israeli companies and a narrow range of agricultural products and building materials.

The West Bank and Gaza have been characterized by underemployment and an exodus of labor, especially people with better skills. While many less-skilled Palestinian workers commuted to Israel to work in construction and agriculture, a large group of highly educated, highly skilled workers left the West Bank and Gaza to seek employment in other countries. During the oil boom of the 1970s, the countries of the Persian Gulf provided an especially attractive market for Palestinian labor. However, worker remittances from the Gulf declined in the late 1980s as the oil boom collapsed. The onset of the first intifada in 1987 and the accompanying Palestinian labor strikes and Israeli security restrictions resulted in a decline in Palestinian employment in Israel and the settlements. New requirements that Palestinian workers in Israel and the settlements obtain work permits limited the extent of the rebound in employment following the end of the first intifada. Palestinian workers suffered a further blow when Kuwait and other Persian Gulf states expelled them during and after the first Gulf War, as a response to support for Iraq by the Palestinian Liberation Organization.

Palestinian Economic Development from the Oslo Accords to 1999[8]

The Oslo Accords brought limited self-rule to the Palestinians as well as expectations of rapid economic development. The Paris Protocol of 1994, one element of the accords, transferred control over much of the Palestinian economy from Israel to the Palestinian Authority (PA). The Paris Protocol also modified the customs union to allow for the free entry of almost all Palestinian goods into Israel. (Remaining restrictions on some agricultural products were completely removed by 1998.) The protocol permitted the use of the Jordanian dinar as legal tender in addition to the new Israeli shekel. It also established the Palestinian Monetary Authority to regulate the financial system, which included reopened Arab banks. Tax collection, which had been a focus of Palestinian

---

[8] This subsection is based on World Bank (1999a, pp. 17–32), UNSCO (2000, 2001a, 2001b), United Nations Conference on Trade and Development (UNCTAD) (1998), and MAS (2001).

resistance during the first intifada, improved: The PA received reimbursements for income taxes collected from Palestinians legally working in Israel, for import duties on goods destined for the West Bank and Gaza, and for value-added taxes on products purchased in Israel by Palestinian firms.

During the post-Oslo period, the public sector grew rapidly because of the establishment of the PA and government institutions. Indeed, most of the growth in Palestinian domestic employment since 1993 is due to growth in the public sector.

However, the Oslo Accords did not markedly alter sovereignty over land and water resources. Negotiations on these issues were postponed until final status talks. Although responsibility for major Palestinian population centers was transferred to the PA, 40 percent of the land in Gaza and 60 percent of the West Bank remained under Israel's direct control, resulting in continued Israeli authority over building, zoning, and land registration. The areas under Israeli control included the Jordan River Valley, which affected development of Palestinian agriculture; and the Dead Sea coast, which affected development of Palestinian tourism and of the chemicals industry. Overall, the unresolved issue of water rights limited the water available for agriculture and raised its cost for industrial and residential purposes.

Israel also retained full control over all borders: Israel effectively controlled the movement of goods and labor among the West Bank, Gaza, and Israel. Continued allocation of land for Israeli settlements and the construction of bypass roads for exclusive use by Israelis further divided the domestic landscape, increasing transportation delays and transaction costs.

Israeli security concerns led to burdensome regulations governing the transportation of goods among the West Bank, Gaza, and Israel (and neighboring countries) and occasionally led to severe restrictions on movement within the territories and to border closures. These measures, a reaction to Palestinian suicide bombings, were first introduced in early 1993 and were used more frequently and broadly in 1996 and 1997. They greatly increased transaction costs for commerce and increased investor uncertainty. Thus, despite the expansion of the domestic banking system and increased donor funds between 1993 and 1996, the real value of private investment spending declined by about 38 percent during the same period.

During this same period, a more restrictive Israeli policy concerning the number of Palestinians working in Israel, also taken in response to suicide bombings, reduced the number of Palestinians employed in Israel or the settlements from about 120,000 in 1992 to fewer then 25,000 in 1996. Border closures were the main factor behind an estimated 18 percent decline in real gross national product (GNP) and a 35 percent decline in per-capita GNP during this same period.[9]

---

[9] By contrast, an increase in private investment between 1998 and 2000, particularly in agriculture and tourism-related industries, coincided with a reduction in border closures and yielded a short period of economic recovery.

Even during the initial period of rapid growth following the signing of the Oslo Accords, increases in industrial output were modest. In contrast, increases in construction activity, particularly construction of infrastructure, were a major driver of economic growth after the adoption of the Paris Protocol. Service sectors also prospered. The positive atmosphere created by the peace process encouraged tourism, expanding employment in hotels and restaurants. However, growth in tourism ended after the suicide bombings and repeated border closures of 1996.

Overall, Palestinian expectations of rapid economic development following the Oslo Accords were largely not borne out, despite greater autonomy. Although real GDP grew 20 percent between 1993 and 1999, per-capita GDP declined by about 8 percent; disposable income, which includes income from abroad and current account transfers, grew only 4 percent (Fischer, Alonso-Gamo, and von Allmen, 2001).

The Palestinian Economy Under the Current Intifada[10]

The second intifada began in September 2000. The period from then through the time of this writing has included Palestinian attacks on Israelis in Israel and the West Bank and Gaza; Israeli military action in the West Bank and Gaza; and Israeli restrictions on Palestinian travel to Israel, between the West Bank and Gaza, and within the West Bank. Since this intifada began, the Palestinian economy has been severely damaged: In 2002, GNI was only 60 percent of its 2000 level. The total losses in GNI from September 2000 to December 2002 ran $5.4 billion, equivalent to the West Bank and Gaza's entire GNI in 1999. The poverty rate rose to 60 percent, up from 20 percent in 1999. Emergency donor aid to the PA has provided some relief through the provision of temporary employment and the maintenance of social services. However, as a result of a 9 percent increase in the West Bank and Gaza's population, real per-capita income in 2002 was only half of its September 2000 level.

This drop in income is mainly attributable to greatly reduced employment of Palestinians in Israel and in Israeli settlements in the West Bank and Gaza, limitations on movement for people and goods within the West Bank and Gaza, and the destruction and depreciation of Palestinian infrastructure. By the end of 2002, the number of Palestinian workers in Israel and the settlements had fallen from 128,000 in 2000 to 16,000. As a result, unemployment at the end of 2002 stood between 42 and 53 percent of the workforce, up from 10 percent in the third quarter of 2000. The closures also affected Palestinian trade: Between June 2000 and June 2002, Palestinian exports declined in value by 45 percent and imports contracted by a third.

Damage from the violence to Palestinian infrastructure (i.e., roads, water, sanitation, power and communications systems, and public buildings) and the commercial sector has been significant. Estimated physical capital losses from the conflict stood at

---

[10] This subsection is based on World Bank (2003c). Timely data on economic conditions in the West Bank and Gaza are quite limited. The current intifada and Israeli responses have limited the functioning of the PA and inhibited data collection and the maintenance of national accounts.

$728 million by the end of August 2002, equivalent to three to four years of public investment since the signing of the Oslo Accords. Destruction of private agricultural and commercial assets accounts for roughly half of this damage.

Principal Challenges and Critical Issues Confronting the Palestinian Economy

Once a final agreement creating an independent Palestine is reached, the new state will need to focus its energies on generating sustained economic growth. If an independent state is created, we expect that it will enjoy very substantial international attention and assistance. This said, the Palestinian economy will face a number of challenges and issues that will affect the economy's ability to generate sustained increases in output. Some of these challenges and issues derive from demographic trends, past economic activities, and the lasting effects of the second intifada. Others will result from the terms of the agreement itself, regarding the geographic shape and extent of the new state and economic and political arrangements. Below we discuss the major challenges confronting the Palestinian economy and identify critical issues for decisionmakers to consider with respect to final status negotiations.

Principal Challenges

Even after a final status agreement, the Palestinian economy will face a number of significant challenges. These include

- threats to security and political stability
- a growing labor force, much of which is currently unemployed
- underdeveloped economic sectors
- underdeveloped economic relations with Arab neighbors
- poor physical infrastructure
- limited private-sector access to capital
- immature governing institutions.

Threats to Security and Political Stability. Clearly, the most important issues affecting the development and growth of the Palestinian economy are security and political instability—particularly in regard to security issues between Israel and the Palestinian state. Economic markets abhor uncertain environments. Businesses and investors desire assurance that their investments will not be subject to unreasonable risk of destruction or expropriation. An environment of insecurity and political instability means that these agents will be less likely to invest, and that economic development and growth will suffer as a result. This sentiment is consistent with attitudes expressed by Palestinian businessmen in the World Business Environment Survey in 2000: Seventy-seven percent of West Bank and Gaza respondents considered "policy instability and uncertainty arising from political conditions in the WBG [West Bank and Gaza]" a moderate or major constraint on expanding business operations and growth (Sewell, 2001, pp. 3–6).[11] In general, scholars of the region attribute the West Bank and Gaza's lackluster economic growth in the 1990s to the uncertain environment resulting from the interim nature of the Oslo Accords. The accords put off the resolution of major Palestinian-Israeli political disputes and failed to stop attacks on Israeli citizens and forestall the imposition of border closures and other severe security measures.[12]

For Palestine, achieving security and political stability depends on the ability of the Palestinian Authority and the Israeli government to craft a mutually beneficial final agreement that embodies effective security arrangements and governance solutions. (These topics are considered in depth elsewhere in this book, particularly Chapters Two and Three.) Overall, the absence of security will inevitably prevent sustained Palestinian economic growth by limiting employment opportunities and access to capital and inhibiting the free movement of people and goods that is necessary for economic success. In contrast, successful Palestinian economic development may help reinforce security and political stability as Palestinians focus their energies on commercial endeavors rather than on conflict with Israel.

Growing Labor Force. The most important asset of an independent Palestine will be its people. The West Bank and Gaza have a large and relatively well-educated labor force. A high percentage of Palestinians are university graduates and a majority of Palestinians speak English, a significant advantage in this age of globalization. In addition, the West Bank and Gaza can draw on members of the Palestinian diaspora, which is well positioned both in the Arab world and in Western countries, for international business contacts, capital, and commercial expertise.

The Palestinian economy of the 1990s, with its periods of high unemployment and lack of private-sector demand for well-educated labor, underutilized this asset. The capital investment necessary to complement an educated labor force was missing. There was also a mismatch between the skills of the Palestinian labor force and those most needed in modern economies. For example, the disproportionately small number of graduates specializing in the sciences and engineering as opposed to graduates specializing in humanities made it more difficult to find jobs for all college graduates.[13]

The Palestinian labor force is projected to rise from 625,000 in 2000 to over 960,000 in 2010—an average annual increase of 5.4 percent. This growth will be even higher if substantial numbers of Palestinian refugees immigrate to the West Bank and

---

[11] Following policy instability and uncertainty as a constraint were corruption (71 percent), inflation (64 percent), the exchange rate (62 percent), taxes and regulations (56 percent), and anti-competitive practices (54 percent).

[12] For more information see Shikaki (2002), Naqib (2002), and World Bank (2002b).

[13] Chapter Eight, Education, expands on this topic.

Gaza and if the currently low rate of labor force participation by Palestinian women increases by more than expected [International Monetary Fund (IMF), 2001].[14] Demand for labor in the Palestinian state will have to grow rapidly over the next 10 to 15 years to accommodate these workers if the state is to avoid widespread unemployment and reduce poverty. This will not be an easy task. Historically, the domestic economy has struggled to provide adequate jobs, even during periods of substantial Palestinian employment in Israel.

Underdeveloped Economic Sectors. A number of important economic sectors in the West Bank and Gaza are underdeveloped. Manufacturing, for example, is relatively small in terms of employment, share of GDP, and exports. The most important manufactured goods in the West Bank and Gaza are footwear, leather goods, apparel, generic pharmaceuticals, furniture, plastics, and wood and metal products. Exported goods consist mostly of unsophisticated, labor-intensive manufactures. For example, the most important export is quarried construction materials. The small volume of exports from the West Bank and Gaza and the relatively limited array of exported goods suggest that Palestinian products are not very competitive on international or domestic markets.

The private sector in the West Bank and Gaza is dominated by small enterprises.[15] These tend to be companies working under subcontracting agreements with Israel, or family businesses that often depend on unpaid family labor. Palestinian agriculture remains very labor intensive. It utilizes few of the agro-technological advances that benefit Israeli agriculture. It serves as the employer of last resort, particularly during times of economic disruption.

Inter-industry linkages, such as among agriculture, agricultural supply industries, and food processing, are very poor in the West Bank and Gaza. Consequently they have inhibited the growth of clusters of integrated industries that would be beneficial for generating economies of scale and scope. Weak inter-industry linkages stem from several causes, including the physical separation of the West Bank and Gaza, historical restrictions by Israel on Palestinian industrial development, and (particularly since the start of the second intifada) limited mobility of goods and people within the West Bank. The result is low domestic value added—products are either exported as raw materials or Palestinian businesses add little value to imported components or raw materials. The low levels of value added by domestic businesses limit the benefits derived from free trade agreements, which often demand that exported goods contain substantial shares of local content.

Consequently, current production patterns are not a good reflection of Palestine's comparative advantage as an independent country. However, current economic activi-

---

[14] This IMF estimate assumes no net migration and that female participation in the workforce remains relatively low but increases from about 11 percent in 1999 to about 24 percent in 2025 (the current level in Jordan).

[15] In 1999, the number of companies employing more than 100 employees was less than 1 percent of the total number of registered companies operating in Palestine, while companies employing less than 20 employees constituted almost 99 percent (Muhanna and Baker, 2001).

ties cannot simply be discarded or radically altered with the promise of a better future because they are the only sectors currently providing employment and business opportunities.

Underdeveloped Economic Relations with Arab Neighbors. As a small and developing country, an independent Palestine would benefit greatly from strong economic ties with other countries, particularly its Arab neighbors, to diversify its trading relationships and spur economic growth. Strong economic relations with Arab countries could facilitate the flow of additional capital into Palestine for expanding current businesses and financing new ventures. Arab investments could also provide additional employment opportunities in the region for Palestinian labor. Such relations are particularly important because they would facilitate more Palestinian trade, increase the number of sources of Palestinian imports, and provide markets for Palestinian exports.

Current economic ties with the West Bank and Gaza's Arab neighbors are weak. In 1998, the West Bank and Gaza's immediate Arab neighbors, Jordan and Egypt, together accounted for only 3.4 percent of the value of merchandise trade transactions (exports plus imports) with Palestinians [United Nations Office of the Special Coordinator in the Occupied Territories (UNSCO), 2000, p. 29]. Although Jordan is the West Bank and Gaza's second-largest trading partner, in absolute terms the volume of trade with Jordan remains small. Despite having signed a trade agreement with the West Bank and Gaza, Jordan has introduced obstacles to trade such as high duties on Palestinian exports and excessive administrative requirements for exporting and importing goods across Jordan's border.[16] As for Egypt, the West Bank and Gaza's ninth-largest trading partner, trade between Egypt and the West Bank and Gaza has been minimal, consisting primarily of imports of Egyptian food and consumer products into Gaza.

There are a number of reasons for weak economic ties between Palestinians and Arab countries: The transportation infrastructure necessary for direct trade (i.e., roads, airports, seaports, and pipelines) is inadequate; Israeli security measures increase the costs of trading with other countries; many Arab countries have high trade barriers, imposing a large number of cumbersome regulations, and have boycotted Israeli (and thus Palestinian) goods; and many Palestinian products are not competitive in low- and middle-income countries because of the West Bank and Gaza's high costs for energy and unskilled labor.

Palestine, Israel, and the international community can mitigate some of these negative factors during final status negotiations. But even if most or all of these issues can be satisfactorily resolved and ties with Arab neighbors strengthened, the overall economic impact could still be quite small. Jordan would be unlikely to absorb a large

---

[16] For example, a truckload of stones imported into Jordan from the West Bank and Gaza would incur a duty of 180 dinar (about $270), which has had the effect in the latter half of 1990s of limiting the importation of stones, a competitive Palestinian product. Soap, another potentially competitive product, has also incurred high duties. Jordan also required Palestinian truck drivers involved in trade to carry Jordanian passports, driver's licenses, and registrations (UNCTAD, 1998).

number of Palestinian exports or workers, considering that its economy is one-tenth the size of Israel's and has similar circumstances to those in the West Bank and Gaza (i.e., few natural resources and a labor force with many low-skilled workers). The larger Egyptian market would presumably present more opportunities, although its low per-capita income levels would permit only modest amounts of Palestinian exports, and high Egyptian unemployment levels would suggest few employment opportunities for foreigners. Rich Gulf countries like Saudi Arabia represent potentially larger markets for Palestinian exports, but they also tend to have rather closed economies.

Poor Physical Infrastructure. Sustained growth in Palestinian per-capita incomes will require a physical infrastructure capable of supporting provision of basic services, developing profitable industries, and transporting goods and people. Such infrastructure includes roads, bridges, and transportation hubs such as seaports or airports for travel and trade within Palestine and with its neighbors and the rest of the world. Palestine needs power plants and electricity grids as well as water and sewage systems that serve both homes and businesses. Palestine also needs a modern telecommunications network, especially to facilitate the development of high-technology sectors, commerce, and tourism.

Palestinian physical infrastructure needs considerable improvement. Existing Palestinian infrastructure has been damaged by military operations during the second intifada and depreciated as a consequence of the economic environment and mobility restrictions (UNCTAD, 2002, p. 4). But even before the intifada, Palestinian infrastructure was in worse shape than in some countries with similar per-capita incomes, despite significant donor assistance. The hilly topography of the West Bank and Gaza and the construction of Israeli settlements and settlement roads have inhibited the development of an adequate Palestinian road network linking population and trade centers. The Palestinian economy depends heavily on Israeli seaports and airports for transport and travel with the rest of the world. The West Bank has no airport and Gaza has one, but Israel closed the airport in 2000 and destroyed the runway in 2002; in any case, the Gaza airport has never had cargo facilities. The construction of an international seaport in Gaza has been put on hold, and the roads and bridges connecting the West Bank to Jordan and Gaza to Egypt are in poor condition.

The Palestinian economy now relies primarily on Israel for electricity. The electricity distribution grid is in poor condition, resulting in substantial electricity losses. These conditions contribute to the West Bank and Gaza having the lowest per-capita energy consumption in the region and the highest electricity costs. Palestinian water quality is declining (as described in detail in Chapter Six). There are no modern sanitary landfills, and sewage systems are rudimentary. Many communities have open sewers.

Introduction of the domestic telecommunications provider PALTEL helped to speed development of that sector. The number of telephone lines more than tripled between 1997 and 2000 (MAS, 2001). Even so, PALTEL is currently prevented by Israel from developing its own international communication services. As of 2000, there were nine Internet providers in the West Bank and Gaza, serving only 60,000 users.

Limited Private-Sector Access to Capital. Significant capital would likely be made available to assist Palestine once it gains independence. Palestinians currently receive substantial financial assistance from outside countries and organizations such as the World Bank; we expect this assistance to continue in the future. Other sources of capital include the Palestinian diaspora and foreign direct investment through multi-national corporations.

An important question is how much of this capital can be accessed by individual businesses seeking to expand and modernize their facilities. The Palestinian financial sector expanded rapidly during the 1990s, attracting almost $3 billion in deposits by 2000. But small enterprises, which dominate the Palestinian economy, had trouble obtaining commercial loans and other financing. The lending-to-deposit ratio was very low; most loans went to state-owned firms and commerce. Long-term loans to finance investment in manufacturing were particularly scarce.

The World Bank notes that the lack of private-sector access to capital is in part the result of the absence of a supportive legal framework and regulatory institutions, as well as the uncertain political and economic environment.[17] The West Bank and Gaza lack the legal framework and supporting institutions necessary to establish and enforce property rights. Regulatory institutions lack mechanisms such as auditing and accounting standards to assess and mitigate risk.

As a result of these conditions, the Palestinian banking sector is highly risk averse: Banks remain relatively liquid, making only short-term loans. Both borrowers and lenders deposit excess liquidity abroad because of the limited number of safe investment opportunities domestically. The deficiencies of the legal framework have caused banks to adopt strict lending requirements such as high collateral and traditional forms of security such as cash, personal guarantors, and real property with clearly held titles—a rarity in the West Bank and Gaza for political and historical reasons. Most business assets such as working capital, equipment, and vehicles as well as immovable assets are unacceptable to banks as collateral because they tend to be unregistered and as such cannot be readily seized.

Immature Governing Institutions. Governing institutions determine the rules by which a country's economic activities take place. A strong system of governing institutions is needed to support business transactions. These institutions create enforceable property rights, provide businesses with transparent information on taxation and registration, and issue clearly defined rules and regulations. These elements help minimize uncertainty and limit political and economic corruption. By so doing, they help to encourage economic activity.

---

[17] For example, in 1999 there was a financial-sector development project proposed by the World Bank (1999c).

Important government institutions in the West Bank and Gaza such as the judiciary are currently weak. To some extent, the weakness of these institutions has impeded economic development. For example, in 1998 the Palestinian Legislative Council approved a law establishing a judiciary independent from the executive branch, a highly progressive move for the Arab world, but the PA did not enact this law until May 2002. The PA's willingness to faithfully implement the law remains unclear (Brown, 2002, pp. 29–31). The existence of special security and military courts continues to threaten the effectiveness of the judiciary by encouraging Palestinians to resolve disputes through means other than the civil courts. The PA has yet to enact a number of laws that would strengthen the enforcement of private contracts and commercial activity, including the Company Law, the Intellectual Property Law, the Secured Lending and Leasing Law, and the International Commercial Arbitration Law (Sewell, 2001, pp. 16–18).

The lack of accounting and auditing standards, as well as the lack of experience on the part of the Palestinian Monetary Authority in regulating and supervising banks, has adversely affected lending. The lack of oversight of PA commercial operations coupled with excessive PA hiring and spending suggest to businesses that the executive branch is neither transparent nor accountable for its actions. At the same time, simply passing laws and creating institutions does not necessarily ensure good governance. The government of a Palestinian state will also need to develop personnel procedures and introduce rewards and penalties that will encourage effective governance. (For more detail on the development of Palestinian governance, please see Chapter Two.)

Critical Issues

The previous discussion highlighted some of the challenges facing the development of a viable economy in a Palestinian state. While addressing these challenges, decisionmakers must consider the critical issues that are relevant to any negotiated final agreement and that markedly affect the path and prospects for Palestinian economic development and growth. These critical issues are

- transaction costs
- resources
- the Palestinian trade regime
- Palestinian employment in Israel.

Transaction Costs. Many of the measures that Israel implemented since the 1990s to prevent violence and maintain security have severely impeded the economic activity in the West Bank and Gaza by imposing very large additional transaction costs on business activities. The complex and cumbersome system of permits, fees, security checks, and special transportation procedures has constrained the movement of both goods and people. For example, regulations that require Palestinian haulers to completely unload their cargo and reload it onto Israeli trucks at the border for passage through Israel have added significant transaction costs to Palestinian commerce because of delays and additional shipping expenses. Closures between the West Bank, Gaza, and Israel have made the movement of goods and people very difficult. A study in 1998 before the second intifada by the Federation of Palestinian Chambers of Commerce, Industry and Agriculture estimates that transaction costs were, on average, 30 percent higher for Palestinian companies than for Israeli companies, and time delays were 45 percent longer (IMF, 2001, p. 73). Not only do these transaction costs make Palestinian goods more expensive (and thus less competitive), they also adversely affect Palestinian industrial supply relationships because of increased risk and uncertainty faced by customers and suppliers.[18]

The physical separation between the West Bank and Gaza and the existence of Israeli settlements in the West Bank and Gaza also result in high transaction costs. Settlements and the network of bypass roads increase travel time within the West Bank and Gaza, especially during periods of Israeli closures. The necessity of passing through Israeli territory to travel between the West Bank and Gaza interrupts the movement of goods and people and increases costs. Also, major travel routes connecting the southern and northern halves of the West Bank pass through Jerusalem, so Israeli security measures for Jerusalem can affect transportation throughout the West Bank. Duplicative layers of bureaucracy impose additional costs as Palestinian companies seek operational approvals from both the PA and the Israeli government.

A Palestinian state that is allocated more territory in the West Bank and Gaza and more sovereignty over this territory would face lower transportation and transaction costs than a more fragmented entity. Dismantling some Israeli settlements, easing or providing access to settlement roads, removing checkpoints, and generally increasing the contiguous nature of Palestinian lands would reduce travel and transaction costs, thereby spurring economic activity.

Resources. The West Bank and Gaza have very few natural resources of commercial value. Current commercial resources are limited to potash, which is used in the production of fertilizer, and quality limestone, marble, sand, and gravel, which are used in the construction industry. Newly discovered (and hence undeveloped) natural gas deposits off the coast of Gaza may be commercially viable, but currently the West Bank and Gaza have no fossil fuel resources; the only potential sources of energy available domestically are solar power and limited hydropower. Palestinian access to clean water is an issue. Although the West Bank borders the Jordan River and sits atop a sizable underground aquifer, these water resources are nearing the point of complete utilization by the West Bank, Gaza, Jordan, and Israel.[19] The West Bank and Gaza do have a favorable climate for agriculture: Crops can be grown year-round. Despite its small size, Palestine offers seven agro-climatic zones with at least 20 different soils supporting about 60 different crops. In addition, major cultural sites are located in Bethlehem, Jericho, and East Jerusalem, while the Dead Sea and the Mediterranean coast offer the potential for recreational tourism.

---

[18] For more details on transaction costs see IMF (2001, pp. 61–82).

[19] See Chapter Six, Water, for more-detailed information.

Broadly speaking, more control of resources and rights would provide Palestine more options for developing its economy. A Palestinian state with more cultural sites could develop a more extensive tourism sector. A Palestine with more water rights in the Jordan River valley could expand agriculture and other industries. And a Palestine with control over its airspace would have the option of building its own airport to transport people and cargo instead of relying on regional facilities. By the same token, one could imagine that a Palestine with little control over its resources would find it much more difficult to develop industry and agriculture.

The Palestinian Trade Regime. Upon achieving statehood, a Palestinian government will need to negotiate trade agreements with its immediate neighbors (Israel, Jordan, and Egypt), with its other Arab neighbors, and with other important partners such as the United States and the European Union. Decisions on the trade regime will have major consequences for future economic development. If the West Bank and Gaza continue to receive preferential trade access to Israel, Palestinian exporters will benefit from the large, proximate Israeli market. Many existing Palestinian firms have contracting and subcontracting relationships with Israeli companies, providing a further reason for seeking to maintain preferential trade relations. If preferential access is discontinued, West Bank and Gaza exporters will have to find new markets.

Because of the current Israeli-Palestinian *customs union* (described above), Palestinian and Israeli goods have free access to each other's markets, common tariffs on other countries' goods, and the same trade policies with respect to external partners. Maintaining a customs union with Israel has some advantages. It would minimize administrative and customs costs because Israeli customs offices would continue to collect and reimburse tariffs on Palestinian imports transiting Israeli ports. It could also strengthen industrial supply relationships between the two countries.

However, maintaining a customs union would also have some disadvantages. It would leave Palestine highly vulnerable to shocks in the Israeli economy and to political relations with Israel. The tariff structure of the union would likely reflect Israeli interests more than Palestinian interests, potentially impeding the development of competitive Palestinian sectors. A future Palestinian state could also lose tax revenues through leakage to Israel of import duties and value-added taxes as is currently the case. If continued close trade links with Israel come at the price of barriers to trade with other potential partners, a future Palestinian government might seek more open trade relations with other partners.

Alternatively, a future Palestinian state may choose to negotiate *free trade agreements* with a number of states, including Israel. Under such a trade regime, Palestine would impose no tariffs on imported goods from all of its trading partners with which it has free trade agreements, including Israel.[20] This would provide Palestine the op-

---

[20] Another possible trade regime would be a *nondiscriminatory trade regime,* under which Palestine would control its own tariff structure and regulations while treating all trading partners equally. The difference here is that Palestine might set nonzero tariffs for different goods. Given the economy's small size and the need to generate as much economic activity as possible, nonzero tariffs would not be recommended. Consequently we do not consider this option in our analysis.

portunity to strengthen ties with other countries in the Middle East, North America, Europe, and Asia, diversifying its exports markets and sources of supply. If Palestine were to eliminate all or most tariffs, which act as a tax on commerce, it would reduce administrative costs since an extensive customs apparatus would not be needed. A completely free trade regime would help Palestine foster use of its comparative advantage in labor, accelerating economic growth.

If Israel were to decide not to provide a future Palestinian state duty-free access to the Israeli market, growth in Palestinian exports would be retarded by the additional costs imposed by Israeli tariffs on Palestinian exports. The reduction in trade could adversely affect Palestinian economic growth in light of Palestine's underdeveloped economic relations with the rest of the world and its lack of transport infrastructure.

Palestinian Employment in Israel. For decades, relatively open Israeli labor markets have allowed Palestinian workers to commute to jobs in Israel and the settlements and return to their homes in the West Bank and Gaza at night.[21] The extent of Palestinian access to employment in Israel and the specifics surrounding this access (e.g., system of permits and lack of access during border closures) will need to be determined in any final agreement.

Easy Palestinian access to the Israeli labor market (in terms of legally sanctioned access either with or without permits) would provide significant employment opportunities for the Palestinian workforce. As we have described, the domestic economy has had difficulty providing full employment for Palestine's current workforce; the IMF projects that the labor force will grow by 40 percent by 2010 (even assuming no influx of refugees). Israel could offer significant additional opportunities for employment. Wages in Israel tend to be substantially higher than those in the West Bank and Gaza, boosting Palestinian incomes. Higher Palestinian incomes translate into higher expenditures, which would fuel the domestic economy.

The primary constraint on Palestinian employment in Israel is security. The Israeli government wishes to ensure that no Palestinian workers in Israel engage in attacks on Israelis. In addition, the Israeli government has frequently used closure of borders or closure of Palestinian towns and cities as a means of combating attacks. Closures make it virtually impossible for Israeli firms to hire Palestinians because employers can never be sure that their employees will be able to make it to work. For Israeli firms to be willing to hire a significant number of Palestinians, Palestinians would have to have relatively unfettered access across Israeli borders. Future Israeli governments may conclude that the security risks of permitting large numbers of Palestinians to work in Israel are so large that the past practice of permitting Israeli firms to employ Palestinian labor is unacceptable. Such a decision would deprive Palestine of this source of employment and income.

---

[21] Beginning in the early 1990s, Israel began requiring Palestinians working in Israel and the settlements to obtain permits as a condition of employment. Also, it is currently illegal for Palestinian workers to remain overnight in Israel.

Economic Scenarios for a Future Palestinian State

The Palestinian economy could develop and grow along very different paths, depending on the conditions that international decisionmakers specify in any final agreement and decisions made by policymakers in the new state. Four critical issues—transaction costs, resources, the Palestinian trade regime, and Palestinian employment in Israel—will shape the conditions under which economic activity occurs in an independent Palestine. In this section we use these issues to construct four scenarios of conditions that Palestine could face with respect to its economic development.[22]

Scenarios of Economic Development

Other studies have examined prospects for economic growth in a newly established Palestinian state. A study by the World Bank (2002c) examines how the Palestinian economy might develop under different scenarios of economic and political relations with Israel, including various trade regimes and degrees of access of Palestinian labor to employment in Israel. The study uses a comprehensive macroeconomic model that incorporates foreign trade and labor markets in addition to growth accounting, providing projections for 2002–2010. A study by the IMF (2001) uses a growth accounting framework to generate economic projections up to 2010, based on different assumptions about access to the Israeli labor market and immigration. The study makes some reasonable assumptions about employment growth, predicts unemployment rates for 2010, and computes the increases in total factor productivity (TFP) needed to achieve acceptable levels of per-capita income.

Our analysis combines these two approaches. Like the World Bank study, we develop plausible scenarios based on the territory encompassed by a new Palestinian state (geographic contiguity) and its economic relations with Israel (economic integration). We discuss these scenarios qualitatively below. Like the IMF study, we use a simple growth-accounting model to project the growth in per-capita GDP and GNI under each scenario for the 2005–2019 time frame based on estimates of growth in employment, TFP, and capital. This quantitative analysis is presented in the next section.

Two points should be made at the outset of our discussion. First, we substantially simplify real-world conditions in our analysis. As the preceding sections suggest, many different policy and investment decisions will shape the future of Palestinian economic development. However, some simplification is necessary to focus on the major drivers of economic development in Palestine and to allow for clear inferences to be drawn. We, therefore, concentrate on the effects of contiguity and integration in the following section but recognize that many other factors, such as the quality of governing institutions, will play important roles also.

---

[22] This is not to suggest that the initial conditions are necessarily fixed in stone. Allocations of rights and institutional arrangements can always be renegotiated in the future should parties deem it beneficial.

Second, we implicitly assume that security is maintained throughout the 2005 to 2019 time frame. In other words, our scenarios are predicated on the notion that economic activity occurs in a safe and stable environment. Lack of security, and resulting responses to it, would inhibit all aspects of Palestinian economic development described in this chapter. Consequently, our conclusions are correctly seen as what might happen in the best case.

Geographic Contiguity

A major determinant of transportation and transaction costs that a Palestinian state will face and the resources that will be available to it will be *geographic contiguity*. We define geographic contiguity broadly to include the amount of territory allocated to the Palestinian state, special sites (such as East Jerusalem and the Jordan valley), the integrity or fragmentation of this territory (perhaps because of settlement roads), and control over elements associated with this territory such as water rights, airspace, and borders.

We consider two possibilities on the geographic contiguity dimension. The *low-contiguity* case reflects conditions that are similar to but still an improvement over the period since the signing of the Oslo Accords. It assumes that for the most part, Israel retains control over East Jerusalem, the existing settlements, aquifers and surface water in the West Bank, external borders, and the customs apparatus. However, Israel would have less authority over the internal situation in the Palestinian state: It could not impose internal closures or curfews or prevent Palestinians from developing their own infrastructure (e.g., water, power, and transportation) should they choose to do so.[23]

The *high-contiguity* case assumes that the Palestinians have (1) more land (e.g., the Jordan valley and the Dead Sea coast), (2) more control over East Jerusalem, (3) more water rights and territorial control, and (4) unfettered passage between the West Bank and Gaza. This case also assumes that most settlements are dismantled or exchanged for contiguous land elsewhere.

Economic Integration

We use an additional composite dimension called *economic integration* with Israel that encompasses the Palestinian trade regime and Palestinian access to Israeli labor markets. In the sense used here, economic integration is similar to "border permeability" or "border openness" used elsewhere in this book.

We consider two possible cases. Under *high economic integration*, cross-border commerce resembles that which existed under the Oslo Accords. This case assumes a customs union (or perhaps a free trade agreement) between Palestine and Israel, a large number of Palestinians are allowed to work in Israel (likely around the pre-intifada

---

[23] Given that the low-contiguity case in our analysis reflects an improvement over the status quo (from the Palestinian perspective), any final agreement that encompasses less land or fewer resources than the low-contiguity case—or that entails limitations on movement of goods and people within Palestinian territory, via closure or curfew—presumably would make it more difficult to sustain economic growth than our analysis suggests.

level of 130,000), and transit and travel procedures in both directions are simple for people and goods.

Under *low economic integration,* cross-border commerce with Israel is impeded by a symbolic or physical wall. This case also assumes that the current customs union with Israel ends and Palestinian businesses do not have favorable access to Israeli markets; that barriers to labor mobility significantly reduce the number of Palestinians working in Israel; and that restrictions are imposed on tourists and others wishing to cross the border. Under both cases, Israel remains an important trading partner, but conditions under high economic integration are more conducive to economic cooperation between Palestine and Israel, providing the possibility of higher trade volumes, more cross-border investment, and more collaboration in tourism and other sectors than in the low economic integration case.

Four Scenarios

The degree of geographic contiguity determines how much control Palestinians will have over resources and movements of people and goods within the new state. The degree of economic integration captures future economic relations between the Palestinian state and Israel. Together, these dimensions create a simple two-by-two framework describing initial conditions confronting the Palestinian state. The likelihood of ending up in any of the four quadrants will vary depending on negotiations to establish the new state and the strategic choices made. It is also possible that the new state could be in more than one quadrant in the first ten years of its existence. This section presents these scenarios without delving into their likelihood, but these issues are discussed in some detail in Chapters Two and Three. As is clear below, there are real consequences to the degree of contiguity and integration of the new state.

As shown in Figure 5.1, these dimensions yield four potential starting points or scenarios for the development of the Palestinian economy and the initial conditions with which the state—with the assistance of external parties—will have to contend. These scenarios are (1) high contiguity/high integration, (2) high contiguity/low integration, (3) low contiguity/high integration, and (4) low contiguity/low integration.

Scenario One: High Contiguity/High Integration. In the first scenario, Palestine consists of a contiguous West Bank with an uninterrupted road and rail link to Gaza. Palestinian territory on the West Bank encompasses significant cultural sites. Palestine has rights to aquifers and other sources of water on its territory. Consequently, transport and transaction costs for businesses and consumers are relatively low. Citizens can move freely within the state and travel to and from Jordan and Israel without much cost or delay. In this scenario, very substantial numbers of Palestinians are permitted to work in Israel, similar to pre-intifada days. Palestine and Israel sign a free trade agreement or agree to continue the customs union.

Figure 5.1
Four Scenarios of Palestinian Economic Development

Economic integration with Israel

		High	Low
Geographic cointiguity	**High**	Lower transaction costs More land and resources Preferential trade with Israel Many workers in Israel	Lower transaction costs More land and resources No preferential trade with Israel Few workers in Israel
	Low	Higher transaction costs Less land and fewer resources Preferential trade with Israel Many workers in Israel	Higher transaction costs Less land and fewer resources No preferential trade with Israel Few workers in Israel

RAND *MG146-5.1*

High contiguity would give Palestinians more options for economic development. Control over major cultural sites would allow Palestinians to collaborate with Israel in attracting and catering to tourists from abroad. Control of the airspace over Palestine would permit Palestinians to choose between constructing their own air cargo facilities or using Israeli airports. Access to higher-paying jobs in Israel would reduce under-employment in Palestine and help to create sustained increases in per-capita incomes; pre-intifada per-capita income levels would return fairly quickly.

Under this scenario, Palestinian employment in Israel rapidly returns to its pre-intifada level. Within Palestine proper, employment growth is concentrated in tourism, construction, and light manufacturing, much of which would consist of subcontracts from Israeli firms. Indigenous economic activity would be skewed toward retailing and wholesaling, transport, agriculture, and the manufacture of labor-intensive consumer goods. Economic activity within Palestine would be bolstered by preferential access to Israeli markets, resulting in a ready supply of inputs and nearby markets for exports and the option of using Israeli seaports, airports, and infrastructure to reach other markets.

Scenario Two: High Contiguity/Low Integration. As in the first scenario, Palestine has significant land and resource rights and goods and people circulate freely in Palestine. The primary difference in this scenario is that economic links with Israel are attenuated. Although Palestinian businesses are able to export to Israel, access to Israeli markets are no better than to other countries or regions with which Palestine has free trade agreements or faces reduced barriers to trade. Palestinian workers, however, have little or no access to the Israeli labor market. Under this scenario, the Palestinian economy could still grow fairly rapidly, but GNI would be appreciably lower than in the first scenario because of the absence of worker remittances from Israel.

In the short term, agricultural production, the manufacture of labor-intensive consumer goods, and services would likely provide most employment and account for most economic output. Palestinian control over natural resources, especially water, would facilitate increases in domestic food production and the emergence of high-value horticultural exports, such as fresh-cut flowers. Agriculture and tourism, which are labor intensive, would help to absorb the thousands of low-skilled laborers no longer able to work in Israel. That said, the domestic economy, at least in the short term, would probably be too small to accommodate the entire Palestinian labor force, considering that roughly 20 percent of it once worked in Israel.

Economic growth would rely largely on the growth of Palestinian exports. Having no tariffs and low transaction costs would help facilitate manufacturers' access to inexpensive inputs, but because Palestinian exports to Israel would now be subject to tariffs (de facto price increases), trade between the two countries would grow more slowly than in the first scenario. Palestinian exporters would have to find new markets in the Middle East, the European Union, and the United States. Export growth would require better infrastructure and unfettered access to a Gaza seaport or to airports capable of handling significant amounts of cargo. Until this infrastructure is completed, increases in per-capita GNI would likely be modest.[24]

Scenario Three: Low Contiguity/High Integration. In the third scenario, Palestine is not contiguous but it is highly integrated into the Israeli economy. In this scenario Palestine will have the ability to leverage Israeli facilities, but construction of infrastructure would still be important to reduce transport times and transaction costs and to improve the environment for economic growth. Within the domestic economy, services such as tourism and retail and wholesale trade would be major employers. The Palestinian economy would also benefit from the wages earned by Palestinian workers in Israel and with Palestinian employment from subcontracting in Palestine. Because of the lack of control over water, the agricultural sector would likely languish. However, there would be opportunities for Palestine and Israel to collaborate on fostering tourism.

The lack of resources and the reinforcement of traditional economic relationships between Palestine and Israel could possibly limit the potential of Palestinian economic development. However, this need not be the case. Presumably, as long as the Israeli economy grows steadily and both Israel and Palestine make a concerted effort to expand trade with other countries, Palestine would be able to sustain economic growth. There would, however, be very high transaction costs to overcome as a result of the

---

[24] We note that factors that may lead to low economic integration with Israel—particularly Israeli concerns about security—are also likely to inhibit the unfettered passage of people and goods between the West Bank and Gaza that we consider to be part of "high contiguity."

lack of contiguity because Palestinian goods and people would have to cross multiple borders. Among other outcomes, this would make Palestinian-produced goods more costly and less competitive on world markets.

Scenario Four: Low Contiguity/Low Integration. Scenario four is characterized both by limited geographic contiguity and by economic separation from Israel. This scenario assumes that the number of Palestinians permitted to work in Israel is severely constrained. Consequently, the Palestinian government would be confronted with the problems of finding employment for the vast majority of Palestinian workers. The absence of major cultural sites or adequate water supply as well as higher transaction costs would adversely affect the state's ability to develop domestic tourism or agriculture.

The scenario also assumes that Palestine would not have preferential access to the Israeli market, so the importance of Israel as an export market and source of imports would decline. Economic activity in the short term would likely center on services, construction (particularly of infrastructure), and efforts to industrialize. Domestic industries in this scenario would develop slowly; it is unlikely that they would grow rapidly enough to accommodate the growing Palestinian workforce. Even if donors funded large-scale construction projects that would employ large numbers of Palestinians workers, it is doubtful that there would be a sufficient number of domestic jobs to significantly cut into unemployment. Growth in per-capita incomes would be slow or stagnant. Foreign donors would probably need to fund significant social welfare programs to feed and cloth large numbers of Palestinians. This scenario is the least favorable for a new Palestinian state: Economic development would likely be stunted and growth in per-capita incomes slower than in the other scenarios.

Even faced with these unfavorable conditions, Palestine might be able to generate appreciable economic growth if the international community were to finance the infrastructure necessary to reduce transportation and transaction costs and create a more favorable environment for business. Ideally, donor-funded projects would attract enough foreign direct investment to spur growth. In particular, Palestine would need a comprehensive network of surfaced roads, a seaport, a modern telecommunications system, and the right to use them. These would be necessary for the efficient movement of people and goods, including imports and exports. At the same time, we emphasize that considerable additional investment would be necessary to help compensate for unfavorable conditions of contiguity and integration, and that even then there would be no guarantee that the economy could overcome the considerable hurdles this scenario would present for achieving sustained economic development.

Summary of Implications

This framework of four scenarios is simply a tool to help decisionmakers consider the consequences of the different forms a final agreement could take. The scenarios illustrate the starting conditions for Palestinian economic development resulting from the specific circumstances negotiated in a final agreement. Each scenario has different implications for Palestinian economic development and the growth of per-capita incomes that can be sustained.[25]

We summarize below the qualitative implications of the four potential scenarios, given their assumptions regarding geographic contiguity and economic integration with Israel:

High-contiguity/high-integration scenario yields rapid economic growth:

- Lower transaction costs and Palestinian control over land and resources result in broad economic development.
- Economic cooperation with Israel provides access to Israel's relatively large market for exports, facilitates joint undertakings in tourism, and preserves subcontracting ties.
- Employment in Israel and worker remittances result in large initial increases in per-capita incomes; continuing access to Israeli labor markets provides ongoing employment opportunities for a growing Palestinian workforce.
- Relatively high increases in per-capita incomes minimize the need for donor assistance, other than for building infrastructure.

High-contiguity/low-integration scenario yields moderate economic growth:

- Low transaction costs and greater resources yield broad economic development, with growth in tourism, agriculture, and construction.
- Less-favorable access to Israeli product markets slows export growth, hurting manufacturing.
- Restricted access to Israeli labor markets reduces growth in incomes and employment.
- Most external assistance is needed in the short term to build and repair infrastructure, thereby creating conditions needed to attract foreign investment and increase exports to markets other than Israel.

Low-contiguity/high-integration scenario yields moderate economic growth:

- High transaction costs and fewer resources result in narrow economic development focusing primarily on services and construction.
- Access to Israeli goods markets facilitates exports and collaboration between Palestinian and Israeli firms.
- Access to Israeli labor markets fosters growth in per-capita incomes and helps to accommodate a growing Palestinian workforce.
- Relatively high per-capita incomes mean donor assistance can target building infrastructure.

---

[25] All scenarios implicitly assume, however, that security and stability are maintained throughout the 2005 to 2019 period for economic development to occur as described.

Low-contiguity/low-integration scenario yields sluggish economic growth:

- High transaction costs and fewer resources result in narrow economic development.
- Less-favorable access to the Israeli market slows growth in exports, hurting manufacturing, but reducing the economy's vulnerability to border closures.
- Restricted access to Israeli labor markets reduces growth in incomes and employment, putting pressure on the domestic economy to accommodate more Palestinian workers.
- Significant donor aid is needed to build infrastructure and to combat poverty through a combination of social support and jobs programs.

Economic Implications of the Scenarios for a Future Palestinian State

The previous section described a series of scenarios, some of which provide a much better basis for sustained growth than others. A highly contiguous Palestine with access to Israeli product and labor markets is far more likely to enjoy rapid sustained growth than a fragmented Palestine cut off from the Israeli economy. In this section, we attempt to quantify the potential differences in economic growth and economic structure implicit in each scenario. For each scenario, we project growth in per-capita GDP and GNI. The differences in outcomes illustrate the economic implications of choices to be made by Palestinian and Israeli decisionmakers and the international community in final status negotiations.

Growth Accounting Model[26]

We estimate the implications of the scenarios for per-capita GDP and GNI by using a simple growth accounting model (see the appendix for details). The model ties growth in the labor force and employment, increases in the capital stock, and rates of growth in TFP to growth in per-capita GDP and GNI. The model is used to project per-capita GDP and GNI for the four scenarios for the 15 years following a final agreement and the establishment of a Palestinian state. We assume the time frame extends from the beginning of 2005 to the end of 2019. During this period, economic development in all four scenarios is assumed to move through three distinct phases:

- 2005–2009—recovery from the intifada and the creation of the foundations for longer-term growth
- 2010–2014—modernization of the economy and development of new economic sectors and markets
- 2015–2019—consolidation of gains and transition to self-sustaining growth.

---

[26] The dollar figures in this subsection are expressed in 2003 constant dollars.

Our model projects rather high annual Palestinian GDP growth rates under all scenarios, ranging from a high of about 20 to 23 percent in 2006 to a low of about 7 to 9 percent in 2019. Although the initial rates appear very high, they are consistent with the experiences of other post-conflict economies. In the first year of peace in Bosnia and Kosovo, GDP rose by three-fifths to two-thirds.[27] The projected rates are *feasible* according to our model. That is, if an independent Palestine achieved the increases in private-sector employment, capital stock, and TFP, these estimated GDP growth rates could ensue. The important questions for each scenario are: What do these GDP growth rates mean for Palestinian per-capita GNI, what private-sector employment growth is needed to drive this growth in GDP, and what is the magnitude of capital investment needed to achieve this GDP growth? We address these questions in turn.

Table 5.1 and Figure 5.2 illustrate per-capita GNI for the scenarios in milestone years. A peaceful, contiguous Palestine with close links to the Israeli economy (high contiguity and high integration) and sensible economic policies offers prospects for very rapid rates of growth. Under this scenario, our model projects per-capita GNI of $3,740 by 2019, over three times the estimated initial level of $1,110 at the end of 2004. Compared to the actual per-capita GNI of $1,890 in 1999, our model suggests that an independent Palestine could surpass pre-intifada levels within 5 years and essentially double per-capita income in 15 years.

Outcomes are not as favorable under the high-contiguity/low-integration scenario or the low-contiguity/high-integration scenarios with year-end per-capita GNI of $3,370, or 9 percent lower. In the first instance, per-capita GNI is lower throughout the entire time period because of limited employment in Israel. In the second, the higher transaction costs involved in doing business in a fragmented state result in slower rates of growth in per-capita GNI.

The low-contiguity/low-integration scenario yields the smallest per-capita GNI of all cases, increasing from $1,110 in 2004 to only $2,810 by 2019 or 25 percent lower than the high-contiguity and high-integration case.

Table 5.1
Estimated Palestinian Per-Capita GNI for 2004–2019 (under each scenario, in 2003 dollars)

Scenario	1999 Actual	2004 Estimate	2009 Estimate	2014 Estimate	2019 Estimate	1999–2019 % change
High contiguity/ high integration	$1,890	$1,110	$2,160	$2,860	$3,740	97.5%
High contiguity/ low integration	$1,890	$1,110	$2,000	$2,640	$3,370	77.6%
Low contiguity/ high integration	$1,890	$1,110	$2,100	$2,690	$3,370	78.0%
Low contiguity/ low integration	$1,890	$1,110	$1,850	$2,310	$2,810	48.3%

[27] Dobbins et al., 2003.

Figure 5.2
Estimated Palestinian Per-Capita GNI for 2004–2019

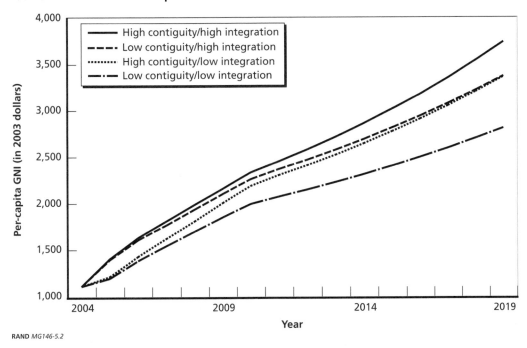

What do these results suggest for the success of an independent Palestine? Although there is no generally accepted definition of what constitutes "success," a few simple criteria can provide some useful perspective. One criterion is whether per-capita incomes return to their pre-intifada levels within a reasonable time frame. Table 5.1 indicates that under every scenario but the low-contiguity/low-integration scenario, pre-intifada per-capita incomes of $1,890 are surpassed within five years. In the low-contiguity/low-integration scenario, however, the 2009 per-capita income of $1,850 indicates that pre-intifada levels are essentially only met.

A second criterion pertains to the long-term footing of the Palestinian state and its ability to recover from the setbacks of the last five years. We can gain insight by comparing the scenarios to a hypothetical Palestine that experienced no second intifada, but that instead saw slow and steady growth in real per-capita incomes between 1999 and 2019. As shown in Table 5.2, the turmoil in the period since the signing of the Oslo Accords provides little historical insight into what conservative, long-term trends in per-capita income for our hypothetical Palestine might look like; consequently we use annual real growth rates of 2 percent and 3 percent for comparison. Steady 2 percent growth from the 1999 base of $1,890 yields a per-capita income of $2,820 by 2019, whereas 3 percent growth yields a per-capita income of $3,420.

Table 5.1 suggests that every scenario but the low-contiguity/low-integration scenario would best both long-term trends by 2019. Thus, according to our model,

Table 5.2
Actual and Estimated Per-Capita GNI Real Growth Rates

Year	Per-Capita GNI Growth (actual)	Time Frame	Per-Capita GNI Growth (assumed)	Per-Capita GNI Growth (assumed)
1994	−4.9			
1995	−9.6			
1996	−9.0	1999–2019	2%	3%
1997	3.4			
1998	7.7			
1999	3.3			
1999 per-capita GNI	$1,890	2019 per-capita GNI	$2,820	$3,420

SOURCES: IMF, 2001, p. 5; and RAND Corporation calculations.

Palestine could potentially grow fast enough by 2019 to make up for the effects of the current intifada. The high-contiguity/high-integration scenario would result in per-capita income about 9 percent higher than that resulting from the 3 percent growth trend. The high-contiguity/low-integration and low-contiguity/high-integration scenarios would yield per-capita income more in line with the 3 percent trend. However, the low-contiguity/low-integration scenario fares less well than the 3 percent trend, and only slightly better than the 2 percent trend.

A third criterion is how well Palestine performs relative to other countries. The World Bank ranks countries by their income levels into one of four categories: lower income (per-capita GNI of $765 or less), lower-middle income ($766 to $3,035), upper-middle income ($3,036 to $9,385), and upper income ($9,386 or above). Palestine's per-capita income of $1,890 in 1999 puts it solidly in the ranks of lower-middle-income countries. But Table 5.1 indicates that Palestine would become an upper-middle-income country by 2019 in three of the four scenarios. In the low-contiguity/low-integration scenario, Palestine would remain a lower-middle-income country although it would be toward the higher end of the range.

Table 5.3 presents the employment projections from the model with respect to potential growth in domestic private-sector employment. It illustrates the average annual increases in private-sector jobs that would be needed to reduce the Palestinian unemployment rate to around 8 percent. The model results show that domestic private employment would have to grow at very rapid rates for this reduction to occur.

Under the high-integration scenarios, domestic private employment would have to grow at an annual average of about 56,400 jobs from 2005 to 2009, or at 15.2 percent per year. This would be followed by more moderate employment growth of 41,100 jobs annually (6.5 percent) from 2010 to 2014, and 46,800 jobs annually (5.5 percent) from 2015 to 2019, yielding an unemployment rate of about 8.2 percent in 2019.

Table 5.3
Estimated Annual Average Domestic Private-Sector Job Growth Needed for Given Unemployment Reduction (under high- and low-integration scenarios)

Scenario	2005–2009 Annual Average Private-Sector Job Growth		2010–2014 Annual Average Private-Sector Job Growth		2015–2019 Annual Average Private-Sector Job Growth		Estimated Unemployment Rate	
	Number of Jobs	Growth Rate (%)	Number of Jobs	Growth Rate (%)	Number of Jobs	Growth Rate (%)	2004 (%)	2019 (%)
High integration	56,400	15.2	41,100	6.5	46,800	5.5	42.8	8.2
Low integration	66,500	17.2	47,900	6.9	52,000	5.5	42.8	8.1

For the low-integration scenarios, domestic private employment would have to grow by about 66,500 jobs per year between 2005 and 2009, or a 17.2 percent annual average growth rate. This is 10,000 jobs per year more than in the high-integration scenarios. More rapid job growth is needed to compensate for lower employment in Israel under low integration. Under these low-integration scenarios, employment growth would moderate to 47,900 jobs annually (6.9 percent) between 2010 and 2014, and 52,000 jobs annually (5.5 percent) between 2015 and 2019. This would yield an unemployment rate of about 8.1 percent in 2019.[28]

Achieving these increases in employment would be a considerable challenge for an independent Palestine. Job growth would have to be even stronger if a large number of refugees were to resettle in the new state. The historical record does not make us optimistic that these rates of employment creation could be achieved: The highest rate of growth in private-sector employment recorded since the signing of the Oslo Accords was only 7 to 8 percent. This employment growth took place in 1998–1999, following a sharp reduction in security restrictions and closures. We could certainly expect rapid increases in employment as the state is inaugurated and constraints on trade and commerce are lifted. But economic growth and investment will have to be very substantial to ensure that high rates of growth are maintained over time.

If Palestine is able to achieve these initial increases in private-sector employment, the prospects rise for achieving growth in per-capita incomes substantial enough to make a very real impact on living standards. However, prospects of employment growth of this magnitude in the low-contiguity/low-integration scenario are poor. Private-sector job growth will be more difficult under this scenario because the state has less control over resources and transactions costs are high. As a consequence, growth in per-capita incomes will suffer.

---

[28] One reason, though not the primary one, why these private-sector growth rates need to be this high is because our model deliberately limits employment growth in the Palestinian public sector to 1 to 2 percent a year. As mentioned earlier, PA employment is already quite high, even by regional standards. High public-sector employment in other Arab countries has contributed to slow rates of growth in private-sector business formation and in TFP because government bureaucracies stifle the creation of new businesses and slow productivity growth through the imposition of regulations designed to extort bribes.

Next we calculate the magnitude of capital investment needed to reach pre-intifada per-capita GNI by 2009 and to effectively double it (in most cases) by 2019. These calculations depend noticeably on the value of the existing Palestinian capital stock, but precise estimates of the capital stock do not exist particularly because of the damage during the intifada. We expect the capital stock to total about $12.1 billion in 2004 (see the appendix for details). Accordingly, we calculate capital stock growth and depreciation in each scenario beginning from this base.

Table 5.4 illustrates the investments in capital stock needed to attain the rates of growth posited in the scenarios over different time periods. Our model indicates that investment in capital stock of $28.7 billion in the ten-year time frame from 2005 to 2014 and $49.9 billion over the 2005–2019 time frame to generate the incomes illustrated in Table 5.1. In other words, investments averaging about $3.3 billion a year would be needed to create a capital stock sufficient to generate per-capita GNI of $3,370 by 2019 under the high-contiguity/low-integration scenario. We have assumed that the volume of investment would rise over time, from $2.6 billion per year for 2005–2009 to $4.2 billion in 2015–2019.

These projections are for total gross fixed capital investment, private and public, in a new Palestinian state needed to generate the posited levels of employment. The investment needed would be higher if a substantial number of refugees resettled in Palestine and additional employment would be necessary. These estimates are totals financed by all sources: domestic savings, direct foreign investment, private borrowing from abroad, loans to the state, and foreign assistance. The international community is not assumed to provide all of this investment. However, it is likely that initially virtually all public-sector and some private-sector investment would be funded by foreign donors. Most of this funding would need to be frontloaded during the 2005–2009 time period so as to create the infrastructure that will be needed for sustained economic growth in Palestinian per-capita incomes. By 2019 most investment would be undertaken by the private sector or financed through tax revenues collected by the Palestinian government.

These levels of investment, although large, are not extraordinarily different from investments and assistance flows provided to Bosnia during the first years following the Dayton Accords. They also are not an estimate of the levels of foreign assistance a new Palestinian state might need. Even at the onset of the new state, Palestinians will be investing their own funds in homes and businesses. As the Palestinian economy gains

Table 5.4
Estimated Palestinian Capital Stock Investment Required in 2005–2019
(under each scenario, in billions of 2003 dollars)

	2005–2009 Total	2005–2009 Average	2010–2014 Total	2010–2014 Average	2015–2019 Total	2015–2019 Average	2005–2019 Total	2005–2019 Average
Each scenario	$13.1	$2.6	$15.7	$3.1	$21.2	$4.2	$49.9	$3.3

NOTE: The five-year totals do not sum to the 15-year totals because of rounding.

its legs, a rising share of this investment will be financed domestically or through direct foreign investment, easing the burden on the international donor community.

The rate of return on this investment is substantially lower for the low-contiguity/low-integration scenario than for the others. An investment of $50 billion between 2005 and 2019 results in Palestinian per-capita GNI of only $2,810 by 2019 in this case. By contrast, the same investment (all else being equal) results in a per-capita GNI of at least $3,370 by 2019 for any of the other three scenarios. According to our model, decision-makers considering the initial conditions for a Palestinian state would be well advised to ensure that Palestine is economically integrated with Israel or provided sufficient contiguity to avoid this suboptimal scenario.

Limitations of the Growth Accounting Model

To some extent the growth accounting model fails to capture the true costs in lower economic output of a noncontiguous Palestinian state. The costs to Palestinian businesses of border closures have been substantial. Even assuming relatively free flows of goods and people among Palestinian territories, if most internal transactions in Palestine entail one or more security checks or border crossings, the increased cost of doing business will throttle growth. This lost economic output cannot be readily measured, but the very sharp declines in per-capita incomes in the West Bank and Gaza over the course of the second intifada illustrate the challenges a noncontiguous state would face.

By the same token, it is difficult to capture in a growth accounting framework the multiplier effects on domestic incomes of wages earned in Israel. The two labor markets are quite complementary: Israel primarily needs less-skilled labor; the West Bank and Gaza has a surplus of less-skilled labor. Demand for well-educated labor such as doctors and engineers is much higher in the West Bank and Gaza.

Within growth accounting models, inputs are fungible: for example, increases in capital can offset slower rates of productivity growth. Although true in a modeling framework, the empirical evidence does not necessarily support this assumption. International assistance programs suggest that unless the institutional arrangements and incentives are present and the necessary human capital available, no amount of investment in physical capital can generate sustained growth. Thus unless the Palestinian government designs and implements the necessary institutional framework and the accompanying controls, sustained growth likely will not materialize. Moreover, growth will not materialize without peace. As demonstrated by Iraq, throwing massive amounts of money at an economy will not generate sustained economic growth in an environment of violence. Although both assumptions are implicit in this model, it bears remembering that good governance and a secure environment are likely to be quite important for economic growth.

Potential Inflows of Foreign Assistance

Virtually all economies, even fairly poor ones, finance most investment from domestic savings. The construction of housing, purchases of motor vehicles, and investments in small businesses all tend to be financed from personal savings. For countries with large expatriate populations, remittances form another important source of investment. Remittances tend to flow into the same types of investments as domestic savings. International borrowing, especially from international financial institutions like the World Bank and from the regional development banks, and foreign assistance that is used for investment are heavily skewed toward public-sector investment. In contrast, foreign direct investment flows to the private productive sector. It is concentrated in sectors such as manufacturing, telecommunications, transport, wholesaling, retailing, and financial services.

The growth accounting model employed above does not distinguish among the sources or destinations of investment. A successful Palestinian state will need to invest in all sectors of the economy and will draw on all sources of investment. However, we believe it is useful to compare the size of these aggregate flows of investment to potential inflows of foreign assistance. Although Palestine will not be able to rely on foreign assistance for all investment, an appreciable share of public investment, especially in the early years, will have to come from international financial institutions or foreign donors. Only after a few years of peace and economic growth and a track record of financial probity will a Palestinian government be able to borrow from commercial lenders.

To roughly size the magnitude of assistance that might become available, we apply average per-capita levels of assistance that went to Bosnia and Kosovo in the first two years of reconstruction to the projected Palestinian population through 2014 to size future levels of assistance analogous to those received by those two entities. We believe the analogies are appropriate. Like the West Bank and Gaza, these two entities suffered considerable damage from conflicts. Both have attracted considerable international interest and assistance. Both have had some success in creating democratic governments and revitalizing the local economies. The entities are somewhat similar in size of population: Bosnia has a population of 4 million; Kosovo, 2.3 million; and the West Bank and Gaza, 3.5 million.

In the first two years following the signing of peace accords in Bosnia and Kosovo, foreign assistance (grants and loans) averaged $714 and $433, respectively, per person per year. Applying these per-capita figures to the projected population of the West Bank and Gaza, an analogous inflow of assistance would run $1.6 billion to $2.7 billion in the first years after the creation of a state, rising to $2.1 to $3.5 billion by 2014 as a result of increases in population (see Table 5.5). Over the ten-year period between 2005 and 2014, flows of foreign assistance to a new Palestine state analogous with those that have been granted Kosovo and Bosnia would run from $18.8 billion to $31.1 billion.

By way of comparison, the World Bank estimated that the total volume of international aid to the West Bank and Gaza was $1,051 million in 2002 and $929 million in 2001; the World Bank reported that the 2001 level represented twice the annual volume of aid prior to the second intifada. Thus aid based on the Kosovo analogy

Table 5.5
Aid Flows Analogous to Those for Bosnia and Kosovo

Year	Palestinian Population	Total Aid (in millions of 2003 dollars)	
		Bosnia Analogy	Kosovo Analogy
2005	3,761,904	$2,688	$1,627
2006	3,889,249	$2,779	$1,683
2007	4,018,332	$2,871	$1,738
2008	4,149,173	$2,964	$1,795
2009	4,281,766	$3,059	$1,852
2010	4,416,076	$3,155	$1,910
2011	4,547,678	$3,249	$1,967
2012	4,676,579	$3,341	$2,023
2013	4,807,137	$3,434	$2,080
2014	4,939,223	$3,529	$2,137
Total	—	$31,068	$18,813

would represent a further 50 percent increase for 2005, relative to the 2002 level of international aid to the West Bank and Gaza, while aid based on the Bosnia analogy would require more than doubling the level of aid received in 2002.

These numbers based on the Kosovo analogy fit comfortably within the projections of the investment needed to rapidly reduce unemployment in Palestine. Those based on the Bosnia analogy exceed the investment projected to be necessary. However, a sizable share of foreign assistance will be used to pay for recurring costs, especially during the first years of the new nation's existence, before tax systems are in place and economic growth provides additional resources that are easier to tax. Thus, per-capita assistance levels such as those provided to Bosnia might be effectively utilized. In any event, the numbers suggest that the challenge facing the international donor community is on the order of the challenges presented by Bosnia and Kosovo. Aid flows exceeding the levels given Bosnia would very likely be difficult for the nascent state to absorb; levels below those provided Kosovo might fail to spur the economic growth that we believe is necessary to make the new state a success.

Best-Practice Economic Policies for Stimulating Economic Growth

Whatever configuration an independent Palestine takes, the Palestinian government in conjunction with external actors—including Israel, other foreign governments, and international financial institutions—will make economic policy decisions that will affect Palestinian development and growth in per-capita incomes. In many instances, some economic policies are clearly superior to others in terms of stimulating economic growth, increasing incomes, and reducing poverty. Below, we provide a menu of best-practice economic policies that would accelerate improvements in economic welfare in a future Palestine.

We have grouped what we see as the key policy options into the following categories:

- fostering free trade
- partnering with neighboring countries
- investing in infrastructure
- easing Palestinian employment in Israel
- expanding access to capital
- choosing currencies
- improving the business climate
- investing in human capital.

Fostering Free Trade

Palestine's key comparative advantage in international trade is its human capital. Thus, regardless of whether or not Palestine retains preferential trade access to Israel, a Palestinian government would maximize gains from trade by making labor-intensive commercial activities located in Palestine as competitive as possible. This could be done through appropriate infrastructure investments (described below) and trade policies.

Competitiveness implies that exporters will not be burdened with paying duties on imported raw materials and components. It suggests that products move swiftly and securely through ports. And it implies that the sources of inputs for Palestinian goods and the destinations for its exports be increased.

We recommend the following:

- Upon achieving statehood, a Palestinian government should adopt a zero- or low-tariff policy, especially for industrial inputs.
- It should also ensure that transshipment costs, customs duties, and customs procedures are as swift, secure, and cheap as possible.
- A Palestinian government should negotiate free trade agreements with as many countries as possible, especially its immediate neighbors (Israel, Jordan, and Egypt), its other Arab neighbors, and other important trade partners such as the United States and the European Union.
- To foster economic growth in Palestine, the Israeli government should provide duty-free access to Palestinian exports. Israel should also encourage Palestine to provide duty-free access to imports from Israel so as to keep Palestinian exporters competitive by ensuring that imported raw materials and components are competitively priced.
- The United States and the European Union should extend current free trade agreements with Israel and Jordan to Palestine.
- Arab states should provide duty-free access to imports from Palestine.

Partnering with Neighboring Countries

Palestine should work with its neighbors to coordinate the development of specific economic sectors. Some sectors would clearly be stronger if multiple countries worked together rather than separately. One example is collaboration with Israel on tourism. Since the signing of the Oslo Accords, a number of hotels and restaurants in the West Bank and Gaza complained that tourists often made only day trips to Palestinian sites while staying and spending their money in Israel. Joint promotion of cultural sites (especially in East Jerusalem) and investment in the surrounding areas and border crossings would help to increase the number of tourists to both countries as well as the amount of money spent in each.

Jordan and Egypt also provide opportunities for cooperation, although it is unlikely that such cooperation would be as extensive as with Israel because these countries are poorer, have similar mixes of production factors (plenty of unskilled labor), and do not have a history of cooperation. Nevertheless, successful Arab partnerships could be built in the areas of tourism, energy, water, transportation, and potentially manufacturing.

We recommend the following:

- In the case of high economic integration with Israel, Palestine should collaborate with Israel to coordinate the development of tourism and other sectors.
- In all cases, an independent Palestine should pursue cooperative ventures with Jordan and Egypt.
- Israel, Palestine, Egypt, and Jordan should seek to make customs procedures as easy and transshipment costs as cheap and swift as possible. These countries should invest in infrastructure at border crossing points (bridges, highways, railroads, and customs points) to ensure that movement and transshipment proceed quickly and efficiently.

Investing in Infrastructure

In light of the poor quality of infrastructure in much of Palestine and the severe damage inflicted on it during the second intifada, a large program of infrastructure construction will be required, regardless of the scenario in which Palestine finds itself. Transportation infrastructure will need to be developed to speed the movement of goods and people. Palestine will need roads, bridges, and transportation hubs, such as seaports and airports, for travel and trade within Palestine and with its neighbors. Investments in electricity, water, and sewage infrastructure will be needed to expand services, thereby improving living conditions and increasing the competitiveness of domestic industries. Investments in communications and information technology will be needed to lay the foundations for the emergence of profitable new industries and for future economic growth.

How extensive these projects need to be, especially with respect to power, water, and sanitation, depends to some degree on the extent of economic cooperation between Palestine and Israel. Since per-capita GDP in Palestine is only one-tenth of Israel's, the Palestinian government will have to prioritize where it spends its limited resources, especially on investment in infrastructure. Where possible, it would make sense to utilize infrastructure in neighboring countries, including Israel. If, for example, the Israeli electricity grid currently serving the West Bank and Gaza provides a quality, cost-competitive service, it would make more sense for Palestine to contract with Israel for these transmission services than to build a new Palestinian system from scratch. The use of Israeli or Jordanian airports is likely to be cheaper than building, operating, and maintaining separate Palestinian facilities. If economic integration with Israel is low, however, Palestine will have no choice but to try to construct its own electric power system and transportation infrastructure, although it is important to recognize that the conditions—particularly relating to security—that would inhibit integration with Israel are also likely to inhibit unrestricted Palestinian development of this type of infrastructure.

Egypt and Jordan could work with Palestine to improve regional infrastructure, especially regarding transportation and energy, which would support economic development broadly and help ease Palestinian dependence on Israel. Oil pipelines to Jordan could be extended to link Palestine with Iraqi or Saudi oil fields. Gas pipelines could be constructed to Iraqi fields. Another possibility would be the creation of a Palestinian electrical grid linked to a regional grid encompassing Egypt, Jordan, Syria, Lebanon, and Israel. This system could be based on existing links (UNCTAD, 1998).

Under all scenarios, projects critical to fostering Palestinian economic growth include

- expanding power, water, and sewage plants
- constructing a Gaza seaport
- ensuring unrestricted access to regional airports, whether they are located in Israel or Jordan, or involve rebuilding the Gaza airport and adding cargo facilities
- developing a corridor linking the West Bank and Gaza
- improving border crossings with Jordan and Egypt.

In addition to the benefits generated by the completed infrastructure, the construction of these projects would benefit the Palestinian economy. Contracting these projects to the domestic private sector would foster development of private Palestinian construction firms and generate employment. Mixed foreign and domestic management of construction projects would facilitate the transfer of project management skills and construction technologies. Such strategies would build the domestic construction industry, bringing it to a level where Palestinian firms could provide construction services to the rest of the world, especially to countries within the Middle East.

We recommend the following:

- In the case of high economic integration, Palestine should leverage Israeli infrastructure wherever possible.
- Israel should encourage the development of common infrastructure with Palestine. Although charges will need to recover the full costs of the service, Israel should price these services as competitively as possible.

- Under all scenarios, Egypt and Jordan should seek to develop common infrastructure with Palestine wherever cost-effective.
- International financial institutions should support cross-border infrastructure projects.
- Whenever possible, donor-financed projects should encourage use of mixed foreign and domestic management of construction projects.

Easing Palestinian Employment in Israel

Whether a final agreement permits significant access for Palestinian labor to Israel or only limited access, it is important that this access be as easy as possible. Employment opportunities in Israel with their relatively higher wages are a much needed source of income that helps to fuel Palestine's domestic economy. Thus, efforts to minimize impediments to Palestinians reaching their jobs in Israel would be beneficial, including streamlining bureaucratic procedures (e.g., to obtain permits) and facilitating easy border crossings.

At the same time, this access should be provided in a manner consistent with Israel's need to maintain security. As mentioned earlier, the primary constraint on Palestinian employment in Israel is security—the Israeli government wants to ensure that no Palestinians in Israel engage in attacks on Israelis and has used border closures and other restrictions to restrain or discourage attacks. So Palestinian cooperation and collaboration with Israel in implementing security measures would help to increase the Israeli government's comfort level and, over time, could potentially help to increase the extent of Palestinian access to Israel.

We recommend the following:

- Palestine should adopt and implement the security measures that would make employment of Palestinians in Israel possible.
- Assuming security measures are adequate, the Israeli government should make it easy for Israeli employers to hire Palestinians by streamlining and reducing the cost of the permitting process.
- Israel should give Palestinian workers expedited access to Israel, including accelerated processing at borders and rapid, seamless transport links to places of employment.
- Provided security has improved, Israel should revamp rules on overnight stays and other strictures so that Palestinian workers have more flexibility to respond to unexpected occurrences such as the need to stay later at work.

Expanding Access to Capital

Increasing private-sector access to capital, which has been limited because of political risk and other concerns, would help spur investment. Palestine could undertake a number of initiatives to strengthen its domestic banking sector, including reforming domestic banking policies and encouraging foreign banks to open branches in Palestine. Such actions could increase financial intermediation and improve the allocation of capital. The World Bank (1999a, pp. 97–109) advocates improving the Palestinian Monetary Authority's (PMA) regulation and supervision of the banking sector by requiring stricter capital adequacy rules, relatively high liquidity ratios, and restrictions on acquiring risky assets. Over the longer term, the PMA could develop mechanisms such as deposit insurance and a discount window to contain bank failures. The mere existence of these regulations and institutions would not guarantee that they would be enforced. However, creating them is a necessary first step for a modern banking system.

Improving the financial system also involves clarifying property rights and improving access to collateral for both borrowers and lenders. The absence of well-defined Palestinian property rights has contributed to disputes between the Israeli and Palestinian communities. The absence of a proper land registry inhibits private-sector borrowing and investment in business by making it difficult to use real property as collateral. A land registration program would facilitate lending and the expansion of residential construction and small business operations.

International programs providing political risk insurance would also help attract both Palestinian and foreign investors to the new state. Political risk insurance reduces the risk to commercial activities stemming from political instability. An insurance program targeted specifically at Palestine and funded by the international community could insure foreign and Palestinian investors against the destruction of property stemming from violence or state expropriation of investment. These guarantees would make it easier for international companies to obtain investment funding. If a separate fund were not set up, guarantees could be obtained from the U.S. Overseas Private Investment Corporation, the World Bank's Multilateral Investment Guarantee Agency, or other such insurance programs.

We recommend the following:

- In accordance with World Bank suggestions, the PMA should tighten lending standards for Palestinian banks and improve oversight procedures.
- International financial institutions should provide training and assistance to the PMA to improve its ability to supervise banks.
- Donors should help the Palestinian Authority create a system of property registration and register all property in the West Bank and Gaza.
- Foreign agencies that provide political risk insurance should offer these services to investors in a new Palestinian state.

Choosing Currencies

As noted above, the Palestinian Authority does not have its own currency but uses three freely exchanged foreign currencies: the new Israeli shekel, the U.S. dollar, and the Jordanian dinar. This tri-currency system appears to have served the West Bank and Gaza very well. Despite very tumultuous situations, inflation has remained lower than that in Israel. Because the current system is relatively successful, the Palestinian economy is small, and foreign trade is a very large share of GDP, there appears to be no need for a separate national currency.

Accordingly, we recommend that a new Palestinian state should not create its own currency, but should continue with the current policy of accepting the Jordanian dinar, the new Israeli shekel, and the U.S. dollar as legal tender.

Improving the Business Climate

Attracting foreign direct investment to Palestine is essential to fostering industrialization and rapid economic growth. When multinational firms locate plants or facilities in a developing country, they bring not only jobs, but also management skills and technologies that spill over into the larger economy. Spillovers occur in a number of ways: when local companies become more efficient by replicating foreign procedures, when local workers leave the multinational firms for local companies, and when multinational firms help improve the capabilities of their local suppliers (Lim, 2001). Foreign direct investment is how countries such as Singapore achieved rapid economic growth.

Improving the transparency and accountability of governance in the Palestinian state would increase investor confidence and encourage flows of foreign capital to fund Palestinian economic development. Improving Palestinian governance involves a broad range of activities, some of which are only tangentially related to economic policy. A number of these key issues and policy changes are addressed in Chapter Two. However, among these policies, one is repeatedly cited: improving the Palestinian legal framework (Sayigh and Shikaki, 1999, 2003; Brown, 2002). These sources and others note the need to strengthen the independence of the judiciary and to eliminate the arbitrary, harsh security courts. Other important measures include improving mechanisms for the resolution of commercial disputes and creating legal guarantees for the repatriation of profits and capital by foreign investors.

Another measure to attract foreign direct investment is to keep the costs of doing business low. One approach is to use economic development zones (EDZs)—enclaves in which customs, registration, and other procedures are simplified and which sometimes offer tax concessions. They are not new to the West Bank and Gaza; they have been discussed throughout the 1990s under the Oslo Accords (and implemented in a limited fashion in Gaza) as a way of marrying Israeli capital with Palestinian labor, providing needed jobs in the West Bank and Gaza while avoiding security concerns associated with thousands of Palestinians crossing into Israel for work. But a bolder program broadly targeted at the entire international community of investors, not just Israeli investment, would prove beneficial in terms of job growth, industrialization, and technology transfer.

However, in Palestine's case, there is little sense in carving out selected areas in which government procedures are expedited. Palestine is so small, geographically (the size of the San Francisco metropolitan area) and economically, that the Palestinian government would be well advised to eliminate tariffs and simplify business registration and other procedures for the entire country, not just special zones. Governments that create simple, low-cost, transparent procedures for registering and regulating businesses have had some remarkable successes in terms of economic development: Witness Hong Kong, Estonia, and Singapore. Such a step would signal to the international investor community that the Palestinian government seriously wishes to attract foreign investment and support the private sector.

Regardless of whether the Palestinian government simplifies regulations for the entire state or just selected zones, regulations should have the following characteristics: They should be designed to help facilitate the movement of people to their jobs and the movement of goods between port facilities and industrial or agricultural centers. Business regulations should be simple and clear.[29] Procedures for settling commercial disputes should be acceptable to the international financial community. Such rules would provide safeguards to foreign investors and address investor concerns about the rule of law and transparency.

We recommend the following:

- The Palestinian Authority should treat the entire country as an EDZ, focusing on expediting cross-border shipping, customs procedures, and administrative procedures for domestic companies and exporters alike.
- The Palestinian Authority should clarify, update, and improve the commercial code immediately.
- The Palestinian Authority should simplify and reduce the costs of registering businesses as soon as possible.
- The Palestinian Authority should consolidate judicial proceedings in civilian courts and improve judicial proceedings and the quality of judges.
- The Palestinian Authority should permit international arbitration and set up other commercial dispute settlement procedures acceptable to the international financial and investment communities.

Investing in Human Capital

There is currently a mismatch between the skills of the Palestinian labor force and those most needed in the sectors of the economy most likely to expand. Most university students study liberal arts subjects rather than engineering or sciences, majors that have been more marketable but less popular. Secondary education suffers from high drop-

---

[29] This is not to suggest that businesses located in EDZs should be exempt from all environmental or other regulations of importance to the community and country. In fact, any program of EDZs that is implemented in Palestine should be cognizant of the issues sometimes experienced in other countries resulting from foreign direct investment, such as environmental pollution, problems with accountability, and the expropriation of resources. We do suggest, however, that businesses should be shielded from excessive regulation, which is a concern given the relative inexperience of Palestinian governing bodies.

out rates and weak vocational training. High dropout rates may stem from the poor quality of vocational training: Students question the benefit for future employment of poorly designed training courses.

As the Palestinian economy develops and modernizes, it will require a skilled workforce ready to participate in a competitive, global environment. Ensuring that the Palestinian workforce is adequately prepared will require significant investments in human capital. Although we discuss reforms of the education system in more detail in Chapter Eight, we note several areas in which reforms would give Palestinian students more-marketable skills:

- Foreign donors should provide tuition assistance and subsidies to encourage enrollments in the sciences and engineering.
- Foreign donors should work with the Palestinian Authority to improve the quality and appeal of vocational training.

Conclusions

In this chapter, we examined possible economic development trajectories in an independent Palestinian state during the 2005 to 2019 time frame. We focused on Palestine's prospects for sustaining growth in per-capita incomes over time. In exploring this issue, we discussed the major challenges that will confront the Palestinian economy, as well as the four critical issues—transaction costs, resources, the Palestinian trade regime, and the access of Palestinian labor to employment in Israel—that will determine the conditions under which the Palestinian economy will function. Using a growth accounting model, we then examined how the four scenarios resulting from different levels of contiguity and integration affect per-capita income. The scenario with the highest resulting per-capita income after ten years (high contiguity and high integration) saw incomes 24 percent higher than incomes in the scenario with the lowest resulting per-capita income (low contiguity and low integration). We also discussed best-practice policy options that could aid the Palestinian economy under any conditions.

Decisionmakers should find our framework and analysis useful in two important respects. First, they provide a rough approximation of the magnitude of investments needed to generate rapid recovery and then growth in per-capita incomes in Palestine. They also provide a useful benchmark for the international community with respect to investment decisions for Palestine. Second, they indicate how different conditions could affect economic growth in a Palestinian state. A contiguous Palestine economically integrated with Israel would likely fare far better than a fragmented state or one that has truncated economic ties to Israel. A less contiguous Palestine that is also oriented away from Israel will have trouble sustaining economic growth. Decisionmakers would do well to avoid this scenario if at all possible.

Appendix 5.A: The Growth Accounting Model

The results described in the section above, Economic Implications of the Scenarios for a Future Palestinian State, are based on a simple growth modeling framework, in which we focus on modeling Palestinian GNI over the period 2005–2019. We define GNI to consist of Palestinian GDP, plus remittances from Palestinian employment in Israel.

Our growth model is intended as a tool for illustrating the economic potential of an independent Palestinian state and the economic opportunity cost of low geographic contiguity and/or low economic integration of this state with Israel. We emphasize that the results from this model follow deterministically from our assumptions about initial levels and trends in Palestinian labor supply and employment rates, capital investment, productivity growth, and the other parameters of the model. Moreover, although our assumptions about these parameters are intended to be realistic, they are not predictive in the sense that we necessarily expect these trends to be realized. Such forecasting, and indeed any type of formal macroeconomic modeling, is outside the scope of this project.

Gross Domestic Product

Our growth modeling assumes an initial (end of 2004/beginning of 2005) level of Palestinian GDP of $3.4 billion, which represents a 30 percent decrease from the 2000 level. This assumption is reasonable considering that, according to the World Bank, Palestinian GDP dropped from $4.7 billion in 2000 to $4.2 billion in 2001 (in constant 2003 dollars). Thus increases to GDP in 2005 and beyond resulting from, for example, infusions of capital begin from this base.

To model Palestinian GDP over the period 2005–2019, we use a Cobb-Douglas production function:

$$\text{GDP}_{ts} = A_{ts} K_t^{\alpha} L_t^{\beta}, \tag{1}$$

where A is total factor productivity (TFP), K is productive capital, L is employment, α is the elasticity of GDP with respect to capital, and β is the elasticity of GDP with respect to labor. The subscript t indexes time (t = 2005 to 2019), while the subscript s indexes scenarios (s = high contiguity/high integration, high contiguity/low integration, low contiguity/high integration, and low contiguity/low integration); parameters that are assumed to be constant across time and/or scenarios lack the corresponding subscript.

Under the assumption that production is characterized by constant returns to scale, $\beta = 1 - \alpha$, and Equation 1 can be rewritten as:

$$\text{GDP}_{ts} = A_{ts} K_t^{\alpha} L_t^{1-\alpha}. \tag{1'}$$

The Cobb-Douglas functional form and the assumption about constant returns to scale are commonly used by economists for national growth modeling.

For this analysis, we must specify the initial conditions for the above variables and parameters (at the end of 2004/beginning of 2005), and then specify how we expect them to change over time in each scenario. In the remainder of this section, we describe the assumptions underlying each variable and parameter in the model. We then report the levels of Palestinian national income that follow from these assumptions.

Total Factor Productivity (*A*)

Growth in TFP refers to the process by which technological or other change raises output per unit of capital and labor. For convenience, and without loss of generalizability, we normalize TFP to take the value of 1 in 2004 under all scenarios. For the high-contiguity/high-integration scenario, we assume that TFP growth starts at 7.0 percent annually in 2005 and declines to 3.0 percent annually by 2019.[30] For the high-contiguity/low-integration and low-contiguity/high-integration scenarios, we assume that TFP starts at 6.0 percent annually and declines to 2.0 percent annually. And for the low-contiguity/low-integration scenario, we assume an initial TFP growth of 4.0 percent annually that declines to 1.0 percent annually. The smaller growth rates primarily reflect the higher transaction costs under these scenarios. Our assumptions about TFP are summarized in Table A.5.1.

Capital Stock (*K*)

We assume an initial capital stock in 2004 of $12.1 billion. Precise estimates of the capital stock do not exist, particularly because of the damage during the intifada. We arrive at our figure from the World Bank's (2002b) average estimate of the 2000 capital stock ($16.3 billion in 2003 dollars[31]) after accounting for (assumed) total losses of $1.6 billion in 2003 dollars[32] from the intifada and 5 percent annual depreciation.

For all scenarios, we assume the same capital stock growth rates. This assumption makes it easier to compare how the four scenarios affect per-capita GDP. We assume a realistic capital stock growth rate of 10.0 percent in the first year of independence, with a significant bump upward to 20.0 percent in the following year.[33] Capital stock growth returns to 10.0 percent in 2007 and remains there until 2010. Between 2011 and 2019, the annual growth rate is at the historical norm of around 7.0 percent.[34]

---

[30] By comparison, the average annual TFP growth in Japan and Germany during the years 1950 to 1973 was 6.4 percent and 5.6 percent, respectively.

[31] The World Bank's estimates of the 2000 capital stock range from $11 billion to $18 billion in constant 2000 dollars. The World Bank assumes that the Palestinian capital stock in 1968 was between 100 percent and 300 percent of GDP, with a median scenario of 200 percent of GDP. The World Bank uses the perpetual inventory method to estimate the change in capital over time, which adds investment and subtracts depreciation, with a depreciation rate of 5 percent. The World Bank reports its assumptions and growth rates in Table VI.1 (2002b), which we use to calculate capital stock in 2000.

[32] The World Bank (2003c) estimated that damage to infrastructure totaled $750 million by August 2002.

[33] Capital stock growth rates are assumed to be net of depreciation.

[34] By comparison, the annual capital stock growth in Japan averaged 12 percent between 1965 and 1970, and then declined to 5 percent for the period 1985 to 1990. This is not to suggest that Palestine will develop along the same

Table A.5.1
Assumptions About Total Factor Productivity (A)

Scenarios	Initial Level (2004)	Annual Average Change (%)		
		2005–2009	2010–2014	2015–2019
High contiguity/high integration	1.0	5.0	3.0	3.0
High contiguity/low integration	1.0	4.3	2.2	2.0
Low contiguity/high integration	1.0	4.3	2.2	2.0
Low contiguity/low integration	1.0	2.4	1.0	1.0

Table A.5.2
Assumptions About Average Annual Change in Palestinian Capital Stock (K)

	2005–2009		2010–2014		2015–2019	
	%	$ (billions)	%	$ (billions)	%	$ (billions)
All scenarios	12.0	$2.6	7.6	$3.1	7.0	$4.2

Our assumptions about the capital stock are summarized in Table A.5.2, based on an initial (2004) capital stock of $12.1 billion. Under these assumptions, total investment would be $13.1 billion between 2005 and 2009, resulting in an average annual increase of $2.6 billion; and $15.6 billion between 2010 and 2014, resulting in an average annual increase of $3.1 billion. The ten-year total would be $28.7 billion.

Elasticity of GDP with Respect to Capital (α)

We assume α to be 0.4 across all scenarios for all years. Correspondingly, we assume β to be 0.6 across all scenarios for all years. These values are identical to World Bank (2002c) estimates and are also common in cross-country growth studies.

Labor Force

As described in the section above, Principal Challenges and Critical Issues Confronting the Palestinian Economy, the Palestinian labor force was approximately 625,000 in 2000, and population growth has caused it to increase rapidly. For purposes of modeling economic growth during the period 2005–2019, we rely on the IMF's (2001) labor force projections for 2000–2005, 2010, 2015, and 2020, using a simple linear projection for the years between those estimated by the IMF.

These projections assume zero net migration. Even so, they yield an average annual labor force growth rate of 4.4 percent throughout the period, high compared to

---

lines as Japan. Rather, the Japanese case is instructive because it presents an example of an economy recovering from the ravages of war. Looking at other countries, capital stock growth in South Korea averaged 15 percent between 1965 and 1970, and then declined to 9 percent between 1985 and 1990. In Singapore, the figure was about 11 percent between 1980 and 1985 and about 8 percent between 1990 and 1998. For reference, the historical capital stock growth (both productive and residential) in the West Bank and Gaza averaged just over 7 percent during the 30 years prior to the second intifada.

Table A.5.3
Assumptions About Average Annual Change in Palestinian Labor Force

	2005–2009		2010–2014		2015–2019	
	%	N (thousands)	%	N (thousands)	%	N (thousands)
All scenarios	23.5	182.4	23.1	222.6	22.4	268.1

SOURCE: RAND Corporation calculations based on IMF (2001).
NOTE: N = number in the Palestinian labor force.

most other middle-income developing countries. The Palestinian labor force—and the requirements of job creation—will obviously rise with immigration, e.g., by Palestinians from the diaspora.

Our assumptions about the Palestinian labor force are summarized in Table A.5.3, based on an initial (2004) labor force of 743,500.

Employment in Israel

Palestinian employment in Israel, and in Israeli settlements in the West Bank and Gaza, has fallen from 135,000 in 1999 to approximately 57,000 in 2003. Given the recent turmoil, we assume an initial level (2004) of 40,000 Palestinians in Israel. We assume that employment in Israel recovers very quickly in the high-economic-integration scenarios: In these scenarios, we assume that 130,000 Palestinians are employed in Israel in 2005, similar to employment levels before the intifada. In the low-integration scenarios, we assume that Palestinian employment in Israel only numbers 20,000 in 2005. In both high-integration scenarios, we allow for 2.0 percent annual growth thereafter; in both low-integration scenarios we allow for slightly higher growth of 3.5 percent.

Table A.5.4 summarizes our assumptions about Palestinian employment in Israel.

Domestic Employment (*L*)

Domestic Public Employment. In calculating GDP via our growth accounting model (Equation 1), we define labor as domestic employment. Domestic employment consists of public-sector employment and private-sector employment.

We assume that initial (2004) public-sector employment is 110,000, which is comparable to the level of employment in the Palestinian Authority in 2000. We assume that public-sector employment increases to 115,000 in 2005, and then increases thereafter by 1.0 percent annually in the high-economic-integration scenarios, and by 2.5 percent annually in the low-economic-integration scenarios.[35]

Table A.5.5 summarizes our assumptions about Palestinian domestic public employment, based on an initial (2004) level of 110,000.

---

[35] The small public-sector growth rate under high economic integration balances the widespread view that the PA is already too large with the view that a growing population and economy would demand an increase in government services. The higher growth rate under low economic integration reflects the fact that the public sector would have to compensate for fewer private-sector jobs under these scenarios.

Domestic Private Employment. Our approach regarding domestic private employment in Palestine is somewhat different than for the other variables we consider here. Our assumptions about all other variables—TFP, productive capital, labor force, private employment, employment in Israel—are informed by empirical data (from the West Bank and Gaza and elsewhere, as appropriate), and they are intended to be realistic. Here, our assumptions are determined by a specific target: to reach about 8 percent unemployment by the beginning of 2020. Given the assumptions we have described about the Palestinian labor force, domestic public employment, employment in Israel, and the current level of private employment in the West Bank and Gaza, we assume growth rates of private employment in an independent Palestinian state that would converge to this target unemployment rate in 2019.

Table A.5.4
Assumptions About Palestinian Employment in Israel

	Initial Level (2005)	Annual Average Change (%)		
		2005–2009	2010–2014	2015–2019
High contiguity/high integration	130,000	2.0	2.0	2.0
High contiguity/low integration	20,000	3.5	3.5	3.5
Low contiguity/high integration	130,000	2.0	2.0	2.0
Low contiguity/low integration	20,000	3.5	3.5	3.5

Table A.5.5
Assumptions About Palestinian Domestic Public Employment

	Annual Average Change (%)		
	2005–2009	2010–2014	2015–2019
High contiguity/high integration	1.7	1.0	1.0
High contiguity/low integration	2.9	2.5	2.5
Low contiguity/high integration	1.7	1.0	1.0
Low contiguity/low integration	2.9	2.5	2.5

Table A.5.6
Assumptions About Palestinian Domestic Private-Sector Employment

	Annual Average Change					
	2005–2009		2010–2014		2015–2019	
	%	Jobs	%	Jobs	%	Jobs
High contiguity/ high integration	15.2	56,400	6.5	41,100	5.5	46,800
High contiguity/low integration	17.2	66,500	6.9	47,900	5.5	52,000
Low contiguity/high integration	15.2	56,400	6.5	41,100	5.5	46,800
Low contiguity/low integration	17.2	66,500	6.9	47,900	5.5	52,000

We assume that initial (2004) Palestinian domestic private-sector employment is 275,000. Given this starting point, Table A.5.6 illustrates the average annual increases in private-sector jobs that would be needed to reduce the Palestinian unemployment rate to around 8 percent, from an initial (2004) level that we assume to be 42.8 percent. Given these high initial levels, the very rapid growth in the Palestinian labor force, and modest growth in Palestinian employment in Israel (even under high integration) and in the public sector, it is clear that domestic private employment would have to grow at very rapid rates to reach the target level by 2019.

Under the high-integration scenarios, we assume that domestic private employment would grow at an annual average of about 56,400 jobs from 2005 to 2009, or 15.2 percent per year; we assume that this would be followed by more moderate employment growth of 41,100 jobs annually (6.5 percent) from 2010 to 2014, and 46,800 jobs annually (5.5 percent) from 2015 to 2019, yielding an unemployment rate of 8.2 percent by the end of 2019.

For the low-integration scenarios, we assume that domestic private employment would grow by about 66,500 jobs per year between 2005 and 2009, or a 17.2 percent annual average growth rate—fully 20,000 more jobs per year more than under high integration, since more rapid domestic job growth is needed to compensate for less employment in Israel. Under these low-integration scenarios, employment growth would slow to 47,900 jobs annually (6.9 percent) between 2010 and 2014, and to 52,000 jobs annually (5.5 percent) between 2015 and 2019. This would yield a slightly lower unemployment rate of about 8.1 percent by the end of 2019.[36]

Given our assumptions about Palestinian employment in Israel, employment in the domestic public sector, and employment in the domestic private sector, we can then calculate expected levels of unemployment. Figure A.5.1 presents estimates of Palestinian unemployment for the years 2004 to 2019 by scenario type. Initial (2004) unemployment across all scenarios is expected to be 42.8 percent. In the high-integration scenarios, unemployment falls rapidly to 27.7 percent in 2005 because of Palestinian access to jobs in Israel. Sharp reductions in unemployment continue to 2010 (to about 9 percent) because of anticipated growth in domestic employment. Unemployment then hovers around the 8 to 9 percent range for the remaining ten years. In the low-integration scenarios, however, unemployment falls only to 41.9 percent in 2005; domestic job increases are offset to some extent by the reduction of Palestinian employment in Israel. A focus on growing domestic jobs between 2005 and 2010 reduces unemployment sharply to 13.4 percent. Over the remaining ten years, unemployment gradually sinks to the 8 percent level.

---

[36] One reason, though not the primary one, why these private-sector growth rates need to be this high is because our model deliberately limits employment growth in the Palestinian public sector to 1 to 2 percent a year. As mentioned earlier, PA employment is already quite high, even by regional standards. High public-sector employment in other Arab countries has contributed to slow rates of growth in private-sector business formation and in total factor productivity as government bureaucracies stifle the creation of new businesses and slow productivity growth through the imposition of regulations designed to extort bribes.

Figure A.5.1
Estimated Palestinian Unemployment for 2004–2019, by Scenario Type

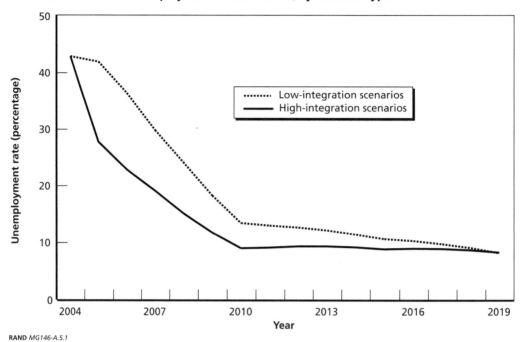

RAND *MG146-A.5.1*

Calculating Palestinian National Income

We calculate GNI for every year from 2005 to 2019 by combining our annual GDP figures with estimated income from Palestinian employment in Israel. We then calculate per-capita GNI by dividing by the projected population for that year.

GDP. We assume an initial (2004) Palestinian GDP of $3.4 billion. For the years 2005 to 2019, GDP is calculated according to Equation 1, given the assumptions above for TFP, capital, labor, and the elasticities of GDP with respect to capital and labor. Table A.5.7 shows the levels of Palestinian GDP resulting from the model for milestone years, as well as their associated average annual growth rates.

In the high-contiguity/high-integration scenario, GDP increases from the initial 2004 level to nearly $7.5 billion by 2009. This increase reflects high annual average GDP growth rates of 23.7 percent from 2005 to 2009, driven by the reduction of barriers to commerce and domestic employment and by large investments into the Palestinian capital stock. Average growth rates slow 11.3 percent and 10.4 percent from 2010 to 2014 and from 2015 to 2019, respectively, indicating the maturing of the domestic economy.

The high-contiguity/low-integration scenario results in higher average growth rates (24.5 percent) from 2005 to 2009 than the high-contiguity/high-integration scenario, and a higher 2009 GDP (of $7.6 billion). This occurs because of the assumption in the model that domestic employment (both private sector and public sector) would need to grow faster in the low-integration scenarios. Nevertheless, over the long

Table A.5.7
Model Results Regarding Palestinian Gross Domestic Product

| | GDP (in millions of dollars) | | | | | |
| | 2005–2009 | | 2010–2014 | | 2015–2019 | |
2004 Initial Level	2009 Level	Annual Average Change (%)	2014 Level	Annual Average Change (%)	2019 Level	Annual Average Change (%)
High contiguity/ high integration						
3,420	7,480	23.7	11,710	11.3	17,810	10.4
High contiguity/ low integration						
3,420	7,610	24.5	11,680	10.7	17,040	9.2
Low contiguity/ high integration						
3,420	7,260	22.4	10,960	10.2	15,910	9.0
Low contiguity/ low integration						
3,420	7,020	21.0	10,180	9.0	14,180	7.9

term this scenario is outperformed by the high-contiguity/high-integration scenario in terms of growth rates and GDP levels.

Both low-contiguity scenarios perform less well than the high-contiguity scenarios, with the low-integration scenario noticeably lagging by 2019 with a GDP that is 20 percent lower than that of the high-contiguity/high-integration scenario.

Remittances. To calculate the contribution of remittances by Palestinians working in Israel to Palestinian GNI, we begin with data on the average monthly wage of Palestinians working in Israel in 1999 (UNSCO, 2001a). We adjust this wage upward to account for moderate growth between 1999 and 2005, and we then convert it into dollars using current exchange rates. Consequently, we take the initial (2004) average wage for Palestinians working in Israel to be $5,370 annually. We increase this wage every year from the initial level by 3 percent. For simplicity, we also assume that 100 percent of the wages go to remittances.

Table A.5.8 shows the total amount of remittances for milestone years and their growth for the three periods of interest. In the high-integration scenarios, remittances jump substantially (61.7 percent) from the initial (2004) level of $215 million to the 2009 level of $877 million. This jump reflects the fact that by 2009 there are assumed to be 100,000 more Palestinians working in Israel than there were in 2004. This growth moderates to 5.6 percent between 2010 and 2014, and between 2015 and 2019, given that the model assumes only small increases in Palestinians seeking employment in Israel over time. By 2019, remittances total just over $1.4 billion.

By contrast, in the low-integration scenarios we assume that the number of Palestinians working in Israel would drop by one-half from initial levels (from 40,000 to 20,000) and then slowly increase. Thus remittances drop to only $143 million by 2009, and increase to only $272 million by 2019.

Table A.5.8
Model Results Regarding Remittances from Palestinians Working in Israel

	Remittances (in millions of dollars)					
		2005–2009		2010–2014		2015–2019	
	2004 Initial Level	2009 Level	Annual Average Change (%)	2014 Level	Annual Average Change (%)	2019 Level	Annual Average Change (%)
High contiguity/ high integration	215	877	61.7	1,122	5.6	1,437	5.6
High contiguity/ low integration	215	143	–6.7	197	7.5	272	7.6
Low contiguity/ high integration	215	877	61.7	1,122	5.6	1,437	5.6
Low contiguity/ low integration	215	143	–6.7	197	7.5	272	7.6

GNI. We then compute Palestinian per-capita GNI by summing GDP and re-mittances for a given year and dividing by the total population. Population estimates come from the IMF's (2001) projections in combination with linear extrapolation. The initial (2004) per-capita GNI is estimated to be $1,110, down from $1,890—which existed just prior to the start of the current intifada. Table A.5.9 illustrates the change in per-capita GNI by scenario from this initial level to 2019.

In the high-contiguity/high-integration scenario, per-capita GNI surpasses the pre-intifada level within the first five years ($2,160) and nearly doubles it by 2019 ($3,740). These results are attributed to the reduction in barriers to commerce because of contiguity and the access to Israeli labor and goods markets.

The high-contiguity/low-integration and low-contiguity/high-integration sce-narios perform less well; although they too surpass the pre-intifada level by 2009, they only grow per-capita GNI by 77 to 78 percent as of 2019. The low-contiguity/low-integration scenario, by contrast, does not reach the pre-intifada level by 2009. By 2019, its per-capita GNI only reaches $2,810—a 48 percent improvement over 1999.

Figure A.5.2 plots per-capita GNI growth between 2004 and 2019 for every sce-nario. In doing so, it allows for ready comparisons of Palestinian performance across different scenarios. The plots in Figure A.5.2 show that high contiguity and high in-tegration would provide the Palestinian state more rapid growth in per-capita GNI than the other scenarios. This growth remains strong throughout the entire 2004 to 2019 time frame. Per-capita GNI levels in the high-contiguity/low-integration and low-contiguity/high-integration scenarios differ somewhat during the first five years of independence, but by 2019 they have essentially converged. The low-contiguity/low-integration scenario performs less well. It is bested by all other scenarios, with

Table A.5.9
Estimated Palestinian Per-Capita GNI for 2004–2019 (under each scenario, in 2003 dollars)

	Actual GNI (1999)	Estimated GNI Per Capita				1999–2019 % change
		2004	2009	2014	2019	
High contiguity/ high integration	$1,890	$1,110	$2,160	$2,860	$3,740	97.5%
High contiguity/ low integration	$1,890	$1,110	$2,000	$2,640	$3,370	77.6%
Low contiguity/ high integration	$1,890	$1,110	$2,100	$2,690	$3,370	78.0%
Low contiguity/ low integration	$1,890	$1,110	$1,850	$2,310	$2,810	48.3%

Figure A.5.2
Estimated Palestinian Per-Capita GNI for 2004–2019, by Scenario Type

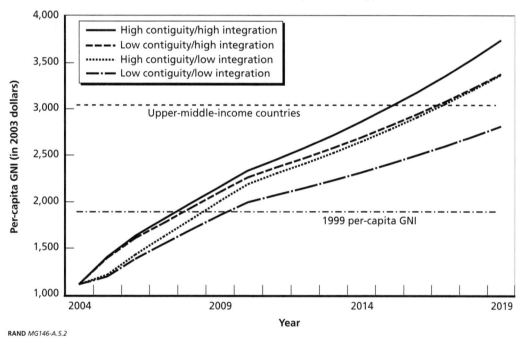

per-capita GNI in 2019 almost $1,000 less than that produced in the high-contiguity/ high-integration scenario.

Figure A.5.2 also allows for comparisons with different benchmarks. It displays the 1999 pre-intifada per-capita GNI ($1,890) and the World Bank's lower bound for designation as an upper-middle-income country ($3,036). The plots show that by 2009 all scenarios but the low-contiguity/low-integration scenario have surpassed pre-intifada levels. Additionally, they indicate that in these same scenarios Palestine will be an upper-middle-income country according to the World Bank by 2017. Under the low-contiguity/low-integration scenario, Palestine remains a lower-middle-income country at least through 2019.

Bibliography

Brown, Nathan J., *The Palestinian Reform Agenda,* Washington, D.C.: United States Institute of Peace, December 2002.

Central Intelligence Agency, *The World Factbook 2002,* Washington, D.C., 2002. Online at http://www.cia.gov/cia/download2002.htm (as of January 22, 2004).

Dobbins, James, John G. McGinn, Keith Crane, Seth G. Jones, Rollie Lal, Andrew Rathmell, Rachel M. Swanger, and Anga Timilsina, *America's Role in Nation-Building: From Germany to Iraq,* Santa Monica, Calif.: RAND Corporation, MR-1753-RC, 2003.

Fischer, S., P. Alonso-Gamo, and U. E. von Allmen, "Economic Developments in the West Bank and Gaza Since Oslo," *The Economic Journal,* Vol. 111, 2001, pp. 254–275.

International Monetary Fund (IMF), *West Bank and Gaza, Economic Performance, Prospects, and Policies: Achieving Prosperity and Confronting Demographic Challenges,* Washington, D.C., 2001.

Krugman, Paul R., and Maurice Obstfeld, *International Economics: Theory and Policy,* New York, N.Y.: Harper Collins, 1994.

Lim, Ewe-Ghee, *Determinants of, and the Relation Between, Foreign Direct Investment and Growth: A Summary of the Recent Literature,* Washington, D.C.: International Monetary Fund, Working Paper WP/01/175, 2001.

Muhanna, Ali, and Ahmed Abu Baker, *Role of Small Businesses in the Palestinian Economy and Impact of Recent Israeli Economic Sanctions and Measures,* Jerusalem, Israel: Federation of Palestinian Chambers of Commerce, Industry, and Agriculture, 2001.

Naqib, Fadie M., *Economic Aspects of Palestinian-Israeli Conflict,* Helsinki, Finland: United Nations University/World Institute for Development Economics Research, Discussion Paper No. 2002/100, 2002.

Palestine Economic Policy Research Institute (MAS), *MAS Economic Monitor,* Issue 7, 2000.

———, *MAS Economic Monitor,* Issue 8, 2001.

Palestinian Central Bureau of Statistics (PCBS), *PCBS Selected Statistics,* 2003. Online at http://www.pcbs.org/ (as of August 19, 2003).

Sayigh, Yezid, and Khalil Shikaki, *Strengthening Palestinian Public Institutions,* New York, N.Y.: Council on Foreign Relations, Independent Task Force Report, 1999.

———, *Reforming the Palestinian Authority: An Update,* New York, N.Y.: Council on Foreign Relations, Independent Task Force Report, January 2003.

Sewell, David, *Governance and the Business Environment in West Bank/Gaza*, Washington, D.C.: The World Bank, Working Paper, April 2001.

Shikaki, Khalil, *Building a State, Building a Peace: How to Make a Roadmap That Works for Palestinians and Israelis*, Washington, D.C.: The Brookings Institution, Saban Center for Middle East Policy, Draft Monograph, Fall/Winter 2002.

United Nations Conference on Trade and Development (UNCTAD), *Palestinian Merchandise Trade in the 1990s: Opportunities and Challenges*, Geneva, Switzerland, 1998.

————, *Report on UNCTAD's Assistance to the Palestinian People*, TD/B/49/9, Geneva, Switzerland, July 26, 2002.

United Nations Office of the Special Coordinator in the Occupied Territories (UNSCO), *Report on the Palestinian Economy*, Jerusalem, Israel, Spring 2000.

————, *Report on the Palestinian Economy*, Jerusalem, Israel, Spring 2001a.

————, *The Impact on the Palestinian Economy of Confrontation, Border Closures and Mobility Restrictions: 1 October 2000–30 September 2001*, Jerusalem, Israel, 2001b.

World Bank, "Arab Republic of Egypt at a Glance," Washington, D.C.: The World Bank Group, August 29, 2003a. Online at http://www.worldbank.org/data/countrydata/aag/egy_aag.pdf (as of September 3, 2003).

————, *Development Under Adversity: The Palestinian Economy in Transition*, Washington, D.C., 1999a.

————, "Israel at a Glance," Washington, D.C.: The World Bank Group, September 11, 2002a. Online at http://www.worldbank.org/data/countrydata/aag/isr_aag.pdf (as of September 3, 2003).

————, "Jordan at a Glance," Washington, D.C.: The World Bank Group, April 22, 2003b. Online at http://www.worldbank.org/data/countrydata/aag/jor_aag.pdf (as of September 3, 2003).

————, *Long-Term Policy Options for the Palestinian Economy*, West Bank and Gaza Office, Washington, D.C., July 2002b. Online at http://lnweb18.worldbank.org/mna/mena.nsf/Countries/West+Bank/D71F9D9035ECF30285256C8A00374436?OpenDocument (as of January 28, 2003).

————, *Two Years of Intifada, Closures and Palestinian Economic Crises: An Assessment*, Washington, D.C., March 5, 2003c. Online at http://lnweb18.worldbank.org/mna/mena.nsf/Attachments/WBGsummary-ENG/$File/WBGsummary-ENG.pdf (as of March 12, 2003).

————, *West Bank & Gaza: Strengthening Public Sector Management*, Social and Economic Development Group, Middle East and North Africa Region, Washington, D.C., 1999b. Online at http://lnweb18.worldbank.org/mna/mena.nsf/Attachments/Strengthening+Public+Sector+(English)/$File/Strengthening+Public+Sector+(English).pdf (as of January 28, 2003).

————, *West Bank and Gaza—Financial Sector Development Project*, Project Information Document, Washington, D.C., Report No. PID4323, September 20, 1999c. Online at http://www-wds.worldbank.org/servlet/WDSServlet?pcont = details&eid = 000094946_9910130708485 (as of January 22, 2004).

———, *West Bank and Gaza Update,* West Bank and Gaza Office, Washington, D.C., August 2000. Online at http://lnweb18.worldbank.org/mna/mena.nsf/61abe956d3c23df38525680b00775b5e/1781eb17c2e717d18527568ef0051cfdc/$FILE/ATT5LGA7/WBGUpdate_April2000.pdf (as of January 22, 2004).

———, "West Bank and Gaza Update," West Bank and Gaza Office, Washington, D.C., August 2002c. Online at http://lnweb18.worldbank.org/mna/mena.nsf/Attachments/August+Update/$File/update+Aug+2002.pdf (as of January 22, 2004).

———, *World Development Indicators 2004,* Washington, D.C., 2004.

CHAPTER SIX

Water

Mark Bernstein, David G. Groves, Amber Moreen

Summary

Clean and sufficient water for domestic consumption, commercial and industrial development, and agriculture is a requirement for a viable Palestinian state. The existing level of water resource development and sharing of water resources between Israelis and Palestinians does not meet this requirement today and is even less likely to do so as the Palestinian population grows over the next several decades. In addition, current water and waste management practices are degrading both surface streams and rivers and underground water resources. In this chapter, we describe the major water resource issues facing the Palestinians, outline policy options to ensure that a Palestinian state has clean and sufficient water by 2015,[1] and present a modeling approach and preliminary results that suggest promising strategies and their costs for addressing these water management issues.

The majority of the Palestinian water supply is provided by springs and wells fed by underground aquifers that are shared with Israel. Current water resource development provides only about one-half of the World Health Organization's per-capita domestic water requirement and limits irrigation and food production. Furthermore, the amount of water extracted by the Palestinians and Israelis from most of the region's aquifers exceeds the natural replenishment rate, signifying that the resources are being used unsustainably. Finally, new natural sources of water are limited; and desalination, the most viable alternative, is still expensive, capital intensive, and sensitive to fuel price volatility.

The long-term challenge for Palestinian water resource managers is to sustainably increase water supply while managing the water demand of the Palestinian population. Options for increasing the water supply include increasing groundwater use accommodated by use reduction by Israel, increasing rain and storm water capture, and increas-

---

We would like to thank Alvin Newman, Chief of the Office of Water Resources at the USAID West Bank and Gaza Mission, and John Pasch, Chief of Party, West Bank Water Resources Program, CH2M HILL, for their time and assistance. We greatly appreciate CH2M HILL's provision of the West Bank Water Management Analysis Tool (CH2M HILL, 2002a), which serves as a basis for much of our analysis.

[1] To be consistent with the rest of the report, cost numbers are presented for ten years through 2014. However, to be consistent with other plans for the region, we use 2015 and 2020 goals for adequate water supplies and minimum levels of consumption, so plans are assumed to run through 2020 even though we only show cost numbers through 2014.

ing desalination capabilities where no other options exist. Demand can be managed through the smart application of water efficiency technologies, water reuse methods, and infrastructure improvements.

Through the use of a water allocation model based on the work of CH2M HILL (2002b), we estimate a base case cost of supplying water and sanitation through 2014 to be over $4.9 billion. We also demonstrate that a more diverse set of water management strategies that includes increased demand management can be more effective and more flexible in meeting future Palestinian water needs. These strategies could reduce costs by as much as $1.3 billion in the base case. If population growth and fuel costs are greater than expected, then costs with standard management strategies could be almost $6 billion. However, our proposed improved strategies provide an even greater benefit, saving almost $2 billion.

Introduction

One of the most fundamental challenges facing the Middle East is ensuring sufficient water for future prosperity. Water security is especially critical for a future Palestinian state: water resources are scarce in the West Bank and Gaza, and supplies must increase to accommodate development. Current consumption from most groundwater sources exceeds the rate of recharge and is unsustainable.[2] According to recent estimates, Israelis and Palestinians are overdrawing from the aquifers underlying the West Bank by more than 170 million cubic meters per year (MCM/yr) (CH2M HILL, 2002a). Overdraft from the Gaza Aquifer exceeds recharge by about 65 MCM/yr (PASSIA, 2003).

Water quality, inadequate water distribution, and sewage infrastructure are also major issues. Water problems in the West Bank and Gaza have already led to significant health problems and hinder efforts to alleviate poverty and to encourage development. The uncertain political environment has significant implications for the water infrastructure. The United Nations estimated that Israeli incursions into the West Bank and Gaza, in just the first quarter of 2002, caused almost $7 million of physical damage to water and sewage infrastructure (UNDP, 2002).

Water management decisions also have strong links to agriculture and energy consumption. For example, the agricultural sector is the primary user of water in the region, and many options for increasing the water supply will be energy intensive. As a result, water resource planning should be undertaken as part of a broader comprehensive planning process that considers the many important interconnections among the water, energy, and agricultural sectors.

---

[2] The process by which surface water flows into aquifers is known as "recharge." The rate of recharge is particularly important because if groundwater withdrawals exceed the recharge rate, the aquifer will be depleted.

We argue that the following should be the four major planning goals for 2015:

1. Increase water availability to meet minimum per-capita consumption while managing demand through efficiency and reuse.
2. Reduce utilization of groundwater resources to sustainable levels.
3. Upgrade and improve the efficiency of the existing water supply and sewage infrastructure.
4. Expand water supply and sewage infrastructure to serve at least 90 percent of the population.

There are many policies that could be implemented to achieve these goals. A prudent planning approach will consider the costs of candidate policies under a wide range of possible water demand and supply scenarios. As we show in this chapter, some policies perform better under uncertainty than others.

Meeting these goals will require overcoming many hurdles, the first of which is negotiating an agreement between the Israelis and Palestinians on the use of shared aquifers. Any proposed water-sharing solution will need to address significant equity issues. Regardless of the solution to sharing water rights, all proposals will ultimately require Israel to reduce withdrawals from aquifers in the West Bank and Gaza to sustainable levels. We assume that the international community will finance alternative supplies to offset water that Israel gives up in any aquifer-sharing agreement. Because desalination is likely the highest-cost option for generating new supplies of water for Israel, we include the cost of desalination to provide an upper bound for our total cost estimates.

In this chapter, we examine potential opportunities and solutions for the water problems in the West Bank and Gaza within the context of the four major planning goals listed above. First, we provide general background on water issues for the Middle East region, to put the West Bank and Gaza issues in context. Second, we outline the historical and current water situation in the Palestinian territories. Third, we describe the major supply, demand, and infrastructure elements of a comprehensive water management strategy. Fourth, we describe our approach to modeling potential policy strategies. Finally, we conclude by discussing some promising options for addressing the water needs of a future Palestinian state.

Water, Agriculture, and Energy in the Middle East

Water Scarcity in the Middle East

The world's supply of renewable fresh water is distributed unequally among the world's population, and many regions suffer from water scarcity. To help characterize water stress (the stress on individuals resulting from different levels of water scarcity), the Swedish hydrologist Malin Falkenmark determined the "minimum level of water needed per capita to maintain an adequate quality of life in a moderately developed country" (Falkenmark and Widstrand, 1992). Falkenmark found that these domestic needs could be met with roughly 100 liters per person per day (or 36.5 cubic meters per person per year), which has become a minimum objective for United Nations planning around the world. Beyond personal needs, Falkenmark found that each new person increases the water demand of the agricultural, industrial, and energy sectors by a factor of up to 5 to 20 times the amount needed for personal needs. Based on these estimates, Falkenmark developed a water stress index with three thresholds, corresponding to different degrees of water shortage (Engelman and LeRoy, 1997).

- "Water stress" includes countries whose freshwater resources are less than 1,700 cubic meters/person/year.
- "Water scarcity" is when freshwater availability falls below 1,000 cubic meters/person/year.
- "Absolute scarcity" is when freshwater availability falls below 500 cubic meters/person/year.

Based on 1996 UN projections, the population living in absolute scarcity could increase from 60 million to 185 million by 2025. In 1995, the Middle East region had an aggregate freshwater availability of 1,420 cubic meters per capita, indicating that it suffers from water stress (World Resources Institute et al., 1998).

Although the Middle East suffers from water stress, the degree of this stress varies substantially between and within countries. The water indices for individual countries in this region, for example, range from less than 100 cubic meters per person (absolute scarcity) to nearly 5,500 cubic meters per person (no water stress) (Saghir, Schiffler, and Woldu, 2000). Figure 6.1 contrasts the available water supply for countries in the

Figure 6.1
Estimated Amount of Water That Could Be Available with Increased Water Resource Development to Select Countries Based on Rainfall, Topology, and Subsurface Characteristics

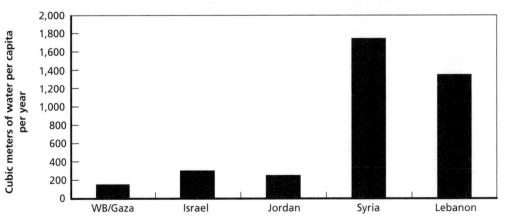

SOURCE: Gardner-Outlaw and Engelman, 1997.
RAND MG146-6.1

region (the numbers representing Syria and Lebanon reflect national figures, not just those portions within the Jordan River basin). The available water resources are determined by a region's rainfall, topology, and subsurface characteristics. Together, these parameters define a basin, which typically consists of a variety of water sources, including surface sources such as lakes and rivers as well as groundwater aquifers.

The Jordan River

The Jordan River, which is approximately 360 km long, flows through Lebanon, Syria, Jordan, Israel, and the West Bank (see Figure 6.2) and supplies more than half of the region's water supply. For Israel and the West Bank, the Jordan River, its tributaries, and the aquifers underlying the area are the only natural sources of fresh water.

The upper Jordan River is fed by three springs: the Hasbani in Lebanon, the Banias in the Golan Heights, and the Dan in Israel. The upper Jordan then flows into Lake Tiberias in Israel from the north. Just south of Lake Tiberias, the Yarmuk River, which is shared by Jordan and Syria, enters the lower Jordan River from the east, as do several other smaller streams. The lower Jordan River flows south from Lake Tiberias toward the Dead Sea and has been significantly reduced in volume during recent years, since no water has been released from Lake Tiberias. At the same time, riverside communities deposit sewage, agricultural runoff, and industrial discharges back into the Jordan River downstream of where they withdraw water from the river. As a result, the dwindling waters of the Jordan River become progressively more polluted and saline as they flow toward the Dead Sea. These practices have reduced the natural surface water flow for the lower Jordan River from about 1,400 MCM per year to 300 MCM per year by the early 1990s (National Research Council, 1999).

Both Israel and Jordan have significant water diversion systems located upstream in the Jordan River basin. These systems transport water to more-distant locations, largely for use in irrigated agriculture. For example, Israel's national water carrier diverts 350 MCM per year of water from Lake Tiberias toward coastal agricultural regions closer to the Mediterranean Sea and the Negev desert. Jordan's East Ghor Canal withdraws 150 MCM per year from the Yarmuk River just before it flows into the Jordan River basin.

Aquifers are rain-fed underground stores of water that can be utilized through wells and springs. Israel, Gaza, and the West Bank are supplied with groundwater from the Coastal and Mountain Aquifers. The Mountain Aquifers that supply much of Israel and the West Bank complements surface water resources. The Coastal Aquifer, while not technically part of the Jordan River basin, is the sole water supplier to Gaza and parts of Israel. The renewable water supply is the sum of precipitation and imports of water, minus the water not available for use through evaporation and exports. Renewable aquifer yields are particularly difficult to estimate because of limited sharing of data, poor measurement techniques, and misclassification of water resources data. However, we use the following estimates for sustainable yield: 339 MCM/yr for the

Figure 6.2
The Jordan River Basin

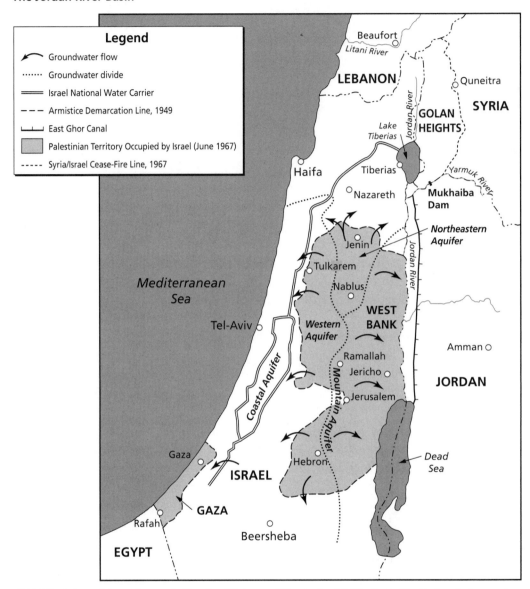

SOURCE: Adapted from Thomas R. Stauffer, *Water and War in the Middle East: The Hydraulic Parameters of Conflicts*, Washington, D.C.: The Center for Policy Analysis on Palestine, (currently The Palestine Center) Information Paper Number 5, July 1996. ©The Jerusalem Fund.
RAND *MG146-6.2*

Mountain Aquifers (CH2M HILL, 2002a), and 55 MCM/yr for the Gaza Aquifer (PASSIA, 2003).

There is significant regional and seasonal variation in rainfall, which affects the amount of water that recharges the groundwater and surface water and sustains rain-fed crops. In the northern sections of Israel and the West Bank, rainfall can be as much as 1,000 mm/yr; in the south it can be less than 30 mm/yr. Almost 90 percent of the land receives less than 300 mm/yr. Most agricultural production in the region occurs in these areas of less precipitation, where the rainfall is technically insufficient for most agricultural purposes. Almost three-quarters of the rainfall occurs from December to February, with almost no rainfall between May and October. High evaporation rates exacerbate the dry conditions by reducing the amount of rainfall available for use and recharge. Only about 20 percent of rainfall can be considered as adding to the renewable water supplies (National Research Council, 1999).

There is also significant annual variation; almost twice as much rain falls in wet years as in average years. As there is little storage capacity other than in aquifers, this variation significantly affects available supplies (National Research Council, 1999). The Middle East has been experiencing a severe drought. Most of the water plans that are developed for the region assume a starting point of normal rainfall; however, in reality, all plans should start with a deficit. In addition, projections of future rainfall assume historical weather patterns, in some cases using 30 years of historical information. However, it is unclear how relevant extended historical observations are, given potential variations in climate. The process of climate change, whether caused by natural variations or human-induced, would likely change both average weather conditions and the variability of the weather (i.e., both the statistical mean and variance would likely change). Such changes would make historic averages misleading, further complicating efforts to address the challenges imposed by water scarcity in the region. Clearly, overcoming the challenges described above will require more than finding solutions under historic average conditions.

Integrated Management

Since water supply consumption and disposal are interrelated, managing water resources in the Jordan River basin requires an integrated approach. Freshwater supplies come from groundwater aquifers, some surface water supplies, and rainfall. Water is consumed for domestic, industrial, commercial, and agricultural purposes. Most municipal and industrial water in the West Bank and Gaza is currently untreated after use. This wastewater is deposited back into rivers, streams, septic systems, and holding ponds, ultimately flowing to the Mediterranean or percolating back into the aquifers. A small volume of treated wastewater is used for irrigation. Finally, irrigation runoff flows back to surface streams and rivers, percolates into the aquifer, or evaporates.

Aquifer Management. Sustainable aquifer management is difficult for several reasons. First, many aquifers underlie several countries, management districts, and/or property owners. Second, the use of aquifers is decentralized and therefore difficult to monitor and control. Finally, although aquifers are a common resource, the benefit of aquifer use accrues to the individual or group that pumps the water, whereas the costs of use are imposed upon all other users. Individuals, therefore, can compromise the resource for all users.

These challenges all exist for the management of the Mountain and Gaza Aquifers. These aquifers underlie Palestinian and Israeli territory, necessitating cooperation to successfully manage the resource. Water is pumped from hundreds of wells owned by individual property owners and municipalities. Finally, aquifer over-pumping has led to the extraction of more groundwater than is replenished.

Overpumping or "groundwater mining" can have several negative consequences. As the water table falls, water must be lifted (i.e., pumped) a greater vertical distance, thus requiring more electricity and possibly larger pumps. Depending on geologic features, the aquifer may also become completely exhausted. As aquifers are depleted they can subside, leading to permanent loss of aquifer storage capacity. In the case of the Coastal Aquifer, seawater may enter an aquifer as the water table drops, decreasing its quality. Termed "saltwater intrusion," this contamination is costly to reverse.

Water Quality. A related and progressively worsening problem is deteriorating water quality. Surface water is contaminated through the release of untreated sewage, industrial effluence, and agricultural runoff. This polluted surface water then percolates into the aquifers, leading to groundwater contamination. In water-scarce regions without proper water treatment facilities, consumption of polluted water leads to significant heath complications.

All natural systems can accommodate some contamination, but as industrial, household, and agricultural uses of water grow, pollution loads in surface waters increase as the remaining flows diminish in response to increased withdrawals. As a result, increasingly large levels of pollutants are discharged into ever-smaller quantities of water. These problems become particularly serious when urban water supplies and waste grow faster than sanitation infrastructures. As surface water quality and quantity decrease, groundwater extractions increase, further exacerbating groundwater overuse.

Groundwater quality problems in the West Bank and Gaza are also significant. Although no water quality database exists, individual studies and monitoring projects indicate severe contamination and water quality problems in all major aquifers. In half of the wells in Gaza, chloride and nitrate levels significantly exceed World Health Organization (WHO) standards for drinking levels.[3] Aquifers in both Gaza and the West Bank have elevated levels of heavy metals and high chemical oxygen demand/biochemical oxygen demand ratios, indicating the presence of non-biodegradable industrial contaminants (METAP, 2001). Intestinal parasites have been found in Lake Tiberias and the Jordan River.

Water and Waste Infrastructure. Although much has been accomplished in providing access to improved water supply and sanitation facilities, many people still lack adequate access to safe drinking water and sanitation. Many people in the Middle East without access to water supplies live in rural areas; however, many residents of poor urban neighborhoods in the West Bank and Gaza also lack access to adequate water

---

[3] Chloride levels exceed 1,000 milligrams per liter (mg/l), and nitrate levels exceed 290 mg/l. The WHO drinking water standard for chloride and nitrate is 250 mg/l and 50 mg/l, respectively.

supplies from piped connections or standpipes. Water supply in many cities is intermittent, with lengthy intervals of no water service. Residents without connections are forced to rely on water delivery.

As in many other developing countries, sanitation tends to receive less attention and fewer financial resources than water supply. The intrusion of raw sewage into ground and surface waters and agricultural reuse of insufficiently treated wastewater have negative environmental and health impacts. Wastewater needs to be adequately treated, regardless of whether it is reused, to avoid degradation of water sources and adverse health effects.

Practically all countries of the region reuse at least some of their wastewater (although reuse in the West Bank and Gaza is limited). In some countries—especially in Saudi Arabia, the Gulf countries, and Israel—a substantial share of the water supplied for municipal and industrial uses is reused in agriculture after treatment.

Links to Agriculture. The agricultural sector is both the leading consumer of water and a major source of water pollution in the Middle East. Irrigated agriculture accounts for 60 to over 80 percent of water use (Saghir, Schiffler, and Woldu, 2000). Therefore, agricultural policy directly affects water demand and consumption. In nearly all countries in the region, public irrigation agencies provide farmers with water at subsidized tariffs. The economic value of water in municipal and industrial uses is many times higher than in agriculture. Irrigated agriculture contributes 5 to 10 percent to GDP in most countries, while industry contributes 20–50 percent to GDP; the service sector, which is concentrated in urban areas, contributes another 30–50 percent. While, on average, irrigation accounts for 7–8 times more water use than do municipal activities, it contributes 4 to almost 20 times less to GDP than do urban industry and services.

Due to heavy reliance on fertilizers and pesticides, agricultural runoff is a significant source of water pollution. Agricultural runoff can lead to nutrient overload and increased salinity in irrigated areas. Salinization reduces yields, decreases soil moisture, and increases susceptibility to erosion. The end result is desertification.

Links to Energy. Worldwide, the Middle East is often viewed as the world's primary supplier of energy. However, the Middle East is also a large and rapidly growing consumer of energy. As with water resources, the countries of the Middle East vary in terms of their domestic energy resources. Many—but not all—have extensive oil and gas reserves. Energy is expensive in countries such as Jordan, Syria, Israel, Egypt, and other North African countries. As a result, the majority of the Middle East's population already faces high energy prices and energy shortages. Since population growth continues to outpace expansion of the energy infrastructure, the region's energy problems are likely to worsen in coming years. The recent discovery of natural gas reserves offshore in the Mediterranean Sea, however, could reduce this energy limitation for Israel and Palestine. Current estimates suggest that Israel and Gaza may have access to 3.5 trillion cubic feet of natural gas reserves off the coast (EIA, 2003b). These reserves could significantly reduce the cost of desalination by lowering energy prices in the region.

Many aspects of water distribution and use are energy intensive. First, water must be procured—water obtained from wells must be pumped to the surface. Next, water must be delivered to demand centers. Although most long-distance water conveyance systems rely on gravity, the water often must be pumped up and over mountain ranges or out of valleys, using much energy. The water also must be treated prior to delivery to end users if the water source is degraded. Tertiary treatments, such as ultraviolet radiation and ozonization, are very energy intensive. Finally, almost all water delivered for domestic and industrial use becomes sewage and must be treated prior to reuse or disposal. Energy requirements for such treatment are considerable.

Israel exemplifies the importance of energy in production and use of water. In 1992 about 9 percent of Israel's electricity was used for water needs.[4] A significant portion of this total is needed to pump water from Lake Tiberias, over a mountain range, and into Israel's National Water Carrier. This requires continuously moving 1.37 MCM of water more than 400 meters vertically each day. Israel's agricultural sector consumes an additional 4.6 percent of the nation's electricity, a large portion of which is used for groundwater pumping and irrigation. Finally, a portion of industrial, commercial, and household electricity consumption is used for groundwater pumping. It is possible that well over 15 percent of Israel's electrical generation capacity (approximately 1,000 megawatts) is used for water, not including treatment of drinking water or wastewater.

Currently, the water system in the West Bank and Gaza is not very energy intensive. Leading proposals for increasing the water supply, such as desalination and wastewater treatment and reuse, however, are highly energy intensive. Ensuring adequate water supplies in the region will require investments not only in new water sources, but also in an expanded electric power infrastructure. Since the vast majority of energy consumed by Palestinians is imported, increases in energy consumption by the water sector will directly affect energy imports, the cost of energy, and ultimately the economy.

Water Issues in Israel and Palestine: The Past and Present

Water issues in the region have been frequently studied, and many such studies have highlighted the vital role that water supply solutions may play in the peace process. Creating a viable Palestinian state will require settling water disputes and ensuring access to adequate amounts of clean water for both Israelis and Palestinians.

Historical Context
Securing adequate water supplies has been an important issue in the region throughout both ancient and recent history. In the last 50 years, the enduring problems resulting

---

[4] Personal communication with Alvin Newman, April 3, 2003.

from the region's water scarcity have been exacerbated by the region's political disputes. The main water issues in the 1950s included: water quotas affecting Israel, Syria, Lebanon, and Jordan; the use of Lake Tiberias for storage; the use of surface water, particularly the Jordan waters and the Litani River (in Lebanon); water importation from the Mediterranean Sea; and the nature of international participation in the region's water use disputes and agreements. These issues continue to drive much of the dialogue surrounding water in the region.

Unilateral water development by every party in the region led to a crisis at the end of the 1960s. After creation of the Israeli state, Israel, Syria, Egypt, the United Nations, and the United States made many attempts to develop a multilateral water management plan among the countries in the region. In 1955, however, the most prominent of these plans (the Unified, or Johnston, Plan) collapsed (Isaac, 1999; PASSIA, 2003). After its failure, unilateral water development and conflicting attempts to divert the Jordan River were followed by military clashes in 1967 (Zahra, 2000).

In the wake of the 1967 Six-Day War, the water conflicts continued. Israel's control of water resources was strengthened, and the Palestinians, as a result of the Israeli's increased control, had access to diminishing amounts of clean water. At this time, the Palestine Liberation Organization began attacking the water infrastructure in the Israeli settlements, and Israel attacked the East Ghor Canal, a part of the Unified Plan that would have supplied 250 MCM/yr to Palestinians. Israel then transferred water authority to the military and took control of the water resources in the area. Palestinian use was restricted to Israeli-established quotas, and Israel forbade unlicensed construction of new water infrastructure.

Agreements made in the early 1990s established the basis for much of the current dialogue surrounding water issues in the region. In 1992, the second round of peace talks resulted in the creation of the water resources working group. This was a step forward; however, the parties were wary of entering into technical agreements in the absence of a political settlement of core issues. In 1993, Oslo I made some progress on water issues. The Declaration of Principles recognized the need for cooperation in managing and developing water resources and allowed the Palestinians to drill new wells, subject to Israeli approval.

Oslo II (the Taba Agreement) strengthened cooperation but produced no tangible changes in the Palestinian water situation. However, in an important move forward, Israel recognized Palestinian water rights in the West Bank for the first time in 1995. The Taba Agreement was supposed to establish future allocation based on "prior use," restricting the Palestinians' agricultural use to only slight growth above about 100 MCM per year. Although the agreement stipulated the development of new water resources and arranged for immediate domestic water needs of roughly 24 MCM per year for the West Bank and roughly 5 MCM per year for Gaza, this quantity represented only roughly 40 percent of the agreed-upon need. Furthermore, remaining water issues were reserved for final status negotiations. These final status negotiations never occurred, and not all of the agreed-upon quantity has been released. Because these issues have not been resolved, Israel continues to consume according to historical use, and the West Bank and Gaza are unable to support their increasing needs.

Current Situation

Palestinian Water Management. The Palestinian Water Authority (PWA) and the National Water Council (NWC) are in charge of implementing any water management strategy. The PWA assumed responsibility as the central water authority within the context of the peace process in 1995. It is responsible for strategic planning, monitoring and oversight, policy implementation, regulation, and water rights negotiations. Its main goal is to ensure the equitable utilization and sustainable management and development of Palestinian water resources. The local ministries, utilities, and water users' associations are responsible for the actual implementation of the PWA's national water plan.

While the PWA is effectively the primary water agency, the NWC is officially the highest body within the Palestinian Authority regarding water issues. The NWC, established in 1996 and chaired by the president of the PA, is composed of the ministers of the five key PA ministries and water experts. Although the NWC has never been convened, it is formally responsible for setting the water policy—defining and endorsing the vision, strategy, and policies for the water sector.

Water Sources. The main sources of water for the West Bank, Gaza, and Israel include groundwater from two main aquifers (Mountain and Coastal) and various springs, as well as surface water from the tributaries of the Jordan River and Lake Tiberias (see Figure 6.2). The Mountain Aquifer is divided into three aquifer basins: Western, Northeastern, and Eastern. The Gaza Aquifer is a subset of the Coastal Aquifer.

Israel's water supply is diverse. Israel obtains water from several aquifers (Mountain, Coastal, Galilee, and Negev) and the Jordan River. It also recycles a substantial amount of wastewater for irrigation. Lake Tiberias is used as Israel's major surface storage, containing roughly 4,000 MCM (National Research Council, 1999). In addition, Israel recently signed an agreement to purchase water from a desalination plant to meet its expected water needs in the future. This plant will produce 100 MCM per year, meeting about 5 percent of Israeli water demands. The expectation of the desalination plant developers is that a power plant, fueled by natural gas, would be built to power the desalination plant.

In contrast, Palestinian water sources are less diverse and severely limited. The West Bank obtains most of its water from the Mountain Aquifers, some from Israel, and some from springs. Gaza's supply comes predominantly from the Gaza Aquifer, with a small supply from Israel. Table 6.1 shows the sustainable water resources (excluding desalination and imports from other regions) and their use by the Palestinians and the Israelis. The "Remaining" water resources are those that could provide new supplies. Negative remaining resources indicated unsustainable use.

Table 6.1
Sustainable and Currently Used Water Resources in the West Bank and Gaza

Resource	Sustainable	Palestinian	Israeli	Remaining
Groundwater				
Western	181	21.4	343.1	−183.5
Northeastern	72.5	15.8	64	−7.3
Eastern	86	25	46.3	14.7
Gaza	55	110	10	−65
Spring flow				
Western	1.2	2.4	N.A.	−1.2
Northeastern	8.4	16.8	N.A.	−8.4
Eastern	49.9	44.8	55	−49.9
Surface water				
Jordan River	120	0	120	0
Wadi flow	168.9	0	N.A.	168.9
Rainfall	125.8	4.9	N.A.	120.9
Wastewater	114.4	9.2	N.A.	105.2

SOURCE: CH2M HILL, 2002a; PCBS, 2003c; and the Oslo Accords.
NOTES: The data used come from the Palestinian Central Bureau of Statistics. There are disagreements and uncertainty about how much water is being pumped from the aquifers. The Israeli Water Commission estimates that the Palestinians draw as much as 320 MCM/yr. Negative remaining resources indicate unsustainable use. N.A. is not applicable.

Inadequate Supply. Palestinians consume, on average, around 55 liters of water per day (l/d)[5] for domestic purposes, or slightly more than half the WHO standard for minimum consumption of 100 l/d. This average consumption estimate masks significant variability. Some surveys have estimated that as much as 10 percent of the population uses less than 30 l/d (PHG, 2003).

In 2001, only 104 MCM/yr of water was consumed by the Palestinian domestic sector (PCBS, 2003b). Assuming system-wide water losses of about 40 percent,[6] it will take an additional 102 MCM/yr to supply the present Palestinian population of 3.4 million with 100 liters of water per day for domestic uses. Meeting the domestic water needs of a Palestinian population of 5.5 million in 2015 under present-day conditions will require an additional 231 MCM/yr of water.

Agricultural water consumption is important to the Palestinian economy. In 2000–2001, agricultural production in the Palestinian territories exceeded $800 million. Fifty-four percent of this production was from cultivation, and 46 percent was from livestock (PCBS, 2003b). According to the PWA, 64 percent of all groundwater extraction was used for the agricultural sector in 2001. Despite the high agricultural water use, only 13 percent of all cultivated land is irrigated. Table 6.2 provides a sum-

---

[5] Domestic consumption estimated from Palestinian Central Bureau of Statistics 2003 data (PCBS, 2003b).

[6] CH2M HILL (2002b) estimates current system-wide water losses to be about 40 percent.

Table 6.2
West Bank and Gaza Agricultural Area and Net Water Demand in 2001

	Area[a] (thousands of hectares)			Water Requirement[b] (1,000 CM/ hectare)	Net Water Demand (MCM)	Gross Agricultural Demand[c]
	Rain Fed	Irrigation	Total			
Vegetables	4.0	13.4	17.4	5.4	72.0	160
(percentage)	(23%)	(77%)				
Field crops	43.7	2.7	46.4	4.8	12.8	28
(percentage)	(94%)	(6%)				
Fruit trees	107.7	8.2	115.9	11.0	89.8	200
(percentage)	(93%)	(7%)				
Total	155	24	180		175	388

[a] PCBS, 2003a.
[b] ARIJ, 1995 and 1996.
[c] Gross agricultural demand includes 40 percent system losses and 25 percent irrigation application losses.

mary of cultivated area and net water requirements by crop type. Fruit trees demand more than half of all water and require more than twice the water per hectare than do vegetables and field crops.

It is estimated that in 2001, because not enough water was available, only 30 percent of irrigation needs were met (CH2M HILL, 2002a). Meeting all current irrigation demand and accommodating growth of irrigated areas will dramatically increase agricultural water demand.

Overuse of Aquifers. There is some disagreement over the sustainable groundwater yields; however, there is little doubt that the Palestinians and Israelis overuse the region's aquifers. The National Academies of Sciences and the studies behind the Oslo Accords estimated that the sustainable yield is equal to the annual rate of recharge and is slightly greater than current use (perhaps as much as 30 MCM/yr for the Mountain Aquifers) (National Research Council, 1999). Recent modeling analysis by CH2M HILL (2002a), however, estimates that the sustainable yields for the Mountain Aquifers are only half the recharge rate—the other half of the recharge is lost to deep percolation and flow out of the basins. We use CH2M HILL's sustainable estimates for the basins of the Mountain Aquifers. As more recent modeling estimates of the Gaza Aquifer do not exist, we use the Oslo recharge value as the sustainable yield. Based on these estimates, all aquifers but the Eastern are in deficit (Figure 6.3). The Gaza and Western Aquifer problems are particularly severe, as use is twice as high as the sustainable yield.

Declining Water Level and Quality. Overuse of the aquifers can cause the water table to fall and springs to dry up. Overuse can also lead to saltwater and wastewater

Figure 6.3
Current Consumption and Sustainable Yields for Major Aquifers

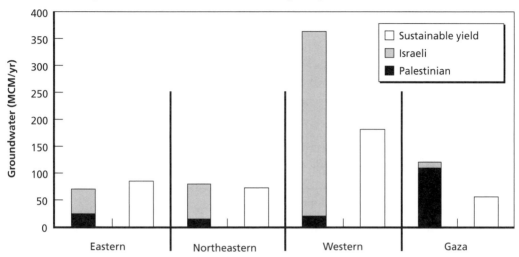

intrusion, reducing the quality of the groundwater. Based on well measurements, the Coastal and Mountain Aquifers' water levels have declined between 1984 and 1998 (EXACT, 2003). Due to significant precipitation in the early 1990s, this decline began to level off in the latter part of the period (1984–1998). However, the drought of the past few years, together with increased groundwater exploitation, is likely to lead to a return to rapidly declining water levels. In the Gaza Aquifer, the groundwater level has remained relatively stable despite heavy overuse, likely due to saltwater intrusion.

Infiltration of untreated wastewater and intrusion of saltwater have reduced water quality in all of the aquifers in the region. The problems are most acute in the Gaza Aquifer as a result of the shallow depth of the groundwater and the almost complete lack of sanitation infrastructure in Gaza. Because the aquifer is close to the surface, polluted water percolates into the aquifer relatively quickly. Significant elevated nitrate concentrations have been found in most of the test wells, attributed mostly to agriculture fertilizers, manure, and disposal of untreated sewage. Near the coast, an observation well showed a consistent 15 mg/l annual increase in chloride concentration from 1984 through 1998. Wells near agricultural areas have also shown chloride increases, perhaps due to infiltration of irrigation water. Wells south of Gaza City had consistent 45 mg/l yearly increases in chloride concentration from 1984 to 1998. Table 6.3 shows some key measures of water quality in the Gaza Aquifer and compares the level of concentration for these chemicals with acceptable guidelines.

The Mountain Aquifers are also showing signs of stress. For example, some 605 water samples taken from the Mountain Aquifers were recently found to have bacterial contamination (EXACT, 2003). Water from 70 springs around Bethlehem was found to be unfit for human consumption; yet this supply continues to be used by house-

Table 6.3
Water Quality in the Gaza Aquifer (in milligrams per liter)

Dissolved Substance	Gaza Concentration	International Standards for Acceptable Concentrations
Sodium	300–1100	20
Chloride	400–1500	250
Calcium	40–120	36
Sulfate	50–400	250
Magnesium	40–120	30
Bicarbonate	300–700	225
Potassium	6–10	4
Nitrate	40–140	45
Fluoride	0.4–2.9	1.5

SOURCE: WHO as cited in Atwan et al., 1999.

holds (EXACT, 2003). Although the Mountain Aquifers do not suffer from seawater intrusion, all aquifers in the region are contaminated with untreated wastewater. The Mountain Aquifers have seen increases in chloride concentrations; in the Northeastern Aquifer sections, concentration has increased at a rate as high as 19 mg/l annually, mostly because of the influences of irrigation and untreated sewage. Concentrations increased significantly during periods of heavy rain in 1992 and 1993, suggesting increased leaching of salts from the soil (EXACT, 2003).

Recent upgrades in the Gaza water supply system were completed through a World Bank project that permitted the Palestine Water Authority to outsource management and operations to a private company. As a result, almost all water for domestic use is treated before consumption. Although treatment helps to reduce chemical concentrations, according to the PWA, the water consumed still does not achieve internationally acceptable levels of quality (see Table 6.3).

The quality of water used for irrigation can also significantly affect crop production. As discussed above, use of fertilizer and pesticides can significantly degrade water and soil quality. As increasingly brackish water is used for irrigation, the soil becomes more saline. Increased salinity can reduce crop yields. In addition, it can degrade the quality of the crops, both in appearance and taste, thereby reducing opportunities for crop exports, as well as the desirability of crops for local markets. Polluted water can even make some crops unfit for consumption, particularly if eaten raw.

Infrastructure. The West Bank and Gaza lack the infrastructure to supply water and to provide proper sanitation. The shortage of capital for new infrastructure and the destruction of existing infrastructure by Israeli forces have exacerbated the problem in recent years. The World Bank estimated the cost of the latest intifada's damage to the water infrastructure at $3.6 million, as of December 2001 (UNDP, 2002). Damage due to more recent conflicts has also been extensive.

Many communities do not have access to a centralized water supply or to sanitation. The Palestinian Hydrology Group's (PHG) ongoing survey of water consumption has so far found that a portion of the population in about 35 percent of communities has no, or almost no, water service. Earlier analyses estimated that roughly 200,000 Palestinians, or 200 communities, were without access to water networks (Naji, 1999; Lein, 2001). CH2M HILL (2002a) estimates that roughly 25 percent of the West Bank population is not currently connected to a piped water source. The Israeli Water Commission estimates this value to be 10 percent. In rural areas, the percentage of homes without a centralized water supply can exceed 60 percent.

Provision of sanitation services is even scarcer: More than half of the communities and 60 to 75 percent of Palestinians have no working sanitation system (Naji, 1999; PHG, 2003; Al-Sa'ed, 2000). In rural areas, almost all homes dispose of their waste in cesspits or open channels.

Closely related to poor infrastructure are losses in the delivery of water or unaccounted for water (UFW). UFW has two causes: physical losses, in which water disappears from the physical infrastructure; and commercial losses, in which water that is not being billed actually does reach water users (Saghir, Schiffler, and Woldu, 2000). Physical losses—mostly leaks, as well as some evaporation—usually account for a significant portion of total UFW. Such losses are caused by inadequate maintenance of pipes and other physical infrastructure, which is often due to institutional and financial weaknesses in public water utilities. Physical losses combined with intermittent supply also affect drinking water quality. Polluted water leaking from broken sewers or from cesspits can be pulled into water distribution pipes, as a result of substantial changes in pressure that occur when supplies are turned on and off (Saghir, Schiffler, and Woldu, 2000). Commercial losses can be due to illegal connections, malfunctioning meters, incorrect meter reading, and faulty billing. As in the case of physical losses, the basic causes for commercial losses are institutional and/or financial weakness of public urban water utilities. In some cases, the utility lacks the management resources to develop a reasonably efficient billing program. In other cases, financial constraints hinder the purchase of equipment and the hiring and training of personnel.

Around the world, water losses can be as low as 8 percent; less than 20 percent is considered adequate in a well-run utility. In the Middle East, losses can be as high as 50 to 60 percent. In the West Bank and Gaza, about 40 percent of all centrally provided water is lost in the conveyance system (Saghir, Schiffler, and Woldu, 2000). Leaks in the sewage system are also substantial and result in losses of approximately 30 percent of sewage conveyed (Naji, 1999).

Health Implications. Inadequate water availability and poor water quality have important health implications for Palestinians. In a recent PHG survey, more than one-fifth of all communities reported that at least 1 percent of the population had water-related health problems. Some communities reported that 17 percent of the population had water-related health problems (PHG, 2003).

Many acute and chronic health problems can be caused or exacerbated by poor water quality and exposure to untreated wastewater. Water scarcity and high salinity can result in kidney dysfunction or failure, which can be exacerbated by the hot weather common in this region (Bellisari, 1994). Chemicals, such as nitrates, found in the water supply cause other water-related illnesses, including diarrhea. The PHG survey found that more than 10 percent of children less than five years old were reported to have had diarrhea episodes during the two weeks previous to the survey. In addition, there are long-term health consequences of ingesting contaminants in the water. For example, high nitrate concentrations can increase anemia and induce spontaneous abortion (Bellisari, 1994). Exposure to raw sewage as a result of the lack of sewage infrastructure also has significant short- and long-term health implications, especially in such vulnerable populations as children and the elderly. Finally, communicable diseases such as hepatitis are "the most prevalent and most serious of all health problems associated with the water supply" (Bellisari, 1994).

Water for a Future Palestinian State: Policy Options

Immediate water issues must be addressed to protect the health and well-being of the West Bank and Gaza population. Current water quantity and quality are insufficient for the population and will not support population or economic growth. New water supplies and demand management need to be developed in parallel and in concert with the design of the water supply and waste systems.

Options for addressing future water scarcity and quality issues for the West Bank and Gaza follow.

Demand Management

Water demand growth can be moderated through sensible policies for managing domestic and agricultural demand and through infrastructure improvements. Improving domestic efficiency and implementing systems to reuse household wastewater from sinks and showers (i.e., graywater) are the two primary methods for reducing domestic demand without compromising water services. Improving irrigation efficiency, providing incentives to switch irrigation from water-intensive crops (such as fruit trees) to less-intensive crops (such as vegetables), and limiting irrigation growth are all effective methods for managing agricultural demand. Finally, reducing water losses from the supply infrastructure can reduce the required supply for both sectors.

Demand Drivers. It is impossible to predict precisely how the many factors driving today's domestic, industrial, and agricultural water demand will affect future demand. Although industrial and commercial demand today is very small, a future state will develop a stronger economy, with corresponding increases in demand for water. Domestic demand, a large component of today's total demand, is driven by two highly uncertain factors—per-capita water consumption and population growth. Per-capita water consumption is currently constrained in most places by supply; more water would be consumed if it were made available at affordable prices. Per-capita consumption in those few municipalities with a reliable centralized water supply is largely determined by household needs, tempered by the cost of the water. This suggests that per-capita consumption will rise initially as supplies are increased. The second determinant, population growth, will be affected by both the internal growth rate in the population and the net inflow of Palestinians (returnees), which is difficult to predict.

The PWA ultimately would like to develop water resources so that supply can meet demand. For planning purposes, however, per-capita consumption targets must be set. The current long-term goal of the PWA is to increase water consumption to 150 l/d (CH2M HILL, 2002a). In the shorter term, we use the intermediate goals of increasing effective consumption to 100 l/d by 2015 and 120 l/d by 2020. As discussed below, investing in domestic water efficiency and graywater reuse can reduce the actual water delivery requirement below this level without affecting service to the consumer.

Demand for agricultural water is uncertain and is tempered by agricultural policies. Consumption depends on how much land is irrigated and the type of irrigation used. It also depends on the types of crops irrigated, and the needs of livestock. Options for managing agricultural demand include upgrading water delivery systems (e.g., lining canals) and improving and maintaining irrigation equipment. Limiting the expansion of irrigated agricultural area and encouraging the shift of irrigation away from water-intensive crops are other important demand-management policies.

Increasing Domestic Efficiency and Implementing Reuse of Graywater. Increased domestic efficiency and water reuse can reduce per-capita domestic consumption without compromising consumer services or public health. The efficiency of domestic consumption can be enhanced by installing water-efficient showerheads, toilets, and faucets. These relatively inexpensive devices can significantly reduce the water consumed by many household activities. A typical household connected to a water system can reduce water consumption by approximately 25 percent by adopting a complete suite of domestic efficiency technologies, including faucet aerators, low consumption showerheads, and low water-use toilets (CH2M HILL, 2002a). The estimated cost for implementing these measures is about $300 per household, with an annual maintenance cost of $30 (CH2M HILL, 2002a) (see the subsection Domestic Efficiency in this chapter for more details).

In addition, minor plumbing modifications can allow much of the graywater in a household to be reused. Possible graywater systems would filter water from sinks and showers and divert it for use in toilets; for washing clothes, windows, and vehicles; and for domestic irrigation. A household retrofitted with a domestic graywater reuse system (where shower and sink wastewater is filtered and reused for toilet flushing, clothes washing, and domestic irrigation) can reduce water use by 40 percent (Libhaber, 2003; Faruqui, 2002; Pottinger, 2003). Graywater reuse is often hindered by fears of negative health outcomes. The graywater systems we propose, however, do not carry many of these health risks—the systems we propose do not reuse toilet water nor do they use graywater for personal hygiene or cooking (Faruqui and Al-Jayyousi, 2002). A case study in Jordan implemented a graywater reuse program in 50 homes and estimated the average annual costs of the graywater reuse system to be $113, which is deemed high because it includes one-time plumbing modifications (Faruqui and Al-Jayyousi, 2002). We used an estimated cost of implementing a graywater system that is about the same as the domestic efficiency measures—about $300 per household, with an annual maintenance cost of $30 (personal communication with Naser I. Faruqui, April 1, 2003; Faruqui and Al-Jayyousi, 2002).[7]

If a household implements both efficiency measures and graywater reuse, the long-term water supply and energy savings continue, since efficiency measures reduce the consumption of freshwater (for showering and cooking) and the consumption of graywater for toilet flushing.

The current insufficiency of domestic water supplies in the West Bank and Gaza has led to a high awareness of the need to use water efficiently and reuse water where possible. Although there is presently no centralized wastewater reuse, Palestinians out of necessity are highly efficient with provided supplies, and reuse water informally within the household. Given the need to reuse with little or no capital investment, many households simply place a bucket underneath the kitchen sink.[8] Once Palestinians are connected to a reliable centralized water supply, however, the incentives to reuse may be significantly reduced. As water service to Palestinians becomes more reliable, building efficiency and reuse into the system will be necessary to moderate water demand to levels appropriate to the available water resources in the region. Because Palestinians already reuse water informally, they are likely to better understand, accept, and support efficiency and reuse measures.

Improving end-use efficiency and ensuring adoption of decentralized reuse technologies will require up-front investments in equipment, information, and education, and will not be simple to implement. The West Bank and Gaza have a surplus of labor that can be trained to install and maintain small-scale water systems.[9] Consumer efficiency and reuse can reduce the total cost of water development and the cost borne by consumers while increasing the security of the water supply. Furthermore, unlike other options to deal with the limited water resources in the regions, extensive planning procedures are not needed prior to implementation. Consequently, these actions can affect demand in the near term.

---

[7] We estimated a graywater system that included only simple filters, not treatment. These numbers are at the high end of the range of costs in the Jordan case study.

[8] Personal communication with Naser I. Faruqui, April 1, 2003.

[9] The training needs for such a workforce may require greater educational investment and thus lead to higher costs for implementing the efficiency and reuse policies.

Limiting Irrigation Growth and Improving Irrigation Efficiency. Increasing the efficiency of irrigation can temper growth in demand for agricultural water. Efficiency can be increased through investment in water-saving technologies such as drip irrigation systems. Drip irrigation is the predominant irrigation method used in the West Bank and currently is about 75 percent efficient. Rehabilitation and enhanced maintenance of these systems can increase efficiencies to 85 percent (CH2M HILL, 2002b). The improved application of irrigation systems will significantly reduce use not only of water, but also of fertilizer and pesticides, thereby reducing runoff and leaching problems.

Managing the growth of irrigation as well as encouraging a shift from water-intensive crops (such as fruit trees) to less-intensive crops (such as vegetables) can also control the agricultural water demand. To illustrate how future demand could vary, Figure 6.4 shows a wide range of future irrigation demands for different rates of irrigation expansion, with or without shifting all irrigated acreage from fruit to vegetables. Each line in the graph assumes different growth rates in irrigation with possible shifts in mixes of irrigation used for agriculture crops from higher-use fruit to lower-use vegetables. Depending on the growth rate and the crop mix, agricultural demand for water could grow more than 140 percent, or decline by over 20 percent by 2020.

Figure 6.4
Scenarios of Irrigation Water Demand for the West Bank and Gaza

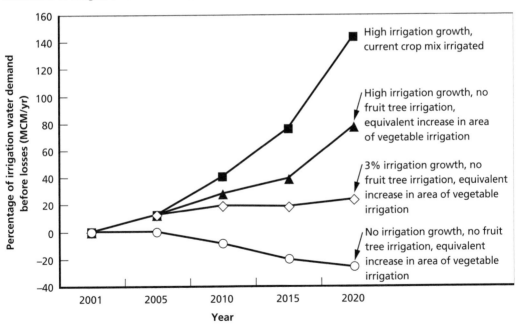

NOTE: Strong growth corresponds to the following inter-period growth rates: 3.0 percent, 4.5 percent, 8.0 percent, and 7.0 percent.

RAND MG146-6.4

Supply Enhancement and Sustainability

In this subsection we briefly describe the major opportunities and requirements for sustainably supplying future Palestinian water demand.

Reducing Withdrawals from Aquifers. The Palestinians and the Israelis are collectively over-utilizing both the Mountain and Gaza Aquifers. Although negotiations between Israel and a future Palestinian state will ultimately determine the quantity of groundwater sustainably available to the Palestinians, it is certain that both the Palestinians and Israelis must reduce their withdrawals in order to retain the Gaza Aquifer as a viable water source. For the Mountain Aquifers, increased Palestinian use of groundwater supplies should be accompanied by concurrent reductions by Israel.

Harvesting Rainwater and Capturing Storm Water. Rainwater harvesting is an important source of water in the West Bank and, to a lesser extent, in Gaza. For many Palestinians, particularly in rural areas of the West Bank where no centralized water distribution system exists, rainwater capture is critical for meeting basic needs. Typically, residents divert rainwater into excavations in the ground (cisterns) and use this water throughout the dry season. Each cistern holds an average of 70 to 100 cubic meters, enough to satisfy minimal requirements during the rainy season and then for an additional three to four months during the dry season (Hunt, 2001). Between 50,000 and 80,000 cisterns in the West Bank currently augment supply (ARIJ, 1995, 1996; National Research Council, 1999; UNEP, 2001).

Investing in rainwater harvesting could supplement centralized water provision. Although installation of rainwater capture systems will be labor and capital intensive, especially in urban areas, increasing national capacity for capturing rainwater could augment by several times the current amount of rainwater captured. To ensure that this water source does not endanger human health, residents will need to be educated about cleaning and maintaining all components of the system. Ensuring the availability of efficient and decontaminated catchments and cisterns to supplement centralized distribution in rural and urban areas will require investments in equipment and education.

Capturing storm water could also augment Palestinian water supplies. Capture requires constructing single or multiple small dams on appropriate wadis. During periods of very heavy rainfall, these dams could provide flood control, as well as supply water for agricultural, industrial, or domestic uses or for aquifer recharge. CH2M HILL (2002a) estimates that up to 148 MCM/yr of storm water runoff is available for capture in the West Bank. The engineering and environmental costs would be high for an ambitious storm water program of this magnitude. As an alternative, CH2M HILL proposes projects that would capture 15 MCM/yr by 2015 and 28 MCM/yr by 2025. We use the latter proposal in the analysis below.

Reclaiming and Reusing Wastewater. Wastewater can be treated and reused to reduce the demands on limited water sources. Treated wastewater can be reused for domestic and agricultural irrigation, industrial uses, domestic toilet water, aquaculture, environmental uses, and/or aquifer recharge. In the near term, agricultural reuse is the most promising of these options because public concern about the safety of treated wastewater for domestic consumption may be considerable.

In Israel, 70 percent of wastewater is already treated and reused for irrigation (National Research Council, 1999). Israel first began to reuse wastewater in the 1970s, primarily for its cotton crop (Juanicó, 2002). Today, reuse is integral to Israel's water management. In fact, Israel uses a higher percentage of wastewater for irrigation than any other country (Shelef, undated). The water reuse techniques that Israel has used so successfully could also be applied to the Palestinian agricultural sector.[10]

The current lack of infrastructure in the West Bank and Gaza provides a unique opportunity to build wastewater reuse into the infrastructure during initial construction. Ensuring wastewater treatment, while admittedly a major undertaking, is critical for protecting human health, current ground and surface water sources, and the environment. As a result, all wastewater in the West Bank and Gaza must be treated before discharge, regardless of whether it is reused. The marginal cost of providing treated wastewater for agricultural reuse, however, is small relative to the cost of initially building the wastewater collection and treatment infrastructure, and much smaller than retrofitting existing infrastructure.

Agriculture is currently the most attractive use of wastewater because (1) the standard of treatment required is lower than for other uses; (2) the nutrients in wastewater can benefit agriculture; and (3) public acceptance is relatively high. Although some wastewater is informally reused for agriculture near the three currently existing wastewater treatment plants in Gaza (Tubail, Al-Dadah, and Yassin, undated), no wastewater in Gaza or the West Bank is officially reused (National Research Council, 1999; CH2M HILL, 2001). CH2M HILL (2002a) reports that up to 85 percent of the municipal and industrial water supply could eventually be treated for use in agriculture. Because of the variation in irrigation demand relative to wastewater production, storage capacity may be required (National Research Council, 1999).

The municipal and industrial sector could also reuse treated wastewater, although it requires more treatment (to potable standards) and conveyance infrastructure than agricultural reuse. The large need for a potable water distribution network provides an opportunity to build dual distribution systems (separate distribution for potable water and reclaimed wastewater) at a cost relatively low compared with retrofitting a distribution system to accommodate dual uses (National Research Council, 1999). Theoretically, centralized wastewater reuse could provide as much as three-quarters of the annual municipal demand (National Research Council, 1999).

Because of current public apprehension about the safety of reusing wastewater, reusing it for irrigation is probably the most tenable option for the next ten years. However, as demand increases and Palestinian industries expand, acceptability and

---

[10] Reuse of treated wastewater must be restricted to the portion of the Palestinian agricultural sector that does not grow crops eaten raw (such as fresh fruit).

cost-effectiveness for non-agricultural uses are likely to increase. If reuse were limited to non-potable uses, the health risks would be insignificant.

Public education and appropriate water pricing could increase public acceptance of wastewater reuse. Use of treated wastewater is currently limited because of both a lack of infrastructure to treat and deliver wastewater to agricultural regions and the low cost of alternative sources of water supply for irrigation. For example, groundwater can be pumped at very low costs from the shallow aquifer in Gaza, and the tariff for surface water provided by the public irrigation system in the Jordan Valley is only $0.02/CM. Under these circumstances, there is little incentive to use reclaimed wastewater, with its associated risks (real and perceived) to health and the marketability of agricultural produce.

Desalination. Desalination is an energy-intensive technology that can produce great quantities of freshwater for use in any sector. Seawater desalinated and treated to potable standards can be supplied directly to the end user. Alternatively, desalinated water can be combined with lower-quality brackish water or contaminated groundwater to yield larger quantities of potable water. In fact, in Gaza, desalinated water with a salinity of 500 parts per million (ppm) is combined with brackish water with a salinity of about 3,000 ppm to yield a blend of potable water with a salinity of 1,500 ppm.[11] The result is a blended water source that can be provided at a lower cost than pure desalinated water.

The cost of desalinated water is high as a result of its high capital requirements and large energy costs. It is usually cost-effective only when surface water, groundwater, or imported supplies are not available. In the Middle East, where water is critically scarce, desalination may play a role in a prudent water management strategy. For Gaza, most analysts would agree that desalination is required to meet the needs of its population. In fact, desalination facilities are already planned in both Israel and Gaza. The Gaza plant, largely financed by the U.S. Agency for International Development, is projected to produce 20 MCM of water per year starting in late 2004 (U.S. Consulate General in Jerusalem, 2002). For the West Bank, desalination is one of several options for augmenting the water supply. Its desirability will largely depend upon its cost relative to other options and the security implications of the required transport of water from the Mediterranean to the West Bank.

A major determinant of the cost of desalinated water is the related energy requirement. Energy costs account for roughly one-third of desalination costs alone, and large amounts of energy would also be required to pump water from a desalination plant on the Mediterranean Sea to the West Bank. If the water is to be used for irrigation, investment and energy costs are lower than for producing potable water because higher salinity (and other contaminant) levels may be acceptable for some crops. Similarly, brackish water is less saline and, therefore, more cost-effective to desalinate than seawater. However, desalinating brackish water is still expensive ($0.50–$1/CM) and en-

---

[11] Personal communication with Alvin Newman, April 3, 2003.

ergy intensive, and the limited sources of brackish water constrain its usefulness as a source. We consider only seawater desalination in this analysis.

Thus, weighing desalination's costs against its benefits is highly dependent on traditional energy costs, the potential presence of renewable solar and wind energy, and the development of less energy-intensive technologies (Abraham, Owens, and Brunsdale, 1999). If the recently discovered natural gas reserves in the Mediterranean Sea can be developed, energy costs may be low enough to make desalination a widespread option. Reverse osmosis is currently the cheapest technology to desalinate water. It is the primary option considered in planning desalination plants.

The scenarios below consider desalination of Mediterranean seawater. We use the cost estimates of CH2M HILL (2002b) for a 50 MCM/yr reverse osmosis plant (~$1.06/CM). Although the operators of the recent Gaza desalination plant expect to produce desalinated water at about half this cost, these low costs have yet to be achieved in practice. If lower desalination costs are achievable in practice, the relative attractiveness of desalination as a new source of water for the region will increase. CH2M HILL suggests that the maximum feasible amount that could be brought on line by 2025 is roughly 390 MCM/yr. Although this option is especially important if groundwater rights are not reestablished, it does present a security risk. A pipeline would be needed to import desalinated water from the Mediterranean Sea, across Israel, and to the West Bank. As a result, large portions of the Palestinian supply would be vulnerable to sabotage and external control by Israel if tensions were to intensify. Although some of this risk could be mitigated through international guarantees or insurance, a high level of political stability is a prerequisite for this water supply option.

Infrastructure Improvements

Expanding Water and Wastewater Infrastructure. Building new water delivery and wastewater infrastructure is a high priority, and in our analysis we treat such infrastructure as a necessity rather than an option. Central provision of water and appropriate sewage services must be extended to the entire population in both the West Bank and Gaza. Transitioning toward a sanitation program is integral to reducing the degradation of aquifers and surface water bodies and eliminating the negative health consequences of unsanitary wastewater disposal. Similarly, transitioning to a central distribution network will eliminate the reliance of the poorest portions of the population on water tankers or degraded water bodies.

The dearth of existing infrastructure presents a unique opportunity to incorporate innovative ideas in water management into the construction of basic infrastructure. For example, expanding wastewater treatment capacity in Palestine will not only eliminate the hygiene and pollution problems associated with raw sewage disposal, but it will also provide a new source of reusable water.

Improving Infrastructure. Due to both the lack of maintenance and the current crisis, much of the crippled existing infrastructure will need to be repaired or rebuilt.

This will entail connecting the quarter of the population currently without access to a centralized water source, connecting most of the Palestinians to wastewater treatment facilities, and repairing the leaky distribution systems.

Currently, it is estimated that 40 percent of water delivered to domestic end users and to agricultural areas is lost (CH2M HILL, 2002b). UFW can be reduced by (1) eliminating illegal use and unmetered connections, (2) reducing errors in metering, and (3) repairing leaks in the distribution system. The first two measures will lead to more efficient water use as previously nonpaying users are charged for the water, and will increase revenues for the water districts. Rehabilitating water networks, locating and fixing system leaks, and lining or piping agricultural water conveyance facilities will be expensive but cost-effective in the long term, by extending the usable amount of each unit of water supply.

Transporting and Distributing Desalinated Water. As discussed below, desalination of water from the Mediterranean Sea may be required to meet the water demand in the West Bank. In this case, a national water carrier may also be required to convey these new large sources. The costs of this infrastructure are included in any scenarios that include desalination for the West Bank.

Another option is to pipe seawater from the Mediterranean Sea or Red Sea to the Dead Sea, where it would be desalinated and used for domestic and agricultural uses. An advantage of this option is that it could replace the need for building a desalination plant on the Mediterranean Sea while also halting the drop in the Dead Sea's water level and the associated negative environmental implications. We do not consider this option in our analysis because it would not likely be in place prior to 2020. However, it should be considered in longer-term plans. Energy costs associated with this plan would amount to 20 to 40 percent of the total cost for importation from both the Red and the Mediterranean Seas. The collocation of power generation and desalination facilities would increase efficiency. Because the Dead Sea is below sea level, hydroelectric power generation from the flow to the Dead Sea could be used to reduce the external energy requirements of the desalination. Such a plan, with desalination plant capacities between 100 and 800 MCM/yr, is estimated to cost between $2 billion and $7 billion (Abraham, Owens, and Brunsdale, 1999; National Research Council, 1999). A conduit to bring the seawater to the Dead Sea is estimated to cost between $1 billion and $5 billion. A conduit from the Mediterranean Sea would be less expensive than from the Red Sea and would have fewer environmental complications (Abraham, Owens, and Brunsdale, 1999). The capital cost of the desalination plant itself is estimated to range between $200 million and $1 billion, or $0.50 to $0.75/CM of plant capacity.

Water importation from other regions has also been discussed as a potential solution to the water crisis in the region. CH2M HILL conjectured that 3.5 MCM/day could be piped from Turkey to supply the water-scarce regions to the south, including the West Bank. Another option would be to import water from Turkey via large tankers or barges. The estimates of the capital costs associated with a pipeline are between

$5 billion and $30 billion, and the annual operation and maintenance costs are estimated at roughly $205 million. The annual costs, assuming approximately $21 billion total capital costs, are $1.07 per CM for capital and $0.16 per CM for operation and maintenance. We do not consider these options as they are currently more expensive than desalination and would require substantial international cooperation.

Modeling Future Water Demand and Supply for Palestine

Palestinian water managers face significant challenges in providing sufficient water supplies to increase domestic consumption to world health standards, to accommodate future population growth, and to support agricultural and industrial growth. Sustainable aquifer use by both Israelis and Palestinians will require cooperation and coordinated management. Failure to do so will degrade much of the Palestinian water supply, increase treatment costs, and decrease agricultural productivity. Increasing water demand must be both managed and met, requiring the development of new sources. Finally, the infrastructure must be upgraded to deliver fresh water to the growing Palestinian population and to collect, treat, and dispose of wastewater.

As described in the section above, Water for a Future Palestinian State: Policy Options, the international community and Palestinian water managers have a variety of options available to them to manage future water demand and develop supplies. Each option has unique costs, and many options have rising marginal costs.[12]

Ideally, Palestinian water managers with the help of the international community would simply choose the least expensive set of demand-managing and supply-enhancing policies that would meet projected future demands. The expected cost of implementing the policy, however, should not be the only consideration. Significant uncertainty surrounds estimates of future supply and demand, the effectiveness of policies, and the costs of policy actions. Some policies will be more robust to unexpected outcomes than others. Furthermore, there are other non-financial costs of different policies (e.g., agricultural impacts) that should be considered when choosing the optimal long-term water management strategy for the West Bank and Gaza.

We generate a few plausible scenarios of water demand and supply from 2001 through 2020, reflecting both uncertain parameters and different potential policies (see Table 6.4). For each scenario, we also estimate the implementation costs from 2005 through 2014 and discuss the implications of each combination of demand management and supply augmentation strategies.[13] Because many parameters driving wa-

---

[12] An example of a policy with rising marginal costs is reducing system water losses. Decreasing losses from 40 to 30 percent is likely to cost less than the reduction from 30 to 20 percent, because the first improvements will often be easier and less expensive than later ones.

[13] We report the costs from years 2005–2014 to conform to cost estimates in other chapters.

Table 6.4
Parameters and Policy Options Modeled and to Consider in Future Analyses

Uncertain Parameters	Policy Options
Modeled	Modeled
Population growth	Domestic efficiency (D)
Energy costs	Domestic graywater use (D)
	Irrigation growth limits (D)
To Consider	Irrigation efficiency (D)
Aquifer recharge and yield	Crop shifting (D)
Policy costs	Rainwater harvesting (S)
Commercial & industrial growth	Storm water capture (S)
	Wastewater reuse (S)
	Desalination (S)
	Increase water system efficiency (I)
	To Consider
	Israeli aquifer use
	Per-capita consumption

NOTE: D, S, and I indicate demand, supply, and infrastructure options, respectively.

ter demand, water supply, and total project cost are uncertain, we test our scenarios against alternative population growth rates and energy prices. This brief sensitivity analysis motivates the need to thoroughly evaluate water management proposals and identifies those management strategies that are robust to these uncertain parameters.

Modeling Mechanics

There are several major modeling steps in generating water scenarios for Palestine. First, future water demands must be forecast. The forecasted demand (from 2001 to 2020) will depend on uncertain parameters such as population growth, as well as policy choices such as the desired per-capita water availability and the amount of water efficiency investment. Next, water sources must be identified to meet this demand.

The first source considered is sustainable groundwater supply. The amount of sustainable groundwater available for Palestinian use is dependent upon aquifer recharge rates and yields and upon Israeli withdrawals. Although the apportionment of the aquifer between the Israelis and Palestinians ultimately needs to be negotiated between the two states, we describe one possible sharing scheme upon which all our scenarios are based.[14] Next, water sources that do not require desalination are specified for each scenario. Any remaining water demand is met by desalination.

---

[14] We anticipate that the chosen aquifer-sharing scheme may not be acceptable to one or both states. Since successful water management will require some investment in desalination for both states, deviations from the proposed sharing scheme simply will shift the relative amount of desalination required for each state.

To estimate the total project costs, we consider the cost of (1) all demand management policies, (2) acquiring water from all sources above the 2001 baseline amount, and (3) all additional infrastructure required for water provisioning and wastewater collection, treatment, and disposal. These cost calculations are based upon a modified version of the West Bank Water Management Analysis Tool developed by CH2M HILL (2002b). We describe the modifications in the Appendix section at the end of this chapter.

Demand

We estimate Palestinian water demand separately for municipal and industrial uses and agricultural purposes. Municipal and industrial demand is composed of domestic, public, and industrial demands, along with system losses. Agricultural water demand includes irrigation and livestock demand, as well as system losses.

Domestic demand is the product of the population and effective per-capita consumption, adjusted for system losses. Current policy guidelines suggest that the effective per-capita domestic consumption rate (the amount of water required to meet basic services without efficiency and reuse) must increase from current levels of about 55 liters per day to about 100 liters per day by 2015.[15] Implementation of domestic efficiency measures and graywater reuse will reduce these net water needs. We model efficiency and graywater policy options in terms of household adoption rates ranging from 0 percent to 90 percent. Public and industrial demands are estimated as a fixed percentage of domestic demand (see the subsection on Municipal and Industrial Demand in the Appendix section at the end of this chapter for details).[16]

Agricultural demand can be defined as the sum of irrigation and livestock demand and physical losses. For the West Bank, we model irrigation water demand by separating irrigation demand growth due to expansion of irrigated lands (assuming the same cropping pattern) and crop shifting away from water intensive fruits toward vegetables. We use PHG estimates of the 1999–2000 cropping and irrigation patterns as a base from PCBS (2003b). The expansion of irrigated land is specified as a percentage growth over each time period. We represent crop shifting by altering the fraction of irrigated land that is growing fruit versus vegetables. Because the water needs are lower for vegetables, crop shifting reduces demand for irrigation water per unit of irrigated area.

For the West Bank scenarios presented here, we started with the West Bank agricultural demand in 2001 and then gradually increased to 2015 to the amount of water that would be used for existing irrigated crops if there were no shortages or rationing. From 2015 through 2020, irrigation demand growth expands by a specified annual percentage rate. The total demand for irrigation water is then equal to the irrigated area times the net irrigation water requirement.

---

[15] According to WHO, 100 l/d is the minimum water requirement for domestic uses for households with connections to a centralized water distribution system (Howard and Bartram, 2003).

[16] Public demand is estimated to be 6 percent of domestic demand for all time periods. Industrial demand increases from 7 percent in 2001 to 13 percent in 2015.

For Gaza, we model irrigation requirements independently of current cropping patterns. For our base case we assume that 2001 water use persists through 2020. For other scenarios, we vary the amount of water made available to irrigation as a function of groundwater use and available treated wastewater.

Livestock water demands make up a small fraction of total agricultural demand. Following CH2M HILL (2001), we assume they will grow from 2001 levels at an annual rate of 3 percent.

Supply

Once water demand is estimated for each time period, supply must be identified to meet this demand. The first new source we consider is new Palestinian aquifer withdrawals, within the renewable limits. For the Mountain Aquifers, we use CH2M HILL (2002a) estimates of renewable aquifer yield. For the Gaza Aquifer, we use the Oslo Accords recharge value as the sustainable yield (see Figure 6.3). Based on a specified schedule of aquifer use by Israel, we compute the Palestinian allocations such that all renewable groundwater is fully used.

Next, we consider sources that do not need desalination. The amount of water available from these sources is determined by the amount of investment in each source, constrained by natural and feasibility limits. Harvesting rainwater can provide additional water to municipalities and is modeled as the percentage of households installing and utilizing cisterns. Storm water capture projects, as described by CH2M HILL (2002b), will provide 15 MCM/yr by 2015. Next, water available to the agricultural sector for irrigation is augmented by treated wastewater. The percentage of sewage that receives additional treatment for irrigation is a policy parameter in our model.

Finally, any remaining demand is met by desalination.

Infrastructure

The model specifies that 90 percent of the population will have access to an improved water network by 2015. This will involve providing water connections to 15 percent of the current population and 90 percent of all future Palestinians. Existing losses to the water system are about 40 percent. We consider various repair schedules that would reduce these losses to as low as 25 percent. Finally, because of the environmental and health consequences of untreated wastewater, our model specifies that no raw wastewater is discharged. This is achieved by providing centralized sewage treatment for the majority of the population (80 percent for the West Bank and 100 percent for Gaza) and septic systems when connection to a central sewer system is infeasible.

Infrastructure requirements vary according to the water management policies used. All new supply options involve considerable infrastructure investment. Most notable is the requirement for a pipeline to transport desalinated water from the Mediterranean Sea to the West Bank.

Project Cost

We use the West Bank Water Management Model by CH2M HILL (2002b) and other sources documented in the Appendix section of this chapter to estimate the cost of implementing all the components of a management strategy from 2005 through 2014. It is important to note that these costs are highly uncertain and are calculated primarily for comparison purposes.

The estimated unit costs for each policy measure for the West Bank (WB) (see Table 6.5) differ from CH2M HILL's estimates only with regard to: (1) rainwater harvesting, because of differences in collection area assumptions and United Nations Environmental Programme (UNEP) capital cost estimates; (2) septic systems and graywater reuse, which are not considered by CH2M HILL; and (3) desalination, because of different energy cost assumptions. While wastewater treatment costs appear different than CH2M HILL's estimates, we have simply separated its estimates into two categories—reuse and treatment.

Costs for Gaza were adopted from the West Bank costs and modified where appropriate. For example: (1) the average household size in Gaza is larger than in the West Bank, leading to lower domestic graywater reuse costs (per capita); and (2) the rainfall in Gaza is significantly less than the mean rainfall in the West Bank, resulting in less water available from rainwater harvesting and thus an increased cost per CM.

The model accounts for the costs of providing new water sources and improving infrastructure. It does not, however, account for reduced costs that arise from some of these investments. For example, graywater reuse and efficiency improvements will decrease the need to empty cesspits, eliminating annual pumping costs of $60 (Faruqui, 2002). Similarly, reuse for domestic agriculture in a pilot project in Jordan provided an additional source of income for households and/or a reduction in food costs totaling an average of about $300 per year, or 10 percent of the household income. Concurrently, the graywater reuse decreased the domestic water consumption by an average of 15 percent and, as a result, lowered water bills by 27 percent. The total net benefit to a household on average was roughly $400.[17] We do not include such cost reductions in our analysis.

Options for the Future

Our analytic methodology allows us to examine a broad range of policy alternatives for meeting future Palestinian water needs. In this section, we first describe several scenarios of demand and supply to 2020, reflecting different policy approaches. For each scenario, we estimate the total cost for the projects from 2005 through 2014 to correspond to the time horizon of the other chapters in this volume.[18] Next we test the sensitivity of these approaches to varying population growth rates and energy prices.

---

[17] Personal communication with Naser I. Faruqui, April 1, 2003.

[18] All total cost estimates are the net present value of the total costs over the planning period of 2005–2014. After 2014, costs will continue to accrue, as capital costs (such as infrastructure) are amortized over the typical life for the capital, and as operations and maintenance costs continue to be realized. A 5 percent discount rate is used for all net present value calculations.

Table 6.5
Capital, Operations, and Maintenance Costs for Water Management Activities for the Original CH2M HILL Model and the Model Used in This Analysis

Policy Action	Capital Costs ($/CM)			Operations and Maintenance Costs ($/CM)			Notes
	CH2M HILL—WB	RAND—WB	RAND—Gaza	CH2M HILL—WB	RAND—WB	RAND—Gaza	
Domestic efficiency	0.15	0.15	0.15	0.11	0.11	0.11	Assumes household consumption of 525 l/d.
Domestic graywater reuse	N.A.	0.11	0.09	N.A.	0.14	0.12	See subsection above on Increasing Domestic Efficiency and Implementing Reuse of Graywater. Differences between Gaza and WB estimates are based on household size differences.
Agriculture system efficiency/rehabilitation	0.21	0.21	0.21	0.08	0.08	0.08	Based on Nuwimeh (near Jericho) village replacement of an open canal with a distribution pipe network; average between Nuwimeh village and estimated WB average.
Irrigation application efficiency	0.00	0.00	0.00	0.38	0.38	0.38	Maintaining drip irrigation systems.
New wells	0.41	0.41	0.41	0.52	0.52	0.52	Costs vary by energy price.
Rainwater harvesting (cisterns)	0.70	0.98	1.95	0.21	0.43	0.86	The quantity collected in Gaza, because of low average rainfall, is estimated to be half of the quantity collected in WB cisterns.
Storm water	0.49, 0.61, 0.76	0.49, 0.61, 0.76	0.49, 0.61, 0.76	0.02, 0.02, 0.03	0.02, 0.02, 0.03	0.02, 0.02, 0.03	Costs for 50, 100, 150 MCM/yr, respectively, of water savings.
Desalination	0.23	0.23	0.23	0.84	0.83	0.83	Costs vary by energy price.
Wastewater reuse	Included in treatment	0.14	0.14	Included in treatment	0.04	0.04	CH2M HILL computes wastewater treatment and reuse together.

Table 6.5—Continued

Policy Action	Capital Costs ($/CM)			Operations and Maintenance Costs ($/CM)			Notes
	CH2M HILL—WB	RAND—WB	RAND—Gaza	CH2M HILL—WB	RAND—WB	RAND—Gaza	
Waste treatment (central)	1.09	0.95	0.95	0.76	0.72	0.72	See System Efficiency Improvements below. CH2M HILL computes wastewater treatment and reuse together. For our analysis, treatment is a given and the amount of reuse is a policy lever.
Waste treatment (septic)	N.A.	0.06	0.06	N.A.	0.05	0.05	See Wastewater Treatment below in the appendix.
System improvements	0.33, 0.42, 0.52	0.33, 0.42, 0.52	0.33, 0.42, 0.52	0.13, 0.16, 0.20	0.13, 0.16, 0.20	0.13, 0.16, 0.20	Costs for 50, 100, 150 MCM/yr, respectively, of water savings.
Distribution	0.17	0.17	0.17	0.02	0.02	0.02	
Transmission ($/CM/km)	0.0010	0.0010	0.0010	0.0002	0.0002	0.0002	Assuming 50 MCM/yr; per unit costs are lower if larger quantities are transmitted.
Pumping	0.0039	0.0039	0.0039	0.0003	0.0003	0.0003	$/CM per meter head.
Mediterranean to West Bank pipeline	0.11	0.11	0.11	0.57	0.57	0.57	

NOTE: N.A. is not applicable.

The Base Case

For the base case, we assume that the population will grow by 3.3 percent in the West Bank and by 4.2 percent in Gaza (Table 6.6).[19] We assume per-capita consumption to rise from 55 l/d to 100 l/d by 2015. Energy costs are expected to increase 1 percent per year, from $0.06/kilowatt-hour in 2001. These electricity costs were estimated by CH2M HILL (2002a) based on the average costs for high-energy users of the Israeli Electricity Corporation.

For the West Bank, we specify that agricultural water deliveries will increase from the current suboptimal levels (see above subsection Demand Management) to optimal levels by 2015, holding the irrigated area constant. Thereafter the irrigated area is specified to grow by 3 percent/year. For Gaza, we specify constant agricultural water use through the modeling period.

The base case policy actions to manage demand and increase supply are conservative. System improvements to reduce losses, domestic efficiency improvements, and cistern expansion are all modest, and no domestic graywater systems are employed. Twenty percent of wastewater is treated and reused for irrigation.

For the base case, we project total water demand in the West Bank to increase from the 2001 amount of 122 MCM/yr to 340 MCM/yr by 2015 and to approximately 422 MCM/yr by 2020 (Figure 6.5). This strong demand growth is driven by both the municipal and industrial (M&I) and agricultural sectors. In Gaza, total water

Table 6.6
Base Case Scenario Model Parameters

Policy	West Bank		Gaza	
	2001	2015	2001	2015
Population growth	3.3% / year		4.2% / year	
Per-capita water consumption (l/d)	55	100	55	100
Energy costs	1% / year		1% / year	
Agricultural irrigation growth	Optimal by 2015		Constant	
Water system losses	40%	29%	40%	29%
Households adopting efficiency measures	0%	12%	0%	12%
Households adopting graywater systems	0%	0%	0%	0%
Households utilizing cisterns	25.5%	35%	25.5%	35%
Percentage of wastewater used for agriculture	0%	20%	0%	20%
Storm water capture (MCM/yr)	0	15	0	0

[19] The 2001 population in the West Bank and Gaza is set to 2.11 million and 1.20 million, respectively, according to PCBS population estimates (2003a). Annual population growth rates are estimated from PCBS "medium projections" for the time period between 2000 and 2020 (see Chapter Four of this book, Table 4.4).

Figure 6.5
Projected Water Demand for the West Bank and Gaza in the Base Case Scenario

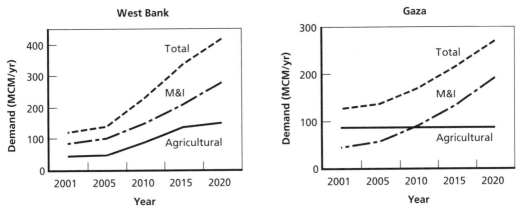

demand also increases dramatically: from 126 MCM/yr in 2001 to 217 MCM/yr in 2015 and then to about 274 MCM/yr in 2020. As agricultural demand is specified to remain constant at 84 MCM/yr (2001 levels), demand growth is driven by population growth and the associated municipal and industrial consumption.

Supply

Baseline. For all scenarios, we start with the 2001 baseline supplies shown in Figure 6.6. Groundwater (springs and wells) supplies 70 percent of the West Bank water supply and 96 percent of Gaza water supply. Purchases from Mekorot (the Israeli water company) provide 26 percent of the West Bank supply. Finally, rainfall capture provides about 4 percent of the West Bank water supply.[20]

Sustainable Aquifer Use. The basis for the analysis is that consumption from the aquifers will be sustainable by both the Israelis and Palestinians. To model different water management strategies and estimate project costs, we choose a possible sustainable aquifer-sharing regime as a starting point. The one chosen is not a recommendation, nor should it be considered an optimal plan. Any actual aquifer-sharing scheme will result from future bilateral agreements. The historical, legal, and ethical issues pertaining to the division of groundwater resources are beyond the scope of this book. We assume, however, that the international community will provide financial support for the Palestinians to develop needed water resources and to increase efficiency and for Israel to develop new water sources to replace reductions in aquifer withdrawals. For simplicity and to provide an upper bound on costs, we choose desalination as the source for new Israeli water.[21]

---

[20] Other estimates suggest that Palestinian water consumption in 2001 was about 20 percent greater than the estimates used here.

[21] Although Israel may also increase its water use efficiency, analysis of Israeli water consumption is beyond the scope of this book.

Figure 6.6
Baseline Water Supplies for the West Bank and Gaza

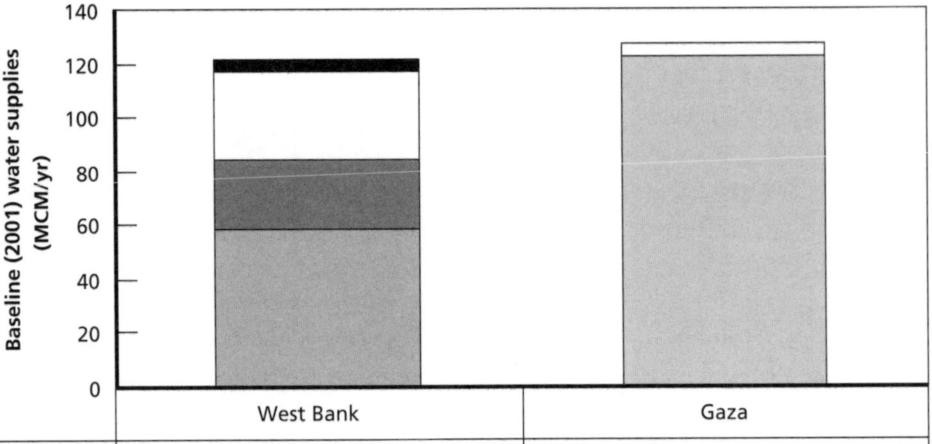

	West Bank	Gaza
■ Rainfall	5	0
☐ Mekorot	32	5
▦ Springs	26	0
☐ Wells	59	122

SOURCE: PCBS, 2003.
RAND MG146-6.6

In this aquifer-sharing scheme, we assume that Israelis gradually stop drawing from the Eastern Aquifer to bring it to balance over ten years. They reduce their use of the northeast and western basins to bring them into balance by 2010 and 2015, respectively. Finally, we assume that use of the Gaza Aquifer is significantly reduced to bring the aquifer into balance. Figure 6.7 summarizes the sustainable aquifer withdrawal schedules used in the model.

This brings the Eastern, Northeastern, Western, and Gaza Aquifers into balance with sustainable yields by 2005, 2010, 2015, and 2020, respectively. Overdraft will occur prior to these years and will exceed 1,500 MCM for the West Bank Aquifers, and just about reach 500 MCM for the Gaza Aquifer. The implications of this overdraft for water quality are uncertain. Substantial degradation, however, is already apparent in the Gaza Aquifer and to a lesser extent in the West Bank. The Israelis and Palestinians may find it necessary to accelerate this schedule to reduce the harmful effects on the aquifers. This would substantially increase the cost of meeting future water needs. It is important to note that this sharing scheme will work only if historical weather patterns prevail. If drought conditions persist in the region, the sustainable levels will change. The costs of unsustainable use of aquifers can be large. A more detailed analysis should consider the increased water treatment and other mitigation costs required if aquifer quality is degraded.

New Supply. Demand is met by existing and new supply and through efficiency. In the base case, new supply for the West Bank includes new groundwater yielded by

Figure 6.7
Current and Possible Sustainable Aquifer Use by Palestinians and Israelis

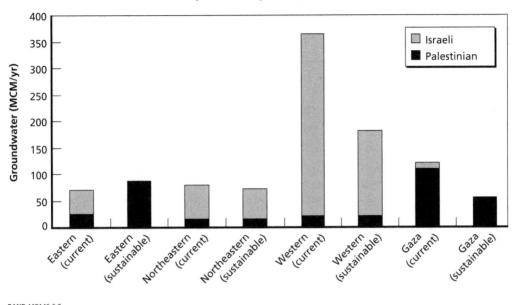

Israel, rainwater capture, some modest storm water capture, treated wastewater, and desalination (Table 6.7 and Figure 6.8). Although by 2015, efficiency accounts for 19 percent of the total water demand, considerable desalination is still required (112 MCM/yr, or 27 percent of total demand). In the agricultural sector (not shown) 15 percent of supplied demand is met by treated wastewater, 11 percent by capture runoff, and 74 percent by groundwater.

For Gaza, groundwater use decreases by about one-half, and the majority of the new water supply comprises treated wastewater (16 MCM/yr) and desalination (143 MCM/yr). System efficiency improvements also stretch the supply by 38 MCM/yr by 2015. Under the base case, in 2015 desalinated seawater meets 56 percent of the total demand and groundwater meets 22 percent (see Table 6.8 and Figure 6.8).

In the base case, Gaza agricultural water use is specified to remain constant over the modeling period, yet groundwater use must decrease by about one-half. These constraints require a considerable amount of desalinated water (about 68 MCM/yr) to be used for agriculture[22] (see Figure 6.9). Agricultural efficiency measures increase the effective use by about 25 MCM/yr from 2001 to 2020. Finally, treated wastewater offsets some (16 MCM/yr by 2015) of the needed new agricultural water supplies.

---

[22] For these scenarios we allocate groundwater to municipal and industrial use first. This results in no available groundwater for agriculture. As we discuss in later scenarios, any non-wastewater supply consumed by the agricultural sector could be used to offset desalinated supplies for the municipal and industrial sectors. So, in effect, any agricultural use of non-wastewater supply increases the desalination requirements for Gaza.

Table 6.7
West Bank Water Supplies for 2001 and
2015 in the Base Case

	2001	2015
	MCM (percentage of total demand)	
Supply	122 (100)	340 (81)
Existing wells	59 (48)	59 (14)
New wells	0 (0)	62 (15)
Springs	26 (21)	60 (14)
Mekorot	32 (26)	0 (0)
Rainwater	5 (4)	13 (3)
Storm water	0 (0)	15 (4)
Reclaimed wastewater	0 (0)	20 (5)
Desalination	0 (0)	112 (27)
Efficiency	0 (0)	80 (19)
Municipal and industrial	0 (0)	42 (10)
Graywater reuse	0 (0)	0 (0)
Agriculture	0 (0)	38 (9)
Total demand	122 (100)	420 (100)

NOTES: Total demand is what would be needed without any efficiency measures in place. Supply plus efficiency equals total demand.

Figure 6.8
West Bank and Gaza Projected Water Supplies in the Base Case, from 2001 to 2020

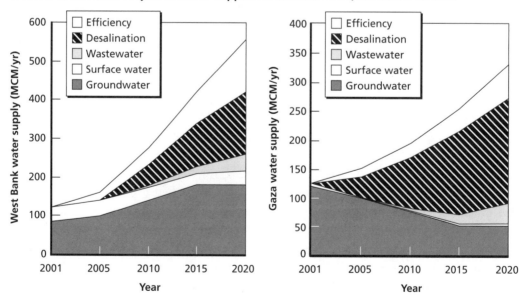

NOTES: Efficiency includes system, domestic, and agriculture efficiency and graywater reuse. Surface water includes rainwater, storm water, and deliveries from Mekorot.
RAND *MG146-6.8*

Table 6.8
Gaza Water Supplies in the Base Case for 2001 and 2015

	2001	2015
	MCM (percentage of total demand)	
Supply	127 (100)	217 (85)
Groundwater	122 (96)	55 (22)
Mekorot	5 (4)	0 (0)
Rainwater	0 (0)	3 (1)
Reclaimed wastewater	0 (0)	16 (6)
Desalination	0 (0)	143 (56)
Efficiency	0 (0)	38 (15)
Municipal and industrial	0 (0)	14 (5)
Graywater reuse	0 (0)	0 (0)
Agriculture	0 (0)	25 (10)
Total demand	127 (100)	256 (100)

NOTES: Total demand is what would be demanded without any efficiency measures in place. Supply plus efficiency equals total demand.

Figure 6.9
Gaza Agricultural Water Sources in the Base Case

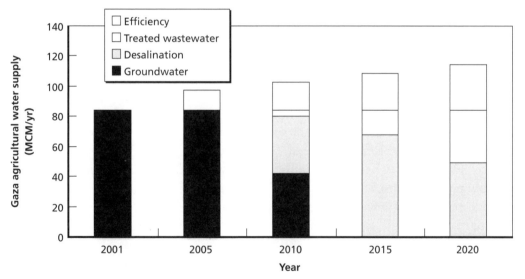

NOTES: The efficiency portion of supply is water that is saved through increased efficiency and improved agricultural techniques. Actual water supplied to agriculture is only the sum of groundwater and treated wastewater.

RAND MG146-6.9

Costs

The total cost for the ten-year period from 2005 through 2014 for upgrading and meeting water needs in the West Bank and Gaza is about $4.9 billion (see Table 6.9). This includes $1.1 billion in aid to Israel for desalination to compensate Israel for reducing its withdrawals from the aquifers. Efficiency costs are modest ($260 million, excluding administration). Wastewater treatment and desalination (along with their share of the administration costs) are the largest single-cost items. Note the high costs of desalination ($900 million) and wastewater treatment ($1.61 billion) for the West Bank and Gaza.

Table 6.9
Base Case Scenario Project Cost from 2005 Through 2014 (in millions of 2003 US$)

	West Bank	Gaza	Palestine	Israel	Total
Domestic efficiency and graywater	76	55	131	0	131
Agricultural efficiency	55	74	129	0	129
Rainwater harvesting	50	39	89	0	89
Wastewater treatment and reuse	581	516	1,097	0	1,097
New wells and storm water	288	0	288	0	288
Desalination	395	503	898	877	1,775
Infrastructure	429	8	437	0	437
Administration	468	299	767	219	986
Total	$2,342	$1,494	$3,836	$1,096	$4,932

Increased Efficiency Scenario

The base case requires significant investment in desalination in order to meet demand. The need for desalination can be mitigated through more aggressive efficiency measures and adoption of alternative new supplies such as rainwater harvesting and reuse of treated wastewater. Efficiency measures are smaller scale, more modular, and can be adopted more rapidly than desalination. The increased efficiency scenario explores one possible policy approach. The scenario is aggressive and it would be difficult to meet the efficiency goals. However, experience in other sectors, such as energy, suggests that this may be feasible. Table 6.10 shows the differences between the base case and the increased efficiency scenario (all other parameters are the same—see Table 6.6).

Demand Projections. Increasing efficiency measures are projected to reduce future water demand substantially. Figure 6.10 shows the projected demand for the West Bank and Gaza in the base case and in the increased efficiency scenario. The efficiency measures in the increased efficiency scenario reduce 2015 demand by 20 percent in the West Bank and 17 percent in Gaza.

Supply. As shown in Table 6.11 and Figure 6.11, efficiency meets about a third of the West Bank water demand, and no desalination (or transboundary pipeline) is required. Reclaimed wastewater supplies 51 MCM/yr (12 percent of the total demand) and rainwater capture supplies 25 MCM/yr (6 percent of the total demand) in 2015.

Table 6.10
Select Policy Options for the Base Case and the Increased Efficiency Scenario (in percentage)

Policy	Base Case	Increased Efficiency Scenario
Households adopting domestic efficiency by 2015	12	40
Households adopting graywater systems by 2015	0	40
Households utilizing cisterns	35	70 (WB) / 35 (Gaza)
Municipal and industrial and agricultural system losses in 2015	29	22
Wastewater reuse for agriculture	20	65

Figure 6.10
Total Water Demand in the Base Case and in the Increased Efficiency Scenario for the West Bank and Gaza

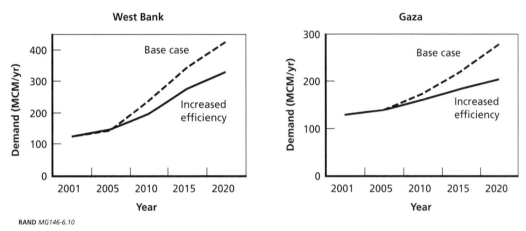

RAND *MG146-6.10*

Table 6.11
West Bank Water Supplies in the Increased Efficiency Scenario for 2001 and 2015

	2001	2015
	MCM (percentage of total demand)	
Supply	122 (100)	272 (65)
Existing wells	59 (48)	59 (14)
New wells	0 (0)	62 (15)
Springs	26 (21)	60 (14)
Mekorot	32 (26)	0 (0)
Rainwater	5 (4)	25 (6)
Storm water	0 (0)	15 (4)
Reclaimed wastewater	0 (0)	51 (12)
Desalination	0 (0)	0 (0)
Efficiency	0 (0)	148 (35)
Municipal and industrial	0 (0)	59 (14)
Graywater reuse	0 (0)	40 (10)
Agriculture	0 (0)	50 (12)
Total demand	122 (100)	420 (100)

NOTES: Total demand is what would be demanded without any efficiency measures in place. Supply plus efficiency equals total demand.

Figure 6.11
West Bank and Gaza Projected Water Supplies in the Increased Efficiency Scenario, from 2001 to 2020

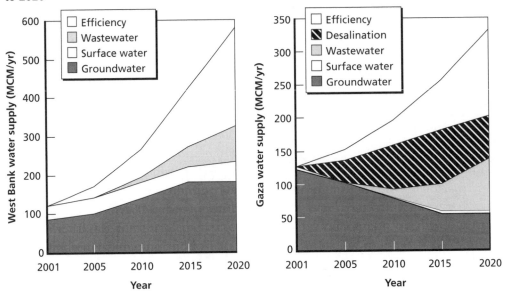

NOTES: Efficiency includes system, domestic, and agriculture efficiency and graywater reuse. Surface water includes rainwater, storm water, and deliveries from Mekorot.
RAND *MG146-6.11*

In Gaza, increased efficiency, domestic graywater reuse, and increased wastewater treatment used for irrigation reduce the need for desalination (from 143 MCM/yr to 82 MCM/yr) (see Table 6.12 and Figure 6.11). By 2015, efficiency in municipal and industrial and agriculture plus graywater reuse meets 29 percent of the total demand. Of the supplied water, 32 percent is desalinated seawater, 22 percent is groundwater, 16 percent is reclaimed wastewater, and 1 percent is from rainwater.

Figure 6.12 shows the projected water supply in 2015 for the West Bank and Gaza in the base case and in the increased efficiency scenario. In the increased efficiency scenario, efficiency and increased used of wastewater replaces much of the desalination required in the base case.

Costs. Pursuing an increased efficiency strategy could reduce the cost of meeting water demand in the West Bank and Gaza from about $4.9 billion to $3.8 billion for the 2005–2014 time period (see Table 6.13). For the West Bank, domestic efficiency and graywater system costs increase from $76 million to $137 million, and rainwater harvesting increases from $50 million to $125 million. This reduction of demand and supply that does not need desalination eliminates the desalination costs ($395 million plus administration) and the associated pipeline infrastructure costs (about $420 million). Another important cost difference is in wastewater treatment and reuse. In the base case, these costs are nearly $600 million for the West Bank. In the increased efficiency scenario, these costs are reduced to just over $500 million, yet the amount

Table 6.12
Water Supplies for Gaza in the Increased Efficiency Scenario for 2001 and 2015

	2001	2015
	MCM (percentage of total demand)	
Supply	127 (100)	181 (71)
Groundwater	122 (96)	55 (22)
Mekorot	5 (4)	0 (0)
Rainwater	0 (0)	3 (1)
Reclaimed wastewater	0 (0)	41 (16)
Desalination	0 (0)	82 (32)
Efficiency	0 (0)	75 (29)
Municipal and industrial	0 (0)	26 (10)
Graywater reuse	0 (0)	24 (9)
Agriculture	0 (0)	25 (10)
Total demand	127 (100)	256 (100)

NOTES: Total demand is what would be demanded without any efficiency measures in place. Supply plus efficiency equals total demand.

Figure 6.12
Total Palestinian Water Supply for 2015 in the Base Case and in the Increased Efficiency Scenario

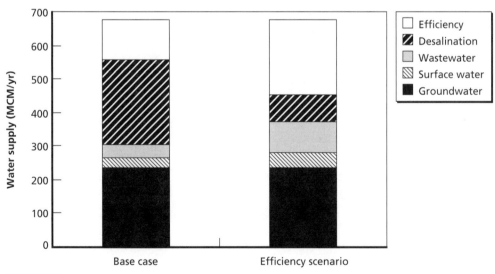

of treated wastewater available for irrigation increases by over 50 MCM/yr. This illustrates the dual saving power of efficiency—savings result from both reduced water demand and reduced wastewater treatment.

Table 6.13
Increased Efficiency Scenario Project Cost from 2005 Through 2014 (in millions of 2003 US$)

	West Bank	Gaza	Palestine	Israel	Total
Domestic efficiency and graywater	137	92	229	0	229
Agricultural efficiency	76	96	172	0	172
Rainwater harvesting	125	39	164	0	164
Wastewater treatment and reuse	518	463	981	0	981
New wells and storm water	288	0	288	0	288
Desalination	0	322	322	877	1,999
Infrastructure	12	8	20	0	20
Administration	289	255	544	219	763
Total	$1,445	$1,275	$2,720	$1,096	$3,816

In Gaza, efficiency measures result in significant savings in desalination costs ($503 million to $322 million). Despite this decrease in cost, more than half of this desalination still goes toward irrigation (not shown in Table 6.13). In addition, groundwater used for irrigation could be reallocated to the municipal regions, thus further reducing the need for desalination as a supply. Our increased efficiency–reduced Gaza agriculture scenario (described below) explores this possibility.

Increased Efficiency–Reduced Gaza Agriculture Scenario

As another policy option, the Palestinian Water Authority might choose to minimize the amount of desalinated water required in Gaza by reallocating all groundwater to municipal and industrial uses. This policy, of course, would have substantial socioeconomic implications in the agricultural sector. It should be viewed only as an extreme policy option and not necessarily the most desirable one. In this scenario, water for irrigation would therefore be supplied only through recycled municipal and industrial wastewater. For this scenario, we use the increased efficiency scenario and modify it for Gaza by eliminating groundwater use for irrigation by 2015. However, because of greater levels of wastewater treatment by 2020, water supplies for irrigation approach the 2001 level (Figure 6.13). Furthermore, by 2020 the effective use is even greater than in 2001 as a result of increased efficiency of water delivery and application in the agricultural sector ("efficiency" in the figure).

A more realistic option, however, might be to transition more slowly away from irrigating with groundwater in Gaza. This would require a larger initial investment in desalination for domestic use in order to accommodate the urgently required reduction in Gaza Aquifer use.

Table 6.14 and Figure 6.14 show the supplies for all sectors in Gaza in the increased efficiency–reduced Gaza agriculture scenario. In contrast to earlier scenarios, only 39 MCM/yr of desalinated water is needed (versus 143 MCM/yr for the base case and 82 MCM/yr for the increased efficiency scenario). Note the large amount of

Figure 6.13
Gaza Agricultural Water Sources in the Increased Efficiency–Reduced Gaza Agriculture Scenario

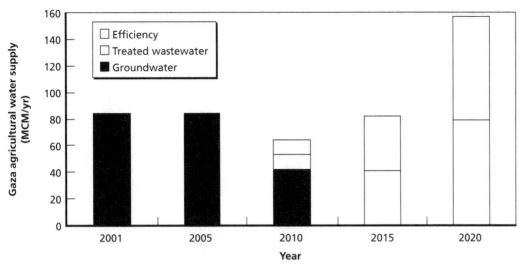

NOTES: The efficiency portion of supply is water that is saved through increased efficiency and improved agricultural techniques. Actual water supplied to agriculture is only the sum of groundwater and treated wastewater.

RAND *MG146-6.13*

Table 6.14
Gaza Water Supplies in the Increased Efficiency–Reduced Gaza Agriculture Scenario, for 2001 and 2015

	2001	2015
	MCM (percentage of total demand)	
Supply	127 (100)	138 (54)
Wells and springs	122 (96)	55 (22)
Mekorot	5 (4)	0 (0)
Rainwater	0 (0)	3 (1)
Treated wastewater	0 (0)	41 (16)
Desalination	0 (0)	39 (15)
Efficiency	0 (0)	117 (46)
Municipal and industrial	0 (0)	26 (10)
Graywater reuse	0 (0)	24 (9)
Agriculture	0 (0)	68 (26)
Total demand	127 (100)	256 (100)

NOTES: Total demand is what would be demanded without any efficiency measures in place. Supply plus efficiency equals total demand.

Figure 6.14
Gaza Projected Water Supplies in the Increased Efficiency–Reduced Gaza Agriculture Scenario, from 2001 to 2020

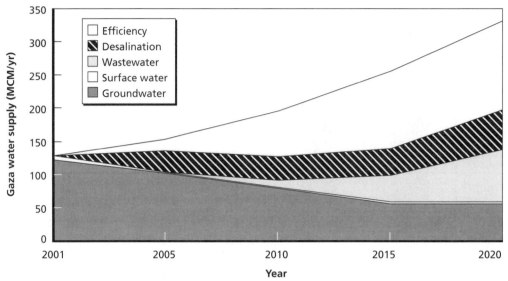

NOTES: Efficiency includes system, domestic, and agricultural efficiency and graywater reuse. Surface water includes rainwater, storm water, and deliveries from Israel.
RAND *MG146-6.14*

water supply that comes from treated wastewater. The cost savings from reallocating all groundwater away from irrigation and toward municipal and industrial uses is about $240 million (not shown in the figure or the table).

There are several important lessons to be learned from this extreme scenario. First, even if groundwater were to be used only for domestic consumption in Gaza, substantial desalination would be required. This implies that any irrigation using Gaza groundwater should be valued at least as high as the cost of providing that water through desalination or at the cost of forgoing domestic consumption. Second, efficiency and wastewater reuse must be aggressively pursued in Gaza. The dual goal of providing for the projected future population in Gaza and supporting an agricultural industry cannot be achieved without bold efficiency and wastewater reuse policies. Finally, the tradeoffs between domestic and agricultural consumption necessitates creating water and agricultural development policies concurrently, using an integrated framework.

Robust Policies

A robust policy is one that is relatively insensitive to major assumptions and unknown parameters. As discussed above, future water demand, available supplies, and costs are all subject to large uncertainties. It is critical, therefore, to evaluate candidate policy strategies against ranges of the uncertain parameters.

There are numerous uncertain parameters that affect the cost estimates. Two important parameters are population growth rates and energy prices. Much of the future water demand is driven by population growth, and the potential return of refugees introduces significant uncertainty into population projections. Energy prices affect the cost of different policies primarily through the high energy requirements of distribution of fresh water, the treatment of consumed water, and desalination.

Table 6.15 summarizes the costs (from 2005 to 2014) for the base case and increased efficiency–reduced Gaza agriculture scenario under the following conditions: (1) expected energy costs and population growth, (2) high energy costs, (3) high population growth, and (4) high energy costs and high population growth. For the high population growth scenarios, population growth in the West Bank and Gaza is set at 4.3 percent per year and 5.2 percent per year, respectively. This population growth rate increase results in 715,000 more Palestinians in the West Bank and Gaza by 2015. At the high end of energy projections, it is possible that energy costs might increase as much as 3 percent per year[23]—based on uncertainty surrounding costs of the potential natural gas discoveries mentioned above.

Table 6.15
Project Costs from 2005 to 2014 for the Base Case and the Increased Efficiency–Reduced Gaza Agriculture Scenario Under Expected Energy Costs and Population Growth, High Energy Costs, High Population Growth, and High Energy and High Population Growth Conditions (in millions of 2003 US$)

	Base Case				Increased Efficiency–Reduced Gaza Agriculture Scenario			
	Expected Energy Costs & Pop. Growth	High Energy Costs	High Pop. Growth	High Energy Costs & Pop. Growth	Expected Energy Costs & Pop. Growth	High Energy Costs	High Pop. Growth[a]	High Energy Costs & Pop. Growth[a]
WB and Gaza	3,834	4,161	4,209	4,569	2,478	2,529	2,678	2,740
WB	2,340	2,553	2,562	2,795	1,443	1,464	1,507	1,527
Gaza	1,494	1,608	1,647	1,774	1,035	1,065	1,171	1,213
Israel	1,096	1,294	1,096	1,294	1,096	1,294	1,096	1,294
Total	$4,930	$5,455	$5,305	$5,863	$3,574	$3,823	$3,774	$4,034

NOTES: Energy costs increase 3 percent per year instead of 1 percent per year under the high-energy-costs conditions. Under the high-population-growth conditions, the population increases yearly by 4.3 percent instead of 3.3 percent in the West Bank and by 5.2 percent instead of 4.2 percent in Gaza.
[a] For the two high-population-growth with increased efficiency cases, graywater system use is increased in the West Bank from 40 percent to 60 percent to accommodate the population growth.

---

[23] Energy cost increases of 3 percent matches the "high oil price" scenario of the Energy Information Administration, *International Energy Outlook 2003* (EIA, 2003a).

Figure 6.15 shows the phasing of costs from 2005 to 2019 for the base case and increased efficiency–reduced Gaza agriculture scenario. The costs increase substantially over time, reflecting the phasing of desalination for both Gaza and Israel. Note that costs under the base case continue to rise rapidly past 2014, whereas the costs in this efficiency scenario begin to level off.

If energy prices are higher than expected, costs might increase about $525 million. In contrast, costs only rise about $250 million under the high efficiency–reduced Gaza agriculture case. This illustrates an important advantage of water efficiency and water reuse—they are less sensitive to volatility in energy price.

In the increased population growth cases, costs increase by $375 million in the base case as opposed to $200 million in the high efficiency–reduced Gaza agriculture scenario. Price rises less quickly under both because each additional person requires less water when efficiency measures are employed and because at these levels increased efficiency can provide effective water more inexpensively than desalination.

Finally, under the worst-case scenario of higher energy prices and greater population growth rates, the project cost could reach about $5.86 billion in the base case but only $4.03 billion in the high efficiency–reduced Gaza agriculture scenario. This potential savings would more than pay for the desalination needed to make up for reductions in Israeli withdrawals from the aquifers.

Figure 6.15 shows the cumulative project costs by period for the base case and high efficiency–reduced Gaza agriculture scenario. For both cases, more than one-half the total costs are realized by 2011, and the costs increase modestly after 2015.

Figure 6.15
Project Cost Phasing for the Base Case and the Increased Efficiency–Reduced Gaza Agriculture Scenario

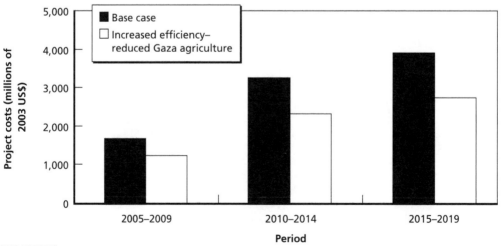

These results suggest that investing in efficiency can be more robust against population growth and energy price uncertainties. These results reflect differences between efficiency/conservation measures and new water source measures like desalination. Depending less on desalination can hedge against price and demand uncertainty.

Finally, the results indicate that a prudent course of action may be to pursue policies that emphasize an increasing amount of efficiency and distributed supply-enhancing options (e.g., rainwater harvesting and wastewater reuse) in combination with desalination (in Gaza). For the West Bank, this strategy may result in delaying the need for desalination indefinitely (as is the case for the increased efficiency scenarios).

Conclusions

Water issues are only some of the many issues that a possible new Palestinian state will have to face, but they are among the most critical. As we have discussed in this chapter, some water issues urgently need attention. Water supplies do not currently meet the growing population's domestic needs, nor are they sufficient for irrigation expansion. Aquifers are already being overused, and they are becoming increasingly contaminated, directly threatening both health and productivity. Finally, the water and wastewater infrastructure is in disrepair, leading to the waste and contamination of scarce supplies. Substantial investment in this infrastructure will be required to support a viable Palestinian state. Efforts to improve the situation are needed now.

Our analysis reveals several major lessons. First, creating a reliable water and wastewater system for a future Palestinian state will be possible only through the use of a variety of policies, including demand management, appropriate agricultural development, infrastructure improvements, enhanced efficiency measures, innovative new supply development (e.g., rainwater harvesting and use of treated wastewater), and desalination. The cost of accomplishing these systems, above and beyond current expenditures, will likely exceed $3.5 billion from 2005 through 2014.

Second, utilizing water resources sustainably will require a substantial reduction in the use of groundwater in both the Mountain and Gaza Aquifers. Because these resources underlie both Israeli and the Palestinian territories, cooperation between Israelis and Palestinians will be required. We have used one aquifer-sharing scheme, but there are many other ways to make this allocation. Deviating from the proposed scheme will alter the total price for the project and require different levels of external sources. Although this determination will ultimately be made through negotiations, we encourage both parties to carefully consider the hydrology of the groundwater basins, the projected needs of the regions' inhabitants, and the total project costs when making these determinations. This chapter provides a framework that can be used to evaluate water management schemes.

Next, although desalination is a promising supply option for a Palestinian state, its high relative costs dictate that its use be accompanied by aggressive demand management and efficiency improvements. Our analysis suggests that desalination will be required for Gaza because of its large expected population and scant groundwater resources. As desalination sources are developed for Gaza, a concurrent goal should be to improve the efficiency of water use to the highest achievable levels.

For the West Bank, however, the water supply options are greater. Although some management plans call for desalinated water to be piped from the Mediterranean Sea to the West Bank, our analysis suggests that in the near term it could be less expensive and more prudent to more fully utilize alternative water sources and demand management in lieu of relying on new desalinated water. This strategy would eliminate the need for a transboundary pipeline for desalinated water transport and increase Palestinians' security and control over their water resources.

Through the evaluation of different scenarios with varying future populations and energy prices, we show some positive features of efficiency and demand management. When employed at appropriate levels, these features can provide a hedge against uncertainty in energy prices and demand. Preparing for uncertainty could significantly increase the chances of a successful future Palestinian state.

Appendix 6.A

The appendix contains additional information regarding the costs and yields of various policy scenarios as well as details of the CH2M HILL model used to estimate project costs.

Demand

Municipal and industrial demand is computed by the following equation:

$$MI = \frac{DD}{(1 - Loss) \times (1 - Pub - CI)},$$

where MI is gross municipal and industrial water demand, DD is gross domestic demand, $Loss$ is physical losses as a percentage of gross municipal and industrial demand, Pub is public water demand as a percentage of consumptive municipal and industrial demand, and CI is commercial and industrial water demand as a percentage of consumptive municipal and industrial demand.

Baseline municipal and industrial demand is derived from actual supply records from PWA as documented by CH2M HILL (2001). Public and industrial water demand is considered to be a percentage of domestic demand. The model also specifies the commercial and industrial demand as percentages of municipal and industrial demand.

Population, a key determinant of projected demand, is projected to grow in Palestine due to internal growth rate (births exceeding deaths) and net inflow of Palestinians. The PCBS forecasts internal growth rates of around 3.3 percent. The net inflow of Palestinians (returnees) is much more difficult to predict as it depends upon numerous characteristics of the Palestinian state including economic prospects and ability to absorb returnees.

Per-Capita Domestic Consumption. We compute domestic demand as the product of the per-capita consumption rate and the projected population. Estimates of gross per-capita supply rates range from 43 l/d to 50 l/d during 1995–1999.[24] Assuming 40 percent physical losses, public demand equal to 6 percent of municipal and industrial demand (excluding losses) for all time periods (CH2M HILL, 2001), and CI consumption of 7 percent of municipal and industrial demand, the 1999 supply rate is estimated to be 50 l/d per person. CH2M HILL uses the baseline of 55 l/d for 2001. The target per-capita consumption rate is 100 l/d by 2015.

Domestic Efficiency. CH2M HILL estimates that typical water-saving household fixtures such as aerators on faucets, low-water toilets, and low-consumption showerheads will reduce daily consumption by 25 percent for consumers connected to a centralized water system with near constant reliability (the objective of Palestinian

---

[24] Source: Table 3 (CH2M HILL, 2001).

water planning). Because most Palestinians do not receive constant and reliable water supplies, current consumption is highly efficient. As a result, CH2M HILL assumes that only 5 to 10 percent of a household's current demand can realistically be reduced via these measures.

While maximum water savings could be significantly higher, we have used 25 percent as a reasonable estimate of water savings. Other sources estimate that efficiency measures could save 15 to 50 percent of a household's consumption (Seckler, 1996). Low-flow toilets alone can reduce water demand by 7 to 15 percent.[25] The use of water displacement devices (such as placing sand-filled containers in the toilet tank) in consort with traditional toilets can save roughly the same amount with nearly no capital investment. Low-flow showerheads can reduce demand by roughly 5 to 15 percent.[26]

We have used CH2M HILL's cost estimates. CH2M HILL estimates that the capital investment necessary to purchase faucet aerators, showerheads, and low-flush toilets range between $168 and $320. These fixtures, assumed to have a lifetime of ten years, will cost roughly $0.15/CM. The yearly operation and maintenance expenditures are estimated to be $30, or $0.11/CM over ten years. These cost estimates are for a household consumption of 787 CM/yr, and estimated savings is 349 CM/yr; a house consuming only 577 CM/yr will have higher costs—$0.20/CM in capital costs and $0.16/CM in operation and maintenance costs.

Domestic Graywater Reuse. Estimates of household water reuse for toilets, domestic irrigation, and washing range from 30 to 80 percent of household consumption (Libhaber, 2003; Faruqui, 2002; Pottinger, 2003). For our analysis, we assume a conservative value of 40 percent. The cost of treating graywater onsite for 20 to 200 people is roughly $50 per capita plus $20–$35 for annual capital and operating expenditures (Al-Sa'ed, 2000). Our model, however, assumes the reuse of untreated graywater for irrigation and toilet water. One case study of wastewater reuse in domestic agriculture in Jordan estimated the average capital cost of graywater systems to be $113. Costs of individual systems ranged from $45 to $229, depending on the system's complexity (Faruqui and Al-Jayyousi, 2002). We assume higher capital costs of $300 to cover any required minor plumbing modifications and small filter needs.[27] We assume annual operation and maintenance costs to be 10 percent of this investment.

---

[25] Since toilet water accounts for 20 to 30 percent of household water use (personal communication with Naser I. Faruqui, April 1, 2003) and low-flow toilets use 33–50 percent of a standard toilet (National Research Council, 1999), low-flow toilets alone can reduce household water consumption by 7–15 percent. Dry toilets, although not estimated in our model, could increase this conservation to 20–30 percent of a household's daily consumption.

[26] Low-flow showerheads save 7.5 liters per minute. Assuming only two 2.5-minute showers per day for a household of seven would equal an annual water savings of 13,700 liters, or 13.7 CM, of annual household use. This is equal to over 5 percent of the water demand of a household of seven consuming 700 l/d. Similarly, if there were 14 minutes of showering daily, low-flow showerheads would reduce water demand by 15 percent.

[27] Personal communication with Naser I. Faruqui, April 1, 2003.

New Supplies

Rainwater Harvesting. CH2M HILL (2002a) estimates that 70,000 cisterns, with an average volume of 70 CM each, account for about 5 MCM of the Palestinians' current consumption. CH2M HILL estimates the upper limit for annual usable rainwater to be about 12 MCM/yr if the collection area for rainwater harvesting were increased to 20 percent of the built-up area. This estimate assumes that the cisterns in this portion of the built-up area each yields 140 CM/yr. The capital cost associated with this collection is estimated to be $0.70/CM of water (or $17/CM of developed capacity),[28] and the operation and maintenance costs are assumed to be $0.21/CM. CH2M HILL estimates that rainfall harvesting could expand at a rate of 0.2 MCM/yr until 2005 and at a rate of 0.6 MCM/yr thereafter.

Our estimate assumes a much larger portion of households will use rainwater capture, but that the yield of the capture systems will be lower. Instead of basing collection area on agglomerated areas as CH2M HILL's analysis did, we estimate rainfall harvest potential based on the total number of households and the percentage of households utilizing cisterns. Following the estimates of the UNEP (2001) and the National Research Council (1999), we assume that each cistern yields 70 CM/yr on average. We estimate the total rainwater supply as the product of the estimated number of households and this average capacity. For the West Bank and Gaza, the number of households is the forecasted total population divided by 6.5 and 7, respectively. For our high-efficiency scenario, we assume that 70 percent of households adopt cisterns by 2015. This results in 23 MCM/yr of new supply from rainwater harvesting in the West Bank.

UNEP (2001) has a detailed analysis of cistern use that estimates lower construction costs than those estimated by CH2M HILL. We have utilized the upper end of the UNEP range of $11–$15 per CM of developed capacity for the initial construction costs and have retained CH2M HILL's estimates of operation and maintenance costs, although we believe these represent the upper range of these costs. Because we estimate a lower yield from each cistern, the costs per CM of water are higher: The capital cost associated with this collection is estimated to be $0.98/CM of water, and the operation and maintenance costs are estimated to be $0.43/CM.

Wastewater Reuse. While none of the currently treated effluent is currently reused, CH2M HILL estimates that 25 percent of the 9.2 MCM currently treated can be reused in agriculture by 2005. It assumes that treatment capacity can increase up to 3 MCM/yr and that land availability and public acceptance will limit reuse to 50 percent of treated capacity in 2025, or 37.5 MCM/yr. The capital costs associated with treatment are estimated to be $1.09/CM, accounting for the purchase of 300 dunums (a dunum is about one-tenth of a hectare) at $7,000/dunum; the associated operation and maintenance costs are estimated to be $148 million, or $0.76/CM over ten years.

---

[28] In other words, a rainwater capture system with 70 CM of capacity would cost about $1,200.

As a result of projections that reuse can become more acceptable to the public (Faruqui, Biswas, and Bino, 2001), our model is optimistic relative to CH2M HILL's assumptions discussed above. We included less conservative estimates of the amount of water that can be reused, based on CH2M HILL's upper-end estimates: We project that about 80 percent of the municipal and industrial demand (after UFW is accounted for) could be reused.

Because all wastewater will be treated regardless of whether it is reused, we attribute only the costs of reuse facilities (conveyance systems, storage reservoirs, and distribution systems) as costs of reuse. As a result, the capital costs are $0.14/CM and the operating and maintenance costs are $0.04/CM. If salinization of soils is deemed a significant problem, additional treatment costs will be incurred. Furthermore, if treatment facilities are not constructed reasonably close to agricultural areas, conveyance costs will increase.

Desalination. CH2M HILL estimates that a reverse osmosis plant desalinating 55 MCM of brackish water [10 grams per liter (g/l) salinity] annually (primarily from the Mountain Aquifers) will cost about $0.23/CM in capital costs and $0.59/CM in operation and maintenance costs over 30 years. A similar plant desalinating seawater (41 g/l salinity) is estimated to have the same capital costs and increased operating and maintenance costs—$0.97/CM. Other sources estimate that desalinating up to 1 billion CM of seawater by reverse osmosis would cost $0.55/CM to $0.65/CM (Abraham, Owens, and Brunsdale, 1999; UNESCO, 2001; Just, 1999) annually, including capital and operation.

Storm Water Capture. Our model uses CH2M HILL's baseline estimates of available storm water runoff: 15 MCM of storm water runoff from the wadis could be available in 2015 at $0.49/CM for capital costs and $0.02/CM in operation and maintenance costs. Only wadis with flows over 4 MCM/yr in the Jordan Valley and over 10 MCM/yr for those flowing into the Mediterranean were considered potential sources for storm water capture.

Water Network
Rectifying the lack of water and wastewater infrastructure, while necessary, will require significant investments.

Extending Centralized Supply. While connecting the entire population to the water network would be ideal, rural areas are difficult to serve; thus, CH2M HILL assumed a final connection status of 90 percent. The capital cost of attaining this 90 percent connection level and building a national water carrier is estimated at $109 million or $0.28/CM. Of this, $0.17/CM is the cost of components of the distribution network, such as pipes, fittings, valves, main transmissions, pumps, booster stations (a total of about $2.8 million), and a reservoir ($1.3 million). The remaining $0.11/CM is the cost of a national water conveyance system—about $13.2 million per year over 30 years. The operation and maintenance cost is estimated to be $324 million, of which

$0.02/CM is estimated to be upkeep on the distribution network and $0.34/CM to $0.57/CM (depending on quantity of water distributed) is estimated for operation of a national water conveyance system.

We have assumed that an expanded network will reach 90 percent of the population. The high operational costs of the national conveyance system are attributed to the energy required for pumping. We have additionally assumed that a national conveyance system (over and above the expanded network) is necessary only to distribute a major new supply, such as the output of a large desalination facility.

System Efficiency Improvements. CH2M HILL estimates that 45 to 60 percent of current supply is from UFW. It estimates that leaks—or physical losses—account for a 40 percent loss (the majority of the observed UFW). Based on UFW rates in the United States, CH2M HILL's model reduced this UFW to 15–20 percent of gross supply, adding an additional usable water quantity of 1.3 MCM/yr. The costs to reduce leaks are $0.33/CM for capital investments—amortized over ten years, including flow measurement and control devices. Of the $3,280,000 estimated for capital costs, 91 percent was estimated for physical improvements; water meter testing, acoustic survey, system layout preparation, hydraulic analysis of the system, and a pilot study each accounted for less than 2 percent of the capital cost, and field survey and site measurements accounted for roughly 3 percent. The operation and maintenance costs were figured as 5 percent of capital investment, and came to $0.13/CM.

We have used the costs as delineated by CH2M HILL. Actual costs, however, are likely to be substantially different. We have, however, varied the amount of UFW remaining to a minimum of 7.5 percent after targeting leak reduction, water meter errors, and detection of unmetered connections (Djerrari, 2003; Tonner, 2003). This projection is optimistic compared with CH2M HILL's analysis but can be achieved. Adequate investment to fix infrastructure problems will drastically reduce leaks, and legal connections for all will drastically reduce illegal use. Water meter errors can be targeted by introducing pressure management modules and changing to volumetric water meters (Nablus Municipality, 2003). Some estimates of the portion of UFW attributable to unmetered connections and illegal use are as high as 55 percent (Nablus Municipality, 2003).

Wastewater Treatment. CH2M HILL estimates that treated wastewater in 2001 totaled 9.2 MCM/yr, or roughly one-quarter of the 35.7 MCM of wastewater produced. By 2025, however, wastewater generation is projected to be about 215 MCM/yr, of which CH2M HILL projects only 75 MCM/yr will be treated. The projected total volume generated is based on the projected supply in 2025 minus the remaining UFW, or 85 percent of the supply. Based on its projection of wastewater generated and treated, CH2M HILL estimates the costs of treating 34.6 MCM/yr to be $33 million for capital costs, such as wastewater conveyance lines, pumping stations, and force mains (but excluding treatment plant costs). Costs to clean blocked lines, replace and repair old lines, and maintain pump stations are estimated at $148 million.

Other cost estimates in the literature are similar to those estimated by CH2M HILL. Secondary-level treatment is estimated to cost $0.5/CM (Faruqui, 2002). The costs reported by CH2M HILL of providing centralized sewer systems, based on a Hebron regional plant, are similar in magnitude to those reported for a Nablus-West Wastewater Treatment Plant (Nablus Municipality, 2003). Because we estimate a more ambitious extension of the wastewater treatment systems to ensure no raw wastewater discharge, we include estimates of septic systems in addition to CH2M HILL's estimates of centralized treatment. To reach households where density is relatively low, on-site and cluster septic systems are likely to be more cost-effective than the centralized approach (North Carolina State University, 1998; EPA, 1997). Capital, operation, and maintenance costs amortized over 20 years can be as high as $50/yr for such systems (North Carolina State University, 1998). Our model estimates that ensuring there is zero raw wastewater discharge for the remaining 15 percent will cost $300 per household including both capital and annual operation and maintenance costs (Al-Sa'ed, 2000; UNEP, 2001). These costs account for the installation of small-diameter gravity sewers and a low-cost anaerobic treatment technology for groups of three homes.

Bibliography

Abraham, S. Daniel, Wayne Owens, and Kenley Brunsdale, *Solving the Problem of Fresh Water Scarcity in Israel, Jordan, Gaza and the West Bank,* Washington, D.C.: Center for Middle East Peace and Economic Cooperation, 1999.

Al-Sa'ed, Rashid, "Wastewater Management for Small Communities in Palestine," Technical Expert Consultation on Appropriate and Innovative Wastewater Management for Small Communities in EMR Countries, WHO conference, Amman, Jordan, November 6–9, 2000.

Applied Research Institute Jerusalem (ARIJ), *Environmental Profiles for the West Bank*, Jerusalem: Applied Research Institute, 1995.

———, *Environmental Profiles for the West Bank*, Jerusalem: Applied Research Institute, 1996.

Atwan, Nawal, Mazen Awais, Peter Boger, Richard Just, Manan Shah, Aliya Shariff, and Mara Zusman, *Allocations of Water and Responsibilities in an Israeli-Palestinian Water Accord*, Princeton, N.J.: Woodrow Wilson School, 1999.

Bellisari, Anna, "Public Health and the Water Crisis in the Occupied Palestinian Territories," *Journal of Palestine Studies*, Vol. 23, No. 2, 1994, pp. 52–63.

CH2M HILL, *Forecasting Assumptions for Water Demand in the West Bank*, draft, CH2M HILL, 2001.

———, Draft West Bank Integrated Water Resources Management Plan, CH2M HILL, 2002a.

————, West Bank Water Management Analysis Tool (V20-CLE_Simplified4), CH2M HILL, 2002b.

Djerrari, Fouad, *Best Practice in Urban Water Resource Management: Contribution of LYDEC in Casablanca*, paper presented at The World Bank Water Week 2003 "Water and Development," Unaccounted for Water Reduction Session, in Washington, D.C., March 4–6, 2003.

Energy Information Administration (EIA), *International Energy Outlook 2003*, Washington, D.C.: Energy Information Agency, 2003a.

————, *Israel: Country Analysis Brief*, Washington, D.C.: Energy Information Agency, 2003b. Online at http://www.eia.doe.gov/emeu/cabs/israel.html (as of May 2003).

Engelman, R., and P. LeRoy, *Sustaining Water: An Update*, Washington, D.C.: Population Action International, Population and Environment Program, 1997.

Environmental Protection Agency (EPA), *Response to Congress on Use of Decentralized Wastewater Treatment Systems*, Washington, D.C.: Environmental Protection Agency, Office of Water, 1997.

EXACT, *Temporal Trends for Water-Resources in Areas of Israeli, Jordanian and Palestinian Interest*, Reston, Va.: U.S. Geological Service, Executive Action Team, 2003. Online at http://exact-me.org/trends (as of May 2003).

Falkenmark, Malin, and Carl Widstrand, "Population and Water Resources: A Delicate Balance," in *Population Bulletin*, Washington, D.C.: Population Reference Bureau, 1992.

Faruqui, Naser I., "Wastewater Treatment and Reuse for Food and Water Security," *UA-Magazine*, Ottawa, Canada: International Development Research Centre, 2002.

Faruqui, Naser I., and Odeh Al-Jayyousi, "Greywater Reuse in Urban Agriculture for Poverty Alleviation: A Case-Study in Jordan," *Water International*, Vol. 27, No. 3, 2002, pp. 387–394.

Faruqui, Naser I., Asit K. Biswas, and Murad J. Bino, eds., *Water Management in Islam*, Tokyo, Japan: United Nations University Press, 2001.

Gardner-Outlaw, Tom, and Robert Engelman, *Sustaining Water, Easing Scarcity: A Second Update*, Washington, D.C.: Population Action International, 1997.

Howard, Guy, and Jamie Bartram, *Domestic Water Quantity, Service Level and Health*, Geneva, Switzerland: World Health Organization, 2003.

Hunt, Steven, *Catching Rooftop Rainwater in Gaza*, Ottawa, Canada: International Development Research Centre, 2001. Online at http://www.idrc.ca/reports/prn_report.cfm?article_num=294 (as of May 2003).

Isaac, Jad, *Water and Palestinian-Israeli Peace Negotiations*, Washington, D.C.: Center for Policy Analysis on Palestine, The Jerusalem Fund for Education and Community Development, August 19, 1999. Online at www.palestinecenter.org/cpap/pubs/19990819pb.html (as of April 1, 2003).

Juanicó, *Wastewater Reuse in Irrigation (Reclaimed Water Reuse): A Proposal from the Academy or a Marked Reality?* Ram On, Israel: Juanicó—Environmental Consultants Ltd., 2002. Online at http://www.juanico.co.il/Main%20frame%20-%20English/Issues/Wastewater%20reuse. htm (as of June 19, 2003).

Just, Richard, *Water Rights in the Jordan Valley*, Princeton, N.J.: Princeton University, Woodrow Wilson School of Public and International Affairs, 1999. Online at http://www.wws. princeton.edu/~wws401c/richard.pdf (as of May 2003).

Lein, Yehezkel, *Not Even a Drop: The Water Crisis in Palestinian Villages Without a Water Network*, Jerusalem: B'Tselem—The Israel Information Center for Human Rights in the Occupied Territories, 2001. Online at http://www.btselem.org/Download/Not_Even_A_Drop-2001.doc (as of May 2003).

Libhaber, Manahem, *Wastewater Reuse for Irrigation, the Stabilization Reservoirs Concept*, paper presented at The World Bank Water Week 2003 "Water and Development" in Washington, D.C., March 4–6, 2003.

Mediterranean Environmental Technical Assistance Program (METAP), *Water Quality Management Country Report—West Bank & Gaza*, Washington, D.C.: Mediterranean Environmental Technical Assistance Program, 2001.

Nablus Municipality, *Water and Waste Water: Nablus Water Project: A Continuing Mission*, 2003. Online at www.nablus.org/structure/water2.html (as of February 17, 2003).

Naji, Fawzy, *Water Crisis in Palestine—Scenarios for Solutions*, paper presented at Palestinian Academic Society for the Study of International Affairs, Jerusalem, February 4, 1999.

National Research Council, *Water for the Future: The West Bank and Gaza Strip, Israel and Jordan*, Washington, D.C.: National Academy Press, 1999.

North Carolina State University, *Choices for Communities: Wastewater Management Options for Rural Areas*, Raleigh, N.C.: College of Agriculture and Life Sciences, Waste Management Programs, 1998. Online at http://plymouth.ces.state.nc.us/septic/98hoover.html (as of February 2003).

Palestinian Academic Society for the Study of International Affairs (PASSIA), *Water: The Blue Gold of the Middle East*, Jerusalem: PASSIA, 2002.

———, *Fact Sheet—Water & Environment*, Jerusalem: PASSIA, 2003. Online at http://www. passia.org/palestine_facts/pdf/pdf2003/sections2/7-Water.pdf (as of July 2003).

Palestinian Central Bureau of Statistics (PCBS), *Population Statistics*, Ramallah: PCBS, 2003a. Online at http://www.pcbs.org/inside/selcts.htm (as of May 2003).

———, *Selected Agricultural Statistics*, Ramallah: PCBS, 2003b. Online at http://www.pcbs. org/inside/selcts.htm (as of May 2003).

———, *Selected Water Statistics*, Ramallah: PCBS, 2003c. Online at http://www.pcbs.org/ inside/selcts.htm (as of May 2003).

Palestinian Hydrology Group (PHG), *Water and Sanitation Hygiene Monitoring Project*, Ramallah: PHG, 2003. Online at http://www.phg.org/campaign/about/about.html (as of March 2003).

Pottinger, Lori, "River Keepers Handbook: A Guide to Protecting Rivers and Catchments in Southern Africa," as excerpted in *New Approaches to Water Supply*, Surrey, UK: International

Rivers Network, 2003. Online at www.thewaterpage.com/river_keepers.htm (as of February 2003).

Saghir, Jamal, Manuel Schiffler, and Mathewos Woldu, *Urban Water and Sanitation in the Middle East and North Africa Region: The Way Forward,* Washington, D.C.: The World Bank, 2000.

Seckler, David, *The New Era of Water Resources Management: From "Dry" to "Wet" Water Savings,* Colombo, Sri Lanka: International Irrigation Management Institute, 1996.

Shelef, Gedaliah, *Wastewater Treatment, Reclamation and Reuse in Israel,* Ramat-Gan, Israel: Bar-Ilan University, undated. Online at http://www.biu.ac.il/SOC/besa/waterarticle3.html (as of June 19, 2003).

Tonner, John, *Desalination Trends,* paper presented at The World Bank Water Week 2003 "Water and Development" in Washington, D.C., March 4–6, 2003.

Tubail, Khalil M., Jamal Y. Al-Dadah, and Maged M. Yassin, *Present and Prospect Situation of Wastewater and Its Possible Reuse in the Gaza Strip,* Amman: MedAqua, undated. Online at http://www.med-reunet.com/docs_upload/wastewater.pdf (as of May 2004).

United Nations Development Programme, *FOCUS,* New York, N.Y.: UNDP, 2002.

United Nations Educational, Scientific, and Cultural Organization (UNESCO), *If Common Sense Prevails,* Paris: UNESCO, 2001. Online at http://www.unesco.org/courier/2001_10/uk/doss04.htm (as of April 2003).

United Nations Environmental Programme (UNEP), *Sourcebook of Alternative Technologies for Freshwater Augmentation in West Asia,* Osaka/Shiga, Japan: UNEP, Division of Technology, Industry and Economics, International Environmental Technology Centre, 2001.

U.S. Consulate General in Jerusalem, *USAID and Palestinian Authority Agree to Major New Water Projects in Gaza,* U.S. Consulate General in Jerusalem, 2002. Online at http://www.uscongen-jerusalem.org/DOCS/PressReleases/PRUSAID040402.html (as of May 28, 2003).

World Resources Institute, UN Development Programme, UN Environmental Programme, and The World Bank, *1998–99 World Resources: A Guide to the Global Environment,* New York: Oxford University Press, 1998.

Zahra, Bader Ali Ahmad Abu, "Water Crisis in Palestine," *Desalination,* Vol. 136, 2000, pp. 93–99.

CHAPTER SEVEN

Health

Michael Schoenbaum, Adel K. Afifi, and Richard J. Deckelbaum

Summary

This chapter examines potential strategies for strengthening the Palestinian health system. We focus particularly on major institutions that would be essential for the success of the health system over the first decade of a future independent Palestinian state. In addition, we recommend several programs for preventive and curative care that are urgently needed and that could be implemented in the short term, with the goal of rapidly improving the health status and health care services of Palestinians.

The health system of a future Palestinian state starts with many strengths. These include a relatively healthy population; a high societal value placed on health; many highly qualified, experienced, and motivated health professionals, including clinicians, planners, administrators, technicians, researchers, and public health workers; national plans for health system development; and a strong base of governmental and nongovernmental institutions.

At the same time, there are important areas of concern. These include poor system-wide coordination and implementation of policies and programs across geographic areas and between the governmental and nongovernmental sectors of the health system; many underqualified health care providers; weak systems for licensing and continuing education; and considerable deficits in the operating budgets of the Palestinian Ministry of Health and the government health insurance system (the principal source of health insurance). There are also important and persistent health problems, including gastroenteric and parasitic diseases, hepatitis A, respiratory infections, and meningitis; high—and rising—rates of malnutrition; and rising rates of chronic disease. Also, access to health care has declined, along with social and economic conditions, since the start of the second intifada in 2000.

We are grateful to Timea Spitka, who served as our project coordinator in Jerusalem; Nicole Lurie and C. Ross Anthony, who served as senior advisors; Meredith L. Magner, who provided research assistance; and Mechelle Wilkins, who provided administrative support. We would not have been able to conduct this work without them. We are also grateful for input and helpful comments on this chapter from Osman Galal, Shimon Glick, Laurie Brand, Ami Wennar, and several Palestinian and Israeli colleagues (who are not named here for reasons of confidentiality).

This chapter describes a number of ways to strengthen the Palestinian health system, to help achieve specific health targets and financial sustainability. Our principal recommendations are as follows:

- Integrate health system planning and policy development more closely, with meaningful input from all relevant governmental and nongovernmental stakeholders.
- Develop viable and sustainable health insurance and health care financing systems.
- Update, standardize, and enforce licensing standards for all types of health care professionals.
- Update, standardize, and enforce standards for licensing and accrediting health care facilities and services.
- Improve training of health professionals, including academic and vocational training programs that are internationally accredited, and implement comprehensive and ongoing programs for continuing medical education.
- Implement a national strategy on health care quality improvement. Systematically evaluate quality improvement projects; disseminate those that succeed.
- Develop and enforce national standards for the licensing, supply, and distribution of pharmaceuticals and medical devices.
- Improve health information systems for tracking data such as health and nutritional status, use and costs of inpatient and outpatient care, health care quality, health system staffing, pharmaceutical inventories, health insurance enrollment, and medical records.
- Improve research and evaluation capacity, including public health, clinical, and biomedical research.
- Improve public and primary health care programs, including an updated immunization program, comprehensive micronutrient fortification and supplementation, prevention and treatment of chronic and noninfectious disease, and treatment of developmental and psychosocial conditions.

While all of these recommendations are important, we suggest that immediate priority be given to the first (improving system-wide coordination and implementation) and the last (improving public and primary health care programs).

In practice, the appropriate strategies for addressing these issues will depend on many factors that are currently unknown, including the borders of a future Palestinian state, its security arrangements and relations with its neighbors, its governance structure, and economic conditions. We therefore discuss policy alternatives applicable to several possible scenarios.

We believe that local stakeholders can and should determine both the overall development process and the details of the health system, particularly given the expertise that already exists in Palestine and among Palestinians living abroad. At the same time, we recognize that successful health system development in Palestine will require considerable outside resources, including technical and financial assistance. We estimate that the Palestinian health system would require between $125 million and $160 million per year in external support over the first decade of an independent state. For comparison, external support for the Palestinian health system averaged around $40 million per year over the period 1994–2000.

Successful development of the Palestinian health system is worthwhile in its own right, and it may be a relatively cost-effective way to help demonstrate the tangible benefits of independence and peaceful relations with neighboring countries. Moreover, health system development is an area where Israel, other neighboring countries, and the larger international community could play a constructive role, especially in areas such as health system planning, licensing and accreditation, development of information systems, and research.

Introduction

Envisioning a successful Palestinian health system is a broad and challenging mandate. Therefore, we started by defining a scope of work that would be both feasible and useful—one that could provide constructive new information to Palestinian stakeholders and other interested parties. We decided to focus primarily on key "macro-level" programs and institutions that we consider to be prerequisites for developing, operating, and sustaining a successful national health system in Palestine. These include policies and programs covering health system planning and coordination across regions and stakeholders; licensing and accreditation of health professionals, facilities, and educational programs; human resource development; health insurance and health care financing programs; pharmaceutical policy; research and evaluation programs; health information systems; disease prevention and health promotion; and public health. We believe that responsibility for the "micro-level" details of health system organization, infrastructure, and operation properly rests with the local stakeholders, including the Palestinian Ministry of Health, the United Nations Relief and Works Agency for Palestinian Refugees in the Near East, relevant private and nongovernmental organizations, and, ultimately, Palestinian consumers who use health care services.

To date, Palestinian stakeholders have produced two detailed national health plans, the first in 1994, published by the Palestinian Council of Health (1994), the second in 1999, published by the Ministry of Health (PA MOH, 1999). These two plans had similar structures, approaches, and goals. (Indeed, many of the goals of the first were repeated in the second because they had not been fully achieved.) The 1999 plan covered the period 1999–2003 and is currently being updated. These national health plans were complemented by the *National Plan for Human Resource Development and Education in Health,* completed in 2001 by the Ministry of Health, the Ministry of Higher

Education (now the Ministry of Education and Higher Education), and the Welfare Association (Welfare Association, PA, and Ministry of Higher Education, 2001a–f).[1] In part, these plans address system-wide development issues for Palestine, and we drew on this information extensively for our analyses. The national health plans also provide micro-level targets in many areas; e.g., the number, type, and geographic distribution of primary care clinics and different types of health care providers. Sample objectives from the 1999 national strategic health plan and the 2001 national plan for human resource development are included in Appendix 7.A of this chapter.

Although we regard the micro-level targets as generally appropriate, it is beyond the scope of this project to affirm their validity. Similarly, we did not perform detailed assessments of prevailing standards of care or quality of care, conduct salary surveys for health care workers in the government sector, assess the suitability of various pilot systems or programs as national models, or conduct similar analyses of particular health system details.

The health system of a future Palestinian state starts with many strengths. These include a relatively healthy population, compared with other countries in the region with similar levels of economic development; many highly qualified, experienced, and motivated health professionals, including clinicians, planners, administrators, technicians, researchers, and public health workers; and a strong base of local institutions. At the same time, there are a number of opportunities to strengthen the Palestinian health system to achieve specific health targets and financial sustainability over time.

Successful development of the Palestinian health system is worthwhile in its own right. It may also be a relatively cost-effective way to help demonstrate tangible benefits of peace. Historically, the health sector has benefited from considerable and ongoing cooperation between Palestinian and Israeli institutions and individuals, in areas such as policy formation and human resource development. Despite the current tensions in the region, we found high levels of support on both sides for continuing and strengthening such cooperation as circumstances permit. If done with appropriate sensitivity to local needs and preferences, and with respect for the extensive infrastructure of Palestinian institutions that is already in place, health system development could also be an area where outside parties—including the United States—could play a constructive role. On the other hand, the social and political costs of neglecting health system development may be significant, particularly given Palestinians' high expectations regarding health and health care.[2]

In the following sections of this chapter, we discuss the goals of a successful Palestinian health system. We describe our methods for conducting the health system analysis and provide brief background information on health and health care in the

---

[1] One of the authors of this chapter, Adel Afifi, was overall project coordinator for the development of the *National Plan for Human Resource Development and Education in Health*.

[2] One factor affecting these expectations is Palestinians' proximity to and experience with the Israeli health system.

West Bank and Gaza. The remainder of the chapter presents specific recommendations for strengthening (and, in some cases, establishing) institutions and programs to promote the current and future success of the Palestinian health system. We conclude with a discussion of costs—the investment that will most likely be required to sustain a successful Palestinian health care system in the first decade of independence.

For ease of exposition, we refer to the West Bank and Gaza as "Palestine." When we discuss Jerusalem, we refer to it explicitly. We refer to the Ministry of Health of the Palestinian Authority as "the Ministry of Health," abbreviated as MOH. We use "the Palestinian government" to refer generically to the current and future governments of Palestine; when we mean the Palestinian Authority, abbreviated as PA, we refer to it explicitly. We abbreviate the United Nations Relief and Works Agency for Palestinian Refugees in the Near East as UNRWA.

In our discussion, we refer frequently to primary, secondary, and tertiary health care. Primary care refers to basic health care that is traditionally provided by physicians trained in family practice, internal medicine, or pediatrics, or by nonphysician providers such as nurses. Secondary care refers to care provided by specialty providers (e.g., urologists and cardiologists) who generally do not have first contact with patients; these providers usually see patients after referral from a primary or community health professional. Tertiary care refers to care provided by highly specialized providers (e.g., neurologists, cardiac surgeons, and intensive care units) in facilities equipped for special investigation and treatment.

All monetary figures are in nominal U.S. dollars (i.e., dollars that are not adjusted for inflation), unless otherwise noted.

What Is a Successful Health System?

A "successful" Palestinian health system should, at a minimum,

- maintain an effective and well-regulated public health system
- provide reasonable access to high-quality preventive and curative services for all Palestinians
- maintain high-quality programs for training health professionals
- achieve health outcomes at the population level that meet or exceed international guidelines, such as those recommended by the World Health Organization (WHO)
- be effective, efficient, and financially viable
- contribute to peace and encompass the possibility of cooperation with neighboring countries on issues of common interest.

There are many ways to achieve these broad goals, ranging from incremental reform to radical redesign. The two national health plans (1994 and 1999) and the

National Plan for Human Resource Development and Education in Health (2001) articulate a vision of how the health system should develop over time, based mainly on incremental rather than radical change. This vision emphasizes public and primary health care as the "cornerstone" of service delivery, with expanded emphasis on health promotion and disease prevention capabilities. The public and primary care systems would be complemented by high-quality secondary and tertiary care systems, but these systems would be developed very carefully, and in a coordinated fashion, to ensure both clinical efficacy and economic efficiency.

In our view, this general vision conforms to the economic realities facing Palestine and to the available evidence from other settings regarding cost-effective health system development. We therefore adopted a similar focus on incremental reforms. In particular, we assume that the government will continue to be responsible for public health; a major provider of health care services; and a major, if not the primary, sponsor of health insurance over at least the first decade of an independent state.[3]

Alternative Scenarios for an Independent State

Our mandate is to describe strategies for strengthening the Palestinian health system to support the success of a future independent Palestinian state. However, the essential characteristics of the future state are currently unknown. In practice, characteristics such as the state's borders, security arrangements, and relations with its neighbors will significantly affect health system development. For this analysis, we therefore consider several possible scenarios for the characteristics of a future state, and we discuss how our policy recommendations might change for each scenario.

Population Mobility

Over the last several years, travel by Palestinians within the West Bank, between the West Bank and Gaza, and to East Jerusalem has frequently been restricted, particularly since the start of the second intifada in September 2000 and with the construction of Israel's separation barrier. Lack of mobility—for people and supplies—has limited patient and provider access to health care facilities, limited the collection of epidemiological and other health-related data, and been associated with declines in nutritional status, among other effects. The geographic closures have been sufficiently long-lasting that all stakeholders in the health system have taken active steps to minimize the short-term consequences, for instance by building new local treatment facilities

---

[3] In interviews with Palestinian stakeholders conducted as part of this analysis, some people expressed support for a transfer of the government's current health care delivery systems and health insurance programs to nongovernmental organizations (NGOs) or the private sector, which would leave the MOH responsible for planning, regulation, public health, provision for the indigent, and other functions for which the private sector is not well suited. Our recommendations do not foreclose such options. However, we think that these decisions must be made locally.

to help meet the acute needs of patients who would have traveled for care under less restrictive conditions.[4]

For purposes of the future health system, the relevant issue is the degree of population mobility that will be possible within a future Palestinian state. We consider two possible scenarios:

- *Unrestricted Domestic Mobility.* This scenario assumes free movement within the West Bank and within Gaza in a future independent Palestinian state. In general, it also assumes that patients would be able to travel between the West Bank and Gaza. Because these areas are relatively distant from each other, primary and secondary care would probably be handled within each area; travel to another area would become important if the patient is referred to a tertiary care center. Similarly, although the status of East Jerusalem is uncertain, we assume that Palestinians will have relatively open access to health care facilities in East Jerusalem.
- *Restricted Domestic Mobility.* This scenario assumes that movement within and between the territories of a future Palestinian state will be restricted (or, in the extreme case, prevented). Various factors could limit mobility, including the degree of territorial contiguity and Palestinian and Israeli security policies. Except as noted, health system development strategies do not depend on the specific cause of mobility restrictions, only on their scope and duration.

In practice, we regard free movement of patients, health professionals, and supplies within Palestine as prerequisites for successful health system development and operation. Restricted mobility would perpetuate and magnify the problems of staffing, supply, and patient access that have prevailed in the Palestinian health system during the second intifada. Moreover, strategies to mitigate these problems would be clinically and economically inefficient, relative to development under free mobility, particularly because the problems inhibit the development and operation of regional referral centers.

As a result, we consider unrestricted domestic mobility to be the default scenario for our analyses. However, at the end of each substantive subsection, we discuss how our recommendations would change under conditions of restricted mobility.

International Access[5]

The extent to which travel is restricted between an independent Palestinian state and other countries, particularly Israel and Jordan, may also significantly affect the future health system. We consider two possible scenarios:

---

[4] There has also been some damage to relevant infrastructure, particularly in conjunction with Israeli military operations in the West Bank during and after March 2002.

[5] Here, "access" refers to the right to travel to and stay in foreign countries, rather than insurance coverage or other factors that affect whether foreign institutions will accept Palestinian patients. As with domestic mobility, international access is likely to be contingent on successful security arrangements.

- *Unrestricted Access.* This scenario assumes that Palestinians face no categorical restrictions on travel to Israel, Jordan, or elsewhere for purposes of receiving health care or for professional training.
- *Restricted Access.* This scenario assumes that access for Palestinians to Israel, Jordan, and elsewhere for purposes of receiving health care or professional training is significantly restricted.

Unrestricted access is clearly preferable for health system development, because it provides additional options for meeting clinical and educational needs. As a result, we consider unrestricted access to be the default scenario for our analyses. However, at the end of each substantive subsection, we discuss how our recommendations would change under conditions of restricted international access.

Other Crosscutting Issues

Other characteristics of a future independent state will also affect health system development in important ways. For instance, any successful health system development depends on effective governance. This extends to all branches of government—i.e., the executive, legislative, and judicial branches. Effective development will also require meaningful inclusion of nongovernmental stakeholders in health system planning, policymaking, and policy implementation. Detailed consideration of Palestinian governance is provided in Chapter Two.

Successful security arrangements between Israel and Palestine are crucial to the successful development of Palestinian institutions. Continued conflict between the two states would, among other consequences, reduce the willingness of international donors to commit staff, money, and other resources to support health system projects; reduce the supply of private capital available for health system development from both local and international sources; encourage emigration of skilled and educated health professionals; and constrain public and private budgets.

Any successful health system development is also contingent on the financial resources available. As we discuss in detail below, a Palestinian health system that can truly be viewed as "successful" along the lines envisioned by our mandate will require considerable outside investment over at least the first decade of independence. The amount of outside resources and the period of time for which they are required depend on the performance of the Palestinian economy. Improved economic conditions will increase the level of both public and private resources available locally. Improved economic and social conditions are also associated with improved population health outcomes, independent of health care use. A detailed consideration of Palestinian economic development is provided in Chapter Five.

For ease of exposition, we do not define specific scenarios for these additional characteristics. However, we considered them in all our analyses and discuss their effects on our recommendations, as appropriate.

Methods

This chapter presents independent analyses conducted by the authors. Information about the Palestinian health system came from published and unpublished analyses by government organizations (e.g., the Palestinian and Israeli Ministries of Health), reports by international organizations (e.g., World Bank, various United Nations agencies, and the WHO), reports by Palestinian and international nongovernmental organizations (NGOs), papers in scientific journals, conference proceedings, working papers, and other formats. We did not collect new quantitative data.

We interviewed many Palestinian, Israeli, and international stakeholders who were experienced with and knowledgeable about, and in many cases have or had responsibility for, important aspects of the Palestinian health system. Interviews were primarily conducted in person during a trip to Palestine and Israel in May 2003. We asked all interview participants to allow themselves to be identified in this book. However, to help ensure that people felt free to express their views fully, interview participants were assured that no comments would be quoted directly or attributed to them in an identifiable way.

Study methods are described in further detail in Appendix 7.B of this chapter, which also includes an alphabetical list of interview participants. The letter of introduction we sent to local stakeholders is included in Appendix 7.C.

As we began this project, we learned that the European Union was sponsoring a comprehensive health sector review on behalf of the Palestinian MOH. That review aims to analyze major areas of the health sector, to assess the constraints resulting from the intifada, and to suggest the elements for a refocused midterm health development strategy. Additional information about that review is included in Appendix 7.D.

Background

This section provides a brief overview of health and health care in Palestine. The information was drawn from a variety of sources, particularly Barnea and Husseini (2002); the annual reports of the Ministry of Health (e.g., PA MOH, 2002a); the first and second Palestinian national health plans (see PA MOH, 1999; Welfare Association, PA, and Ministry of Higher Education, 2001a–f); Giacaman, Abdul-Rahim, and Wick (2003); the scientific literature; and data compiled at the Health Inforum web site (http://www.healthinforum.net/).[6] These and other references are provided in the bibliography.

We note that systematic collection of health data has been difficult since the start of the second intifada; we therefore report the most current information available to us at the time of this writing.

---

[6] Health Inforum describes itself as the "information body linked directly with the Core Group of the Health Sector Working Group." It was formed in 2001 through the collaboration of the World Health Organization, the Italian Cooperation, USAID, Maram, UNSCO, and UNDP.

Health Status

Life expectancy at birth in Palestine is about 70 years (as of 2000), higher than all neighboring countries except Israel. The infant mortality rate is approximately 23 per 1,000 live births, less than half the rate during the 1970s and comparable to or lower than rates in neighboring countries other than Israel (the Israeli rate is 6 per 1,000 live births). The maternal mortality rate was 19 per 100,000 births in 1998–1999, also down by more than half since 1980. The Palestinian maternal mortality rate is considerably better than those in Jordan, Iran, and Egypt, but some four times the Israeli and Kuwaiti rates (see Table 7.1).

Palestinian health indicators have improved significantly over time. Since the 1970s, standards of living and hygiene improved steadily, as did access to health care. For instance, the fraction of households with three or more people per room declined from 47 percent in 1975 to 28 percent in 1992 in the West Bank, and from 47 percent to 38 percent in Gaza. Similarly, by the mid-1990s, more than 90 percent of homes had electricity (up from around 25 percent in 1972–1975), and more than three-quarters of Palestinian households had access to clean, chlorinated drinking water (up from under one-quarter in 1972–1975). Access to primary health care services also improved significantly since 1970, as both the Israeli administration (before 1994) and the PA (from 1994 onward) expanded the number and geographic distribution of primary care and maternal and child health clinics.

Another factor contributing to lower infant mortality rates is the substantial expansion over time in the fraction of births occurring in a health facility or attended by a trained health professional: In 2001, 82 percent of Palestinian births occurred in a hospital, and 95 percent were attended by a health professional. The long-standing

Table 7.1
Basic Health Indicators, Palestine and Elsewhere (1998–1999)

	Life Expectancy at Birth (years)	Infant Mortality Rate (per 1,000 live births)	Mortality Rate for Children Under Age 5 (per 1,000 live births)	Maternal Mortality Rate (per 100,000 live births)
Palestine	70	23	28	19
Israel	78	6	6	5
Jordan	68	30	36	41
Egypt	67	51	69	170
Kuwait	68	12	13	5
Qatar	72	15	18	10
Iran	69	29	33	37
Yemen	58	87	121	350
United States	77	7	8	8
France	78	5	5	10

SOURCES: United Nations Children's Fund, 2000; PA MOH, 2002a.

strength of the Palestinian immunization program also played an important role in improving child health. Immunization rates among children for the major vaccine-preventable diseases (e.g., polio, measles, mumps, rubella, diphtheria, tetanus, pertussis, and most recently hepatitis B) have exceeded 95 percent since the mid-1980s; as a result, incidence of these diseases has been low or zero since the 1980s. Also, from 1986 to 1998, infants and pregnant women attending government maternal and child health centers and village health rooms received vitamin and mineral supplements (iron and vitamins A and D for infants, and iron and folate for women). These supplements helped improve infant growth patterns and reduce malnutrition and susceptibility to infectious disease.

Some indicators, such as immunization coverage and the fraction of births occurring in medical facilities, have declined since the beginning of the second intifada, primarily because of travel restrictions for providers and patients. However, the magnitude of these changes is currently unknown.

Incidence of gastroenteric and parasitic diseases has also declined significantly since the 1980s, and outcomes have improved. However, these conditions remain important health problems, primarily because of hygienic conditions (which have deteriorated since the start of the second intifada). Other areas of concern include hepatitis A, which is endemic in Palestine; respiratory infections; and meningitis. To date, vaccines for hepatitis A, haemophilus influenza B, and varicella have not been added to the Palestinian immunization program.

Acute and chronic malnutrition are also relatively prevalent, as are anemia and other micronutrient deficiencies. Nutritional status has declined in the last few years, as measured by indicators such as anthropometric status of children, anemia levels, and reported nutrient intake. Factors that might contribute to declining nutritional status include declining economic conditions, particularly since the outbreak of the second intifada, and the cessation in 1998–1999 of routine vitamin and mineral supplementation for infants and pregnant women in the government health system.[7]

As the role of infectious disease has declined in Palestine, the relative importance of noncommunicable and chronic illness has risen. As in most countries, stroke, ischemic heart disease, hypertension, diabetes, and cancer together account for more than half of adult mortality, and incidence and prevalence rates for these conditions have been rising over time. Among infants and children, one-third of deaths are due to accidents (of all kinds), more than any other identifiable category of causes.

Health status in Palestine is described in detail elsewhere, particularly in annual reports published by the MOH. However, data regarding inequities in health status between rural and urban residence, between refugee and nonrefugee populations, and

---

[7] Declines in nutritional status have been documented in several recent studies, which differ primarily in their estimates of the magnitude of the decline. Another recent survey, conducted by the WHO, found that other health status indicators had not declined significantly during the second intifada but cautioned that such declines might be forthcoming if social and economic conditions continued to decline.

by geographic region are relatively limited. Our recommendations for improving data collection are discussed below under "Strengthening Key Institutions, Policies, and Programs."

Health System Organization

Before 1994. Prior to being occupied by Israel in 1967, Gaza was administered by Egypt, while the West Bank and East Jerusalem were administered by Jordan. Health institutions in each area operated independently from each other. Gaza followed Egyptian protocols for medical licensing and other relevant issues, while the West Bank followed Jordanian protocols.

Between 1967 and 1994, these areas were both administered by the Israeli Defense Ministry. Gaza and the West Bank had separate chief medical officers and administrative structures, and they continued to follow different protocols in certain health policy areas, particularly those relating to medical licensing and supervision of health facilities. While many aspects of health policy were standardized for both the West Bank and Gaza, there were also some differences between the two areas, including differences in vaccination programs, maternal and child health programs, primary care services, and health insurance. As we discuss further below, the policy differences between Gaza and the West Bank remain relevant today.

Since 1948, UNRWA has been charged with providing basic health services to registered Palestinian refugees, including in the West Bank and Gaza. Refugees eligible for UNRWA services include those Palestinians (and their descendants) who were displaced from their homes because of the war between Israeli and Arab armies in 1948. Currently, approximately 75 percent of Gaza residents and 30 percent of West Bank residents—a total of some 1.5 million people in those areas—are designated as refugees. During most of the period of Israeli administration, UNRWA headquarters were in Vienna, Austria, and most planning for UNRWA health programs in Palestine was done there. UNRWA headquarters were subsequently moved to Amman, Jordan.

As described by some of its top Israeli managers, the objectives of the Israeli administration were to provide good health care, given the available resources; to minimize the risk of political unrest; and to provide a stable basis from which to negotiate a political solution.[8] The top managers of the government health system were Israeli physicians appointed by the Israeli Defense Ministry, with supervision from the Israeli Health Ministry. High-level planning was directed by the Israeli administration, generally via joint committees with senior Palestinian health officials. Most staff of the government health sector were Palestinian, including administrative and clinical personnel. Some independent review was provided by visiting experts from the WHO, the International Committee of the Red Cross, and other organizations.

---

[8] These objectives are described by Yitzhak Sever and Yitzhak Peterburg in Barnea and Husseini (2002). Both served as chief medical officers with the Israeli Civil Administration, in the West Bank and Gaza, respectively.

Israel aimed at financial self-sufficiency of the government health sector. Approximately half of the total health budget came from Palestinian taxes (and health insurance premiums) during the 1970s, rising to 75–100 percent during the 1980s and early 1990s. Consistent with these financial goals, the government health system placed a heavy emphasis on public health and primary care, particularly immunization programs for vaccine-preventable illness, and maternal and child health programs. Between 1970 and 1993, the number of government maternal and child health clinics increased by 488 percent, while the number of general government clinics increased by 63 percent.

In contrast, relatively little capital investment was directed toward secondary and tertiary care. For instance, the number of government hospital beds in the West Bank and Gaza increased by just 13 percent between 1970 and 1993. Similarly, in 1992, approximately 10 percent ($5.9 million) of the government health budget for Palestine went to development; the rest went toward operating expenses.[9] Hospital development efforts were focused on strengthening personnel and capacity in key departments, particularly anesthesia and internal medicine; also, all regional hospitals developed fully operational renal dialysis units during this period, and several hospitals were developing tertiary care services such as cardiac and neurosurgery.

Transfer to the Palestinian Authority. Following the Oslo Accords in 1993, Israel and the Palestinians negotiated the transfer of responsibility for health services and health policy from Israeli administration to the newly formed PA. The PA assumed health sector responsibility for Gaza and Jericho in May 1994 and for the rest of the West Bank at the end of that year.

The Palestinian health system is commonly described as consisting of four "sectors": the government sector, led by the MOH; the private sector; the NGO sector; and the sector run by UNRWA. The MOH serves as the principal administrative and regulatory body for the Palestinian health system, although responsibility for some relevant areas is also held by other ministries, including the Ministry of Finance (e.g., for budgeting), the Ministry of Planning (e.g., for infrastructure development programs), and the Ministry of Education and Higher Education (for academic and vocational training programs). The MOH manages public health services and delivery of primary, secondary, and tertiary care in government facilities. The MOH organizational chart from the second Palestinian national health plan (published in 1999) is reproduced as Figure 7.1.

Health Care Infrastructure

Table 7.2 provides data on some key indicators of health system infrastructure and capacity in Palestine, along with some international comparisons. The role of the government

---

[9] The Israeli administration published data on government health sector expenditures for the West Bank from 1990 ($26.7 million, $34 per capita) through 1993 ($37.2 million, $37 per capita). Relatively little public data were available for other periods, or for Gaza. Moreover, budget records were not among the information provided to the MOH by Israel when responsibility for the health system was transferred to the PA.

Figure 7.1
Ministry of Health Organizational Structure

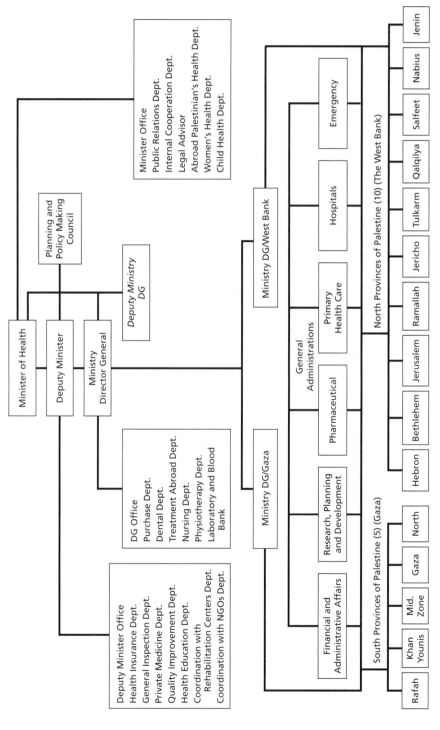

SOURCE: PA MOH, 1999, p.43.
NOTE: Our understanding is that this organizational chart remains generally accurate, although some details may have changed since it was produced.

Table 7.2
Health System Infrastructure, Palestine and Elsewhere (2000–2001, unless otherwise noted)

	Palestine	Israel	Jordan	Egypt	European Union	United States
GNP per capita	$1,771	$16,710	$1,650[c]	$1,080[c]	$22,363	$35,182
Health system spending per capita	$111[a]	$1,671	$139	$45[f]	$2,123	$4,887
Health system spending as a percentage of GNP	6%	10%	8%	4%[g]	10%	14%
Hospital beds per 100,000 population	137	614	160[d]	210[d]	622	360
Hospital occupancy rate	76.9%[b]	93%[b]	70%[g]	55%[e]	78%[b]	67%
Physicians per 100,000 population	84	377	165[d]	76	349	240
Nurses per 100,000 population	120	590	250[c]	N.A.	668	810
Dentists per 100,000 population	9	114	49[c]	6	64	60
Pharmacists per 100,000 population	10	62	N.A.	6	79	62

SOURCES: World Bank, 1998, 2003b; World Health Organization, 2001, 2004; The Hashemite Kingdom of Jordan, 2004; Gaumer et al., 1998; Medistat, 2003; Partnerships for Health Reform, 1997; PA MOH, 2002a; European Commission and Eurostat, 2001; Barnea and Husseini, 2002; Organisation for Economic Co-operation and Development, 1997, 2004; Centers for Disease Control and Prevention, 2003.

NOTES: N.A. = not available. As described elsewhere in this chapter, gross national product (GNP) per capita has since fallen substantially as a result of the second intifada.

[a] Data are from 1997.
[b] Occupancy rate is for MOH hospitals in Palestine and for acute care hospitals elsewhere.
[c] Data are from 1996.
[d] Data are from 1998.
[e] Data are for all hospitals in 1996.
[f] Data are for 2002.
[g] Data are for government hospitals in 1996; occupancy in private hospitals for that year was 49 percent.

sector in health care delivery—relative to that of the NGOs, private, and UNRWA sectors—is presented in Table 7.3.

Health System Funding and Expenditures

The annual operating budget for the MOH peaked at around $100 million in 1997 but has declined fairly continuously since then because of declining revenue from health insurance premiums and a general budget crisis. At least up to 2000 and the second intifada, government revenue for the health sector came from general taxation (60 percent), health insurance premiums (25–30 percent), and patient cost sharing (10–15 percent). In 1998, government health spending was $88 million, of which

Table 7.3
Distribution of Capacity Across the Sectors of the Palestinian Health System (2001)
(in percentage)

	Government	UNRWA	NGOs	Private
General hospital beds	53	1	37	10
Specialized hospital beds	75	N.A.	13	12
Maternity hospital beds	31	N.A.	33	37
Primary health clinics	61	8	30	N.A.
Health employees	56	7	30	7
Expenditures (1997)[a]	33	11	16[b]	40[c]

SOURCES: PA MOH, July 2002a; World Bank, 1998.

NOTE: N.A. = not available.

[a] Includes capital expenditures.

[b] Combines international donors and NGOs.

[c] Includes household expenditures and private capital investments.

$39 million was spent on salaries, $25 million on drugs and medical supplies, $9 million on treatment abroad, and $14 million on other operating costs.[10]

Overall, Palestinian health system spending was estimated to be around $320 million in 1998, including infrastructure development.[11, 12] In addition to the $88 million spent by the MOH, spending on health care in the private sector was approximately $90 million per year, while NGO spending on health care was estimated to be around $70 million.[13] UNRWA spending on health in Palestine was around $18 million in 1998.

The remainder of national health expenditures—some $54 million in 1998—came from other sources, particularly international donors.[14] Between mid-1994 and mid-2000, international donors disbursed approximately $227 million in health development assistance to Palestine, excluding humanitarian assistance. This averaged about

[10] The component for salaries has been the largest, and fastest growing, part of MOH spending, with the number of MOH employees more than doubling between 1993 and 2001, from 4,020 to 8,285. This was driven in part by a doubling of the number of government outpatient clinics and increases in hospital capacity during this period.

[11] We use 1998 as a reference point here because relatively detailed data were available to us for that year and because financing in subsequent years was significantly distorted by the second intifada. Additional information on health system spending is provided in the "Cost" subsection of this chapter.

[12] Palestine spent approximately 6 percent of gross national product (GNP) on health in 1998. The fraction of GNP spent on health in Israel was somewhat higher (10 percent). More important, Israeli GNP per capita—and thus health spending per capita—was more than nine times higher than that in Palestine (World Bank, 1998; PA MOH, 2002a). Moreover, Palestinian national income and health system spending have fallen considerably since 2000; this is discussed further in the "Cost" subsection of this chapter, and in Chapter Five.

[13] Publicly available data on private-sector and NGO spending on health are limited, so these estimates may be somewhat inaccurate.

[14] All of these figures exclude East Jerusalem. Estimates for the amount contributed annually by Palestinians in East Jerusalem to Israeli national insurance—which includes health insurance—range from $30 million to $40 million.

$38 million per year, more than six times the governmental development budget during the last years of Israeli administration. Although detailed data on the distribution of international donations between infrastructure development and ongoing expenses are unavailable, donors have certainly preferred to direct donations toward the former, and they have been particularly reluctant to fund the operating expenses of the government sector. For example, of the $224 million in donor commitments made to health sector development to cover the period 1994–1997, only 5 percent ($12 million) was specifically designated for recurring costs; 24 percent of the total commitments was specifically designated for other purposes, mostly equipment and construction, while the designated purpose for the rest was mixed or unspecified.[15]

A schematic for the flow of funds in the health system is reproduced as Figure 7.2.

Patient Benefits and Costs

Government Health Benefits. Under PA administration, the entire Palestinian population, regardless of health insurance or refugee status, is entitled by statute and government policy to immunizations, prenatal and postnatal care, preventive and curative care for children until age three, basic preventive services, hospital care, and community mental health services, without patient cost sharing. The predominant source of health insurance in Palestine is currently the government insurance program, which covers primary, secondary, and tertiary curative care. Palestinians who officially reside in East Jerusalem (i.e., those with a Jerusalem identity card) participate in the compulsory Israeli health insurance programs and receive care under those systems. Participation in the government plan is mandatory for government (i.e., PA and municipal) workers and for Palestinians working in Israel. Other people may join the government program voluntarily as individuals, households, or groups organized around a firm or workplace.

The current government health insurance program is modeled closely on the system originally introduced by Israel. However, the MOH deliberately reduced insurance premiums after 1994 to promote enrollment. This strategy was generally effective: enrollment increased from 20 percent of households in 1993 to 55 percent in 1996. Enrollment subsequently declined because of a budget crisis in the government health sector and worsening economic conditions. However, premiums were recently waived for large segments of the population, particularly the households of people who lost jobs in Israel since the onset of the second intifada or who have been hurt in clashes with Israel, and enrollment has consequently increased.

Until the outbreak of the second intifada, health insurance premiums for government employees and participants via workplace groups were 5 percent of a worker's base monthly salary, with a monthly minimum of $8.50 and a maximum of $16.[16]

---

[15] We lack similar data on the distribution of actual disbursements, as opposed to donor commitments.

[16] Premiums and cost sharing are paid in Israeli shekels (NIS). Costs in U.S. dollars are based on a rate of $1 = 4.74 NIS, the rate at the end of March 2003.

Figure 7.2
Flow of Funds in Palestinian Health System

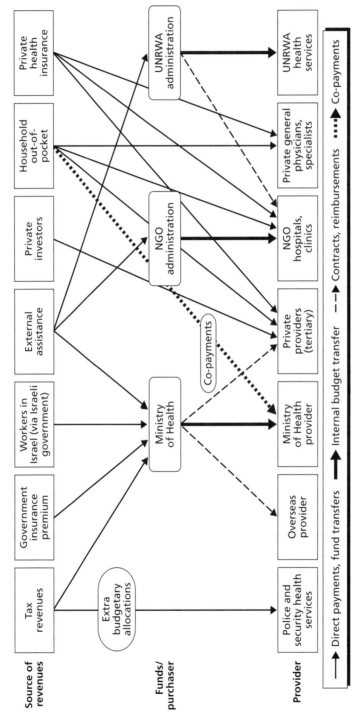

SOURCES: World Bank, 1998, p. 24. Also appears in Barnea and Husseini, 2002, p. 184.

NOTES: Several sets of arrows are missing from this figure. For instance, arrows should run from the MOH to NGOs and the private sector. As described below, government health benefits do not cover some care from such providers when patients are referred because a covered service is not available in the government system. Also, an arrow should run from UNRWA to the MOH. As also described below, UNRWA pays government insurance premiums for some UNRWA beneficiaries.

Private participants were charged $10.50 per month for individual coverage and $16 for household coverage.[17] Palestinians working in Israel were charged $20 per month, a small part of which was deducted by Israel to pay for care provided there. Parents over age 60 could be covered for an additional $3 per month in premium payments. Health insurance premiums were waived for households that met "hardship" criteria, with the MOH assuming responsibility for them.[18]

When economic conditions declined significantly after the outbreak of the second intifada, enrollment in the government health system also fell. Correspondingly, the fraction of the MOH operating budget that came from health insurance premiums fell from 40 percent in 1999 to 24 percent in 2001. This revenue source was then substantially reduced when the PA decided to waive government health insurance premiums for large segments of the population, as a result of the emergency conditions associated with the second intifada.[19] As of this writing, insurance premiums remain waived.

Even for people whose premiums have been waived, some co-payments remain. Under the government health insurance program, patients are charged $0.21 per laboratory test and for imaging services. If a private provider refers patients to the government sector for care, patients are charged $4 per referral by the government insurance program, although apparently this charge is often not enforced. Pharmacy co-payments are described below. With the exception of these charges, there is no cost sharing for outpatient and inpatient care in the government sector under the government insurance plan, nor for care in the NGO or private sectors (or in foreign institutions) for patients who receive appropriate referrals from the government system. In theory, the government system pays for care in the NGO and private sectors only when an appropriate referral has been obtained. Referrals are supposed to be provided only when needed services are not available from government providers.

Under the pharmacy benefit of the government insurance program, patients are charged $0.63 per prescription for medications ($0.21 for children up to age three). Patients obtain prescription drugs from government clinics; in general, drugs obtained from private pharmacies are not covered by the government plan. The MOH developed a national essential drug list, which was released in 2002. In principle, all the drugs on the list—and only the drugs on the list—are available to patients in the gov-

---

[17] For comparison, Palestinian gross national income was around $1,800 per capita in 2000 and $1,070 per capita in 2002, based on data from the MOH.

[18] Hardship cases included indigent households and those that met certain other criteria, such as households headed by widows. In 1998, before the second intifada and the waiving of premiums for many people, approximately 20 percent of participants in the government health insurance system were hardship cases; 30 percent were required to participate as government employees; 20 percent were required to participate as workers in Israel; and 30 percent were enrolled on a voluntary basis, as individuals or via group contracts.

[19] Enrollment in the government insurance system increased again when premiums were waived, to some 80 percent of the population. However, the MOH budget has not been increased to fully reflect the associated liabilities for the government health system. We discuss health insurance in greater detail in "Strengthening Key Institutions, Policies, and Programs" below.

ernment health sector. In practice, not all covered drugs are consistently available in all geographic areas, because of factors including insecure supply, poor distribution, and the MOH planning process. However, purchase of drugs from private pharmacies is not covered by the government health plan, even if the drugs were prescribed by but were unavailable in the government health system. We discuss pharmaceutical policy in greater detail in "Strengthening Key Institutions, Policies, and Programs" below.

The MOH is the main provider of hospital beds, particularly in Gaza. The MOH is also the main provider of primary care, operating a large network of primary care clinics, maternal and child health centers, and village health rooms. Immunizations are provided by the MOH at its primary care sites and in UNRWA clinics, as well as via traveling immunization teams for areas that lack on-site services.

Health care providers in the government sector are salaried public employees. Providers in UNRWA and most NGOs are also salaried employees. Private practice has expanded since 1994 but is still fairly limited, especially in Gaza.

United Nations Relief and Works Agency. UNRWA's health services focus on disease prevention and control, primary care, family health, health education, physiotherapy, school health, psychosocial support services, and environmental health. There is no patient cost sharing for these services, which are provided mainly through a network of UNRWA outpatient clinics throughout the West Bank and Gaza, primarily in areas with significant concentrations of refugees. UNRWA also provides some secondary care; patients must pay 25 percent of the cost of care (10 percent in hardship cases) for these services, which are provided through one UNRWA hospital, in the West Bank, and in public and NGO hospitals with which UNRWA contracts for inpatient care. In general, UNRWA does not cover care for chronic and noncommunicable diseases. For some conditions, particularly cancer, UNRWA "sponsors" patients' care by covering the cost of enrolling the patient in the government health insurance program.

UNRWA's budget is determined by the United Nations General Assembly. However, in practice the budget allocation is not always fully funded by donor countries. For example, in 1998, donor countries provided $18 million (72 percent) out of an approved health budget of $25 million for Palestine.

Since this analysis is framed in terms of a future independent Palestinian state, it is worth commenting on the likely role of UNRWA in that context. Nearly all Palestinian stakeholders whom we interviewed thought that the role of UNRWA in Palestine would be eliminated with a final political settlement and the establishment of an independent state, and that the UNRWA system would probably be transferred to the MOH eventually.[20]

Use of UNRWA services does not affect eligibility for government health insurance and services.

NGOs and the Private Sector. Nongovernmental organizations have played a very important role in all levels of the Palestinian health system, during both the Israeli and

---

[20] Since UNRWA's services are financed by international donations, the MOH and donor countries would need to work together to ensure that such a transfer does not cause a financial shock to the Palestinian health system.

Palestinian administrations. Although some international NGOs operate in Palestine, the role of indigenous NGOs is at least as great. NGOs include organizations with social, political, and religious motivations. Historically and today, NGOs in Palestine have provided services including outpatient and inpatient care, psychosocial support, rehabilitation, health education, and emergency care. They have also been active in health promotion and health education, consumer activism, health planning, infrastructure development, human resource development, and other aspects of the health system.

NGO development was particularly significant during the first intifada and the period immediately preceding the Oslo agreement (1987–1993), when NGOs were one feasible outlet for developing national institutions. Following the transfer of the health system to the MOH, international donors shifted substantial resources from the NGO sector to the government sector, a trend that was somewhat reversed following the start of the second intifada.

Private investment in the health sector was relatively limited before 1994 but grew considerably between 1994 and 2000. The private health sector now includes clinics and hospitals; pharmacies; laboratories; radiology, physiotherapy, and rehabilitation centers; and medical equipment manufacturing facilities. In addition, there is a growing domestic pharmaceutical industry, which produces approximately 700 different products and supplies substantial amount—estimated to be around one-half—of the Palestinian demand for prescription drugs. There have been some attempts to establish private health insurance programs, but private coverage has never exceeded 2–3 percent of the population. Private insurance plans have essentially been eliminated by the economic hardships accompanying the second intifada. However, private expenditures on health remain considerable (see Table 7.3).[21]

Strengthening Key Institutions, Policies, and Programs

For each of ten key areas, we present background information and our recommendations. We also briefly describe the effects of alternative scenarios. Our major recommendations are summarized in Table 7.4.

Health System Planning, Policy Development, and Policy Implementation

Background. During the period of Israeli administration (1967–1994), planning for the government health sector was led primarily by Israelis, with some Palestinian participation in policy formation and with Palestinian administrative support. Examples of joint policy development include the 1985 Adler Committee on health planning for the West Bank and standing committees such as the Child Health Committee in Gaza. Planning for UNRWA was mainly conducted at UNRWA headquarters in Vienna for

---

[21] The Palestinian Central Bureau of Statistics (2000b) estimates that 3–4 percent of household income is spent on health care (including health insurance premiums) (Barnea and Husseini, 2002).

Table 7.4
Recommendations for Palestinian Health System Development

Area	Recommendation
Health system planning, policy development, and policy implementation	The Palestinian government should integrate health system planning and policy development more closely, with meaningful input from and coordination with all relevant governmental and nongovernmental stakeholders.
Health insurance and health care finance	The Palestinian government should develop viable and sustainable health insurance and health care financing systems.
Licensing and certification of health professionals	Palestinian standards for licensing and certifying all types of health professionals should be updated, standardized, and enforced.
Licensing and accreditation of health care facilities and services	Palestinian standards for licensing and accrediting health care facilities and services should be updated, standardized, and enforced.
Human resource development	Palestinian institutions should implement a human resource development strategy for the health professions to ensure an adequate supply of appropriately trained personnel for the Palestinian health system.
Health care quality improvement	A national strategy on health care quality improvement should be developed and implemented, with systematic evaluation of quality improvement projects and dissemination of those that succeed.
Policies on prescription drugs and medical devices	Policymakers should implement national strategies on the licensing, supply, and distribution of pharmaceuticals and medical devices to ensure a stable and adequate supply of safe and cost-effective products.
Health information systems	Palestinian policymakers should develop comprehensive, modern, and integrated health information systems.
Research	Palestinian policymakers should develop national strategies regarding public health, health services, clinical, and basic science research.
Programs for rapid improvement	The MOH should implement comprehensive programs to improve nutritional status, including food fortification, micronutrient supplementation for high-risk groups, and promotion of healthy dietary practices.
	The national immunization program should be updated, and the costs of purchasing and distributing vaccines should be explicitly covered by the government budget.
	The MOH and other stakeholders should expand the scope of available primary care services and expand access to comprehensive primary care.
	The MOH and other stakeholders should develop comprehensive strategies for addressing psychosocial needs, particularly those relating to the exposure of children to violence.

all five areas of UNRWA activity (Syria, Lebanon, Jordan, West Bank, and Gaza), with some local Palestinian input. Government and UNRWA activities were coordinated to some degree, but many policies varied between these two sectors. The Israeli administration exercised some control over the NGO sector's infrastructure and programs. However, in many respects, NGOs explicitly aimed to compete with the government in the health sector for political reasons; coordination with the government was correspondingly low.

When Palestinian national health planning started in the years prior to the Oslo Accords, its leaders followed a process that was explicitly designed to be inclusive. The first national health plan called for the creation of a "health council" to oversee the health system, with the responsibility of developing strategic plans for future action, developing policy across both public and private health care programs, and monitoring and evaluating progress in meeting policy targets, among other functions. The plan called for this council, referred to as a "central authority," to involve all relevant stakeholders in its activities, including "the private sector, the nonprofit sector, the university system, businesses, organized labor, and the voluntary sector," as well as local communities, and to ensure that these stakeholders participate in a meaningful way (Palestinian Council of Health, 1994).

In 1992, the Palestine Liberation Organization authorized the establishment of the Palestinian Council of Health, which completed the first Palestinian national health plan and acted as the national planning body until the MOH was established. This council included representatives from numerous NGOs, as well as private providers, academics, UNRWA, and other relevant stakeholders, all of which were involved in the council's activities.[22] Many council participants expected that this organization would serve as the "central authority" referred to in the first national health plan, once it became clear that responsibility for the Palestinian health system would be transferred to the PA under the Oslo Accords in 1994. As the MOH became established, however, many of the council's responsibilities—along with much of its staff—shifted to the new MOH. Although the council was not disbanded, it quickly stopped functioning as the national planning and coordination body for the health system.

As we have noted, national health planning has continued under the MOH, and the planning process has involved representatives from NGOs, the private sector, UNRWA, and the donor community. However, there is no systematic national process for ensuring that health system development is tailored to the goals articulated in the national health plan or other relevant planning documents. The MOH has had limited success exercising its managerial authority over the health system, and neither the MOH nor any other national institution provides effective overall coordination. Instead, there is a general lack of coordination in policy development and implementation across parts of the PA, between the West Bank and Gaza, and across the four major sectors of the health system (government, NGO, private, and UNRWA). Organizations across the four health sectors compete in an effort to advance their own priorities, rather than pursuing system-wide or national priorities; there is no consistent national process for reviewing new infrastructure projects to ensure that health infrastructure is developed efficiently; there are no modern standards for many key aspects of health

---

[22] Participation by Palestinian staff of the (Israeli) government health system was initially limited, for political reasons.

system operation and minimal enforcement of the standards that do exist.[23] In addition, consumer input to the planning process has been limited.

In our view, the lack of coordination in policy development and implementation has limited progress toward achieving the health and health system targets specified in the national health plans, reduced the financial viability of the health care system, and undermined public confidence in the government health system and possibly in the government generally. These conditions apply in some degree to nearly all aspects of the health system, including the development and operation of public health programs and clinical infrastructure, health care finance, and the pharmaceutical sector. One possible exception is human resources and health education, where the MOH and the Ministry of Education and Higher Education have recently established a body with authority to accredit any new health-related academic or vocational training program.

Recommendation: The Palestinian Government Should Integrate Health System Planning and Policy Development More Closely, with Meaningful Input from and Coordination with All Relevant Governmental and Nongovernmental Stakeholders. There are many ways to improve health system planning and coordination. However, effective planning and coordination processes are likely to share the features described below.

The planning and coordination processes should be implemented by a governmental authority. Nongovernmental stakeholders can help inform planning and the policymaking process, but they cannot independently develop national policy. National health planning, policymaking, and coordination across stakeholders should be led by a governmental body, with its responsibilities defined by legislation and/or regulation. Relevant areas of responsibility include

- overall responsibility for promoting the health of Palestinians
- establishment of national health priorities and targets
- financing of public health
- assurance of access to health care at the primary, secondary, and tertiary levels
- epidemiology and health status monitoring
- environmental quality and food and water safety
- safety and efficacy of pharmaceuticals and medical products
- maternal and child health
- control of communicable diseases
- control of noncommunicable diseases, injuries, and conditions
- legislation, licensing, and regulation of health care facilities and personnel (including educational standards)

---

[23] In some ways, competition between NGOs and the government sector has intensified since 1994. Now, as under Israeli administration, some NGOs compete with the government sector, for ideological reasons and because of a scarcity of resources. Additionally, the MOH has competed with certain NGO activities, perhaps in an effort to establish authority over a health system in which several major NGOs were already well established when the MOH was created.

- promotion of quality and equity in health care
- collection of national health accounting data and other data necessary for health system planning, policy development, and policy implementation.

It might seem that the most obvious entity for leading the planning process, and for coordinating across stakeholders, is the MOH. The MOH has led many of the health system planning efforts since 1994; it has considerable relevant expertise among its staff; and, at least in principle, the MOH already has responsibility for system-wide planning and coordination and at least some of the authority to carry it out. On the other hand, the MOH has had limited success to date in developing, implementing, and enforcing policy for the health system as a whole. For example, the MOH Health Sector Working Group—which includes the MOH, the Ministry of Planning, several international donors, the WHO, and other stakeholders—advises the MOH regarding policy development. But its decisions are not binding on the participating organizations, let alone on nonparticipating stakeholders. In addition, the MOH operates independently in Gaza and in the West Bank in many respects, even before the second intifada.

There are presumably many reasons for this, which will need to be addressed if an integrated planning process is to succeed. For instance, the MOH may have lacked the resources or expertise to implement effective planning and coordination at a national level; it may have lacked the necessary statutory authority; and/or it may have lacked the political will or ability to exercise such authority. Most interview participants favored the last of these explanations. In practice, the PA as a whole and most of its departments, including the MOH, have suffered from a weak level of authority over the sectors for which they are responsible; inefficient management practices; and autocratic, inconsistent, and nonparticipatory decisionmaking processes. The issue of Palestinian governance is discussed in more detail at the end of this chapter, and in Chapter Two.

The MOH serves as a health care delivery system as well as a planning and regulatory body, creating the potential for conflicts of interest in the planning and policymaking process. It may therefore be beneficial to minimize the extent to which individuals or departments within the MOH have responsibility for both health care delivery and health system planning and policymaking. Options for distinguishing the two include creating a separate division within the MOH to be responsible for the government delivery system, creating an entirely separate agency with such responsibility, and privatizing health care delivery. Such options would need to be evaluated locally.

As an alternative method of broadening the policymaking process, national planning and coordination could be led by a new governmental body. The MOH would naturally play a significant role in this body, which would also include participants from the Ministries of Planning, Finance, and Education and Higher Education, and possibly other key players. To date, cooperation between the MOH and these other ministries regarding health policy has been limited, and effective cooperation may be more likely if all ministries jointly contribute to a new planning and coordination body.

Effective health planning and coordination also require appropriate oversight. The national planning and coordination body should ultimately be accountable to the prime minister; to the elected legislature, which defines the scope of the authority; and to the judicial system, which helps ensure that the body neither neglects nor exceeds its mandate. Many health systems have also developed formal processes for soliciting public input into planning and policymaking and an ombudsman process to help address consumer grievances.

Additional recommendations for strengthening the planning process are described below.

Health Planning Targets Should Reflect International Standards and Local Conditions. In many countries, and internationally, national targets for population health status, access to care, health care quality, and other indicators of health system performance play a vital role in guiding health system planning. Previous national health plans have included targets in some of these areas, framed largely in terms of local conditions. These targets should be revised and expanded on an ongoing basis, and they should reference—although not necessarily be identical to—international guidelines such as those developed by the WHO. Potential frames of reference for refining Palestinian targets include the WHO's Health for All in the 21st Century [online at http://www.who.int/archives/hfa/ (as of February 2004)] and the U.S. Healthy People 2010 targets [online at http://www.healthypeople.gov (as of May 2004)], in addition to data on health and health care in Palestine.

The Planning Process Should Be Inclusive. National health system planning should include meaningful participation by representatives from the NGO, private, and UNRWA sectors, in addition to government participants; from relevant professional associations (e.g., for physicians, nurses, pharmacists, etc.); from relevant academic institutions; from international donors; and especially from consumers and the community. In addition to ensuring consumer representation in national planning bodies, making meetings open to the public and including public hearings and a public comment period as part of policymaking are good strategies for promoting more comprehensive and effective consumer participation. Laws defining patients' rights can also strengthen the role of consumers in the planning and policymaking process; in Palestine, a draft patients' bill of rights was proposed by the Palestinian Council of Health, but no such policy has become law.

Formal participation by all stakeholders is likely to enhance the political and social legitimacy of the planning process and its outcomes, which in turn helps facilitate implementation of the plans.

Interview subjects expressed concern about the potential that the planning process might be "captured" by a small number of established stakeholders, or be dominated by specific personalities. Such issues are common to policymaking and regulatory bodies, and the planning process should be designed to reduce the chance of such outcomes.

Planning and Policymaking Should Be Integrated. The planning process should be comprehensive in scope and yield specific and measurable national targets for health status and health system development (in many ways, the previous national health plans have included such targets). These targets should guide policymaking for the health system.

In practice, the strategies for integrating planning and policymaking will differ for different stakeholders. In the government sector, the MOH and other ministries can be directed by statute or executive order to pursue such integration. It is important that health system budget allocations conform to and support national health development targets.

Government control over the policies of nongovernmental stakeholders is necessarily more limited; in particular, it is easier for the government to *prevent* donors or other organizations from implementing a particular project than to *compel* these organizations to implement a particular project. As a result, both regulatory oversight and positive incentives may be needed to increase integration with national plans. On the regulatory side, NGOs, private providers, or international donors can be required to seek approval for major capital investments, to ensure that infrastructure is developed in accordance with national plans; such an approval process should have established and transparent guidelines, and it should be binding. (This issue is further discussed under "Licensing and Accreditation of Health Care Facilities and Services" below.)

With respect to incentives, the MOH can use the coverage and payment rules of the government insurance programs to influence the scope and quality of service delivery in the private and NGO sectors; and it can increase commitment to the national health plans by including nongovernmental stakeholders in the planning process, as discussed above. Another possibility would be to establish an advisory panel of independent, international experts, which would advise the MOH and the national planning and coordination body and help provide support for policy decisions that are beneficial but may be unpopular.

Policy Implementation Should Be Strengthened. In the Palestinian health system, as in many other health systems, planning has frequently functioned better than policy implementation, and many of the aims of current and prior health plans have not been achieved. In our view, effective strategies for national health planning and coordination require that responsibility for implementing policy decisions be explicitly assigned to the appropriate stakeholders, with ongoing monitoring of implementation and appropriate incentives for successful performance. Subsequent recommendations in this chapter focus on the need to strengthen and maintain the skills of health system managers, evaluate new programs and policies, and collect comprehensive data about the health system.

Nearly all our interview participants expressed the view that the Palestinian government should *immediately* create a national planning and coordination authority with "teeth"—the power to ensure that health system policies and development projects conform to the national health plans. Although recognizing that such a body would influence and probably change how most health system stakeholders function, most interview participants considered its creation to be a necessary condition for addressing key problems in public health, health care access, health care quality, and financial viability of the health system. To the extent that opinions differed, they did so primarily with respect to the details of how such a planning body would be established and how it would function. However, even stakeholders in NGOs, the private sector, academic institutions, and international donor organizations agree that the planning body should be created under the auspices of the government, despite expressing concerns about the capabilities and the motivations of the MOH and the PA.

Effects of Restricted Domestic Mobility. Restricted mobility within Palestine would seriously inhibit essentially all aspects of health system planning, policy development, and policy implementation, as experience during the second intifada has shown. Since the start of the second intifada, the MOH has attempted few major development initiatives; those that have been attempted, such as a World Bank project on health information systems, have been delayed considerably; and coordination between MOH activities in the West Bank and Gaza has declined (from a level that was itself problematic). Continued restricted mobility would inhibit or prevent policymakers from meeting; inhibit or prevent oversight of health system functioning, including all types of data collection; and make implementation of new policies and programs more difficult and more costly.

Effects of Restricted International Access. Restricted international access would not necessarily inhibit the process of health system planning, policy development, and policy implementation, unless access by Palestinians to outside expertise and other resources is also restricted. However, it would affect the outcomes of the planning and policymaking process, by requiring that clinical and educational needs be met domestically. We discuss this further below.

Health Insurance and Health Care Finance

Background. During the period of Israeli administration, health insurance coverage was available primarily via the government health insurance plan; there was no private (commercial) health insurance, and informal insurance arrangements operated by NGOs were very limited. (Of course, the UNRWA health system functions as a health service benefit program for registered refugees.) Participation in the government plan was restricted to the groups who were required to enroll—i.e., government workers and Palestinians working in Israel. Under Israeli administration, the insurance program was priced to be largely self-funding, so that the annual premium corresponded to the average annual cost of covered services used by members. The Israeli administration had relatively strong control over the services offered in the government sector.

Nearly all Palestinians with health insurance obtain it through the MOH's insurance program. After 1994, some private health insurance was introduced, but these plans—which never enrolled more than 3 percent of the population—basically ended with the second intifada.

Although the government health plan is still closely based on the system that was introduced by Israel, the MOH has made several important changes. Perhaps the most fundamental change was to allow voluntary enrollment by individuals and households and by employee groups that were not required to participate. At the same time, insurance premiums were reduced to promote enrollment.

The effects of such reductions on financial viability could have been positive if they had substantially increased enrollment by healthy people. However, allowing voluntary enrollment created the risk of adverse selection—in other words, that the people who chose to enroll were disproportionately sick. The risk of adverse selection was reinforced by the fact that people could enroll at almost any time, creating an incentive for healthy people to stay out of the system—and avoid paying insurance premiums—until they become sick or injured. As a particularly stark example, UNRWA pays to enroll people in the government insurance program when they are diagnosed with cancer; this is, in effect, an institutionalization of adverse selection.

Expansion of eligibility and reduction of premiums were intended to expand health insurance coverage and help reduce unmet need. In practice, however, the net effect of these changes was to increase the government system's liabilities more than it increased revenue, deepening the operating deficit that has existed since 1994 and threatening the survival of the system. Subsequent economic crises—and, of course, the decision after 2000 to waive premiums entirely for many people—have exacerbated the financial problems of the government insurance system.[24]

In contrast to the enrollment rules and premiums, the benefit structure of the government health plan has changed very little over time. Members face no cost sharing for outpatient office visits, but co-payments are required for diagnostic services such as laboratory tests and imaging. Many health insurance plans in other countries work in exactly the opposite fashion, the rationale being that patients have relatively strong control over the decision to see the doctor, but relatively weak control over the diagnostic services the doctor prescribes. The government plan also requires co-payments for prescription drugs but not for inpatient care with appropriate referral; both are features that have been widely adopted in foreign health insurance plans. Moreover, the "gatekeeping" aspect of the referral system for inpatient care is not always applied rigorously, and patients who seek such a referral are generally able to receive one.

The government health system does not include systematic utilization review for outpatient care, such as requiring primary care referral for specialty care. We recognize

---

[24] We note that even waiving the health insurance premiums has not led to universal insurance coverage, one stated goal of the national health plans. Coverage is estimated to be around 80 percent at the time of this writing, apparently because not everyone who is eligible has actually enrolled. When premiums were required, health insurance coverage peaked at 55 percent of households, including families whose insurance coverage was sponsored by the government under the hardship program—also far short of universal coverage.

that the potential effect of primary care gatekeeping is likely to be muted, at least in the short run, by the current shortage of specialists in many clinical areas. Patients in the government health sector (and in UNRWA) have little ability to choose providers, except by opting to receive care in a different sector.

The government plan covers care only from government providers, unless patients are specifically referred to private or NGO providers, or to providers abroad, for care that cannot be provided in the government sector. The reliance on government services has both clinical and financial motivations. The former reflect concerns about inconsistent quality and lack of government oversight in the private and NGO sectors. The latter reflect a desire to avoid the open-ended liabilities that might arise from paying NGO and private providers on a fee-for-service basis, while government providers are salaried. In practice, however, the government sector has been unable to meet the demand for its services, particularly following the large increase in insurance enrollment since premiums were waived. At the same time, the MOH lacks the economic resources—and the statutory authority—to shift some of this excess demand to the private or NGO sectors. The result has been considerable overcrowding of government facilities and a perceived decline in quality of care—while simultaneously some private and NGO facilities are underutilized.

Several other factors affect care in the government sector. For instance, as is true in many developing areas, the government salary structure serves as an incentive for public providers to maintain private practices on the side, by choice or out of economic necessity. This dual role may distract public providers from the responsibilities of their government positions and create other conflicts of interest. The relatively centralized management structure of the public sector offers few positive incentives to facility administrators and individual clinicians to provide health care efficiently. For example, senior hospital staff are generally appointed by the MOH rather than by the hospital director. Hospital managers are not provided with specific budgets for operating their facilities, and accountability by hospital managers for the use of pharmaceuticals and other consumables in their facilities is often weak. At the same time, all health care sectors lack modern health information systems, particularly relating to hospital discharge data and other indicators of health system performance. This makes it very difficult to implement an efficient system of local accountability, since it inhibits planning and evaluation of facility performance.

Overall, the government health sector has operated at a deficit since its inception in 1994. Government liabilities have considerably exceeded the sum of health insurance premiums and general tax revenues allocated to the health sector. Communication between the MOH and the Ministry of Finance (which determines or at least administers budget allocations) is poor, and there have been periods of crisis (e.g., in 1997) when the Ministry of Finance did not allocate the expected budget to the MOH. The PA effectively doubled enrollment in the government health insurance system when it recently waived premiums, but these increased liabilities were not reflected in the budget planning process. Indeed, it appears that the government did not explicitly account for the liabilities it incurred when it lowered insurance premiums in the mid-1990s to promote enrollment in the government program.

System-wide, a substantial part of the cost of health care services has been borne by patients in the form of out-of-pocket spending. However, there is a perception of considerable unmet need for health care in Palestine—even while all sectors of the health system (except perhaps the private sector) have received considerable external subsidies. The operating budget of the MOH has been directly supported by foreign donors and indirectly supported by the high volume of services provided in other sectors to patients who are formally entitled to receive the care in the government sector. Similarly, with the exception of patient cost sharing, the entire UNRWA sector is externally financed by design (UNRWA also subsidizes the government system, to the extent that it provides services that patients would otherwise be entitled to receive from the government system). Finally, most NGOs subsidize the care they provide with funding from local and foreign sources.[25]

Recommendation: The Palestinian Government Should Develop Viable and Sustainable Health Insurance and Health Care Financing Systems. Addressing these complex issues is difficult in any health care system. However, successful policies are likely to include some common features, as described below.

The Planning Target Should Be Universal Health Coverage. Most health systems that are regarded as "successful," in the sense intended by our mandate, have achieved universal—or close to universal—health insurance coverage. The previous national health plans have included the goal of universal health insurance coverage in Palestine. We think maintenance of this goal and good faith efforts to achieve it are important for social and political reasons—a view supported by all our interview participants.

Interview participants (and the policy literature) suggested a range of possible strategies, without any obvious consensus. Some participants thought that achieving this goal needs to be deferred for the foreseeable future and favored continuing the current government system and its provision for voluntary enrollment. Others favored mandatory and universal participation in a national insurance program but differed in how comprehensive the benefits of such a program should be. For instance, one option might be to provide a "core" benefit, available to everybody, that covers a basic set of services (e.g., public health, preventive care, and basic curative services). People could supplement this core benefit, if they chose, by purchasing more comprehensive private coverage. Opinions also differed on the appropriate role for government versus private insurance. As is always the case in insurance, the risk-pooling benefits of universal government coverage are likely to trade off against the restricted choice and potentially

---

[25] We note that market-based health reform strategies often seek to promote competition, particularly on the basis of cost and quality. One implication of the significant level of subsidies in the Palestinian health system is that the competition across and within sectors of this system is not necessarily market based. In particular, UNRWA, NGOs, and international donors are not simply making "investments" in the business sense.

poor quality that arise in such a system. In our view, these issues need to be resolved locally.

Demand-Side Incentives for Efficient Health Care Use Should Be Improved. We assume that the government insurance program will be maintained in the future, in some form. However, its benefit structure should be updated to encourage both patients and providers to use care more efficiently. On the demand side, available evidence from developed and developing countries suggests that modest levels of patient cost sharing for many types of health care services help control health care costs without adversely affecting health outcomes (appropriate co-payment levels would be determined locally).Similarly, there is evidence that utilization review and care management techniques can help control costs and/or improve outcomes, particularly among patients with chronic medical conditions (such as diabetes, asthma, hypertension, and heart disease) that commonly involve acute complications and hospitalization. Updated cost-sharing and utilization review mechanisms should be based on international evidence and local economic circumstances.

Government policies currently provide universal entitlement to preventive health services without patient cost sharing. In general, the scope of preventive services is relatively comprehensive for children, particularly up to age three. However, there is considerable room to expand the scope of such services, for both children and—perhaps especially—adults. As we discuss further below, government strategies regarding nutritional status require updating and expansion, particularly for high-risk groups. (The MOH released a new national nutrition strategy in July 2003; it is too early to know what its effects will be.) With respect to the general adult population, available epidemiological evidence suggests high and increasing prevalence of chronic diseases—notably diabetes, hypertension, and heart disease—for which primary and secondary prevention efforts can be quite effective. Although these conditions are associated with considerable expenditure on tertiary care, health education and prevention efforts for these conditions are relatively underdeveloped. Increased prevention efforts in these and other areas have the potential to reduce total health care costs.

Supply-Side Incentives for Efficient Health Care Use Should Be Improved. The MOH (or the national health planning authority) should improve incentives for the efficient supply of health services, particularly in the government sector. These improvements should include better management practices for government health facilities—e.g., by implementing formal budgeting processes, holding facility managers accountable for clinical and financial performance, and providing local staff with greater authority and autonomy. Other possible steps include giving individual providers incentives to meet specific evidence-based performance benchmarks and minimizing conflicts of interest between government providers' public and private practices. We note that performance incentives do not necessarily have to be monetary; other possible incentives include peer recognition, training or research support, and additional vacation time.

Effective implementation of such strategies is likely to require improved information systems, which we discuss in greater detail under "Health Information Systems" below.

Coverage Rules for Tertiary Care Referrals Should Be Specific, Publicized, and Implemented Consistently. Tertiary care capabilities in Palestine are currently limited. Additional tertiary care capabilities, including development and operation, are expensive, and the cost to the MOH of referring patients for treatment abroad—whether to Israel, neighboring countries such as Jordan or Egypt, or to Europe—is also considerable. Given scarce resources, the MOH has worked to reduce the rate of such referrals by expanding local capacity and by making referral criteria more restrictive. In general, such efforts are likely to be beneficial for the health system overall. However, both strategies should be implemented systematically and transparently.

Strategies for expanding local capacity should reflect both the relative cost and the relative quality of treatment abroad. In particular, the Palestinian population is relatively small, and there are likely to be many conditions for which the national incidence rate will be below the minimum volume necessary to sustain a clinically successful treatment program. It may be both clinically and economically efficient to develop tertiary care "centers of excellence," focusing on high-impact conditions that are also relatively prevalent. In any case, development of tertiary care facilities should conform to the strategies and targets determined by the national health planning process.

Referrals for care abroad could also be more systematic and cost-effective. The MOH is likely to benefit from negotiating bilateral agreements with foreign countries or institutions regarding referral of Palestinian patients. The MOH has already negotiated some agreements with foreign institutions, but our understanding is that these agreements do not specify the rates that the MOH will be charged for care. Future agreements should include rate schedules for specific types of care.

Israel is one obvious place to refer Palestinian patients, for reasons of geography and of health system capacity and quality. Indeed, the MOH has referred many patients to Israeli institutions since 1994 and continues to do so. Several interview participants pointed out, however, that Israeli institutions charge the MOH the equivalent of "tourist" rates for Palestinian referrals; i.e., higher rates than these institutions charge for treating the members of Israeli health insurance plans. Although this may reflect economic realities, most notably the risk of nonpayment or incomplete payment, we recommend that the referral terms be renegotiated to be more favorable to Palestinian patients. In our view, this would benefit all parties.

Criteria for determining whether patients are referred outside the government health system, domestically or abroad, should be detailed, transparent, and applied consistently.

Policymakers Should Consider Covering Care in the Private and NGO Sectors. As described above, the government health insurance program does not generally cover services provided outside the government health sector. At the same time, many government facilities are already operating at the limits of their capacity, and they are certainly not adequate for meeting the needs of the entire population. The MOH will therefore need to expand the government health sector significantly, and/or expand the role of private and NGO providers under the government insurance program, as it works toward achieving the national goal of comprehensive universal health insurance coverage.

Private and NGO providers currently represent a substantial part of health system capacity (see Table 7.3). To the extent that these providers meet appropriate criteria regarding quality and costs, it is likely to be more efficient for the MOH to purchase care from them than to replace them. In particular, policymakers should avoid devoting scarce development resources to building redundant capacity—i.e., building or expanding government capacity in areas where private and NGO capacity is available and adequate. We recommend against having the government sector provide all care, because such a monopoly might weaken incentives for quality and efficiency.

Such expansion may be more feasible and appropriate in the context of improved national planning, policy development, and policy implementation, as discussed above; strengthened national licensing and certification standards (discussed further below under "Licensing and Certification of Health Professionals" and "Licensing and Accreditation of Health Care Facilities and Services"); transparency in financial accounting for all stakeholders; and cost-control mechanisms for care in the private/NGO sectors, such as standardized fee schedules for specific health services, primary care gatekeeping, and preauthorization requirements for care from nongovernment providers. Particularly in the context of such developments, the MOH could use inclusion in the government health benefit as an incentive to private and NGO providers to promote quality and efficiency.

Policymakers Should Develop Contingency Plans Regarding East Jerusalem. As we have described, Israel currently has responsibility for the health system in East Jerusalem. Residents of East Jerusalem are covered by the compulsory Israeli national health insurance program and are thus enrolled in one of the four Israeli "sick" funds that cover primary, secondary, and tertiary care. Health care providers and facilities in this system are governed by Israeli protocols.

This chapter would be incomplete without some consideration of the possibility that responsibility for the health system of East Jerusalem will shift to the government of a future independent Palestinian state. In particular, patterns of health and health care use and costs in East Jerusalem are currently closer to Israeli standards than to those in Palestine. On the one hand, without substantial outside subsidies, the Palestinian health system will certainly lack the resources to maintain current levels of provider reimbursement and overall spending for Palestinians in East Jerusalem. On the other hand, significant reductions in reimbursement levels and overall spending in East Jerusalem are likely to cause considerable harm to its health care infrastructure. The MOH and other relevant stakeholders (e.g., other ministries, health care providers in East Jerusalem, the Israeli Ministry of Health, and international donors) should consider specific strategies for incorporating the health system of East Jerusalem into the broader Palestinian health system.

Several interview participants raised the possibility that net contributions by Palestinian residents of East Jerusalem to the Israeli health insurance programs have been positive (i.e., contributions have exceeded the cost of health care use). This could arise, for instance, for groups that are younger than the population average. They argued that, if this were true, Palestinians who had historically been covered by Israeli insurance have an entitlement to continued participation in the Israeli system. The rationale is that national social insurance involves risk sharing between healthy and unhealthy people not just at a point in time, but over time as well (i.e., as people age, they use more health care for age-associated reasons). We did not evaluate this issue here.

The Palestinian Government Should Work with Other Stakeholders, Particularly International Donors, to Establish Stable and Adequate Health System Funding. Since 1994, local resources have not been sufficient to sustain the Palestinian health system at current levels, which in any case do not meet our mandate of a truly successful Palestinian health system. Some of the policy options described above have the potential to reduce costs and/or increase efficiency, and thus to promote financial viability. Nevertheless, we believe that achieving a successful Palestinian health system will require considerable outside resources for the foreseeable future. (We discuss levels of external support in the "Cost" section below.) Given the current and likely future role of the government sector, many of these resources will need to be directed to the government health system for the overall health system to function successfully.

However, as prior analyses of the Palestinian health system have emphasized, such an approach conflicts directly with the policies and priorities of many international donors, who strongly favor channeling resources through NGOs rather than through government entities, and who also favor making capital investments rather than supporting operating budgets. In recognition of the limitations of these strategies, in July 2003, the U.S. government authorized $20 million of direct support to the PA, the first such payment since the PA was established.[26] Additional direct cooperation between the Palestinian government and international donors is needed to facilitate successful future health system development and operation.

Effects of Restricted Domestic Mobility. Health insurance benefits should reflect patients' abilities to reach appropriate health care facilities. For instance, if patients cannot travel to distant government facilities, it may be necessary for the government health benefit to cover care in the NGO and private sectors on more than the current

---

[26] Of this total, $11 million were slated for specific infrastructure projects, including the repair of municipal water and sewage systems; road repair and reconstruction; repair of electrical distribution lines; and rehabilitation of municipal schools, clinics, courthouses, and other public buildings. Up to $9 million were intended to ensure the continued provision of electric, water, and sewage utility services.

exceptional basis. If mobility is restricted, however, even such expanded coverage will leave many people with inadequate access to care, particularly secondary and tertiary care in rural areas. We discuss the implications of restricted mobility on access to care and health infrastructure development further below under "Licensing and Accreditation of Health Care Facilities and Services."

Restricted domestic mobility would also significantly impair health system management. While it would necessarily increase the authority of local managers—something we recommend, in principle—it would inhibit national systems of oversight and accountability. On a related issue, restricted mobility would inhibit or prevent the collection of most types of health system data; we discuss this further below under "Health Information Systems."

More generally, restricted mobility is likely to limit the economic viability of a Palestinian state and correspondingly reduce the resources available for health system development. In principle, this could be offset by additional external resources. However, the availability of certain sources of funding, particularly private investment, is likely to be positively related to the economic viability of the state.

Effects of Restricted International Access. Health insurance policies regarding referrals for care abroad will obviously depend on whether and to where such referrals are possible.

On a related issue, if the Israeli labor market is open to Palestinian workers to any significant degree, we recommend that the Palestinian health planning authority (or the MOH in its absence), the Israeli Ministry of Health, and other relevant organizations develop coordinated policies regarding health insurance coverage and health care for Palestinians working in Israel.

Licensing and Certification of Health Professionals
Background. According to the second national health plan, there are approximately 2,000 physicians in Palestine. Since the only Palestinian medical school, at Al-Quds University, was established in 1994 and graduated its first class in 2001, essentially all practicing physicians in Palestine were trained elsewhere.[27] Although we know of no systematic inventory of where physicians practicing in Palestine were trained, it is clear that their training has varied widely and may be incomplete and out-of-date in many cases. For instance, many Soviet medical graduates who emigrated to Israel in the 1990s required additional training before qualifying for an Israeli medical license, suggesting that the many Palestinian graduates of Soviet medical schools might also require additional training to meet appropriate practice standards.

Historically, and today, Palestinian physicians must receive a license to practice. In both the West Bank and Gaza, candidates are required to pass examinations in order to be licensed, although procedures differ in these two areas. The West Bank's licensing protocols are modeled on those in Jordan, while Gaza's protocols are modeled on those

---

[27] Indeed, a number of Al-Quds medical graduates are currently receiving postgraduate training abroad.

in Egypt. However, these licensing criteria have not been consistently applied since the PA assumed responsibility for health care in 1994; as a result, some physicians received licenses without meeting the minimum criteria. Moreover, physicians and other health professionals are licensed for life; and they are not required to participate in continuing education to maintain their skills, nor to demonstrate continued proficiency as a condition of maintaining their medical license.

As a related issue, the institutions controlling subspecialty certification are weak or absent. Subspecialty certification is particularly problematic in Gaza, partly because Egyptian protocols regarding subspecialty training are relatively weak and partly because there have been few attempts to enforce existing standards. As a result, many physicians in Gaza represent themselves as subspecialists of various types without having completed adequate subspecialty training.

To our knowledge, no systematic and ongoing program of continuing medical education (CME) currently exists in Palestine; hence, even providers who would voluntarily participate in CME may have difficulty doing so. Although many training programs have been offered over the past decade, sponsored by many different organizations, they have typically been conducted once or twice, not on a systematic, ongoing basis to successive cohorts of providers. We also know of no standard processes for suspending or revoking a medical license in case of malpractice or professional misconduct, or for individual or class-action lawsuits in such cases.

In our interviews, several people proposed reasons why continuing education has not been established despite widespread consensus regarding its importance. These included the economic cost of participating in training and possible provider reluctance to let their patients know that they were receiving continuing education (e.g., because this might undermine patients' confidence).

With few exceptions, conditions are similar for nurses, pharmacists, and other health professionals: Initial training often needs to be improved; standards of licensing are weak and/or inconsistently enforced; and licenses are valid for life, without any requirement to participate in continuing education programs. As is the case with physicians, no institutionalized CME programs are available for nurses, pharmacists, and other health professionals on even a voluntary basis.

Information from published reports and our interview stakeholders supports the view that weak licensing requirements and the lack of CME combine to reduce quality of care, in some cases to unacceptably low levels. Moreover, as is true in many countries, Palestinian consumers have difficulty distinguishing high-quality providers from those who are unqualified—a difficulty compounded by the fact that existing licensing standards are inconsistently applied and that there are no systematic legal remedies for addressing acute problems.

Recommendation: Palestinian Standards for Licensing and Certifying All Types of Health Professionals Should Be Updated, Standardized, and Enforced. Effective licensing and certification programs are likely to share some common features, as described below.

Licensing and Certification Standards Should Be Valid Measures of Providers'
Qualifications. The purpose of these standards is to ensure that all licensed providers
have demonstrated the knowledge and skill to provide effective care. It obviously follows from this that licensing and certification standards should be valid measures of
this knowledge and skill—both at the time of initial licensing and over time.

In principle, licensing exams and subspecialty certification criteria could be developed locally, based on international standards; or exams and criteria from elsewhere
could be used directly (e.g., those from Jordan, which are already used in the West
Bank). Given the limited size of the Palestinian health system, particularly in subspecialty fields, we recommend the latter.[28]

The Licensing and Certification Processes Should Be Implemented with Govern-
mental Authority. In most health systems, licensing of physicians, nurses, pharmacists,
and other health professionals is a government function. In Palestine, this function
would most naturally be implemented by the MOH, but it could also be implemented
by an independent organization or by another body with MOH oversight. Practices
vary with regard to subspecialty certification, which is sometimes implemented by
government and sometimes by an independent body under government authority. The
appropriate model for Palestine should be determined locally.

In any case, licensing and certification standards should have the force of law—
i.e., practicing without a license, or violating the terms of the license, should lead to
civil and/or criminal sanctions. In addition, there should be established procedures for
suspending or revoking licenses in the case of malpractice or misconduct.

Licensing and Certification Standards Should Apply to All Palestinian Providers.
A single set of standards for the West Bank and Gaza and for all sectors of the health
system would minimize the cost of these programs and maximize their benefit for consumers. Different standards add complexity and cost, impose unnecessary constraints
on practice patterns if providers are licensed in one area or sector but not another, and
confuse consumers.

Adequate Levels of Accredited Continuing Education Should Be a Condition of
Maintaining the License/Certification. Effective licensing and certification standards
require the availability of high-quality continuing education programs for all types
of health professionals. These programs can be implemented by the MOH, NGOs,
academic institutions, and others; and by domestic or international organizations.[29]
However, all continuing education programs should be relevant to local conditions,

---

[28] For instance, in the United States, subspecialty certification standards are developed by professional organizations
for each subspecialty. In Palestine, however, the total number of subspecialists in many fields is too small to support
an effective professional association for each field.

[29] In our interviews, various people reported that the organizations they represented were interested in developing
and offering ongoing continuing medical education (CME) programs if the policies of the MOH and the relevant
professional associations supported such training.

and they should be accredited. We discuss accreditation of training programs in detail below.

One factor that has inhibited the development of continuing medical education in Palestine is the economic burden CME imposes on providers. Such education could be required and uncompensated (in effect, a "cost of doing business"). Alternatively, providers could receive some compensation for participation, at least initially. The issue of compensation is presumably most acute for nonsalaried providers in the NGO and private sectors (government and UNRWA providers are generally salaried). This issue can best be resolved locally as part of the policymaking and implementation process.

Palestinian organizations, like those in other countries, have begun to use distance learning methods for training in health and other areas. Expanded use of such methods may facilitate the quality of continuing programs (e.g., by providing easier access to outside experts) and reduce their costs.

The Licensing and Certification Standards Should Include Explicit Policies Regarding Current—and Potentially Underqualified—Providers. Any time that new licensing standards are introduced, there is a question of how these standards will affect providers who were licensed using prior standards. Palestinian policymakers will need to determine whether and how existing providers should be required to meet whatever new licensing requirements are developed, whether they should be permitted to relicense on a voluntary basis, or whether they should be totally or partially exempted under a "grandfather clause." If existing providers are not required to comply with new standards, an alternative might be to develop conventions for naming the new credentials that could be used only by providers who meet the new standards.

Of these options, mandatory relicensing is likely to have the biggest effect on improving providers' knowledge, and consumers would need to recognize only a single licensing standard. However, it may be politically difficult to implement, involve relatively high training costs, and risk producing a shortage of providers (e.g., if many existing providers are unable or unwilling to qualify). Voluntary relicensing is likely to be easier to implement than a mandatory program; and the effects of such a program could be enhanced through consumer education about the new standards as a signal of provider quality, and/or through financial incentives from the MOH and other payers for relicensing. These issues should be resolved locally.

We note that many of the issues covered in this subsection were examined in greater detail in the *National Plan for Human Resource Development and Education in Health*. In general, we consider the goals and strategies outlined in that plan to remain relevant, and we refer readers to that report for additional details (Welfare Association, PA, and Ministry of Higher Education, 2001a–f).[30]

---

[30] Dr. Afifi, one of the authors of this chapter, was overall project coordinator for the development of the *National Plan for Human Resource Development and Education in Health*.

Effects of Restricted Domestic Mobility. Limited population mobility would make it difficult to implement and enforce appropriate standards of licensing and certification. By inhibiting access for both faculty and students, it would also prevent the development and implementation of high-quality continuing education programs. These effects could be mitigated with additional financial resources to pay for operating local-area licensing, certification, and training. However, doing so would be costly, and it is unlikely that enough appropriate personnel would be available to implement these programs in all areas.

Effects of Restricted International Access. Licensing, certification, and continuing education activities are generally implemented domestically. However, restricted access could limit access by Palestinians to outside expertise and other resources, and thus inhibit the development and implementation of effective licensing and certification programs.

Licensing and Accreditation of Health Care Facilities and Services

Background. As with the process for licensing health professionals, the processes for licensing and accrediting health care facilities and services in Palestine should be strengthened. In general, the MOH has authority to review and approve new infrastructure development projects that are proposed for the health system and also to set standards for the operation of existing facilities and services. However, the MOH has exercised this authority in a very limited fashion. Current standards for licensing new projects and for reviewing existing facilities and programs are relatively weak, and they are inconsistently applied and enforced. Moreover, many practices continue to differ between the West Bank and Gaza.

As a result, new infrastructure projects do not always conform to the health development targets of the national health plans, or to any other coordinated national strategy, and low-quality facilities and services are allowed to operate, with little pressure to improve. For example, the European Hospital in Gaza was built despite the fact that it did not conform to national development strategies for inpatient care. Following its completion in 1997, it remained unused for more than three years because the MOH lacked the money and staff to operate it.

Many types of health services fail to meet consistent standards. For example, the law prohibiting pharmacists from dispensing medication to patients without a physician's prescription is rarely enforced. As another example, an increasing number of ambulance services operating in Palestine do not meet national (or other internationally accepted) standards for training, equipment, and overall quality. The Palestine Red Crescent Society (PRCS) has statutory authority to set standards for ambulance services. However, to be effective, these standards must be enforced by the government, which has generally not happened. PRCS has offered to provide equipment and supplies to ambulance services that voluntarily conform to the PRCS national standards, but this strategy has also not generally led to compliance. Similarly, the PRCS has developed practice guidelines for prehospital emergency care, while the MOH and other stakeholders are currently developing a parallel set of standards.

A somewhat related issue is the long-run integration and operation of the new infrastructure that has been developed in the context of the second intifada and the associated geographic closures. Although the local facilities developed since 2000 have helped to increase access to health care under conditions of closure, under conditions of peace many of these facilities may not be clinically effective or economically efficient because of low patient volume. If free travel is allowed in a future independent Palestinian state, policymakers will need to determine how (or whether) to integrate these new facilities into the national health system.

Recommendation: Palestinian Standards for Licensing and Accrediting Health Care Facilities and Services Should Be Updated, Standardized, and Enforced. Successful licensing and accreditation systems are likely to include some common features, as described below.

New Infrastructure Development Should Be Consistent with National Strategies and Targets. To promote efficient infrastructure development, many health systems require that new health system infrastructure projects be licensed. To be successful, such a process should have specific and transparent guidelines, such as requiring that new infrastructure projects be consistent with national development targets. Licensing requirements should be binding, regardless of funding source or sponsoring organization. As discussed above, this process would fall under the national health planning authority.

The Licensing and Certification Processes Should Be Implemented with Governmental Authority. As described under "Licensing and Certification of Health Professionals," this function can be carried out directly by the government, or by an independent body under government authority.

The Licenses/Accreditation of Facilities and Programs Should Be Reevaluated Periodically. As with health care providers, a policy of licensing facilities and programs "for life" is unlikely to maximize their effectiveness and efficiency. Facilities and programs should therefore be reevaluated periodically. Every effort should be made to strengthen those that do not meet current standards; in extreme cases, however, the authority should exist to close facilities and programs temporarily. Evaluation standards should be specific, transparent, and national; and they should be applied consistently to government, private, NGO, and UNRWA facilities and programs. Evaluation of government and UNRWA facilities by an independent body may help reduce conflict of interest.

Licensing and Accreditation Standards Should Be Valid Measures of Facility and Program Performance. The purpose of these standards is to ensure that all approved facilities and programs are providing care that is adequately effective and efficient. The standards should be valid measures of such performance.

The Government Health System and Other Payers Should Consider Explicit Incentives to Promote Quality. Many health systems are using, or are considering the use of, financial incentives for health care facilities and programs that meet certain performance benchmarks. Such strategies may complement national licensing and accreditation standards, which are generally designed to ensure that institutions meet a minimum threshold of quality. We discuss these and other strategies further under "Health Care Quality Improvement" below.

Effects of Restricted Domestic Mobility. Limited population mobility would make it difficult to implement and enforce appropriate standards of licensing and accreditation. As discussed above, it would also require significantly different health infrastructure development strategies. In particular, it would require much greater emphasis on local delivery of clinical services. However, it would be difficult or impossible to provide all needed services in all areas, particularly secondary and tertiary services; moreover, the costs associated with developing many local facilities would be higher than that of a system based on fewer referral centers, and clinical quality is likely to be lower because of low patient volume.

Even assuming contiguous Palestinian territory in the West Bank and unrestricted access to East Jerusalem, the Palestinian health system is likely to face the challenge of a physically separate Gaza. If so, national health planners will need to determine whether it is more efficient to develop separate secondary and tertiary care capabilities in Gaza and the West Bank, versus investing in patient transport systems, international referral, or other strategies. In any case, we recommend that Palestinian health planners focus on developing national institutions with common standards and programs across all Palestinian territories.

Effects of Restricted International Access. Licensing and accreditation are generally implemented domestically. However, restricted international access for patients could affect strategies for infrastructure development. Given the size of the Palestinian population and the current capabilities of its health system, a strategy of domestic provision of all types of health care—including secondary and tertiary services—is unlikely to be economically or clinically efficient. Developing an infrastructure to deliver all types of care domestically (rather than referring some patients to foreign institutions for specialty care) is likely to result in higher costs and lower quality.

Human Resource Development

Background. Along with licensing and certification procedures, Palestinian educational programs need to be strengthened for all types of health professionals, including clinicians, pharmacists, health system administrators, public health workers, research and evaluation staff, and other relevant personnel. In many of these fields, the supply of appropriately trained professionals for the Palestinian health system is currently inadequate.

As noted above, there is one medical school in Palestine, which currently admits 40–50 new undergraduate students per year. The medical training program needs to be strengthened academically to meet international standards, with respect to both basic science and clinical education. Although some internship posts are available in Palestinian institutions and more are being developed, postgraduate medical training in Palestine is currently very limited. Our interview participants noted that Palestinian medical graduates must go abroad to receive suitable subspecialty training in nearly all fields, including primary care subspecialties such as general internal medicine and family practice.

Overall, the number of physicians per capita generally conforms to targets set in the national health plans. However, the supply of highly qualified physicians is limited, particularly in many medical subspecialties. Specific areas of shortage mentioned by interview participants included psychology, psychiatry (particularly child psychiatry), neurology, and oncology (particularly radiation oncology), among others.

There are also two dental schools in Palestine, which were established more recently than the medical school. Training programs in other clinical areas, including nursing, pharmacy, midwifery, medical social work, and psychology, were established before the medical school. Together, the capacities of these programs come closer to meeting Palestinian national needs in their respective areas than does the medical school. However, there is a shortage of qualified professionals in many areas, including dentistry, nursing, midwifery, and psychosocial medicine, and there may be some degree of excess in pharmacy (or at least in the current number of private pharmacies).[31] Moreover, there was widespread consensus among those we interviewed that the quality of all types of training programs needed to be improved.

We were unable to assess the supply and quality of training of other health professionals, such as administrators, public health workers, and research and evaluation staff. However, it is likely that these areas also require strengthening. We emphasize the importance of focusing on training in each of these areas as part of any national human resource development program in health, particularly since these areas are often underemphasized relative to training programs for clinicians.

Finally, successful human resource development for the Palestinian health system is likely to require improved salary and working conditions, particularly in the government sector. Interview participants who were *not* themselves public employees consistently commented on the acute lack of resources in the public sector for recruiting and retaining highly qualified staff. Limited resources, along with weak civil service institutions and the perceived lack of a stable career path for public health sector employees, may be causing some qualified staff to move from the government sector to the private sector, to NGOs (particularly those with international funding, some of which offer salaries that vastly exceed the government pay scale), or abroad. A related problem suggested by our nongovernmental interview participants is that the organizational structure of the MOH, particularly the fragmentation of responsibility across departments, negatively affects employee performance and willingness to remain in the public sector.

---

[31] Validating these perceptions was outside the scope of our analysis.

Recommendation: Palestinian Institutions Should Implement a Human Resource Development Strategy for the Health Professions to Ensure an Adequate Supply of Appropriately Trained Personnel for the Palestinian Health System. Successful strategies for achieving this goal are likely to include a number of features, as described below.

Existing Educational Institutions and Programs Should Be Accredited, Using Appropriate International Standards. Many countries have implemented minimum accreditation standards that medical, dental, and nursing schools and other educational institutions and programs must meet for their programs to be allowed to operate and for their graduates to be eligible for professional licensing and certification. These accreditation standards are implemented with government authority, but they can be defined and assessed by governmental or nongovernmental organizations.

In Palestine, the Ministry of Education and Higher Education has responsibility for authorizing the establishment of new educational programs and for monitoring existing programs. However, health education programs have not consistently been held to high standards of quality, neither at the time they were established nor over time. This has a number of implications, including the likelihood that graduates' initial training may be inadequate and that graduates may have limited access to further training—particularly abroad—because their initial degrees do not meet international standards.

Addressing shortcomings in educational quality will require development and application of appropriate accreditation standards. These standards should be based on appropriate international models. International standards are likely to be useful in their own right, and adherence to international standards facilitates educational exchange for undergraduate and graduate training.[32]

We expect that many educational programs will require strengthening to meet accreditation standards. Strengthening domestic training programs will require a national investment strategy to recruit and retain suitable faculty and to build, maintain, and operate the infrastructure necessary to support training. Programs that repeatedly fail to meet accreditation criteria should be closed until the standards are met.

Under conditions of peace, Israel is likely to be a valuable source of technical assistance, particularly regarding faculty development and research. Israeli institutions have played this role successfully in the past, and Israeli stakeholders consistently reported that their institutions would be willing to do so in the future, circumstances and resources permitting.

The MOH and the Ministry of Education and Higher Education have recently established a body that must authorize any new health-related academic or vocational training program in health. This approach is consistent with the recommendations outlined in this chapter. This body is relatively new, so there has not yet been an opportunity to evaluate its performance systematically.

---

[32] In the absence of a suitable Palestinian accreditation program, the medical school at Al-Quds University has directly pursued accreditation by British and U.S. institutions. It is also currently pursuing accreditation by Israel; because of the location of the medical school, Israeli policy requires such accreditation.

Existing Health Education Programs Should Meet Minimum Accreditation Standards Before New Programs Are Established. New programs are likely to compete with existing programs for scarce human, physical, and financial resources, risking a reduction in overall quality and limited success in achieving the programs' objectives. Perhaps the most salient example of this is the medical school at Al-Quds University, which was opened in 1994 without its own teaching and laboratory facilities, equipment, library, complete curriculum, or adequate faculty and staff. Indeed, the school was established despite a recommendation by the Palestine Council on Higher Education (later the Ministry of Higher Education, and now the Ministry of Education and Higher Education), based on a feasibility study and internal workshop, that the opening of a Palestinian medical school be delayed. In our view, the medical school has had limited success in achieving the goals for which it was established, which included improvement of health care quality, CME, and clinical research in Palestine. Whether it will achieve the goal of producing competent physicians to serve the Palestinian population is still unknown because the first cohorts of graduates have not yet completed their training.

It may be beneficial to delay the establishment of new degree-granting educational programs in health until the corresponding existing programs have been evaluated by the Ministry of Education and Higher Education and after strategies are in place to strengthen these existing programs in accordance with appropriate accreditation standards. (By "corresponding" existing programs we mean programs that grant the same or similar degrees as a proposed new program or that are required for the proposed new program to function effectively; for instance, a doctoral program in pharmacy would require a successful undergraduate pharmacy program.) In the meantime, resources that might otherwise have been devoted to establishing new programs should be devoted to strengthening those that already exist and to developing the infrastructure needed to support future expansion of training capacity.

Policymakers Should Develop Incentives to Ensure an Appropriate Supply of Qualified Professionals. The Palestinian health system is likely to benefit from the creation of a student loan program for study in accredited health training programs. We understand that many qualified students currently face significant financial barriers to continuing their education and that Palestinian university students are disproportionately concentrated in the humanities (versus the sciences), in part because the educational fees are lower in those fields. To the extent that training in the health professions represents a good long-term investment—i.e., via more job opportunities and higher earning potential—both the students and Palestinian society would be better off if loans for such study were available.

Loan programs and other forms of support may be particularly valuable in fields where there is an acute shortage of qualified personnel (based on national targets or on operational conditions). The specific fields to be supported should be updated over time to ensure that those with present shortages do not become oversupplied. Under free labor market conditions, labor shortages in particular fields may be self-correcting over time (e.g., because high demand and correspondingly high salaries induce people to enter those fields). However, the large Palestinian government sector may dampen some of these incentives. Also, many Palestinians face liquidity constraints in pursuing education—i.e., they are unable to borrow enough money to pursue relatively expensive training, even if that training would pay off over their professional career.

Palestinian training programs should also be adjusted (for instance, by shifting resources to other areas) in the event of an oversupply of qualified personnel in particular health fields. In addition, the government health system should use flexible compensation and contracting arrangements to reflect the relative demand for personnel with different types of training.

The Public Sector Should Be Able to Attract and Retain an Adequate Number of Appropriately Qualified Staff. Given the current and likely future role of the government as a provider of care in Palestine—and given its administrative, regulatory, and enforcement responsibilities—it is essential that the MOH and other relevant government institutions be able to attract and retain suitably qualified professionals. This may require increasing the salaries of health professionals in the government sector. It may also require changing the civil service law, which is currently relatively weak; ensuring a stable career path for government employees in the health sector; and developing merit-based hiring, retention, and promotion criteria that are consistently applied.

We recognize that any efforts to improve labor conditions in the MOH are likely to have implications for all ministries and public employees. Such changes may be most plausible in the context of broader civil service reforms.

Managers in All Health Sectors Should Receive Appropriate Training, Initially and on an Ongoing Basis. To function effectively, health system managers need to be able to use modern systems for planning, budgeting, procurement, accounting, data collection and analysis, and other key functions. These skills must be continuously maintained and updated. Effective training programs in these areas should be established and strengthened.

Policymakers or Local Institutions Should Develop Cooperative Agreements with Foreign Institutions Regarding Training and Academic Exchange. For a health care system and population the size of Palestine's, any efficient human resource development strategy will include having some people train abroad, rather than attempting to develop all necessary training capacity domestically. In this context, the Palestinian health system is likely to benefit from the development of bilateral agreements with foreign countries and/or institutions to designate training slots for suitably qualified Palestinian students and to enable periodic exchange of faculty.

With respect to training abroad, appropriate institutions should be developed to increase the likelihood that Palestinian students trained abroad will return to work in Palestine, at least for some period of time. There are various international models for this, many of which are already being used by Palestinian organizations that help sponsor foreign training.

Under conditions of peace, training in Israel is likely to be a very cost-effective option for Palestinians, and the exchange may itself contribute to the peace process. In the past, many Palestinian health professionals have received such training; indeed, some Palestinians are currently training in Israeli institutions. Palestinians training in Israel may be able to live at home, or at least to travel home frequently and cheaply. In addition, Palestinians trained in Israel (rather than in other countries) may be more likely to return to Palestine when their training is completed.

Basic Science Education Should Be Improved. Chapter Eight provides information about primary and secondary education in Palestine. One finding described in Chapter Eight is especially salient here: the need to strengthen science education at all levels of the Palestinian education system, including primary and secondary schools. This would help ensure that future cohorts of Palestinian graduates have the qualifications to pursue health-related training if they choose. Strengthening public education programs is particularly important for poor students, whose opportunities are otherwise especially limited.

Effects of Restricted Domestic Mobility. For human resource development, the problems associated with restricted mobility are analogous to those for the development of health care facilities, services, and programs. Specifically, implementation and enforcement of appropriate licensing and accreditation standards are more difficult; and it is more difficult and costly to develop high-quality education programs if the mobility of students and faculty is restricted.

Effects of Restricted International Access. Licensing and accreditation are generally implemented domestically. However, restricted international access for students and health professionals is likely to hinder strategies for human resource development. It is unlikely that the medical, nursing, public health, and other manpower needs of the new state can all be met domestically at appropriate levels of quality. Meeting these needs is likely to require access to educational institutions in Israel, Jordan, and other countries for Palestinian students and health professionals who seek advanced training (as well as access to Palestine by foreign health professionals who might provide training in Palestinian institutions).

Prior to 2000, for instance, there was regular cooperation between Israeli and Palestinian institutions regarding training of health professionals. Nearly all official cooperation ended following the outbreak of the second intifada, although some activities continue on a personal level. Israeli interview participants told us that their institutions would welcome the resumption and indeed expansion of such cooperation with their Palestinian counterparts, circumstances and resources permitting.

Over time, it is also possible to imagine flows of students into Palestine and flows of Palestinian faculty to foreign institutions. Indeed, the latter, and to some degree the former, already takes place.

Health Care Quality Improvement

Background. Although formal assessment of the quality of health care in Palestine was outside the scope of this analysis, available evidence suggests that patient satisfaction with the Palestinian health care system is low. Patients generally regard health care services in Palestine as inferior, and those who can afford to do so seek care in Jordan, Israel, and elsewhere. Patient satisfaction with private and NGO services is higher than with the government sector, particularly in the last several years when the PA's waiving of government health insurance premiums led to a doubling of enrollment without a corresponding increase in capacity. In our experience, opinions among providers and other health system leaders mirror those of patients. Our interview participants consistently emphasized the need to improve health care quality with respect to primary, secondary, and tertiary care and in all sectors of the health system.

Before and after 1994, many health care quality improvement (QI) projects have been undertaken in Palestine. Some projects were relatively independent, implemented by one organization or facility and often the result of the personal initiative of individual providers. Others were part of systematic QI efforts. These efforts have improved care in specific clinical areas, in specific institutions, and in the health system overall. Indeed, Palestine was one of the first developing areas where modern QI practices were shown to be effective.

Systematic efforts by Palestinian authorities predate the creation of the MOH, beginning with the establishment of the Central Unit for Quality of Health Care within the Palestine Council of Health in 1994. This unit developed the *Strategic Plan for Quality of Health Care in Palestine* and the *Operational Plan for Quality of Health Care in Palestine,* the overall goals of which were to introduce and institutionalize the use of modern QI methods in the government health sector and in the Palestinian health system generally.

When the Central Unit for Quality of Health Care was discontinued in June 1995, its responsibilities were assumed and expanded by the Quality Improvement Project (QIP) within the MOH. The QIP operated dozens of successful QI projects in several demonstration sites and worked to expand the number of facilities in which it operated. It also provided formal training in QI methods to several hundred health professionals. By the late 1990s, however, the QIP had ceased to function effectively because of lack of institutional support within the MOH and travel restrictions within Palestine. The World Bank's current health-sector development projects in the West Bank and Gaza include QI components.

Although QI projects continue throughout the health system, they are no longer part of a coordinated national process. In general, QI interventions such as clinical practice guidelines or clinical pathways, provider reminder systems, or quality-based financial incentives are not widely used in the Palestinian health system; nor are institutional processes such as continuous QI or total quality management. However, some efforts are currently under way to increase use of evidence-based protocols and guidelines in Palestine, particularly regarding nutrition, diabetes, and maternal and child care. This work has been funded by international donors and is supported by the MOH.

Quality improvement depends on reliable evaluation. A number of organizations within the Palestinian health system have capabilities in program and policy evaluation, including the MOH; Al-Quds and Birzeit Universities and other academic institutions; the Health Development, Information and Policy Institute (HDIP) and other NGOs; and others.[33] However, these existing capacities are weak in a number of important ways. For instance, the number of professional positions available to trained health researchers is relatively limited, so there is insufficient capacity to address all relevant issues. In addition, as is true in many other settings throughout the world, new health-related policies and demonstration programs are often implemented without an explicit evaluation component, and the results of many initiatives are not systematically documented or published.

Recommendation: A National Strategy on Health Care Quality Improvement Should Be Developed and Implemented, with Systematic Evaluation of Quality Improvement Projects and Dissemination of Those That Succeed.

Every health care system faces challenges in institutionalizing health care QI processes. However, successful strategies typically include some common features, as described below.

Quality Improvement Efforts Should Be Coordinated. National QI efforts should be coordinated to enhance their efficiency and to facilitate evaluation. In addition, priorities for QI should be consistent with national health planning targets. The national strategic plan for QI should be updated.

Facilities and Programs Should Adopt Systematic, Modern Quality Improvement Processes. In many settings, one key component of QI efforts is adoption of an institutional QI process, e.g., one that uses the principles of total quality management. An institutional process helps create a framework of responsibility within the facility or program for choosing and implementing QI projects and makes such activities part of an organization's core functions.

Quality Improvement Projects Should Be Evidence Based. There is a considerable and expanding literature regarding the efficacy, effectiveness, and cost-effectiveness of various QI strategies in health care. Although findings in other geographic areas or practice settings may not always apply to Palestine, this evidence base is likely to provide a valuable frame of reference for local QI efforts, particularly if interventions are carefully adapted to local circumstances.

Quality Improvement Projects Should Be Evaluated, and the Results Should Be Publicized. While some QI projects in Palestine have been formally evaluated, many have not. When programs are evaluated, the results are often not widely disseminated

---

[33] HDIP maintains an annotated bibliography of journal articles and other reports on health and health care in Palestine (see Barghouthi, Fragiacomo, and Qutteina, 1999; and Barghouthi, Shubita, and Fragiacomo, 2000).

or publicly accessible. Systematic evaluation of QI interventions would help develop an evidence base of best practices in Palestine, which would help guide future health system planning and development. In addition, such evidence would also serve as a useful reference for QI efforts in other developing areas.

Successful Quality Improvement Projects Should Be Supported and Disseminated. In many settings, even successful demonstration projects are not sustained in place after the demonstration period, nor are they widely disseminated. Patients, providers, and other health system stakeholders are likely to benefit if the QI process in Palestine includes explicit strategies for sustaining and spreading QI projects that are found to be cost-beneficial or relatively cost-effective from a societal perspective.

Effects of Restricted Domestic Mobility. Like health system planning and policy development, the ability to carry out and evaluate QI activities would be significantly inhibited under conditions of restricted mobility.

Effects of Restricted International Access. QI activities are generally implemented domestically. However, the development of QI programs would be inhibited if staff responsible for QI activities were unable to travel internationally for training and professional collaboration.

Policies on Prescription Drugs and Medical Devices

Background. Following several years of development, the MOH distributed the first national drug list in 2003. Development of the list was informed by several sources, including the essential drug lists developed by the WHO. The new list is likely to be of considerable value to the Palestinian health system, particularly the government sector, by helping to define its pharmaceutical policy in a public and systematic way. However, the national drug list was distributed without corresponding training for clinicians and pharmacists in how to use the list. In addition, there is currently no systematic process in place for updating the national drug list, although there are several reasons to expect that such updating will be beneficial. Most obviously, new and more effective drugs are frequently introduced. In addition, there is a constant stream of drugs coming off patent. Such drugs should be evaluated for possible inclusion in the formulary. One example is the antidepressant fluoxetine (brand name Prozac), which was on patent and not on the national drug list when the list was originally developed. Although fluoxetine has subsequently come off patent, it remains off the list.

In addition, both the content of the national drug list and the amount of each drug that is purchased and distributed by the MOH were largely based on historical prescribing and consumption patterns in Palestine, with relatively little explicit consideration of scientific evidence on effectiveness, cost-effectiveness, or patterns of microbial resistance. As a result, if past prescribing and consumption patterns were clinically or economically inefficient, the current national drug list—and MOH purchasing policies—are likely to reflect these inefficiencies.

Distribution of pharmaceuticals in the government sector is currently uneven, with excess supply of many drugs in some places (particularly urban centers) and shortages elsewhere. The MOH and the World Bank are currently developing improved pharmaceutical data systems, focusing on inventories and expiration dates. Such systems are likely to be beneficial, particularly if they are integrated with data on geographic patterns of morbidity and patterns of pharmaceutical prescribing and use. However, such data systems do not currently exist.

Although there is a considerable domestic pharmaceutical industry, there has been little coordination between the MOH and pharmaceutical suppliers regarding the domestic supply of drugs on the national drug list—even regarding drugs with a short shelf life and those that are required for treatment of life-threatening conditions. However, a promising recent development is the coordination between the MOH and the United States Agency for International Development (USAID) to develop a program of local procurement of some of the products on the national drug list, with the explicit intent of building strategic reserves for particular medicines.

The uncertain supply of necessary drugs from domestic or foreign sources has created problems for some patients when importation and/or local distribution of pharmaceuticals has been disrupted, as has occasionally occurred since 1994 and particularly since the outbreak of the second intifada.

In 2002, some international donations of pharmaceuticals to the MOH included products that were not on the national drug list. However, the MOH rejected some donations for clinical and policy reasons. International donations also apparently included some products for which there were actually domestic suppliers, effectively undermining Palestinian producers. To our knowledge, the MOH does not have a formal policy for how to handle such donations.

Although responsibility for the Palestinian health system was transferred to the PA in 1994, the PA and MOH do not have complete authority over pharmaceuticals and other medical products. In particular, all such products imported into Palestine must be registered in Israel, using Israeli standards. In our view, this policy results in both potential costs and benefits for Palestine. On the one hand, this policy is likely to raise the cost of pharmaceuticals in Palestine by limiting potential foreign suppliers to those who have incurred the cost of registering in Israel. On the other hand, it may help ensure the quality of imported drugs. In addition to possible clinical benefits, the local pharmaceutical industry might benefit by closing the Palestinian market to low-quality—and very low-priced—competition.

In our interviews, Israeli stakeholders expressed the expectation that Israeli restrictions on Palestinian imports would be eliminated with the establishment of an independent Palestinian state. The MOH currently has a process for licensing pharmaceuticals and other medical products that are locally produced, but it is not as comprehensive as the Israeli process. In any case, the capacities of this process would need to be expanded significantly if responsibility over imported products were also transferred to the PA.

Recommendation: Policymakers Should Implement National Strategies on the Licensing, Supply, and Distribution of Pharmaceuticals and Medical Devices to Ensure a Stable and Adequate Supply of Safe and Cost-Effective Products. Successful strategies in this area are likely to include some common features, as described below.

There Should Be a Systematic Process in Place for Updating the National Drug List. To remain clinically relevant and cost-effective, drug formularies need to be updated periodically to reflect current evidence on clinical efficacy and cost-effectiveness of new and existing drugs, and changes in the supply and cost of particular drugs. Since the national drug list is binding only for the government sector in Palestine, it may be most appropriate for the updating process to be led by the MOH. We recognize that effective implementation of this process is likely to require improved health information systems, particularly regarding microbial resistance (discussed further in the following subsection).

Products on the National Drug List Should Be Consistently Available Throughout the Government Health System. Consumers and providers are likely to regard the health system as deficient if the drugs to which people are formally entitled as part of their health insurance benefit are not consistently available. A reliable supply will require efficient distribution methods, which in turn will require improved health information systems.

Training for Pharmacists and for Clinicians Regarding Pharmaceuticals Should Be Strengthened. Our interview participants mentioned a number of quality issues, including prescribing without appropriate clinical indications, dispensing without a prescription, dispensing drugs that are past their expiration date, and prescribing and dispensing without adequate instructions for patients. We have already discussed recommendations for improving licensing and continuing education for clinicians, pharmacists, and other health care professionals. Here, we emphasize that initial and continuing training programs regarding pharmaceuticals should focus particularly on the content of the national drug list to ensure that clinicians can prescribe and pharmacists can dispense all these medications appropriately—a level of skill that is not currently universal.

Policymakers Should Review and, If Necessary, Update the National Prescribing Law. The national health plans and many of our interview participants referred to the need for an updated national prescribing law. One specific provision called for in the national health plans is mandatory generic substitution. Although such provisions have been beneficial elsewhere, these and other details should be resolved locally.

It is apparently common practice for pharmacists to dispense prescription medications to patients without a physician's prescription. This is officially prohibited, and this prohibition should be enforced consistently. At the same time, some interview participants suggested that it might be cost-effective for pharmacists to have discretion in recommending specific medications, conditional on receiving diagnosis information and recommending that a patient receive prescriptions from a physician. Such a policy might be beneficial, particularly given the current lack of uniform training and licensing standards among physicians and pharmacists in Palestine.

The National Programs for Licensing Pharmaceuticals, Medical Devices, and Medical Consumables Should Be Strengthened. Every health system should have specific procedures for licensing drugs and other medical products to determine which products may be sold and to ensure that they are safe and effective. As we have described, the Palestinian health system currently relies on Israel to perform much of this function, as part of the agreements in the Oslo process. It may be efficient for the Palestinian health system to incorporate the licensing determinations of Israel or other third parties into its own policies. If so, however, this decision should be made explicitly by local policymakers. Even then, new and expanded responsibilities are likely to fall on the Palestinian health system, and its capabilities in this area will need to be strengthened and expanded.

Effects of Restricted Domestic Mobility. Efficient distribution of pharmaceuticals would be significantly inhibited under conditions of restricted mobility, as has been the case during the second intifada. As discussed above, licensing and education activities would also be inhibited.

Effects of Restricted International Access. Restrictions on international trade would inhibit efficient and clinically appropriate pharmaceutical policies by restricting access to imported pharmaceuticals and to the raw materials needed for domestic pharmaceutical production, and by inhibiting Palestinian exports. Licensing of pharmaceuticals and medical devices would mostly be implemented locally. However, those programs would be inhibited if staff responsible for them were unable to travel internationally for training and professional collaboration.

Health Information Systems

Background. For this analysis, we define "health information systems" relatively widely to include all types of data that are directly relevant to health system planning, operation, and evaluation. These data encompass vital statistics; epidemiological data, including but not limited to nutritional status, vaccine coverage, microbial resistance, behavioral risk factors, incidence of infectious disease, incidence and prevalence of chronic illness, and disease registries; hospital cost and discharge data; data on cost and use of ambulatory care; inventory and consumption data for pharmaceuticals and other medical products; health insurance registry; tracking systems for international referrals; and medical records.

Many of these types of data are currently collected in some fashion in the Palestinian health system. For instance, vital statistics are maintained by the Palestinian Central Bureau of Statistics, which shares these and other data within the government and with outside parties. Many types of epidemiological monitoring have been conducted by the Palestinian Central Bureau of Statistics and the MOH, including population- and clinic-based surveys of nutritional status and vaccine coverage, tracking of infectious disease, and data on the incidence and prevalence of noncommunicable and chronic diseases. Anthropometric status has been included in pediatric medical records in the government health system since the 1980s. Some data are available on use of inpatient and outpatient care, particularly within the government health system.

These data have supported previous national planning efforts, policy development, research, and evaluation. However, the success of future health system development efforts will require significant strengthening of existing systems, the introduction of new data capabilities, and more systematic use of data in informing health system policies and operation.

Perhaps most important, existing data systems have not been developed in an integrated, coordinated fashion. Many types of data that are essential for effective health system planning and operation are not consistently available, including national health accounts that cover all health sectors, comprehensive chronic disease registries, and data on pharmaceutical prescribing and use. Even vital statistics data, which are relatively well developed, have important limitations. For instance, births are recorded by the father's name and are not easily linked to the records of the mother. A related issue is that many types of data are collected in some parts of the health system but not in others and/or are collected in different—and incompatible—formats in different locations. Also, many types of data are recorded on paper rather than electronically.

Some efforts to strengthen particular information systems are currently under way. For instance, Birzeit University and the MOH have developed and are implementing updated pediatric medical records, which improve on previous charts by including screening tools for various developmental conditions. Ongoing, population-based nutritional monitoring is being conducted or supported by various organizations, including Birzeit University, Al-Quds University, Johns Hopkins University, CARE, Maram/USAID, the United Nations Children's Fund, the Palestinian Central Bureau of Statistics, and the Food and Agriculture Organization of the United Nations. The World Bank is currently sponsoring a major project with the MOH to strengthen various health information systems, including national registries for health insurance and international referrals; clinical information (on a pilot basis); and a central repository for health data, which will track data on vaccinations, pharmaceutical inventories, incidence of reportable infectious disease, and—in a subsequent phase—hospital discharge data based on the discharge system of the European Hospital in Gaza.

Since its creation in 2001, the Health Inforum has served as an information clearinghouse for the Palestinian health sector.[34] Among other things, Health Inforum maintains a database of health development projects in Palestine. The materials available through Health Inforum were invaluable for our analyses.

---

[34] See http://www.healthinforum.net/.

These various efforts should be continued and supported—but these efforts alone are unlikely to meet the information needs of the Palestinian health system.

Recommendation: Palestinian Policymakers Should Develop Comprehensive, Modern, and Integrated Health Information Systems. Successful health information systems are likely to include a number of common features, as described below.

Data Should Be Collected on Incidence and Prevalence of Noncommunicable Diseases and on Behavioral Risk Factors. Currently, available data suggest that incidence and prevalence of noncommunicable diseases are high and rising rapidly, including diabetes, hypertension, heart disease, and cancer. However, data on these conditions are incomplete as a result of considerable undiagnosed morbidity and a lack of comprehensive population-based screening or surveys in these areas. Also, to our knowledge there is currently no national cancer/tumor registry or registries for other relevant diseases (including for inheritable genetic conditions, some of which are relatively prevalent in Palestine). Accurate data in these areas are essential for effective health system planning and operation.

The Palestinian health system is also likely to benefit from a surveillance system of behavioral risk factors, including cigarette smoking, diet, and physical activity. There was a consensus among interview participants that health promotion and disease prevention efforts need to be strengthened. For instance, several interview participants mentioned that levels of obesity have apparently been increasing among Palestinians, even during periods of economic crisis; another pointed out that the MOH incurs substantial costs for treating diabetes but currently spends very little on diabetes education. Comprehensive surveillance of behavioral risk factors would help to target and implement interventions.

Data Should Be Collected on Nutritional Status, Food Availability, and Food Security. As we have already noted, nutritional status has been and continues to be a key area of concern in Palestine. A number of new data collection initiatives have been implemented in the area of nutritional status, food availability, and food security, including ongoing monitoring reported on a biweekly basis in the Inforum newsletter. Effective monitoring of these issues should be institutionalized. Such data are likely to facilitate health planning and program evaluation.

Health Manpower Registries Should Be Established. Policies to strengthen licensing, certification, and continuing education of health professionals are likely to require national registry systems for all types of health professionals. These systems could track the licensing and certification status of all health professionals eligible to work in Palestine across all sectors of the health system. They could also track participation in continuing medical education.

National Health Accounts Data Should Be Strengthened. The MOH, the Palestinian Central Bureau of Statistics, Health Inforum, and other sources have worked to create comprehensive and consistent accounts of health system revenue and spending. However, available data need to be improved, particularly regarding international donations (currently, better data are available on pledges than on disbursements) and the private and NGO sectors. The Italian Cooperation is currently sponsoring a project to improve national health accounts.

Hospital Cost and Discharge Data Systems Should Be Strengthened. Stronger national hospital data systems, including systems that capture patterns of cost and use (i.e., discharges), are likely to facilitate improvement of health system management practices. The World Bank and the MOH are planning a development project in this area based on the discharge system of the European Hospital in Gaza. In addition to a hospital discharge system, the Palestinian health system is likely to benefit from a national hospital cost accounting system to be used by both public and private hospitals in Palestine.

Data Should Be Collected on Outpatient Costs and Health Care Use. The MOH and other organizations currently collect and report data on the use of many types of outpatient care. These data are reported, for example, in the annual MOH reports on health in Palestine. However, current data are fairly limited, particularly with respect to costs and services provided in the private and NGO sectors. Enhanced data in these areas are also likely to facilitate health system planning and program evaluation. Comprehensive monitoring of outpatient use and costs may be expensive, and policymakers should balance the benefits of ongoing monitoring against the costs of data collection.

Medical Records and Clinical Screening Systems Should Be Strengthened. As noted above, the MOH and the World Bank are currently piloting an improved clinical information system in a small number of clinics, and the MOH and Birzeit University are developing new pediatric charts. Screening of newborns for phenylketonuria (PKU) and congenital hypothyroidism began during the 1980s, but screening for congenital hip dislocations, heart defects, thalassemia, and other congenital conditions is less common. Similarly, screening of adults for chronic disease risk factors is not currently widespread.

New charts and clinical information systems will require systematically training clinic staff to use the new systems. Improved screening and diagnosis must be accompanied by appropriate follow-up services when problems are detected; these should include treatment referrals, patient education, and social support services.

Pharmacy Data Systems Should Be Strengthened. Improved data on pharmaceutical inventories and use will help to strengthen national pharmaceutical policy. The MOH and the World Bank are currently piloting an information system for primary care clinics that includes a prescription drug module.

Regional and International Systems for Data Exchange Should Be Strengthened. Health in Palestine is closely bound to health in Israel, Egypt, Jordan, and other countries in the region, because many population health issues are common across the region and/or have the potential to cross borders. As a result, these and other relevant countries are likely to benefit from development of ways to rapidly and accurately exchange epidemiological data, particularly regarding infectious disease. Some such mechanisms are currently in place, particularly between the MOH and Israel. However, these mechanisms require strengthening and expansion.

Health Data Should Be Used More Systematically to Inform Policymaking and Management. In general, Palestinian health information systems are likely to be most useful if they are computerized. We recognize that this is likely to involve considerable investment, and that planners must evaluate technologies carefully to maximize the efficiency and sustainability of national data systems.

Effects of Restricted Domestic Mobility. Restricted mobility would inhibit or prevent the collection of most types of data described in this subsection.

Effects of Restricted International Access. Regional and international systems of data exchange will be more difficult to implement effectively if Palestinian professionals have limited access to foreign countries, particularly Israel or Jordan. Other health information systems are mostly implemented domestically.

Research

Background. Several universities and NGOs in Palestine currently conduct public health and health services research. However, these existing capacities are weak for the same reasons that evaluation capacity is weak. (Evaluation capacity was discussed above, in "Health Care Quality Improvement.") Moreover, there are currently few established clinical or basic science research programs in Palestine. The lack of such programs is likely to limit medical education and efforts to improve clinical care, particularly secondary and tertiary care.

Recommendation: Palestinian Policymakers Should Develop National Strategies Regarding Public Health, Health Services, Clinical, and Basic Science Research. Such strategies are important complements to the national health plans and the *National Plan for Human Resource Development and Education in Health*. Indeed, there is explicit overlap with components of these plans.

We recognize that the Palestinian health system faces significant resource constraints and that efforts to develop research capacity must be realistic and appropriate in this context. However, systematic expansion of research capacity is likely to have a number of benefits for the Palestinian health system. For instance, in addition to producing output that is scientifically valuable per se, clinical research programs are likely to contribute to the training of future clinicians and health system leaders. They may help foster international respect for Palestinian institutions, as the Israeli Weizman Institute of Science illustrates with respect to Israeli institutions. Research programs may also help generate revenue.[35] In addition to the Weizman Institute, other local models

---

[35] Interview participants particularly mentioned inheritable genetic disorders as an area where there might be considerable demand—and external financing—for scientific collaboration with international institutions, because of the relatively high prevalence of some such conditions among Palestinians.

might include the Lebanese Council for Scientific Research and the Jordanian Higher Council of Science and Technology.

Strategies to develop health research capacity in Palestine will require cooperation among government, academic institutions, NGOs, and international donors. Cooperation regarding research and training with centers of excellence in Israel and other neighboring countries is also likely to be very beneficial.

Many Palestinians with relevant skills currently live abroad, and efforts should be made to recruit members of the Palestinian diaspora to visit or work at Palestinian research institutions. Also, Palestinian research programs are likely to benefit considerably from international partnerships, for instance with Israeli and Jordanian organizations; among other benefits, such partnership may help attract external research funding.

Effects of Restricted Domestic Mobility. The effect of restricted mobility on research programs will vary by the type of research. In particular, research involving population-based data collection will be inhibited. Basic science and some clinical research depends less on population access and would correspondingly be less affected (although, of course, the researchers themselves need to be able to reach their jobs). As described above, restricted mobility will inhibit the economic viability of a Palestinian state and correspondingly reduce the resources available for research.

Effects of Restricted International Access. As with other areas of human resource development, successful development of Palestinian research capability will require that Palestinian students and faculty have access to foreign institutions and that Palestinian institutions be able to recruit foreign faculty (and, to a lesser degree, students).

Programs for Rapid Improvement

Background. As we noted at the beginning of this chapter, our principal analytic focus is on the institutions that would be needed for the successful operation of the Palestinian health system over the first decade of a future independent Palestinian state. Given this mid- to long-term policy perspective, we have so far included relatively little discussion of the type and quality of health services being provided in Palestine. We believe that strengthening the "macro-level" institutions on which we have focused will ultimately increase the efficiency and effectiveness of health care and improve health status throughout Palestine.

In this subsection, however, we diverge from our general approach and consider several specific programs that would directly and rapidly improve the health and health care of Palestinians. There are several reasons for this shift in focus. Rapid improvements are, of course, worthwhile in their own right. In addition, improving health conditions in the short run may also help to achieve longer-run development goals.

At a macro-level, social conditions in Palestine since 1994—including health— have not improved as much as many people had hoped or expected. Many factors have contributed to this lack of improvement, including political and armed conflict, but also ineffective governance and weak policy development and implementation. The lack of improvement has certainly undermined support for the PA and its institutions and for the peace process overall. Indeed, many interview participants and other observers suggested that the slow improvement in quality of life for many Palestinians contributed directly to the outbreak of the second intifada.

At a more micro-level, a dual strategy of pairing short- and longer-term development efforts may contribute to staff and organizational morale. Interview participants noted that boosting morale is particularly important for organizations that place heavy emphasis on humanitarian assistance in response to current conditions. Indeed, we encountered many organizations that were pursuing projects with various planning horizons, from immediate humanitarian aid to multiyear efforts to develop human and physical infrastructure. Overall, we were consistently impressed by the scope of both short- and long-term development projects that we observed.

In sum, whatever the strengths of the Palestinian health system, there are clearly acute areas of need, and all stakeholders are likely to benefit by addressing them effectively and rapidly. In this context, we make the following recommendations.

Recommendation: The MOH Should Implement Comprehensive Programs to Improve Nutritional Status, Including Food Fortification, Micronutrient Supplementation for High-Risk Groups, and Promotion of Healthy Dietary Practices. Available evidence suggests an urgent need to improve nutritional status in Palestine. Studies have shown persistently high levels of anemia at all ages, based on blood testing and dietary intake studies; malnutrition, particularly among children via anthropometric monitoring; vitamin A deficiency, based on dietary intake studies (a blood study of vitamin A is currently pending); and other nutritional problems. Moreover, there is some evidence that the rates of micronutrient deficiency and malnutrition have increased since the outbreak of the second intifada. Poor nutritional status is a well-recognized cause of short- and long-term health problems across the lifespan, including complications of pregnancy, birth defects, heart disease, cancer, osteoporosis, and other conditions. It also impairs children's psychomotor development and later educational performance, including delay in school enrollment, increased absenteeism, impaired concentration, and increased susceptibility to infectious disease—issues that are less commonly emphasized in the development of nutrition policies.

Although a number of efforts to strengthen nutritional status—and the nutrition policies of the MOH—are currently under way, these efforts needed to be consolidated, expanded, and institutionalized. Such efforts will require cooperation among the MOH, UNRWA, and other stakeholders to develop and implement coordinated, comprehensive national programs to improve nutritional status in Palestine, particularly among children and women of childbearing age. Based on scientific evidence, these programs should include fortification of common foodstuffs with vitamins A and D, iron, and folic acid (folate); and provision of vitamin and mineral supplements to children at least through age two and to childbearing women before, during, and after pregnancy. The government health system provided such supplements to infants in the past, but this practice was discontinued in the mid-1990s. The need for supplements prior to pregnancy would be reduced by an effective national fortification program that includes folate.

Recommendation: The National Immunization Program Should Be Updated, and the Costs of Purchasing and Distributing Vaccines Should Be Explicitly Covered by the Government Budget. Immunization programs have been one of the great strengths of the Palestinian health system since the 1970s, with high coverage of a progressive program of vaccines. However, the Palestinian vaccination schedule needs to be updated somewhat, particularly to reflect the availability of new vaccines such as hepatitis A, haemophilus influenza B, and varicella. Each of these is now included in the Israeli vaccination program.

For several years following 1994, the MOH budget explicitly provided for purchase and distribution of all vaccines covered by the national immunization program. However, this practice was discontinued in response to budget pressures, and the immunization program has subsequently relied on international donations of vaccines. In our view, the latter practice is unlikely to guarantee the continuous availability of high-quality vaccines to the Palestinian health system, and the former policy should be reinstated.

Recommendation: The MOH and Other Stakeholders Should Expand the Scope of Available Primary Care Services and Expand Access to Comprehensive Primary Care. As we have described, primary care is the current and intended future cornerstone of the Palestinian health care system. However, certain aspects of primary care—as it is commonly defined—require considerable strengthening. These include health promotion and disease prevention, which also need to be strengthened in schools and elsewhere in society; screening and diagnosis, particularly of child developmental disorders and adult chronic and noncommunicable diseases; reproductive health services, including family planning; and psychosocial support and mental health care, for which there are both considerable societal need and a particular shortage of appropriately trained providers. Efforts to strengthen these areas will require cooperation across stakeholders, including the MOH, UNRWA, relevant NGOs, and international donors.

The relative importance of the primary health care delivery system has increased since the outbreak of the second intifada, because primary care clinics are widely distributed and thus relatively accessible during periods of restricted mobility. Geographic closures have also strengthened the role of nurses and other nonphysician professionals, because these staff tend to live closer to the primary care clinics and have been more consistently available to patients than physicians during periods of closure. Some interview participants regarded the resulting change in practice patterns as beneficial for patients, even if it arose for negative reasons. However, interview participants expressed concern that, when closures lift and economic conditions improve, the MOH and other providers are likely to shift resources away from primary care and toward secondary and tertiary care. In our view, such a shift would be both clinically and economically undesirable for the Palestinian health system.

In the short run, efforts to strengthen health promotion and disease prevention could include additional training and empowerment of health educators, social workers, skilled lay people such as village health workers, community groups, and others. However, the number of such people is currently limited and should be increased over time. Key substantive issues to be addressed include public health issues such as sanitation and water quality; traffic, home, and workplace safety; diet and nutrition; physical activity; cigarette smoking; domestic violence; and clinical issues such as developmental disorders, psychosocial problems, and chronic illness.

There is also a need to strengthen treatment programs—sometimes referred to as "tertiary prevention"—for chronic diseases, particularly diabetes, heart disease, and hypertension. As we understand it, these areas have received relatively little emphasis from NGOs and international donors. However, they represent a considerable and increasing fraction of the overall burden of disease among Palestinians. Moreover, there is increasing scientific evidence that many of these conditions can be effectively—and cost-effectively—managed in primary care.[36]

Recommendation: The MOH and Other Stakeholders Should Develop Comprehensive Strategies for Addressing Psychosocial Needs, Particularly Those Relating to the Exposure of Children to Violence. There is an urgent need to strengthen psychosocial support to help mitigate the consequences of the physical, economic, social, and political stressors that have been prevalent in Palestine. Perhaps most notably, there has been considerable exposure to violence from armed conflict, particularly since the start of the second intifada. Yet there is very limited capacity in the health system—and in the education system and other parts of society—to address the developmental and other consequences of these stressors.

One important step is to strengthen psychosocial support and mental health care in primary care, as noted above. However, successful efforts to address psychosocial needs should extend beyond the health care delivery system. In particular, psychological and developmental problems are stigmatized in Palestine, as elsewhere. Patients and family members may not recognize such problems or view them as treatable, and they may be reluctant to seek care in any case. Providers may not diagnose problems correctly, particularly if patients present with somatic complaints; and they may not recommend effective treatment. For these and other reasons, successful strategies are likely to require community-wide collaboration, involving various parts of the health system, the school system, religious institutions, community groups, and other stakeholders. They should include screening, outreach, and other proactive strategies. Proactive strategies are generally valuable for addressing psychosocial problems and particularly for

---

[36] These issues are also discussed above, in the context of health care finance and quality improvement.

treating psychological trauma; indeed, relatively few trauma victims receive effective care in the absence of outreach programs.

Several relevant programs already exist, including clinic- and school-based programs to address issues among children. These efforts should be continued, but most such programs that we know of are small (one notable exception is the Classroom-Based Intervention program, sponsored by USAID). More generally, we note that the WHO began a new program in 2003 focusing on improving mental health in Palestine. Addressing unmet psychosocial needs will require major increases in qualified personnel, including psychiatrists, psychologists, social workers, school counselors, and qualified lay workers. It will also require the development, dissemination, and support of effective intervention strategies for addressing particular problems, such as psychological trauma among children.

Effects of Restricted Domestic Mobility. Restricted mobility would inhibit successful achievement of all the recommendations in this subsection. Both nutrition and immunization initiatives require transport of supplies and personnel, which will be more difficult under restricted mobility. Similarly, training—whether of health professionals or of consumers—will be more difficult to implement successfully.

As we have described, the role of primary care increases under conditions of restricted mobility, because primary care facilities are more widely accessible. Under such circumstances, however, primary care clinics will necessarily emphasize curative care, and there is likely to be little opportunity to expand the scope of care in the areas described above. Similarly, it will be more difficult to expand systems of psychosocial care under conditions of restricted mobility, because training, planning, and implementation will be inhibited. Moreover, as discussed above, restricted mobility is likely to reduce the economic viability of the state, and with it the resources available for expanding health system capacity.

Effects of Restricted International Access. All the services discussed in this subsection would mainly be provided domestically. However, as with other areas of health system development, the expanded capabilities recommended here will be easier to achieve if Palestinian health professionals have access to technical assistance from abroad and to training in foreign institutions.

Priorities and Timing

As we have described, we believe that the specific priorities for health system development should be determined locally. To this end, we have focused on describing institutions, policies, and programs that are essential for local stakeholders to be able to undertake such priority setting effectively.

In this context, we believe that Palestinian health system development efforts should begin with our first area of emphasis: establishing a planning and coordination authority with adequate power to develop and implement national policy for the Palestinian health system. Indeed, nearly all our interview participants expressed the view that this should occur immediately, not just when an independent Palestinian state is established.

The planning and coordination body would be responsible for reforming policies regarding health insurance and health care finance. It would also oversee the establishment and strengthening of the key institutions described in most of our other recommendations, i.e., licensing and certification of health professionals; licensing and accreditation of facilities, programs, and educational institutions; implementation of national quality improvement strategies; oversight of pharmaceuticals; and collection of national health data.

While we recognize that resources will be scarce, we believe that these institutions are all essential for the successful development of the Palestinian health system. However, the level of available resources will certainly affect the policies and priorities that these institutions pursue. For this reason, among others, we recommend that major new infrastructure projects be deferred until the relevant institutions are in place to ensure that projects are consistent with national priorities and can be implemented effectively.

With respect to research, we believe that efforts to establish research capabilities could begin at any time and that these capabilities should grow slowly but steadily. Finally, the "rapid improvement" recommendations made in the last subsection should be implemented as soon as possible because they have the potential to produce tangible improvements in quality of life for many Palestinians.

Cost

One objective of RAND's project is to estimate the costs involved in strengthening the institutions of a future independent Palestinian state. A general estimate is provided below. However, a detailed estimate of the costs associated with implementing the recommendations made in this chapter is outside the scope of our analysis. Such an estimate will depend on the specific policy choices that local stakeholders make to address each recommendation, which of course are currently unknown, and on details of the current system that were unavailable for this analysis. For instance, the cost of licensing and accrediting health care facilities or educational programs will depend on the licensing and accreditation standards that are ultimately selected for Palestine and on the extent to which current facilities and programs fall short of those standards. Although we could estimate the cost of the licensing and accreditation process per se, using this cost alone is likely to be misleading. The costs of upgrading to meet new standards are likely to dwarf the costs of reviewing programs and of approving or denying their license/accreditation.

In this section, we therefore consider health system development costs from a macro perspective. Our policy recommendations in this chapter focus primarily on incremental reforms to the Palestinian health system, rather than on radical restructuring. As a frame of reference for considering the scale of future investments in the Palestinian health system, we therefore consider two kinds of information: recent levels of per-capita health system spending in Palestine and the level of health system development efforts since 1994.

In 1998, prior to the second intifada, total annual Palestinian health spending was estimated at $100–$111 per capita. Since the start of the second intifada, economic conditions have declined dramatically. Health sector spending has correspondingly declined, although exact data on current per-capita health sector spending are not available. For present purposes we assume a current level of spending of $67 per person per year, 60 percent of the pre-intifada level.[37]

According to World Bank data for 1997–2000, annual per-capita spending of $111 is very close to the average expenditure of $116 observed among "middle income" countries, as defined by the World Bank; higher than the level observed among "lower middle income" countries ($72); and about one-third the level observed among "upper middle income" countries ($309). Palestinian gross national product per capita ($1,771 in 2000) compares similarly with that of "middle income" countries ($1,860), while "lower middle income" ($1,230) and "upper middle income" ($4,550) countries vary accordingly. In terms of other countries in the region, per-capita health spending of $111 is higher than that reported for Syria ($30) and Egypt ($51), but it is lower than per-capita spending in Jordan ($137), Saudi Arabia ($448), Lebanon ($499), and Israel ($2,021).

The 1998 level of per-capita spending corresponded to total annual health sector expenditures of $320 million to $344 million (given a population of approximately 3.1 million). Of these expenditures, approximately $40 million per year came in the form of international aid. International donations to the Palestinian health system totaled approximately $227 million between 1994 and 2000, an average of $38 million per year. For comparison, disbursement of international donations across all sectors in Palestine was $3.1 billion over the same period, an average of $512 million per year. Thus, slightly over 7 percent of total international donations were directed to the health system. Since the start of the second intifada, considerable international contributions to the health sector have continued, but their focus has shifted a great deal toward humanitarian relief. Detailed information on the distribution of health sector expenditures between operating expenses and capital investment is unavailable; based on available data, however, we estimate that capital investment was on the order of $40 million to $50 million per year.

---

[37] Based on data from PA MOH, 2003a, Palestinian gross national income (approximately equivalent to GNP) was $1,070 per capita in 2002, 60 percent of the level reported for 2000. To our knowledge, the MOH has not reported national health expenditures for 2001 or 2002; for present purposes, we assume that per-capita health spending has fallen in proportion to national income.

In this context, we estimate that a constructive level of external support for the Palestinian health system over the first decade of an independent state would be $130 million to $165 million per year, in year 2003 U.S. dollars. Over the ten-year period 2005–2014, this level of external support would total $1.3 billion to $1.65 billion.

This estimate is based on the assumption that the Palestinian health system will require a relatively large amount of resources in the first year or two of an independent state to restore per-capita spending to pre-intifada levels and beyond. At a conceptual level, at least, we regard the pre-intifada level of spending as a sustainable baseline under conditions of peace.

In terms of health sector improvement, we estimate that such contributions would support increasing annual per-capita health sector spending from the estimated current level of $67 to between $122 and $197 per person per year. This estimated effect on per-capita spending assumes that increases in external contributions following the establishment of an independent Palestinian state would be accompanied by increases in other health sector funding (i.e., taxes, insurance premiums, co-payments, and private investments/donations). The higher per-capita spending estimate ($197) assumes that these other funding sources would grow enough to keep the fraction of total health sector spending contributed by external funding at the 1998 level (13.2 percent, or approximately $45 million in external funding out of total health sector spending of $340 million). The lower per-capita spending estimate ($122) assumes that domestic funding sources would rise disproportionately more slowly than external sources, and that the latter would make up three times that proportion of new health sector spending.

Estimated effects on per-capita spending assume an initial population of 3.5 million people (i.e., approximately the current level), and a population growth rate of 4 percent per year, consistent with conditions described in Chapter Four. If the annual rate of population growth were 3 percent, this level of external support would increase per-capita spending to between $130 and $217 per person per year (maintaining all other assumptions). Our estimates do not account for "health care inflation"—i.e., the tendency (particularly in developed countries) for health care costs to increase, principally because of the introduction of new products and procedures.

Our estimates are informed by, and broadly consistent with, previously published estimates of the resources needed for health sector development. In particular, in the Palestinian development plan, 1999, the PA estimated that donations of about $60 million per year would be needed for development of the government health sector during 1999–2003. This is about half again as much per year as the average annual level of donations during 1994–2000, and more than twice the annual level of donations that went to the government sector during that period (the rest went to NGOs and UNRWA). A separate calculation for the health system overall, presented in Barnea and Husseini (2002), estimated that the shortfall between health system revenues and the expenditures needed to maintain the system at 1998 levels was between

$50 million and $100 million per year for 2001–2004. The amount increases over time because of population growth.[38]

If spent effectively, external support of $130 million to $165 million per year should yield tangible improvements in the Palestinian health system. In terms of per-capita spending, the Palestinian health system would remain below those of some of its more economically advanced neighbors, such as Lebanon, Saudi Arabia, and Israel. Further donations might raise the standards of the health system further. At the same time, this level of external support is three to four times the average annual level of international donations from 1994 to 2000. We believe that the Palestinian health system would have difficulty successfully absorbing international donations of much more than this, and that higher donations would risk waste and disruption (e.g., because of capacity constraints in human and physical capital). Over time, as the Palestinian health system—and the Palestinian economy—becomes more advanced, its ability to absorb and use outside investments efficiently will increase.

We note that, if responsibility for the health system of East Jerusalem were transferred to a future Palestinian state, additional resources would be needed to maintain current patterns of care and reimbursement in East Jerusalem. This issue requires separate analysis that is outside the scope of this chapter. Similarly, water and sanitation infrastructure is excluded from this analysis, but it is discussed in detail in Chapter Six.

Finally, we have based these analyses on data regarding total and per-capita health system spending for Palestine and other areas. We could not determine definitively whether these data capture spending in all areas addressed in this chapter. If particular areas, such as educational programs for health professionals or research, are generally excluded from these data, our estimates of constructive levels of external support for the Palestinian health system would correspondingly need to be revised.

Discussion

In this chapter, we have described a variety of options for strengthening particular aspects of the Palestinian health system, with the goal of improving health and health care for the Palestinian people in the context of an independent Palestinian state. Our recommendations (summarized in Table 7.4) were developed based on considerable input from Palestinian, Israeli, and international professionals who are currently involved in the Palestinian health system or were involved in the past.

Considerable effort will be required to implement the recommendations we have described. In our view, however, such developments are well within the reach of the Palestinian health system, assuming that the larger political and security environment

---

[38] These estimates were prepared prior to the second intifada. Since then, tax revenues, health insurance premiums, and household incomes (which support patients' out-of-pocket spending) all decreased substantially. Deficit estimates under these circumstances would have been correspondingly higher.

is favorable and that resources are available. Whenever interview participants described a particular policy or project that they felt was important for the Palestinian health system, we asked what they thought would be required to achieve it. Interview participants consistently expressed the view that the necessary human resources existed in Palestine (and among Palestinians living abroad) or could be created relatively quickly—as long as there was a political will among Palestinians to do so, adequate financial resources were available, and the geographic closures ended. We could not verify this view independently. However, the many positive aspects of health and health care in Palestine certainly provide evidence of the considerable skill and motivation of Palestinian health professionals and other stakeholders.

Role of International Donors

International donors have made considerable contributions to the development of the Palestinian health system. In order for the development efforts we have described to be feasible, international donors will need to remain involved for the foreseeable future. Indeed, they will probably need to increase their levels of investment in the health system.

At the same time, we believe that the returns on this investment, in terms of health status and satisfaction with the health system, are likely to be increased if the actions of the donor community are guided by effective local institutions. To this end, care should be taken to use international support to enhance but not replace the responsibility of the MOH and other national institutions for the Palestinian health system. In particular, international support for the Palestinian health system should be closely related to the priorities and targets described in this chapter, to minimize conflict between the national agenda—which is ultimately a government responsibility—and the agendas of particular donors or NGOs. In turn, international donors could use progress toward reforms described in this chapter as benchmarks to gauge whether the MOH and other key institutions are performing effectively.

Limitations of Our Analysis

We recognize that this analysis has a number of important limitations. We sought input from a relatively large number of people involved in or knowledgeable about the Palestinian health system, including people from each sector of the health system, academia, international donor organizations, and relevant Israeli institutions. However, our list of interview participants was neither representative nor exhaustive. For instance, because of travel and time restrictions, we had limited in-person contact with MOH personnel; much interaction took place by telephone. We did not interview health care providers employed in the government health sector or representatives of consumer groups or community organizations. We did not speak with any representatives of Islamic organizations, although Islamic NGOs do play an important role in delivering health care and other social services in Palestine.

The input we received was generally consistent across interview participants. However, it is certainly possible that the stakeholders we did not meet would have provided different information. In addition, we did not attempt to validate the accuracy of the information provided by interview participants, beyond comparing comments to information from other interviews, to published reports, and to our own prior experience. Moreover, many of the reports we reviewed were written by one or more of our interview participants, so that these different sources of information were not entirely independent.

In Closing

Our analysis is intended to inform the health system development efforts of a future independent Palestinian state. Outside analyses—including those conducted by international donors and by research organizations such as RAND—can be valuable. However, we believe that successful health system development in Palestine requires that local stakeholders be committed to and in control of both the overall development process and its substantive details.

Appendix 7.A:
Selected Objectives from Prior Palestinian Health Plans

Table 7.A.1 presents objectives from several different substantive areas to illustrate the types of goals included in previous national health plans. Goals are for the period 1999–2003.

Table 7.A.2 presents strategies in the previous national health plan's three main substantive areas. Goals are for the period 2001–2006.

Table 7.A.1
Selected Objectives from the 1999 *National Strategic Health Plan*

Area	Recommendation
Health planning and projects management	Develop national sustainable capacity in health planning, policy development, and project management
	Create an information base for health planning and projects management
	Develop measurable indicators to monitor and evaluate planned activities and programs
	Validate community participation, involvement, and ownership initiated during the process of developing the five-year health plan in all Palestinian districts
	Assist in the development of an organized national system for coordination of health developmental activities
	Develop rational master plans for different categories of hospitals and primary health care facilities
	Develop a national accreditation system for planning health sector facilities
Health management information systems	Develop nationwide computerized communication links facilitating the operation of an effective health management information system to be connected to the national information system that links all Palestinian ministries
	Serve the Palestinian community by a system that collects, tabulates, stores, and makes available information on demography, health status, and health resources for policymakers in the health area
	Develop a well-functioning computerized medical information system at district, regional, and central levels by establishing medical information systems in the West Bank and strengthening the existing one in Gaza
	Develop and implement an extensive training program for selected health personnel representing major health care professions from different settings, including the MOH, hospitals, and primary health care
Health promotion and education: chronic heart disease/stroke	Reduce by 40 percent the level of ill health and death caused by heart disease and stroke
	Reduce by 60 percent the risks associated with heart disease by modifying specific human behaviors
Health promotion and education: maternal and child health	Reduce infant mortality from 24.2 in 1997 to 15 deaths per 1,000 live births
	Reduce maternal mortality and morbidity by 50 percent
	Reduce prenatal and neonatal deaths by 50 percent
	Increase by 50 percent the utilization rate of maternal and child health services, especially postnatal care, throughout Palestine
	Increase vaccination coverage to 100 percent, especially tetanus toxoid for teenagers

SOURCE: PA MOH, 1999.

Table 7.A.2
Selected Objectives from the 2001 *National Plan for Human Resource Development and Education in Health*

Area	Recommendation
Planning for health care human resources in Palestine	Conduct national health planning for the various health professions
	Prepare and/or update databases on health care human resources in Palestine
	Develop national and institutional capacities in health planning and development
	Develop and utilize scientific research in health planning and human resource development and promote decision-linked research in human resource development
	Explore fields of cooperation in planning and human resource development at the national, regional, and international levels
	Improve the image of some health-related professions (e.g., nursing, midwifery, and occupational therapy)
Education and training of human resources	Develop and implement an accreditation system for formal education/training programs of health human resources
	Conduct continuing education activities involving the different health professions' categories based on continuing education priority needs as indicated in Welfare Association, PA, and Ministry of Higher Education, 2001a–f
	Provide scholarships within the next five years for priority specialty qualifications in selected health professions
	Strengthen available academic programs and start new programs according to priorities indicated in Welfare Association, PA, and Ministry of Higher Education, 2001a–f
	Start, upgrade, and develop databases on formal degree-granting educational programs in health
	Utilize technology and varied nontraditional teaching-learning methodologies in educational programs
	Develop continuing education potential
	Strengthen clinical/practical training to support educational programs in health
	Develop a remedial training program for physicians and programs for other health care professionals who need such training
Management of health care human resources	Develop conducive managerial practices in health care human resource development
	Ensure availability of necessary protocols/guidelines/rules and regulations related to human resource development
	Strengthen professional unions/associations and health-related councils to promote human care resource development
	Promote an organizational climate that enhances continuing education and human resource development

SOURCE: Welfare Association, PA, and Ministry of Higher Education, 2001a–f.

Appendix 7.B:
Methods

The analyses underlying this chapter were mainly conducted between December 2002 and July 2003.

First, we reviewed previously published academic research and policy analyses regarding health and health care in Palestine to understand the history of the Palestinian health system and the current status of health and health care in Palestine.[39] These materials were available in the form of books, journal articles, reports by government organizations (i.e., the Palestinian and Israeli Ministries of Health), reports by international organizations (e.g., the World Bank, various United Nations agencies, the World Health Organization), reports by Palestinian and international nongovernmental organizations, scientific publications, conference proceedings, working papers, and other formats. We reviewed all such information that we could obtain, with the goal of identifying priorities for health system development in Palestine over the next decade.

Second, we identified and contacted local stakeholders in Palestine and Israel whose input we wanted regarding this analysis, based on their expertise in the organization, operation, and financing of the Palestinian health system. We interviewed each of these experts several times by telephone. Given our project mandate, each person was asked to identify priorities for health system development in Palestine over the next decade. We discussed these issues iteratively with each expert, along with issues we identified from our literature review. We did not use an interview guide for these discussions.

In addition, we asked each expert to recommend additional people whom we could ask for information regarding the Palestinian health system and our analysis. We specifically asked to be referred to people in all sectors of the Palestinian health system; relevant Palestinian and Israeli academics; and people from relevant international organizations, particularly key donors to the Palestinian health system.[40] We tried to contact everyone to whom we were referred. In addition, we decided that it was important to interview certain categories of stakeholders to whom we had not already been referred. They fell into two broad categories: international organizations, particularly donors, and Palestinian women active in health care delivery and health policy. We identified people in these categories through a combination of referral and independent research.

---

[39] We include a partial listing in the bibliography. See also the HDIP annotated bibliography of journal articles and other reports on health and health care in Palestine (Barghouthi, Fragiacomo, and Qutteina, 1999; and Barghouthi, Shubita, and Fragiacomo, 2000).

[40] The European Union is sponsoring a comprehensive health sector review on behalf of the PA MOH that overlaps in time and subject with RAND's analysis. We discuss this in additional detail in Appendix 7.D.

In March and April, 2003, we contacted the people to whom we had been referred by fax, mail, email, and/or telephone. We provided materials describing this project, including its background and aims, along with a preliminary list of health system development priorities and a general set of questions we wanted to discuss with them (a sample letter of introduction is included as Appendix 7.C of this chapter). We asked people to meet with us during a visit to Palestine and Israel in May 2003. We scheduled meetings with everybody who said they would be available. No person whom we approached about this project explicitly refused to meet with us, although some people were unavailable for various reasons.

In March 2003, we also held a two-day meeting at RAND's office in Washington, D.C. During that meeting, we discussed the information in the written materials we had reviewed, and we discussed our analysis plans and the strategy for our upcoming trip with several Palestinian and Israeli experts.

In May 2003, Drs. Schoenbaum and Deckelbaum traveled to Palestine and Israel for two weeks.[41] Together with Timea Spitka, we met with the majority of the local stakeholders to whom we had been referred. Nearly all meetings took place face-to-face in Jerusalem or Ramallah. Because Gaza was closed to foreigners during the entire period of this visit, meetings with the Palestinian Ministry of Health in Gaza, and with other relevant stakeholders of that area, had to be postponed or canceled. Where possible, these interviews were conducted by telephone instead, and we were subsequently able to meet with one Gaza contact in Washington, D.C.

In each interview, the questions listed in the letter of introduction served as a general interview guide (see Appendix 7.C). Interview questions were open-ended, so as not to constrain the scope of the information that people provided. Interview participants were asked to base their responses on their own expertise and experience.

Interview participants were asked to allow themselves to be identified in this chapter. However, to help ensure that people felt free to express their views fully, interview participants were assured that no comments would be quoted directly or attributed to them in an identifiable way. We took written notes during all meetings, which we subsequently transcribed. Only we and Timea Spitka had access to the meeting notes. The list of interview participants is included at the end of this appendix.

All interview participants received a draft version of this chapter and were invited to submit comments prior to publication. They were told that we would seriously consider all comments but not necessarily implement them in the final book. This chapter, along with the rest of this book, was also reviewed in accordance with RAND's usual quality assurance procedures.

---

[41] Adel Afifi was also scheduled to participate in this trip, but he was unable to do so because of a family emergency.

The following people were interviewed for this chapter:

Hani Abdeen, Al-Quds University

Ziad Abdeen, Al-Quds University

Haidar Abdel-Shafi, Palestine Red Crescent Society

Yehia Abed, Maram

Mahmoud Abu-Hadid, Al-Quds University

Fathi Abumoghli, Palestine Ministry of Health (in association with the World Bank)

Zeid M. Abu Shawish, Palestine Ministry of Health

Hikmat Ajjuri, Palestinian Council of Health

Mamdouh M. Aker

Younis Al-Khatib, Palestine Red Crescent Society

Mirca Barbolini, European Union

Mustafa Barghouthi, Union of Palestinian Medical Relief Committees

Tamara Barnea, JDC-Brookdale Institute

Sherry F. Carlin, United States Agency for International Development

Ellan Coates, Maram

Khuloud Dajani, Al-Quds University

Nahil Dajani, Dajani Maternity Hospital

Rajai Dajani, Dajani Maternity Hospital

Anwar Dudin, Al-Quds University

Rita Giacaman, Birzeit University

P. Gregg Greenough, Johns Hopkins University

Arafat S. Hidmi, Makassed Charitable Society

Rafaella Iodice, European Union

Emil Jarjoui, Palestine Liberation Organization

Anne Johansen, World Bank

Salam Kanaan, World Bank

Umaya Khamash, Maram

Rana Khatib, Birzeit University

Bassim Khoury, Pharmacare PLC

Hanan Halabi, Birzeit University

Samia Haleleh, Birzeit University

Abdullatif S. Husseini, Birzeit University

Rafiq Husseini, Welfare Association

Ajay Mahal, Harvard University

Faris Massoud

Rashad Massoud, University Research Co. LLC

Shlomo Mor-Yosef, Hadassah Medical Organization

Salva Najab, Maram

Joumana Odeh, Happy Child Center

As'ad Ramlawi, Palestine Ministry of Health

Ann Roberts, Maram

Yitzhak Sever, Israel Ministry of Health

Mohammad Shahin, Al-Quds Medical School

Varsen Aghabekian Shahin, Al-Quds University

Toufik Shakhshir

Munther Al Sharif, Palestine Ministry of Health

Hossam K. Sharkawi, Palestine Red Crescent Society

Raghda Shawa

Husam E. Siam, UNRWA

Ricardo Solé Arqués, World Health Organization

Suzy Srouji, United States Agency for International Development

Theodore Tulchinsky, Hebrew University School of Public Health

Henrik Wahlberg, World Health Organization

Laura Wick, Birzeit University

Appendix 7.C:
Letter of Introduction Regarding RAND's Health System Analysis

<date>

Dear Sir or Madam:

We are writing to you on behalf of RAND, an independent, non-partisan research organization based in California. With the support of private donors, RAND is analyzing important parameters for the success of a future independent Palestinian state. RAND will distribute the findings from this research to key policy-makers in the United States, Palestine and Israel.

As part of this larger project, our working group is leading an analysis of the Palestinian health system. Our goals are: 1) to understand the strengths and gaps of the current system, with respect to organization, human and physical infrastructure, and financing; 2) to identify major priorities for future development and investment, over approximately the next ten years; and 3) to estimate the financial cost of reaching various development goals.

We are currently planning to visit the region in May to meet with key Palestinian, Israeli and international stakeholders. We would like to speak or meet with you as part of our work. In the meantime, we would like to provide more information about our project and RAND.

About RAND and RAND Health

RAND is an independent, non-profit research organization, with headquarters in Santa Monica, California, and other main offices in Washington, Pittsburgh, and Leiden (the Netherlands). RAND was established in 1948. RAND's mission is to improve policy and decision-making through research and analysis. RAND has a staff of more than 1600. 85% of the research staff hold advanced degrees, with more than 65% having earned PhDs or MDs. RAND's areas of expertise include health, education, international relations, international development, civil and criminal justice, national security, population studies, and science and technology.

The largest single program within RAND, and the largest private health care research organization in the United States, is RAND Health. RAND Health has helped shape private- and public-sector responses to emerging health care issues for more than three decades. Our research has changed how health care is financed and delivered, in the United States and internationally, by providing evidence on:

- the effects of health insurance design and payment policies on health costs and health status
- the measurement of health care quality for physical and mental illness

- the gaps between the medical care people *should* receive and the care they *do* receive
- the cost-effectiveness of interventions to improve health care quality

Every RAND publication, database, and major briefing is carefully reviewed before its release, to ensure that the research is well-designed for the problem, based on sound information, relevant to the client's interests and needs, balanced and independent, and that the research adds value to the research area.

Additional information on RAND is available at http://www.rand.org/, and on RAND Health at http://www.rand.org/health_area/.

About RAND's Palestine Project

RAND's Center for Domestic and International Health Security (part of RAND Health) and its Center for Middle East Public Policy are undertaking an unprecedented multidisciplinary analysis of the parameters central to the success of an independent Palestinian state, over the state's first 8–10 years. The analysis includes consideration of economic, demographic, governance, education, health, public safety, security, and natural resource issues. Where appropriate, the analysis includes consideration of policy alternatives that reflect choices that might face the key participants in the process of creating such a state.

This study adopts a long-term perspective, recognizing that many short-term problems will also have to be solved in the process. It assumes that a successful Palestinian state should ultimately bring stability for Palestinians, Israelis and the region. It also assumes that substantial resources will be required from various sources in order to establish and support the institutions and infrastructure necessary for a successful independent Palestine, and it seeks to estimate the necessary resources associated with key policy alternatives. *By identifying the needs for a viable state and quantifying the costs of such a development, the parties will have a realistic appraisal of what is possible and what it will cost.*

RAND's research on Palestine is being led by a multidisciplinary team of investigators, including: Drs. Kenneth Shine and Jerrold Green (co-Project Directors), Michael Schoenbaum (leader, Health working group), Glenn Robinson (leader, Governance working group), Robert Hunter (leader, Security working group), Jack Riley (leader, Public Safety working group), Mark Bernstein (leader, Natural Resources working group), Cheryl Benard (leader, Education working group), Brian Nichiporuk (leader, Demographics working group), and David Gompert and Richard Neu (senior advisors).

RAND's Palestine project is funded by private donations.

Additional information on RAND's Center for Domestic and International Health Security is available at http://www.rand.org/health/healthsecurity/, and on the Center for Middle East Public Policy at http://www.rand.org/nsrd/cmepp/about.html.

About RAND's Analysis of the Palestinian Health System

RAND's analysis of the Palestinian health system is being led by Drs. Michael Schoenbaum (economist, RAND), Adel Afifi (neuroscientist, University of Iowa), and Richard Deckelbaum (pediatrician and nutritionist, Columbia University); and advised by Dr. Nicole Lurie (senior natural scientist at RAND and former U.S. Principal Deputy Assistant Secretary of Health).

The overall goals of our analysis of the Palestinian health system are: 1) to understand the strengths and gaps of the current system, with respect to organization, human and physical infrastructure, and financing; 2) to identify major priorities for future development and investment, over approximately the next ten years; and 3) to estimate the financial cost of reaching various development goals.

We recognize that there is a well-established Palestinian national health planning process. This process has led to several National Health Plans that contain detailed targets for improving health status and for developing health manpower and physical infrastructure. Evaluating each of those specific targets is outside the scope of RAND's project. At the same time, one emphasis in all the information we have gathered so far is that there is room to strengthen key Palestinian institutions, particularly relating to planning and coordination—and that such strengthening could considerably improve the health system's performance.

Our project therefore focuses on key institutions and programs that are necessary for the Palestinian health system to operate successfully, and options for strengthening these institutions. These include:

- **National health planning authority,** with responsibility for policies including division of responsibility across public, private, NGO and UNRWA sectors; authorization (certificate of need) for new buildings and expensive equipment; accreditation guidelines for providers, facilities, and education programs; clinical quality improvement; and health care finance
- **Licensing and accreditation bodies,** including for health care providers, delivery facilities, laboratories, educational programs, pharmaceuticals and medical devices
- **Policies for health insurance and finance,** including effective financing mechanisms; defined benefit and payment schedules; and incentives for quality, efficiency and health promotion
- **Prescription drug policy,** including a cost-effective national essential drugs list, policies regarding generic substitution, and efficient purchasing mechanisms
- **Health information systems,** for tracking elements including health and nutritional status, outpatient care, hospital discharges, health care quality, health system staffing, and billing and payments
- **Health manpower strategy,** including strategies to strengthen existing training programs and to meet needs that are currently unmet
- **Research and evaluation capacity,** including health policy and evaluation and biomedical research

In addition, we will examine:

- **Fast-track public and primary health care interventions,** to address current deficiencies and ensure a stable basis for population health that supports longer-term health planning

We recognize that the current security closures and travel restrictions have implications for the Palestinian health system. As above, however, the overall focus of this project is on fostering the success of a future independent Palestinian state. For purposes of this project, we therefore do *not* focus on short-term strategies for operating the health system under the current conditions. Instead, we focus on longer-term health system development, under the assumption of unrestricted travel within the West Bank and Gaza.

Planned Trip to the Region

We are preparing for a trip to Palestine and Israel in May, during which we will meet with key Palestinian, Israeli and international stakeholders regarding the Palestinian health system. *We would like to speak with you about your work, and meet if possible.* In our meetings, we will ask people to address the following issues:

1. Which health policy issues require most urgent attention? What five policy changes *can* and *should* be implemented *immediately?*
2. Based on your knowledge of the institutions described above, how well do those institutions currently function in the Palestinian health system? Which institutions particularly need to be strengthened? How could they be strengthened?
3. Have we left out any key institutions that need to be strengthened in the Palestinian health system? Which?
4. What are the major barriers that affect successful development of the Palestinian health system?

Finally, we will want to collect information on the potential costs of implementing various policy options. We will also have other questions related to your area of expertise.

We understand that other organizations are studying the Palestinian health system and providing technical assistance, including the European Union's health sector review on behalf of the Palestinian Ministry of Health. Although our mission is to conduct independent analyses, we will coordinate with these other projects as much as possible.

We will contact your office about meeting with us in May. If you have questions about this project or would like additional information, please feel free to contact any of us directly using the contact information listed above; or through our representative in Jerusalem, Ms. Timea Spitka, at <telephone number>. Thank you.

Respectfully yours,

Michael Schoenbaum, PhD	Richard Deckelbaum, MD	Adel Afifi, MD, MS
Leader, Health Working Group	Consultant	Consultant

Appendix 7.D:
Integration with Prior and Concurrent Health Sector Analyses

As we began this project, we learned that the European Union (EU) was sponsoring a comprehensive health sector review on behalf of the Palestinian MOH. This review is being led by the EU, with participation by the World Bank, the WHO, the British Department for International Development, the Italian Cooperation, and possibly others.

Based on draft documents about the health sector review that were provided to RAND in April 2003 and on conversations with participating organizations, we understood the general objectives of the EU health sector review to be similar to those of RAND's project—i.e., to understand the current Palestinian health system and propose options for developing the sector over the coming decade. However, the EU and RAND efforts differ on several dimensions.

The EU review is being conducted on behalf of the Ministry of Health by representatives of organizations that have also been major donors, lenders, and/or providers of technical assistance to the Palestinian health system. At present, the EU project is limited to the health sector.

RAND's review is being conducted independently, and RAND has had no involvement, advisory or otherwise, in the Palestinian health system. In addition, RAND's analysis of the health system is part of a larger, multisector study of policy options for a future Palestinian state.

Overall, however, we view the respective projects as strongly complementary. Following conversations and correspondence with the EU and other members of the review team, we agreed to pursue ongoing communication with the EU team regarding our work plan, analyses, and findings. We interviewed representatives from several of the participating organizations during our visit to Palestine and Israel in May, as listed in Appendix 7.B. The projects have otherwise been conducted independently. Analyses for this chapter were scheduled to be completed before the EU health sector review.

More generally, there have been a number of previous analyses of the Palestinian health system conducted by researchers, NGOs, international donors, and of course the Palestine Council of Health and the MOH. We recognize that most or all of the issues we address here have been addressed in previous plans and analyses. We have tried to apply an independent perspective and to build on and extend previous work to maximize the relevance of this analysis.

Bibliography

Abdeen, Z., et al., *Nutritional Assessment of the West Bank and Gaza Strip,* mimeo, Jerusalem, September 2002.

Abdeen, Z., G. Greenough, R. Qasrawi, and B. Dandies, *Nutrition & Quantitative Food Assessment, Palestinian Territories, 2003,* Jerusalem, 2004. Online at http://www.healthinforum. net/files/nutrition/Nutrion_Quant_Food_Ass03.pdf (as of October 2004).

Abdul-Rahim, H., N. Abdu-Rmeileh, et al., "Obesity and Selected Co-Morbidities in an Urban Palestinian Population," *International Journal of Obesity,* Vol. 25, 2001, pp. 1736–1740.

Abdul-Rahim, H., G. Holmboe-Ottesen, et al., "Obesity in a Rural and an Urban Palestinian West Bank Population," *International Journal of Obesity,* Vol. 27, 2003, pp. 140–146.

Abdul-Rahim, H., A. Husseini, E. Bjertness, et al., "The Metabolic Syndrome in the West Bank Population—An Urban Rural Comparison," *Diabetes Care,* Vol. 24, No. 2, February 2001, pp. 275–279.

Abdul-Rahim, H., A. Husseini, R. Giacaman, et al., "Diabetes Mellitus in an Urban Palestinian Population: Prevalence and Associated Factors," *Eastern Mediterranean Health Journal,* Vol. 7, No. 1, 2, 2001.

Afana, A.H., et al., "The Ability of General Practitioners to Detect Mental Disorders Among Primary Care Patients in a Stressful Environment: Gaza Strip," *Journal of Public Health Medicine,* Vol. 24, No. 4, December 2002, pp. 326–331.

Al-Khatib, A., and S. Salah, "Bacteriological and Chemical Quality of Swimming Pool Water in Developing Countries: A Case Study in the West Bank of Palestine," *International Journal of Environmental Health Research,* Vol. 13, 2003, pp. 17–22.

Al-Khatib, A., et al., "Water-Health Relationships in Developing Countries: A Case Study in Tulkarem District in Palestine," *International Journal of Environmental Health and Research,* Vol. 13, June 2003, pp. 199–206.

Aoyama, A., *Toward a Virtuous Circle: A Nutrition Review of the Middle East and North Africa,* Washington, D.C.: World Bank, August 1999.

Aqel N. M., et al., "Gaza's Health Services," *The Lancet,* Vol. 2, No. 8567, November 1987, pp. 1090–1091.

Arab Medical Welfare Association, *Medical Bulletin Continuing Medical Education,* Vol. 1, No. 2, Ramallah, 1999.

Arafat, C., and N. Boothby, *A Psychosocial Assessment of Palestinian Children,* Tel Aviv, Israel: USAID, 2004. Online at http://www.usaid.gov/wbg/reports/Final_CPSP_Assessment_ English.pdf (as of October 2004).

Barghouthi, M., L. Fragiacomo, and M. Qutteina, *Health Research in Palestine: An Annotated Bibliography,* 4th ed., Ramallah: Health Development Information and Policy Institute, 1999.

Barghouthi, M., A. Shubita, and L. Fragiacomo, *The Palestinian Health System: An Updated Overview,* Ramallah: Health Development Information and Policy Institute, March 2000.

Barnea, T., and R. Husseini, eds., *Separate and Cooperate, Cooperate and Separate: The Disengagement of the Palestine Health Care System from Israel and Its Emergence as an Independent System,* Westport, Conn.: Praeger, 2002.

Beckerleg, S., et al., "Purchasing a Quick Fix from Private Pharmacies in the Gaza Strip," *Social Science and Medicine,* Vol. 49, No. 1, December 1999, pp. 1489–1500.

Belgian-Israeli-Palestinian Cooperation Project in Applied Scientific Research, Training and Education, *Policies and Strategies of Future Israeli-Palestinian Academic Cooperation Draft Report on Public Health,* mimeo, November 1999.

Centers for Disease Control and Prevention (CDC), *2001 Health Data,* 2003 reprint. Online at www.cdc.gov/nchs/data/hus/tables/2003/03hus106.pdf (as of June 2004).

Cockcroft, A., *West Bank and Gaza Service Delivery Survey: Health and Basic Education Services,* Washington, D.C.: World Bank, December 1998.

de Jong, J. T., et al., "Lifetime Events and Posttraumatic Stress Disorder in 4 Postconflict Settings," *Journal of the American Medical Association,* Vol. 286, No. 5, August 1, 2001, pp. 555–562. Comment in *Journal of the American Medical Association,* Vol. 286, No. 5, August 1, 2001, pp. 584–588.

Donati, S., R. Hamam, and E. Medda, "Family Planning KAP Survey in Gaza," *Social Science and Medicine,* Vol. 50, No. 6, March 2000, pp. 841–849.

Economic Cooperation Foundation and Palestinian Council of Health, *Building Bridges Through Health, Israeli-Palestinian Cooperation in Health, Medicine and Social Welfare,* 1999 Report, February 2000.

———, *Building Bridges Through Health, Israeli-Palestinian Cooperation in Health, Medicine and Social Welfare,* 2000 Report, February 2001.

European Commission and Eurostat, *Euro-Mediterranean Statistics,* Luxembourg: European Committees, 2001.

Gaumer, G., et al., *Rationalization Plan for Hospital Beds in Egypt,* Partnerships for Health Reform Technical Report No. 29, Bethesda, Md.: Abt Associates, 1998. Online at http://www.phrplus.org/Pubs/te29fin.pdf (as of August 2003).

Giacaman, R., H. Abdul-Rahim, and L. Wick, "Health Sector Reform in the Occupied Palestinian Territories (OPT): Targeting the Forest or the Trees?" *Health Policy and Planning,* Vol. 18, No. 1, 2003, pp. 59–67.

Giacaman, R., and S. Halileh, "Maintaining Public Health Education in the West Bank," *The Lancet,* Vol. 361, No. 9364, April 2003, pp.1220–1221.

Halileh, S., "Israeli-Palestinian Conflict. Need for Medical Services for Palestinians Injured in West Bank Is Urgent," *British Medical Journal,* Vol. 324, No. 7333, February 9, 2002, p. 361.

Halileh, S., et al., "The Impact of the Intifada on the Health of a Nation," *Medicine Conflict and Survival,* Vol. 18, No. 3, July–September 2002, pp. 239–247.

The Hashemite Kingdom of Jordan, *Human Resources,* "A Healthy Population," Jordan, 2004. Online at http://www.kinghussein.gov.jo/resources4.html (as of January 28, 2004).

Health, Development, Information, and Policy Institute (HDIP), *Coordinating Primary Health Care,* Policy Dialogues Series, No. 3, Ramallah, June 1997.

———, *The Future of Hospital Services in Palestine—A Coordination Workshop on Hospital Care,* Ramallah, September 1999.

———, *Health Care Under Siege II: The Health Situation of Palestinians During the First Two Months of the Intifada,* Ramallah, December 2000.

———, *Health Insurance and Health Service Utilization in the West Bank and Gaza Strip,* Ramallah, February 1998.

———, *Sharing Responsibility,* Policy Dialogues Series, No. 2, Ramallah, December 1996.

———, *Towards Better and Cost-Effective Hospital Care,* Policy Dialogues Series, No. 4, Ramallah, July 1998.

"Health Without Borders in the Middle East," session proceeding presented at the Annual Conference: Health and Politics in the 21st Century of the Israel National Institute for Health Policy and Health Research, Jerusalem, 2001.

Husseini, A., H. Abdul-Rahim, et al., "Prevalence of Diabetes Mellitus and Impaired Glucose Tolerance in a Rural Palestinian Population," *East Mediterranean Health Journal,* Vol. 6, No. 5–6, September–November 2000a, pp. 1039–1045.

———, "Selected Factors Associated with Diabetes Mellitus in a Rural Palestinian Community," *Medical Science Monitor,* Vol. 9, No. 5, 2003, pp. CR181–CR185.

———, "Type 2 Diabetes Mellitus, Impaired Glucose Tolerance and Associated Factors in a Rural Palestinian Village," *Diabetic Medicine,* Vol. 17, 2000b, pp. 746–748.

———, "The Utility of a Single Glucometer Measurement of Fasting Capillary Blood Glucose in the Prevalence Determination of Diabetes Mellitus in an Urban Adult Palestinian Population," *Scand J Lab Invest,* Vol. 60, 2000c, pp. 457–462.

"In Shift, U.S. to Aid the Palestinian Authority," *The New York Times,* Late Edition—Final, July 8, 2003, Sec. A, p. 6.

International Crisis Group, *Islamic Social Welfare Activism in the Occupied Palestinian Territories: A Legitimate Target?* International Crisis Group Middle East Report No. 13, Amman/Brussels, 2003.

Khamis, V., *Political Violence and the Palestine Family: Implications for Mental Health and Well-Being,* mimeo, 2000.

Lennock, M, *Health in Palestine: Potential and Challenges,* mimeo, March 1997.

Lewando-Hundt, G., Y. Abed, M. Skeik, S. Beckerleg, and A. El Alem, "Addressing Birth in Gaza: Using Qualitative Methods to Improve Vital Registration," *Social Science and Medicine,* Vol. 48, No. 6, March 1999, pp. 833–843.

Lilienfeld, L., J. Rose, and M. Corn, "UNRWA and the Health of Palestinian Refugees. United Nations Relief and Works Agency," *New England Journal of Medicine,* Vol. 315, No. 9, August 28, 1986, pp. 595–600.

Madi, H., "Infant and Child Mortality Rates Among Palestinian Refugee Populations," *The Lancet,* Vol. 356, No. 9226, July 22, 2000, p. 312.

Massoud, R. F., "A Study of the Financial Statement of Health for the West Bank and Gaza," Harvard School of Public Health, Harvard University, mimeo, 1993.

Medistat, *Medistat—Country Profiles, Egypt,* West Sussex, U.K.: Medistat, Espicom Business Intelligence, April 2003. Online at http://www.espicom.com/web.nsf/structure/TocsMedistat01/$File/egypt.PDF (as of February 2004).

Organisation for Economic Co-operation and Development (OECD), *OECD Health Data 2004,* 1st edition. Paris: Organisation for Economic Co-operation and Development, 2004.

———, *OECD Health Data 1997,* Paris: Organisation for Economic Co-operation and Development, 1997.

———, *Requirements and Guidelines for the Accreditation of Nursing Education Programs in Palestine,* April 1996.

Palestine Red Crescent Society, *Operating Under Siege,* Ramallah, January 2001–December 2002.

Palestinian Authority, *Palestinian Development Plan, 1999–2003,* January 1999.

Palestinian Authority, Palestinian Council of Health, and PA MOH, *The Strategic Plan for Quality of Health Care in Palestine,* mimeo, December 1994.

Palestinian Authority Ministry of Health (PA MOH), *Health Indicators, Palestine 2002,* July 2003a. Online at http://www.healthinforum.net/files/moh_reports/HealthIndicators 2002.pdf (as of July 2003).

———, *Health Status in Palestine. Annual Report 2001,* July 2002a.

———, *National Strategic Health Plan, 1999–2003,* 1999.

———, *Nutrition Strategies in Palestine,* July 2003b.

———, *Palestine National Cancer Registry—Cancer Incidence in Palestine 1998–1999,* December 2001.

———, *Palestinian Drug Formulary,* 1st ed., 2002b.

———, The Status of Health in Palestine, 1998.

———, *The Status of Health in Palestine: Annual Report,* June 1997.

Palestinian Authority Ministry of Health and Al-Quds University, *Report on Iodine Deficiency Survey in West Bank and Gaza Strip,* April 1997.

Palestinian Authority and the United Nations Children's Fund, *The Situation Analysis of Palestinian Children, Young People & Women in the West Bank and Gaza Strip,* August 2000.

Palestinian Central Bureau of Statistics, *Health Survey 2000—Executive Summary,* November 2000a.

———, *Health Survey 2000, Main Findings,* November 2000b.

———, *Nutrition Survey 2002—Press Conference on the Survey Results,* 2002.

Palestinian Council of Health, *The Nursing Human Resource in Palestine,* January 1997.

Palestinian Council of Health et al., *Palestinian-Israeli Cooperation in Developing Occupational Health and Safety Services in Palestine,* February 2000.

————, *Workshop Proceedings: Regional Workshop on Substance Abuse,* October 1999.

Palestinian Council of Health, Planning and Research Centre, *The National Health Plan for the Palestinian People: Objectives and Strategies,* Jerusalem, April 1994.

Partnerships for Health Reform, *Jordan Embarks on Health System Reform to Preserve Health Gains and Expand Coverage,* Jordan: Partnerships for Health Reform, September 1997. Online at http://www.phrplus.org/Pubs/pib10.pdf (as of February 2004).

Primary Health Care Preventive Medicine Department, *Palestine Annual Communicable Disease Report,* Ramallah, 1999.

Ramlawi, A., *Preventive Medicine Team. Brucellosis Prevention and Control Program: (KAP) Knowledge—Attitude and Practice in Palestine*, Palestinian Authority Ministry of Health, 2000a.

————, Preventive Medicine Team. Viral Hepatitis Survey 2000, Palestinian Authority Ministry of Health, 2000b.

Reinhardt, U. E., P. S. Hussey, and G. F. Anderson, "Cross-National Comparisons of Health Systems Using OECD Data 1999," *Health Affairs* (Millwood), Vol. 21, No. 3, May–June 2002, pp. 169–181.

Schnitzer, J., and S. Roy, "Health Services in Gaza Under the Autonomy Plan," *The Lancet,* Vol. 343, No. 8913, June 1994, pp. 1614–1617. Comments in *The Lancet,* Vol. 344, No. 8920, August 1994, p. 478; *The Lancet,* Vol. 343, No. 8913, June 1994, pp. 1581–1582.

Schoenbaum, M., T. Tulchinsky, and Y. Abed, "Gender Differences in Nutritional Status and Feeding Patterns Among Infants in the Gaza Strip," *American Journal of Public Health,* Vol. 85, No. 7, July 1995, pp. 965–969.

Shani, M., and T. Tulchinsky, "Health in Gaza," *British Medical Journal,* Vol. 307, No. 6902, August 21, 1993, p. 509. Comment in: *British Medical Journal,* Vol. 308, No. 6921, January 8, 1994, p. 137.

Stene L, R. Giacaman, H. Abdul-Rahim, A. Husseini, K. Norum, and G. Holmboe-Ottesen, "Food Consumption Pattern in a Palestinian West Bank Population," *European Journal of Clinical Nutrition,* Vol. 53, 1999, pp. 953–958.

————, "Obesity and Associated Factors in a Palestinian West Bank Village Population," *European Journal of Clinical Nutrition,* Vol. 55, 2001, pp. 805–811.

Thabet, A. A., Y. Abed, and P. Vostanis, "Emotional Problems in Palestinian Children Living in a War Zone: A Cross-Sectional Study, *The Lancet,* Vol. 359, No. 9320, May 25, 2002, pp. 1801–1804. Comments in: *The Lancet,* Vol. 359, No. 9320, May 25, 2002, pp. 1793–1794; *The Lancet,* Vol. 360, No. 9339, October 5, 2002, p. 1098; *The Lancet,* Vol. 361, No. 9353, January 18, 2003, p. 260.

Tulchinsky, T. H., "Medical Services in Gaza," *The Lancet,* Vol. 1, No. 8530, February 1987, p. 450.

Tulchinsky, T. H., Y. Abed, G. Ginsberg, S. Shaheen, J. Friedman, M. Schoenbaum, and P. Slater, "Measles in Israel, the West Bank and Gaza: Continuing Incidence and the Case for a New Eradication Strategy," *Reviews of Infectious Diseases,* Vol. 12, 1990, pp. 951–958.

Tulchinsky, T. H., Y. Abed, S. Shaheen, N. Toubassi, Y. Sever, M. Schoenbaum, and R. Handsher, "A Ten Year Experience in Control of Poliomyelitis Through a Combination of Live and Killed Vaccines in Two Developing Areas," *American Journal of Public Health,* Vol. 79, No. 12, December 1989, pp. 1648–1652.

Tulchinsky, T. H., A. M. Al Zeer, J. Abu Mounshar, T. Subeih, M. Schoenbaum, et al., "A Successful, Preventive-Oriented Village Health Worker Program in Hebron, the West Bank, 1985–1996," *Journal of Public Health Management and Practice,* Vol. 3, No. 4, 1997, pp. 57–67.

Tulchinsky, T. H., S. El Ebweini, G. M. Ginsberg, Y. Abed, D. Montano-Cuellar, M. Schoenbaum, et al., "Growth and Nutrition Patterns of Infants in Association with a Nutrition Education/Supplementation Program in Gaza, 1987–1992," *Bulletin of the World Health Organization,* Vol. 72, 1994, pp. 869–875.

Tulchinsky, T. H., and J. Shemer, "Health Services in Gaza Under the Autonomy Plan," *The Lancet,* Vol. 344, No. 8920, August 1994, p. 478. Comment in *The Lancet,* Vol. 343, No. 8913, June 1994, pp. 1614–1617.

United Nations Children's Fund, *The State of the World's Children,* New York, 2000. Online at http://www.unicef.org/sowc00/ (as of February 2004).

United Nations Office for the Coordination of Humanitarian Affairs, "Humanitarian Monitoring Report: Commitments Made by the Government of Israel to Ms. Catherine Bertini, Personal Humanitarian Envoy to the Middle East for the Secretary General," Jerusalem, June 2003. Online at http://www.healthinforum.net/files/misc/Humanitarian%20Monitoring%20Report–June03.pdf (as of February 2004).

United Nations Relief and Works Agency for Palestine Refugees in the Near East, *Annual Report of the Department of Health,* Amman, Jordan, 2001.

The United States Agency for International Development (USAID) West Bank and Gaza, *Health and Humanitarian Assistance Portfolio Overview,* Washington, D.C.: USAID, May 22, 2003.

Welfare Association, Palestinian Authority, and Ministry of Higher Education, *National Plan for Human Resource Development and Education in Health, Overview Volume,* Jerusalem: Welfare Association, 2001a.

———, *National Plan for Human Resource Development and Education in Health, Report #1: Planning, Accreditation and Licensure of Health Professionals in Palestine: Suggested Models,* Jerusalem: Welfare Association, 2001b.

———, *National Plan for Human Resource Development and Education in Health, Report #2: Appraisal of Palestinian Educational Programs in Health,* Jerusalem: Welfare Association, 2001c.

———, *National Plan for Human Resource Development and Education in Health, Report #3: Appraisal of CE [Continuing Education] Infrastructure in Major Health Service Provider Organizations in Palestine,* Jerusalem: Welfare Association, 2001d.

———, *National Plan for Human Resource Development and Education in Health, Report #4: Appraisal of CE [Continuing Education] Needs of Graduates of Educational Programs and Practicing Professionals in Health,* Jerusalem: Welfare Association, 2001e.

————, *National Plan for Human Resource Development and Education in Health Report #5: Professionals, Sub Plans,* Jerusalem: Welfare Association, 2001f.

World Bank, *Competitiveness Indicators,* 2003a. Online at http://wbln0018.worldbank.org/psd/compete.nsf/ (as of August 2003).

————, *Project Appraisal on a Proposed Credit in the Amount of US$7.9 Million to West Bank and Gaza for a Health System Development Project,* Washington, D.C., November 8, 1999.

————, *West Bank and Gaza: Medium-Term Development Strategy for the Health Sector,* Washington, D.C., August 1998.

————, *World Development Indicators 2003,* CD-ROM, Washington, D.C., 2003b.

World Food Program (WFP), *Emergency Food Security Needs Assessment: 2004 Update Assessment,* Jerusalem, Israel: World Food Program 2004. Online at http://documents.wfp.org/stellent/groups/public/documents/ena/wfp036508.pdf (as of October 2004).

World Health Organization (WHO), *Country Statistics, United States,* Geneva, Switzerland: World Health Organization Headquarters, 2001.

————, *Essential Drugs and Medicine Policy,* "WHO Model List of Essential Drugs," 11th ed., Geneva, Switzerland: World Health Organization Headquarters, 1999. Online at http://www.who.int/medicines/organization/par/edl/infedl11alpha.html (as of February 2004).

————, *Essential Drugs and Medicine Policy,* "The WHO Model List of Essential Medicines," 12th ed., Geneva, Switzerland: World Health Organization Headquarters, 2002. Online at http://www.who.int/medicines/organization/par/edl/eml12.shtml (as of February 2004).

————, *European Health-for-All Database,* Copenhagen, Denmark: World Health Organization, Regional Office for Europe, 2004. Online at http://hfadb.who.dk/hfa/(as of February 2004).

————, *Severe Mobility Restrictions in West Bank and Gaza Force Palestinian Population to Change Health Services,* press release, Jerusalem: WHO Office for the West Bank and Gaza, August 2003a. Online at http://www.healthinforum.net/modules.php?name = News&file = article&sid = 118 (as of February 2004).

————, *Survey on Access to Health Services in the Occupied Palestinian Territories—Preliminary Results and Comments,* Jerusalem: WHO Office for the West Bank and Gaza, August 2003b.

CHAPTER EIGHT

Education

Charles A. Goldman, Rachel Christina, and Cheryl Benard

Summary

Building an excellent education system will be key to Palestine's prosperity and stability in the coming years. The new state will have a strong base of human capital, and maximizing investments in that capital should be a national priority. Maintaining the relevance and resonance of the education system to its sociocultural context should be equally important. Indeed, addressing these two foci in tandem will be essential to positioning Palestine as a powerful player in the region's knowledge economy.

In this chapter, we offer a framework for understanding what an excellent education system looks like and what it must achieve. We trace the development of Palestinian education and assess the extent to which its current status does or does not align with that model. Next, we briefly examine a set of core planning documents related to the development of the education system after autonomy, comparing their content and focus with our theoretical framework. We then offer our recommendations for areas in which the Palestinian education system can maintain and develop its strengths, focus greater attention, or reconsider its directions. Finally, we offer some cost estimates for the development of a successful, high-quality Palestinian education system, within the demographic and economic constraints identified in Chapters Four and Five.

The success of every education system depends on achievement in three key areas: access, quality, and delivery. In these respects, the future Palestinian state will begin with a number of strengths. Access strengths include a commitment to equitable access and success in achieving gender parity, strong community support for education, and leadership that supports both system expansion and system reform. Quality strengths include awareness of the importance of early childhood experiences to later academic achievement, willingness to engage in curricular reform, strong interest in and resources for improving pedagogy, commitment to improving the qualifications and compensation of staff, and the perception of schools as a key location for the development of students' civic skills and engagement. Delivery will be supported by relatively strong management ability and established transparency, as well as solid data collection systems and cooperation with other entities.

Nevertheless, the system also faces significant challenges. In the area of access, these include the lack of a generally enabling environment, inadequate basic facilities and supplies, unsafe schools and routes to schools, lack of special education options for students with special needs, lack of nonformal options[1] for school-age students who are not enrolled in school, and a lack of lifelong learning opportunities. Quality challenges include a lack of clear goals and expectations for the system; minimal accountability; a need to fully integrate the system's stated principles of democracy, tolerance, and equity into curricula and instruction; limited relevance of secondary, vocational, and tertiary (higher education) programs to Palestine's economic needs; limited research and development capacity and activity; low staff compensation and an emerging administrative "bulge"; and difficulty monitoring process and outcomes. Delivery is hobbled by a severely underfunded and donor-dependent system and because data on the system are not effectively linked to reform.

Our recommendations for the system over the next ten years focus on the following:

- Maintaining current high levels of access, while also working within resource constraints to expand enrollments in secondary education (particularly in vocational and technical education and the academic sciences) and early childhood programs.
- Building quality through a focus on integrated curricular standards, assessments, and professional development, supported by long-term planning for system sustainability and improved accountability.
- Improving delivery by working with donors to develop streamlined and integrated funding mechanisms that allow the administration to focus on the business of meeting student needs, informed by strong evaluation and backed by significant sustained investment.

We estimate that the Palestinian education system will require $1 billion to $1.5 billion per year in financing[2] (including both donor and national investments) over the first decade of statehood if it is to operate at a level of excellence that will support national ambitions for development. We do, however, offer some compromises to reduce that cost should it be necessary to do so.

---

[1] Nonformal education is a structured program of education or training that supplements, complements, or compensates for the programming offered in the standard sequence of formal (government or private) education in a particular country, when students are unable to access or benefit from those formal programs.

[2] All cost estimates are presented in constant 2003 U.S. dollars unless otherwise noted.

Introduction

Quality education is essential for human development. At its best, education allows individuals to acquire skills, knowledge, and attitudes that translate into improved material circumstances, and it provides them with political, social, and economic resources that support their overall well-being. It builds critical understandings of government, economy, and culture and provides opportunities for individuals to better both themselves and their communities through participation in and reform of existing systems. It offers insights into and connections across societies that enrich individual experience and contribute to common understanding.

These effects cross generations, as educated citizens raise healthier, more-educated families in improved economic and social conditions. They cross cultures, as educated individuals and groups interact with one another in increasingly global forums. They cross traditional barriers of ethnicity, gender, and class, as institutions subject to scrutiny by informed stakeholders become increasingly accountable and responsible.

For societies emerging from conflict, these visions for the role of education are particularly powerful. The rehabilitation of the school system in these contexts serves as both a symbolic marker of the return to normalcy and a platform of hope for the future. This is likely to be particularly true in Palestine, where education is an integral part of national identity and a source of community pride, and where the education system generally enjoys the confidence of the population. Palestinian schools and universities will clearly have important roles to play in the transition to and establishment of statehood—not simply by delivering services, but also by providing continuity and stability balanced with relevant reform.

This chapter examines the potential of the Palestinian education system for fulfilling those roles and offers recommendations for maximizing its success. First, we propose a framework for understanding what a successful education system entails and what it must achieve. Then, we trace the development of Palestinian education and assess the extent to which its current status does or does not align with that model. Next, we briefly examine a set of core planning documents related to the development of the education system after autonomy, comparing their content and focus with our theoretical framework. We then offer our recommendations for areas in which the Palestinian education system can maintain and develop its strengths, focus greater attention, or reconsider its directions. Finally, we offer some cost estimates for the development of a successful, high-quality Palestinian education system, within the demographic and economic constraints identified in Chapters Four and Five.

Throughout the chapter, we use current Palestinian terms to refer to the configuration of the system: "basic education" for grades 1–10, "secondary education" for grades 11–12, and "tertiary education" (also called "higher education") for education following the completion of grade 12 (including vocational and technical programs provided by community colleges, four-year degrees offered by colleges and universities, and graduate study).

We note at the outset that asking the Palestinian education system to meet or rise to standards of excellence within the short time frame of this exercise presents a daunting challenge. The system has many strengths and has demonstrated notable durability and vigor even under the constraints of successive external administrations and violent upheavals. However, the intifada context within which Palestinian educators and students are currently operating provides a very poor resource and infrastructure base for future development. Equally if not more important, the psychological and social climate of fear and uncertainty has provided little support for learning over the past four years, and the system will face the long-term challenges of responding to the needs of the significant numbers of staff and students who have experienced trauma.

This analysis, therefore, proposes what is essentially a best-case scenario for the development of the Palestinian education system. Our recommendations provide starting points that are not, considering all evidence, unreasonable. However, we emphasize that the system will need significant and sustained support from the Palestinian community and from international actors to achieve them as outlined here.

What Is a Successful Education System in the 21st Century?

Planning for a successful Palestinian education system requires both a general understanding of what "works" in education and specific attention to the supports and constraints within which a uniquely Palestinian system will operate. Efforts to rehabilitate the system and move it forward can then be made with these frameworks in mind. Here, we outline basic characteristics of quality education, drawing initially on UNESCO and World Bank models produced through processes of international analysis and consultation. These models examine education at a system level, with the understanding that specific applications of their principles will vary from one system to another. They also set high expectations for system components, many of which will not necessarily be achievable in the first ten years of Palestine's independent statehood. Articulating an ideal framework, however, provides a standard against which achievements can be judged and a starting point for system transformation.

In addition to these broad international indicators of system success, our framework also incorporates concerns specific to the Arab world (which is and will remain the dominant cultural and economic frame for Palestine), as articulated in the United Nations Development Program's Arab human development reports (UNDP, 2002 and 2003) and the Arab states' regional framework for action (UNESCO, 2000 and 2004a; UNESCO/ARABEFA, 2001) under the Education For All initiative. Across the region, education is viewed as one of the key instruments of reform, development, and renaissance. However, while there is broad agreement that change is necessary, the reshaping of the nature and content of Arab education systems to achieve those goals is the subject of great debate. It is significant that the 2003 *Arab Human Development Report* is subtitled *Building a Knowledge Society* and that a core issue with which it wrestles is the status and future of the region's education systems. That document's struggle to articulate a framework for authentic, relevant, internally driven, and sustained reform represents the context within and against which Palestinian efforts will take place, and we bear it in mind throughout this chapter.

Across the multiple perspectives on which we draw, there is general agreement that the success of an education system rests on *access, quality,* and *delivery.* We use the rendering of these terms in the World Bank's 1999 *Education Sector Analysis* as a starting point for our examination of successful education systems (World Bank, 1999a).[3] We then elaborate on the original model as described below, paying particular attention to the potential of these three factors to support learning in domains that Delors and colleagues at UNESCO have referred to as *learning to know, learning to do, learning to live together,* and *learning to be* (Delors et al., 1996). System outcomes, of course, will vary, based on the nature of access, quality, and delivery in particular contexts.[4]

Access

Access refers to the extent to which a system provides members of a society with opportunities to learn, in terms of both the structure of schooling and the environments that support high-quality learning experiences. Principles underpinning access include the following:

- Adequate shelter, good nutrition, and good health enable learning. Students' home environments should support educational achievement.
- Learning does not begin with school entry. Appropriate development opportunities for younger children should be made available and considered an important component of the education system.
- Parents or guardians and communities should encourage participation in schooling and support learning.
- On both the local and national levels, the attitude toward education should be positive. Leadership at all levels should be interested in, supportive of, and willing to devote resources to education.
- The educational system should be accessible to all, without regard to gender, religion, ethnic identity, rural or urban location, settled or transient status, level of income, or level of ability.

---

[3] Annex One of this World Bank document (p. 47) provides the initial model from which we worked.

[4] Indeed, the success of an education system is largely dependent upon the extent to which it is part of an accountable, relevant, and sustainable overall national development plan. This chapter does not propose education reform as a panacea for development ills, but rather as one important component of multi-sectoral efforts to address them.

- Schools should be within reasonable physical proximity of students' residences.
- Schools should have adequate supplies and materials, and facilities should be appropriate for educational purposes.
- The school environment itself, and the routes children take to and from school, should be safe and free of the threat of violence.
- Appropriate, high-quality nonformal education services should be provided for school-age children who are not formally enrolled in school.
- Lifelong learning opportunities should be provided to support and enhance the formal school system.

Quality

Quality spans inputs, processes, and outcomes of education, with particular attention to curriculum, staffing, and teaching and learning at the classroom level. Quality principles include the following:

- Clear goals and expectations for the educational system should be established and supported by leadership.
- The curriculum should be relevant to the needs of the individual, the state, and the region. Education should provide the competencies necessary to succeed and thrive in a global economy.
- Schools should promote skills and attitudes that support the development of students into engaged citizens who contribute to the well-being of their own countries and of the world. Religious, ethnic, and political tolerance; protection of minorities and the vulnerable; and the free exchange of ideas and opinions are important core values for education that support national development and global integration.
- The education system should be flexible and responsive to the needs of both state and local communities, and should include capacity for research and development.
- Staff should be highly motivated, with solid initial training, continuing professional education, and good pay and career development opportunities.
- The teaching and learning process should be well-matched to the system's requirements.
- Evaluation of the education system should address both processes and outcomes, with strong ongoing monitoring for quality assurance and improvement.

Delivery

Delivery addresses the institutional mechanisms in place for assuring high-quality education that is accessible to all. Important delivery considerations include governance, resources, and information management, as discussed below.

- Governance of the educational system should be characterized by clear responsibilities and accountability, flexible analysis and planning capacity, and appropriate decentralization of decisionmaking.
- Schools should be able to count on dependable financial resources, including an appropriate level and allocation of public funds. School administrators, as well as local and state governing bodies, should press continually for efficient and effective use of resources.
- Reporting and information systems should be sufficient to provide administrators and leaders with the necessary information to encourage effectiveness and efficiency, but should not be allowed to become excessive or onerous. Systems should provide regular monitoring and feedback, to improve performance and policymaking.

Issues Crossing Multiple Domains

Within this general framework, a number of issues cross the access, quality, and delivery domains. These issues include educational relevance, the competencies needed to function successfully in the global economy, and gender equity, and all are core concerns in Palestinian development. We address these concerns briefly here at a conceptual level and will revisit them when we recommend next steps for the system.

Relevance

In contexts of political and social transition, education's potential to both preserve and revitalize culture makes it a key focus of debate. For Palestine, these issues are particularly acute, as educators strive for autonomy in an environment where it has hitherto been unknown.

Much has been written about the tension between integrating with increasingly global economic, political, and cultural systems and maintaining cultural uniqueness. In societies like Palestine, where policymakers must juggle both significant internal diversity and strong external influences, defining relevance is particularly complicated. The Ministry of Education (MoE) cites as a key goal and challenge: "maintain[ing] a balance between the promotion of national values and openness to world cultures so as to be able to effectively contribute to the evolution of world civilization" (Palestinian MoE, 2000). Resistance on principle to any external input is both impractical (given the system's inability to finance itself) and unreasonable. However, redirecting such input through local negotiation and prioritization can produce a healthy "vernacularized" (Appadurai, 1996) system that addresses both internal and external concerns.[5]

The Arab development report of 2003 argues that "the potential for developing the knowledge capabilities of Arab countries is enormous—not only because of their

---

[5] See also Hall (1991); Henry et al. (1999); Lingard (2000); and Luke and Luke (2000).

untapped human capital, but also because of their rich cultural, linguistic and intellectual heritage" (UNDP, 2003, p. ii). Tapping that potential will be a key task of Palestinian education, requiring a delicate balance between inward reflection and outward engagement so that Palestinians are "immersed in the global knowledge stream" but not "swamped or drowned" (UNDP, 2003, pp. i–ii).

Global Competencies

Closely linked to the debate over relevance are questions about what kinds of technical competencies are necessary for individuals and societies to compete and collaborate at a global level. For the Arab world in general, and for Palestine in particular, three specific concerns seem to be emerging:

- Vocational/technical education's lack of appeal, relevance, and quality.
- Tertiary education's bias toward humanities and social sciences and lack of capacity for research and development.
- Limited and uneven use of information technology to support instruction and learning.

As Gill and Fluitman (2002) note, vocational education provides an important complement to academic secondary and postsecondary training, and, when well-designed and integrated with the labor market, it is a vital contribution to economic development. Unfortunately, it is often a neglected stepchild of the education system: underfunded, anachronistic, and unappealing to large numbers of students. Creating flexible, responsive, and state-of-the-art vocational training structures and curricula that link to career opportunities and evolve as the labor market changes is a challenge for systems with already limited financial resources, but it is also an imperative (UNDP, 2002). Partnerships with private-sector businesses can alleviate some of the fiscal pressures on the system, as well as guide it toward more relevance and adaptability, but care should be taken that such arrangements do not serve corporate interests above those of the student population as a whole.

Tertiary education in much of the Arab world is notably weak in the sciences (UNESCO, 2000; UNDP, 2003). This weakness is often a function of cost: facilities and equipment for science instruction and research are expensive. However, student preferences for humanities, social science, and education are also shaped by early education experiences: tracking (channeling of students into strictly separated arts or sciences streams) in secondary school and high-stakes matriculation examinations reduce the population eligible for more intensive college- and university-level sciences, and low-quality science and mathematics instruction in the early years further reduces the pool that will have the option to pursue these fields in tertiary study (Birzeit University, 2002; Hashweh, 2003). Finally, the preference for teaching the sciences in English at the tertiary level prevents broader enrollments, because many students are not prepared to function in a second language at that level. It also raises issues about both the quality of foreign language instruction at lower levels—which is often low, particularly in lower-income schools—and the desirability and long-term sociocultural outcomes of constraining higher-level knowledge content and usage in this fashion.[6]

Access to and facility with information technology is rapidly becoming an essential indicator of development potential. For societies poor in natural resources, investment in human capacity serves as a means of entering and competing in the international arena, but knowledge capital is limited by the extent to which its owners can reach and manipulate computers, the Internet, and other electronic media.[7] For countries building knowledge economies, education becomes the key means of providing this access equitably to all members of society. The wealthy may be able to provide for themselves in this arena, but the majority of Middle Eastern populations cannot afford the initial and follow-up costs of computing and other information technology at the household level (UNDP, 2003, pp. 63–64; Burkhart and Older, 2003). Failure to embed new technology within the educational system and to routinize and facilitate its use by students and teachers risks pushing most students to the wrong side of the "information divide" and has negative long-term implications for regional and international competitiveness.

Gender Equity

The importance of the education of girls and women to development is well documented.[8] Investments in female education substantially benefit individuals, families, and societies, and such benefits include economic, political, and social components. Indeed, while the economic benefits of educating girls are the most commonly cited, effects in other arenas are at least as profound and bear particular relevance in societies like Palestine where the participation of women in the labor force is limited and a source of internal debate.

At the individual level, education not only provides access to employment opportunities, but provides girls with "an expanded sense of [their] own potential, increasing [their] self confidence, [their] social and negotiation skills . . . and [their] ability to protect [themselves] against violence and ill health" (Bellamy, 2004, p. 7). The knowledge and life skills that schooling provides are valuable risk reducers in a range of family and social arenas.

At the family level, a mother's education has lasting effects on the health of her children, on their own levels of education, and on the well-being of her family.[9] For

---

[6] See UNDP (2003) for a thoughtful discussion of these tensions and the importance of maintaining and developing Arabic as a language of instruction.

[7] See Delors et al. (1996) for exploration of the equity and interdependence issues involved in harnessing the power of "universal communication" for education.

[8] See, for example, UNICEF (2004), UNESCO (2004b), and World Bank (2001).

[9] See UNICEF (2002), cited in Bellamy (2004) p. 18.

example, across the developing world, each extra year of maternal education has been estimated to reduce the mortality rate for children under five by 5–10 percent (Herz et al., 1991, p. 19). Educated women have demonstrated a greater propensity for dedicating family finances to investments and expenditures that benefit the health and education of their family and their children, and they have both more knowledge and greater access to resources in these areas. When educated mothers participate in the labor force, these benefits are multiplied by increases in family income.

At the social level, gross domestic product per capita increases as primary enrollment ratios for girls increase, and increasing gender parity in education is linked to lower socioeconomic development costs overall and faster economic growth (World Bank, 2001). Increasing the education of women also provides them with greater opportunities for engagement in politics and administration. The presence of greater numbers of women in formal political and administrative positions has been found to decrease corruption and reduce levels of violence (Dollar, Fisman, and Gatti, 1999).

While these links among girls' education, family, and social well-being have resulted in a greater emphasis on girls' education in international development circles, gender equity in education is not simply a matter of ensuring enrollment parity (which Palestine, significantly, has already largely achieved). The quality of the education that girls and boys receive also has significant effects on their life chances, and too often quality indicators (including curricula and pedagogy) favor boys. Greater attention to what girls are learning and how they are being taught is imperative if equity concerns are to be fully addressed.

It is important to note that education for boys is worthy of attention as well. Gender equity demands high-quality experiences for both boys and girls. There is evidence linking education for boys to a variety of positive outcomes beyond improved employment opportunities. In the West Bank and Gaza, for example, enrollment rates of children and youth are more than 10 percentage points higher when the father has at least secondary-level education (Jacobsen, 2003, p. 98). Unfortunately, when education for boys is discussed, the current debate tends to focus on whether there is a relationship between education and the propensity to radicalization and violence. Like girls, boys deserve more thoughtful analyses of ways in which what and how they are learning can contribute to their own and their societies' well-being.

In sum, we suggest that the excellence of an educational system can be assessed in three areas: access, quality, and delivery. However, system characteristics in each of these areas affect those in the others, and their interplay can either strengthen or weaken the system as a whole. Crosscutting issues of a system's local relevance, the extent to which it is globally competitive, and the ways in which issues of gender are addressed should also be considered when assessing system quality or contemplating reform. In what follows, we use this framework to appraise the challenges and the potential of the present Palestinian system and to offer recommendations that reflect targets of excellence that can support the new state's ambitions for becoming an important and independent part of the region's political economy.

Historical Development of Palestinian Education (1517–2004)

Any proposals for the development of Palestinian education must take into consideration the system's unique history and the resulting competencies and deficiencies in access, quality, and delivery to which it has been subject. When viewed in terms of the framework we have provided above, Palestinian education has consistently exhibited three features:

- Steady expansion of *access,* both horizontally (in terms of class, gender, and the urban-rural divide) and vertically (in terms of increasing access to higher levels of education along these same dimensions).
- Struggles to achieve and maintain *quality* while expanding access.
- Inconsistent *delivery*, due primarily to constraints on administration and funding.

In this section, we trace these trends from the Ottoman administration of Palestine to the present, with particular attention to the significant effects on Palestinian education of external forces. We note that these effects have both supported and inhibited the growth of the system, and that they are likely to linger well into the early years of a Palestinian state. The high value Palestinians place on education and their efforts to maintain educational progress in the face of political and economic upheavals have given the system durability, but also a certain amount of detachment from other development challenges. The willingness of outside agencies and donors to support and develop Palestinian education has also had a dual effect. It has sustained the system and provided a degree of linkage to international standards, but it also has reduced its autonomy. Building on the system's durability and maximizing the positive effects of its international connections, while supporting autonomy and local relevance, will thus be a core challenge for the emerging Palestinian state.

Education Under the Ottomans (1517–1917)

Formal, "modern" education in Palestine began to take shape during the Ottoman era. In this period, access was limited, quality was uneven, and delivery was split across a variety of institutions. The majority of schools were the traditional village *kuttab*,[10] which

---

[10] A *kuttab* is a traditional school with a strong religious focus that also teaches basic literacy and numeracy. The instructor is usually a local religious figure. Girls may be taught with boys or taught separately by the instructor's wife. Although still common in many parts of the Middle East, the *kuttab* is not a feature of the current educational system in Palestine (a preschool operated by a mosque or an Islamic social service organization is not technically a *kuttab*).

taught minimal literacy and provided an introduction to the Qur'an and religious practice for both boys and girls (although female enrollment was limited). However, a small number of government schools were also established, to train future bureaucrats or to offer Islamic religious instruction in a controlled environment. During the second half of the 19th century, private schools were increasingly opened as outreach arms of Christian missionary organizations or under indigenous sponsorship; these schools included the first institutions established especially for the education of girls. Government schools used Turkish as the language of instruction, while *kuttab* and private schools used Arabic, with the sponsoring country's language (e.g., English, German, or French) as the secondary language in missionary institutions. In none of the schools of this period was education developed specifically for Palestinian students, nor was it designed to serve as the foundation for a uniquely Palestinian state. Ottoman education prepared Ottoman citizens, private schools guided indigenous elites toward a Euro-American modernism, and the *kuttab* provided a basic literacy and religious training for a broader Muslim identity rather than for Palestinian nationalism.

The British Mandate (1917–1948)

Ottoman administration of Palestine was followed by the British Mandate. Access improved and delivery was streamlined as the total number of schools grew under British administration, but quality varied significantly across institutions. Village schools were largely folded into the state school system, and secular education became increasingly dominant. Attempts were made to declare education to be compulsory and to expand the participation of girls, although neither effort was very successful. Private schools remained the choice and largely the territory of the elite.

Developments in this period essentially set the framework for the next 50 years of Palestinian education. Expanded access, secularism, and bureaucratization were accompanied by strong external influence on the system and a general disconnection from the needs and concerns of ordinary Palestinians. By 1948, the system was

> increasingly designed to serve the entire population but starved of the resources to meet that mission; administration was highly centralized; control of the system was politically sensitive, chiefly on nationalist grounds; the curriculum was largely imported and ignored Palestinian national identity; and the public system was supplemented by an extensive private system. (Brown, 2003, p. 146)

1948–1967

Access to education continued to expand in the years between the end of the British Mandate and the Israeli occupation of the West Bank and Gaza. However, delivery of educational services was significantly complicated during this period, often with negative effects on quality. Two important structural and institutional changes occurred, with lasting effects on the system.

Egyptian and Jordanian Administration. The 1948 war resulted in Jordanian administration of the West Bank and Egyptian administration of Gaza. These governments implemented their own curricula, textbooks, teacher certification procedures, and administrative regulations in the areas that fell under their control. The Palestinian education system thus developed a two-tiered structure, with next to no coordination between the agencies serving Palestinians under the two administrations.

Establishment of UNRWA. A third educational delivery institution also emerged, with the establishment of the United Nations Relief and Works Agency for Palestine Refugees in the Near East (UNRWA) in 1949. Founded to meet the needs of Palestinians displaced in the 1948 war, UNRWA continues to serve those individuals and their descendants today. Along with other social services, the agency provides schooling through grade 10, teacher training, vocational training, and college scholarships for refugees in the West Bank and Gaza, as well as for those in Jordan, Lebanon and Syria. UNRWA is also a significant employer and has served as one key point of connection between the international community and Palestinian educators and students. While the agency has historically coordinated its service provision with the governing powers in the territories in which it operates, it has had access to additional resources and opportunities as a result of its international sponsorship, which has provided additional support for quality.

1967–1987

The 1967 war resulted in the occupation of the West Bank and Gaza by Israel and further complicated delivery of Palestinian education. While the Israelis retained the Jordanian and Egyptian educational systems in their general form, the military and later civil administrations assumed direct oversight of system components thought essential to maintaining stability within the West Bank and Gaza. Israeli authorities reviewed texts and curricular materials for use in Palestinian government schools; oversaw the hiring of educators, system staff, and administrators; licensed private schools; and issued permits for new school construction and existing expansion (Brown, 2003; Rigby, 1995). The Israeli administration also managed the educational budget for government schools in the territories (UNRWA school budgets continued to be derived from international contributions to the agency).

The education system continued to expand quantitatively during this period, with particularly notable growth in the availability of tertiary education. University education was no longer limited to the elite; increasing numbers of low-income students, rural students, and those from refugee camps also gained access to tertiary schooling (Baramki, 1987; Paz, 2000). These university-educated Palestinians contributed to the development of an active civil society during this period, as the number of student groups, research centers, the media, youth organizations, and similar institutions expanded rapidly.

The expansion of access, however, was not paralleled by a proportional increase in funding, and quality concerns deepened (UNESCO, 1995). As the population grew, demand outpaced supply, and the system became significantly under-resourced. Schools began to operate on multiple shifts, equipment and educational resources were scarce, and teachers and administrators were often unqualified or underqualified. Curricula were not updated to parallel revisions in Egypt and Jordan, with the result that Palestinian educational content did not keep pace even with that of its closest neighbors. Government schools were reputed to provide the lowest quality education, although they served the largest number of students. UNRWA schools, second largest in terms of overall enrollment, were able to access the agency's fiscal and human resources to help support their services, and the far smaller network of private elementary and secondary institutions was able to leverage international connections to support some innovation and quality improvement (Rigby, 1995). In general, however, an inverse relationship between access and quality developed during this period, and resolving this dilemma will be one of the system's most difficult future challenges.

The First Intifada (1987–1993)

The military, security, and political ramifications of the 1987–1993 intifada further eroded the Palestinian education system's capacity to deliver quality services. However, this period was also notable for a degree of innovation and flexibility in curriculum and pedagogy that provided a base for independent development after autonomy in 1993 (Graham-Brown, 1984).

Palestinian schools became active centers of political resistance[11] during the intifada—a function that led to significant disruption of education. From 1987 to 1991, it was not uncommon for schools to miss as much as half of their instructional time because of closures and strikes (Al-Haq/Law in the Service of Man, 1988; Rigby, 1995, p. 15). Palestinian universities were closed by Israeli administrative order from 1988 to 1990, gradually reopening from May 1990 to October 1991 (Essoulami, 1992; B'Tselem, 1990).

The infrastructure and resource problems of the system were exacerbated by the political conflict. As the formal system declined, however, communities organized emergency alternatives to fill the gaps created by these outages in services, and an active and dynamic network of nongovernmental and alternative providers of educational services, training, and innovations began to develop (Mahshi and Bush, 1989; Fahsheh, 1993). Questions about the appropriate nature of and control over Palestinian education were central to the conflict, and debates around these issues during

---

[11] Schools observed national strikes in protest of the occupation and served as rallying points for demonstrations, while teachers and students engaged in unsanctioned study of curricular elements prohibited by formal policy (including Palestinian history and geography). Universities provided a base for student political activism and loci of interaction with the international community around issues related to the occupation. See, for example, Baramki, 1987; Mahshi and Bush, 1989; and Fahsheh, 1993.

the intifada set the stage for much of the Palestinian planning in the early autonomy period (Rigby, 1989).

Early Autonomy (1994–1999)

The education system serving Palestinians in the West Bank and Gaza (with the exception of schools in East Jerusalem) was transferred from Israeli control to that of the Palestinian Authority (PA) in 1994, as a condition of implementation of the Oslo Accords. Between 1994 and 1999, a number of important steps were taken toward system rehabilitation.

Improvement of service delivery was the primary focus of development efforts. The disjointed structures of the Egyptian- and Jordanian-based systems in Gaza and the West Bank were streamlined and combined, and a new Palestinian matriculation examination was designed and implemented. An Education Management Information System was also developed for MoE use.

An independent Curriculum Development Center was established, with responsibility for curriculum design, production, and implementation later transferred to a curricular unit in the MoE. Curricula and texts were borrowed from the national curricula of Jordan and to some extent Egypt while a Palestinian national curriculum was being developed.[12] Phase-in of the new national curriculum and ongoing review and development began in 1996.

Short- and long-term plans for the development of the system were formulated, and attention was paid to the need to build both long-term and short-term institutional capacity. Relationships with donors and other external bodies were cultivated and expanded, and accountability was acknowledged as a system priority. In general, the MoE was perceived by international partners and by the local population to function well and to operate, to the best of its ability, with reasonable transparency and expertise (Birzeit University, 2003; Jerusalem Media and Communication Centre, 2001; World Bank, 1999b and c).[13]

Planning, however, was stymied by fiscal realities, and access and quality remained significant problems for the system. Rapid population expansion as a result of immigration following autonomy—the student population increased from 650,000 to 1 million between 1994 and 2001 [Palestinian Central Bureau of Statistics (PCBS), 2001b and 2004a]—led to crowded schools and forced the ministry to focus on facilities and infrastructure at the expense of quality improvement. Donor commitments notwithstanding, the necessary funds for the construction of additional government

---

[12] These materials were issued with PA-authorized covers but were not products of the PA's curriculum unit. International concerns about anti-Israeli and/or anti-Jewish content in these materials appear to be being gradually addressed as the PA develops and implements its own curricula, as we discuss later in this chapter.

[13] These observations are intended as relative; lack of qualifications among decisionmaking staff, reported nepotism, and questionable appropriations of funds have been matters of concern across all Palestinian ministries.

schools and the improvement of existing ones were not fully forthcoming, and the schools remained overcrowded and under-equipped.

Nongovernmental schools continued to play a key role in Palestinian education, with varied relationships to the state system. UNRWA continued to operate schools through grade 10 for refugee students in the West Bank and Gaza, adopting the Ministry of Education's new curriculum and scheduling. Interface between the UNRWA system and the Ministry of Education, however, was not seamless, and planning for the eventual absorption of UNRWA services into the government framework under a final settlement was only sporadic. Private schools increased in number with the return of expatriate Palestinians and international interest in supporting innovation in Palestinian education, although their planning and development was subject to MoE approval and licensing. Opportunities for preschool education, almost entirely nongovernmental, also increased, although only 29 percent of the age group of four- to five-year-olds was utilizing these services in 2003–2004 (Palestinian MoE, 2004c, p. 7).

Al-Aqsa Intifada (2000–2004)

The ongoing intifada has significantly eroded the progress of the 1994–1999 period, undermining even the system's most notable and durable achievements in access, quality, and delivery.[14] These issues are discussed briefly below and in greater detail in the section of this chapter on "Strengths and Challenges Regarding Future Development."

Access to education has been limited by damage to the educational infrastructure across all levels of the system, by the seizure of property by Israeli forces, and by restrictions on the movement of students, teachers, and administrators. The Ministry of Education reports that 295 schools, 11 higher education institutions, and seven MoE administrative complexes have been shelled or damaged since 2000, with consequences including structural damage from shelling and bulldozing and damage to or destruction of furniture, computers, teaching materials, and administrative records. Forty-eight schools have been turned, temporarily or permanently, into Israeli military bases or detention centers, while ten schools and two universities have been closed by Israeli military order (Palestinian MoE, 2004b and 2004c).

Quality has eroded in the absence of consistent access and reliable funding streams and the presence of an overwhelming atmosphere of violence and fear. Student achievement has slipped notably, particularly for students in high-conflict locations, and the need for both academic and psychosocial support services is high (Palestinian MoE, 2004c; Save the Children, 2001; UNRWA, 2003a). UNRWA schools, for example, now offer programs of compensatory education in Arabic, English, and math

---

[14] Although much debated in the public realm, "responsibility" for the conditions we describe in this section is irrelevant for the purposes of this exercise. Planning for the development of any emergent Palestinian state's education system requires an acknowledgment that this system faces notable material and sociopsychological deficits resulting from the events and climate of the 2000–2004 period.

for students suffering from anxiety, phobia, withdrawal, depression, sleep disturbance, and diminished concentration. UNRWA has provided these services to approximately 120,000 of its 250,000 students over the past three years (Nasser, 2004), but demand has been greater than the agency's capacity to provide assistance.

Delivery of education has been hampered by constraints on the movement of people and goods and by the uncertainty of the policy environment. Attempts at better integrating the split systems of the West Bank and Gaza and planning for the integration of the Ministry of Education and UNRWA systems have been interrupted, resulting in the continuing cost burden of maintaining duplicate, parallel administrations. Similarly, efforts to build infrastructure across the system and upgrade facilities have been slowed or in some cases halted. Most important, long-term planning has been set aside in favor of crisis response, and the ambitious efforts of 1994–1999 to coordinate system restructuring and reform have come largely to a halt.

The system deficits resulting from these broad contextual factors are exacerbated by the ongoing construction of the separation wall in the West Bank. Costs to the Ministry of Education and to Palestinian families are both direct (in terms of the need to establish new schools and hire new teachers in areas cut off from established services) and indirect (in terms of forced relocation, absence, increased dropout rates, and increased travel by students and teachers needing to pass through or around the wall to attend their schools or institutions of tertiary education). As of October 2003, 22 localities had been separated from their schools by the wall (PCBS, 2003a), and its completion will isolate many more.

The PA requested $31 million in emergency humanitarian aid to education ($21 million for primary and secondary education and $10 million for tertiary education) in 2003–2004, a significant addition to the roughly $52 million in long-term development aid it was already administering (PA, 2003, pp. 16 and 17). In July 2002, UNRWA requested an additional $56 million for physical repairs and for interim programs for children unable to reach their schools, such as kits for emergency homeschooling (UN, 2002). Additional UNRWA emergency appeals [for an additional $9.4 million in aid for remedial and vocational education, extracurricular programs for school children and youth, and psychosocial counseling in 2003 (Nasser, 2004; UNRWA, 2003b and 2003c), and $5.9 million in 2004 (UNRWA, 2004)] have been necessary to continue to provide support and basic services as conditions in Gaza, in particular, worsen.[15]

---

[15] As of September 30, 2004, UNRWA's emergency appeals (including those for education) for 2004 remained underfunded by slightly over $119 million, and emergency education activities had been scaled back as a result (Nasser, 2004).

The Palestinian Educational System Today

Planning Palestinian educational development through the first ten years of statehood requires an analysis of the current system's strengths and weaknesses, and the implications of their configuration for short- to-medium-term system outcomes, as we will discuss. First, however, we provide more detail on the current characteristics of the system to explain its classification in the target areas. Data in this section reflect 2003–2004 conditions where possible and appropriate. Where 2003–2004 data are not available, numbers typically refer to 1998–1999, the last fiscal year of relative system stability prior to the crisis conditions of the current intifada.

Structure

The Palestinian education system currently includes ten years of basic schooling (four years of lower elementary school and six years of upper elementary school) and two years of secondary schooling.[16] Secondary schooling is either academic (with students tracked into arts or science, depending on academic performance and the recommendation of teachers[17]) or vocational (in commercial, agricultural, industrial, religious law, or tourism tracks, with options that allow for continuing to tertiary education or terminating studies after grade 12). For those who hope to continue to tertiary education, secondary schooling concludes with the *tawjihi* examination, the results of which largely determine students' access to the postsecondary institutions and fields of their choice. The minimum *tawjihi* score needed for tertiary education admission varies annually, and departments within tertiary institutions set their own internal standards, with sciences typically requiring higher scores than nonscience departments, and universities requiring higher scores than community colleges.

Indigenous tertiary education options for Palestinians currently include eleven universities and five colleges. Three universities are in Gaza, and the remaining eight universities and five colleges are in the West Bank. Universities and colleges offer four-year baccalaureate degrees and, at seven institutions, graduate programs. There are also twenty community colleges in the West Bank and five in Gaza. These institutions offer higher technical and vocational training that lasts for two years and leads to various diplomas. Finally, Al-Quds Open University maintains fifteen regional centers in the West Bank and five in Gaza, and awards undergraduate degrees through distance learning.

Palestinian schools include both single-sex and coeducational institutions (there were 674 of the latter in 2003–2004—about 23 percent of the total number of schools) (Palestinian MoE, 2004a). Coeducational schools are more common at the elementary level (social preference is for separated schooling at the secondary level) and in the elite

---

[16] UNRWA schools provide only academic basic and limited vocational secondary options. UNRWA students who wish to enroll in academic secondary school must transfer to government or private schools in 11th grade.

[17] Tracking streams were eliminated in the first curriculum revision in 1996, but reintroduced in 2003–2004.

private sector. Universities may be coeducational or offer a range of single-sex options for students (e.g., classes are held on certain days of the week for males and others for females).

Scope and Enrollment

As of 2004, there were 2,956 basic and secondary schools and kindergartens in the West Bank and Gaza (2,254 in the West Bank; 702 in Gaza) (PCBS, 2004a). Of these, 1,580 basic and secondary schools and two kindergartens were run by the Ministry of Education, and 272 basic schools were run by UNRWA. An additional 845 kindergartens and 257 schools were privately run. School facilities served 1,017,443 pupils (West Bank: 601,941, Gaza: 415,502), with about 69 percent in government schools, 25 percent in UNRWA schools, and 6 percent in private schools. A total of 70,225 students were enrolled in kindergarten over that period (about 29 percent of the age-eligible population) (PCBS, 2004a).

Gross enrollment in basic education is near-universal, and the average persistence to grade five was at 99 percent in 2001 [United Nations Children's Fund (UNICEF), 2001; PCBS, 2001a]; the net enrollment rate (representing children enrolled in age-appropriate schooling—number of enrolled same-age children divided by all school-age children, and excluding those children who are not the appropriate age for their grade) was 93.7 percent for that same period (Palestinian MoE, 2004c, p. 10). These numbers are high for the region and for developing countries overall, and they are roughly equal to rates in developed countries.[18] Secondary education enrollment is also high, with gross rates of 80 percent for males and 86 percent for females in 2000 (UNICEF, 2000). Again, this rate is much higher than the regional average and approaches the 90 percent average of the developed world. Overall, roughly one-third of the total West Bank and Gaza population is presently in basic or secondary school [UNESCO, undated(a)]—a figure that is expected to increase over the next 20 years and that is characteristic of the very youthful population of Palestine.

As enrollment figures (see Table 8.1) demonstrate, the school system has achieved near-parity by gender; in fact, more girls than boys are enrolled in secondary schooling. This higher female enrollment is increasingly characteristic of the Middle East, where many male youth choose work over secondary schooling. Nonetheless, boys are much more likely to attend private schools (among which are numbered the "best" of the Palestinian educational institutions [Brown, 2003; Palestinian MoE, 2000]) than are girls. Indeed, while the high enrollments of girls are a system strength, questions remain about what kind of schooling they have access to, and the quality of education that they receive, as we discuss below.

A total of 98,439 students were studying in universities and colleges during 2003–2004, and 5,892 were at community colleges during that period (PCBS, 2004c). There

---

[18] For this and all other comparative data, comparison sources are UNDP, 2003; UNESCO, 2004; UNICEF, 2004; and World Bank, 2004.

Table 8.1
Number of Students in Basic and Secondary Schools by Region, Supervising Authority, Stage, and Gender, 2003–2004

Region	Supervising Authority	Grand Total			Basic			Secondary		
		Total	Males	Females	Total	Males	Females	Total	Males	Females
Palestinian Territory	Total	1,017,443	512,490	504,953	916,837	463,806	453,031	100,606	48,684	51,922
	Government	706,187	352,350	353,837	609,604	306,079	303,525	96,583	46,271	50,312
	UNRWA	251,584	124,313	127,271	251,584	124,313	127,271	NA	NA	NA
	Private	59,672	35,827	23,845	55,649	33,414	22,235	4,023	2,413	1,610
West Bank	Total	601,941	302,736	299,205	542,520	274,331	268,189	59,421	28,405	31,016
	Government	489,621	245,858	243,763	433,989	219,707	214,282	55,632	26,151	29,481
	UNRWA	59,909	25,920	33,989	59,909	25,920	33,989	NA	NA	NA
	Private	52,411	30,958	21,453	48,622	28,704	19,918	3,789	2,254	1,535
Gaza	Total	415,502	209,754	205,748	374,317	189,475	184,842	41,185	20,279	20,906
	Government	216,566	106,492	110,074	175,615	86,372	89,243	40,951	20,120	20,831
	UNRWA	191,675	98,393	93,282	191,675	98,393	93,282	NA	NA	NA
	Private	7,261	4,869	2,392	7,027	4,710	2,317	234	159	75

SOURCE: PCBS, 2004b.

is near gender parity in enrollment at this level as well, for both types of postsecondary education.

Governance

The Ministry of Education[19] is responsible for primary oversight of Palestinian government and private schools. Although the intent is a unified system, administration is conducted from duplicate centers in Ramallah (for the West Bank) and Gaza City (for Gaza), because of constraints on the movement of staff and resources in the current political context. Seventeen regional directorates oversee the delivery of government and private educational services. The MoE also provides curricula and examinations for schools administered by UNRWA, but it is not responsible for financing or management of those schools. UNRWA schools operate with the same framework of courses, grades, and semesters as the government schools, but the agency hires, trains, and pays its own staff and is accountable to the United Nations, not to the PA.

The MoE also collaborates with other government agencies in the development and administration of education and training programs for school-age and out-of-school populations. These bodies include the Ministry of Social Affairs; the Ministry of Health; the Ministry of Labor; the Ministry of Youth, Sports and Culture; and the General Personnel Council.

Policy mandates parent councils at each MoE school (not in the UNRWA or private institutions), but the role of these bodies is unclear, and there is no evidence that they have in fact been constituted across the system.

Preschool and Special Services

Preschool services are provided by private day-care centers (which are licensed and overseen by the Ministry of Social Affairs) and by kindergartens that are licensed but not typically funded by the Ministry of Education. These facilities tend to be clustered in and around urban centers and to be patronized by the children of financially better-off families.

Special education services are provided by both the Ministry of Education and UNRWA for their respective student populations. There are no available data on the exact number of Palestinian students with special education needs, but it is probable that the majority of those with such needs are not being served. In East Jerusalem, for example, only 400 out of 20,000 school-age Palestinian children were identified as needing special services (Gumpel and Awartani, 2003), an exceptionally low figure that is probably linked to lack of capacity for diagnosis. (The majority of students served are those with readily apparent physical disabilities.)

Counseling and psychological services are also provided in both MoE and UNRWA schools, although the scope and content vary. All UNRWA schools are

---

[19] The Ministry of Higher Education was formally separated from the Ministry of Education in 1996 and then reabsorbed into the MoE in 2003.

served by the agency's emergency trauma support program, and many receive additional support through targeted programs of psychological intervention.[20] MoE schools are served by a small, experimental cadre of school counselors, funded by external contributions.

Grade Repetition and Dropout Rates

Grade repetition rates in 2002–2003 were 1.4 percent for the basic and 1.3 percent for the secondary stages of school, with boys averaging higher rates than girls in both stages (1.5 percent versus 1.2 percent and 1.4 percent versus 1.1 percent, respectively). These rates are low compared with others in the region and with those of developing countries as a group. Palestinian dropout rates are also low through the basic grades, but rise to 3.7 percent overall at the secondary level. At the primary level, dropout rates are a bit higher for boys, with an average of 0.9 percent versus 0.6 percent for girls; at the secondary level, however, dropout rates are lower for boys (2.6 percent) than for girls (4.8 percent)[21] (PCBS, 2003c).

Classroom Context

Demographic pressure on the Palestinian education system is high (see Chapter Four for details on population growth and projections). In the absence of sufficient funding for system expansion, student-to-teacher ratios and classroom density ratios have continually increased, although both are higher in UNRWA schools than in government schools. During the 2002–2003 school year, student-teacher ratios averaged 35.9 to 1 in UNRWA schools, 27.2 to 1 in government schools, and 16.6 to 1 in private schools (PCBS, 2004c).[22]

Classroom density ranges from a high of 43.4 students per classroom in UNRWA schools, to 34.7 in government schools, to a relative low of 24.4 in private schools (PCBS, 2004a). Faced with high demand and limited supply, UNRWA schools have also taken the additional step of moving to multiple shifts (see Table 8.2). In partial double shifts, some of the classrooms operate on a double shift while the majority of the other classrooms operate on a single shift. In full double shifts (one in the morning and one in the afternoon), all or most of these classrooms operate on a double shift under the administration of one headmaster or headmistress, or two different schools use the same school premises.

Eighty government schools (11.4 percent of the total) were also operating on double shifts in 2003–2004 (Palestinian MoE, 2004c, p. 15).

---

[20] It should be noted that funding for these programs is always in jeopardy because of the agency's financial shortfalls.

[21] We discuss factors influencing this pattern of female dropout later in this chapter.

[22] The student/teacher ratio does not include kindergarten.

Table 8.2
UNRWA Schools by Number of Shifts Operated, 1998–1999

	West Bank	Gaza
Elementary (grades 1–7)		
Single shift	12	15
Partial double shift	3	1
Full double shift	14	105
Preparatory (grades 8–10)		
Single shift	51	29
Partial double shift	6	1
Full double shift	12	17
Total		
Single shift	63	44
Partial double shift	9	2
Full double shift	26	122

SOURCE: UNRWA (2004b).
NOTES: The number of schools on a partial or full double shift have increased since 1999, but current figures are not publicly available. Although newly standardized education system descriptions do not include a separate "preparatory" (formerly grades 7–10) cycle, UNRWA cycle descriptions tend to continue to reflect past practice (as well as the current allocation of students to buildings by grade).

Teacher Characteristics

Palestinian students at all levels may be taught by either men or women, although female teachers are found in boys' secondary classrooms only in private schools, and kindergarten teachers are almost exclusively female. There is an overall cultural and policy preference for matching the gender of staff to that of students at the secondary level, and the presence of male teachers in girls' classrooms is primarily a function of the imbalance of qualified male-to-female staff ratios at that level, not a preferred policy choice.

Data from 1997 on staff distribution (see Table 8.3) illustrate the difference by gender as the educational level increases. This pattern does not appear to have reversed in the 1997–2004 period, although exactly comparable data are not publicly available. Gender imbalance remains particularly noticeable among tertiary education staff, with 2,959 males and 425 females out of a total of 3,384 university instructors in 2002–2003 (PCBS, 2004a and 2004c).

Teacher levels of degree achievement also vary notably by gender and degree level, as reflected in Table 8.4.[23]

---

[23] These configurations of staff may have implications for quality, particularly the quality of education received by girls, as we discuss below.

Table 8.3
Teachers and Principals by Level and Gender, 1996–1997

	Teachers				Principals			
	Male	Female	Total	Percentage Female	Male	Female	Total	Percentage Female
Preschool	5	2,372	2,377	99.8	17	561	578	97.1
Basic	8,116	7,785	15,901	49.0	523	506	1,029	49.2
Basic and secondary	4,140	3,243	7,383	43.9	243	151	394	38.3
Secondary	411	158	569	27.8	20	9	29	31.0

SOURCE: PCBS and Palestinian MoE (1997).

Table 8.4
Distribution of Basic and Secondary Teachers by Education Level and Gender, 1998–1999

Education Level	Male	Female	Total	Percentage Female
Secondary or less	289	454	743	61.1
Lower diploma (two years)[a]	5,702	7,091	12,793	55.4
Bachelor's degree	7,591	5,885	13,476	43.7
Higher diploma (one-year postgraduate)	111	33	144	22.9
Master's degree and above	240	65	305	21.3

SOURCE: PCBS, 1999b.
[a] Lower diploma is a technical term for a two-year degree, similar to the U.S. associate's degree.

Financing

Palestinian education is financed through a mixture of direct budget appropriation, donor support, and, at the tertiary education level and in private schooling, student fees. National budget allocations are used almost entirely to cover salaries; most other costs (including development, research, training, and equipment) are covered by external funding (PA, 2000, p. 10), which may be project or task specific or may cover multiple activities in a subfield. This international support is a mix of grants and loans.

UNRWA schools are funded from the agency's budget, derived from contributions from United Nations member states. The agency has been struggling with a significant budget shortfall of between $50 million and $70 million annually since 1993 (UN, 1999), which has limited its ability to implement programming.

Between 17 and 18 percent of the PA 2004 budget is allotted to education,[24] up from 13 percent in 1999–2000 (PA, 2000, p. 10). This nearly 20 percent commitment

---

[24] Presentation by Dr. Akram Hammad, Deputy Financial Manager, Ministry of Education during the December 17–18, 2003, Mezan Center for Human Rights conference on the Palestine Authority's 2004 Budget. See http://www.mezan.org/site_en/budget_confrence/1st_day.php.

is comparable to spending in other Middle Eastern states, and well above the developed country average of 4 percent in 2001 (UNICEF, 2004).

Strengths and Challenges Regarding Future Development

When measured against the ideals for access, quality, and delivery, the current status of Palestinian education raises significant concerns. Many of these concerns are due to the present environment of crisis and as such may be ameliorated significantly by a transition to statehood and relative stability. Others, however, are more embedded and will require

Table 8.5
Current Status of Palestinian Education

	Present	Limited but Emerging	Limited and Declining	Absent
Access				
Enabling environment (shelter, nutrition, and health)			X	
Quality early childhood opportunities		X		
Parent and community support	X			
Supportive leadership	X[a]			
Equity in access	X			
Physical proximity of schools to residences	X[b]			
Adequate and appropriate facilities and supplies			X	
Safe schools and routes to schools				X
Quality nonformal education for school-age students				X
Lifelong learning opportunities				X
Quality				
Clear goals and expectations			X	
Relevant curriculum with local, national, and global content		X		
Schools that support civic development and engagement		X		
Flexible system, including research and development			X	
Motivated, trained, and well-compensated staff		X		
Pedagogy that matches system goals		X		
Process and outcome evaluation and monitoring		X		
Delivery				
Accountable, flexible, and responsive governance		X		
Sufficient funds				X
Adequate data for system improvement				X

[a] As we discuss below, support at the policy level is not necessarily consistent with action at the implementation level; this is thus only a relative strength of the system.
[b] Strength in this area is challenged by the isolation of communities from schools in the area of the West Bank separation wall, as noted in the "Historical Development of Palestinian Education (1517–2004)" section of this chapter.

substantial, sustained efforts to be resolved. The system also has a number of strengths, which will provide bases for action following statehood if they can be preserved.

Mapping the current state of Palestinian education against our earlier set of indicators of a successful education system (see Table 8.5) creates a portrait of a system that is mixed on access (but with significant strengths in that area), struggling on quality (but with general upward momentum), and weak in delivery (mostly as a result of a lack of sufficient and reliable funding).

Foundations to Build On: Strengths of the System

Clearly, Palestinian education has a number of strengths that will provide a solid foundation for the system in the first years of statehood. In this subsection, we explore these strengths in more detail and consider what their value to a new Palestinian education system might be.

Identified system strengths include the following:

Access
- Commitment to equitable access and success in achieving gender parity
- Strong community support for education
- Leadership that is supportive of both system expansion and system reform
- Awareness of the importance of early childhood experiences in developing school readiness.

Quality
- Willingness to engage in curricular reform and vigorous debate around the nature of that reform
- Strong interest in improving pedagogy and a range of resources for doing so
- Commitment to improving the qualifications and compensation of staff
- Perception of schools as a key location for the development of students' civic skills and engagement.

Delivery
- Management ability and transparency
- Solid data collection infrastructure and collaboration in analysis.

Access Strength: Equity and Universality of Access. The high level of access to education across all sectors of society has produced levels of literacy and of overall education in the population that are among Palestine's greatest assets in the transition to statehood. Literacy stood at 96.3 percent for men and 87.4 percent for women over age 15 in 2003; these figures are notably higher than those for the Arab states as a group, developing countries overall, and lower-middle-income countries as a group, and they approach overall literacy rates in developed countries as a group (PCBS, 2004a; World

Bank, 2004). The significant gains made in educating girls and women are one of the system's particular strengths. Indeed, female literacy rates in Palestine "increased 8-fold" between 1950 and 1990 (Heiberg and Øvensen, 1993) and girls rose from 3.5 percent of the total school population in 1950 to 49.9 percent in 1999 (UNRWA, 2004b; Birzeit University, 2002, pp. 29 ff). These figures represent a level of female participation far above that of many of Palestine's neighbors. This initial footing of broad access and gender equity bodes well if it can be maintained and if quality can be addressed with equal vigor.

The high level of access to Palestinian tertiary education can also be an asset to the system if these institutions are developed appropriately. If tertiary sector growth occurs in consort with careful cross-sectoral planning, it can be a strong contributor to the development of indigenous research and development capacity and to the expansion of the Palestinian knowledge economy. Indeed, Palestinian knowledge capital will likely be the new state's greatest resource. (For more detail on the Palestinian economy, see Chapter Five.) Seven percent of the total population had tertiary education as of 2003 (PCBS, 2003b), and the high levels of advanced education among some groups in the Palestinian diaspora have the potential to also contribute significantly to development if enabling conditions are created following statehood.[25]

Access Strength: Strong Community Support for Education. In a context of uncertainty and social upheaval, the consistency and variety of community support for education in Palestine are notable. This support is both principled and practical: Education is seen as a key point of leverage for individual and national development (Van Dyke and Randall, 2002; Birzeit University, 2002 and 2004), and there is a strong tradition of the community providing resources to supplement the low-quality education provided by governing authorities, as we discuss below.

Educational NGOs and other civil society groups have long served as active and generally constructive partners of the Palestinian education system, supplementing gaps, improving quality, and providing coping mechanisms when the regular systems broke down or were impaired by periods of conflict. In fact, community actors and their supporters claim that nongovernmental and civil-sector educational institutions were

> behind all of the concrete positive developments in the period 1967–1994 . . . [including] (1) the introduction and spread of higher education, (2) the spread and the improvement of the quality of early childhood programs, (3) the spread and the improvement of the quality of adult education programs, (4) the spread of programs of education for children with special needs, (5) the introduction of pilot programs to improve the quality of formal schooling, and (6) activities designed to . . . network with educational institutions abroad (Mahshi, 2000, p. 5).

---

[25] UNDP's successful recruitment of expatriate Palestinian professionals to provide short- or long-term technical assistance for Palestinian development following the 1993 Oslo Accords is one institutional example of such contributions (see United Nations Development Programme/Programme of Assistance to the Palestinian People, undated).

In an environment of open debate around educational development, these organizations can serve as partners in setting priorities and negotiating action. They also provide important complementary capacity to governmental institutions, in both the short and long terms.

More broadly speaking, the generally high value placed on education in the Palestinian community, and that community's historic willingness to sacrifice and adapt as necessary to attain greater access and quality (see, for example, Fahsheh, 1993; Heiberg and Øvensen, 1993; Mahshi and Bush, 1989), can provide a cushion of trust to support experimentation and innovation in the early years of statehood. Community awareness of educational issues is generally high, and opportunities for engagement already exist, particularly through the media (as in the case of the monthly educational supplement to the *Al-Ayyam* newspaper that is prepared by the Palestinian Educational NGO Collaborative). Communities have also shown willingness to contribute significant resources to the development of education, particularly in the early childhood sector, where many kindergartens are community sponsored or supported (Christina, 2004). This extant capacity for community involvement could be tapped to build partnerships for development in the future.

Access Strength: Supportive Leadership in the Ministry of Education. The MoE has supported reform efforts by soliciting a variety of input to the educational development process, both through the activities of personnel who represent a range of positions and by opening its work to community scrutiny (Lempinen, 2002). Indeed, of all Palestinian government institutions, the MoE enjoys one of the most positive reputations for interaction with community groups, critics, and activists (Birzeit University, 2002).[26] These processes resulted in the "Five Year Plan for 2000–2005," an integrated, cross-sectoral plan for educational development judged to be reasonable and professional by local and international observers (Birzeit University, 2002, p. 100). This initial footing of trust and general openness provides a critical foundation for dialogue about change and (if it can be maintained) for working productively across actors in the education sector to implement reform plans in the future.

Access Strength: Awareness of Early Childhood Education and Development As a System Support. Although access to early childhood services in Palestine is limited, and access to quality services more so, there is an awareness at both the policy level and within the community of the importance of this sector to later student success that bodes well for system development. As Christina (2004) notes, early childhood NGOs, both indigenous and international, are active and vocal, particularly around crucial issues of quality and developmental appropriateness, and services for the group of children under six have boomed in the past decade. While limited Ministry of Education

---

[26] Again, this positive reputation is relative to the negative reputation of some of the other government offices. The quality of this reputation is also lower at the implementation level, in schools and the regional directorates, than at the policy level, which presents a challenge to change.

and Ministry of Social Affairs budgets have to date prevented government sponsorship of early-childhood programs (with the exception of two model kindergartens), cross-MoE collaboration in the National Plan of Action for Palestinian Children provides an important foundation for later action in this arena (PA, 1996 and 1999).

Quality Strength: Willingness to Reform Curriculum and Efforts to Do So. PA schoolbooks and the values being taught in the Palestinian curriculum have come under sustained scrutiny and been the subject of considerable controversy, but the willingness of the Palestinian educational community to engage in a process of both internal debate and external collaboration is notable and indicates an engagement with issues of quality and purpose that will be essential to the success of any state system of education.

The curriculum development process was initiated in 1995 through the work of the independent Palestinian Curriculum Development Center (PCDC), a collaborative effort of local experts funded largely by the Italian government. In general, the result of these efforts (PCDC, 1996) has been judged acceptable by most neutral observers,[27] and it has been found to be compatible with the integration of Palestine with the international community and markets (Moughrabi, 2002). However, the later incorporation of the curriculum development project into the Ministry of Education has slowed the progress of reform and, according to local critics, retained a traditionalist bias in the depiction of gender roles (Jerbawi, 2002, as cited in Moughrabi, 2002; Birzeit University, 2002) and discouraged the development of critical thinking (Birzeit University, 2002).

Politically, the curriculum, including the language and images used in textbooks, is likely to continue to generate disagreement, both among Palestinians and internationally. Concern that educational resources will be used not to promote but to hamper the development of stable and peaceful relations with the new state's neighbors are frequently aired, with critics focusing primarily on the content and focus of the history, geography, and religion curricula. However, neutral analyses appear to indicate progress, if somewhat erratic, in the integration of themes of tolerance, pluralism, and nonviolent resolution of conflict (see, e.g., Firer and Adwan, 2004; Georg Eckert Institute, 2004;[28] and Pingel, 2003). Even the system's critics seem to agree that "the new textbooks, in contrast to the old Jordanian and Egyptian ones, no longer contain any of the prejudices generally derogatory to the Jews or Israelis, or anti-Semitic stereotypes" (Livnat and Rasmussen, 2002). Certainly there is considerable pressure within the Palestinian and international educational community for a curriculum that is supportive both of internal democratic development and the stable integration of Palestine

---

[27] See, for example, Brown (2003); Morena (2001); Livnat and Rasmussen (2002); and Israel/Palestine Center for Research and Information (2003).

[28] A range of reports on current texts is available through the comparative textbook analysis project of UNESCO and the Georg Eckert Institute; see http://www.gei.de/english/projekte/israel.shtml.

into the region (Brown, 2003; Moughrabi, 2001 and 2002; Van Dyke and Randall, 2002; and Velloso de Santisteban, 2002).

Preparing curricula when borders are unclear, conflict is ongoing, and future circumstances are uncertain is a daunting task. Cultivating pride and national identity in Palestinian children while also addressing concerns about responsible global citizenship are significant challenges. The successful management of these issues in both political and in pedagogical terms will be critical for the development of a stable and democratic Palestinian state, and it will be an essential test of the education system's strength and resilience in the face of change.[29]

Quality Strength: Strong Interest in Improving Pedagogy and a Range of Resources for Doing So. A vigorous debate exists within the Palestinian community about ways to move the education system forward and align it more closely with international standards of best practice for pedagogy (Coalition of Palestinian Educational NGOs, 1999; Christina, 2004; Nasru, 1993; PCDC, 1996; Rigby, 1995; and Van Dyke and Randall, 2002). Participants in this debate include intellectuals; prodemocracy activists with an interest in educating critical, participatory youth; education specialists (many with international training and experience and a desire to import state-of-the art learning methods); and reform-minded teachers (Brown, 2003, pp. 151 ff). These parties have developed connections with regional and international nongovernmental organizations and other actors in the educational development field, and they provide a rich resource base for indigenizing good practice.

Quality Strength: Commitment to Increasing Staff Qualifications and Compensation. Increased standards for preservice teacher training (the minimum requirement for new teachers in both MoE and UNRWA schools has been raised to a bachelor's degree), and efforts at expanding in-service training programs through the Ministry of Education and UNRWA have provided important foundations for quality development in Palestinian education. UNRWA schools, in particular, benefit from the focused in-service training programs of the agency's Educational Science Facilities in Jordan and the West Bank and from school-level programming designed by the Institute of Education at UNRWA headquarters in Amman. These institutions offer regular short courses and (in Jordan, but accessible to teachers from the West Bank and Gaza) a three-year in-service program to upgrade staff to the bachelor's level. Six hundred preservice and 334 in-service teachers were enrolled in programs in the West Bank and Gaza in 2004 (UNRWA, 2004c).

Movements toward greater salary parity between UNRWA teachers and those in government schools have also alleviated to some extent the tensions between staff in the

---

[29] We note that the potential for education to serve as a mediating engine of democratization is sharply limited by context. "Progressive" curricula are challenged by the Palestinian experience of multiple forms of authoritarianism and violence, and their effect on youth is confounded by other social pressures (as we discuss in the section of this chapter on challenges to education). Willingness to reform curricula is thus only a relative strength of the system; even under the assumption of a cessation of hostilities with Israel, educational efforts must be tied to broader changes in the discourse and practice of governance in a context of economic improvement.

two sectors, although a gap remains (UNRWA salaries are higher). The PA is also, in principle, committed to raising teacher salaries[30] to more accurately reflect the professional status of employees in the face of high costs of living. Such a move would provide both an incentive for high-achieving youth to enter teaching and an alternative to lucrative private tutoring that currently diverts teachers' energy from their primary jobs.

Quality Strength: Vision of Schools As Civic Development Centers. Players in Palestinian education clearly conceptualize schools as centers of civic development and the cultivation of social responsibility (see, for instance, Coalition of Palestinian Educational NGOs, 1999; Moughrabi, 2002; Nasru, 1993; Van Dyke and Randall, 2002). While there are varying visions of those responsibilities and of appropriate civic participation, interest in maximizing the role of schools as shapers of civic identity and action is a strong resource for future system development. Civics has already been introduced into the curriculum, and the development of that component and related pedagogy for the system at large will be an important support for the MoE goal of the education system's "evol[ution] into a major social institution contributing to democracy and the transfer of cultural experiences" (Palestinian MoE, 2000).[31]

Delivery Strength: Management Ability and Transparency. By and large, Palestinian education is considered to be well-managed, and its reputation is better than that of the education bureaucracies of many other Arab states (see, for example, Ahed-Ahmad, 2002, p. 11). Those responsible have shown a willingness to confront the system's problems, to diagnose them accurately, and to make plans to resolve them,[32] although the MoE's ability to follow through on these plans has been much more limited, for a number of reasons (see below). Indeed, the "education sector seems to be a step ahead of other sectors in the country" (Lempinen, 2002, p. 7) in terms of management capacity.

These impressions are shared by both Palestinians at large and by the international community. A 2001 study concluded that "the MOE is regarded [by Palestinian educational experts and teachers] as effective and its Five Year Plan is so far considered to be proving successful" (Jerusalem Media and Communication Centre, 2001). Palestinian public opinion data, which rank educational institutions as the institutions most trusted by the Palestinian people, also support a view of the education system as reliable (Birzeit University, 2003 and 2004). The World Bank, traditionally cautious in its praise, has lauded the ability of the Ministry of Education to focus its resources intelligently and to do the best job possible given its financial constraints (World Bank,

---

[30] In practice, teachers have been jailed for striking to demand those higher wages, have taken pay cuts along with other civil-sector employees, and have had salaries unpaid for periods during budget crises. This is thus only a relative strength, and change is dependent on broader developments in the economy and in governance.

[31] This process is subject to the constraints discussed above and the later sections of this chapter on challenges to educational development.

[32] We chart the content of a number of these plans in Table 8.6.

1999b and c). This international and intercommunity confidence will provide an important boost to the system in the transition to statehood.

Delivery Strength: Established Data Collection Systems and Ongoing Analytical Efforts. The data collection and management system that links the Ministry of Education to the Central Bureau of Statistics is solid. Analytical efforts through the MoE, the Bureau of Statistics, and the Child Statistics Project provide an initial foundation for policy and practice changes.

Challenges

While the strengths of the Palestinian educational system are notable, particularly in the wake of years of struggle to maintain and enhance the system, it also faces a number of pressing concerns that will significantly affect development over the coming years. Here, we discuss these challenges and their implications for the system in greater detail, paying particular attention to those that may be rapidly ameliorated following a final settlement and those that will present longer-term problems.

Key concerns related to the current system include the following:

Access
- Lack of a generally enabling environment
- Inadequate basic facilities and supplies
- Unsafe schools and routes to schools
- Lack of special education options for students with special needs
- Lack of nonformal options for school-age children who are not in school or who are attending only part time
- Lack of lifelong learning opportunities.

Quality
- Lack of clear goals and expectations for the system, and little accountability
- Interest in pedagogical reform not matched by progress
- Limited relevance of secondary, vocational, and tertiary programs
- Limited research and development capacity and activity
- Low staff compensation; administrative "bulge" emerging
- Difficulty monitoring process and outcomes in a crisis climate.

Delivery
- Severely underfunded and donor-dependent system
- System data not linked to reform.

Access Challenge: Lack of Enabling Environment. With the Palestinian economy in disarray, standards of health, shelter, and nutrition are low and declining, particularly in Gaza and in West Bank villages. With research indicating the importance of physical, psychological, and environmental health to school success, rising levels of malnutrition, homelessness, and general poor health (Abdeen et al., 2002) in the population are reasons for concern.

Indeed, the current economic conditions, although beyond the control of educational policymakers, create a context in which children dropping out of school becomes a necessity for many families. There is already a tendency to move boys from private schools to public schools to save tuition, and Palestinians who send their children to schools that charge fees are more likely to take their daughters out of school than their sons when finances are an issue (PCBS, 1998, pp. 5–57; UNICEF and Birzeit University, 2003). As family incomes continue to drop, young men leave school to seek any kind of immediate work, and young women are encouraged to marry (Farah, 2000). If these trends continue, they will eventually lead to a decline in the overall level of skills and education, and a downgrading of Palestine's human resources, as well as a regression from gender equity.

Pressure to choose work over school is a concern both for children's rights and for Palestinian social and economic development over the long term. In 2002, 2.8 percent of Palestinian children aged 10–17 were in the labor force. Half of these children worked for more than six hours a day (PCBS, 2004d, p. 16). These children were typically working instead of attending school. Indeed, in a 2003 study, 70 percent of working children were reported to be dropouts (UNICEF and Birzeit University, 2003, p. 24). These overall numbers represent the children who have *found* work. However, the number of children "looking for and ready to work" has in fact increased significantly in recent years, with a jump from 17.7 percent of those aged 10–17 in 2000, to 34.3 percent in 2001, to 41 percent in 2002 (UNICEF and Birzeit University, 2003, p. 16). While these figures are still relatively low for developing countries, they set a precedent for dropping out that is not consistent with Palestine's aspirations for developing its knowledge capital.

These numbers also have ominous implications for stability and social cohesion in a fledgling Palestinian state. Research indicates that while a family's stated reason for obliging or allowing a child or youth to drop out of school may be related to a concrete alternative plan, particularly to work, such a plan materializes only in about half of all cases. Approximately half of female dropouts marry or work within their own home to help the family, and only about half of male dropouts participate in the labor force (Egset, 2003, pp. 110 ff); the other half remains idle. This group, with neither education nor employment, presents a challenge to development and a potential social crisis.[33]

Access Challenge: Inadequate Facilities and Supplies. The present infrastructure for Palestinian education is severely degraded. An UNESCO assessment prior to the outbreak of the current intifada noted that,

---

[33] For more discussion of the implications of such a "security demographic," see Cincotta, Engelman, and Anastasion, 2003.

> [t]he present state of schools in the Gaza Strip is poor. . . . many school buildings have deteriorated so much that they need to be demolished or reconstructed, or completely renovated. With the [continuous growth] of the school population, additional schools will have to be built to relieve pressure on existing ones. Many schools in the West Bank are accommodated in rented buildings which were not built for educational purposes and many of the facilities are unsuitable" (UNESCO, 1997).

Infrastructure damage during the intifada, described above, has further eroded the capacity of the system to meet students' basic needs.

Although the Ministry of Education constructed 125 new schools and 1,824 school additions and renovated an additional 412 classrooms between 1994 and 1999, increasing the number of government schools by 10.4 percent (Palestinian MoE, 2004c, p. 16), this expansion nevertheless fell short of that needed to accommodate the growth in the school-age population over that period. The responses to this capacity problem have included enlarging class sizes and running schools in shifts. Neither of these approaches is optimal, and (as further explained below) the second appears to be more problematic than the first.

Observers note that UNRWA schools, with their high student/teacher ratio, nonetheless achieve better results (in terms of literacy and school persistence, as well as test scores) than government schools with slightly smaller class sizes, and they conclude that UNRWA's teacher training and teacher commitment may help compensate for large class size (Heiberg and Øvensen, 1993). Running schools on multiple shifts is more constraining. Accommodating double shifts requires changes to the curriculum, with the most commonly cut subjects being physical education, art, and computer training. The loss of these subjects has significant negative implications. Physical education and art instruction can play important compensatory roles in a context of restricted movement and omnipresent political violence and are known to be helpful to children in coping with stress and trauma (Arafat, 2003, p. 7). The achievement of computer literacy is considered to be a significant component of modern education, and one that will be important to future Palestinian development (Birzeit University, 2002; Palestinian MoE, 2000).

Access to technology and to basic educational resources is also a problem (Birzeit University, 2002; Palestinian MoE, 2000). Laboratory supplies and equipment are in scarce supply, and libraries in many Palestinian schools are under-equipped and often used as classrooms for lack of alternative space. Students from under-resourced schools are less prepared to enter scientific or technical tracks at the tertiary level, compounding the problem of lack of tertiary education relevance to the needs of the economy. In addition, while these resources are available in many private institutions, their absence from schools attended by less-privileged students raises equity concerns across the system. While the Ministry of Education has expanded computer access to 600 schools through 2004,[34] fully articulating computer use with instruction and supporting more than basic computer literacy for students are challenges for the system.

Access Challenge: Unsafe Schools and Routes to Schools. Palestinian schools have suffered significant damage during the four and a half years of the current intifada, and concerns about the safety of children have contributed to dropout, particularly among girls at the secondary level. Secondary schools tend to be further removed from the students' residences; thus, they have been more affected by curfews and the insecurity of travel than the primary schools, which tend to be located in the students' villages or neighborhoods. The state of crisis has therefore contributed to a (it is hoped, temporary) reduction in gender parity, because when secondary schools become more difficult or dangerous to reach, parents are more reluctant to expose their daughters to risk than they are their sons (Save the Children, 2001). Indeed, concerns that schools cannot be reached safely may be the deciding factor in cases where families are already less inclined to support the continued education of girls, whose primary schooling is considered sufficient to equip them to be wives and mothers, and whose employment may be seen as infeasible or undesirable (Farah, 2000). Should this trend continue, the consequences on development of lower levels of education for girls and women would be serious, as discussed above.

In addition, the lack of safety takes a significant psychological toll on students and school staff. Pervasive fear, feelings of hopelessness, and lack of trust are psychological outcomes of the climate, and these have measurable effects on learning (Save the Children Alliance, 2001). The long-term implications of children's exposure to violence are of concern: Research on the educational outcomes of Palestinian children in school during and after the previous intifada indicates that the physical and psychological damage they suffered notably affected their learning and their social and interpersonal skills (Mansour, 1996; Baker, 1990). An entire generation of Palestinian young adults currently has experienced the traumas of the intifada of 1987–1993, with observable effects (Awwad, Dubrow, and Pinek, 1998; Garbarino and Kosteiny, 1996; Thabet, Mousa, and Kostanis, 1999); a second generation is now being exposed to even greater traumas, also with observable effects. A recent study by the Gaza Community Mental Health Center indicated that 55 percent of children in two of the most troubled areas of Gaza demonstrate signs of acute posttraumatic stress disorder, while 35 percent display moderate signs. Thirteen percent of the children in the study had registered a "sharp increase in mental and behavioral problems" (including problems in school) following Israeli bombardment of their neighborhoods (Gaza Community Mental Health Program, 2002). Peter Hansen, UNRWA's director general, refers to a "a tidal wave of traumatized children" (Hansen, 2003) moving through the system; the implications of this trend for internal and regional stability and for the development of human capacity in a Palestinian state are troubling, to say the least.

---

[34] See Palestinian MoE, undated.

Access Challenge: Lack of Special Education Services. The lack of capacity for diagnosis of children with special needs is a particular weakness of the system, given the concerns about physical and behavioral health impacts on education noted above. A significant number of Palestinian children are likely to suffer from undiagnosed physical, learning, or behavioral disabilities, which may lead to the poor performance that is cited by many of those leaving school as a key factor in the decision to drop out (PCBS, 1998, pp. 49–50). Social discomfort with identified disability is a contributing factor, but the lack of explicit programming for students with special needs and public awareness campaigns for such programming limits access for what is likely to be a significant segment of the population. Gifted students are equally unserved (Palestinian MoE, 2004c).

Access Challenge: Lack of Nonformal Education for School-Age Students. Programs of nonformal education for school-age children not currently (regularly) attending formal schooling (for example, working children, child detainees, and young mothers) are largely lacking from the MoE's current efforts. Working children note difficulties in attending school regularly and a lack of sympathy and flexibility on the part of teachers as key reasons for dropping out (UNICEF and Birzeit University, 2003). Young mothers typically lose opportunities for schooling with their peers, and those who wish to return to school are usually limited to adult education programs later in life. The child detainee population is small (248 pupils in long-term detention in 2002, and 561 in the justice system overall during that period) (PCBS, 2004d, p. 15), but it is a largely unacknowledged population in the MoE's documentation. For all of these groups, nongovernmental programs sponsored by external donors are the primary means of continuing education. Instability in such funding due to shifting trends in development practice and reductions in international assistance commitments more generally makes these opportunities uncertain, and a lack of common planning and shared standards for quality across nongovernmental programs raises equity concerns (Palestinian MoE, 2004c, p. 16).

Access Challenge: Lack of Lifelong Learning Opportunities. Lifelong learning opportunities are important in Palestine for two primary reasons: Dropouts who wish to return to education or upgrade their skills have few options (although those options are increasing), and illiteracy among older adults remains a problem.

Although Palestinian literacy rates overall are high, there is a substantial proportion of the older population, mostly female, that remains unable to read, write, or conduct basic mathematical operations. The literacy equivalency rate (the rate among females in relation to the rate among males, for all ages 15 and above) is 86.4 percent (Palestinian MoE, 2004c). As is the case in the rest of the Arab world, however, Palestinian illiteracy "is generally being eliminated through the education of the young, and not through effective adult literacy campaigns" (UN, 2000, p. 46). New curricula for adult education are being developed through the MoE, which as of 2002 was operating 58 literacy centers serving 1,600 students (Palestinian MoE, 2004c, p. 12), but most adult literacy efforts remain under the sponsorship of the nongovernmental sector.

Interface between these institutions and the formal education system is limited, and standards are not coherent (Palestinian MoE, 2004c).

Quality Challenge: Lack of Clear Goals, Expectations, and Accountability. Although management capacity at the Ministry of Education is in principle fairly strong (a notable number of upper-level staff have advanced degrees in education, and there has been an effort to invest in developing policy capacity), day-to-day policymaking, in the words of the World Bank, "tends to be ad hoc" (World Bank, 1999c, p. 46). There has apparently been limited success over the past several years in adhering to standards and processes for decisionmaking. This situation has largely but not entirely come about because the MoE has been operating in crisis mode since 2000, adapting to volatile immediate circumstances rather than planning for the long term in a coherent fashion. Efforts to articulate system priorities and translate them into medium- and long-range plans have been stymied by the emergency conditions, and the ambitious vision embodied in the MoE's five-year plan of 2000 has been supplanted by the need to build bulwarks against continuing system decline.

Crisis conditions and limited capacity have also meant that expectations for system performance are still unclear. A rational and coherent set of learning standards for students does not yet fully underpin the curriculum, although expectations for outcomes by grade-level are under development. While decentralization of responsibility to schools is promoted and the Ministry of Education has mandated greater involvement of community members through the formation of parent-teacher councils for schools, there are no functional incentives or sanctions for school performance. The gaps in these areas between principles and practice make increased system accountability and related reform difficult.

Quality Challenge: Interest in Pedagogical Reform Not Matched by Progress. While both UNRWA and the MoE have placed pedagogical improvement on their lists of priorities and while they have begun to address teacher qualifications as a basis for that improvement, much remains to be done, particularly in MoE schools. The proportion of teachers meeting the qualification requirement of a bachelor's degree is still only around 50 percent for MoE staff (Palestinian MoE, 2004c, p. 17; similar figures are not available for UNRWA teachers). While those with lower credentials may be aging out of the system, upgrading teacher education remains a significant challenge. Promotion standards for MoE teachers are minimal (World Bank, 1999c, p. 46), and in-service training has yet to reach the majority of that staff. UNRWA efforts, with a smaller pool of staff to serve initially, have been more successful (UNRWA, 2004c). In addition, research indicates that rote learning, authoritarian teacher-student relationships, and an absence of techniques that promote critical thinking and engaged learning remain the norm (Khaldi and Wahbeh, 2000; Moughrabi, 2002).

Quality Challenge: Limited Relevance of Secondary, Vocational, and Tertiary Programs. Significant problems of relevance pervade the secondary, vocational, and tertiary sectors of Palestinian education. These issues cut across public and private institutions and UNRWA, reinforcing each other to create highly unbalanced outcomes for the upper levels of the education system.

The core of the problem appears to be the vocational sector, which is generally held by Palestinian and international education experts to be one of the primary areas of weakness in the system as a whole and which appears to serve as much as a relief for unemployment as a contributor to national development (Birzeit University, 2002, p. 89). Programs are outdated, poorly linked to the labor market, and under-resourced (the World Bank bluntly states that "funding for public vocational training centers is insufficient to provide even minimal acceptable quality") (World Bank, 1999c, p. 43). In addition, they are poorly coordinated. As Kouhail notes,

> "[a] person can train to become a carpenter in more than 20 institutions. . . . One can become a carpenter in nine months, 11 months or 24 months. A person may train for carpentry in vocational secondary schools, or in a train-ing center run by UNRWA . . . or quite a number of private institutions, each one using different curricula" (Kouhail, undated, p. 5).

The result of this sectoral disarray is that vocational programs in general are unap-pealing to students (Jacobsen, 2003, p. 92). Indeed, only 3.9 percent of Palestinian sec-ondary students chose a vocational secondary option in 1999–2000 (PCBS, 1999a).

Vocational enrollment at the tertiary level is also limited. In 2001–2002, 73 per-cent of students graduating from secondary school were accepted into institutions of tertiary education—64 percent of those at universities and 9 percent at colleges (Hashweh, 2003, p. 6). These figures represent a strong preference among Palestinian students for study at universities or colleges rather than at vocational or technical in-stitutions. This preference is historic, and the gap appears to be increasing, rather than decreasing, as indicated in Figure 8.1 (Palestinian MoE, 2003).

This large proportion of students entering universities and colleges creates a greater number of bachelor's degree graduates than the labor market can absorb.

The tertiary sector also has problems of relevance and appeal. Sixty-nine percent of Palestinian tertiary education students were enrolled in the social sciences, humani-ties, and education in 2001–2002, with only 24 percent choosing the sciences (natu-ral sciences, mathematics, computer sciences, medical professions, engineering, and agronomy) as an area of specialization (Palestinian MoE, 2003). Women are particu-larly absent from these fields, although their levels of enrollment are close to those of men overall (PCBS, 1998, pp. 60–63).

This imbalance is partly the result of tuition variations in tertiary education based on the field of study. Tuition is significantly lower in the liberal arts, which do not require expensive labs and equipment. The tracking system in secondary school also contributes to the imbalance, which pushes students (again, particularly girls) out of science specializations early in their academic careers and does not provide them with

Figure 8.1
Newly Enrolled Students in Higher Education Institutions, 1994/95–2001/02

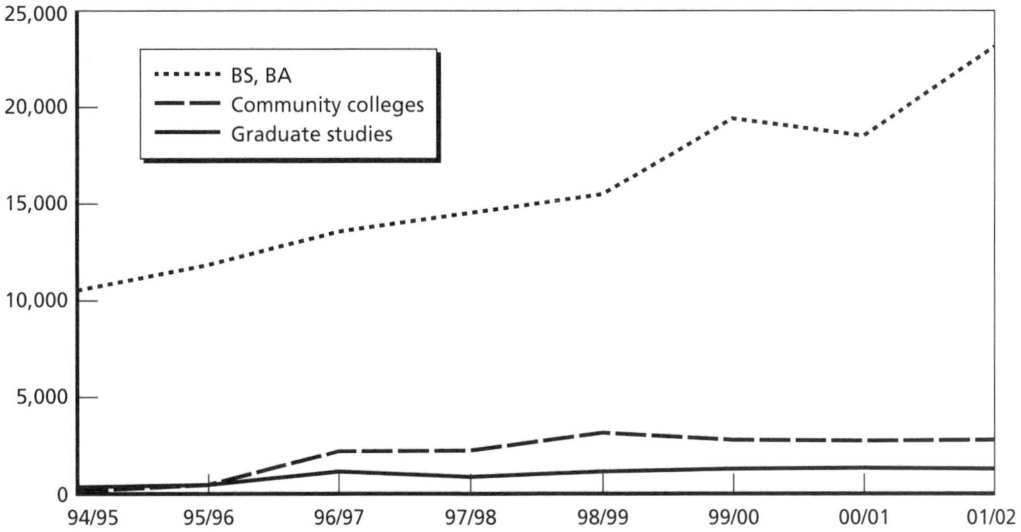

SOURCE: Palestinian Ministry of Education and Higher Education. "Higher Education Statistics," 2003. Online at www.moe.gov.ps/Downloads/prosure.pdf (as of September 2004).
RAND MG146-8.1

opportunities to build the skills and knowledge base to reenter those areas in the university should they wish to do so (PCBS, 1998, pp. 50–56). Basing departmental admissions in large part on *tawjihi* scores also narrows the pool of entrants, because science faculties tend to require higher scores for admission than nonscience areas. Finally, the reliance on English as the dominant language of instruction in the sciences and a low capacity for English instruction at the basic and secondary stages further limit the eligible population for the sciences at the tertiary level.

These weaknesses highlight internal inefficiency and indicate the potential for the Palestinian education system to generate a large pool of educated unemployed or underemployed. However, the broader question of how directly and how strongly education is linked to earnings and social mobility in Palestine is equally important. Indeed, framing the question this way uncovers some interesting anomalies and raises more-substantive questions about education's contribution to development (Jacobsen, 2003, p. 93). For example, in the early 1990s[35]:

> 24% of the heads of households [in Gaza] with post-secondary education [were] among the poorest one third and 39% [were] among the top one

---

[35] Patterns appear not to have changed substantially since that time, although exactly comparable data are not available.

third. . . . In Arab Jerusalem, of those household heads who have no education at all, a full 44% of them [were] also among the richest third of the
population (Heiberg and Øvensen, 1993).

These data support assertions that in Palestine, as in much of the Middle East, kin-
ship ties and the social placement of a family are as or more helpful in gaining employment and opportunities as skills. In the absence of a fully merit-based system of employment, education's power to support mobility is, and will continue to be, limited.

Quality Challenge: Limited Capacity for Research and Development. Crises in
tertiary education financing (see below) and limitations on the import of technology
and equipment limit the extent to which Palestinian universities can serve as sources of
research and development. Human resources are available, but laboratories are under-
equipped, information technology resources are tenuous, and infrastructure for experimentation is lacking. Conditions for conducting field research are also highly problematic.
These gaps in the system are not consistent with the visions in Palestinian plans (Kouhail,
undated; Palestinian MoE, 2000) for the state's development as a knowledge economy.

**Quality Challenge: Low Staff Compensation Overall; Administrative "Bulge"
Emerging.** While the MoE has a stated commitment to implementing teacher raises
in line with the civil service law, salaries in government schools remain well below
levels needed to support most Palestinian families. Average government teacher salaries are about $400 per month, and average salaries in UNRWA schools are slightly
higher. Private school employees can earn significantly higher wages than those working for the government or UNRWA, but salaries are inconsistent across the private
sector. Even prior to the current intifada, teacher salaries were only slightly above the
poverty line of $400 a month for a family of six (PA, 2000); declining economic con-
ditions since 2000 have placed additional stress on families in this income bracket.

One result of poor compensation is that teachers often take on second jobs to
provide additional income. These efforts tax teacher energy and divert attention from
school responsibilities. In some cases, these jobs are unrelated to education. Many
teachers, however, turn to private tutoring to add to family resources. This trend toward tutoring is negative for a number of reasons. First, like any other second job,
it diverts teacher energy and time from classroom responsibilities and from out-of-
classroom preparation and evaluation. Second, it inequitably distributes resources to
those students able to pay for greater instruction, undermining system equity along
class (and possibly gender) lines.

Finally, there appears to be a trend toward increasing administrative appointments (which are typically more highly paid than teaching positions) relative to those
of teaching staff (World Bank, 1999c, pp. 46–48). This is partly because of the need
to develop the capacity of the MoE and its directorates in areas that had not traditionally been staffed or were understaffed (such as special education, counseling, and
kindergarten oversight). As the World Bank notes (1999c, pp. 46–48), rational growth

in these areas and across the administrative structure is necessary, but expansion of the educational bureaucracy beyond levels of efficiency threatens the system's internal alignment and the equitable distribution of resources.

Quality Challenge: Insufficient Monitoring of Process and Outcomes. Although the MoE's Assessment and Evaluation Center has begun an effort to track student performance in math, Arabic, and science, the examinations are still in their infancy and remain not fully supported by a coherent and challenging set of learning standards. Process evaluations of Palestinian education are essentially nonexistent, and there is little technical support and no concrete incentives for the practice changes promoted in teacher and administrator professional development.

Delivery Challenge: Underfunded, Donor-Dependent System. Current levels of funding for Palestinian education are barely maintaining the system's essential functions, and it is unlikely that even with greater internal efficiency the funds available to improve the system would substantially increase. Projected population expansion and an assumption by the PA of fiscal and structural responsibility over time for services now provided by UNRWA will further strain the system's budgets. Indeed, the World Bank has estimated that by 2020, the recurrent costs of basic and secondary education will range between 30 and 60 percent of the PA budget (World Bank, 2000, p. 1).

Tertiary funding presents an additional challenge. The tertiary education sector was initially supported with foreign donor resources, but when these were reduced in the 1990s, tertiary education became largely tuition based. As poverty has increased and the job market for graduates has collapsed, this system has become nearly untenable. Indeed, the 2002 UNDP (p. 106) human development report states flatly that "there are questions about the ability of the Palestinian higher education sector to survive."

External donors provide major financial support for the operation and development of the Palestinian education system across all educational levels. These donors include bilateral governmental aid agencies, multilateral organizations, and major established youth or education-related NGOs. A broad range of small NGOs and large numbers of religious, cultural, welfare, and political clubs, groups, and associations also contribute to some extent. Subsidies and scholarships, many from Arab countries and notably from Saudi Arabia,[36] have helped the tertiary sector to struggle along, but these stopgap measures do not put the universities on a solid financial footing. Certainly, a Palestinian state will not be able to fund its education system without the larger external donors, at least not in the near term. The small NGOs and the scholarship assistance to tertiary education have been and can continue to be important resources. However, there are pitfalls inherent in relying on external support to such an extent.

Although donors provide essential resources and funds, augment capacity, and assist in the development of transparency, a donor-driven system is not ideal for a

---

[36] In 2002, Saudi Arabia agreed to pay 75 percent of the tuition and fees for third- and fourth-year college students. See Del Castill (2002).

number of reasons. Sustaining donor interest and trust requires a substantial effort and diverts institutional resources away from the design and provision of education and toward the cultivation and management of donor partners. Donors often have specific areas of interest or constituent pressures that restrict how their funds may be used, and these priorities tend to drive rather than support educational development, with the result that recipient partners are less able to determine the shape and direction of the system than they might like (Patrick, 1998). Cobbling together donor-selected projects or responding to donor trends to form a coherent education system can be complicated and undermines efforts of central planning, coordination, and standardization. Previous efforts to develop a single system of project design, funding, and oversight for Palestine have been less successful than hoped and raise concerns about the utility of future international contributions (Brynen, 2000).

Indeed, the international community has notably reduced its commitment to the funding of educational development projects in Palestine over the last decade (Brynen, 2000), and long-term funding is not guaranteed. Major bilateral and multilateral donors are likely to be generous over the short and perhaps the middle term, but only if there is some assurance that their contributions will lead to a self-sustaining system in the future. Arab states are also eager, in principle, to help make a success of long-awaited Palestinian statehood but have been less forthcoming in actual disbursal of funds. Given their own social and economic problems, even nominal enthusiasm may not be sustainable over the long term.

Delivery Challenge: Limited System Data Are Not Linked to Reform. While steps have been taken to establish a strong and reliable data collection and analysis infrastructure (see "Quality Challenge: Insufficient Monitoring of Process and Outcomes" above), there are practical constraints on the collection of that data in crisis conditions, and the acute effects of the intifada on student and teacher populations create anomalies within the system. In addition, data use beyond the policy level is extremely limited. Decisionmaking at the school level is not data driven, and the capacity for many educational personnel to understand and use data for planning and school improvement is low. Finally, data on stakeholder satisfaction and perceptions of the system are limited and inconsistent, with no recurrent, systematic efforts to provide the community with a voice in the process.

Planning for the Future: Efforts to Date

Palestinian education has been the subject of a number of domestic and international analyses and planning efforts, both prior to and post-autonomy.[37] These documents

---

[37] See, for example: Palestinian Ministry of Higher Education, PA, and World Bank (2002); World Bank (1993 and 1999c); Kouhail (undated); Palestinian MoE (2000); UNESCO [1995 and undated(a) and (b)]; UN (1996); Nasru (1993); and PCDC (1996).

are generally serious efforts to build on strengths of and address concerns about the system's weaknesses and are valuable resources for approaching statehood. While planning at the Ministry of Education has been stymied by political and economic circumstances and the evolution of government infrastructure, its efforts and those of the Ministry of Labor and former Ministry of Higher Education (now absorbed into the Ministry of Education) have already laid the groundwork for much of what will need to be done once stability is achieved. In Table 8.6, we summarize the foci of the PA main educational planning efforts, relative to the indicators of system success identified in our analytical framework.[38]

Clear expectations, supported by curriculum and instruction that are both locally relevant and internationally resonant, in a context of sufficient material and administrative resources to allow staff to focus on educating students are common ambitions across the range of major educational providers. This articulation of development priorities bodes well for the system and represents a strong policy platform on which to build.

Moving Forward: Recommendations for a Strong Education System in a Palestinian State

Clearly, Palestinians understand their greatest challenges, and they have developed a series of responses that are both reasonable for the near term and optimistic about the potential of education to contribute to a strong, healthy, and independent state over time. Indeed, our recommendations for approaches to be taken in the early years of statehood echo many of those already extant in government planning documents. Where we differ is in framing a set of recommendations that explicitly support the development of an "excellent" Palestinian education system—not one that is more cautiously cast as "good enough" for a society emerging from conflict. Moving away from minimal system maintenance and crisis management is essential if Palestinian education is to serve as both a catalyst for development and a source of internal stability. While we appreciate the challenges of implementing reform and the need to remain within saturation levels of capacity and funding, setting high standards and targets provides both a vision for future success and an indication by the government that it takes its commitments to its citizens seriously.[39]

Based on the system's strengths to date and the challenges facing its development, we recommend that near-term efforts focus on three goals:

---

[38] We have not marked areas that were noted as concerns (for instance, the general environment and the safety of schools) but for which substantive plans for improvement were not or could not be made.

[39] The cost estimates we present following this section reflect this commitment to excellence. In costing, we do, however, offer a set of possible compromises, on the understanding that they would also be likely to turn the "excellent" Palestinian education system we model here into one that is "good."

Table 8.6
Palestinian Education Planning Foci

	Five-Year Plan for Basic and Secondary Education, 2000[a]	Proposed Direction for Higher Education/ Higher Education Financing Strategy, 2002[b]	Vocational Technical Education and Training Plan, 1995[c]
Access			
Enabling environment (shelter, nutrition, and health)			
Quality early childhood opportunities	X		
Parent and community support	X		
Supportive leadership			
Equity in access	X	X	X
Physical proximity of schools to residences	X		
Adequate and appropriate facilities and supplies	X	X	X
Safe schools and routes to schools			
Quality nonformal education for school-age students	X		
Lifelong learning opportunities		X	X
Quality			
Clear goals and expectations	X	X	X
Relevant curriculum with local, national, and global content	X	X	X
Schools that support civic development and engagement	X	X	
Flexible system, including research and development		X	X
Motivated, trained, and well-compensated staff	X	X	X
Pedagogy that matches system goals	X	X	X
Process and outcome evaluation and monitoring	X		X
Delivery			
Accountable, flexible, and responsive governance	X	X	X
Sufficient funds	X	X	X
Adequate date for system improvement	X	X	X

[a] Palestinian MoE, 2000.
[b] Palestinian Ministry of Higher Education, PA, and the World Bank, 2002.
[c] Kouhail, undated.

- Maintaining currently high levels of *access*, while also working within resource constraints to expand enrollments in secondary education and early childhood programs.
- Building *quality* through a focus on integrated curricular standards, assessments, and professional development, supported by long-term planning for system sustainability and improved accountability mechanisms.
- Improving *delivery* by working with donors to develop streamlined and integrated funding mechanisms that allow the administration to focus on the business of meeting student needs, informed by strong evaluation and backed by significant sustained investment.

Maintaining and Expanding Access

As we have noted, the high levels of access to and participation in education at all levels are the Palestinian education system's greatest strength. Near-universal enrollment in basic education provides strong support for literacy and a solid foundation in skills that will be important for future social and economic development. High levels of access to secondary and tertiary education are a springboard for the development of a knowledge economy in Palestine and a potential source of significant indigenous development capacity.

Access to basic education should be maintained at its current level of near universality,[40] with development efforts at that level focused on meeting the unique access needs of students with special needs (currently notably underserved). Collaboration with the Ministries of Health and Social Affairs is encouraged for the development of programs of early diagnosis and intervention, as well as the provision of services. Previous success in raising vaccination rates through school and health sector cooperation provides a foundation for such efforts.

Access to secondary and tertiary education is complicated by quality and delivery factors, including the availability and appeal of vocational and technical training and the relevance of current tertiary education options to individual and societal development goals. Over-enrollment in the humanities and social sciences at the tertiary level and a strong preference for university study rather than other forms of tertiary education have resulted in a large number of highly educated unemployed, and they limit Palestine's ability to meet technical and service needs. Lower levels of female participation in secondary and tertiary science specializations are also a concern.

While investment in tertiary education is important, increasing the extent to which students are able to choose and complete quality secondary education (as preparation for tertiary schooling or for workforce entry) is essential if the potential of the

---

[40] Maintaining access should include efforts to reduce dropout rates, with a focus on school quality issues. However, as many dropouts cite noneducational factors (such as the need to find jobs to help their families) in their decision, expectations for rate reduction solely through school improvement should not be high.

tertiary sector to support development is to be fully tapped. We therefore recommend focusing access development efforts on secondary education programming, with a particular focus on the vocational and technical sector and the academic sciences. Specific quality choices that will support greater student preference for these options, once they are available, are discussed below. Costs of expanding access may be partially reduced by public-private partnerships with local industry and business (carefully designed, these efforts can also increase the relevance of programming and the employability of students upon completion).

A final area of access investment should be the development of the early childhood sector, which provides an important initial support for student learning and socialization. Addition of a kindergarten year to the public education system would bring the Palestinian system into line with those of more-developed states considered to be of excellent quality. As noted, public demand is high, and resources to support such efforts are present and available in the nongovernmental sector. These resources include facilities—contract, rental, or purchase of which by the Ministry of Education in the short term would provide immediate access and reduce cost.

All access development activities should be conducted in the context of a commitment to solid infrastructure. Adequate and appropriate classrooms, laboratories/workshops, libraries, and information technology resources must be available in all schools. System development should prioritize current efforts to upgrade facilities, with a significantly greater investment in infrastructure in the near term to repair and fully resource existing institutions and build sufficient new facilities to meet immediate needs and plan for projected growth.

Building Quality

Quality improvement in education requires integration and coordination of efforts to upgrade both services and staffing; attempts to address "problem" issues independently provide little support for overall systemic improvement and sustainability. In the Palestinian case, setting standards, developing assessments, and training and retraining staff have all begun but have not had the kind of sustained and substantial financial and logistical support that is needed for them to have deep and complementary effects on quality—partly because accountability mechanisms are largely lacking in the system. Coordinated long-term planning that links these efforts and provides significant allocation of funds to support them is essential to building an excellent Palestinian education system.

Highest-Priority Quality Recommendations: Standards, Assessment, and Professional Development Within an Accountability Framework. Standards for student learning across the system are in development. Efforts to ensure that those standards are internationally competitive and supportive of overall system goals—and that curricula reflect them—need to be prioritized. Outside interest in the Palestinian curriculum is unlikely to subside, and the PA will need to continue to participate in and support both local and international efforts at objective assessment of curricular content. The transparency of the curriculum development process to date should be supported as the remaining subjects and grade levels are brought on line. To support reflection on the performance of the system and improvement over time, efforts to develop assessments that are fully aligned with the learning standards should be a priority.

Standards and assessments for vocational and technical education are no less important than those for general education. The Ministry of Education should continue its efforts in collaboration with the Ministry of Labor to align program standards and content across providers and to raise expectations for learning and performance within the sector. To support relevance and integration, collaboration with private-sector businesses is important in this process.

Standards implementation will have little effect, however, if staff are not prepared to work effectively within the framework of expectations set by developers. Capacity development of teaching staff must therefore be a priority. While the MoE has provided training to thousands of teachers since 1994, the quality of that training and its ultimate consequences are uncertain. In particular, a lack of sustained technical support for the implementation of changes in pedagogy is likely to limit the extent of change in classrooms. Fully funding efforts to support reformed pedagogy at the school level—through such approaches as embedded training, teacher-to-teacher programs, or frequent follow-up—will be key to ensuring that the expectations for student learning are met. This is particularly true in the areas of participatory teaching and learning and of active, student-led investigation, which are articulated as goals but are rarely part of the culture of schools. Here, again, rich resources already exist in the local community, and efforts to work in closer collaboration with NGOs and other actors involved in rethinking pedagogy should be increased.

The capacity of staff in the regional directorates and in school administration to assist in the implementation of these policies is still limited, when compared to that of upper-level MoE staff. Building knowledge, skill, and will among these core constituencies will be essential to long-term embedding of educational change. Such efforts should not result in the expansion of the educational bureaucracy, however, as we note in our recommendations on delivery; rather, the focus should be on developing the instructional leadership and support capacity of current principals and regional supervision staff.

The development of a broader pool of quality instructors in English, the sciences, and information technology—three of the weakest yet most important areas of the system—is also essential. Such a process is complicated by the low salaries paid to teachers, which can prevent university graduates in noneducation fields from choosing teaching as a career option. Although the majority of system expenditures are already devoted to teacher salaries, compensation that allows staff in all areas to make teaching their only job and incentives that make the profession appealing are important investments in long-term system development and in the building and maintaining of quality. Special investment (through salary bonuses or other incentives) in teachers of English, science, and technology may be effective as an additional recruiting tool and should be considered.

These efforts all require a context of increased accountability, with clear incentives for school performance that support changes in practice that have been shown to benefit students. Mechanisms for holding staff and schools accountable for performance and tracking their attention to system-wide and school-specific goals must be put into place if reform is to be systematic and productive.

Other Quality Priorities: Improving Quality for Both Genders and Improving Tertiary Education. Differential choices and experiences of girls and boys within Palestinian education are partly due to broader cultural preferences, but they are also shaped by institutional practices. From the significant differences in access to private schools by gender, to curricula that retain explicit and implicit biases against girls and women, to differences in pedagogy for boys and girls, to the tracking of female students away from the sciences and the tracking of boys into vocational education, quality is a gender issue. However, understanding of the mechanics of these system characteristics is still far more inferential than substantiated by research. More study of the barriers to and facilitators of female and male performance within the system is necessary, and it should be a core component of planning efforts related to curricula, pedagogy, and system structure.

Tertiary education quality is hampered by limited resources and a lack of productive exchange and cooperation within the tertiary education sector and/or with external partners. Programs that are heavily focused on the humanities and social sciences are cheaper to run but of inconsistent quality, and a focus on these areas limits the extent to which universities and other tertiary education institutions can contribute to a vibrant Palestinian economy and to the research and development base in Palestine and in the region—a contribution that could be important both to national development and to the positioning of Palestine as a knowledge exporter in the future. Such development efforts, however, should be undertaken with a long-term perspective, because the system needs strengthening in many other ways to support such development.

Developing more-sustainable financing for the tertiary education sector should be a priority, but care should be taken not to bias the system in favor of higher-income students (as discussed, one of the system's strengths has been its historic accessibility to students from all socioeconomic backgrounds). Subsidies for high-cost, high-priority specializations may be one way of balancing national need with student preferences and of minimizing the class effects of greater reliance on fees or loans to fund the sector (this of course presumes equity by class across the lower levels of the system, so that all students have access to the preparation needed to excel in these specializations).

Access should never be expanded at the expense of quality, particularly as increasing proportions of costs are passed on to students. Development of reasonable and coordinated accreditation for programs and a system of alignment that allows for comparison across institutions is essential, and tertiary education expectations should be informed by learning standards for lower levels of the system.

Investment in technology and research infrastructure is also essential to raising the quality of the Palestinian tertiary education system. Public-private partnerships here—as in secondary-level vocational and technical education—are an important potential source of support for such efforts, although government oversight of such partnerships is necessary to keep the system focused on its primary clients (students). One key concern is the intellectual infrastructure for research and development. Limited availability of high-quality research in Arabic and weaknesses in instruction in English across the system undermine the quality of degrees in science and technology fields. Palestinian participation in regional efforts to upgrade Arabic-language research and development, increase translation of foreign-language research into Arabic, and broaden publication of research by local scholars will both enhance local capacity and extend the reach of the state's knowledge market.

Improving Delivery

The Ministry of Education's first priority must be meeting student needs—i.e., delivering high-quality services in a timely and accessible manner. Unfortunately, the government's dependence on donor financing for much of the system, which is unlikely to decrease in the near future, can make maintaining such a focus difficult. As discussed, conflicting donor interests, requirements, and procedures are significant burdens on the system, and they require the dedication of staff time to "donor management." Working with donors to standardize and streamline funding and reporting procedures must be an essential component of system development.[41]

Such efforts should not, however, result in lower standards of transparency. The respect that the Palestinian education system enjoys among donors for its relative cleanness of funding and allocation is an important point of leverage internally and externally, and efforts to pare down budgeting and accounting complexity must protect that reputation.

Indeed, strengthening the system's evaluation mechanisms should be a focus of delivery efforts in the near term: Better evaluation will both encourage confidence and support program development. While the first priority should be the development of capacity at the system level, longer-term investment in initiatives that support data analysis and utilization at the school level can eventually shift some cost and control to that key constituency. Such efforts would be consistent with the system's broader goals of encouraging participation in public decisionmaking by a wider range of societal actors, and they will be important components of a developed accountability system.

Absorption of UNRWA schools and staff into the government system will need to be planned and conducted to maximize the retention of UNRWA's human and physi-

---

[41] These efforts can also help to counter the bureaucratic bloat that appears to be beginning to emerge in the Ministry of Education.

cal resources. Equalizing salaries across sectors and facilitating the transfer of UNRWA staff to comparable positions when possible will be key to the success of this effort. The Ministry of Education should make every attempt to capitalize on UNRWA training infrastructure, which is currently of higher quality than that of the PA. Indeed, depending on the pace of system integration, shared training experiences for UNRWA transfers and Ministry of Education staff can serve as supports for system development that also function as induction and acculturation exercises. Absorption of UNRWA expertise should not be limited to school-level operations; MoE-level operations would benefit from the participation of the agency's trained administrators, staff developers, and public relations staff.

The foundation for the delivery of quality services to all students, however, is adequate funding, and the government's first priority should be soliciting and maintaining the budget required to support an excellent education system. Although current spending on education as a proportion of the national budget indicates its high priority, that investment must be increased and must be kept at sufficiently robust levels to meet both infrastructure and development/innovation needs of the system. To compensate for the substantial deficits in the current system, donors who hope to see a successful transition to statehood will need to increase their contributions in the early years.

Costs of Building a Successful Palestinian Education System

Spending on education has been a priority for both the PA and the United Nations, through UNRWA. The level of resources devoted to this sector has resulted in impressive achievements in educational services and participation, particularly considering the difficult circumstances that prevail in the Palestinian territories.

The world-class, universal education system described in this chapter is characterized by very high enrollment rates, measured as a percentage of the usual age group for each level of schooling. It also offers safe, high-quality facilities for learning and well-trained, motivated teachers. This preferred system relieves overcrowded classrooms and schools, allowing elementary and secondary class sizes to fall to levels prevailing in other countries with highly developed education systems (roughly 20 to 30 students per class). The preferred system also allows most school buildings to operate on a single shift per day, in contrast to the present situation.

Here, we first estimate approximate resources required to fund the system at a world-class, universal level (see Table 8.7). Then we compare these estimates to recent education spending in Palestine. We conclude with a discussion of possible compromises if full funding is not realized in the new state.

To estimate total required funding, we also need estimates of likely student enrollment under the assumption of a high-quality, well-functioning education system. The

Table 8.7
Estimated Spending Requirement Per Student

Year	Primary	Secondary	Tertiary
2004	$755	$841	$1,553
2005	$712	$820	$1,510
2006	$690	$776	$1,445
2007	$669	$755	$1,402
2008	$647	$733	$1,337
2009	$625	$712	$1,294
2010	$652	$722	$1,351
2011	$637	$735	$1,348
2012	$644	$747	$1,366
2013	$651	$732	$1,356
2014	$657	$743	$1,371

appendix provides a more detailed explanation of these enrollment projections. We include one year of kindergarten in the primary enrollments.

All of these enrollment estimates are reported in Table 8.8. As the columns show, enrollments in general are projected to increase substantially over this 11-year period at all levels, primarily because of rapid youth population growth and secondarily to modest increases in educational participation.

Table 8.8
Estimated Enrollment

Year	Enrollment (number of students)		
	Primary	Secondary	Tertiary
2004	987,062	100,606	110,771
2005	1,116,841	104,051	120,727
2006	1,180,119	112,738	124,861
2007	1,244,611	121,666	135,286
2008	1,311,157	130,760	145,999
2009	1,380,356	140,043	156,912
2010	1,438,274	149,506	168,052
2011	1,502,996	156,234	179,407
2012	1,570,631	163,264	187,481
2013	1,641,309	170,611	195,917
2014	1,715,168	178,289	204,733

NOTES: The sources and methodology are described in the appendix. Primary enrollments include one year of kindergarten.

Multiplying the per-student funding requirements in Table 8.7 by the estimated enrollments in Table 8.8 yields the total estimated funding required for successful development, shown in Table 8.9. The annual funding required remains approximately level because of two offsetting effects over this period. Initially, the spending required per student is higher (see Table 8.7) because we allow more capital spending in the early years after statehood. Later on, spending required per student declines, but the enrollments increase. The decrease in spending per student offsets the increase in students enrolled, resulting in an annual funding requirement that remains more or less level over most of the period, at approximately $1 billion to $1.5 billion.

These estimates assume that there is no significant effect from net migration over the period 2004 through 2014. In the event that migration flows are significant during this period (as predicted in the Demography chapter) and result in more children of school age, the spending requirements will increase correspondingly from the levels estimated here.

We now compare this funding requirement with recent spending history. Because of the great disruptions since 2000, we use 1996–1999 figures for comparison. Using PA figures for estimated spending from all sources (public, private, and international), we see in Table 8.10 that total spending was roughly $250 million. Thus, our estimates of education funding required by a new Palestinian state are about four times the recent spending level.

In terms of spending per student, Table 8.10 shows that primary and secondary education averaged about $220 per student and tertiary about $1,400. The relatively high tertiary spending per student is a result of the emphasis on universities rather than community colleges. Comparing current spending with our estimates of required spending per student in Table 8.7, we see that our estimates are roughly two to three times higher than recent spending levels for primary and secondary but only slightly higher for tertiary. We would, however, expect significant increases in tertiary enroll-

Table 8.9
Estimated Total Education Funding Required for Successful Development (millions of dollars)

Year	Primary	Secondary	Tertiary	Total
2004	$745	$85	$172	$1,002
2005	$795	$85	$182	$1,062
2006	$814	$88	$180	$1,082
2007	$832	$92	$190	$1,114
2008	$848	$96	$195	$1,139
2009	$863	$100	$203	$1,166
2010	$938	$108	$227	$1,273
2011	$958	$115	$242	$1,315
2012	$1,012	$122	$256	$1,390
2013	$1,068	$125	$266	$1,459
2014	$1,127	$132	$281	$1,540

Table 8.10
Education Spending in Palestinian Territories (All Sources), 1996–1999

Year	Education Spending (All Sources)				Estimated Spending Per Student	
	Current Dollars (millions)	2003 Dollars (millions)	Primary and Secondary (millions of dollars)	Tertiary (millions of dollars)	Primary and Secondary (dollars)	Tertiary (dollars)
1996	$214	$240	$170	$70	$240	$1,709
1997	$220	$243	$171	$72	$219	$1,423
1998	$246	$268	$188	$80	$224	$1,418
1999	$240	$258	$180	$77	$203	$1,166

SOURCES: Palestinian Ministry of Higher Education, the PA, and the World Bank, 2002, and authors' calculations.
NOTES: All figures are in 2003 U.S. dollars except "Current Dollars," which reports actual annual spending without adjusting for inflation. The U.S. GDP price deflator was used to adjust to 2003 dollars. "Education Spending (All Sources)" indicates that spending from public, UNRWA, and private sources is included in the amounts.

ments with more students attending lower-cost community colleges and a significant number at the more expensive universities.

Palestinians already have an education system that is very good when compared with societies with similar levels of income and development. To achieve an excellent universal education system in a new state will require even more funding than present or recent levels. The figures here do not specify how that funding should be provided (i.e., from the state budget, from international sources, or from private payments such as tuition), but the following observations are relevant to funding decisions.

In the face of budget pressures, the PA has turned to private payments for tuition, especially at the tertiary level. Once employment possibilities improve to the point where students can earn reasonable incomes during and after tertiary education, this can be a viable strategy for at least some of tertiary financing. Income potential after tertiary education and a reasonable financing system would allow students to take out loans to pay for tertiary education and repay the loans during working years. But until that point is reached, high tuition payments will necessarily drive down enrollments, degrading the functioning of the system.

Without substantial international funding, at least during the early years of statehood, the new state will almost certainly not be able to afford the kind of system described here. A number of compromises are possible, which would make delivery of education cheaper, but all will entail reductions in quality. Strategies to reduce funding requirements include the following:

1. Use existing buildings with less-extensive renovation and reconstruction than supposed here.

2. Focus tertiary education on less-expensive community colleges with one- and two-year programs, rather than four-year university programs.
3. Keep large class sizes, or even increase class sizes.
4. Continue to run two shifts per day in many schools to stretch the use of the capital resources available.
5. Ration access to fewer students than otherwise would wish to take advantage of the system.

As stated, each of these will significantly compromise the quality of the education system and lead it to fall short of the goals described in this chapter. If funding is insufficient, however, we recommend that they be considered in the order in which we have listed them. In the event of insufficient funding, we would expect the development of a good Palestinian education system with less than universal service, somewhere between the present system and the ideal of an excellent, universal system envisioned in this chapter.

Summary and Conclusion

The development of a strong education system will be essential to the success of any Palestinian state. This chapter has outlined a framework for excellence within which such a system might be conceived and suggests measures for achieving it. Specifically, we recommend the following steps as the system moves toward independence and sustainability:

Access
- Maintain access to basic education at near-universality.
  - Focus on students with special needs, in collaboration with the Ministries of Health and Social Affairs.
  - Reduce dropout rates by addressing school quality issues cited as factors in school leaving.
- Develop programs that increase access to secondary education.
  - Focus on quality of vocational and technical education and the academic sciences.
  - Expand public-private partnerships with industry and business in vocational-technical programming.
- Add a kindergarten year to the public education system.
- Prioritize efforts to upgrade facilities across levels of the system.
  - Focus near-term investment on infrastructure repairs, resourcing, and new construction.

Highest Quality Priorities

- Ensure that learning standards are internationally competitive and aligned with curricula and assessments, and that curricula reflect system goals of internal stabilization and democratization and external integration.
    - Collaborate with the Ministry of Labor to align vocational and technical standards and ensure their high quality.
- Place priority on pedagogical development of teaching staff.
    - Fully fund and staff efforts to support reformed pedagogy at the school level.
    - Work in closer collaboration with NGOs and other educational actors involved in rethinking pedagogy.
- At the administrative level, focus on developing the instructional leadership and support capacity of current principals and regional supervisory staff.
- Develop a broader pool of quality instructors in English, the sciences, and information technology.
    - Compensate all staff at levels that make second jobs unnecessary.
    - Consider salary bonuses or other incentives for these high-need fields.
- Develop mechanisms for holding staff and schools accountable for performance and attention to goals.

Other Quality Considerations

- Devote research resources to better understanding barriers to and facilitators of student performance by gender; incorporate findings into development of curricula, pedagogy, and system structure.
- Develop more-sustainable funding for tertiary education.
    - Consider loans, balanced with subsidies for high-cost, high-priority specializations.
- Align programs across tertiary education institutions to support exchange and continuity within the sector.
- Develop expectations for tertiary education performance that link to the standards and goals of the lower levels of the system.

Delivery

- Increase spending on education as a proportion of the national budget, and maintain levels robust enough to meet both infrastructure and development needs of the system.
- Work with donors to streamline and standardize funding and reporting mechanisms.
- Strengthen evaluation mechanisms within the system, with a priority focus on system-level structures and long-term investment in initiatives for data analysis and utilization.

- Structure absorption of UNRWA schools and staff to maximize retention of UNRWA's human and physical resources.
  - Capitalize on UNRWA training infrastructure.
  - Ensure that UNRWA expertise is reflected at the ministry level, not only in schools.

We believe that these measures are not unreasonable and that they would provide the Palestinian state with the broad educational capital it will need to move into a position of strength in the region and in the world. However, in the context of both notable strengths and significant challenges to the current system, patience and sustained support from external partners will be required to allow reform to take hold. Without such support, the system's potential cannot be achieved.

Appendix 8.A: Methods for Estimating Education Costs

Per-Student Expenditures

Since the majority of education spending is for the salaries of teachers and administrators, education costs are closely related to national salary levels across countries. A standard way of expressing education costs is by computing the ratio of education spending per student to GNI per capita (which is an approximate way of indicating the average national salary level per worker). UNESCO computes this education spending ratio for countries where data are available.

The aspirations for the Palestinian education system will require spending at levels comparable to countries with excellent education systems. To estimate this level, we present UNESCO data for selected countries in Table 8.A.1. Ideally we would use countries with similar economic and social context (and similar teacher salaries) that already have highly developed education systems. In the immediate region, only Israel both fits this category and supplies data to the United Nations. Other regional countries that would be useful comparisons include Egypt, Lebanon, the United Arab Emirates, Bahrain, and Saudi Arabia, but these countries do not report these data to the United Nations.

Since we have data for only one country in this category, we look at data for regional countries with moderately developed education systems. Three of these coun-

Table 8.A.1
Education Spending Per Student As a Percentage of GNI Per Capita, 2001

Education Level	Primary	Secondary	Tertiary
Within region comparison, highly developed education systems			
Israel	21	22	30
Within region comparison, moderately developed education systems			
Jordan	16	19	(not available)
Iran	12	12	40
Oman	13	21	50
Outside region comparison, highly developed education systems			
Austria	24	29	45
France	18	29	30
Germany	17	22	43
Japan	22	22	18
Sweden	24	27	50
Switzerland	23	28	53
United States (public only)	21	24	27
United States (public and private)	23	26	48

SOURCE: Authors' calculations from UNESCO (2004a) statistics. See text for explanation.
NOTES: Public expenditures only, except where noted. Elementary and secondary education are typically split 6 to 6 or 5 to 7 in most systems, compared with 10 to 2 in Palestine.

tries report data: Jordan, Iran, and Oman. We would want to set the spending ratio for Palestine at or above these levels, especially for primary and secondary education.

We also look at countries in other regions of the world with well-developed education systems. Because the spending ratios are scaled to national salary levels, they can be used as an approximate guide to spending in any well-developed system. Table 8.A.1 presents a number of such countries that report data. All of these figures are based on public expenditures only. To assess the limitations of the public-only figures, the authors estimated the figures in the United States for both public and private expenditures and report these figures in the last row of the table. The United States has relatively little private education in the primary and secondary sectors, and these figures increase only a little when private expenditure is included. There is much more private activity in tertiary education, so those figures increase a good deal.

We select ratios of 23 percent, 26 percent, and 48 percent for Palestine (for each sector, respectively), which are fully consistent with the data shown in the table. These are intended to represent both public and private expenditures in a new state.

We make two significant adjustments to these base figures: one adjustment to recognize the large investments in capital stock that will be required and another adjustment for differences between the time transition path of salary levels and the path of GNI per capita.

Many of the countries in Table 8.A.1 have low rates of population growth and well-developed capital stocks of buildings and equipment. Therefore, these countries do not need to spend as much on capital as the new Palestinian state will require. In Palestine, the population will be growing rapidly, at perhaps 4–5 percent per year (see Chapter Four for more detail on population growth predictions). Furthermore, as we describe above, the existing capital stock is substantially depleted because of damage or depreciation, and it is inadequate to meet the needs of the growing population.

To estimate capital requirements, we examine data from the United States on the ratio of capital to current expenditures. In the United States, about 12 percent of the spending on education is for capital purposes, representing the renewal of existing buildings and equipment and a modest amount of construction in areas with population growth. However, this flow of investment assumes a steady state, with a stable capital stock that is gradually depreciating and being replaced. As noted above, these initial conditions do not apply in Palestine, which needs heavy initial investment to establish an adequate base of infrastructure. Given the useful lifetime of buildings and equipment, we assume that the full costs of constructing the capital stock are perhaps 10 to 20 years worth of "steady-state" expenditures (in other words, the capital stock is renewed every 10 to 20 years). Under this assumption, the initial infrastructure needs of the Palestinian education system represent 120 to 240 percent of spending levels listed in Table 8.A.1. Thus, if the capital stock could be established immediately, initial spending would have to be 220 to 340 percent of the figures in Table 8.A.1 (i.e., at the low end, 100 percent of the spending for the steady-state expenditure, plus 120 percent for the initial investment in infrastructure). In practice, the Palestinian state will have to spread this investment over at least several years; the state will not have the capacity to undertake all of the construction in one year. In addition, even steady-state spending on capital is likely to be somewhat higher than the U.S. ratios, given the growth of the youth population in Palestine.

To make this adjustment, we set spending ratios 50 percent higher than the Table 8.A.1 amounts in the first year and gradually reduce the spending ratio linearly until it reaches the Table 8.A.1 level in year 11. The cumulative effect of this adjustment is to generate enough capital spending to accommodate the construction and purchasing needs consistent with the preceding assumptions.

The second adjustment we make accounts for differences in the likely transition path of salaries, including teacher salaries, versus GNI per capita, during the first few years after statehood. GNI per capita has declined markedly during the 2000–2004 period during the al-Aqsa intifada as a result of severe economic dislocations. The government and UNRWA salary schedules for teachers have not been much affected during this period of dislocation. In practice, however, teachers often simply have not been paid or have been paid partial salaries. In view of this situation, we project that salary levels after statehood would be equal to the present official schedule (which is the level that was actually paid up to 2000). We then expect salary levels to start increasing a few years after statehood as the economy grows and salaries in all sectors begin to rise.

Even under the most favorable future economic conditions described in Chapter Five, it will take three to four years after statehood until GNI per capita recovers to the pre-2000 level. Furthermore, (official) teacher salaries are currently high for a low-income country, consistent with the high priority on education in Palestinian society. Since our education spending factors are based on countries where teacher salaries are closer to one to two times the level of GNI per capita, we adjust the early years of GNI per capita after statehood until the estimates reach a level where teacher wages would be no more than about twice GNI per capita, rather than four or five times GNI per capita in the unadjusted estimates. We make this adjustment so that there are no decreases in teacher salaries from one year to the next.

Using the most favorable economic scenario in Chapter Five, the "high-contiguity/high-integration scenario," the level where GNI per capita equals twice the teacher salaries prevailing prior to statehood is first reached in 2009. So for our calculations, we base education spending on the wage and price levels that would prevail in 2009 for all years prior to 2009. Later years follow this same scenario, as shown in Table 8.A.3. We could achieve the same effect by adjusting the spending factors in Table 8.A.2 upward for the years from 2004 to 2008, but we consider the former approach a more straightforward way of explaining and calibrating the adjustment.

If actual GNI per capita varies from these supposed trajectories, especially in later years, that would have a material effect on the accuracy of our spending estimates.

Table 8.A.2
Projections of Spending Per Student as a Percentage of Palestinian GNI Per Capita

Year	Primary	Secondary	Tertiary
2004	35	39	72
2005	33	38	70
2006	32	36	67
2007	31	35	65
2008	30	34	62
2009	29	33	60
2010	28	31	58
2011	26	30	55
2012	25	29	53
2013	24	27	50
2014	23	26	48

To compute estimated spending requirements per student, we multiply the spending factors in Table 8.A.2 by the adjusted GNI per capita in Table 8.A.3. The result is shown in Table 8.7 above. Again, these figures represent spending from all sources: public, private, and international.

Table 8.A.3
Adjusted GNI Per Capita Used to Represent Wages and Prices

Year	Estimated	Adjusted
2004	$1,105	$2,157
2005	$1,400	$2,157
2006	$1,627	$2,157
2007	$1,804	$2,157
2008	$1,985	$2,157
2009	$2,157	$2,157
2010	$2,330	$2,330
2011	$2,452	$2,452
2012	$2,577	$2,577
2013	$2,712	$2,712
2014	$2,857	$2,857

SOURCE: Based on Chapter Five estimates for the high-contiguity/high-integration scenario.

Enrollments

Primary and secondary participation rates have been very high, as noted earlier in the chapter, so we see no need to make further adjustments. We therefore use the extant PA estimates of projected enrollments, which include primary and secondary students through 2010. After 2010, we use a youth population growth figure of 4.5 percent per year, based on the demography analyses in Chapter Four.[42]

For tertiary enrollments, we base the estimates on the previous year's secondary enrollment (see Table 8.A.4). Secondary school covers two grades, whereas tertiary covers between two and four years plus additional enrollments for older learners and postgraduate studies. To achieve high enrollment in tertiary education, we estimate that the enrollments would reach 1.2 times the previous year's secondary enrollment (since secondary education includes only two grades and tertiary can include 2–4 or more, it is logical to see somewhat greater enrollments in the tertiary than secondary levels). These figures are generally consistent with, and slightly higher than, enrollment levels before the al-Aqsa intifada.

Table 8.A.4
Estimated Enrollment

Year	Enrollment (number of students)			
	Kindergarten	Primary	Secondary	Tertiary
2004	70,225	916,837	100,606	110,771
2005	80,618	1,036,223	104,051	120,727
2006	92,550	1,087,569	112,738	124,861
2007	106,247	1,138,364	121,666	135,286
2008	121,972	1,189,185	130,760	145,999
2009	140,024	1,240,332	140,043	156,912
2010	146,325	1,291,949	149,506	168,052
2011	152,909	1,350,087	156,234	179,407
2012	159,790	1,410,841	163,264	187,481
2013	166,981	1,474,328	170,611	195,917
2014	174,495	1,540,673	178,289	204,733

NOTES: For primary and secondary enrollment from 2004 to 2010 and kindergarten enrollment for 2004, PA 2003. For 2011–2014, primary and secondary enrollment is assumed to increase at 4.5 percent per year. For kindergarten 2005–2014, enrollment is estimated as described in the text. Tertiary enrollment is estimated from previous year's secondary enrollment, as described in the text. The stage lengths are kindergarten, 1 year, primary, 10 years, secondary, 2 years, and tertiary, variable. The information in this table is also shown in Table 8.8, where Kindergarten and Primary are combined into a single Primary column.

---

[42] We note that a growth rate of 4.5 percent in the school-age population is toward the lower end of the range considered in Chapter Four. Higher growth rates would increase the student population and thus the financial costs of successful development.

Bibliography

Abdeen, Ziad, et al., *Nutritional Assessment of the West Bank & Gaza Strip*, CARE International, Johns Hopkins University, and Al Quds University, September 2002. Online at http://www.usaid.gov/wbg/reports/Nutritional_Assessment.pdf (as of September 3, 2004).

Ahed-Ahmad, Basima, "Achievements of the Palestinian Assessment and Evaluation Center," *Education Update*, Vol. 5, No. 3, New York: United Nations Children's Fund, 2002.

Al-Haq/Law in the Service of Man, *Punishing a Nation: Human Rights Violations During the Palestinian Uprising, December 1987–December 1988*, Boston, Mass.: South End Press, 1988.

Appadurai, Arjun, *Modernity at Large: Cultural Dimensions of Globalization*, Minneapolis, Minn.: University of Minnesota Press, 1996.

Arafat, Cairo, and Neil Boothby, *A Psychosocial Assessment of Palestinian Children*, United States Agency for International Development, 2003.

Awwad, Elia, Nancy Dubrow, and Bojo Pinek, *Palestinian Adolescents Survey in Gaza: Childhood Exposure to Violence: Psychological and Behavioral Aftermath in Adolescence*, Jerusalem: United Nations Development Programme, 1998.

Baker, Ahmad, "The Psychological Impact of the Intifada on Palestinian Children in the Occupied West Bank and Gaza: An Exploratory Study," *American Journal of Orthopsychiatry*, Vol. 60, No. 4, 1990, pp. 496–505.

Baramki, Gabi, "Building Palestine Universities Under Occupation," *Journal of Palestine Studies*, Vol. 17, No. 1, 1987.

Birzeit University, Development Studies Programme, *Poll No. 17: An Opinion Poll Concerning the Performance of Palestinian Institutions, Their Service Provision, Their Role in the Development Process, and International Funding*, Birzeit: Birzeit University, Development Studies Programme, June 28, 2004. Online at http://home.birzeit.edu/dsp/opinionpolls/poll17/ (as of September 3, 2004).

———, *Poll No. 11: Living Conditions, Emergency Assistance, and Reforming Palestinian Institutions*, Birzeit: Birzeit University, Development Studies Programme, March 12, 2003. Online at http://home.birzeit.edu/dsp/DSPNEW/polls/poll_11/ (as of September 3, 2004).

Birzeit University, Development Studies Programme, and the United Nations Development Programme, *Palestinian Human Development Report 2002*, Birzeit: Birzeit University, Development Studies Programme, 2002. Online at http://home.birzeit.edu/dsp/phdr/2002/ (as of September 3, 2004).

Brown, Nathan, "Democracy, Nationalism and Contesting the Palestinian Curriculum," in *Palestinian Politics after the Oslo Accords*, Berkeley, Calif.: University of California Press, 2003.

Brynen, Rex, *A Very Political Economy: Peacebuilding and Foreign Aid in the West Bank and Gaza*, Washington, D.C.: United States Institute of Peace, 2000.

B'Tselem, "Closure of Schools and Other Setbacks to the Education System in the Occupied Territories," *B'Tselem Information Sheet,* Jerusalem: B'Tselem, September–October 1990.

Burkhart, Grey, and Susan Older, *The Information Revolution in the Middle East and North Africa,* Santa Monica, Calif.: RAND Corporation, MR-1653-NIC, 2003.

Christina, Rachel, "Contingency, Complexity, Possibility: NGOs and the Negotiation of Local Control in Palestinian Early Childhood Programming," in Margaret Sutton and Robert F. Arnove, eds., *Civil Society or Shadow State? State/NGO Relations in Education,* Greenwich, Conn.: Information Age Publishing, 2004.

Cincotta, Richard, Robert Engelman, and Daniele Anastasion, *The Security Demographic: Population and Civil Conflict after the Cold War,* Washington D.C.: Population Action International, 2003.

Coalition of Palestinian Educational NGOs, *Training for Transformation and Palestinian National Development: Alternatives to Support Strong Educational Programming,* Ramallah: October 1999.

Del Castill, Daniel, "Saudi Arabia Helps Palestinian Colleges," *Chronicle of Higher Education,* October 4, 2002.

Delors, Jacques, et al., *Learning: The Treasure Within: Report to UNESCO of the International Commission on Education for the Twenty-First Century,* Paris: UNESCO, 1996.

Dollar, David, Raymond Fisman, and Roberta Gatti, *The 'Fairer' Sex? Corruption and Women in Government,* Washington, D.C.: World Bank, Policy Research Report 4, October 1999.

Egset, Willy, "The Labour Market," in Laurie Blome Jacobsen, ed., *Finding Means: UNRWA's Financial Crisis and Refugee Living Conditions, Volume 1, Socio-Economic Situation of Palestinian Refugees in Jordan, Lebanon, Syria and the West Bank and Gaza Strip,* Oslo, Norway: Fafo Institute for Applied International Studies, Fafo Report 427, 2003.

Essoulami, Saïd, *Israel/Palestine: Cry for Change,* London: ARTICLE 19, the Global Campaign for Free Expression, January 1992.

Fahsheh, Munir, *West Bank: Learning to Survive,* in Cyril D. Poster and Jurgen Zimmer, eds., *Community Education in the Third World,* London: Routledge, 1993, pp. 17–28.

Farah, Randa, *A Report on the Psychological Effects of Overcrowding in Refugee Camps in the West Bank and Gaza Strip,* prepared for the Expert and Advisory Services Fund—International Development Research Centre, Ottawa, Canada, April 2000. Online at http://www.arts. mcgill.ca/MEPP/PRRN/farah.html (as of September 3, 2004).

Firer, Ruth, and Sami Adwan, *The Israeli-Palestinian Conflict in History and Civics Textbooks of Both Nations,* Falk Pingel, ed., Hannover: Hahnsche Buchhandlung, 2004.

Garbarino, James, and Kathleen Kosteiny, "The Effects of Political Violence on Palestinian Children's Behavior Problems: A Risk Accumulation Model," *Child Development,* Vol. 67, 1996, pp. 33–45.

Gaza Community Mental Health Program, *Study on the Psychosocial Effects of Al-Aqsa Intifada: Significant Increase in Mental Disorders and Symptoms of PTSD Among Children and Women,* Gaza: Gaza Community Mental Health Program, 2002.

Georg Eckert Institute for International Textbook Research, *Reviews of Current Israeli and Palestinian Textbooks,* Braunschweig, Germany: UNESCO and Georg Eckert Institute, 2004.

Gill, Indermit, and Fred Fluitman, eds., *Skills and Change: Constraints and Innovation in the Reform of Innovation in the Reform of Vocational Education and Training, Synthesis of Findings,* Washington, D.C.: World Bank and International Labour Organization, 2002.

Graham-Brown, Sarah, *Education, Repression, Liberation: Palestinians,* London: World University Service, 1984.

Gumpel, Thomas P., and Sana Awartani, "A Comparison of Special Education in Israel and Palestine: Surface and Deep Structures," *Journal of Special Education,* Spring 2003.

Hall, Stuart, "Old and New Identities, Old and New Ethnicities," in Anthony D. King, ed., *Culture, Globalization and the World System: Contemporary Conditions for the Representation of Identity,* London: Macmillan, 1991, pp. 41–68.

Hansen, Peter, "Picking Up the Pieces in Gaza," *International Herald Tribune,* June 23, 2003.

Hashweh, Maher, et al., *An Assessment of Higher Education Needs in the West Bank and Gaza,* submitted by The Academy for Educational Development to the United States Agency for International Development, September 2003.

Heiberg, Marianne, and Geir Øvensen, *Palestinian Society in Gaza, West Bank and Arab Jerusalem,* Oslo, Norway: Fafo Institute for Applied International Studies, Fafo Report 151, 1993.

Henry, Miriam, Bob Lingard, Fazal Rizvi, and Sandra Taylor, "Working With/Against Globalization in Education," *Journal of Education Policy,* Vol. 14, No. 1, 1999, pp. 85–97.

Herz, Barbara, et al., *Letting Girls Learn: Promising Approaches in Primary and Secondary Education,* Washington, D.C.: World Bank, World Bank Discussion Paper No. 133, 1991.

Israel/Palestine Center for Research and Information, *Analysis and Evaluation of the New Palestinian Curriculum: Reviewing Palestinian Textbooks and Tolerance Education Program,* submitted to the Public Affairs Office, U.S. Consulate General, Jerusalem, March 2003.

Jacobsen, Laurie Blome, "Education and Human Capital," in Laurie Blome Jacobsen, ed., *Finding Means: UNRWA's Financial Crisis and Refugee Living Conditions, Volume 1, Socio-Economic Situation of Palestinian Refugees in Jordan, Lebanon, Syria and the West Bank and Gaza Strip,* Oslo, Norway: Fafo Institute for Applied International Studies, Fafo Report 427, 2003.

Jerbawi, Tafida, *Women in the Palestinian Curriculum,* Ramallah: Women's Affairs Committee, 2002.

Jerusalem Media and Communication Centre, "The Palestinian Education System," Jerusalem: Jerusalem Media and Communication Centre, June 2001. Online at http://www.jmcc.org/research/reports/educate01.htm (as of September 9, 2004).

Khaldi, Musa, and Nader Wahbeh, "Teacher Education in Palestine: Understanding Teachers' Realities and Development Through Action Research," Paper presented at Selmun Seminar Conference: *Teacher Education in the Mediterranean Region: Responding to the Challenges of*

Societies in Transition, Al-Qattan Centre for Educational Research and Development, Ramallah, October 2000.

Kouhail, Hisham, "Vocational Technical Education and Training in Palestine: A Proposal for a National Strategy," Ramallah: Ministry of Higher Education and Palestinian Authority, undated. Online at http://www.crm.hct.ac.ae/events/archive/tend/004kuheil.html (as of September 3, 2004).

Lempinen, Jyrki, *Palestine (Gaza and West Bank) Country Report,* Helsinki, Finland: Ministry of Foreign Affairs, Education and Training Sector, October 2002.

Lingard, Bob, "It Is and It Isn't: Vernacular Globalization, Educational Policy, and Restructuring," in Nicholas C. Burbules and Carlos A Torres, eds., *Globalization and Education: Critical Perspectives,* New York, N.Y.: Routledge, 2000, pp. 79–108.

Livnat, Limor, and Anders Fogh Rasmussen, "Education for Peace—or War?" *The Jerusalem Post,* October 11, 2002.

Luke, Allen, and Carmen Luke, "A Situated Perspective on Cultural Globalization," in Nicholas C. Burbules and Carlos A Torres, eds., *Globalization and Education: Critical Perspectives,* New York, N.Y.: Routledge, 2000, pp. 275–298.

Mahshi, Khalil, "The Palestinian Ministry of Education and Non-Governmental Organizations: Cooperation and Possible Partnership," Paper presented to the International Conference on Palestinian Government/NGO Relations: Cooperation and Partnership, Ramallah, February 2000.

Mahshi, Khalil, and Kim Bush, "The Palestinian Uprising and Education for the Future," *Harvard Educational Review,* Vol. 59, No. 4, 1989, pp. 470–483.

Mansour, Sylvie, "The Intifada Generation in the Classroom," *Prospects,* Vol. 26, No. 2, Paris: UNESCO, June 1996, pp. 293–310.

Morena, Elisa, "Israel or Palestine: Who Teaches What History?" *Le Monde Diplomatique,* July 2001.

Moughrabi, Fouad, *Educating for Citizenship in the New Palestine,* Ramallah: Qattan Center for Education Research and Development, 2002. Online at http://www.qattanfoundation.org/research/cur1.pdf (as of September 3, 2004).

———, "The Politics of Palestinian Textbooks," *Journal of Palestine Studies,* Vol. 31, No. 1, 2001, pp. 5–19.

Nasru, Fathiyeh, *Preliminary Vision of a Palestinian Education System,* Birzeit: Center for Research on and Documentation of Palestinian Society, 1993.

Nasser, Maher, Chief of United Nations Relief and Works Agency for Palestine Refugees in the Near East Liaison Office (New York), "Education Emergency Activities," email to Deanna Weber Prine of the RAND Corporation, sent October 13, 2004.

Palestinian Authority (PA), *Emergency and Public Investment Plan, 2003–2004,* Ramallah: Ministry of Planning and International Cooperation, 2003.

———, *Education For All: 2000 Country Assessment, Palestine,* Ramallah: United Nations Educational, Scientific and Cultural Organization, 2000. Online at http://www2.unesco. org/wef/countryreports/palestine/contents.html (as of September 3, 2004).

———, *Agenda for Social Renewal: The National Plan for Palestinian Children, Revised and Updated,* Ramallah: Ministry of Planning and International Cooperation, 1999.

———, *Agenda for Social Renewal: The National Plan for Palestinian Children,* Ramallah: Ministry of Planning and International Cooperation, 1996.

Palestinian Central Bureau of Statistics (PCBS), "Education—Current Main Indicators," findings from the Educational Institutions Census 2003/2004, 2004a. Online at http://www. pcbs.org/educatio/edu_main.aspx (as of September 3, 2004).

———, "Number of Students in Schools by Region, Supervising Authority, Stage and Sex, 2003/2004," Palestinian Central Bureau of Statistics, 2004b. Online at http://www.pcbs. org/educatio/yb0204_educ3.aspx (as of September 3, 2004).

———, "Number of Students, Graduates and Teaching Staff in Universities and Community Colleges by Sex, 1994/1995–2002/2003," findings from the Educational Institutions Census 2003/2004, Palestinian Central Bureau of Statistics, 2004c. Online at http://www.pcbs. org/pcbs/educatio/educ9.aspx (as of September 3, 2004).

———, *Palestinian Children—Issues and Statistics, Executive Summary,* Palestinian Central Bureau of Statistics, February 2004d. Online at http://www.pcbs.org/child/pdf_file/echild5. pdf (as of September 3, 2004).

———, "Impact of the Separation Wall on the Socioeconomic Conditions of Palestinian Households in the Localities the Wall Passes Through," Palestinian Central Bureau of Statistics, October 2003a.

———, "Percentage Distribution of Persons (15 Years and Over) By Educational Attainment, Region and Sex, 1995, 1997, 2000, 2001, 2002, 2003," Palestinian Central Bureau of Statistics, 2003b. Online at http://www.pcbs.org/educatio/educ11.aspx (as of September 3, 2004).

———, "Repetition and Drop-Out Rates by Region, State, and Sex, 2002–2003," Palestinian Central Bureau of Statistics, 2003c. Online at http://www.pcbs.org/pcbs/educatio/yb0204_ educ9.aspx (as of September 3, 2004).

———, "Fourth Annual Statistical Report, 2001: Palestinian Children—Issues and Statistics," Palestinian Central Bureau of Statistics, 2001a. Online at http://www.pcbs.org/pcbs/child/ rep_2001.aspx (as of September 3, 2004).

———, "Number of Pupils in Schools and Kindergartens by Region and Stage, 1994\1995– 2001\2001," Palestinian Central Bureau of Statistics, 2001b. Online at http://www.pcbs. org/abs_pal/abs_pal2/qudsb/3.4.3.htm (as of November 17, 2004).

———, "Palestinian Children—Issues and Statistics, Annual Report 1999, Executive Summary April 1999," Palestinian Central Bureau of Statistics, 1999a. Online at http://www. pcbs.org/pcbs/child/exc.aspx#Child%20Education%20Reality (as of September 3, 2004).

————, "Distribution of Teachers by Qualification and Sex—1998/1999," Palestinian Central Bureau of Statistics, 1999b. Online at http://www.pcbs.org/educatio/project_educ13.aspx (as of September 3, 2004).

————, "Women and Men in Palestine, Trends and Statistics," Ramallah: Palestinian Central Bureau of Statistics, 1998.

Palestinian Central Bureau of Statistics (PCBS) and the Palestinian Ministry of Education (MoE), *Educational Statistical Yearbook 1996–97,* No. 3, Ramallah, June 1997.

Palestinian Curriculum Development Center (PCDC), ed., *A Comprehensive Plan for the Development of the First Palestinian Curriculum for General Education,* Ramallah: Palestinian Curriculum Development Center, 1996.

Palestinian Ministry of Education (MoE), "Basic Education Figures," 2004a. Online at http://www.mohe.gov.ps/English/Education_figures_eng.htm (as of September 3, 2004).

————, *Assessment 10: The Impact of the Israeli Occupation on Palestinian Education 28/09/00–14/6/04,* Ramallah: Palestinian Ministry of Education and Higher Education, 2004b.

————, *Education for All Summary Report,* Ramallah: Palestinian Ministry of Education and Higher Education, 2004c.

————, "Higher Education Statistics," 2003. Online at www.moe.gov.ps/Downloads/prosure.pdf (as of September 3, 2004).

————, *Five-Year Education Development Plan 2000–2005: General Education in Palestine,* Ramallah: Palestinian Ministry of Education and Higher Education, 2000.

————, "Istikhdam Techologiya Al Maaloumat Fi Wazarat Al Tarbiya Wa Al Taalim Al Ali–Mukhtabarat Al Hasoub" ["Use of Information Technology in the Ministry of Education and Higher Education—Computer Laboratories"], Ramallah: Palestinian Ministry of Education, Technology Summary, undated. Online at http://www.moe-tech.net/accomplishments/acc1.html (in Arabic) (as of September 3, 2004).

Palestinian Ministry of Higher Education, the Palestinian Authority, and the World Bank, *Palestinian Higher Education Financing Strategy,* Washington, D.C.: World Bank, August 2002. Online at http://lnweb18.worldbank.org/mna/mena.nsf/Attachments/MOHE+Strategy/$File/MOHESR.pdf (as of September 3, 2004).

Patrick, Stewart, "The Check Is In The Mail: Improving the Delivery and Coordination of Post-Conflict Assistance," New York, NY: New York University, Center on International Cooperation, December 1998.

Paz, Reuven, "Higher Education and the Development of Palestinian Islamic Groups," *MERIA Journal,* Vol. 4, No. 2, June 2000.

Pingel, Falk, ed., *Contested Past, Disputed Present: Curricula and Teaching in Israeli and Palestinian Schools,* Hannover: Verlag Hahnsche Buchhandlung, 2003.

Rigby, Andrew, *Palestinian Education: The Future Challenge,* Jerusalem, Israel: Palestinian Academic Society for the Study of International Affairs (PASSIA), 1995.

————, *The Intifada: The Struggle Over Education,* Jerusalem, Israel: Palestinian Academic Society for the Study of International Affairs (PASSIA), 1989.

Save the Children Alliance, West Bank and Gaza, *Palestine: The Education of Children at Risk,* Save the Children Alliance, 2001. Online at http://earlybird.qeh.ox.ac.uk/cgi-bin/ps/saxon.pl?psychsoc.7.xml?copyright.xsl (as of September 9, 2004).

Thabet, Abdel, Aziz Mousa, and Panos Kostanis, "Post-Traumatic Stress Reactions in Children of War," *Journal of Child Psychology and Psychiatry,* Vol. 40, 1999, pp. 385–391.

United Nations (UN), "Additional 56 Million Dollars Needed for Relief Works in Palestine," United Nations Press Release, New York, N.Y.: United Nations, July 2, 2002.

————, Economic and Social Commission for Western Asia, *Women and Men in the Arab World: A Statistical Portrait,* New York, N.Y.: United Nations, 2000.

————, "Report of the Commissioner-General of the United Nations Relief and Works Agency for Palestine Refugees in the Near East," New York, N.Y.: United Nations, October 1, 1999.

————, United Nations Special Coordinator for the Palestinian Territory, *United Nations Education Strategy for Palestine,* Gaza City: United Nations Special Coordinator for the Palestinian Territory, United Nations, 1996.

United Nations Children's Fund (UNICEF), *The State of the World's Children 2004: Girls, Education and Development,* New York, NY: United Nations Children's Fund, 2004. Online at http://www.unicef.org/files/SOWC_O4_eng.pdf (as of September 3, 2004).

————, *Analysis of Multiple Indicator Cluster Surveys and Demographic and Health Surveys,* New York, NY: United Nations Children's Fund, Division of Policy and Planning, Strategic Information Section, 2002.

————, "Statistics for the Occupied Palestinian Territories," New York, NY: United Nations Children's Fund, 2001. Online at http://www.unicef.org/infobycountry/opt_statistics.html (as of September 3, 2004).

————, "Statistics for the Occupied Palestinian Territories," New York, NY: United Nations Children's Fund, 2000. Online at http://www.unicef.org/infobycountry/opt_statistics.html (as of September 3, 2004).

United Nations Children's Fund (UNICEF) and Birzeit University, Development Studies Programme, *The Children of Palestine in the Labor Market,* Ramallah: Birzeit University, Development Studies Programme, 2003.

United Nations Development Programme (UNDP), *Arab Human Development Report 2003: Building a Knowledge Society,* New York, NY: United Nations Development Programme/Regional Bureau for Arab States, 2003.

————, Regional Bureau for Arab States, *Arab Human Development Report 2002: Creating Opportunities for Future Generations,* New York, NY: United Nations Development Programme/Regional Bureau for Arab States, 2002.

United Nations Development Programme/Programme of Assistance to the Palestinian People, *Palestinian TOKTEN,* undated. Online at http://www.palestiniantokten.org/ (as of November 18, 2004).

United Nations Educational, Scientific, and Cultural Organization (UNESCO), *EFA Global Monitoring Report 2003/4: Regional Overview: The Arab States,* New York, N.Y.: UNESCO, 2004a. Online at http://www.unesco.org/education/efa_report/zoom_regions_pdf/arabstat.pdf (as of September 3, 2004).

———, *Gender and Education for All: The Leap to Equality,* New York, N.Y.: UNESCO, EFA Global Monitoring Report 2003/2004, 2004b. Online at http://portal.unesco.org/education/en/ev.phpURL_ID = 23023&URL_DO = DO_TOPIC&URL_SECTION = 201.html (as of September 3, 2004).

———, *Education for All in the Arab States: Renewing the Commitment (The Arab Framework for Action to Ensure Basic Learning Needs in the Arab States in the Years 2000–2010),* adopted by the Regional Conference on Education for All for the Arab States, Cairo, Egypt: UNESCO, January 2000. Online at http://www.unesco.org/education/efa/wef_2000/regional_frameworks/frame_arab_states.shtml (as of September 3, 2004).

———, "Developing Education in Palestine," *UNESCO Newsletter,* September 1997. Online at www.unesco.org/iiep/eng/newsletter/1997/jule197.htm (as of September 3, 2004).

———, *Primary and Secondary Education in the West Bank and Gaza Strip: Overview of the Systems and Needs for Development of the Ministry of Education,* Paris: UNESCO, June 1995.

———, "Developing Education in Palestine: A Continuing Challenge," New York, N.Y.: UNESCO,, undated(a). Online at http://www.unesco.org/education/news_en/131101_palestine.shtml (as of September 3, 2004).

———, *Palestine: Priority Projects for Educational Development,* Paris: UNESCO, undated(b).

UNESCO and ARABEFA, *Education for All in the Arab States: Issues, Priorities, and Follow-up Mechanisms,* Beirut, Lebanon: UNESCO, June 2001.

United Nations Relief and Works Agency for Palestine Refugees in the Near East (UNRWA), *UNRWA Emergency Appeal for 2004 (January–December 2004),* Gaza City: UNRWA, 2004a. Online at http://www.un.org/unrwa/emergency/appeals/7th-appeal.pdf (as of September 3, 2004).

———, *Statistical Profiles,* Gaza City: UNRWA, 2004b. Online at http://www.un.org/unrwa/publications/pdf/education.pdf (as of September 3, 2004).

———, *Teacher Training,* Gaza City: UNRWA, 2004c. Online at http://www.un.org/unrwa/programmes/education/teacher_training.html (as of 17 November 2004).

———, *UNRWA in Figures: Figures as of 30 June 2004,* Gaza City: UNRWA, 2004d. Online at http://www.un.org/unrwa/publications/pdf/uif-june04.pdf (as of 17 November 2004).

———, *13th Joint Meeting: UNRWA/Arab League Council of Education for the Children of Palestine,* Gaza City: UNRWA, December 2003a.

———, *UNRWA Emergency Appeal for 2003 (January–June 2003),* Gaza City: UNRWA, 2003b. Online at http://www.un.org/unrwa/emergency/appeals/5th-appeal.pdf (as of September 3, 2004).

————, *UNRWA Emergency Appeal for 2003 (July–December 2003),* Gaza City: UNRWA, 2003c. Online at http://www.un.org/unrwa/emergency/appeals/6th-appeal.pdf (as of September 3, 2004).

Van Dyke, Blaire G., and E. Vance Randall, "Educational Reform in Post-Accord Palestine: A Synthesis of Palestinian Perspectives," *Educational Studies,* Vol. 28, No. 1, 2002, pp. 17–31.

Velloso de Santisteban, Augusto, "Palestinian Education: a National Curriculum Against All Odds," *International Journal of Educational Development,* Vol. 22, 2002, pp. 145–154.

World Bank, *World Development Indicators,* Washington, D.C.: World Bank, 2004.

————, *Engendering Development: Through Gender Equality in Rights, Resources, and Voice,* World Bank Policy Research Report, New York, NY: Oxford University Press, 2001.

————, *Comprehensive Development Framework for Palestine, Basic and Secondary Education,* Washington, D.C.: World Bank, working draft, 2000.

————, *Education Sector Analysis,* Washington, DC: World Bank Education Section, Human Development Department, 1999a.

————, "Strengthening Public Expenditure Management in West Bank and Gaza, Palestinian Education: A Sector Review," Washington, D.C.: World Bank, March 1999b.

————, "Strengthening Public Sector Management: West Bank and Gaza," World Bank report number 20002, Washington, D.C.: World Bank, Social and Economic Development Group, Middle East and North Africa Region, January 1, 1999c. Online at http://www-wds.worldbank.org/servlet/WDS_IBank_Servlet?pcont = details&eid = 000094946_00011405343316 (as of September 3, 2004).

————, *Developing the Occupied Territories: An Investment in Peace,* Washington, D.C.: World Bank, 1993.

CHAPTER NINE

Conclusions

If a state of Palestine is created, it is essential that it be successful. The purpose of this book is to describe steps that Palestinians, Israelis, Americans, and members of the international community can take to ensure that a new independent Palestinian state is successful.

An independent Palestinian state will begin with a number of strengths. These include a population that is devoted to the success of their state and, according to polls, willing to live side by side and in peace with Israel. This population is relatively healthy and well-educated, compared with other countries in the region with similar levels of economic development; moreover, both the health and education infrastructures have proven themselves to be flexible and adaptive, even in the face of severe social, political, and economic strain. Particularly notable is the strong degree of gender parity in education outcomes. In health, education, and other areas, a Palestinian state will be able to draw on a strong base of governmental and nongovernmental institutions and on many highly qualified professionals. An independent Palestinian state will also surely be created with strong political and financial commitments from the international community to the state's success.

At the same time, the new state will face significant challenges. Most fundamentally, the state must be secure within its borders, provide for the routine safety of its inhabitants, be free from radical subversion or foreign exploitation, and pose no security threat to Israel—conditions that have been lacking since at least the start of the second intifada in 2000. The state must establish and maintain effective governance, rather than the corrupt, nonrepresentative, and authoritarian rule that has characterized the period since 1994. The state will face a large and rapidly growing population, with a very high dependency ratio (i.e., the ratio of children and elders to workers) and the likely immigration of large numbers of Palestinians from abroad.

Other key challenges considered in this book include the implications for the new state of how Palestinian borders, the status of Israeli settlements, and the status of Jerusalem are resolved in settlement negotiations; the need for strong economic development, starting with a recovery from the economic decline that has accompanied the second intifada; the need for adequate, safe, and reliable supplies of water; and the need to strengthen and expand the health and education systems, with respect to financing, physical infrastructure, and human resources.

In the remainder of this chapter, we briefly summarize the conclusions reached in this book. Specifically, we discuss conditions affecting the success of a future independent Palestinian state. We then describe options for Palestinians and the international community to leverage the likely strengths of an independent Palestinian state and address the challenges it will face. Finally, we summarize the potential financial requirements for establishing and sustaining a successful Palestinian state.

Requirements for Success

The requirements necessary to maximize the chances of Palestinian success can be broken into three time frames: immediate (requirements at the state's founding that will affect long-term viability), near term (actions that the international community and Palestinians must undertake in the early years of statehood to assist the process), and near to longer term (actions that must be undertaken after statehood to better institutionalize a successful state). Using these three phases, we can trace the key requirements needed to meet the four criteria we use throughout this book to measure the new state's success: good governance, economic viability, security, and health and well-being (see Table 9.1).

Table 9.1
Important Factors for a Successful State of Palestine

Success Criteria	Important Factors		
	State Founding	State Enabling	State Maturation
Good governance	Land contiguity Border permeability Land size Refugee issues Status of Jerusalem Settlements	Good governance	State legitimacy Administration of justice Health and education Dependency on aid
Economic viability	Land contiguity Border permeability Land size Water Refugee immigration Settlements	Aid Investment Desalination plants	Good governance Regulatory regime Investment climate Administration of justice Water Health and education Dependency on aid Property rights
Security	Land contiguity Palestine security roles Border permeability Refugee immigration Settlements	Counterterrorism Security cooperation Administration of justice Police training	Palestinian police and security Administration of justice Dependency on aid
Health and well- being	Water	Aid for health enhancement and educational reform	Health and education Dependency on aid

State Founding

To thrive, an independent Palestinian state must be designed at its founding to maximize the chances for success. After studying various options, we concluded the following relative to state success:

- **The more contiguous Palestine's lands, the more likely Palestine will succeed.** Contiguity of territory within the West Bank and unrestricted access between the West Bank and Gaza will facilitate almost every aspect of Palestinian life—including economic development, health and education, governance, and security.
- **The more open Palestine's borders, the more likely Palestine will succeed.** Prosperity depends on the relatively free flow of people, goods, and services across all borders (Israel, Jordan, Egypt, and, by extension, the international community).
- **The greater the legitimacy of the new government in the eyes of its citizens—and the more transparent, accountable, and participatory it is—the more likely Palestine will succeed.** Legitimacy will depend on a number of factors, including good governance, territorial contiguity, and land area approaching the size of that in 1967.
- **The more immigrants, and the more rapidly Palestine receives immigrants, the less likely it will succeed.** Refugees can bring valuable skills to the new state. But too many refugees received too quickly will overburden the economy and sap scarce resources.
- **The more Israeli settlements within Palestine, the less likely Palestine will succeed.** Israeli settlements on Palestine's side of the border will complicate the security arrangements between the two states and will disrupt territorial contiguity.
- **The more water Palestine has, the more likely Palestine will succeed.** Close cooperation with Israel will be needed to assure an adequate supply of water. Lack of high-quality water will endanger the population's health and impede economic development.
- **The more involved the international community, the more likely Palestine will succeed.** Given the breakdown of trust between Israelis and Palestinians, the international community will likely need to participate in the design and implementation of the security arrangements agreed to by the parties as well as provide significant economic assistance.

State Enabling

Maximizing the chances of success for the State of Palestine will require a significant international investment of both capital and manpower during the first decade of statehood. The following "state-enabling" correlations pertain to the first decade of Palestinian statehood:

- The more the international community and Palestinians insist on good governance within Palestine, the more likely good governance will be practiced.
- The more willing the international community is to commit financial resources to Palestinian development and security, the more likely Palestine will succeed.

State Maturation

If Palestine is to enjoy long-term success, it will need more than a good initial design and strong international backing. For a mature Palestine to succeed, the Palestinians themselves will need to make smart policy choices.

- The more Palestine bears the responsibility for its security, the more likely Palestine will succeed.
- The more effective, transparent, and accountable the administration of justice in Palestine, the more likely Palestine will succeed.
- The better the health and education of Palestinians, the more likely Palestine will succeed.
- The longer Palestine remains financially dependent on the international community, the less successful it will be as a state.

Options for Facilitating Success

This book has described a number of options for strengthening the institutions of a future Palestinian state in order to help ensure the state's success. These include steps that can be taken—many even before the establishment of a new state—by Palestinians, Israel, the United States, and the international community.

Promoting Security

Since security will present the new state with its most immediate challenges, this is also the area where international assistance can provide the most immediate benefits. The long-term goal should be to engender Palestinian self-sufficiency in dealing with internal security matters and Palestinian bilateral cooperation with its neighbors, especially Israel.

The United States and the international community should help to develop a Palestinian internal security system capable of providing public order and stability. Support for administration of justice and the restructuring, equipping, and training of security services are the most urgent tasks. Support for administration of justice would foster an independent judicial system; provide investment capital for reconstructing courthouses and police stations; and supply equipment and materials necessary for training, such as legal texts, computers, and other office equipment. Regarding security services, the focus should be on helping to restructure and streamline the multiple services that now exist and provide training, equipment, and long-term monitoring. In the near term, outside assistance might also encompass the deployment of international police and help in the vetting and recruiting of judges, attorneys, police officers, and others involved in the administration of justice.

Addressing Population Growth

It is likely that the Palestinian population growth rates will continue to fall as the new state succeeds economically and as opportunities for women increase, as has been true elsewhere in the world. Falling fertility rates will likely continue only if economic progress is achieved in the future, which will depend on international private and public investment.

It is likely that there will be considerable immigration to a new state by Palestinians currently living abroad. Based on assumptions about which groups of Palestinians will be most likely to return and under what conditions, we estimate that this immigration may include 500,000 or more people during the first decade of independence. Ultimately, the number of Palestinians returning will depend upon the terms of the final statehood agreement and on social, political, and economic developments in the new Palestinian state. Detailed assessment of the likely scope and impact of immigration is outside the scope of this book.

Developing a Vibrant Economy

Perhaps the most important factor in the economy of the new state will be a high degree of both internal contiguity and economic integration with Israel. A highly contiguous Palestine—one with fewer impediments to the movement of goods and people—would have lower transaction costs and a broader base of economic activity. Also, a Palestine that has permeable borders economically and liberal trade policies with Israel would enable Palestinians to access lucrative employment opportunities in Israel as well as provide customers for Palestinian raw materials and intermediate goods exports.

Palestine should pursue a number of best-practice policies to encourage economic development and growth in per-capita incomes. Clearly these policies should involve efforts to repair and invest in Palestinian infrastructure pertaining to transportation, water, power, and communications; this infrastructure forms the basis of any functioning economy.

But these policies should also involve efforts to nurture economic activity. Critical areas include fostering free trade between Palestine and elsewhere by minimizing the costs of commerce; joining with Palestine's neighbors to develop specific economic sectors; expanding access to capital through a program of industrial and economic development zones, reformed domestic banking policies, and an international insurance fund; and improving the business climate through increased transparency and accountability of Palestinian governance. In light of this array of challenges, an independent Palestine will need significant assistance from the international community over an extended period of time.

Improving the Quantity and Quality of Palestine's Water

There are many possible strategies that could be adopted to assure that the water supply, a critical resource, meets the future needs of a Palestinian state. We assess that the most successful strategies would include some of the following elements: (1) an increased allocation of the region's water resources to the new Palestinian state, (2) external financing for the development of infrastructure to produce and procure new water supplies and treat wastewater, (3) substantial investment in water saving and reuse technologies, and (4) a revised agricultural policy that favors the irrigation of high-value crops. Without these actions, continued water scarcity, substandard quality, and inadequate wastewater treatment will dramatically restrict economic development, hinder health improvements, and possibly contribute to continued insecurity in the region.

The analysis presented in this book highlights the need for serious and sustained cooperation between the Palestinians, Israelis, and donor countries in the development of an equitable, sustainable, and adequate water supply and treatment system for a new Palestinian state. Without joint management between the Palestinians and Israelis of the region's groundwater, the quality and quantity of this water will continue to decrease. Without substantial external investment, the financial resources to procure new water supplies and modernize water use in Palestine will not be available. Finally, without sensible planning by all parties, the risk of costly future water shortages will remain unacceptably high.

Improving Health Care

The most immediate priorities for strengthening the Palestinian health system are (1) to strengthen system-wide coordination and implementation of planning, policies, and programs and (2) to improve public and primary health care programs, including an updated immunization program, comprehensive micronutrient fortification and supplementation, prevention and treatment of chronic and noninfectious disease, and treatment of developmental and psychosocial conditions. Other critical improvements include the development of viable and sustainable health care financing systems; updated, standardized, and enforced licensing and accreditation standards for health care professionals, facilities, and training programs and for pharmaceuticals and medical devices; and improved health information systems and research and evaluation capacity.

The details of health system development must be determined by local stakeholders, including governmental and nongovernmental institutions and, ultimately, Palestinian consumers. At the same time, health system development is an area where Israel, other neighboring countries, and the larger international community could play a constructive role, especially in health system planning, licensing and accreditation, development of information systems, and research. Moreover, as we discuss below, a truly successful Palestinian health system will require considerable outside investment over at least the first decade of independence.

Improving the Education System

Building an excellent education system will be key to Palestine's prosperity and stability in the coming years. The state has a strong base of human capital for development, and maximizing investments in that capital should be a national priority. In the near term, the focus should be on (1) maintaining currently high levels of access to education, while also working within resource constraints to expand enrollments at the secondary level (particularly in vocational and technical education and the academic science track) and in early childhood programs, (2) building quality through a focus on integrated curricular standards, assessments, and professional development, supported by long-term planning for system sustainability, and (3) improving delivery by working with donors to develop streamlined and integrated funding mechanisms that allow the administration to focus on meeting student needs, informed by strong evaluation and backed by significant sustained investment.

Specific ways to meet these goals should be determined through processes of consultation and participation involving the Palestinian community, the government, and international donors. Significant resources for system development already exist in local NGOs, universities, and other educational research institutions, and these should be incorporated into any national plan. International support for education has historically been strong, and both traditional partners and new collaborators can provide valuable conceptual and practical assistance to the system over the coming decade. Costs of building an excellent system will be high, and this international partnership will be essential to achieving funding targets for both capital and recurrent costs.

Financing Successful Development

This book includes estimates of the financial costs associated with implementing each chapter's recommendations. Because these estimates are approximate and are not based on detailed cost analyses, we intend them as a guide regarding the scale of financial assistance that will be required from the international community to help develop a successful Palestinian state. More precise estimates will require formal cost studies (involving detailed needs assessments), which were outside the scope of the present project. Moreover, we did not estimate the costs of all the major institutional changes and improvements in infrastructure that would be required for a successful Palestinian state.

The individual cost estimates use some common methodological approaches. Except for a few minor cases, all estimates are presented in constant 2003 U.S. dollars. In no case did we attempt to adjust the estimates for future trends in inflation or exchange rates. In all cases, we report results for the first ten years of a Palestinian state, assuming

2005 as the initial year. Unless otherwise noted, we converted data on historical expenditures in dollars to 2003 dollars using the U.S. GDP deflator. We focus on the real costs of implementing our recommendations, considering changes in relative prices. In particular, we assume that productivity increases would counterbalance increases in dollar wages. Our cost estimates account for natural population growth (at annual rates of 3–5 percent), but we have assumed zero net migration. In the event of substantial immigration to an independent Palestinian state, most of the cost estimates would need to be increased to meet the specified development targets for a larger population. The main exception would be the costs for security, which are determined by the security environment and are not directly proportional to the population.

Costs to Implement the Recommendations Described in This Study

As described in the Introduction, we use two approaches to estimating costs: the analogy approach (i.e., using costs of similar programs elsewhere to estimate the likely costs of these programs in Palestine) or parametric estimation (i.e., using relationships between costs and input variables based on historical data from similar projects to create a mathematical model for estimating costs in Palestine). In each case, the details supporting these estimates are provided in the relevant chapters.

Internal Security. We specify a variety of components that would be required for robust internal security. We estimate the costs of these components using analogies based on recent experience with the creation of new internal security institutions in Iraq. This approach results in a cost estimate for establishing and operating the institutions of internal security of $7 billion to $7.7 billion over ten years.

Water. The cost estimate is based on a previously developed model, which we have modified based on our best judgment for various scenarios. One of the benefits of a well-developed model is the ability it provides to examine multiple scenarios. The cost of our base case is $4.93 billion for the ten-year period from 2005 to 2014. However, in an alternative scenario, a combination of higher energy costs and increased population growth raises this estimate to $5.86 billion. Cost numbers for models based on improvements in the efficiency of water use combined with reducing agricultural use of water in Gaza range from $3.57 billion for the base case to $4.03 billion for an alternative scenario in which energy costs are relatively high and the population increases more rapidly.

Health. We use historical Palestinian data as a starting point and develop an incremental cost estimate for external support needed to increase health system spending to a satisfactory level, given health system development needs, population growth, and declines in spending during the second intifada. The total incremental cost ranges from $1.3 billion to $1.65 billion for the first ten years of statehood (2005–2014).

Education. We use UNESCO data on the ratio of education spending per student to GNI per capita in three categories of countries (those similar to Palestine with high-quality education systems, those similar to Palestine with moderate-quality education systems, and those with different socioeconomic contexts *and* high-quality education systems) to propose base spending ratios for Palestine, which are multiplied by adjusted GNI per-capita figures for Palestine over the relevant time frame. (Base figures are adjusted for the large investments in capital stock that will be required and for differences between the time transition path of salary levels and the path of GNI per capita.) Palestinian enrollment projections through 2010 are used, supplemented by a youth population growth rate of 5 percent per year for 2010–2014, to calculate annual spending per student and total annual cost. Total annual cost for the Palestinian education system ranges from $1 billion to $1.54 billion for 2005–2014. We do not distinguish between donor and national investments.

Other Key Infrastructures. It is important to note that significant investment will be needed in a number of additional areas, for which detailed analysis was outside the scope of this book.[1] While we have not attempted to identify every additional program or investment necessary for a successful state, we provide brief information here about five additional areas where considerable investment will be needed to promote successful development: the Palestinian road network, including a road to connect Gaza and the West Bank; a commercial seaport in Gaza; rehabilitation and expansion of the airport in Gaza; upgrading and expanding the electric power grid; and improving and expanding the Palestinian housing stock. We present a summary discussion here; additional information is in Appendix 9.A.

- *Road Improvements.* A good system of roads is essential to efficiently move people and goods within a Palestinian state and between Palestine and its neighbors. The West Bank and Gaza currently have an extensive system of roads, but this infrastructure needs both improvement and expansion. A Palestinian state will also require suitable transportation links between the West Bank and Gaza that ensure Israel's security. Plausible estimates of the cost of a road linking the West Bank and Gaza range between $500 million and $1 billion, but we also found estimates ranging between $200 million and $10 billion.
- *Gaza Seaport.* Currently, all seaborne shipments of goods and services entering or leaving the West Bank and Gaza go through Israeli ports. If security concerns are resolved, a future Palestinian state would likely build a port in Gaza to facilitate trade. A plausible lower bound estimate of the cost of constructing such a port is $62 million—the value of a contract tendered in 2000 to build a seaport in Gaza. That seaport project was suspended because of the second intifada.
- *Airport.* The government of a Palestinian state may choose to construct an airport capable of handling commercial aircraft. The existing Gaza airport, built in 1998 at a cost of $64 million, was damaged by Israeli forces during the second intifada; in 2003, the cost of repair was estimated at $35 million. To our knowledge, the

---

[1] Doug Suisman, Steven N. Simon, Glenn E. Robinson, C. Ross Anthony, and Michael Schoenbaum, *The Arc: A Formal Structure for a Palestinian State*, Santa Monica, Calif.: RAND Corporation, MG-327-GG, 2005.

Gaza airport was never equipped to handle substantial commercial traffic, which would require additional investment.

- *Electric Power Grid.* In a 1999 needs assessment, the World Bank master plan "identified investment requirements over the next ten years (exclusive of generation and new transmission lines) totaling more than $600 million" for Palestine.[2] The costs of building generating capacity and new transmission lines would be appreciably more than this figure, especially if Palestine were to replace Israeli generating capacity with indigenous plants.

- *Housing Stock.* Very limited investments have been made in Palestinian housing since the beginning of the second intifada. Square meters per capita—one measure of the adequacy of housing stock—is low in the West Bank and Gaza, even compared with other Middle Eastern countries; and the number of people per room is relatively high. Improvements in the housing stock will involve repairing the existing stock and building new residences to provide for population growth and to reduce crowding. A companion RAND report will explore options for addressing housing and related requirements of a burgeoning Palestinian population.[3]

Decisions on the timing, size, and priority of major infrastructure investments will need to be made at a national level. In almost all cases, the Palestinian state will need financing from foreign donors and lenders for all large infrastructure projects. Financing will necessitate feasibility and cost studies. Consequently, foreign donors and lenders will be heavily involved in discussions concerning priorities and the design and construction of investment projects.

Additional Areas of Investment. The chapters on governance and demography do not contain explicit cost estimates. However, the activities and policies discussed in these chapters will require additional expenditures. Below are some areas where costs are likely to be incurred.

- *Governance.* This chapter identified some of the issues involved in creating a democratic state with an efficient, responsive government in Palestine. This will entail real financial costs, for conducting elections and establishing and operating the legislative and executive branches of government, among other costs. The chapter does not estimate the costs of these institutional changes, which would be in addition to those discussed above. Some instances of institutional change discussed in that chapter, however, are explored from different angles in other chapters. For example, the Internal Security chapter includes the costs of a judicial system,

---

[2] World Bank, *Project Appraisal Document on a Proposed Trust Fund Credit in the Amount of $15.0 Million to the West Bank and Gaza for an Electric Sector Investment and Management Project,* Report No. 19603-GZ, August 12, 1999, p. 17.

[3] Suisman et al., 2005.

while the Health chapter discusses needs associated with health system development, including strengthening the Palestinian Ministry of Health.

- *Demography.* This chapter describes demographic trends. While population growth substantially affects the costs of providing government services—for example, health care and education—it does not entail specific costs in and of itself. The chapter also discusses potential immigration to a Palestinian state of Palestinians living in other countries. These inflows could add substantially to the total population in ways that are hard to forecast because of uncertainty about the number and characteristics of the immigrants. In general, substantial immigration to a Palestinian state would increase the costs of achieving the development goals we describe.[4]

- *Economic Vitality.* Finally, the Economics chapter estimates levels of capital investment needed for successful development. Specifically, this chapter includes projections of increases in employment and economic output based on an annual level of capital investment of around $3.3 billion per year for a cumulative total of some $33 billion over the first decade of independence (and $50 billion over the period 2004–2019 considered in the chapter).

Using an accounting growth model at this assumed level of investment and assuming the changes in the Palestinian labor force and in total factor productivity specified in the Economics chapter, the model yields projections of future employment and Palestinian national income per capita. The capital costs of the estimates above (e.g., water projects, health and education infrastructure, roads, the seaport and airport, and the electric power systems) would be subsumed in these projections of gross fixed capital investment. However, operating costs, such as salaries of workers at water treatment plants, are not.

Much of this investment will be provided by the Palestinians themselves, especially investment in housing. It is hoped that rapid economic growth will generate revenues that can be applied toward a variety of state building investments, reducing the amount that must be raised from international donations. Nonetheless, a substantial share of this investment in gross fixed capital is likely to be financed from abroad, especially in the early years.

Donor Funding and the Costs of Creating a Viable Palestinian State

This book provides a number of cost estimates of individual elements of a Palestinian state. However, it does not provide an estimate of the likely *total* costs of creating the new state. Nonetheless, some of the projections and estimates help explore these costs.

---

[4] As above, cost estimates in other chapters consider natural population growth but assume zero net migration. The cost estimates for several chapters, including Chapter Three, are directly proportional to population size (so that a 10 percent increase in population would increase costs by 10 percent, given the methods used in those chapters); this is also true for education costs, but with respect to specific age subgroups rather than the population overall.

The Economics chapter estimates that gross fixed capital investment of $3.3 billion per year will be needed over the first decade of statehood to generate the posited gains in employment. This aggregate figure includes all investment, whether funded by domestic or foreign sources. It exceeds the individual estimates of costs for the seaport, airport, connecting road, and improvements in the electric power system; the capital costs of expanding water and sewage systems; and even the costs of improving health care and education—many of which are *operating* rather than *investment* costs. Thus, this economic analysis of the Palestinian economy indicates that the individual cost estimate totals reasonably align with overall investment needs.

Although both cost-estimating approaches (analogical and parametric) help us estimate the financial challenge of creating a new state, neither approach distinguishes between resources provided by the Palestinians themselves and those that may be requested from foreign donors. To roughly determine the magnitude of funding that might be requested, we have resorted to the use of "reasonable" analogies: the amount of foreign funding that has been required to reconstruct Bosnia and Kosovo.

Like Palestine, these two entities suffered considerable damage from conflicts. Both have attracted considerable international interest and assistance. Both have had some success in creating democratic governments and revitalizing the local economies. In the first two years following the signing of peace accords in Bosnia and Kosovo, foreign assistance (grants and loans) averaged $714 and $433, respectively, per person per year. Applying these per-capita figures to the projected population of Palestine, an analogous inflow of assistance would range from $1.6 billion to $2.7 billion in the first year, rising to $2.1 to $3.5 billion by 2014 as a result of increases in the population (see Table 9.2). Over the ten-year period between 2005 and 2014, total flows of foreign assistance to a new Palestinian state analogous with those that have been granted to Kosovo and Bosnia would run from $18.8 billion to $31.1 billion. These dollar totals include all areas estimated in our study plus some others (e.g., transportation) that were beyond the scope of the present study.

By comparison, the World Bank estimated that the total volume of international aid to the West Bank and Gaza was $1.051 billion in 2002 and $0.929 billion in 2001.[5] Thus the amount of aid required in Palestine based on the Kosovo analogy would represent more than a 50 percent increase for 2005, relative to the 2002 level of international aid to the West Bank and Gaza, while aid based on the Bosnia analogy would require more than doubling the level of aid received in 2002.

Although large, this magnitude of costs is certainly sustainable through concerted international cooperation.

---

[5] The World Bank figures are in then-year U.S. dollars; World Bank, *West Bank and Gaza Update*, April–June 2003.

Table 9.2
Aid Flows Analogous to Bosnia and Kosovo

Year	Estimated Palestinian Population	Total Aid (millions of 2003 dollars)	
		Bosnia Analogy	Kosovo Analogy
2005	3,761,904	2,688	1,627
2006	3,889,249	2,779	1,683
2007	4,018,332	2,871	1,738
2008	4,149,173	2,964	1,795
2009	4,281,766	3,059	1,852
2010	4,416,076	3,155	1,910
2011	4,547,678	3,249	1,967
2012	4,676,579	3,341	2,023
2013	4,807,137	3,434	2,080
2014	4,939,223	3,529	2,137
Total		31,068	18,813

In Conclusion

At the time of this writing, the prospects for establishing an independent Palestinian state are uncertain. U.S. attention, without which a negotiated settlement between Palestinians and Israelis seems unlikely, has been primarily focused on Iraq to date. Nevertheless, a critical mass of Palestinians and Israelis—as well as the United States, Russia, the European Union, and the United Nations—remain committed to the goal of establishing a Palestinian state. Additionally, U.S. experience in Iraq and Afghanistan can only reinforce the value of having plans in place for the eventuality of an independent Palestine. The death of Yasser Arafat in November 2004, which spurred both Palestinians and the wider world to focus on the future of the region, may yet turn this eventuality into a more imminent reality.

Our book is not a prediction that peace will come soon. We firmly believe, however, that thoughtful preparation can help make peace possible. And when peace comes, this preparation will be essential to the success of the new state. This book is designed to help Palestinians, Israelis, and the international community—the United States, its Quartet partners, and Palestine's Arab neighbors—prepare for the moment when the parties are ready to create and sustain a successful Palestinian state.

Appendix 9.A: Major Infrastructure Investments

This appendix describes how we assessed the potential costs of developing the Palestinian road network, including a road to connect Gaza and the West Bank; a commercial seaport in Gaza; rehabilitation and expansion of the airport in Gaza; and upgrading and expanding the electric power grid. Detailed examination of these areas was outside the scope of this project.

Road Improvements

A good system of roads is essential to efficiently move people and goods within a Palestinian state and between Palestine and its neighbors. The West Bank and Gaza currently have an extensive system of roads, but the quality varies considerably. Palestine will need both more and better roads.

The West Bank and Gaza will also need suitable transportation links. Currently, Palestinians cannot move freely between the two areas. However, because road or rail connections would cross Israeli territory, they would have to be designed to ensure Israel's security.

A number of proposals have been made for a road and/or train connecting the West Bank and Gaza. One proposal envisages constructing an elevated road traversing the 47 kilometers from Beit Hanoun to Dura, referred to as the southern safe passage route. According to former Israeli Prime Minister Ehud Barak, the high end estimated cost of an elevated roadway of 47 kilometers is $10 billion. A traditional road would be considerably cheaper, potentially as little as $200 million, according to the Palestinian Economic Council for Development and Reconstruction. Israeli newspaper *Ha'aretz* cites another estimate by the Israeli Public Works Authority of $1 billion for a connecting road, which we consider to be a more realistic estimate than either of the two extremes.[6]

An alternative approach to using these estimates is to estimate the cost of constructing a road running through Israel lined on both sides by a security fence. We have created our own rough cost estimate assuming that the road would have to be lined on both sides with a security wall akin to the West Bank separation barrier currently being built by Israel. The cost of that barrier is reported to be approximately $2.2–$3.3 million per kilometer.[7] Assuming that this is an appropriate costing analogue, fencing both sides of a 47-kilometer road would cost between $207 and $310 million; this would be in addition to the costs of constructing the road itself and the costs of over- or underpasses connecting Israeli territory north and south of the road. Depending on

---

[6] Akiva Eldar, "There Is No Such Thing as a Magic Bridge," *Ha'aretz*, October 6, 1999.

[7] "Cost of Fence Could Rise to NIS 15 Million Per Kilometer," *Ha'aretz*, February 23, 2004.

the number of intersections, the costs of building these passages could add appreciably to the total costs.

Gaza Seaport

Currently, all seaborne shipments of goods and services entering or leaving the West Bank and Gaza go through Israeli ports. If security concerns are resolved, a future Palestinian state would likely build a port for Gaza to facilitate trade. On April 20, 2000, before the second intifada, a contract for the development of a 20,000-square-meter Gaza seaport was tendered.[8] A Gaza port would be designed to handle commercial vessels of up to 35,000 deadweight tons, with a total throughput of one million tons a year.[9] While this volume is smaller than Israeli ports—Ashdod and Haifa have annual throughput of 16.5 million and 15 million tons of cargo, respectively[10]—it would probably be adequate for the needs of a Palestinian state during its first decade of existence. Construction costs for a port of this size were estimated at $62 million in 2000.[11] We note that the actual costs of such large public infrastructure projects are often higher than initially estimated. Construction was expected to take 25 months to complete; for this reason, and because the Palestinian government might choose to invest in a larger port, this cost estimate should be viewed as a lower rather than a midpoint estimate.

Airport

The government of a Palestinian state may choose to construct an airport capable of handling commercial aircraft. An airport was built in Gaza in 1998 at a cost of $64 million.[12] The runway was 3,080 meters in length and could accommodate aircraft up to and including wide-bodied jumbo jets.[13] However, the airport was heavily damaged by Israeli forces during the second intifada, and it will require significant repair before it can be used again. In the summer of 2003, the Palestinian Authority's Transport and

---

[8] The Economist Intelligence Unit, *Country Profile: Palestinian Territories*, London, p. 23.

[9] "Dutch to Build Harbor at Gaza," *Dredging News Online,* Vol. 1, No. 28, May 26, 2000; and The Economist Intelligence Unit, *Country Profile: Palestinian Territories*, London, p. 23.

[10] Lloyds Register, *Fairplay Ports and Terminals Guide,* CD-ROM, 2003.

[11] "Full Steam Ahead at Gaza Port," *Middle East Economic Digest,* May 12, 2000. Construction of the Gaza seaport never began because of the second intifada.

[12] "Palestinians Get Their Wings," *The Economist,* November 7, 1998, p. 46.

[13] See http://www.gaza-airport.org/about1.html.

Communications Minister cited the figure of $35 million as the estimated outlay to repair and reopen the airport.[14] To our knowledge, the Gaza airport was never equipped to handle substantial commercial traffic, which would require additional investment.

Electric Power Grid

In a 1999 needs assessment, the World Bank master plan "identified investment requirements over the next ten years (exclusive of generation and new transmission lines) totaling more than $600 million" for Palestine.[15] The costs of building generating capacity and new transmission lines would be appreciably more than this figure, especially if the Palestinians were to replace Israeli generating capacity with indigenous plants.

---

[14] "Israel Said to Agree 'in Principle' to Gaza Airport Rehabilitation," *BBC Monitoring*, July 9, 2003.

[15] World Bank, *Project Appraisal Document on a Proposed Trust Fund Credit in the Amount of $15.0 Million to the West Bank and Gaza for an Electric Sector Investment and Management Project*, Report No. 19603-GZ, August 12, 1999, p. 17.

Index